Lawma

BRU

Lawman

BRUT

Translated, with an introduction
and notes, by Rosamund Allen

*Reader in English, Queen Mary and
Westfield College, University of London*

St. Martin's Press
New York

Introduction, translation and notes © J. M. Dent Ltd 1992

First published in the United States of America in 1992

Printed in Great Britain

ISBN 0-312-08576-1

Library of Congress Cataloging-in-Publication Data

Layamon, fl. 1200.
    [Brut. English]
    Brut / Lawman : translated with an introduction and notes by
Rosamund Allen.
      p. cm.
    Translation of: Brut.
    ISBN 0-312-08576-1
    1. Brutus the Trojan (Legendary character)—Romances. 2. Great
Britain—History—To 1066—Romances, 3. Romances, English—
—Modernized versions.   4. Arthurian Romances.
5. Britons—Romances.
I. Title.
PR2023.A2A34   1992
821'.1—dc20
                                      92-16866
                                         CIP

CONTENTS

	Page
Preface	ix
Abbreviations	x
Introduction	xiii
Bibliography	xxxvii

THE TEXT	*Line Numbers*
LAWMAN	1
The History of the British	
ÆNEAS	45
ASCANIUS	110
BRUTUS	152
LOCRIN	1054
GWENDOLINE	1247
MADAN	1265
MEMBRIZ and MALIN	1271
EBRAUC	1306
LEIL	1385
RUHHUDIBRAS	1399
BLADUD	1417
LEIR	1450
CORDOILLE	1861
MORGAN	1877
CUNEDAGIUS	1931
RIWALD	1938
GURGUSTIUS	1952
GORBODIAGUS	1957
IUDON	1992
DUNWALLO MOLINUS	2035
BRENNES AND BELINUS	2143
GURGUINT	3037

Contents

GUENCELIN	3133
MARCIE	3159
SILLIUS/RUMMARUS/DAMUS	3163–69
MORPIDUS	3170
GORBONIAN	3257
ARGAL	3264
ELIDUR	3279
LADOR/MORGAN/ANMAUNUS	3418–22
IWALLO	3436
RIME/GORONCES/CATULUS/COILLUS/POREX	3443–8
CHERIN/FULGENIUS etc.	3449–68
URRIAN/ELIUD etc.	3469–75
MERIAN	3476
BLEDON/CAP etc./BLADGABREAT	3482–97
ARKINAUS/ALDOLF/REDION etc.	3498–3512
PIR/CAPOR/ELIGILLE/HELI	3513–23
LUD	3524
CASSIBELLAUNUS	3568
TENNANCIUS	4501
CYMBELINE	4520
WITHER	4584
ARVIRAGUS	4653
MAURUS	4934
COIL	5027
LUCES	5033
BASIAN	5213
ALLEC	5329
ASCLEPIDIOT	5358
COEL	5417
TRAHERN	5601
OCTAVES	5672
MAXIMIEN	5808
GRACIEN	6107
CONSTANTINE	6432
CONSTANCE	6619
VORTIGERN	6854
VORTIMER	7309
VORTIGERN (2)	7523
AURELIUS	8061
UTHER	9064
ARTHUR	9944

Contents

CONSTANTINE	14298
CONAN	14357
VORTIPORUS	14369
MALGUS	14379
CARRIC	14400
GURMUND	14641
CADWAN	14965
ALFRIC AND CADWAN	14996
CADWATHLAN AND EDWIN	15027
[OSWALD]	15618
[OSWY]	15701
[OSRIC]	15854
CADWALADER	15865
ATHELSTAN	15941
Notes	411
Emendations to the Caligula MS	470

PREFACE

I gratefully acknowledge permission granted by the Council of the Early English Text Society for use of the edition of the *Brut* edited by G. L. Brook and R. F. Leslie, on which this translation is based, and the Trustees of the British Library for permission to consult B.L. Manuscripts Cotton Caligula A.ix and Cotton Otho C.xiii which contain Lawman's *Brut*. All who work on Lawman's *Brut* owe an incalculable debt to its first editor, Sir Frederic Madden of the British Museum, who, devoting 'the leisure hours of many years of toil and anxiety to the work' produced an accurate (and twice corrected) edition of the two British Library manuscripts, with elaborate notes, glossary and glossarial notes, and a literal translation, with suggestions for emending both manuscripts; for all this he lacked a good dictionary, since ten years were to pass before Dean Trench persuaded the Philological Society to begin compiling material for the *OED*; MS O has deteriorated since then, and Madden's edition is the source for many readings; admiration and gratitude for Madden's work must be unqualified. It was Madden's literal translation which formed the text for the translation of Lawman's *Brut* in Everyman's Library, number 578, there entitled *Wace and Layamon: Arthurian Chronicles*, edited, and the Wace section translated, by Eugene Mason: the 1912 edition was reissued with an introduction by Gwyn Jones in 1962. Mason only presented the Arthurian section and its immediately preceding context, beginning with Constantine's arrival from Brittany, at line 6388. I have not been able to include the Wace text as well as the complete Lawman poem for reasons of space, but the notes include comparison and contrast with this major source of Lawman's poem.

This project received wholehearted support from Jocelyn Burton, then General Editor of the Everyman Library at J. M. Dent Ltd., and later from Malcolm Gerratt: their help and encouragement were invaluable.

I thank colleagues and former colleagues: Julia Boffey, Lucinda Rumsey and Jim Bolton, also Lesley Johnson and Victoria Sellar, who between them read the translation and introduction and pointed out many errors and awkward readings; for all those which still remain I am of course wholly responsible. I also thank Dr Paul Brand, for information on early thirteenth century law, Margaret Savage, for material on Hadrian's Wall, and my husband, Stephan Sulyák, who helped with the word-processing and printing (and the household chores: incalculable aid!). One last debt: George Kane taught me Middle English from the extracts from the *Brut* in *Early Middle English Texts*, so beginning my fascination with the poem.

Abbreviations

The following abbreviated titles are used in the Introduction and in the Notes which follow the Text; full bibliographical references are given in the *Bibliography*.

ASC	*The Anglo-Saxon Chronicle*
Bede	Bede's *Ecclesiastical History*
BBIAS	*Bibliographical Bulletin of the International Arthurian Society*
Bennett *MELit*	J. A. W. Bennett, *Middle English Literature*
B–H	Blenner-Hassett, *The Place-Names in Lawman's 'Brut'*
B&L	*Laȝamon: Brut*, ed. Brook and Leslie
B&S	*Early Middle English Verse and Prose*, ed. Bennett and Smithers
B&W	*Laȝamon's Arthur* ed. Barron and Weinberg
Brook	*Selections from Laȝamon's 'Brut'*, ed. G. L. Brook
D&W	*Early Middle English Texts*, ed. Dickins and Wilson
DEPN	*Dictionary of English Place-Names*
EETS	Early English Text Society
ES	*Englische Studien*
Engl. Studies	*English Studies*
GoM	Geoffrey of Monmouth: *History of the Kings of Britain*
H	*Layamon's Brut: Selections*, ed. J. Hall
Hall [*EME*]	*Selections from Early Middle English* ed. J. Hall

LeedsSE	*Leeds Studies in English*
LMDA	Sir Thomas Malory, *Le Morte Darthur*
Le Saux, Sources	F. Le Saux, *Layamon's 'Brut': The Poem and its Sources*
M/ Madden	*Laȝamon's 'Brut'* ed. Sir Frederic Madden
MÆ	*Medium Ævum*
MED	*Middle English Dictionary*, ed. Hans Kurath and Sherman Kuhn, (Univ. of Michigan Press, Ann Arbor, 1954–)
Mg	*The Chronicle of Robert Mannyng of Brunne*
MHRA	*Bulletin of the Modern Humanities Research Association*
MP	*Modern Philology*
MS C	British Library Manuscript Cotton Caligula A.ix (used as the base text for this translation).
MS O	British Library Manuscript Cotton Otho C.xiii (referred to in the Notes and used to correct some readings of C in text; see **Emendations**)
NM	*Neuphilologische Mitteilungen*
N&Q	*Notes and Queries*
OED	*The Oxford English Dictionary*, (Oxford, 1933)
Poole, *1087–1216*	A. L. Poole, *Domesday Book to Magna Carta: 1087–1216*
PMLA	*Publications of the Modern Language Association of America*
RES	*The Review of English Studies*
Salter, *E&I*	E. Salter, *English and International*
Serjeantson	Mary Serjeantson, *History of Foreign Words in English*
SN	*Studia Neophilologica*
Tatlock, *Legendary History*	J. S. P. Tatlock, *The Legendary History of Britain*
Thorpe	*Geoffrey of Monmouth: History of the Kings of Britain*, trans. L. Thorpe
VCH	*The Victoria County History (of Worcester)*

Further abbreviations:

b	born
c	(preceding a date) *circa*, approximately

13thc	(or other numeral) thirteenth century
d	died
gl	glossed (as)
L 16095	Lawman's *Brut* line ref.
W 14866	Wace, *Roman de Brut* line ref.
ME	Middle English
OE	Old English
om	omitted
OW	Old Welsh
prec	preceding
s.a.	*sub anno*, under the entry for this year
sp	spelling, spelled as
sb	substantive, noun
s.v.	*sub verbo*, under this word/item
trans	translated, translator

INTRODUCTION

Lawman

Most early medieval texts are anonymous and our only knowledge of the author is the quasi-authorial narrator in the work. Sometimes we know the author's name, but no more, or perhaps a few details which tell us nothing about the circumstances in which he lived and worked. This is the case with Lawman, who tells us his name, recorded as *Laȝamon* and *Laweman* in the two extant manuscripts of his poem, and gives us information (which cannot be exact) about his sources and working methods, but then is silent about the things we would most like to know: about his patron if he had one, or if he did not, his personal reasons for his choice of subject-matter; and how long he spent writing the work. If, as he claims in line 14, he did travel far and wide gathering information, then he must have spent around a decade on his book, and he must have had a high degree of self-motivation – or a very demanding patron.

Earlier Versions of British History: Geoffrey and Wace

Lawman's *Brut* is the story of Great Britain from its foundation under the eponymous figure 'Brutus', who was supposed to have descended from the Aeneas Virgil celebrates, who escaped from Troy, to the transference of power to the 'Angles' under Athelstan, by which time the 'British', Brutus's descendents, had been relegated to Wales and Cornwall or had emigrated to 'Little Britain': Brittany.

The story was not Lawman's own, but it was not very ancient either: almost certainly most of the narrative had been invented by Geoffrey of Monmouth. Geoffrey wrote in the Latin narrative style of medieval historians, producing a blend of apparently factual statement and political rhetoric, which in the main he inserted into the protagonists' mouths, but occasionally displayed as an authorial indulgence. Although Geoffrey claimed that his *History of the Kings of Britain* (*Historia Regum Britanniae*) was translated from 'a very ancient book' ('*vetustissimus liber*') in 'the British tongue', lent him by Archdeacon Walter, it is very unlikely that what he wrote was anything more than an ingenious compilation of genuine history and sheer inspired invention. He used such authentic sources as Caesar and Bede, the sixth century Welshman Gildas and so-called 'Nennius' from the ninth century, and seems to have known oral Welsh or Breton tales of Arthur; he even seems to have used material from his own contemporary historiographers, William of Malmesbury and Henry of Huntingdon. Walter the Archdeacon certainly existed: he was a fellow-member of Geoffrey's college of secular Canons of St Augustine, at St George's in Osney, outside Oxford, but his book, whether in Welsh, Cornish, or Breton, is reckoned by most (but not all) scholars to be imaginary.

Geoffrey was a 'maker of history'. It is from Geoffrey that we learn of King Arthur's personal history and his place in British 'history': he is not mentioned by Bede, is little more than a name in the *Annales Cambriæ* (*Annals of Wales*) and early Welsh Triads, but after the more expansive treatment of him in 'Nennius's ninth century *History of the Britons*, Arthur becomes famous in Welsh saints' legends and poetry as a great ruler. It was Geoffrey who made him into an historical figure. C. S. Lewis thought Geoffrey's style execrable, but the story line is actually quite gripping, and he has a good sense of formal structure.

Geoffrey's work must have been completed by the end of 1138; in January 1139 an astounded Henry of Huntingdon, who had previously declared that no information on the early history of the Britons was available, was handed a copy of Geoffrey's book in the monastic library of the Abbey of Bec in Normandy which he was then visiting (Tatlock, *Legendary History*, pp. 433–4). William of Malmesbury and Henry of Huntingdon seem to have accepted Geoffrey's work as surprising – because hitherto unknown – but true. Many people continued to accept it as history until the eighteenth century; sixteenth and seventeenth century plays were written about Leir, Ferrex and Porrex, and other characters from Geoffrey's *Historia*; the poet Milton contemplated an Arthuriad.

The first major sceptic was William of Newburgh in the 1190s, who was caustic in his condemnation of Geoffrey's fraudulent 'pseudo-history', but by then it had gone through at least one redaction in its original Latin, and had been translated into Latin hexameters (late 12c), Anglo-Norman French and Welsh. By the end of the Middle Ages there were, in addition, a Latin metrical version (*c1250*), two more French metrical versions, and in English a modified version in Robert of Gloucester's Chronicle and two English versions derived from Geoffrey via Wace. Geoffrey had struck a popular chord. There are at least two versions of Geoffrey's prose text extant: one assumed to be original and one which is now called 'The First Variant', which omits certain small details found in the first version. Another view is that this variant *is* Walter's 'very ancient book'. The textual history of Geoffrey's book, now under investigation, is still uncertain; the *Historia* was enormously popular and much altered in dissemination and translation.

For his translation into French, Wace used the Variant version of Geoffrey's work for the first half, and then used the original from the point where Merlin appears. Wace came originally from Jersey and had studied in the Île-de-France and at the Abbey of Caen. In another work, *Le Roman de Rou*, he calls himself 'clerc lisant' which is usually interpreted as 'tutor, teacher'; like Geoffrey and Lawman he was a cleric. Wace was a careful worker who supplemented Geoffrey's *Historia* with details from more reliable historians like Bede, and shows a true historian's accuracy in dating the completion of his work: 1155. The date is significant; Wace wrote some fifteen to twenty years before Chrétien began writing his vernacular verse romances about Arthur's knights. Two details he added to Geoffrey's account of Arthur were prolific growth points in those later romances: a brief mention of the Round Table, constructed to avoid disputes over precedence (W 9747–60), a symbol of chivalric endeavour (W 10285, 13269*f*); and the claim of the British that Arthur is to return again from Avalon (W 13279–90), both perhaps taken from Celtic traditions.

Instead of Geoffrey's Latin prose, which invited a monastic readership, Wace wrote in French octosyllabic couplets. Geoffrey had spanned the divide between story and history: some of what he wrote was true (Caesar did invade Britain, as did Severus; a Constantine was declared emperor while in Britain, and a Belinus had attacked Rome, although he was not British; Penda and Oswald were real enough). But Geoffrey was strongly influenced by the kind of popular narrative which within half a century was to give rise to vernacular romance: his tale of Baldulf's entry into York disguised as a *mimus*, and his account of how Brian entered Edwin's court disguised as a beggar, are clear instances of influence from popular tale.

Wace carried this elaboration of history further by 'dramatising' the narrative, presenting clearly visualised and motivated action, which is given a depth of perspective in time and place by being firmly located in a tangible world, where people create events by interaction with others, and by reaction to the situations they find themselves in. It is often said that Wace added a dimension of courtesy and magic to Geoffrey's more factual narrative, where speech is showily formal and has little to do with character. Wace's characters are undoubtedly more 'free-standing' than the decorated frieze-strip of Geoffrey's narrative, and it is this autonomy of character which gives the impression of a greater grace and more civilised behaviour. Wace's people decide for themselves, with us an onlookers; one of Wace's favourite phrases is 'if you had been there you would have seen/heard . . .'. Another is 'ne sai', 'I do not know', which gives perspective, reminding us that Wace is writing long after the events have been half-forgotten, and also creates an impression of realism, a sense that those who people the narrative have their own lives and motives about which the author is often ignorant. Geoffrey's characters, on the other hand, are the exemplars of Geoffrey's own opinions on government, law and the maintenance of society.

Geoffrey seems to demonstrate that the Celtic element in the population had a past as well documented and as instructive as the English and the Norman. But some readers, then and now, detect Norman political models in this probably half-Celtic, half-Norman cleric which dominates his presentation of history: people are at their best when subject to a strong king with creative and constructive ideas about building towns, roads and castles, and about initiating and maintaining laws. Wace was less partisan; his *Roman de Rou*, patronised by Henry II, is a history of the Normans, and like his contemporary Gaimar he may have planned, but not lived to complete, a trilogy of histories of the three nations: Welsh, Normans and English. Gaimar's *Brut* is no longer extant. Wace seems to be much more interested than Geoffrey in personal motivation, in the importance of the individual as catalyst in the great changes and developments of society. His interest in emotions, those of his characters and ours as we participate in their dramas, mark him out as a creative artist.

Lawman's Version of the Story of Britain

Wace was still alive in 1174, but had died before Lawman began writing: Lawman writes of him in the past tense (L 21). Exactly how long after Wace's death Lawman 'took up his quills' (L 26) and began his redaction of Wace's version of the *Historia* is still a matter of dispute. In his Prologue, Lawman gives us a piece of information about Wace which that author himself had not divulged: that he presented his book to Queen Eleanor 'who was the queen of Henry the great king' (L 22–3), and critics have tried to use this information to date Lawman's poem, or rather, the Prologue, which was probably written after the rest of the work was complete. The Eleanor to whom Wace presented his work must have been Eleanor of Aquitaine, whose second husband was Henry II of England. In 1216 another Henry came to the throne, the nine-year-old Henry III, for whom the great old soldier William Marshal, Earl of Pembroke, acted as Regent, aided by the papal Legate, Cardinal Guala. It is argued that, had Lawman been writing after Henry III's accession, he would have distinguished the earlier Henry in some way, and that therefore Lawman's *Brut* must date from between Henry II's death in 1189 (because the past tense is used of Henry and Eleanor in line 22) and Henry III's accession in 1216. Two objections can be made to this: the first, a minor point, is that the expression 'who was Henry's Queen' seems to signify that Eleanor herself was dead (she died, in France, in 1204); the second is that Henry is indeed distinguished by an epithet: Eleanor was queen of 'the high/great king' (*þes heȝes kinges*); this might well be a means of distinguishing a man famous for his legal and administrative reforms from a mere boy, and could extend the period of composition to the time when Henry III assumed his majority, 1227. But had Lawman been writing as late as 1236, when Henry III himself married a queen called Eleanor, presumably he would then have distinguished the early Henry and Eleanor more specifically from the later.

Attempts to date the poem by Lawman's doubt about the continued payment of Peter's Pence (L 15964) do not identify any precise date: in 1205 John refused to send the collected monies to Rome, but payment also ceased in 1164 and 1169; the allusion could even relate to the period of the Interdict, 1208–14.

It looks as if Lawman wrote either during the reign of John, or while Henry was still a child; in other words, between 1199 and, say, 1225. Indeed, it might have taken him more than a decade to produce the 16,000 long lines of the *Brut*. It is clear that Lawman admires a king who is strong and consistently motivated, (even if this means that at times he is severe in administering justice and its penalties) and one who is in harmony with his barons and his clergy. Perhaps it is not impossible that the vagaries of John's temperament and the vicissitudes of his reign, with the loss of Normandy in 1204, the Papal Interdict imposed from 1208 and not formally lifted until 1214, and the baronial demands which culminated in Magna Carta in 1215, could have led Lawman to postulate an ideal monarch markedly distinct from the actual king. Nevertheless, King John was popular in the West, and was actually buried in front of the high altar in Worcester Cathedral in 1216 (Poole, *1087–1216*, p. 486). The Interdict may itself hold the clue to dating Lawman's *Brut*: during this period no priest could say mass, preach, hear confession, baptise, marry or conduct a funeral for his parishioners; this must have left the clergy with time on their hands, which Lawman might have filled constructively by writing the *Brut* – but this is mere surmise. It is, however, interesting that when translating Wace's account of the apostasy under Gurmund, Lawman adds a line declaring that no bells were rung and no masses said all through Britain, exactly as happened during the Interdict (L 14693).

Who, then, could Lawman have been? He tells us in his Prologue that he was a priest, and had a living at Areley in the diocese of Worcester. There are still some stones and one round-headed window dating from the twelfth century in St Bartholomew's Church at Areley King's, which must have been there in Lawman's time (*VCH: Worcester*, (1901–24), vol. iv, p. 228). The rectors of Martley presented to the living of Areley Kings in the thirteenth century, and Elizabeth Salter shows that Areley Kings was part of the manor of Martley which passed from the King's hands in 1196, first, in part, to Philip de Aire and then entirely to the de Frisa or de Frise family in 1200; they kept it until 1233 when it passed to the Despensers (Salter, *E&I*, p. 67, citing *VCH: Worcester*, vol. iv, pp. 227–30); Madden says the estate went to the de Fruges family, in 1205 (*Brut*, I, x, n. 2), and adds the information that the advowson of Martley was, since the time of Domesday, in the possession of the Abbey of Cormeilles near Lisieux in Normandy (*Brut*, I, x, n. 2). The Prior of Newent, the English cell of Cormeilles, occasionally presented to the living, (*VCH, Worcester*, vol. iv, p. 295) but quite possibly Lawman had an Anglo-Norman monk as his rector, since alien priories continued to present to English livings after the loss of Normandy in 1204.

It is important to see Lawman in the context of his parish near the Welsh marches and in his diocese of Worcester. Although Tatlock asserts that Lawman was an obscure cleric living in a rural backwater

(*Legendary History*, pp. 509, 514), in fact he lived only ten miles north of the important ecclesiastical centre at Worcester; during the decade from 1208–18 successive bishops of Worcester were called upon to share in pronouncing the Interdict and in supervising the nine-year-old king Henry III, and to direct the burial of King John in front of Worcester Cathedral High Altar and beside his patron saint, Wulfstan. It was at Worcester that the great Welsh Prince Llywelyn did homage to the infant King Henry III in March 1218, in return for confirmation of the lands he had conquered from the Anglo-Normans. Llywelyn was a supremely good statesman and soldier, and maintained peace among the princes of South Wales until his death in 1240 (Poole, *1087–1216*, pp. 300–1). In Llywelyn, Lawman might well have seen a second King Arthur or another Cadwathlan, with the inept King John, who had planned a campaign against the Welsh, and had antagonised his own barons into inviting Louis of France to take the kingdom, in the rôle of the Saxons Colgrim or Edwin.

The long tenure of Bishop Wulfstan in the see of Worcester must have produced a painful transition when Norman episcopal control supervened in 1095; the bishops of Worcester at the turn of the twelfth century were especially uncongenial to native English clerics and layfolk: over the nine years from 1190 three Normans held the see, the last of whom, John de Constantiis, removed from the cathedral the relics of the English Archbishop Wulfstan, just around the hundredth anniversary of his death. Mauger his successor, who appealed to the Pope to be admitted to the see despite his illegitimacy, was a money-grabber: he had Wulfstan's relics restored to the cathedral and arranged his canonisation in 1203, less out of devotion to the English saint (Norman prelates generally scorned native saints) than out of greed for the income from pilgrims to the shrine, which he was using to defray the costs of rebuilding after a fire in the precinct in 1202 until compelled by the Worcester monks to divide the proceeds. Mauger tried to bully the monks at Evesham, but then fled from King John's anger during the Interdict, abandoning his flock; he died in France in 1212. The next bishop but one abused Saint Wulfstan's relics by personally cutting the bones to fit the new shrine prepared for the rededication of the cathedral in 1218; Wulfstan avenged himself: the bishop died six days later. This kind of behaviour from his ecclesiastical superiors may well account for Lawman's reference to the malicious Normans (L 1030, 3547; see *VCH: Worcester*, vol. ii, pp. 11–13).

The Manuscripts of Lawman's Brut

The *Brut* is extant in two manuscripts, both in the British Library. MS Cotton Caligula A ix is a quarto volume of 285 leaves, its first half containing the *Brut* on 192 folios written in double columns, mostly of 34 lines, by two scribes who exchanged stints once, the second resuming and completing the copying, and so transcribing about nine-tenths of the whole poem; there are marginal Latin glosses in black ink offering historical summaries and corrections of Lawman's poem, and the names of the characters in red where they occur in the text; the MS has been corrected by a contemporary of the two scribes and further corrected by a later hand (Le Saux, 1; B&L, I, ix). The other manuscript, MS Cotton Otho C xiii is also in double columns and was originally 155 folios written by one scribe. Only 145 folios survive, many greatly damaged in the fire at Ashburnham House in 1731 and deteriorating when Madden was working on the MS, which he had rebound (*Brut*, I, xxxvi–viii).

Because MS O, before it was damaged, was a condensed version of the work, some 3,000 lines shorter than C and omitting many of the rhetorical expressions, poetic descriptions and archaic diction of MS C, it was assumed until the 1960s that MS O was fifty years or so later than C. When Neil Ker pointed out that MS C dated from the middle rather than the early thirteenth century, two things became clear: first, MS O was not merely a modernised *Brut*, updated after expressions and grammatical structures in the original had become obsolete, but a conscious representation of the material from a factual rather than an imaginative standpoint; second, because neither extant manuscript was as early as the beginning of the 1200s, as had been thought, it was quite possible that Lawman himself was writing as late as the mid-thirteenth century. One reason that the poem had previously been thought to date from the mid- to late twelfth century was its archaic language: MS C preserves with reasonable accuracy declined forms of the definite article, and strong adjectives, with traces of grammatical gender in nouns, features which had been levelled in most parts of the country by the early thirteenth century. Otho is an inferior version of the poem, partly written from memory and by a scribe who was not sympathetic to Lawman's aims and methods. There are about 80 half-lines in O not present in C, some of them probably authentic. MS C is probably more faithful to Lawman's original, even though it may have been copied half a century after Lawman wrote.

Whenever Lawman was writing, from the ninth decade of the twelfth century to the middle of the thirteenth, he was using a self-consciously archaic spelling and grammar, perhaps to give an 'antique flavour' to his history, yet his diction was mainly colloquial and up-to-date, with some older compounds which had survived from Old English, and some new compound forms which he either invented on older patterns or imported from current speech to give sonorance and dignity to his account of the great deeds of great men in British history.

The Audience of The Brut

Lawman tells us he was the son of *Leouenað*, and enjoyed his situation, near to Redstone (where the parishes of Astley and Areley meet), and there he 'read Book' (probably the Missal at Mass or his breviary, L 1–5). But this identification is contradicted by MS O in which we are told that his father was *Leucais* and that he lived at Areley 'with the good knight', where he read 'books'. In MS C he is a simple country priest (although the illuminated letter A which begins MS C contains a miniature of Lawman habited as a Benedictine monk), in MS O a learned man, for his time, and presumably a household chaplain. The two states are not incompatible, successively or even perhaps simultaneously. The difference of rôles in the two manuscripts suggests a significant distinction in the aim of writing. A chaplain to a household was presumably assigned a certain topic by a patron and wrote for the entertainment or instruction (or both) of a mixed audience, the household as a whole if the work was read aloud, particular literate members of it if the book was passed around in manuscript, a single auditor, perhaps, if the writer were a tutor. In the simplest form of the relationship presumably the patron would furnish the many parchment sheets needed for a huge work like Lawman's *Brut*. A parish priest in a rural area was not very likely to be writing for his rustic parishioners, and unless he wrote the work for the secular priests of neighbouring parishes, or a college of Augustinian canons, or, (like Mannyng who also translated Wace's *Brut* in 1338) for the lay brothers of a monastic community, it is hard to surmise what the purpose of writing and what the actual or envisaged audience could have been. From the little that Lawman tells us of his 'splendid idea' of writing a history of England (L 6–7), he could have been writing for his own entertainment and with no audience in mind but himself.

For the first thousand lines or so Lawman's *Brut* does not appear to be directed towards any specific audience. Then begins a sporadic use of the second person singular pronoun: *þu*. Grammatically, Lawman is conducting a dialogue between himself and one other person; however, the obvious potential for declaming many of the speeches which he adds to Wace's narrative, makes it unlikely that Lawman wrote for a solitary reader. Yet who could have wanted to hear the poem, at this length, and in English? Anyone interested in the customs and ancient history of the country and sufficiently literate to be able to read for himself a work as idiosyncratic as the *Brut*, would either be from the clergy, and therefore capable of reading Geoffrey's Latin and Wace's French, or at least from the administrative class, the estate bailiffs and stewards, who by the thirteenth century were learning French for business purposes, and could at least have managed Wace in the original. I think we must assume that Lawman did indeed write for a patron, for the household of a man of some status but certainly not of the Norman ruling class. It is possible that he was a merchant, of English stock, for whom the traditions of his country, and especially its place-names, were important: Lawman's second person singular address frequently occurs at the explanation of a place-name, and several of these are Lawman's own insertions. In the tale of Brian in the *Brut*, Brian adopts the disguise of a merchant; this is not necessary to the plot, since Brian's main and effective disguise is that of a beggar, and the account of Brian's base in Southampton, already in Lawman's time a major port, with a detailed description of the cellar in which he conceals his stock, are quite irrelevant but intriguing details, perhaps a touch of realism to please the patron. Another possibility is that the poem was written with an old soldier in mind: when Arthur has conquered Gaul he sends his veteran soldiers home to retirement, to pray for the undoubted sins their martial life-style will have led them to commit (L 12029–39): his command that they should love God so as to deserve Paradise is not in Wace (W 10135–8). There may also be a mild admonition to young men in his audience when Lawman suggests that Carrais drew his army from those who refused to stay at home and work (L 5270–1); in contrast to the neglect with which daughters were often treated, Lawman insists that Ebrauc's thirty daughters were all well clothed and cared for (L 1362). The poem could have belonged to a family.

There is, then, an enigma about Lawman's status, audience and aims which is partly resolved if we accept MS O, line 3, and assume that he was the chaplain to a household, perhaps tutor to the sons of the family, and that parts of the book might be read aloud to them, while others could be read to the head of the household (or handed over to him if he was literate). There was already something of the compendium in Geoffrey's original work, and Lawman broadened its scope even further, even catering for women and young people in the readership. Clearly he had been reading the romances which had been produced in the seventy-odd years since Geoffrey wrote, and in his presentation of the story of Brian, Lawman highlights even more than Wace the romance motifs and themes. In the latter part of his poem especially, Lawman makes frequent use of the romance narrative transition 'now let us turn to'. This allusion to romance techniques, together with Lawman's rather clumsy attempt to deal with female fashion in the account of Arthur's Crown-wearing at Caerleon, the generally compassionate tone of much of the narrative, and his enhancement of the women characters, make it not impossible that he wrote with some particular women in mind; even the apparently disparaging comment on women's ingenuity which he offers in speaking of Gornoille would not be out of place in a family setting, where it becomes a piece of friendly banter. The noticeably moralising tone of many of Lawman's comments would fit this family setting, as would the generally didactic colouring of the material. Lawman's main contribution to the story of Britain is to present a picture of 'merry Britain' where law and order create a world in which populations thrive and society achieves stability and security. His Arthur is one of many lawgivers, who hands on the tradition he inherited to his successor, and his Gawain, markedly distinct from the source character, praises the delights of God-given peace, when men do better deeds (L 12457).

Lawman's own interest in the law is apparent from his allusions to laws and law-makers. In Geoffrey's narrative there were already many references to law, most notably in the accounts of Dunwallo Molmutius and of the great law-giver Queen Marcia; these reflect Geoffrey's Norman interest in government and also his aim of gaining support from the aristocracy, especially Robert of Gloucester and the Empress Matilda. The many women in Geoffrey's work who take the throne or who are instrumental in running affairs are probably part of Geoffrey's political message in support of Matilda's cause. In his version, Lawman enhances this emphasis on the organisation of society, and it is even possible that he worked in some way with legal transactions or records: perhaps his name 'Lawman' is not in fact his given name but a cognomen, reflecting his interest in the past and its customs (*MED* s.v. *laue* 9 b. 'national custom'); its spelling may well be a deliberate evocation of the OE form of this title, rather than 'Scandinavian', as Tatlock maintains (*Legendary History*, p. 529). Perhaps this spelling was Lawman's deliberate imitation of the Anglo-Saxon form of the word: the OE term *laʒmann*, probably a late loan from Norse *lǫgmaðr*, was used in the very specialised senses of 'one of [?twelve] permanent 'judges' in the five boroughs of the Danelaw, and also, in the tenth century *Ordinance of the Dunsætas* (see *OED* s.v. *lawman*), of the 'finders of law', six experts in Welsh law and six in English in the border region of rural Hereford called 'Archenfield'. But probably in more general use a *law-man* was 'one of a number of local magistrates administering justice in a borough or town' (*MED* s.v. *laue-man*); three men of the thirteenth century are on record with 'Lawman' as a surname, and the *MED* cites Lawman's own name as an instance of the cognomen. Paul Brand has explained (in a private communication) that we know little of early thirteenth century local courts: the 'suitors' to manorial courts, such as that at Martley, or the hundred courts (in Lawman's area this was Dodingtree) were experienced in the unwritten customs of the land. Such men were important receptacles of knowledge, since little written law as such was in force in England *c*1200; it was Magna Carta in 1215 which set the mark for the later thirteenth century preservation of law in its original form. But if 'Lawman' was an honorary title, it must have acquired the familiarity of a personal name or 'Lawman' would not have asked for prayers for his soul under this name.

Lawman's Verse Style

In return for writing his poem Lawman expected gratitude and payment in the form of prayers from readers who did not know him personally; in other words, he expected to be read by posterity. He had written a long poem which he assumed would have a lasting appeal.

He had every reason for his self-confidence: the *Brut* is a well constructed narrative. Its episodes, discrete units which probably constituted sections for an evening's reading (Barron-Le Saux, 'Narrative Art', 28), are presented at a controlled pace. His tone is more solemn than Wace's, and he frequently directs the action with a conventional 'voice-over' of somewhat trite but stern moralising; he attempts to lighten this with humour in rather poor taste (which perhaps appealed to some of his audience). Yet the characters' motives are not left obscure, nor does Lawman obtrude on their dilemmas to reduce them to the level of moral exempla. There is a delicate tact in his narrative method: if it is only occasionally that we see into characters' minds, as in the case of Androgeus, nevertheless people are often presented in close-up, and without the distancing effect of irony, which gives the narrative immediacy and dramatic power; this makes fully credible even outrageous events, like Uther's impersonation of Gorlois, or startling confrontations like Tonwen's appeal to her sons. By contrast, where the historical montage is moving much faster and the narrative is focussed on more distant views of a swift succession of events or actions, Lawman pinpoints salient features in a clearly visualised setting without clogging the pace with detail. He is especially good at the technique which allows the reader to 'follow the gaze' of his characters as they appraise their situation or re-live their past (for example, Brutus, and later Belinus, surveying their territory; Merlin's mother recalling her seduction; Brian and his sister encountering each other at Edwin's court).

The narrative mode of Lawman's poem is a compound of chronicle, romance, saint's life and sermon; in some sections the reader is especially conscious of romance procedures, and in the last fifth of the work hagiography is prominent. Several of Lawman's characters deliver sermons, and his lay leaders address their auditors using the oral techniques of an expert preacher. Lawman seems to have been familiar with the formal procedures of all four of these literary kinds. He has a certain number of set themes among which Ringbom identifies 'feasts' and 'voyages' (with the sub-theme 'arrivals'). To these may be added 'battle-conflict' and 'death'. When these themes recur, Lawman recounts them in formulaic diction, in phrases which are very similar but not necessarily identical in each occurrence. Nor are these 'formulaic' phrases confined to set pieces like battles; there are some 128 such 'epic formulas' which recur throughout the poem in roughly similar circumstances, few if any deriving from Old English, but all with that kind of 'archaic dignity' which Lawman must have considered appropriate to his material.

In addition, Lawman gives his tone epic dignity by using compounds; there are over 400 compound nouns in the *Brut*, only about 50 of them Old English poetic compounds, and many composed by Lawman himself, it seems, to convey two major topics: warfare and 'the people'. He also has a number of formulas denoting sub-themes, on the effects of warfare: notably, the cut and thrust of swords, the breaking of shields and armour, and the falling of the dead and the shedding of blood. Lawman has been called bloodthirsty and savage, perhaps because these phrases seem to occur so often. Yet in fact he abbreviates the high point of Geoffrey's narrative, Arthur's war against the Emperor of Rome, and he cuts down battles and the technicalities of warfare (Le Saux, *Sources*, 33, 42). Although there are over thirty occurrences of the formula 'the fated/dead fell there', this is no gloating over gore, but rather, as it recurs it becomes a world-weary acknowledgement of the effects of human aggression. In battle description the formulas operate as a distancing device: malice and mortality are an unvarying element in human history; the tone is one of sadness rather than exultation. Far from rejoicing in martial heroism, except where pagans or traitors are being finished off, Lawman's verse technique undercuts these achievements by making each battle sound very like the last. The only obvious difference may well be the rousing speech which precedes the fight, where he does make distinction, for example, between the stirring rhetoric of Arthur and the crude threats of the emperor.

There is an archaic resonance in Lawman's diction which derives from his use of phrases which are found in Old English prose and poetry; presumably Lawman has imported some of these as literary loans, not necessarily from the Old English works in which they are now extant, but from similar works which he may well have read in some monastic library, perhaps in Worcester Cathedral. Such words as *geddian* 'to speak' (L 1676, cf. *Beowulf* 1253) and poetic compounds like *mod-kare* (L 1556, cf. *Beow* 3553) and *sæ-werie* (L 2306 cf. *Beow: sæ-mēþe*) or *wunsele* (L 7836, 8784; cf. *Beow* 1383) were presumably not in everyday speech, but it is possible that such phrases as *hine braeid sæc* (L 3324, cf. ASC s.a. 1003 *gebræde he hine seocne*) and Lawman's favourite *sæht and sibbe* (cf. ACS s.a. 1140 *sib and sæhte*) could have been in colloquial use, at least in the vocabulary of the English story-teller. More difficult to explain are the verbal and situational parallels between L 13802–13804 and *The Battle of Maldon* (see Notes), and the presence of a passage very reminiscent of Wulfstan's most famous sermon in L 2013–18; Madden and others see a strong resemblance between the Old English *Battle of Brunanburh* and Lawman's diction. Whether or not there are conscious loans from Old English texts, such traditional use of language gives an antique flavour to the *Brut* (Stanley, 'Antiquarian Sentiments', 27–30).

The Arthurian section of Lawman's *Brut* is especially noted for its 'long-tailed' or epic similes. There are eight of these in the section covering the war with the Saxons and especially the battle of Bath. Although it has been suggested that Lawman must have used a particular source for this section (Davies, 'Laȝamon's Similes'), these similes are merely longer than others which occur throughout the poem and all resemble instances in both Geoffrey and Wace in which a hero is likened to a fierce animal and his foes to hunted prey (see Le Saux *Sources*, 206–13); moreover, extended similes even more elaborate than this are a feature of Latin heroic poetry of the late twelfth and early thirteenth centuries, in works known or dedicated to patrons on both sides of the English Channel; they also feature, of course, in Virgil and Statius, who were the inspiration of those medieval Latin poets (Salter, *E&I*, 63–5). Like his use of formula and poetic compound, Lawman's similes are a stylistic enhancement of his theme.

All these stylistic features serve to highlight Lawman's main interest: people. His most impressive style demonstrates his admiration for great leaders, but by less flamboyant means he can also show a sensitive awareness of the special problems of women. But the world of artefacts interests him less: he omits the technical details of siege-warfare, musical instruments, ships under sail, and courtly past-times like gambling, which Wace controls with narrative skill and decorum. Perhaps Lawman did not know the equivalent terms in English; perhaps the concepts were not always familiar to his audience; perhaps borrowing Wace's terms would have been the only way of conveying his substance, and the French words would have clashed with his designedly 'English' lexis. Perhaps his audience would simply not have been interested.

Whereas in the later thirteenth and fourteenth centuries writers gave their work a courtly tone by using loan-words taken over from French, Lawman uses very few French-derived words in the *Brut*, even though he was translating from a French poem: Madden counted under 50 words of French origin in MS C, and no more than 70 in the MS O adaptation (*Brut* I, xxii, and notes 3 and 4; Serjeantson, *History of Foreign Words*, pp. 117–18). Quite possibly, Lawman considered using French terms for that technical detail and courtly settings would clog the narrative and slow the pace and so distract from his theme, the people of this island.

Lawman has a different concept of 'Britain' from Geoffrey and Wace. Geoffrey inverts the accepted view of England as seen from the standpoint of English history, by placing the English in the novel rôle of interrupters rather than initiators of political history; Wace also sees British history as a sequence of successive political supremacies, but Lawman's emphasis is on continuity. He is more interested in the 'ordinary people' (cf. Le Saux, *Sources*, p. 80), the bedrock of the population which changes far less than the rulers. This he demonstrates in narrative content and technique, and in diction. His rulers constantly confer with their subjects at the 'hustings', a kind of informally constituted parliament not confined to the upper classes (Gillespy, 'Comparative Study', p. 398–401; Le Saux *Sources*, p. 225). We find repeatedly in the *Brut* that Lawman adds direct speech to Wace's narrative: his characters confer and consult. Prominent in the narrative method of the *Brut* is the 'messenger theme', whereby Lawman adds the figure of a messenger who moves between two characters and gives a verbal report, in place of Wace's bald statement that information was given. This has the effect of showing that ordinary people are essential even in the high enterprises of the great (Le Saux, *Sources*, pp. 48–9). Lawman's use of the word *leod(e)* is ambiguous: the word can mean 'men', 'people' or, in Lawman's use, 'the land, nation'. The concept of an 'English' nationhood developed steadily from the loss of Normandy in 1204, and in his use of this word Lawman seems to evince a sense of national identity: the beautiful country promised to Brutus and surveyed by him with delight is home for a group of peoples whose identity it epitomises; that identity is threatened by invaders, and it is invasion and civil war rather than martial prowess for its own sake on which Lawman focusses in his battle-scenes; if there is a 'hero-figure' in the *Brut* it is 'this land' rather than any individual. The 'land' is a metonymic expression for everything which is 'us' to Lawman and his audience; great rulers enhance its people's reputation and protect them, evil ones and traitors prey off the populace or bring in alien favourites. Lawman is not interested, for example, in Wace's explanation of Modred's attitude to Arthur nor in his remorse (W 13054, 13073–6): his actions betray and endanger the people, and Lawman simply condemns him outright (L 12728–34; 13925).

Lawman's alliterative technique has strong affinities with the alliterative prose of homilists like Ælfric of Eynsham (Frankis, 'English Sources'), and Wulfstan the writer of *Sermo Lupi*; indeed, there seems to be an echo of this sermon in Lawman's *Brut*. In addition, there are phrases and longer passages reminiscent of parts of the Anglo-Saxon Chronicle, of Ælfric's work, and perhaps of the

Blickling Homilies. There are two passages, prayers by Arthur and Gawain, which also seem to contain echoes of Old English religious verse (lines 12760–3 and 14077–8; see Le Saux, 213–17).

Already in Old English verse and rhythmic prose authors brought rhyme into play, and, especially after the first thousand lines, Lawman regularly produces the kind of full rhyme found in the OE *Rhyming Poem* and sporadically in texts like *The Battle of Maldon*. *The Proverbs of Alfred* is a twelfth-century poem which combines alliteration with rhymes in a manner very similar to Lawman's *Brut* (Salter, *E&I*, p. 54). Furthermore, Lawman utilises another word-echo device which derives from the rhetorical prose of the early Middle Ages: the matching of word-endings, particularly case-endings of declined words, a rhetorical device known as *similiter cadens* (cf. Madden, *Brut*, I, xxiv, n. 2). It is commonly said that Lawman wrote alliterative verse, and it is true that many of his half-lines are linked by alliteration. However, very many do not present this 'initial rhyme', but have either full rhyme in our sense, that is, the stem vowel and following consonant are identical, or have the 'closing rhyme' of identical or rhyming grammatical endings; for example 12626 *swein: þein* and 12684 *comen* (pret.pl.): *to hireden* (dat.sg.). Still more lines have an identical stem vowel in the two halves ('assonance') with *similar* consonants, that is liquids (*r, l*) or nasals (*n, m*); an example is 12609 *honden* ('hands'): *worden* ('words'), where the stem vowels *o* probably rhyme and the inflexions *-en* certainly do. Or, and this is something we would no longer consider rhyme, they have identical or nearly identical consonants with distinction of vowels: 12717 *stille: halle*; 12688 *londen: þusende*. The resulting verse is something between the long line of Old English verse, with medial caesura, and the short octosyllabic couplet of much French narrative verse. Madden printed the short lines individually, like couplets; Brook and Leslie, in the *EETS* edition on which this translation is based, followed editors of extracts from the *Brut* like Emerson, and Brandl and Zippel, and print long lines with medial caesura, with some 'short' lines where the scribes (or perhaps in some cases Lawman himself) did not write a full line.

Whatever presentation of the verse the editors use is not important: in the original Lawman must be read with ear rather than eye: the speaking voice, or perhaps one should say, the preaching voice, is dominant, with the natural intonation of colloquial English (Bennett, *ME Lit*, p. 83), even where the words are archaic or the construction grandiose. It is for this reason that I have tried to translate into the speech rhythms Lawman used, and tried wherever possible to echo his 'rhymes'. A prose rendering makes Lawman sound all too like Geoffrey of Monmouth, and inevitably misses some of Lawman's poetic fervour, his enthusiasm for human endeavour, that continuing ambition which created our past and will always fire great achievements – or indeed misfire into disasters, as Leir's father Bladud crashed when he tried to fly, and as Morpidus died when he took on a monster single-handed.

Lawman's Sense of History

Why Lawman should have chosen to present this exciting narrative of the deeds, and, in his version in particular, the words of ancient British men in an archaic idiom modelled on the language of their Saxon conquerors is something of a puzzle. In all likelihood he chose this old-fashioned form of the language because it was redolent of days gone by, and because those days represented a time when the Anglo-Saxons, like the ancient Britons before them, had had a flourishing culture, literate, administratively sound, and independent of the kind of foreign influence and organisation which had overtaken them with the arrival of the Normans. The Anglo-Saxons had used their own native language where the Norman tradition favoured Latin for many of the official records of Church and State, among them the annals and chronicles of monastic historians. The Anglo-Saxon Chronicle, begun under the auspices of King Alfred in the late ninth century, was kept up until the middle of the twelfth century in Peterborough, but had been discontinued (after being translated into Latin in some cases) in other centres. What Geoffrey of Monmouth did for the Britons in recording/inventing their past, Lawman continued by identifying the plight of the Britons under Saxon rule with the situation in England under the Normans, who antagonised the English by spurning their saints, traditions and language. He did this through his use of the older English tongue in its former role: historical record.

Geoffrey, Wace and Lawman were typical of the period of the high Middle Ages in their interest in the past, and particularly the pagan past; a similar tendency is at work in the activities of Snorri Sturluson in thirteenth century Iceland, and in Chaucer's tales with a classical and Celtic pagan setting. Against the backdrop of a belief system which does not automatically reward the good and punish the bad after death, the actions of men, for good or ill, take on new dimensions: people may act well because it serves their reputation or helps others; they may equally, however, choose to act selfishly with little expectation of reprisal, unless chance or a man of extreme courage appears to redress the balance – or to gain his own advantage from political chaos. Even the great (nominal) Christians like Arthur lived in a world threatened by pagan incursions, and in this they formed rôle-models for later Medieval Europe, threatened by Muslim invasion, from the south and west via North Africa and Spain in Lawman's time, and by 1260 a new threat was developing in the east, with the Ottomans in Turkey and the Tatars in Hungary.

But Lawman lacked the precise sense of structure which is clear in Geoffrey of Monmouth, who modelled his work on Bede and Caesar, and to some extent on the Old Testament. Geoffrey shows a nation emerging from one dominant individual, reaching its apogee, and declining largely because of the extradition of its best men and women to people Brittany, a European version of the Babylonian captivity of Israel, from which the Britons were still expecting a release, perhaps in the form of Arthur's Return. Wace does not share Geoffrey's chauvinistic concern with the British versus all other comers, but does exhibit the developing interest of the twelfth century in the significance of the individual and presents his characters against the background of social customs, leisure activities and artefacts. It is, inevitably, for the most part his own culture he depicts. Lawman is different again: since his principal interest in this shifting kaleidoscope of people, races and events is their common interest in the land itself, he suppresses specific detail by using formulaic expression. Even Geoffrey's hero Arthur is presented from the more distant perspective of his liegemen, who fear his anger, and of the weak, who seek his protection, and are kept in comfort and content in his retinue. Lawman's greatly expanded treatment of Arthur resembles the fuller accounts of the kings of Scandinavia, which developed at about the same time from synoptic histories of limited scope into long, imaginative rather than historical biographies: 'the vertical narrow run of historical sequence broadens into a fuller presentation' (Einar Sveinsson, *Njáls saga* [Lincoln, Nebraska, 1971]); Lawman was following a current trend in Northern Europe.

Lawman's knowledge of history was less extensive than Geoffrey's and Wace's. Although he claims to have used Bede's *Ecclesiastical History*, he seems not to have used it even for the story of Pope Gregory and Saint Augustine's Conversion of England; apart from Wace, he claims one other source, an unidentified book which he ascribes to Albin and Augustine. This may have been the original Latin version of Bede's *Historia,* for which Albin supplied Bede with material and in which Augustine is the main character in Book I; if so, it was a book he did not (could not?) read, or he would have described it more accurately (but see notes to lines 16–19). Lawman based his *Brut* on Wace's *Roman,* which he translated by taking up large amounts of copy and rendering it freehand, largely from memory. Sometimes he re-orders Wace's text, or omits matter (Tatlock, *Legendary History* p. 489), and occasionally mistranslates (Madden, *Brut,* I, xiv, n. 3), but most of the time he amplifies, by adding speeches and episodes, and making his account more emphatic, explicit and solemn than Wace's (Le Saux, *Sources,* pp. 42–58). He may also have added some material from local legends of saints like Oswald and Augustine, and may perhaps have found someone to translate for him the Welsh triadic poems and perhaps the *Armes Prydein.* Lawman is not a historiographer, and the mention of Bede's name near the beginning is the closest he gets to history. And yet there is a historical relevance in Lawman's work: it lies in his emphases, what he finds significant in his material: the mores of his own times and his sense of the importance of the family and kinship group. His sense of 'England' is made all the more relevant by the loss of Normandy to the French in 1204, forcing the Anglo-Norman magnates to give up their lands in Normandy if they wished to remain in England.

Lawman's Importance and his Achievement

It was Archbishop Usher who first read Lawman in post-medieval times: in 1639 he referred to the names in Lawman's account of the conversion of Lucius's Britain. Lawman was mentioned or quoted about ten times in the eighteenth and nineteenth centuries, but it was Madden's splendid three-volume edition in 1847 which made the whole text available to post-medieval readers. It was also Madden who emphasised the linguistic importance of Lawman's poem, to some extent over-insisting on the early ('Semi-Saxon') state of the English language pre-1230 and minutely examining and correcting in footnotes and Appendix the grammatical features of the language of Lawman's scribes.

Articles on Lawman's language are still appearing, and to some extent this has distracted attention from his creative imagination, his control of narrative pace, ability to select salient details of the action from his source(s) and to give a recognisably 'human', often domestic, setting for the narrative, particularly in the more extended episodes such as Locrin's affair with Astrild, Cordoille and Leir, Brennes and Belinus, Cassibellaune, Ursula's Fate, Uther's seduction of Ygerne, and St Augustine. Many of these episodes are much expanded from Wace, and there are incidents which do not appear in Wace at all.

Especially significant are the 'supernatural' additions in the Arthurian section: the fairies who attend Arthur's birth, the elvish smith who made Arthur's corslet, the marvels of Britain, Arthur's nightmare about Modred, and the mysterious Argante and the boat with two women in it which appears at his end to take him to Avalon. Merlin figures more prominently than in Wace: he is sent for twice, to aid Aurelius and later to help Uther, and Lawman continues to refer to Merlin's prophecies as a device to enhance Arthur's status, after Merlin has disappeared from the narrative, at Arthur's birth, the founding of the Round Table, before the Roman War and at his death. Wace candidly refuses to include the Prophecies in his translation, and only alludes to them at Arthur's death, which he claims Merlin had said would be doubtful. Lawman cannot have derived his knowledge of the Prophecies of Merlin from Wace.

In the first half of this century critical opinion, following Imelmann, maintained that Lawman's *Brut* derived immediately from an expanded version of Wace's *Roman de Brut* to which material had been added from Gaimar's lost 'History of the Britons'. Until Visser's *Vindication* (1935), Lawman was regarded as a mere translator. But Madden, and recently Le Saux, have suggested that Lawman used other materials, both written and oral, for his sources. He took from Celtic oral tale the account of Taliesin and probably his expanded treatment of Merlin. He seems to have known Geoffrey of Monmouth, or at least the Prophecies of Merlin, perhaps in an Anglo-Norman version, and may have read Geoffrey's late work, the *Vita Merlini* ('Life of Merlin'; Le Saux, *Sources*, p. 110–16). He talks of books he has found on Dunwallo and on the origin of the name Walbrook, the state of Caerleon, and Carric's change of name. He may indeed have looked at many books, yet in the newly literate world of twelfth and thirteenth century vernacular poetry, it had become conventional for a writer of romance to talk of the books which were his source, and the ethos and the style of vernacular romance have influenced Lawman strongly, especially in the later sections of his work, from Constance to Cadwalader.

It is now generally considered that Lawman was a creative artist who may have 'compiled' his material from various Welsh, French, English and Latin sources, both oral and written; in fact, critical opinion has swung to another extreme, of regarding Lawman as a trash-bin rummager for any old bits of fact and fiction. Perhaps it is judicious to regard him as a sensitive writer who invented a great deal of his narrative by subconscious associations and by conscious derivation from narrative commonplaces.

However much Lawman may have derived from sources other than Wace, which today can only be guessed at, it remains true that his presentation of his material often shows the mark of genius. The *Brut* is both an interesting picture of how an educated man in the early thirteenth-century thought of his nation's past, and a illuminating portrait of the world of the thirteenth century itself. Lawman was a cleric who wrote a translation of a pseudo-history in a strangely contrived idiolect, yet it is not as cleric, historian or grammarian that he is really to be appreciated, but as a poet of genial pragmatism; his sternness is part of his age: in lawless times *justise* meant physical punishment as well as justice and authority. He was the first poet to tell of Arthur and the British past in English, and as far as we know the first poet to write a long narrative poem in English since the Norman conquest, and one of the first to bring the secular literature of the French aristocrats to the English. He is best read as a writer who knew how to provide an instructive message for the youth of his age out of the lessons of the past, yet who never forgot that his narrative (*spell*) was also for entertainment.

A Note on the Translation

Lawman's *Brut* is extant in two manuscripts, both formerly in the collection owned by Sir Robert Cotton, and both now in the British Library. The more complete is BL MS Cotton Caligula A ix, [C], from which this translation has been made. The other manuscript, BL Cotton Otho C xiii, [O], is incomplete today because it was badly damaged in the fire at Ashburnham House in 1731, but has always been shorter than the Caligula text: from the outset it was prepared as an abridgment of Lawman's original. Both manuscripts derive from a shared ancestor which had already acquired erroneous readings, but presumably MS C resembles Lawman's original better than MS O, and I have therefore translated this, the longer version of the *Brut*. The errors and inadvertent omissions by the scribes in MS C can sometimes be corrected by reference to MS O; these emendations are enclosed in square brackets in the translation, and in such cases the readings of both C and O are listed in the *Emendations*.

A translator who wished to reproduce in modern English stylistic effects to match Lawman's would have to imitate Pope's poetic diction, Spenser's archaic forms, and Hopkins's compound words, while at the same time capturing the idioms and rhythms of colloquial speech in the racier outbursts of the characters and some of the narrator's more intimate observations. The modern requirement of consistency of tone makes such a mode of presentation impossible. I have left some of the inversions of object and verb which Lawman regularly uses, to indicate the artificial nature of his formal style. I have retained as much as was practical of his rhyme and alliteration, which Lawman seems to have used not for decorative effect but as aids to comprehension when the work was read aloud, much as similar devices had done in Ælfric's sermons two hundred years earlier, and also perhaps to encourage accurate copying, by blocking scribes' attempts at rewriting and simplifying lines in transmission. The alliteration and rhyme in the original speed rather than impede the flow of the narrative, and occasionally provide opportunity for witty contrast and pun, as in the joke about Englishmen's tails (line 14772), and the savage pun on *iqueme* and *aquele* in line 8807. Modern English is far less inflected than Lawman's and the 'light rhyme' on identical inflexional endings, which he often used to give balance, is impossible, although sometimes I have tried to echo it by matching form-words such as prepositions or pronouns in similar clauses but without rhyme (e.g. 4765 *about it: all of it*), or I have used 'eye-rhyme' (489 *killed: kindred*, 539 *have: live*). But rather more often I have used sound echo which will only be obvious if the reader remembers the sound rather than the appearance of the words (for example, 6904 *learn: worthy*).

A translator into modern English cannot use alternative pronunciations, whereas Lawman can rhyme *man* with *Lateran* and *mon* with *on*; we are also unaware of the licence by which Lawman (like other Middle English writers) regards *long* and *lond/land* as a rhyme. A close (-ish) translation cannot match all the aural devices Lawman uses, and I have tried simply to give an indication of the kind of sound pattern he creates; after the first few hundred lines he settles into a fairly regular metre in which the end of the second half of the long line echoes the end of the first half more times than not (even if that echo is confined to a single phoneme: [*i*] in 8312 *king: him*, and [*n*] in 8323 *mon*: *Drihten*), unless additional sound-echo in the form of alliteration is present elsewhere in the line. Often Lawman uses both end-rhyme and alliteration, and I have tried to give an impression of this, and of the variation in his line lengths.

It was to give some idea of the rich aural effects in Lawman's *Brut* that I chose to make a 'verse' translation, but I have tried not to depart too far from the sense of the original merely for the sake of metre; this is not, however, in any sense a close translation which can be used as a crib.

The author of the *Brut* is usually known as Laȝamon in England, and as Lawman, its modern equivalent, in America. He seems to have chosen an archaic spelling for his name (or title) reminiscent of the Old English etymon *laȝu* (pl. *laȝa*) 'law'. 'Layamon' is an inaccurate version of his name, often used by modern critics because the special symbol 'yogh' does not occur in modern printers' founts and 'y' is one of its modern equivalents; in this word, however, the modern equivalent is 'w', giving 'Lawemon', and I have further modernised his name to 'Lawman'. His contemporaries would probably have pronounced it 'Lau-a-mon', the first syllable like *-lou-* in 'loud', with a medial vowel resembling the unstressed indefinite article 'a'.

Queen Mary and   R. S. Allen
Westfield College,
June 1990

BIBLIOGRAPHY

Complete editions of Lawman's *Brut*

Laȝamon's 'Brut', or Chronicle of Britain: A Poetical Semi-Saxon Paraphrase of *The Brut of Wace*, ed. Sir Frederick Madden (London, 1847¹; Osnabrück, 1967²); 3 vols.

Laȝamon: Brut, edited from British Museum MS. Cotton Caligula A.ix and British Museum MS. Cotton Otho C. xiii, ed. G. L. Brook and R. F. Leslie, *EETS* OS 250, 277 (1963, 1978); 2 vols.

Selections

Laȝamon's Arthur: The Arthurian Section of Laȝamon's 'Brut', ed. and trans. W. R. J. Barron and S. C. Weinberg (Harlow: Longman, 1989). [Lines 9229–14297, with facing-page translation, Introd. and Notes].

Layamon's 'Brut': Selections, ed. J. Hall (Oxford, 1924). [Lawman; Leir; Brennes and Belin: conquest of Rome; Merlin and Stonehenge; Arthur and Childric; The Round Table; Arthur's Dream; Gurmund; Brian; Cadwalader. Notes, Glossary]

Selections from Laȝamon's 'Brut', ed. G. L. Brook (Oxford: Clarendon Press, 1963); rev. John Levitt (University of Exeter, 1983²). [Arthur's Begetting, Early Reign; Origin of Roman War; The Morte; Notes, Glossary, Introduction by C. S. Lewis]

Extracts included in anthologies

Alexander, M., and F. Riddy, eds., *The Middle Ages* (700–1550) Macmillan Anthologies of English Literature, I (London, 1989), p. 121–9. [Arthur's Death, from Brook].

Bennett, J. A. W., and G. V. Smithers, eds., *Early Middle English Verse and Prose* (Oxford, 1966). [Arthur's Dream; Notes, Glossary].

Brandl, A., and O. Zippel, *Middle English Reader* (Berlin, 1916). [Opening; Modred's Treason; Arthur's Last Battle: MS C, (also O variants), Wace and Geoffrey].

Dickins, B., and R. M. Wilson, eds., *Early Middle English Texts*

(London, 1951). [245 lines: Opening (MSS C & O), and five short extracts from Arthurian section; Notes, Glossary].

Emerson, O. F., *A Middle English Reader* (London, 1929). [Arthur's Last Battle; glossary, some notes].

Hall, Joseph, *Selections from Middle English 1130–1250* (Oxford, 1920), 2 vols. [Text vol. i: Vortigern and Rowena; Notes vol. ii, pp. 450–79].

Garbáty, T. J., *Medieval English Literature* (Lexington, 1984). [Opening; Murder of Gracien; Birth of Arthur, Fairy Gifts; Plot against Uther; Arthur Battles the forces of Colgrim; Childric; Battle of Bath; Round Table; Giant of Brittany; Lucius; Arthur's Dream; Last Battle; Marginal Gloss].

Kaiser, R., *Medieval English* (Berlin, 1958³), pp. 332–40. [Opening, Brutus, Bladud and Leir, Godlac, Round Table, Arthur's Death, Conclusion; some readings from O].

Mätzner, E., *Altenglische Sprachproben* (Berlin, 1867): I, pp. 19–39.

Morris, R. and W. W. Skeat, *Specimens of Early English* (Oxford, 1898²). [Hengest and Horsa, pp. 64–86; notes p. 309].

Translation

Eugene Mason, *Wace and Layamon: Arthurian Chronicles*, Translated, with an Introduction by Gwyn Jones, Everyman's Library 578 (London: Dent, 1962²). [Trans. of MS C Lawman's *Brut* lines 6388–14297, from Madden, with Wace's *Brut*, lines 6424–13298b trans. from Bibliothèque Nationale MS, fonds français 1416].

Lawmans's source material and other chronicles

WACE
Le Roman de Brut de Wace, ed. Ivor Arnold, S.A.T.F. (Paris, 1938, 1940); 2 vols.

GEOFFREY OF MONMOUTH:
Geoffrey of Monmouth: The History of the Kings of Britain, trans. Lewis Thorpe (Harmondsworth: Penguin, 1966).

The Historia Regum Britanniae of Geoffrey of Monmouth, I, Bern MS 568, II, First Variant Version ed. Neil Wright (Cambridge: D. S. Brewer, 1985, 1987).

Geoffrey of Monmouth: A Variant Version ed. Jacob Hammer (Cambridge, Mass., 1951).

Hanning, Robert W., *The Vision of History in Early Britain from Gildas to Geoffrey* (New York: Columbia U. P., 1960).

ANGLO-SAXON:
Bede: A History of the English Church and People, trans. Leo Sherley-Price, rev. E. Latham (Harmondsworth: Penguin, 1968²).
The Anglo-Saxon Chronicle, trans. G. N. Garmonsway, Everyman's Library 624 (London: Dent, 1972²).

MIDDLE ENGLISH
The Chronicle of Robert Manning of Brunne, 1338, ed. F. J. Furnivall (London, 1887); 2 vols.

Information on Lawman's language and metre

Amodio, Mark C., 'Laȝamon's Anglo–Saxon Lexicon and Diction', *Poetica*, 28 (1988), 48–59.
Blake, Norman 'Rhythmical Alliteration', Modern Philosophy, 67 (1969), 118–24.
Friedlander, C. van D., 'Early Middle English Accentual Verse', *MP*, 76 (1979), pp. 219–30.
Glowka, A.W., 'Prosodic Decorum in Laȝamon's *Brut*, *Poetica* 18, (1984), 40–53.
Jack, G., 'Relative Pronouns in Laȝamon's *Brut*, *LeedsSE*, XIX, (1988), pp.31–66.
Le Saux, F., 'Transition or Rejection? French Cultural concepts in Layamon's *Brut*', Summary of Paper read at 15th International Arthurian Congress, *BBIAS*, XL, (1988), pp. 341–2.
Noble, J., 'Variation in Laȝamon's *Brut*', *NM*, 85 (1984), pp. 92–4.
——'The Larger Rhetorical Patterns in Laȝamon's *Brut*', *English Studies in Canada*, 11 (1985), 263–72.
Sauer, H., 'Laȝamon's Compound Nouns and their Morphology', in *Historical Semantics, Historical World-Formation*, ed. J. Fisiak (Berlin, 1985), pp. 483–532.
Serjeantson, M., *A History of Foreign Words in English* (London, 1935).
Tatlock, J. S. P., 'Epic Formulas, especially in Laȝamon', *PMLA*, 38 (1923), 494–529.
——'Layamon's Poetic Style and its Relations', The Manly Anniversary Studies in Language and Literature (Chicago: Univ. of Chicago Press, 1923), 3–11.

Background and reference

Alcock, L., *Arthur's Britain* (Harmondsworth: Penguin, 1971).
Blenner-Hassett, R., *A Study of the Place-Names in Lawman's 'Brut'* (Stanford University Pubs. 1950); Language and Literature, 9.
Ekwall, E., *The Concise Dictionary of English Place-Names* (Oxford, 1960⁴).

Poole, A. L., *From Domesday Book to Magna Carta, 1087–1216*: Oxford History of England III (Oxford, 1955²). [For information on Lawman's own time].

Literary and source studies

Allen, R. S., 'Female Perspectives in Romance and History', in M. Mills et al., eds, *Romance in Medieval England* (Cambridge: D. S. Brewer, 1991), 133–47.

——'"Long is Ever": the Cassibell aunus Episode in Three Versions of the "Brut"', *New Comparison*, 12 (1991:2).

Barron, W. R. J., *English Medieval Romance*, Longman Literature in English Series (London, 1987), pp. 134–7.

Barron, W. R. J., and F. Le Saux, 'Two Aspects of Laȝamon's Narrative Art', *Arthurian Literature* ix (Cambridge: D. S. Brewer, 1989), pp. 25–56.

Bennett, J. A. W., *Middle English Literature*, ed. and completed by Douglas Gray (Oxford, 1986), pp. 68–89.

Brewer, D., *English Gothic Literature*, Macmillan History of Literature (London, 1983), pp. 9–14.

Davies, H. S., 'Layamon's Similes', *RES* (n.s.) 11 (1960), pp. 129–42.

Donoghue, Daniel, 'Laȝamon's Ambivalence', *Speculum* 65 (1990, 537–63).

——'Animals Tethered to King Arthur's Rise and Fall: Imagery and Structure in Lawman's *Brut*', Mid-Hudson Language Studies, 6 (1983), 19–27.

Everett, D., 'Laȝamon and the Earliest Middle English Alliterative Verse', *Essays on Middle English Literature* (Oxford, 1955), pp. 28–45.

Frankis, P. J., 'Laȝamon's English Sources', in *J. R. R. Tolkien, Poet and Storyteller: Essays in Memoriam*, ed. M. Salu (Ithaca, N.Y., 1979).

Gillespy, F. L., 'Layamon's *Brut*: A Comparative Study in Narrative Art', *University of California Publications in Modern Philosophy*, 3 (1916), pp. 361–510.

Imelmann, Rudolf, *Laȝamon: Versuch über seine Quellen* (Berlin, 1906).

Johnson, Lesley, 'Tracking Laȝamon's *Brut*', *Leeds Studies in English* (n.s.) 22 (1991), 139–165.

Keith, W. T., 'Layamon's *Brut*: The Literary Differences between the Two Texts', *Medium Ævum* 29 (1960), pp. 161–72.

Kirby, I., 'Angles and Saxons in Laȝamon's *Brut*', *SN*, 26 (1964), pp. 51–62.

Le Saux, F., *Laȝamon's Brut: The Poem and its Sources*, Arthurian Studies xix (Woodbridge: D. S. Brewer, 1989).

——'Laȝamon's Welsh Sources', *English Studies*, 67 (1986), 385–93.

Lewis, C. S., 'The Genesis of a Medieval Book', in *Studies in Medieval and Renaissance Literature*, ed. W. Hooper (Cambridge, 1969), pp. 18–33.

Loomis, R. S., *Arthurian Literature in the Middle Ages* (Oxford, 1959), pp. 104–11.

Morris, R., *The Character of King Arthur in Medieval Literature*, Arthurian Studies iv (Cambridge: D. S. Brewer, 1982).

Pearsall, D., *Old and Middle English Poetry* (London, 1977), pp. 80–1, 108–12.

Pilch, H., *Laȝamons Brut: Eine Literarische Studie* (Heidelberg, 1960).

Ringbom, Håkan, *Studies in the Narrative Technique of 'Beowulf' and Lawman's 'Brut'* (Åbo, 1968).

Salter, Elizabeth, *English and International: Studies in the Literature, Art and Patronage of Medieval England* (Cambridge, 1988), pp. 48–70.

Schirmer, W., 'Layamon's *Brut*', *MHRA* (1957), pp. 15–27.

Shichtman, Martin B., 'Gawain in Wace and Laȝamon: a Case of Metahistorical Evolution', in *Medieval Texts and Contemporary Readers*, ed. L. A. Finke and M. B. Shichtman (Ithaca, 1987), pp. 103–19.

Stanley, E. G., 'The Date of Laȝamon's Brut, *N&Q*, 213 (1968), pp. 85–8.

——'Laȝamon's Antiquarian Sentiments', *MÆ*, 38 (1969), pp. 23–37.

Swanton, M., *English Literature Before Chaucer*, Longman Literature in English Series (London, 1987), pp. 175–86.

Visser, G. J., *Laȝamon: An Attempt at Vindication* (Utrecht, 1935).

Willard, R., 'Laȝamon in the 17th and 18th Centuries', *Texas Studies in English*, 27 (1948), 239–78.

Wyld, H. C., 'Layamon as an English Poet', *RES*, 6 (1930), pp. 1–30.

The Text

*Signals a note in the NOTES TO THE TEXT.

†Signals an emendation entered within square brackets, which is explained in the EMENDATIONS TO THE CALIGULA MS.

THE HISTORY OF THE BRITISH
from MS. Cotton Caligula A.ix

There was a priest living here, who was known as
    Lawman;[*]   LAWMAN
He was the son of Liefnoth – the Lord have mercy on him! [*]
He had a living at **Areley**, at a lovely church there,
Upon the River Severn bank – splendid he found it –
Right beside Redstone, where he recited his Missal.
    There came to his mind a most splendid idea,
That he would tell of England's outstanding men:
What each had as name and from what place they came,
Those earliest owners of this our England,
After the great Flood that came from the Lord God,   10
Which killed all living creatures that it met with here,
Saving Noah and Shem, Japhet and Ham,
And all their four wives who were on the Ark with them.
    Lawman went travelling the length of this whole land,
And secured the splendid book which he took as source-text:
He took up the 'English Book' which Saint **Bede** had created, [*]
A second he took in Latin created by Saint Albin,
And our dear Augustine who brought the Christian faith in,
A book he took as third source, and set by this his whole course:
A French cleric composed it,   20
Wace was what they called him, and very well he wrote it,
And he gave it to her highness, Eleanor of Aquitania;
She was the queen of Henry, the king of such high fame.
Lawman laid out these books, and he leafed through them,
Gazing at them gratefully – the Lord be gracious to him!
Quill pens he clutched in fingers, composing on his parchment,
And the more reliable versions he recorded,
Compressing those three texts into one complete book.
Now Lawman makes entreaty to each and every good man
(For almighty God's sake)[†]   30

I

Who may read this book and learn its revelations,
That in the form prescribed he should recite the set of prayers
For Lawman's father's soul, who first gave him being,
And for his mother's soul who bore him as a male-child,
And lastly for his own soul, that it may be the safer. Amen.
   Now speaks with inspiration he who lived as priest,
Exactly as the book explains, which he took as example.

WHEN the Greeks had tragically made conquest of Troy-town,
Laying the land waste, eliminating people,
And all for the avenging of **Menelaus's** queen,   40
(She was named **Helena**, alien woman,
Whom **Paris Alexander** with practised treason won):*
For her in a single day one hundred thousand died.
Out of the fighting, which was most ferocious,
Aeneas the Duke with anguish escaped;   AENEAS
He had but the one son who with him was salvaged,
– **Ascanius** he was known as – he had no children more.
And this Duke with his dependents to the sea withdrew:
With family and retainers who followed the Duke there,
With people and property which he led to the seashore,   50
Twenty great shiploads he gathered and filled there,
And the ships went far and wide across the wintry sea.
From storms and sharp weather they suffered much torment,
And with the greatest trouble they managed to make landfall:
In Italy they came up on land, where in our time now Rome stands;
Not for many years beneath the sun was Rome as yet won.
And now the Duke Aeneas with all his dependents
Had forayed afar across that far flood,
Doubled round many headlands, lacked all decision.
In Italy he came ashore, which gave him much comfort,   60
In that land he found much food, and behaved there most honour-
    ably,
And with tribute and with treasure, he treated for peace.
In the Tiber he went to land, where sea washes that stream,
Very close to that same spot where now Rome itself stands.
The king of that land bore the name of **Latinus**:
Noble was he and wealthy and in counsels most wise,
By age then encumbered (according to God's wish).
   There Aeneas came and the aged king he greeted,
Who received him respectfully, with all his retainers.

Much land he gave him, and of more made promise,   70
Along all the sea-coast, far and wide stretching;
The queen felt anxiety but had to allow it.
The king had but one daughter, and he loved her most dearly:
To Aeneas he betrothed her, to have as his wife,
And after his reign's end, all his own royal lands,
For he had not a single son, the sadder were his feelings;
The young girl was called **Lavinia** – she would later be the people's
    queen –
Lovely was the lady, and likeable to all men.
But there was a man named **Turnus** who was Duke of Tuscany,
And he loved that fair one much, and proferred her his faith
That he would wish to have her as his own most high queen.   81
Then there came news to him (as far and wide was known)
That the king Latinus had given his Lavinia,
His most beloved daughter, to Aeneas as a bride.
Then Turnus was grief-struck and gloomy in his spirit,
For he had very deeply loved her and promised loyal affection.
Turnus started warfare, he was tortured by the insult,†
With Aeneas he had a fight which was furiously fierce,
Hand-to-hand in fight fought those high-ranked men,
Grief was on the battle-ground where Turnus fell,   90
Hacked apart by sword-blades – and so his human strength subsided.
    Aeneas most lovingly took Lavinia as wife:
He was king and she queen and the kingdom they governed
In peace and in plenty, and both with passion loving.
When Aeneas had taken Lavinia and so gained the land's people,
He constructed a strong castle with stout stone-built walling;
Lavinia was his beloved's name, so the castle he called Lavinium;
This was all in her honour; highly he esteemed her.
Four years was their wedded life, in equal worth and welfare,
After the fourth year passed he had died – his friends were deeply
    saddened.
Queen Lavinia was then carrying a king's child in her body;   101
The widowed Queen soon afterwards had a son for consolation:
Silvius Aeneas, for his ancestor, they named him,
Ascanius his brother, who with his father came from Troy-town,
With very great reverence this royal child regarded
(Ascanius was the baby's brother, but they did not share a mother,
His mother was called **Creusa**, the daughter of King **Priam**,
Whom his father Aeneas, forlorn, lost in Troy:

3

In that very skirmish his foes snatched her from him).
   Ascanius ruled this land of renown for many
      days and years, ASCANIUS
And he founded a great fort, as Alba Longa it was famous.* 111
This fort was well finished within a few years;
He gave it to his stepmother in affection for his brother,
And the castle of Lavinium, and tracts of land with it,
Which his father had constructed while he was still alive.
This land he allowed her till she ended her life there.
But she took off the statue they regarded as god*
Which Aeneas with his retinue carried out of Troy;
In Alba Longa [s]he stationed it, but it soon flitted from there,†
Off back again on the full wind away the Devil ferried it. 120
   Courageous Ascanius, who was in the king's place,
For thirty-four long years ruled over that land
And those who lived there, in content.
Then came his life's ending, little though he liked it.
To Silvius his brother, the son of Lavinia,
He bequeathed all that land which their father Aeneas had once held
    in hand.
   Just the one son had Ascanius who was also known as **Silvius**;
This child carried his uncle's name, but short years he survived,
For his own son subsequently shot him to death. 129
When this child was grown handsome he fell in love with a girl:†
She was Lavinia's relative – most covertly he loved her –;
Things turned out there just as almost everywhere:
That this same young woman was expecting a baby.
Ascanius was still alive then, the duke over all that land.
The circumstance was understood, that the woman expected a
    child;
Then summoned Ascanius, the lord and the leader,
Throughout all that land those who knew the witchcraft song.*
He wished to work out, through those wicked agents,
What sort of thing it would be the woman had in her womb.
They cast in all their lots: the Devil was among them, 140
And found by those evil arts songs of great anguish:
That the woman had conceived a son, it was a curious child,
Who was destined to destroy both his father and his mother:
Through him they were to die both, and undergo their deaths,
And through his parents' death he'd be driven from the land,
And after long delay to reverence would attain.

Those lots had then all been cast: and so it came to pass.
When the time arrived and the infant boy was born,
In that fortress – the female passed away.
The child was delivered safely in his mother's distress.   150
They gave the child the name **Brutus**: indeed the babe did not die.
   This child lived on and flourished and loved and   BRUTUS
     followed virtue;
He went when he was aged fifteen off into the woodlands,
And his father with him, a fateful trip he made there:
They found a great supply of stags huge in size;
The father went round them – though there was no need –
Driving them towards his son (to his own disaster):
Brutus notched his arrow:
He aimed towards the antlered deer – but what he hit was his own
     father,
Right through the breast-bone! Brutus was anguished at it: 160
Anguished was he in life when his father lay in death.
When news came to his kindred (whose family he came from)
That it was he who'd loosed the shaft and slaughtered his own father,
They drove him into exile out of that land,
And he departed sorrowing over the sea-surges,
Into the Greeks' land, where he found his kindred
From the Trojan people who in suffering were scattered,*
Their queen came from **Helenus'** line, the son of old King Priamus,
And many people from his state, but all of them were slaves,
And from his own family, many an offspring of kings;   170
Many years had gone by since his people arrived there:
The men had matured and the women grown gorgeous,
And their flocks were very fruitful.
   Brutus had only been in that land for just a little while
Before he was popular with all the people and won a great deal of
     support,
For he was very amiable, able to please all men,
He was very generous – on this depends allegiance –
And everybody liked him there, whoever set eyes on him,
They gave to him their treasure and treated him most kindly,
They said to him, as wise advice, and with secret whispers,   180
That if he were so daring as to hazard acting,
And would then convey them out of that same country,
Out of their slavery, so that they would be free,
Then they would appoint him duke, and director of the people:

'We have seven thousand sturdy warriors,
Not counting women, who cannot handle weapons,
Children and herdsmen who are to keep our cattle,
For many things we will endure and suffer want in our existence,
If only we in freedom could flee from all our foes.'
All who were at this council believed those confidences.   190
     In Greece there was a young man thirty years of age,
Known as **Assaracus**, of very noble kindred,
[His father was a great knight, but he was also very strong in
          might]†   192a
His father was of Greek descent, but his mother was from Troy,
And she was a concubine, her value less considerable.
Nonetheless it fell out, within a few years,
That the father perished and abandoned all his people.
He gave Assaracus his son three splendid castles
And all the land lying round them that belonged to them.
Assaracus had a single brother but he was born in wedlock;
According to the heathen custom which they had in that land   200
This boy had the father's lands, and he disliked his brother
Because he governed the strong castles on the strength of his father's
          gift;
His brother would have snatched them from him, but could not
          succeed.
Slaughter and dissention arose, and many spiteful blows.
Assaracus was a good knight: against the Greeks he made many a
          fight
But with very much support from his mighty tribe,
From the males of Troy-town related to his mother:
Because of their relationship love was strong between them.
Assaracus gave counsel, in very covert secrecy,   *Assaracus's*
That the folk of Troy-town should firmly press forward,   *Advice*
And taking that knight, Brutus, should make him their Duke.   211
And all their allegiance he accepted graciously:
He sent his instructions wide throughout that nation,
Ordering his race to assemble and to muster to himself.
Weaponed men and women, the wealthy and the wretched,
All of them he summoned and sent into woodlands,
Except seven thousand fighters whom he stationed in the forts.
Then he sent riding unreckoned numbers,
To requisition food and arms, for urgent was their need;
And all the less important men he placed beyond the mountains,   220

He himself, with his forces, before them and behind them.
   Then he came to the conclusion, after consultation,
Of sending a communiqué most sensibly compiled,
Saluting King **Pandrasus** with well-selected words,
And forwarded the missive to him, framing this message:
'Because of the worldly shame and of the outstanding blame
Which the Dardanian tribes, from whom we descended,
Live in, in this place, to the people's disgrace
(In servile status they are doing slaves' duties),
They have therefore assembled from the aforesaid tribe,   230
In order that this same folk may take their freedom from you.
They have all made decree that I am duke over them.
In my forts I have stationed seven thousand fighters;
Up in the mountains I have many thousands:
Sweeter for them to subsist on roots of the woodlands,
Just as wild swine do that go rootling through the groves,
Than suffer any longer under servitude with you;
If they would like their liberty, you need not look astounded:
They are asking you in friendship that you should set them free.
These words they send you, just as the writing states,   240
Asking to settle wherever it would suit them,
In peace and in plenty; and they would proffer you their friendship.
If you will not accept this, then things will go worse for you.'
   The king seized the written note, and wrathfully surveyed it:
Strange did it seem to him, speech of such a kind;
When at last he spoke, threats were what broke out:
   'To their own disadvantage they have done such acts –
My slaves among my subjects to make me myself subservient!'
   To far parts of that land he sent (for he was the people's sovereign)
Telling them to come to court, both rich men and beggars,
All of the male sex who could manage weapons,   250
On pain of life and limb. All the population
On horseback and on foot, hurried to assemble.
The king threatened Brutus, as he did Assaracus
That he would encompass them with their hated enemies;
If he could subdue them all by his forces' strength,
They should all be hanged aloft on the highest trees.
   Brutus had reports – it really was the case –
That King Pandrasus was coming towards him
With a very large force (but some of them were fated);   260
Brutus made a decision which was best for them:

He took his fiercest men who were valiant on the field,
He went off to the woodlands, into the wilderness,
To that same way, along which he knew so well
The king and his forces would be moving forwards.
    Brutus had choice champions ready for his purpose,
Three thousand with him, advancing on that throng;
The king came riding by, with his resplendent band,
Brutus attacked them with his grim assault-force,
He sought out those Greeks with sharp steel-edged weapons: 270
The Greeks were not alerted to their own danger,
And turning their backs, those fearful men fled.
There was a stream called Achalon a short distance from them,
They hurled themselves into it in many thousands.
Brutus in pursuit of them was constantly pressing them;
With sword and with spear-point he quite scattered that king's army:
On land and on water he laid them down low.
The king himself fled: he could see his friends falling.
Very many men were slaughtered there in many different ways.
The king had just one brother, he hadn't any other,   280
His name was **Antigonus**: in the Greeks' land he was noted.
He saw his brother's forces, and how they were all faring
On water and on land in most unlucky plight.
Antigonus with his armoury and with his assault troops
Bore down upon Brutus, bent on his destruction:
Together they clashed with very great courage.
Any onlooker present might well observe there
Frequent disasters, downfalls a-plenty:
Many a head, many a hand, falling to the feet;
Many there were fighting, many seeking flight there;   290
Many there were falling through their unfriendly actions.
The Trojans went on striking all the Greek men who came near them:
Brutus seized Antigonus, the brother of King Pandrasus,
Conducting him away with him, delighted to have got him;
He had him safeguarded in specially stout fetters,
And also his companions, who along with him were captured.
    The news came to Pandrasus and it was not pleasing to him,
That Antigonus his brother was in miserable bonds.
The king sent out his word to the limits of his kingdom,
And ordered each able man, whether he came on mount or ran,   300
To come as his escort to the castle of Sparatin:
There was no castle as strong in all the Greeks' lands.

He thought that it was fact (but in fact it was not so)
That Brutus had incarcerated in that same castle
The men captured in battle, and was keeping them alive there,
And was there himself among them because they were worth so
    much.
But Brutus had a better plan, and so things went better for him:
Promptly into that castle he put six hundred of his knights;
He himself with his hostages hastened to the woods.
The king towards the castle went marching with his men,   310
And laid siege to it; his loathed enemies were inside it.
He positioned his troops on all sides around.
Often they rushed down with battering-rams there,
With steel-tipped planks and with stiff assaults,
With baulks and with boulders they raised bitter conflict;
Under balls of Greek-fire the fated men fell there;*
There was copious blood-shed; slaughter was rife there.
    The knights in the castle withstood them with courage:
The warriors of the king could not kill them off,
But from his own men the king lost very many thousands.   320
The king grieved at heart for the loss of his good men:
He returned for one more effort and attacked the castle
And the people in it, and when he would have conquered it,
He would execute them all or burn them all alive there.
He had a great ditch excavated which was extremely deep
All around his forces, and fenced it in with thorns,
And sheltered within it, to experience the outcome.
The king was most enraged and made a powerful oath:
He would never depart from there until his enemies lay dead.
In the castle there were many men and much provision was
    needed: 330
The food supplies ran out, so many were being supported.
They took one errand-runner, most able in extremity,
And sent him to their leader for whom they all had heart-felt love;
Him they sent greeting with their own good words,
Begging him to come and help them with all of his forces:
All the time they were unscathed they were his stalwart men.
    Brutus made his mind up in this great necessity,
And with a steadfast spirit these words he spoke:
'He gives himself assistance who aids his own supporters:
So will I do mine, as I am man alive!'   340
    Now there was a well-born man there, **Anacletus** by his name,

Captured with the king's brother and lying there in bonds;
Brutus strode towards him with determined steps,
By the hair on his head he seized him, just as if he wished to kill him,
And upon the man's neck he set his naked sword-blade,
And Brutus the noble announced in these words:
'Scoundrel, you'll be dead unless you do as I say,
And your leader too, unless you listen to my words;
But if you are willing, you may well help both the two of you.'
   'Lord,' replied Anacletus, 'I'll act just as you require;   350
I'll help my prince and myself with all of my powers.'
'Do that,' said Brutus, 'It will be the better for you.
You shall have life and limb and both be my well-loved friends.'
   Brutus swore to him on oath that never would he break faith.
Brutus announced this – of all knights he was the best:
'Tonight, Anacletus, my dear friend, you are to travel,
(Best would be at that time when people go to bed)
You are to go away from here towards the king's army.
When you come upon those knights who watch over the king
There you'll find seven hundred, and those soldiers are most
      brave;   360
Call them over to you and cunningly speak to them:
"I am Anacletus and from affliction I've escaped,
Out of the bondage which Brutus had imposed on me.
And I can say one other thing: here I've brought the brother of the
      king,
Out of the dungeon of that house of death
Which Brutus had thrust him in, because tomorrow he would have
      hanged him.
But I have secured him in this wood secretly.
Knights, hurry with me! Leave the king sleeping,
And let us go successfully, every bit as silently,
As if we were going stealing;   370
And I will then conduct you straight to my commander,
Inside the woodland, where he lies beneath the twigs.
And if then you could but bring that man to meet our king,
This bringing would much please him, and you'd be better for it,
Because he is his brother, and he hasn't any other."'
   He was known to those knights, and they recognised him there,[*]
So they assumed his tales were totally true,
But they were utterly treacherous, since he was traitor to his people.
There is nowhere any man so wise that he can't be taken in.

Anacletus went in front, with the knights all following,   380
Marched along a brook valley, as Brutus had instructed:
Brutus had his force both in front and behind them;
It was a long path and deep and the [rocks] around were steep.[†]
    Brutus rushed upon them with redoubtable force:
The entire party he seized, not a sole one left behind;
Some he slew, some he bound, the best he retained alive,
Disposing there of all of them as he deemed was best.
Brutus took his forces and divided them in four parts,
And instructed all his men to earn true acclaim there:
The young men and the old men, all were to excel: 390
Redoubtable warriors, resisting their enemies,
In the greatest haste were to march to the king;
'And I forbid here my loyal retainers
(By the great love they bear me, which lies between us)
That any of them be so rash or so unreasonable
As to exchange words or to utter any speech,
Before they can hear my horn with high spirit being blown.
For I myself will take the lead to the tent of the king.
As soon as I get off my steed, then I will sound attack;
As soon as you can hear it, my stout-hearted warriors,   400
Strike at them bravely and wake them from their sleep!
Let all those Greek men go down to the ground,
Fall there, all fated, since they're fully our foes.'
    All of those fighters did as Brutus had told them,
And he himself took the lead to the tent of the king;
From his horse he bounded, his horn powerfully sounded,
The Trojans all heard it, and moved towards the Greeks:
They woke them up fully, with their frightening slaughter!
Heads went falling on the field, the fated men all fell there –
Many hands, many feet: so their forces declined.   410
Tens of thousands fled from there, trailing their intestines,
And Brutus with his comrades captured the king.   *Pandrasus's*
Quite safe and quite sound he shouted aloud: *Capture*
'I hold this people's king, conquered are his soldiers!
Leave no one breathing to break for the woods!
Meanwhile this same king I will conduct myself.'
There Brutus seized everything spread before him.
    He relieved Sparatin, his own high castle.
Next morning when it was day and the night departed
Brutus summoned his troops (all were totally his allies)   420

He commanded all his loyal forces, through the love they had for him,
That they should take the [carnage] and carefully get it buried:[†]
Into deep pits they should place all the dead.
It was swiftly accomplished as many thousands assisted.
All the acquired property he shared among his knights,
And all his beloved men he favoured with his friendship.
When all this had been done, he did something still more:
He got someone to climb aloft and to shout out loudly
That on the very next day his most noble men should come
And all his highest men should attend the hustings. 430
And this they then did: joy was there on that day.
The warriors came together, all those warlike knights,
And their leader spoke, and in this way said to them:
'Listen my champions, listen my beloved men,
Tell me in discussion the decision which you want:
I have this tribal-king tied up in my fetters,
And his brother also – we are the better for it –
His liege men being slain (he loathes me the more for that!)
And all his possessions donated to my princes;
If you, my chief advisers, choose this decision, 440
I with my sword will swipe his head off now:
If it's as you desire, I shall make him expire;
But if you advise me, I shall set him free,
Provided he gives me great gifts, gold and silver,
All of his riches, as condition of his reprieve.'
Then those redoubted knights gave their response:
Some did consent to it, that they should indeed kill him,
Brutus should possess that land and be the people's king there;
But some spoke otherwise; so their speeches proceeded:
'Give us the king and all his gold and the riches of his land, 450
Give us purple garments, give us horses, splendid clothes,
Give us just a corner from his kingdom's land,
Give us hostages too that this will be completed.'
There was many a great man there who could give little counsel,
Whether it were preferable to stay or to proceed.
While they were in doubt like this, a cry came from **Membricius** –
He was an important man, and had a splendid presence,
Wise and aware, and knew well how to declare –:
'What are you saying, fellow knights, what are you saying, fighters?
Out of the whole lot of you, there's none gives good advice, 460
Of those who have so far declared what we had better do.

If you would listen to me, Brutus my own lord,
And if you all believe my much better counsel,
Then I will state to you the most suitable advice.'
Then the entire assembly cried: 'We're all eager now to hear it.'
   Then said Membricius in a loud voice: *Membricius's*
'Let us get from the king gifts which are really good: *Advice*
First of all agreement that he will set us free;
Straightaway after we ask for his daughter,
That he should give her to our lord, Brutus, as his bed-mate;   470
That he should give us from his corn so much that we would be
    contented,
Gold and great treasure and his good horses,
And all the best foodstuffs which his followers have,
And all the seaworthy ships which there are in his land,
Together with all that's needed to make the ships move,
By way of mariners and weapons, so we may proceed well,
Sail off over the sea to where we may succeed,
And voyage a great distance before we disembark,
Exploring deep into that land, to establish there a nation
Where it will be convenient. A king let us make now   480
Of Brutus our leader, who is much the best of us,
Making **Ignogen** our queen, the present king's daughter.
But if we should agree to remain here with the Greeks,
They are utterly our enemies, since with them we're at enmity,
Having slaughtered their relations (under earth they're sleeping):
We are loathsome to them because of their great loss.
They're intent on betraying us by means of hostile tricks,
And they will be the better off, the worse we become;
With our weapons we have killed so many of their kindred,
With our own hands slain many thousands of them.   490
To expect conciliation will be death for our community:
If we should believe them, it will be to our great loss;
If their numbers increase, they will cut back ours.
   Firmly I declare this, because I know it's fact:
There is none so well-born, there is none so base-born
Who did not have some friend whom we have felled to earth.
Therefore if it suits you who are sensible in judgement,
Let us leave this country where we loathe all those who live here:
We'll lift all their property and leave them very little;*
They'll live very abjectly in all their impoverishment,   500
And we'll go off in grandeur if we value what's good sense,

Because we'll carry off with us all this country's wealth,
And leave them wretchedly behind for [want] to accompany them:†
Room is given to the rich to rush ahead of wretches.'
    These words were uttered, the utterance approved.
Then might a person hear, if he were present,
Much discussion, much din, many men's delighted shouts.
And in these words all cried out: 'Membricius tells the truth.'
And everybody loved it, so good was his lesson.
Then they had the king drawn out of his dungeon,   510
And his brother with him, both of them together,
In iron fetters, there in front of Brutus.
They shouted out to him, and hostile words they spoke,*
Saying that he ought to be hanged high on a tree-top,
Or by wild horses torn apart with horrendous torments,
If he would not let them freely flee from off his land;
He must give them all his wealth that he could get hold of,
And all his ships which were any good, floating on the sea-flood,
And his daughter Ignogen, to be their duke's own queen.
    Then the king thought carefully what might be his strategy;   520
He was weary of his life, the news was most unwelcome,
He was anxious about death, disturbed in his feelings.
Pandrasus answered them, with downhearted speeches:
'You call for my daughter so lissom, and yet you hold me in prison,
With Antigonus my brother, in most awful tortures,
And you have slain my true men, and yet desire my treasures,
And my dearest daughter, for the hand of a man so dire;
But he must needs bow down who is already fast bound.
Your request I you allow, reluctant though it makes me,
But if you should wish to stay, here within my nation,   530
A third of my whole land I would bestow on Brutus's hand,
And free all his followers and make friendship with them,
And my daughter Ignogen would I give to your duke;
And we should remain by this means just like dear relations,
Leading our lives and going along together.'
Brutus responded, he was born as [lord and] duke,†
'We shall not agree to this: we want to go away,
And you must very promptly protect yourself from death:
Give us what we want to have, if you wish to live.'
    The king sent a command throughout all the Greeks' land: 540
From what he owned they should bring to him there every thing,
And should stock his ships with food, down beside the sea-flood,

So that all that was needed should be notably provided,
If they wished to free their leader from his hated foes.
All his men acted as the king instructed:
The ships were got ready, filled with goods to the gunwales,
The king gave Brutus his daughter, his own very dear child;*
The whole agreement was fulfilled. Then the forces marched
    forward,
Right ahead to the sea-coast went those splendid men;
Great acclaim and rejoicing accompanied Duke Brutus;   550
Brutus took Ignogen and led her on board ship.

    They laid in their lines, and lifted their masts up,   *Brutus*
Wound up their sails, had wind where they wanted: *Departs*
Sixteen times twenty vessels ventured from the haven,
And four great merchant ships, loaded to the gunwales
With the best weapons which Brutus possessed.
They sped from the shore-strand and left the Greeks' land,
Making a way on the wide sea where wild waves were stilled.†
For two whole days and two nights they were on the sea,
On the second day by evening they sailed in to shore: 560
Logice the isle was called – it had no inhabitants,*
No weaponed men nor women, just ways through the wilderness:
Outlaws had ransacked that whole land and killed all those who lived
    there,
So it was all plundered, deprived of provisions,
But so abounding with wild animals that it amazed them all,
And all the men of Troy-town went off towards the beasts,
Taking from those wild things everything they wanted,
[Carrying] off towards the ships [as much as ever they] wished.†

    They discovered on the island a well-defended stronghold:
All the walls were tottering, the halls had tumbled down,   570
They found only one temple, made entirely of marble,
Grandiose and glorious, and dedicated to the Devil;
Inside it was an idol in the image of a woman,
Beautiful and very high, and in a heathen style her name,
Diana, was written; the Devil had adored her:
She performed amazing feats (the Devil had assisted);
She was queen of all the wood groves which grow upon this earth;
In those heathen cults she was held as a high deity;
Those who associated with her were especially clever men:
Things which were to come to pass she'd make quite clear to
    them†

By means of signs or else of dreams whilst they were all
    sleeping. 581
While those on that island were dwelling as a tribe
They worshipped at that idol and the Devil took the praise.
    Brutus heard the message through his mariners,
Who'd been to that coast before and well knew the customs.
Brutus took twelve wizards who were all his wisest men,
And one priest of his own faith such as was found in heathen days:
Gerion was that priest's name and he came from noble stock;
He went to the place in which Diana was positioned:
Brutus went into the temple, and those twelve men with him, 590
And made all his men remain outside there.
In his hand he bore a bowl, made of solid gold,
There was milk in the bowl, and a little wine too:
The milk had come from a white hind, shot by Brutus's own hand.
On the altar he kindled there an admirable fire;
Nine times around that altar fire he circled as the rites require:
He called upon the lady for he loved her in his heart;
With most placating words he summoned up her powers,
Often kissing the altar with decorous gestures;
He poured the milk into the fire with peaceable phrases: 600
'Lady Diana, beloved Diana, lofty Diana, help me in my need.
Guide me and govern me through your vigorous skills
As to where I can travel and take this tribe of mine
To a splendid land where I could settle down.
And if I could conquer that land and my people possess it,
I would erect in your name an excellent temple,
And for you I will hallow it with the highest worship.'
So Brutus spoke.
Then he took the hide which came from the white hind,
Before the altar he spread it out, as if preparing his couch. 610
He went down on his knees on it and then he lay right down,
And so began to slumber, and afterwards to sleep.
    As he lay asleep there, in dream he seemed to see
That Diana his lady gazed lovingly towards him;
With an attractive smile, she amicably promised,
Graciously laying her hand on his head there,
And spoke to him like this, as he lay asleep there:
'Beyond France, in the west, you'll find a welcome landfall: *Diana's*
The sea surrounds that place; in it you shall be blest: *Prophecy*
Full of birds, full of fish, and the finest beasts live there,* 620

There is woodland and water, and extensive wilderness;
The land is very welcoming, with wells of sweet water.
Living in that country there are very powerful giants;
Albion the land is called, but no men are living in it.
There you will multiply and a new Troy you'll make there,
And from your own race royal children will arise.
Your glorious descendants will rule in that land,
Throughout the world highly honoured; and you'll be healthy and
    fit.'
    When Brutus awoke he felt most elated;
He pondered on his dream and how the lady addressed him   630
With very much affection; he announced to his people
How the lady had seemed to address him as he dreamed.
He thanked her profusely with most pleasant words,
Vowing her a promise (and certainly performed it)
That he would be attached to her and build for her a temple,
With her likeness in bright gold, when he came to land,
And all his whole life he would fulfil her wishes.
    They said goodbye to her and went on board ship.
They had winds, they had currents, which carried them well; *†
For thirty nights and thirty days they journeyed onward
    always,   640
Along Africa's coast they held course, bearing north by west at full
    force,
Over the Lake of Silvius, and over Lake Philisteus, *
By Ruscikadan took the open sea, by the mountain of Azare;
On that sea they found outlaws and pirates, the fiercest there were at
    that date;
Fifty ships full of them – these foes were far too many –;
Against Brutus they fought and felled some of his men,
But Brutus had the upper hand: the doomed he killed, the living he
    bound,
And many kinds of wealth Brutus won there for himself:
Reserves of riches and of food: his renown grew more resplendent;
Brutus had no man so humble that he did not wear gold and purple.
    From there they voyaged on for very many days: 651
Over River Malvan sailing far along, in Mauritania they came to
    land: *
They journeyed far throughout that land, and slaughtered those who
    lived there.
The food and the drink, which they could find there,

17

They ferried this to their ships, and reckoned it of the finest.
They took from that country everything they fancied,
Then they hastened onwards with their hearts on high:
They had won bountiful property. Then they came to the bounds
Which Hercules had erected with his enormous strength:
These pillars were very long, made of marble stone most
      strong;*   660
This landmark left by Hercules showed that all surrounding
      territories
(Very broad and very long) were entirely his own land.
   There they encountered the mermaids, which are beasts of cunning
      escapades: *
They really seem like women, but from the waist they
      look like fish;   *Mermaids*
So alluring is their song that, however much the day's been long,
No man is ever weary while such singing he is hearing.
Half human it is, half fish in fact; it has the Devil's aspect:
Because its acts are so entrancing, many men cannot evade it.
Brutus heard mention from those who were his mariners
Of the evil escapades practised by the mermaids.   670
He commanded that cables be fastened, sails tied down to topmast,
And set the ship before the wind, scudding over salt-waves.
The mermaids swam across and surrounded them on all sides,
Holding them up totally with their hateful teasing;
All the same, Brutus drove past without any disaster,
And proceeded on his course: his ships were making progress.
   A helmsman gave a welcome shout that he had Spain in sight;
They moved into harbour: the men were all delighted,
And pushed off towards land, where they found pleasant people,
Four tribes of them, totalling many thousands,   680
Good warriors all, who were valiant in battle,
And these were their relations; so much the better for them!
These four tribes of men had all fled from Troy,
With **Atenor** leading them, an elder in the nation, *
And he with those forces fled out of Troy,
When the Greeks conquered it with all that great carnage.
Corineus had become their duke when Atenor died;
Corineus was a strong man and he had massive bones:
He was as fierce, he was as strong, as if he were a giant.
   The message came to Corineus that Brutus had come there,   690
He was quite delighted: he had never been so glad yet.

They approached each other and many times they embraced.
Brutus, with him speaking, told that he travelled one land seeking,
Which he could colonise with his comely people.
Corineus responded: 'I will come with you, indeed,
With my servants and retainers, and go shares in it with you,
And look to you as lord, and esteem you as leader.'
The agreement was ratified and [rigorously kept].
   They voyaged from Spain straight on to Brittany.
(Armorica they called that country, where now it is called
     Brittany). 700
Poitou they left on their right hand as they arrived in that   *Brittany*
   land,
On a very lovely river where the Loire enters the sea there;
For a week and one more day, Brutus in that harbour lay,
And sent men throughout that land and surveyed those who lived
   there.
   To **Goffar** king of Poitou this was far from pleasing,
When he saw such spies in bands exploring all his lands.
The king ordered his wise men, whose eloquence was great,
To travel to the sea-coast where the troops were camped,
And ascertain from those men what they were after then,
Whether they wished to keep the peace and appear before
   the king, 710
Or whether they wished most wickedly to oppose the king.
Numbert was the dignitary who had to take this dictum.
Corineus had gone to the woods to chase the wild beasts there,
With his horns and with his hounds and with five hundred nobles.*
On his way they encountered Numbert, the king's emissary for that
   part;
Numbert shouted out to them, in a powerful voice:
'Where do you come from, knights? What you're doing isn't right!
You're hunting in the royal park, and you shall perish for it! 719
You treat the king with great contempt: for this we shall have you
   condemned;
His animals are prohibited: for this we shall leave you stiff and dead.'
   Corineus got aggrieved at this, and going over to him
Uttered the following words with rage and with fury:
'Sir, you're very stupid, threatening like this;
If the king has really forbidden this, he'll never flourish for it,
But for all his prohibition, I shall not stop my action
Of taking his harts and taking his hinds and every creature I can find.'

Now the enraged Numbert, that royal park's manager,
Was holding in his hand a massive bow to bend,
And he notched up the string: sorrow came at once.
He set an arrow on it and in enmity he drew it;   730
And let the arrow slide along Corineus's side.
Corineus, swerving, avoided the bow-shot,
And leaped towards Numbert as if he were a lion,
Gripping hold of the bow with enormous force.
He struck Numbert with the bow and his skull broke in pieces,
So his blood and his brains were both spattered there.
His partners departed in hostile panic
To the court of King Goffar, and divulged to him news most dire
Of the slaughter of Numbert, who was his own royal steward.

The king was most distressed and in deep depression,   740
And sent out emissaries through all his territories
To muster his army: men were now doomed to die.
The army was assembled and they advanced in haste
Towards Brutus the lucky lodged in camp by the sea.
Brutus was very ready (he was ruled by his intellect),
And had dispatched spies to the king's courtroom,
To learn of his manoeuvres and where he made plans to fight.
The spies went their way, and were quickly back again,
And came back to their leader where he lodged beside the harbour,
Giving him this information, as indeed it was [the case]:†   750
'Hail, to you, Brutus; you are the highest of us!
King Goffar has already assembled his army,
An army huge and powerful, and proud words he's spoken,
That they will exterminate everything alive,
Scuttle the ships and so drown the women.
They intend not to leave any one of us living.'
   Brutus took all his young people and on board ship he packed
      them,
And all that he had then he gave to his men,
And to them declared Brutus the lucky:
'You, my beloved men, listen well to what I say: 760
Never disembark, never come from shipboard before I send a secret
      password
Whether I succeed in getting the upper hand over the king.'
Brutus took his vanguard and marched them straight forward   *Battle*
On to the exact route which he'd been instructed   *with*
The king would travel over with all his crowds of troops.   *Goffar*

20

So together they clashed, and boldly they attacked,
There was very fierce fighting; those fated then fell.
Many a strong man was struck through with steel;
All day long lasted that fight: there fell many a good knight.

    Corineus came collecting spoil and declared to himself: 770
'For shame, Corineus! Weren't you a special champion?
Now show your own strength and your special power,
And fell to the ground all these Poitevin folk!'

    Corineus rushed in on them like a rime-grey wolf
Designing against sheep-flocks destruction to wreak.
He drew with his right hand a sword both huge and very strong:
Everything he hit with it fell down there in a heap;
However strong the warrior, even in his war-mail,
If he but touched him with that sword, never again did he stand up.
When Corineus had hacked apart two hundred with his
      sword,   780
The sword snapped off there in his hand, right up against the hilt;
Corineus got worked up then, and cried out in these words:
'A curse upon whichever smith once with his hands you smithied!'
Corineus started staring round; the soldier was storming now with
      rage
And snatched from out of one man's hand a battle-axe most massive:
All he came close to he crushed to pieces with it.

    The king set off in flight and all his forces followed,
And Corineus came after them most courageously,
Calling out to them there, that keenest of champions:
'Goffar and your forces, why are you seeking flight?   790
You shouldn't dash away like that if it's us you want to drive off!
You'll have to make a stronger fight before we run away in flight!'

    Neither walking nor riding did any dare wait for him.
The king had one servant, battle-hardened, who was known as
      Suard;
He could see Corineus coming along after him:
Suard had as his companions three hundred cavaliers:
He returned immediately and unfearingly fought back.
But not for very long could Suard remain standing:
For Corineus beat him down with his battle-force.
He struck Suard on the head, sent him reeling groundwards,   800
And sliced him in the middle, in two pieces, by his ribs.
There was no man sufficiently sturdy to withstand him any longer:
Corineus beat them all to pulp, their bones and all their ribs,

21

Driving them right across that land; many thousands there lay dead.
The forces fleeing Corineus then encountered Brutus,
And these two killed everyone that they came near to.
    When Goffar understood he'd lost, he only just escaped:
He fled from his land and left his liegemen behind,
Finding shelter in France where he found himself friends,
With the emperor there and his twelve companion peers,   810
Telling them of the outrage which Brutus had inflicted.
In France there were counted twelve loyal companions;
In French they called them 'douzepers' – they were very doughty
        men;
'Kings' people called them, and they could prove their name.
They made promise to King Goffar they'd volunteer to avenge him,
Avenge him on his enemies so that he'd feel the [easier].†
They sent posts throughout France to call up their forces;
For seven whole nights they were summoning warriors,
While Brutus led his army in Armorica's country,
Feeling most elated at all his great acquisitions.   820
Through that land he proceeded and all the towns he burned,
Plundered the entire land, drawing it into his own hand.
All that land he surveyed and all of it subdued.
    As he advanced with his army he arrived at a hill,
It was lovely and lofty and he looked it over well;
He consulted all his men about constructing a castle there.
Once erected, there it stood: a fort impregnable and good,
And only a short while later King Goffar came marching after,
With vast numbers of forces from all the folk of France,
And from all those territories which are tributary to France.   830
When King Goffar then caught a glimpse of the castle
He was so much dismayed that his sense quite deserted him:
He hustled that way quickly with his heroic army;
They divided in twelve sections and [advanced] on every side,†
While the Trojan men came out towards them,
And at once from the Frenchmen to the ground they felled three
        thousand.*
The French were being stormed, but all the same they made a stand,
And then with scorn those scoundrels began to drive them back
        again!*
Brutus and his companions they drove into the castle,
And in that very same assault slew some of his supporters   840
And all that day they raged and made a rush at the castle,

22

Until there came the night, bringing limit to their might.
In the castle was consternation: at midnight they had
    consultation:
They wanted to send Corineus out into the woodland
With all of the people that he had in his platoon:
They slipped out as secretly as if they were going stealing,
Into a woodland thicket which was off to the west.

    Brutus was in the castle and was guarding it well.
In the morning when the dawn came and day came to mankind
Brutus was as battle-mad as the wild boar gets[*]   850
When the hounds have him at bay out in the woodlands.

    Brutus ordered his men to put on their mail-coats,
And to take their best weapons, since they would have to fight.
Up they wound their castle-gates and courageously went out,
Sallied forth upon the French, who in turn set upon them:
There was very furious fighting and on both sides it was fierce,
Many ranks of the forces there and many a rider died.

    Now a cousin there of Brutus, who was by name called **Turnus**,
Was so desperate for battle that he doomed himself:
He massacred the Frenchmen in many kinds of ways: 860
With his own hands alone he slaughtered many hundreds,
But he ventured too far away from his friends;
The enemy approached him upon every side,
With weapons wounded him there and afterwards they slew him.
Brutus found him dead there and back to the castle carried him,
And inside it he buried him alongside a stone wall;
Because of this same Turnus, Tours was the name it
    took,[*]   *Turnus's*
And all that land was called Touraine because of   *Death*
    Turnus's death.

    Brutus burst out, emboldened for battle,
Wanting to avenge his wrongs and his friend well-loved and
    young.   870
Together they clashed and grievously attacked:
There halberds were hacked; there horror was mounting,
And fighting uncontrolled: the fated then fell there.
That fight was very savage; then from the woodland came Corineus
With numerous forces to give Brutus full support.
On the one side was Brutus, on the other Corineus,
They sent flying out their very sharp spears;
They destroyed all the French they were able to find,

And laid that place waste and slaughtered the people.
No man has been born yet, none so wise was ever met,   880
Who could for that day's toll reckon up the dead,
How very many thousands there were laid upon the ground.
    Then Brutus blew horns and summoned his forces,
Speaking with them together of many great issues,
And made one resolve: they were ready to go.
They had loudly proclaimed and pronounced through that army
That Brutus the lucky was to leave for the sea.
So they went to their ships with all they had won there,
Both with silver and with gold which had once been King Goffar's
And also that of the Frenchmen who had perished in the fight.   890
They sailed out from the harbour: the soldiers were rejoicing:
Wind blew as they wanted; the wild fish were playing;
The water was very smooth, the soldiers contented;
The troops travelled on until they touched the mainland
At Dartmouth haven, in Totnes; Brutus was glad at this.*   *Arrival*
The ships ran aground on the sand: the whole company went   *in*
        on land: *Britain*
So Brutus had the favour which Diana had promised him
On Logice once, the isle, where they had paused a while.
There was much merrymaking among the men then,
Giving thanks to God with most grateful words   900
That such times of joy they now had at command.
    They found in that country twenty gigantic creatures,
Their names I've never heard tell of in song or in story,
Except the name of one of them, the captain of them all:
Gogmagog he was called, the one who was the chief,*
God's own adversary, but the Evil One did love him.
Brutus and his doughty men detected all those demons,
And dispatched their steel-tipped shafts straight towards those devils.
They did not like the arrows and they loped off to the mountains,
And in deserted places in hollow caves they dwelt.   910
    It happened one fine day that Brutus and his followers
Were doing their devotions with devout observance,
With food and drink oblations and with joyful festal song,
With silver and with gold which each took in his hand,
With steeds and with vestments: there was joy among the settlers;
More than ever before in their life that band of men was blithe.
    Then tumbling from the mountains came down a full twenty
Of giants both long and massively strong.

All together they tugged out tree-trunks of great girth,
Galloped over to Brutus's men and there maimed them badly: 920
In a very short space they'd slain five hundred apace,
With stakes and with stones they made sudden raiding,
And the brave Trojan men with force hit back again:
They sent their arrows flying and put the giants to flight;
And they let slip at them spear-heads keen-slicing:
When they thought they were fleeing, that was when they were fated;
Nineteen of them they slaughtered; **Gogmagog** they captured,
And alive he was brought face to face with Brutus.
Brutus had him close-fettered, as well as could be,
So they could test out his tremendous power,   930
By wrestling in front of Brutus: Gogmagog with   *Gogmagog*
    Corineus.
    Brutus adjudicated atop the high downs,
Right up on the sea-cliffs the people assembled.
Out stepped Corineus and squared up his shoulders,*
And the giant also, and everyone could see it.
There were men with weapons, there were many women,
There were many crowds at that wrestling-match.
They wrapped arms round each other and got themselves ready,
Breast against breast: then bones started cracking;
They lunged out with their legs (the lads were really strong)   940
Their skulls scraped together (spectators stared intently)
Often they were leaning as if about to lie down,
As often they leaped up as if about to dash off;
Looks of deep loathing they let flash from their eyes;
They were gnashing their teeth just like wild boars in fury;
One moment they were blanched and breathing horrid frenzy,
The next they were florid, aggressively twisting,
Each of the two concerned to conquer the other
By ruses and by rushes and by unrivalled powers.
Gogmagog devised a plan and pushed at Corineus,   950
Forwards with his breast, bending him right back,
Breaking down the backbone four of his ribs.
Gruesomely he crippled him, but no way did he complain.
Hardly anyone surmised Corineus would survive;
But all the same, to himself he mused what could be his ruse,
Got his courage back again and straightened his arms,
And pulled at Gogmagog so his back snapped in pieces,
Grabbed him by his girdle and grimly heaved him up;

The crag where their cliff-top fight took place was very high:
Corineus threw him downwards and thrust him off with force,   960
Headlong from the cliff-face so all his bones were crushed,
And the gremlin split apart before he reached ground level.
And so the hateful monster was hustled off to Hell.
To this day, and so for ever, that cliff has always taken
Its name in every language from Gogmagog's great leap.
And so by this policy those giants were destroyed.
   Now to Brutus's hand was allocated all this land;
In this way the Trojan soldiers had surmounted all their   *Settlement*
   troubles.
Then they were happy in their minds and hearts.
Then they built their houses and held themselves secure;   970
They laid out their towns, started tilling the soil:
Corn seeds they sowed, meadow-leas they mowed;
Everywhere they tilled it, just as they intended:
Since all was their own prize everywhere they cast their eyes.
   When Brutus arrived here this land was called Albion;
Now Brutus was quite sure it should not be called that any more,
But settled a name on it based on himself:
He was called Brutus and this land he named 'Brutain',
And the Trojan people who had taken him as leader
After 'Brutain' called themselves 'Brutons'.   980
And still the name has stuck, and in some places it lingers.
Brutus gave Corineus, who was his [special] champion,†
One section of his lands and placed it in his hands:
Its lord was called Corineus, and that land 'Corinee',
Then through the habits of the later inhabitants
They called it 'Cornwall' (concerned as they were with folly).
Their native speech, the Trojan tongue, subsequently they called
   'Brutonish',
But English people have altered it since **Gurmund** came into this land:
Gurmund drove out the Britons and his folk were called Saxons;
From one end of Almaigne the Angles took their name,   990
And from Angles came the Englishmen and 'Engle-land' was what
   they dubbed it.
Then the English overcame those Britons and brought them down
   much lower,
And never since have they been superior or had any say in matters.
   'Brutain' went to Brutus and Cornwall to Corineus:
Brutus took all his friends who came among his forces,

Endowed them all with land where they most of all desired it.
Corineus summoned to him all his special followers:
To all he gave lands where they especially liked.
That people grew and prospered, for each had what he wanted.
That nation in a few years had grown to be so numerous   1000
That there was now no limiting this people who were thriving.
    Brutus began reflecting, beholding all these people,   *The*
He beheld the mountains, beautiful and mighty,   *Countryside*
He beheld the meadows which were most magnificent,
He beheld the waters and the wild creatures,
He beheld the fishes and all the birds and fowl,
He beheld the grasslands and the lovely groves,
He beheld the woodland flowering and beheld the cornfields
    growing;
All this he saw in the country and his heart was light and happy;
Then he reflected on Troy-town where his tribe had suffered
    terrors.   1010
    He continued round this country and he viewed the countryside:
He found one pleasant spot upon a stretch of water,*
And there he erected a very rich city,
With living-rooms and halls and with high stone walls.
When the city was ready it looked really splendid,
The city was very well made: a ready name for it he had;
He gave it as its glorious name, great 'Troy the New',
To commemorate his kindred from whom he had come down.
Later the land-dwellers, very long after,
Set aside the old name and '**Troynovant**' named it then.   1020
With the passage of many years it later came to pass
That there came to power a high king from Brutus's kin,
Who was called **Lud**, and this city he loved greatly;
The king dwelt in this city for very many winters.
He had it called 'Lud' aloud among his land's people:
Commanded them to pronounce 'Kaerlud' after this king.
Later came another fame, and new information,
That men were calling it 'Lundin' throughout all the land.
And then there came English men and they called it '**Lundene**';
And then came the French race who gained it by fighting,   1030
With their language habits, and they called it 'Lundres'.
So has this city fared since its early erection,
So has this island passed from hand to hand,
Such that all the boroughs which Brutus established,

And all their good names which in Brutus's day were famed
Have quite disappeared through dispersal of peoples.
    When Brutus had completed that high city he called New Troy,
And had ordered many people to proceed towards it,
He entrusted the town to them and equipped it with the best,
And gave them legislation in the form of good laws.   *Laws*
He instructed that it should be love which linked them
      together,   1041
Each upholding others' rights, both by day and by night,
And if any refused, he was to be punished,
And for great crimes committed, a man must be hanged.
From such good edicts they developed great respect,
And became upright men, and loved reasonable words.
    For twenty-four years this land lay in [Brutus's] hands,*†
And from Ignogen his queen he had three sons good and fine.
When their father died they all met to decide,
And so buried him within the borough of New Troy-town,   1050
Which their father had constructed with considerable joy.
Then those three brothers met together each with other,
All in concord and with love this land they divided.
    The eldest of the brothers, who was named **Locrin**,   LOCRIN
He was the wisest, he was the wariest,
He was the strongest, and of sturdy intellect.
He had as share the south land, which from him was called Logres,*
And **Cambert** was an other, he was the second brother:
To his share came the land which took the name of Cambria,
And this is that wild land which the Welsh people love,*   1060
Since then it has been called Wales because of Queen Galoes,
And because of Duke Gualun, 'Welshmen' they are known as;
The third had **Albanac** as name, whom **Humber** was to bring to
      shame:
Albanac took his land in the northern end,
To which now our people give the name of Scotland,
But Albanac in his own day gave it the name of Albany.
Locrin's limit ran south and eastwards; Albanac had the parts
      northwards;
Camber had all to himself the land to west of Severn.
When those three brothers ruled this land, those who lived here loved
      them,
With serenity and civil peace for seventeen long years.*   1070
    Once those seventeen years were passed, speedily after

Came travelling to this territory an alien tribal king,
Who had the name **Humber**, the king of the Huns;
Evil were his habits, his henchmen were very bold;
He had laid waste many lands, and conquered those who lived there,
And many hundred islands more which lay beside the sea-shore,
Nearly every one of them from here to Germany.
   King Humber and his entire fleet with all his forces on
      board ship,   *Humber's*
Arrived in Albanac's own land and fought against his   *Invasion*
      liegemen
With fire and with warfare and with frequent wretchedness.   1080
Albanac pressed towards him with great military power,
And so they encountered: great champions fell there.
All Albanac's forces sank down on the field,
Save one or two who sought flight to the wood-fastness;
And there was Albanac himself slaughtered in the fighting.
And such damage in that land did Humber the severe
That those forces who escaped the fight fled out of the country
Into Brutus's land, to Locrinus the strong:
They told him truthfully most terrible tales:
How his brother Albanac was dead; and how Humber destroyed
      him.   1090
   Together came in full trust those two remaining brothers,
Locrin and Camber, and all their loyal men,
With each of the knights they could summon to fight.
They marched toward Humber in such heavy strength
That Humber was utterly enraged: the land to him was all engaged;
He crossed the Scottish Water with his deadly warriors: *
By battling intensely they wanted to win Britain.
Locrin and Camber came up against them:
They displayed their weapons: distress fell on the people;
Humber came to tribulation (the British were triumphant)   1100
All his men were lost to him there through Locrin and Camber,
While Humber in distress flung himself in deep water
In which he was drowned and his followers with him:
Because of King Humber's death, it had the name Humber.
   With a very mighty army Humber had harried Germany,
And had much destroyed that land, and the people much diminished;
He took from that population three very pretty girls:
The first was named **Astrild**, a noble king's daughter,
The loveliest of all women living in the world then.

These girls were stowed on shipboard along with Humber's soldiers
Who guarded Humber's best goods while he went off to
      battle.   1111
When Humber was dead, drowned in the Humber,
Locrin and Camber came up to those ships
To appropriate the objects which King Humber owned;
In the throng of mariners they discovered those three maidens:
Locrin set eyes on Astrild and with love-looks her beheld;   *Astrild*
He gathered her into his arms and gladness filled his heart;
And he whispered to her: 'I'll see to your welfare:
You're a lovely lady, and I'd like to have you
(With highest reverence) as my royal queen;   1120
For as long as I live no other will I have,
For you make me more happy than I had ever hoped to be.'

    Now Corineus was still alive then, he who was Duke of Cornwall,
And he had only one daughter but he loved her very dearly;
Locrin was under a contract, that he would have her as his consort,
And he had given her his pledge on it in the presence of his courtiers. *
But for love of this Astrild he was about to desert her.

    This news came to Corineus, he who was Duke of Cornwall,
That his beloved daughter was unloved by Locrin;
Corineus was dismayed, and depressed in spirit: 1130
He travelled to this country until he came to Locrin,
Carrying on his upper arm an enormous gisarm. *
He stood in front of Locrin and looked at him with loathing;
Corineus the champion came out with these words:
'Tell me, Locrinus, tell me, loathsome man,
Tell me, now, you madman – may you be miserable!
No one is to save you now from a scandalous death –
You have my daughter (and she my darling child)
And myself insulted: and for that you're going to suffer.
I came to land with your father, and I led his forces: 1140
Much toil, much trouble, many a sorrowful combat,
Many a grim onslaught, many a great blow struck,
Many a wound, many a marvellous fight
Did I endure on the field, in front of Brutus;
He was my dearest friend, my most doughty leader.
So for this I shall fell you. For sure, he never was your father:
For if you were Brutus's son you would never treat me with such
      shame;
For love of him I laid dead many a giant upon the ground;

And all my industrious labour you would repay with brazen insult:
Deserting the lovely one and fine, my own daughter
    Gwendoline,   1150
All for this alien, this girl they call Astrild.
You've no idea what land it was she left when she came here,
Nor which king is her father, nor which queen her mother,
And now for the love of her you'll get something which you won't
    like:
You shall be struck to pieces with my own sharp axe.'
Corineus raised it aloft and slammed down his axe, *
Smashing into a massive stone where Locrin was standing;
The stone totally shattered, and Locrin started back.
The bystanders rushed forward, those on either side,
And pulled them apart; there was panic in the army: 1160
There were many proud words.
    Then the most senior men strode to an assembly:
They held a special husting, the highest of those heroes.
Said they would not tolerate, just for alien treasure,
That there should be this quarrel between Corineus and Locrin:
'But we will give counsel, this advice we confer:
That we give to Locrin Gwendoline to be our Queen,
And keep all the oaths we made to Corineus and Locrin,
And preserve the people's love with most profound intent,
And send Astrild away, out of this country.'   1170
Locrin had to approve of this, as it was his people's advice:
So he took Gwendoline and had her as his wife,
And he told them this (though it was not true)
That now Astrild would be sent right out of the country.
But this he did not do at all, planning to deceive them,
But took one of his retinue, whose loyal faith he knew,
And commanded him most secretly to steal away from court,
And commanded him to go to the town then called Troynovant
(Which in our language was given its present name of London)
And there, in great haste above everything else,   1180
Fashion an earth-house, attractive and fine: *Astrild's*
The walls made of stone, the doors of whale-bone,   *Earth-House*
And make it in a pleasant place, away from people's prying.
And put inside plenty of coal and sufficient clothing:
Coverlets and purple cloths and plenty of golden coins, *
Plenty of wine, plenty of wax and plenty of welcome things.
And then afterwards straight, moving always at night,

31

And by secret devices, convey Astrild inside it.
All this did that noble man, as Locrin had instructed him
(After all, every good man ought to do his lord's command!)   1190
    Seven years was Astrild in that same earth-house,
Without ever going out of doors or anyone knowing her in there,
Except for King Locrin and his companion with him.
Whenever he went to Troynovant, then he said to poor Gwendoline
That his god there he wished for one week to revere
In devout seclusion: he did not dare do other
Lest someone found out what he wanted there.
Gwendoline believed him (telling lies was his talent);
Meanwhile Locrin was so rampant that he made his Astrild pregnant,
And Gwendoline also: he had got her pregnant too.   1200
Astrild had a daughter in her earthen house:
She was baptised in the rites which they observed in those times,
And was called **Abren**; there was no prettier child then;*
While Gwendoline had a son (she felt the prouder of him):
Madan he was known as, the king's noble son;
This child grew and flourished and everybody loved him.
When he had learned to walk, and to talk to people,
King Locrin took him, his lovely son Madan,
And sent him to Corineus, away to his country,
So that he should train him well and teach him etiquette,   1210
And this he did most earnestly as long as he was able.
    And then the time came gliding which for each man waits in hiding:
Corineus the mighty was meeting his life's end.
This the king had heard: to him it was consoling.
When he knew for certain that Corineus was dead,
He took from his forces twelve faithful men,
To conduct Gwendoline into her father's land,
Into Cornwall, to her own countrymen.
So Gwendoline was in her home and with her, her son Madan;
And greatly she complained of it to all those companions   1220
Whom her father had commanded in the course of his lifetime.
    She assembled together all her friends and relations,
And all of the knights whom she could summon to fight;
And all the folk she knew well who were her firm friends,
And those she did not know came across to her
From different lands, for silver and for gold,
And readily she gave it to those good champions,
And asked them in return for it to avenge all her wrongs.

King Locrin had openly taken Astrild to him:
He found her desirable and adopted her as his Queen: 1230
Out of this delight came many great disasters.
Men notified Locrin, who was king of this nation,
That Gwendoline and her army were advancing in this country
To avenge all her harm on the King and the Queen.
The king with his army advanced to oppose her,
And they joined battle together just beside a river,
The waters of the Stour; that fight was very stern.*
In Dorsetshire Locrin suffered his death:
An arrow hit him in the heart so that he heaved his last:
There he was fated, and many of his forces, 1240
And the survivors fled away and made a panic flight.
   Gwendoline had the upper hand and obtained for herself all this
      land:
So she advanced on the castle where Astrild lay inside,
She seized Astrild and Abren and got men to bind them,
And had them thrown down into very deep water;
There they both drowned and suffered their deaths.
   So Gwendoline now was the nation's lady.   GWENDOLINE
Then she issued an edict (with an element of wit)
That in future those same waters where Abren had been drowned
Should be known as Avren because of Maiden Abren, 1250
And for love of Locrin, who was her king and lord,
Who engendered Abren upon the woman Astrild.
So then she had disposed of the King, the new Queen and their child.
And Avon still is the name of that stream, which at Christchurch
      enters the sea.
   Gwendoline was very strong, now she had all Britain in her hand,
And she was very well advised, and to each man she gave his rights;
Right through her land each man could travel even were he carrying
      gold.
Ten years she was with Locrin, and would often grieve and would
      repine;
For fifteen years and nine days after Locrin had died
All Britain she ruled as well as the best, 1260
In peace and in plenty: there was joy in the people.
Then she put into Madan's hand all the king his father's land;
To Cornwall she returned, which her father had once ruled,
And she lived there in that place: the people were the more
      content.

Then Madan her son took a wife, and most gracious she   MADAN
    was.
By her he had two boys but both of them were most vicious:
Membriz they called the elder, **Malin** the younger.
But for forty years their father Madan with honour ruled his realm,
But when his life's end approached, he thought he had found the best
    action:
To both his sons he gave command of all his rich royal lands.   1270
But when their father was dead, wickedly both the sons acted:
Between them rose conflict and crime, and they were both in contest;
Slaughter came and much sorrow, all because of their   MEMBRIZ
    sinning.   *and*
But Membriz committed evil (he was a traitorous criminal):   MALIN
With Malin his brother he made peace and to keep
    concord made promise,
And so he chose a day when their distinguished men should come,
Peace and a pact to ratify between him and his brother.
    On the day that had been set together they all met;
Membriz had no sooner made that peace than he stirred up unrest:
He created much sorrow indeed, for there his brother he slaughtered.
And so he won all of this land: it lay at his sole command.   1281
Membriz hated all his kin: not one of them could please him.
The rich he turned into paupers, the humble cursed him roundly;
Any man too noble whom he dared not topple,
He would give draughts of poison so that at once he died.
He took a very gracious wife; just one single son he had by her,
Ebrauc, that was his name and everywhere he was known.
    Membriz did an evil deed, but worse still would befall him;
Evil things were to his taste; he totally spurned his consort:
He took his serving-men to bed and women quite avoided.   1290
Twenty years he ruled this land and ruined those who lived here.
But then there came a time for him when his troubles found him out:
When he went off to the woods to his own disaster,
To go hunting after deer, which was how he met his death.
    In the wood he found a most beautiful hind:
The hunters all pursued it with their horns and loud clamour;
So quickly did they give chase the king got completely lost,
And no longer even had one of all of his men;
He went into a valley where he discovered woe
In the form of a pack of wild, rabid wolves;   1300
They leaped upon him on every side,

And tore the king apart and tugged his limbs in pieces,
And his horse as well, until dead they both fell.
    That was the fate of Membriz who betrayed his brother Malin.
Just one son he had by his self-same queen,
Who was called Ebrauc, most admired of all the kings   EBRAUC
Who ever have to govern land or command those who live there.
All his kin he honoured, the rich ones and the humble:
The rich he allowed to be quiet; the humble had all they required.
He had the land cultivated; serving-men came to support him.   1310
There was bliss in the country at all kinds of things;
He maintained firm peace and no man broke his faith.
    His strong knights were good: fierce in their knighthood
They kept desiring war: for that their Lord disliked them;
The king knew all this well though he did not dare to tell;
By the seaside he arranged for strong ships to be prepared;
After a short span the ships were all ready,
And in them he placed his powerful knights,
And sent them off to France with a massive army,
And they ravaged France and very far beyond it,   1320
And all the territories tributary to it:*
Vast was the treasure which they had captured,
And home again they came all safe and unharmed.
And this was the first king who ever went raiding,
Who went abroad to raid out of this land;
For a very long time after all those living here
Were exeedingly rich from all that plundering.*
    An idea then came to Ebrauc the famed
That he would construct two strong townships.
He took his forces and marched forth and made his way due
      north,   1330
On this side of Scotland; there he took his station.
First he constructed a town and he called it **Kaer Ebrauc**;
The second on a hilltop; Adud he named that one.*
Then it was called Kaer Ebrauc; afterwards it was called Eborac;
After that came foreign men and 'Eoverwic' they pronounced it;*
And those northern men, not long ago at all,
Through their carelessness, they called it York.
Then the king marched further north yet and he founded a new town,
Upon the mount of Angnetes, marvellously pretty:
Maidens' Castle it was called (I do not know who it was
      named for).*   1340

Ebrauc lived for a very long time and ruled the land with glory;
For sixty years he was king; in peace he held his kingdom,
But he had many different wives who increased his descendants:
He had twenty surviving sons, and each had a separate mother.
He fathered thirty fine daughters, all of them pretty females.
Hear now the names of all his sons as I announce them to you:
1 **Brutus Vaert-Escut**; 2 Margadud; 3 Sisilvius; 4 Regin; 5 **Bladud**;*
6 Morvit; 7 Lagon; 8 Ebedloan; 9 Ricar; 10 Spaden; 11 Gaul;
    12 Pardan;
13 Aeldad; 14 Gangu; 15 Kerin; 16 Luor; 17 Ruc; 18 Assarac;
    19 Buel; 20 Hector.
That was the list of all the sons of noble King Ebrauc.   1350
Now listen to his daughters' names (all of them were born nobly):
The eldest was called **Gloigin**, then came Ocidas, Ourar, Ignogen;
5 Guardid; 6 Radan; 7 Guendlian; 8 Angarad; 9 Guenboden;
    10 Methelan;
11 Malure; 13 Ecub; 13 Zangustel; 14 Scadud; 15 Kambreda;
    16 Methahel;
17 Gaz; 18 Echem; 19 Nest; 20 Gorgon; 21 Wladus; 22 Ebraen;
    23 Blangru; 24 Egron;
25 Bedra; 26 Aballac; 27 Eangnes; 28 **Andor**; 29 Scadiald; 30 **Galoes**
(It was after this, Galoes that Wales took its name):
Galoes was lovelier than all of the others,
Dearest to the king of the sisters and of the brothers;
And the best educated was An[d]o[r]; she knew well about
    etiquette;†   1360
Gloigin they called the one who was eldest; she was also in all ways
    the noblest.
[They were all well clothed;] they were all well cared for.†
    King **Silvius** of Lombardy was the closest relative they had;
With all pomp he sent post-haste to King Ebrauc in this country,
Asking him to send to him all of his daughters,   *Lombardy*
And he would bestow them all on his noblest men,
Very noble knights from the Trojan nations
Who lived in Lombardy, from their own strain, though streams did in
    fact divide them;
And as the women of Lombardy were quite repulsive to them,   1369
Therefore the king was sending for these girls to give to his noblemen.
That's what he did, and so it was done: the Lombards came to grief
    for it!
So then King Silvius had his way, and wielded power in Lombardy

And all his Trojan relatives attached themselves to him;
Some of the brothers who were sons of Ebrauc came over there with
      their sisters:
They got themselves weapons, they got themselves ships, they got
      themselves men who could defend them;
They sent over the entire country to get themselves a great army;
Then those knights who came from Britain marched out from
      Lombardy to Germany:
Assarac who came out from this land his brothers called 'comman-
      der'.
They marched with vigilance and with wisdom so long that they came
      to Germany's kingdom.
Huge castles they embarked on; they slaughtered and they burned
      down; and that land they obtained.
  Ebrauc their father held this land: sixty years he held   **1381**
      command.
He had retained here with himself the eldest of his sons;
His fame was widespread and good: he was called **Brutus Vaert**
      Escud;
Twelve years he ruled this land of kings when his father left it to him;
One son he had who was called **Leil** who held this kingdom   LEIL
      after him
For fully twenty-five years after his father's days;
He constructed a great town, lovely and gracious:
To commemorate Leil the king, Kaer Leil they called it;
In all the north region no town had such perfection.*
King Leil ruled this land firmly; he made laws which were very
      stern;   **1390**
But towards his life's end he lost all his good luck
When all his noble earls and all his great barons
Created much unrest: they refused altogether to keep the King's
      peace;
They had for their own king nothing but blatant scorning,
And every reckless person indulged his selfish passions;
Then the king became sick from overpowering sorrow,
And soon after that came the day when the king dead lay.
  This king had just one son who was a very good man,
He was also a good knight, known as **Ruhhudibras**;   RUHHUDIBRAS
The knight took up rule and the kingdom as well,   **1400**
And for thirty-nine long years he ruled the people,
After his father, who was Leil, had departed this life.

He settled this land, he worked for peacefulness,
He established strong laws; he was stern with the foolish
But he loved those people whose lives were law-abiding;
Every single good man he honoured with property;
He enforced peace and truce upon pain of limb and life.
He established a noble town which he called Winchester;
This act he found so fulfilling that he then founded Canterbury,
And Shaftesbury Castle on the downs of Waladon.   1410
Never since has there come any stranger thing
Than for a huge eagle to speak, on the castle as it sat,
Where King Ruhhudibras himself was able to hear,
And all of his knights who were there with him.
This bird bore witness of the king's demise;
Soon after Ruhhudibras died: his people were distressed.

    His son was called **Bladud**; he was a very busy man;   BLADUD
He was strong and very big-built, a mighty man and rich;
He knew the wicked arts and with the Devil he would speak,
And all he ever desired the Devil would tell him.   1420
This same king Bladud made the town of Bath,*
By very great ingenuity with a stone engine,
As huge as a wooden beam, which he laid in a running stream;
This same thing makes the water hot, and healing for people.
Opposite the bath he put up a temple in the name of one divinity,
(You who want to hear her name: **Minerva** she was known as);
For her he had a reverent love and he called her 'lady';
In the temple he had burning a brazier of fire
Which never lost its flaring light in winter or in summer,
But always the fire was tended, as the king instructed,   1430
In honour of his lady whom he loved in his heart.

    What this King Bladud did was widely celebrated.
When he had done this thing then he thought up another:
He boasted that he would fly in the air like a bird,*
So that all folk could witness it, and observe his flying.
He made himself a feather-coat (for which he had great disgrace);
He marched off to London with many of his people;
He then put his feather-coat on and thereupon his flight began:
With his magic flight he soared up to the sky,
He floated very high: to the clouds he was drawing nigh –   1400
The wind gusted against him and his flying grew feeble,
The strings all snapped which he was strung up with,
He was dashed to the dust: the king was doomed.

High up on a spot situated in London
Was the temple of Apollin who was a tremendous fiend:
The king fell on the roof of it and into pieces split.
And so this kingly realm of its king was bereft;
Twenty years had Bladud had this kingdom in his hand,
After his father Ruhhudibras who the rich king Leil's son was.

    Bladud had just one son: **Leir** he was called.   LEIR
After his father's day he held this distinguished land   1451
For his lifetime; his rule lasted sixty years.
He founded a noble town by his notable skill,
And caused it to be named simply after himself:
Kaer Leir the town was called (the king really loved it)*
Which we in our language now pronounce '**Leicester**';
Long ago in the olden days it was a very handsome town,
But then there settled on it very much sorrow,
So that it was all destroyed through the inhabitants' death. *

    Sixty years did Leir have this whole land in his control.   1460
The king had three daughters by his distinguished queen;
He had no son at all (about that he felt sadness)
To uphold his honour, but just these three daughters:
The eldest daughter was called **Gornoille**, the second **Regau**, the third
    Cordoille,
Who was the youngest sister, in beauty fairest of them all;
She was as beloved to her father as his own dear life.
Then the king grew elderly and enfeebled in his strength,
And he considered carefully what was the remedy
For his dominion after his death.
He said to himself (and this was quite wrong):   1470
'I will divide my realm among all my daughters,
And give them my kingly land, divide it for my children.
But first I shall find out which one is my best friend,
And she shall have the best part of my precious land.'
So the king reasoned, and accordingly summoned
Gornoille; he called his gracious daughter
Out of her bower, to her dear father.

    In this way the old king spoke, as he sat in regal state:
'Tell me, Gornoille, with your true words,
Very dear you are to me, how much you love me;   1480
What value do you rate me at, to get rule in this kingdom?
Gornoille was very wary (as are women almost everywhere)*
And she replied by lying to her father who was king:

'Dear father, darling, as I hope for God's favouring,
So help me, Apollin, for my faith is all in him,
You alone are dearer to me than all this entire world,
And once more to you I'll emphasise: you are dearer than my life;
And this I'm telling you as truth; you surely can believe me.'
Leir the king believed in his daughter's lying,
And this was the answer the old king gave his daughter: 1490
'I tell you, Gornoille, beloved darling daughter,
God shall reward you well for this kind of greeting:
Through being so old, I've become much less bold,
Yet you love me exceedingly, more than any one living;
My desirable lands I shall in three parts divide:
Yours is the best part, you are my precious daughter,
And you shall have as lord the best of all my thanes
Whom I can detect in all of my kingdom.'
   Next the old king spoke with his [second] daughter:†
'Dear daughter, Regau, what good reasoning can you make
      me?   1500
Declare before my doughty men how dear I am to your heart!'
Then [she] answered with witty words [but not with her heart]:†
'All that is alive is not to [me] so dear†
As to me is but one of your limbs compared with my own life.'
But she did not speak sincerely, any more than her sister;
All her lying her father believed.
Then the king answered (his daughter had cajoled him):
'The third part of my land I present into your hands;
You shall take the lord who is most beloved by you.'
   Even then the people's king would not put off his silliness: 1510
He gave orders to call before him his daughter Cordoille;
Of the three she was the youngest, with ready truth the strictest,†
And the king loved her more than both the two others.
Cordoille heard all that lying which her sisters spoke to
      the king,   *Cordoille's*
Made a loyal promise to herself that she would not tell him   *honesty*
      lies:
To her father she would say the truth, whether he were glad or sad.
Then the old king spoke (unreason went with him):
'Now I will hear too, Cordoille, from you,
How dear, so help you Apollin, is to you this life of mine?'
Then loudly answered Cordoille, and she did not say it
      quietly: 1520

40

With joking and laughter to her well-loved father:
'You are dear to me as my father, and I to you as your daughter;
My love for you is loyal and true, since I'm closely related to you,
And as I hope for favour, I will say you one thing further:
Just so much value you're rated at as you are [ruler] of,[†]
And just so much as you possess, men will love you for it,
For at once his price is lowered, the man who little owns.'
So spoke the young girl Cordoille, and then she sat very still.
    Then the king grew very angry, being not at all appeased,
And thinking in his mind it was all her lack of manners,   1530
That she estimated him so low that she would not esteem him
As had her two sisters, who both spoke lies in unison.
King Leir blanched as white as if he were a bleached cloth,
So were his face and his flesh, for he was madly fuming;
With the fury he was so astounded he fell down unconscious;
As he slowly got to his feet the girl was really frightened;
When the great outburst broke it was evil that he spoke:
'Attend now, Cordoille, as I tell you how I put you in my will:
Of my daughters you were my dearest; now you are loved by me the
        least;
You are never going to hold one bit of my land.   1540
Between my real daughters I shall divide my realm,
And you are to be worthless and wallow in wretchedness;
Never did I dream that you would so despise me!
For that you shall be as dead, I find: go from my sight and from my
        mind!
Your sisters are to have all my kingdom: this conforms to my will;
The Duke of Cornwall is to have Gornoille,[*]
And the King of the Scots have Regau the sweet,
And I here give them all the riches that I am ruler over.'
    And everything the old king did, just as he'd decided.
Often had the girl been sad, yet never till then were things so
        bad;   1550
She was [anguished] in heart at her father's anger.[†]
She went off to her room where she spent much time in gloom,
Because she would not lie to her beloved father.
The girl was very discomfited because her father dismissed her,
And took the best course by remaining in her room,
And there endured mind-grief and mourned incessantly.
And so for some time things stayed the same.
    In France there was a king, noble and courageous,

Aganippus he was called, he was a commander of champions.
He was a young king, but he had as yet no queen;   1560
By his messenger he sent over into this land,
To Leir the king, and greeted him lovingly,
Asking him to do his will by giving him Cordoille,
And he would have her as a most high queen,
And do first at her request what would to her be dearest;
Much had travelling men talked about the maiden's
Lovely face and friendliness, (so they informed the French king),
Of her very great beauty, of her great dignity,
How she was patient, lovely in her deportment:
No other in King Leir's land was such a gracious woman;   1570
And King Aganippus greeted King Leir like this.
The king considered carefully what action he should try;
He had a missive composed, and carefully had it inscribed,
By his messenger had it sent into the land of the French.
In this way the king's letter ran (it was widely published):
    'The King of Britain, by the name of Leir,
Greets Aganippus, commander of France:
Honour be yours [for] your achievement,[†]
And your fine letter, intended to bring me your greeting;
But I wish to make you aware by what I write here,   1580
That in two parts I've divided my desirable land,
And bestowed it on my two daughters both of whom are very dear;
I have another daughter, the third, but it's not my concern where she
    lurks,
Because she derided me and she declared me despicable,
And she was utterly disdainful about my old age;
She made me so very angry that adversity shall attend her;
Of all my lands, and of all those who live there,
Which I ever acquired, or ever may acquire,
I tell you most truly, she shall never have a tittle.
But if you want to have her because she's an honest girl   1590
I will preserve her for you, and send her to you in a ship,
In the clothes she stands up in: she gets no more from me.
If you're prepared to take her, then this same I will offer.
I have told you my reasons; "may you prosper" is my benison.'
    This letter came to France to the fair-minded king;
He had it read to him; precious were its symbols to him.
Then the king mused that this must be a mean trick
By which King Leir her father wasn't going to let him have her,

And much the more madly he pined for that maiden,
Saying to his barons, this very busy king: 1600
'I am enough of a wealthy man not to want any more now,
And King Leir is not going to take that girl away from me:
No! I want to have her as my high queen;
Let her father have all his land, all his silver and his gold;
I'm not asking for any property: myself, I have got plenty,
Only that girl Cordoille: then I shall have my wish fulfilled.'
With written word and oral he sent back to this land,
Asking Leir to send across his daughter who was gracious,
And he would readily receive her and great respect would show her.
And then the aged king took his admirable girl   1610
In the clothes she stood up in, and let her sail off
Over the sea-current: her father was severe.
The French king Aganippus received this female child,
(His people all consented) and he crowned her as his queen.
And so she stayed and lived there, beloved of the people,
While her father King Leir lived on in this land,
Having given to his two daughters all his desirable lands.
Gornoille he gave to Scotland's king:
He was called **Maglaunus**, and mighty strength was his.
To the Duke of Cornwall he gave his daughter Regau.   1620
    Next it befell then, immediately after,
That Scottish king and the Duke were speaking together;   *Conspiracy*
In very secret conclave they took as counsel
That in their own hands they would have all this land,
And allow King Leir as fee for the time he was living
Both by day and by night a retinue of forty knights,
And they would provide him with hawks and with hounds
So that he could journey over all the country,
And live in delight all the time he was alive.
So they discussed it and afterwards performed it.   1630
And King Leir [liked] it at first — but later on he suffered.†
So Leir proceeded to the Scottish people,
To Maglaune his son-in-law and to the elder daughter.
The king was received there with very much reverence,
And he was well supplied with forty knights in attendance,
With horses and with hounds, with all that he had need of.
    Next it befell then, immediately after,
That Gornoille considered carefully what might be her   *Gornoille*
    policy;

43

She had a very low opinion of her father's honoured state,
And began to moan about it to Maglaune her husband.   1640
And said to him in bed as they lay together:
'Tell me, my lord, most beloved of men to me,
It seems to me my father has now lost his spirit,
He has no dignity, he's losing his mind;
It seems to me the old man will be senile before long.
Here he keeps forty knights every day and every night,
He has here those henchmen and all their serving-men,
Hounds and hawks – and we're hard done by through it;
They contribute nothing, and they cost us a lot,
And all the goods we give them they cheerfully receive them,   1650
And give us no thanks at all for everything we do;
What's more they insult us badly by beating up our men;
My father's got too many of these idle men:
Let's pack a quarter of them quickly off the premises,
He's got plenty with thirty thrusting to the tables.
We've got cooks ourselves to scurry to the kitchens,
We've got porters ourselves and plenty of cupbearers,
Let's send some of this horde to hurry off where they want;
As my hope is for God's favour I won't put up with it any longer!'
    Maglaunus was listening as his queen carried on like this,   1660
And he made response to her with really moral words:
'Lady, you're saying very wrong things; haven't you got enough
    belongings?
Just give your father a happy life: he isn't going to live very long!
Just think: if kings from abroad were to hear the message
That we treated him like that they'd take us to task for it.
Let's leave him in charge of his men as he chooses
(And this is my own advice) since soon after this he'll die,
And anyway we've got our hands on half of his royal lands.'
Gornoille said at this: 'My lord, hold your peace!
Let me plan all this, and I'll provide the arrangements!'   1670
She sent word in her scheming to the knights' lodging,
And ordered them to go away as she refused to give food any more
To many of the henchmen, many of the serving-men
Who had come to that place there along with King Leir.
    King Leir heard of this, and was furious about it;
Then the king lamented with low-spirited words,
And this is how he spoke, sorrowful at heart;
'A curse on the man who rules land and is respected

Who hands it over to his child while he himself could hold it,
For often it happens that he afterwards regrets it.   1680
Now I will depart from here directly for Cornwall;
I shall talk reasonably with Regau my daughter
Who had Duke **Hemeri** and my desirable land.'
      Away the king went down to the southern end,
To Regau his daughter, as he'd run out of good advice.   *Regau*
When he came to Cornwall his reception there was regal,
And for all of the half year with all his household he was there.
Then Regau said to her Duke Hemeri:
'Lord, listen to me: it's the full truth I'm telling, see?
We've made a great mistake here by taking in my father   1690
With his thirty knights: it isn't convenient.
Let's get rid of twenty; ten are quite enough,
Seeing all they eat and drink, and they bring nothing in.'
Then said Duke Hemeri (quite betraying his old father):
'As sure as I stand here alive he won't have more than five!
That's quite enough retinue, he hasn't got anything to do,
And if he wants to leave over it, let's push him out at once.'
And as they had discussed, so they dispatched things:
They took from him his retinue and all his royal attendants,
Refusing to leave with him more knights than five.   1700
      When King Leir saw all this his life was a misery;
He lost all his composure and he bitterly complained,
Speaking these words with a sad and serious face:
'Woe to wealth, o woe: how you betray many a man!
When most trust of all he puts in you, then is the time you prove
            untrue.
It was not long ago, and fewer years than two,
That I was a rich king in charge of my knights.
Now things have happened to me that I sit here empty,
Of all wealth deprived – I'm weary of my life.
I was with Gornoille, with my gracious daughter,   1710
Lived in her country with my thirty knights,
And still I could be living, but then began travelling,
I thought that I would do well so, but now worse things I undergo;
I shall go back to the Scots, to my sweetest daughter,
Craving pity of her, since she will not respect me,
Beg her to admit me with my five attending knights;
There I will live out my time and endure these torments,
Just for a little while, I shall not live very long.'

King Leir then set forth for his daughter settled in the north;
Just for three whole nights she sheltered him and his knights,   1720
On the fourth day she swore, by all of heaven's power,
That he must not have more than a single knight there,
And if that displeased him, let him go wherever pleased him.
Often had King Leir been sad but never till then were things so bad.

Then the old king spoke – anguished was he in his heart –
'Woe to death, woe to death! Why will you not destroy me?
Cordoille spoke true, as I know now I must rue,
My youngest daughter who once was dear to me,
Then so hateful she was to me because she told me truthfully
That worthless is he and valued low, the man who all too little
    owns,   1730
And I could not be rated more than the worth of what I ruled.
All too true spoke that young woman: with her there goes much
    wisdom.
While I had my royal lands all my liegemen loved me,
For my lands and for my money all my barons knelt at my knee;
Now I am in dire poverty; for that, not a single man loves me.
But my daughter told me the truth: now I believe her well enough,
And both her two sisters said to me lies,
"That they had so much love, I was more loved than their life";
And my daughter Cordoille spoke words of deep profit,
That she loved me in fairness as one should a father;[†]   1740
How could I ask for more from my daughter dear?
Now I will set forth and be ferried over sea,
And hear from Cordoille what may be her will.
Her honesty put me in a rage, and now because of that I'm in disgrace,
For now I'm forced to plead for what before I simply scorned;
She can't treat me any worse than to turn me off her land!'

Leir went to the sea-side with one single servant,   *Leir*
He went aboard a vessel and no one knew him at all;   *in*
The sea they crossed over and quickly took harbour;   *France*
Off then went King Leir with no more than one servitor.   1750
They enquired after the queen so they could come to her quickly:
Those living there directed them to the land's queen.
King Leir went into a field and rested on the fallows,
And went off his servant, who was loyal and obedient,
Up to Queen Cordoille; he said, quiet and still:
'Fair Queen, may you prosper! I am your father's server,
And your father has arrived here: of all his land he is deprived there.

Your sisters have both now broken faith with him:
He comes very poor into this land of yours:
Help him! You can and must – he is your father – as it is just.'   1760
   For long Queen Cordoille sat very silent and still;
She flushed red there on her seat just as if with wine replete,
The servant knelt there at her feet – and straight after he felt better
For when the outburst broke it was good things that she spoke:
'Lord Apollin, thanks I render that to me here comes my father;
I hear news which I love, that my father is alive.
For I shall give him good help and wise (I would rather die otherwise).
Be attentive to me, servant, and hear my instruction:
I will give in your keeping a casket most rich;
Silver coins in it secure, a hundred pounds of them, for sure.   1770
I shall entrust to you a steed, a good one and powerful,
To transport this treasure to my dearest father,
And tell him that I greet him with most gracious greetings,
And urge him to go swiftly to some noble town,
And find himself rooms in the richest of [lodgings],†
And first for himself get whatever was his favourite,
Of food and drink and decent clothes,
Of hounds and hawks and splendid horses;
Let him have in his house forty household knights
Rich and well born, resplendently clad.   1780
Make him a good [bed], frequently bathe him,†
Give him blood-letting, little and often.
When you need more silver, seek for it from myself,
And to him I shall send good plenty from these parts.
But he must not make known where it was he lived before,
Not to knight nor servitor nor ever any master.
   'When forty days are gone then he may be known again
As my beloved lord, who is Leir in his own land,
Come across the salt-stream to oversee his dominions.
I shall receive the news as if I knew nothing of him,   1790
Leave to go and meet him with my own lord,
Rejoicing at my [father's] fortunate arrival;†
Let no man ever know other than that he's newly come,
And send this in writing to my lord the king.
So take now this property and see that you act properly;
And if you spend it as I say it shall be for your good some day.'
   The servant took the property and set off towards his   *Restoration*
   lord,

And to Leir the king he gave these tidings,
As he lay in the field, resting on the fallows.
At once amid rejoicing the old king's wretchedness was
    relieved,   1800
Uttering these words in the truest of tones:
'After evil there comes good; happy he who has got it.'
They went off to [a noble] town as the queen instructed,[†]
And they did everything as she devised.
    And forty days further on when time had elapsed
King Leir took the knights whom he liked the most,
And saluted Aganippus, his beloved son-in-law,
And in the message which he sent said he'd come into his land
To exchange words with his daughter who to him was very
    dear.
Aganippus gave a smile when he heard of Leir's arrival,   1810
And set off to meet him with all his attendants,
And Queen Cordoille went; and so Leir was content.
They came to meet each other and over and over again they kissed,
They went to the palace; great pleasure it gave the household:
There was trumpet song and pipes sounding along,
And all of the halls had rich cloth on the walls;
All the food trestles were groaning with gold,
And [rings of bright gold] each man had on his hands.[†]
With fiddles and with harps happy men chorused.
The king set men on the city wall to shout the news aloud
    to all,   1820
Saying that King Leir had come into their land:
'Now Aganippus commands (as he is in control of us)
That to King Leir you all show your submission,
Who is to be lord over you within all this land
For just as many years as he wishes to dwell here,
While Aganippus our own king is to be his underling.
Whoso wishes life and liberty, let him keep this amity,
And whatsoever refusal brings instant reprisal;
Thus he warns every man that he observe this command.'[†]
Then responded the populace 'We agree to implement,   1830
In thought and in word, the will of our lord.'
Throughout all that same year in this way did all those there,
In the greatest concord, in great conciliation.
    When that year had wholly gone, then Leir wished to go home,
To leave there for our own land, and asked for that king's leave.

King Aganippus answered him like this:
'You are not to travel far without extensive forces;
Now I will lend to you, from my own land's people,
Five hundred war-ships, all filled with knights,
And all which must be deployed for them on the voyage.   1840
And your daughter Cordoille, who is queen of this my land,
With extensive forces, she shall voyage with you,
And proceed thus to that place where you were the people's king.
And should any there be found who against you take a stand,
Depriving you of all your rights and of your kingdom's might,
Boldly do you fight them, and fell them to the ground,
And take possession of that land and set it in Cordoille's hand,
So that she may have it all, after your days.'
    So spoke Aganippus, and King Leir did all this,
And all he performed as his friend had instructed.   1850
To this land he proceeded, with his precious daughter;
He made peace with the best, those who wished to be obedient,
And felled everyone of those who fought against him,
And his entire kingdom he won back to his own hand,
And gave it to Cordoille, who was the Queen of France;
And so for some time things stayed the same.
King Leir in his own land lived for just three years;
Then came his ending-day and dead the king lay.
In Leir-chester his daughter had him laid out,
In Janus's temple, just as the book tells it,*   1860
And Cordoille held this land with superior strength: CORDOILLE
For fully five years she was queen here,
And meanwhile the French king made his fatal passing,
And to Cordoille came the word that she had become a widow.
    Then came a missive to Scotland's king*
That Aganippus was dead and King Leir had died.
He went through all Britain, down into Cornwall,
And told the Duke, who was strong, to make trouble in the south
        land,
As he up in the north lands, which he would acquire:
For it was a great disgrace, and also most infuriating,   1870
That ever a woman should be king in this land,
And their sons be bereft, who were much her betters,
Coming from the elder sisters, and ought to have the ascendency:
'No more shall we endure it: all the land we shall obtain;
[We shall have the land and put it in our children's hand]†   1874a

49

They began warfare: wretchedness came at once,
And the queen's sisters' sons summoned their forces;
Their names sounded like this: **Morgan** and **Cunedagius**.   MORGAN
Often they led their forces, often did they fight;
Often they were victors, and often vanquished.
Then came last of all what to them was most likeable: 1880
They killed off the British and they captured Cordoille,
Put her in close-quarters in a torture chamber,
And drove their aunt demented more than they should have,
So that the woman grew so enraged that on herself she turned her
     outrage,
And taking a long knife she deprived her own self of life.
This was an evil way so to make herself away.
     Then all this royal land was in Morgan and Cunedagius's hand;
They seized upon this land and by fighting conquered it.
Then the brothers divided all this desirable land:
Cunedagius had all the west, and Morgan had the north and
     east,   1890
And so they held all this land, for two whole years, in their hand.
When the two years had departed, then their minds divided:
Morgan was in Scotland, with the northern end in his hand;
Down in Cornwall Cunedagius had many a good rich house.
Morgan in his household had very many knights
Who did not love those living here: loathsome to them they were.
These men spoke to Morgan and they slighted his knighthood;
This is how they spoke to him, those uncivil men:
'Lord Morgan, why won't you travel, and stir up your troops,
And travel through all Britain's land and take it into your own hand?
For we are much disgraced, and our feelings are infuriated   1901
That you are sharing this land, which should all be in your own hand;
You are someone very clever and the son of the elder sister,
And you share the land with your cousin – you haven't any courage!'
     So those traitors talked, and stirred trouble with words
So long they badgered him that he believed them;
He gathered his forces, which were frightfully huge,
Marched across the Humber and created havoc:
He ravaged, he burnt, he slaughtered,
They killed, they captured all they came close to.   1910
The word came south quickly for it was known widely:
Morgan was leading a huge army and to the people doing great harm.
Then news came to Cunedagius that his cousin Morgan did all this;

Then he fell in a rage, making these remarks:
'A curse on you ever, avarice, many a man you entice;
Through you my cousin Morgan has lost all his morality,
But he shall pay the penalty, as I hope to live.'
Round all his countryside Cunedagius sent out letters,
And gathered many poeple and prepared all his army.
He marched off courageously towards his cousin Morgan;   1920
When it came to fighting, Morgan fled away,
From region to region, and he rushing after him:
Into Wales he fled, and he came following after,
And there overtook Morgan with very great strength,
And lopped off his head there – which was bad luck for him!
And slaughtered all his men whom they could get near to,
Except for such wretches as escaped alive to safety.
They took Morgan's corpse and laid it on the earth;
And well did they bury him who once was lord of Wales.
Because of Morgan all that land was known as Margan,[*]
[And now and evermore it has that name there].[†]   1930a
    Cunedagius had all this land, and over it he was   CUNEDAGIUS
      lord;
For thirty-three long years he ruled in this realm
In peace and in plenty, to his friends' pleasure.
In the days of Cunedagius who was king of this people
Romulus and Remus were founders of Rome:[*]
(Both of them were brothers, but the one slew the other).
After thirty years there came the day when Cunedagius dead lay;
He had one resolute son whose name was **Riwald**:   RIWALD
He was wise, he was handsome and he ruled this very kingdom;
Everyone loved him who lived in the land.   1940
    In that same time there occurred a strange signal,   *Plagues*
Such as never came before nor ever since to this place:
From heaven there came a miraculous flood; for three days it rained
    down blood;
For three days and three nights (it was a quite tremendous plight).
When the rain had gone there came another signal hard upon it:
Black flies came flying here and floated in men's eyes,
In their mouths and in their noses so that their very lives were lost.
Such a swarm of flies there was that they swallowed the corn and all
    the grass.
Wretched were all the people who lived in the land.
After this came such a fearsome plague that very few were left alive;

And then came a harsh event: that King Riwald was dead.   1951
   King Riwald had but one son, **Gurgustius** was his   GURGUSTIUS
     name;*   (*etc*)
His lands he held for half a year, and then he heeled over.
After him came **Sisillius**, and he soon died off here.
Then came **Lago**, who only lived eight weeks,
And then came **Kin[e] Mark**, and he was king for thirty weeks;†
And then came **Gorbodiagus** who was a good king   GORBODIAGUS
     for five years;
This king had two sons, and both of them accursed;
The elder was called **Fereus** and the younger called **Poreus**.
These two brothers were so crazed and so contrary   1960
That they were totally at enmity; they were totally opposed,
And each hated the other, as in no way should any brothers,   *Fereus*
And both in [envy and in] hate they lived here in this state,†   *and*
So that Gorbodiagus their father of his own sons was   *Poreus*
     frightened,
For often in his very hall they would fall to brawling.
The elder said that all this land he would hold in his own hand,
The younger gave him this for answer: 'I'll kill you first here with my
     spear!
Before you get it for yourself while I am still alive.'
Poreus had a heart so base and did so much his brother despise
That he wanted to betray him by some kind of means.   1970
Fereus heard this recounted, by reliable witness,
That his brother wanted to kill him, and he was deeply concerned.
He went away across the sea, which seemed to him the best,
And fled into France, onwards, to the king who was called S[i]ward;†
He begged him for protection, promised to obey him,
Be to him a loyal knight, both by day and by night.
The king was glad at his coming, and at the knights who came with
     him,
And retained him in his retinue and reverently used him.
   For fully seven years with the king he remained there;
The king found him companionable, and so did the queen.   1980
When the seven years had elapsed, then he asked to leave,
As he wished to travel into this our land.
The king lent him a force of his bravest fighters,
And himself a message sent widely through that land,
Mustering all the knights whom he could get to fight,
And so he assembled his very huge horde,

And transported them safely here to this country.
At once they began fighting and felling the population,
And his brother Poreus was advancing to oppose,
And in the fierce fighting there they felled Fereus,   1990
And all of his army they laid to the earth.

 Their mother was **Iudon**, the famed and magnificent,   IUDON
And she was deeply distressed at the dreadful disaster
That of her sons the younger had slaughtered the elder;
For her, the dead one was more dear, the live one was more dire;
The live one was for her so dire that she thought to deprive him of life.
Poreus lay in his bedroom and a grave plight he was in:
He lay there softly and was sleeping soundly;
His mother came slipping in with sinister powers,
With [six] other women, with six long knives;[†]   2000
And so the cursed mother murdered her own son:
She slit his throat across (may she be for ever lost!),
The cursed mother: with her sword she sliced him up,
And sliced off completely each limb from the other.

 Then there was much discussion all through that kingdom
Concerning Queen Iudon who killed her own son,
And of the sorrow which was seen in the land.
Then was deceased Fereus and so too was Poreus,
And the mother deprived of dominion in the land.
Then there were none of that kindred who could rule in this kingdom,
Neither woman nor weaponed man, except the grieving
  Iudon;   2011
But good men came together and drowned her in the sea-depths.[*]
Then first here there was discord: everywhere they broke concord;[*]
Serious were the pains endured through severe plundering;
Each man robbed the other, even if it were his brother;   *Civil*
Disturbance in the country and disaster to the weak;   *War*
Here was hunger and hatred, here the greatest of all harms;
Here there was much mortality so that few were left alive.
Four men here were powerful and they had extensive forces;
They oppressed all the others and abased their station.   2020
So they spoke together, and the high men said
That they had the intention to divide this land between them.
So they decreed it, and afterwards they did it.

 In Scotland the king was **Stater**, in Logres it was **Piner**;
Cloten had all Cornwall and **Rudauc** had North Wales,
But Cloten had the greatest right to have the whole realm,

But the rest were rougher and also they were richer
In gold and in great wealth and in good lands;
Cloten they completely shunned, and scoffed at his enmity.
Cloten had Cornwall which he held well in peace;   2030
Cloten had one son, a splendid man entirely:
He was handsome, he was huge, in fighting he was famous,
As a knight he was bold and in giving bountiful;
Good habits and kind he had in his mind;
His name sounds like this: **Dunwallo**
    Molinus,   DUNWALLO MOLINUS
The most handsome man who ever ruled this kingdom.*
Once he could bear weapons and well master his horses,
He swept the length of this land as if he were a lion.
He struck down king Piner, he killed all his people,
And those who withstood he brought down to his boot;   2040
And all of Logres land he acquired for his own hand.
Then he changed direction and drove directly into Wales,*
Where he found King Rudauc who was rough in fighting;
Towards him also sped there the king of Scotland, Stater.
They talked there of truce, of tranquillity and treaty;
On oath they declared that they would never deceive.
  So they made their pact, and back proceeded Dunwallo,
With his great army to Cornwall his country.
Then news came to Stater that Dunwale was very far:
With a huge force of Scotsmen he surged into this land;   2050
Rudauc with his Welshmen (the mob was by so much the more)
Into this land they flooded and the folk here they slew;
Far and wide they raced, towns they set ablaze;
A great deal they laid waste with horrors of the worst.
The news came to Dunwale, where he was in Cornwall,
Of what Rudauc was doing here, as was also Stater.
Then Dunwale declared, as a very valiant man:
'Now they have broken truce with all their treachery.
By Apollin's mercy I'll no more believe their loyalty;
Now let [us] rush and run raging against them:†   2060
Under this heaven let right make decision.
Have my message sent throughout all my lands,
And command each good man who is glad to keep peace,
And all who hold land of me to come here at once,
And send travelling men to other territories
My land to help me uphold, for silver and for gold,

And I will carry my right into strong fight
Against these sworn brothers who are both of them forsworn,
For often is he overwhelmed who stands in the wrong,
And never can a perjurer long enjoy privilege.'   2070
　　When Dunwale had spoken all men praised his opinion.
He summoned his army, such as was never in the country
Since the time that Brutus's men came travelling here.
He recruited his ranks and rode on in great state
Towards the two kings, and found them in the forest.
They engaged battle and bravely they fought;
The fated all fell there, their faces grew pale;
All the soil of the fields there was spattered with blood.
Many a hardy man there was hacked down with swords.
Dunwale in that fighting was fantastically brave;   2080
The fighting was very strong, very severe and very long;
Dunwale in the fight had very good knights,
Wise men and wary, and many they felled.
Dunwale considered carefully what was his strategy.
He took from his army six hundred knights
From the best rank of all, and in battle the boldest,
And said to them this, in his secret council:
'Let us take these weapons which are lying by this wall,
And hold before our breasts our very broad shields,
And let us go around the sides, as if we were some of theirs,   2090
And all the while shall our forces be fighting on steadily.
When Stater's band see our fine shields
Coming in haste, it will greatly console them;
Through the weapons they'll suppose that those are their companions.
We shall be making ready and will kill King Rudauc,
And directly after, right there, we shall kill King Stater.
With strength we shall proceed straight through our opponents,
And fell all our foes, since all of them are fated!'
　　This was Dunwale's declaration, as a most valiant man,
And everything was performed just as he instructed.   2100
They took up the shields which were lying in the fields,
Broad ones and good and covered with gold,
And sought out the kings where they were in the combat.
The kings were satisfied, [the sight was agreeable],[†]
Judging from those shields that these were their soldiers.
As soon as Dunwale came close he gave orders to [set on] those,[†]
'Slay them with your swords, since they're all of them forsworn!'

Rudauc they killed and Stater they captured,
And dismembered him then, drawing one limb from the other.
Their spears were sturdy and his corpse was target
    practice.   2110
At once they continued towards their companions,
And when they encountered, as opponents they attacked.
The kings were both dead, and their doughty men divided;
The knights were in despair now their fame had departed,
And Dunwale's men slew all they came close to;
All the army they felled to the earth,
Save for one man, badly wounded, who painfully escaped.
    So Dunwale had this land, all acquired by his own hand.
And then he was a great king: wide spread good reports   *Laws*
    of him:*   *of*
The books bear record in unbounded examples;   *Dunwallo*
This was the first man whom they put a golden crown
    on,
Here within Britain since Brutus's men came here.   2122
He made such a peace, he made such a truce,
And laws which were good and [long] afterwards stood;†
He established a settlement and with oaths he secured it,
So that each peasant at his plough had peace like the king him-
    self;
Each wayfaring man, should he have killed or have stolen,
If he could get into a borough and find himself bail,
Then and constantly he must be given clemency
To hasten to his home and have what he owned,   2130
And if any did him injury that man was to be punished,
And so each first offence the king himself forgave.
The king made many laws which we still have in this land,
And all laws which were good and in his days stood.
Forty years he ruled this land and in joy it rested in his hand;
Then the king died: sad were his people.
Together came his leaders, and to burial led him,
Within London city they laid him well to rest,
In a noble temple, with gold they entombed him.*
    That king by his wife had two sons still alive,*   2140
The elder was called **Belin** and the younger was **Brennes**.
These brothers were reconciled through reliable advice:
Belin gave his beloved brother a share of his land
Beyond the Humber, to hold it in homage,

North towards the sea, and well might it suit him.   BRENNES
And for this he became his vassal and had to vow him homage.   *and*
Belin held this southland and Cornwall in his hand,   BELINUS
And Wales along with it, and fairly he ruled it.
For five years they held this land like this, and love there was between
    them,
So that each one loved the other just as he should his brother.*   2150
   But Brennes had evil men who abused his honour,
Each day they waylaid him with wicked instructions,
That he should break that agreement he had with his brother.
He had a retainer, in that faction a leader
Who was stirring up sedition; and with Brennus he spoke on:
'Tell me, my lord, most beloved of men,*
Why put up with it that Belin, who is your own brother,
Has so much of this land, and you have so little?
Did you not have both one father, and both of you one mother,
Both the same nurture? It's known among the people.   2160
Now lies all this great land in Belinus's own hand,
And you are his man and his knight: this is wrong and no way right.
Were you a concubine's son that you want to be outdone?
Or are you such a cowardly knight that for land you don't care in the
    slightest?
Or do you expect to die quite soon, and desert all your dependents?
Forget your promise, forget your vow, for all these people are angry
    with you.
Hearken to your men's advice, and they are willing to help you.
It seems amazing to us that you won't assert yourself.
   'You are a far better knight to win a combat and a fight,
And you are much braver and also much stronger.   2170
Cheflon you conquered and Scotland from him snatched,
He was king of Moray, who fought with you valiantly:*
First you overcame him, and afterwards you killed him,
And all his army which he brought into the country.
But well I can believe it that we are loathsome to you,
So that you hold back your thoughts from your household men;
But not for any such contempt would we conspire against you,
Not for one moment as we stand here present!
Now act as we instruct, and you yourself conduct
Twelve of your advisers, of your ablest men,   2180
And set sail now tonight, off to Norway straight,
To **Alfing** the king: you will be a welcome visitor,*

And greet the land's king and all those who live there.
  'The king has a daughter who to him is very dear;
Ask for her in your urgent need to have her as a queen.
When he sees you, a handsome knight, he will give you her at once,
      outright.
Then you must beg the king to lend you an army,
To lead to your own land to embolden your liegemen;
Ask for every single knight whom there in any way you might
Get, for silver and for gold, to come with you to this land.   2190
And we shall meanwhile guard well your kingdom.
Most discreetly you're to do these very same deeds,
So that Belin doesn't know, and he is your own brother.
But go quickly and come back soon, and so we say to advise you.
  'When you come returning home we shall all be ready
With our tremendous army to travel through the country,
To avenge your wrongs upon Belin who has branded you with
      shame.'
So spoke **Malgod**; as a traitor he was good!
The rest gave him the same advice – may they know universal malice!
  When Brennes had heard the words of his housemen,   2200
He brightened in mood: this advice he found good,   *Brennes*
And he gave them this response: 'I'll follow your advice.'   *in*
He prepared all his knights and they travelled on by nights,   *Exile*
So far that they arrived at the court of King Alfing.
The king they gave greeting and all his good men,
And the king replied to him extremely politely.
Then Brennes spoke up and stated his errand,
That he desired the king's daughtrer, to have her as a queen,
And the king agreed to all that he had asked for:
Gold and great wealth, valuables and forces.   2210
Then Brennes felt very bold, in spirit he felt blithe: *
The young girl he wedded and took her to his bed.
Seven nights he stayed there; it felt to him like seven years
Before he could return to combat with his brother.
They were raving in their mind [those who] thus him advised.†
  Brennes was in Norway, Belin was in this land;
Belin heard it said, through some trustworthy saying,
Of his brother's wiving and what motives moved him,
And of the special need which in Norway he could meet.
Belin thought quite hard about such behaviour,   2220
And these words he said (the saying was trustworthy):

'Accursed ever be the brother who betrays the other!
Where are you, my knights? where are you my champions?
Where are you, my dearest men: now we must depart!'
   They marched off down to Humber lands: the castles there were
     strong;
Of those castles they took all, and strengthened their walls.
He bad them blow their trumpets, and captured all the boroughs
Which were on his brother's lands: those he had in his own hands.
He put in food as needful, and weaponed men were plentiful,
So that he could hold them against Brennes's onslaught.   2230
All his knights and he set off towards the sea;
They camped beside the shore-line and kept watch intently.
   Brennes was in Norway, and of this he knew nothing:
He thought that his brother knew nothing of his behaviour.
He took his leave from Alfing, the Norwegian king,
Who gave him ready answer: 'I wish you constant welfare,
And my daughter, **Delgan**, who to me is very dear.'
   The young queen realised then, that she would have to journey:
Now she had had a lover, and this man had deeply loved her;
He was the king of Denmark, and dear he was to her heart.   2240
He was a very good knight: **Godlac** he was entitled.   *Delgan*
Then Delgan the queen sent a message into Denmark,   *and*
And dispatched it to Godlac, her dearest and good man,   *Godlac*
Secretly inscribed runes she sent to him to read,
And told him that to Brennes, a king who came from Britain,
She had now been wedded and he'd taken her to bed,
Entirely unwillingly, and about this she was unhappy,
And he was now about to lead her to the land of his own people:
She had no more than three nights' space before she must set sail.
'Soon now it may turn out that I must travel from here: 2250
May you have joy and peace: we can never more converse,
So I am sending you this greeting, with my own gold ring.'
   When Godlac saw this note he was anguished, without doubt,
Silently he fell into a swoon as he sat there on his throne;
They threw on to his face cold water from the well.
When the king gained consciousness he was in grave distress;
He burst out right there with 'Where are my knights?
Let's put out speedily to sea, my splendid fighters!'
Godlac in great haste made his war-grim hosts
March towards the sea, and found there ships in plenty;   2260
He formed a mighty sea-fleet and they travelled with the tide

Towards that same harbour from which Brennes had set course.
    When Brennes came on the open sea he encountered his enemy:
Ship rushed against ship and all collapsed in splinters;
Prow against prow: the weaker was toppled;
Many a breast there was pierced with broad spear;
Helmets there rang; men were down flung;
Disaster fell thickly and Brennes fled quickly,
With Godlac in pursuit: many ships there he caught.
He could see a ship scudding, and silken was its sail-cloth;   2270
He called out to his fighters: 'Oh, now, you blighters!
That there's the queen's ship shooting in front of us;
You catch up with it, and if you can seize it,
I'll love you for ever as long as I live!'
With all their strength they oustripped it and the queen they gripped
    then.
Godlac killed the shipmen and they seized the gold and treasure,
And conducted Queen Delgan back to Denmark at once.
He intended to keep her at his own pleasure,
But quite other it was settled [very soon after].[†]
Godlac gathered speed, and glad was his heart,   2280
Thinking he'd have Delgan as his queen in Denmark;
But he met a great hindrance which he found most hateful:
Atrocious weather overcame them; the whole sky grew dark,   *Storm*
The wind swung against them and stirred up the sea,
The choppy waves churning like towns which were burning;
The rigging was stripped; disaster fell thickly;
The ships sank;
Fifty three ships there sank to the depths;
In the tumultuous seas the sails all turned round.
    Godlac had a good ship, but this did not give him joy;   2290
He considered carefully what might be the remedy:
He grabbed a battle-axe, massive and very sharp:
He hewed down the mast, in two pieces in the middle,
And let the sail and mast together lie there on the waves.
This Godlac spoke, and sorely was he grieving:
'Every able-bodied man help us to survive!
As long as we get ashore, no matter now which country!'
They travelled with the weather and they just did not know whither;
After five days' journey they landed in this country.
Up came the king's coastguards who were watching the shore,   2300
And captured King Godlac, and Delgan his queen.

They gave them this harsh ultimatum: 'You are all of you dead men,
But if you will declare to us we may yet spare you this:
Where have you come from and what did you want here?'
Godlac answered with gracious expression:
'We are sea-weary men and what we say we shall mean,
But these men don't know at all wherabouts we've made landfall,
And this beach we do not know where we have landed now,
Not this land nor those who live here, nor even who their lord is,
Nor do we know this also, if it's our enemies we speak to.   2310
But I ask you kindly, sirs, please conduct us to the king,
And I will give him news of happy things and sad ones.'
    And the coastguards led them to their own land's king,
Godlac and [the] queen, their possessions and his men,[†]
And they told him he was in Britain, in King Belin's land.
As soon as he came to the king, most sensibly he called to him:
'Good health to you, King Belin, you are Brennes's brother,
And I am called Godlac and I once was lord of good men,
King I was in Denmark, and this woman is called Delgan.
Brennes came to Norway, over to King Alfing,   2320
And the king gave him Delgan, who was already my own dear one.
Messengers came to me with tales, telling me true stories,
When Brennes wanted to depart and drag away my dear one;
I flung off to meet him with forty sturdy ships,
And with as large an army as the ships could carry.
    'Now what I tell you is a wonder: his ships were seven hundred,
And I began a fierce contest, and Brennes started fleeing;
His men were in my power, and many did I slaughter,
And there I captured Delgan, who once had been my dear one.
Now I'm telling you the truth: he's still alive, your brother,   2330
He was heading for the land, and safely got to harbour,
And then I saw the queen's ship shoot past on the waves,
And I flung after it, and I fought and won it.
And then I knew delight, as I'm breathing and have life!
Once I was on the open sea, adversity befell me,
The weather grew so wild, and the sea was raging,
And drove me into this land, left me in this country.
Now show me your pity, since you have power over me!'
    The king had them held captive in comfortable confinement,
In a strong castle, where he had them closely guarded.   2340
A bare four weeks after these [things] had befallen,[†]
Brennes came riding right into Scotland,

With four hundred ships: many folk were fated.
He sent off a message-bearer to Belin his brother,
Ordering him quickly to give him back his queen,
And also King Godlac who had slaughtered his good men,
And if he refused, then he would be the worse:
'In his lands I will go and kill all I can find,
With fighting and with fire; this firm agreement I'll keep:
Unless he will release to me what I require of him,   2350
And retreat from my land and go to his own realm,
And give me back my boroughs and my best castles,
Fortresses and towers, which he holds from me unfairly.'
   So off sped the messenger to the King Belinus,
And gave him this bad command from Brennes his brother,
And Belin then refused him all that he insisted on,
Such things he'd not abide just as long as he could ride!
The messenger sped back again and made report to Brennes.
Brennes in terrific rage summoned all his troops,
Supplying all his soldiers as if they set off to war;   2360
There was mustering of his knights as if they were off to fight.
Belin on his side started off in haste to meet him,
And great anger was there beneath the wood of Kalatere,*
Where they had their meeting, and most uncivil greeting;
Together they came, and at once they were groaning;
With fury they were fighting, by thousands they were falling:
Strongly fought King Belin, so did his Britons,
They were very brave men defending their own country.
   Brennes broke away from them and with his folk he fled,
Right off towards the sea in great uncertainty,*   2370
And Belin went after them, laying them all low:
Sixty thousand he laid to the ground.
Brennes found a ship standing by the bank,
He got himself inside it with twelve of his men,
Those were the survivors of his entire [force].†
Over the sea he was ferried, away towards France,
And those badly wounded men went into the woods.
When this affair was over, and Brennes had fled away,
Belin held a hustings of his earls in the town of York;
He requested that his powerful men provide him with right counsel:
What should best be done by him with that selfsame man,   2381
Namely with King Godlac, whom [he] held in chains,†
Since Godlac had sent him word, through a wise man,

That if he would ease him of his odious bonds,
Then he would be his vassal with all his force of men,
And he would give him all the gold which he had in Denmark's land,
And every year he would send three thousand pounds,
And would provide him with hostages he would find for him,
As long as he would let him leave, him and his companions,
And his dear beloved, for the land of Denmark.   2390
King Belin allowed him the agreement that he asked for,
And courteously let him go, and his companions too.
Belin had the hostages, and the handsome presents,
And his homage, which he had won with honour,
And Godlac led away the very lovely woman,
Whom very dear he'd bought: now to enjoy her was his thought.
    Belin held this realm for very many years,
And most generously all his people justly led;
He made a very powerful peace and his people kept it well;
There were in this land here laws which were good,*   2400
And all loved that king who was alive then in this land.
When Belin had in his hand all of the Britons' land
He travelled over all of it and established laws;
He viewed all the woods and the wilderness,
The meadows and the moorlands and the high mountains,
The boroughs and the villages, and eagerly beheld it.
The king thought carefully what could be his strategy:
He began to build a street, big, wide and straight,   *Belinus's*
Splendid and very long, right through all this kingdom,   *Streets*
And the king and all his folk called it '**Foss Way**';   2410
It runs from outside Totnes until it comes to Caithness:*
Totnes is in Cornwall, Caithness to Scotland falls.
Another street he made, very handy, from Southampton to Saint
    Dewy;
Then a third he carved, which cut this land in half.
When these streets were laid, laws for them the king made,
Saying that if any on these streets made affray, then would the king
    take his life away,
But whoever met another there, he should greet him well and fair.
These were the king's streets, which I have called to mind.
    In France meanwhile was Brennes, who was this king's brother;
In his heart he harboured rage, in his mind he felt disgrace   2420
That he had lost his kingdom and his queen whom he had loved,
And felt very ashamed that he had been so scorned.

He remained in France, with his twelve retainers,
He served the king, who was well contented with him,
And all those who lived in France, they loved Brennes much,
For Brennes obtained much property and plentifully shared it,
He was not a greedy man, but rather very generous;
He was a most courageous man and courtly were his actions,
And often things went well for him, which made him yet more
    welcome;
Then he became famous there and everywhere familiar,   2430
And the king loved him, and everyone who lived there.
Then he took his retainers with him and he requested the monarch
That he should support him, with his good people,
In getting back his land from Belin his brother.
This the king did promise, and fulfilled likewise; *
Then he asked leave to go, and his way led him further
To **Seguine**, who was lord of Burgundy,
And of the Breton lands which lie beyond the sea strand.
   Politely he addressed the duke when he sought his protection,
Saying he would obey him, acknowledge him as overlord,   2440
Loyally bow to him, and acknowledge him as leader.
At this the duke rejoiced, and respectfully received him;
Brennes was very gifted and his grace was the greater:
Brennes knew about hounds, Brennes knew about hawks,
With his own hands he knew how to handle the harp;
Because of his clever skills the courtiers loved him,
To his lord he was as welcome as if he were his very son.
The Duke had a daughter, who to him was very dear,
But he had not a single son, and at this he was saddened.
The Duke observed Brennes, who had a handsome body, *   2450
And spoke to him then, of his most sincere thoughts:
'Brennes, you are handsome, and you are high born,
And you're a very accomplished knight, and most acceptable to me;
You came across the sea's stream, you are a king's offspring,
You are so genial with me and I genuinely love you,
Everything which I promise you, I'll perform it for you:
I will give you my daughter, who is to me extremely dear,
And after my days, my own desirable lands,
For it is most agreeable to all of my barons
That things should be arranged like this, and that you should receive
    this.'
Then Brennes replied with submissive expression: 2461

'I give you thanks for this, and all your good people,
For this great respect shown when you grant me such a good.'
All this was done as the duke had decreed:
There was bliss at the court there when Brennes took this maid;
In very great respect he remained there with the duke.
When the first year had quite elapsed, then the duke was dead,
And Brennes took the territory [into his own hand];[†]
And all the people liked him there as much as their own life,
Because he guaranteed good peace, and was gracious with
      his men.   2470
He had vast tracts of land which all lay in his own hand,
And he had a very good wife, and he loved her as his life.
    Within a very few years, Brennes began thinking,
Of [how] his brother Belin of his land bereft him.[†]   *Brennes*
A message then he sent throughout Burgundian land,[†]   *Invades*
[And from far and wide he assembled his force]:[†]   2475a
The force was so enormous that it was innumerable.
He came into Normandy and there he took to sea,
And travelled in safety into this country:
Brennes disembarked on land with his large force.
The tale came to Belin which told him the truth,   2480
That Brennes his brother had come to his realm,
With innumerable forces had arrived on his shores.
Belin had men summoned throughout all his land,
And called up every champion who lived on this island
To come to him in his need and drive out the aliens.
The army was mustered and onward it marched,
And they came very close, [but one mile lay between them].[*†]
    As yet still lived [their mother], a woman wise and brave;[†]
Her name was **Tonwen**, she bore Belin [and Brenne];[†]
This old queen was so wise that she knew how to cope: 2490
She put on her a kirtel which was quite torn to pieces,[*]
And she kilted the hem till it came close to her knees;
She walked on her bare feet (she did all this for the best),
And came up to the army which had come to this country,
And enquired after Brennes, where he was among his forces.
[She was shown] where he was arming, as if intending to fight,[†]
And all of his men were donning their iron mesh.
They directed her so far, that she came upon him:
Right up to him she ran, between her arms she held him,
Again and again hugged him, again and again kissed him,   2500

[And these words she said to her beloved son]:[†]   2500a
'Oh, what is it you want, Brennes? What base strife are   *Tonwen's*
    you stirring?   *Appeal*
If you kill your brother, you will not be getting another:
There will never be but you two, and my sons are both of you.
Think about your honour! Think about your mother!
Think what I am telling you – you are my dear child.
Look, here are the nipples which you once sucked with your lips.
See, here is the very woman who bore you into the world;
See, here is the very womb in which you lay so long;
See, here is that very same body. Now do not do me such disgrace
That, because of your fight, I stab myself with a knife!   2510
    'Now it's going on seven years since you were last here,
And all agreements you have broken with your own brother;
You had become his man, and he loved you like his son;
You swore him deep oaths that you would not deceive him.
You are wrong, and he is right, and it's this that brings you in this
    plight.
And then you passed over sea, all without permission,
Over to Alfing, and took the young daughter of the king.
And so you wanted, with your army, to advance upon this country,
And do yourself the dishonour of fighting with your brother,
(If the King of Denmark had not disrupted you)   2520
And then you did come, and had disaster,
And went abroad again, and come back now with advantage:
Now you are the ruler of lands, things will go the less well for us:
With these foreign [folk] you will kill your own kindred;[†]
No knight should ever ravage where once he ruled at home,
Nor ever visit evil upon his own acquaintance.
Oh dear son, Brennes, bring down your fierce thoughts,
Cast aside your war costume and your scarlet shield,
And your spear so long, and your sword so strong,
And believe your mother, and love your own brother.'   2530
    Her tears were running over her cheeks;
Brennes saw all that, and was saddened in his heart.
He let go of his great spear and it fell over to the ground;
He shot his rich shield far out in the field,
Away he threw his good brand, and off with that byrny!
Brennes and his mother gently made their way
Into a broad field, and Belin came towards them.
Then wept this brother, and so did the other;

Then the mother spoke, mildly with her mouth:
'The two of you are my dear sons, now do go together,   2540
And be reconciled, and always be happy.
Kiss and embrace, and acknowledge your kinship;
You are both courageous knights; once I was queen:
This is no indignity your mother asks of you two!'
There they kissed each other, those who were king's children:
In front of the two armies they re-formed their friendship.
Brass trumpets were blown, there was bliss among the people,
There were songs from singers, and pipes blown by pipers;
There was so much merriment that no more might be.

And that was how Brennes was reconciled with his brother.   2550
They sent an invitation to their dear inhabitants   *Reconciliation*
That all should come to London, with forty pounds as penalty,
To hold there a hustings before Belin the king.
When all those lieges were assembled in London,
There was King Belin and all of his kingdom,
The Britons and Scots and many handsome thanes;
There was the Duke of Burgundy, Brennes by name,
And both the brothers were happy at heart,
And all the two armies of many a country.

The kings sought proposals from their prominent men,   2560
For they wished with their forces to push forward through France.
In France there were laws which were strange in those days,
And strange reports came, for there were four kings.
Belin said to Brennes 'Let us go speedily
Off towards France and win it by fight.'
They blew their brass trumpets and bade muster their armies,
And went to the sea and crossed over well: *Invasion*
With nine hundred vessels they came into harbour;*   *of France*
They came to the land and they overwhelmed people.

Then came the tidings to those four kings   2570
That King Belin had come and Duke Brennes with him,
With innumerable forces to make conquest of France.
Together those kings came and vows they then made
That they would live together or lie dead,
And each of them the other would consider as brother:
With oaths they made the promise and fully performed it.
They summoned their forces, which were phenomenally great,
And they marched briskly towards Belinus.
Brennes with his army was in front of Belin.

Together clashed those kings with their battle-captains,   2580
Force against force furiously fought,
The Scots and the Britons, both there together,
Belin their lord marching before them,
Brennes beside them with his Burgundian folk.
They struck together: helmets there rang;
Broad spears broke, shields there shivered,
Red blood was shed, bold warriors fell,
There was much grinding of teeth; slaughter had come there.†
The hills and the dales were concealed by the dead.

    Belin lifted his helmet and called out to Brennes: 2590
'Can't you see, dear brother, how the French begin to totter,
While the army from our land is still standing whole?
Let us get ready with our grim onslaughts,
And make an assault on them with point and with edge!'
Brennes was very brave and this he applauded:
All of them they slaughtered whom they could get near to,
And those four kings they laid to the ground;
Any noble who fled away, into a castle made his way,
And our men went after him with spear and with sword.
(There was no other course if he would not crave peace);   2600
That castle they seized, and himself and his men they slew.
And so they penetrated the country of France.

    In that same year Belin became emperor,
And his brother Brennes, both of them together,
Because they had won France by all their fighting,
And all the free territories which are tributory to France.
When they had a great realm thus released into their hand,
Then they laid their heads together, these lucky brothers,
And declared that they wished to hold a hustings
Of all of those loyal [people] who loved their own laws,†   2610
And of all those lands which lay now in their hands,
And by decision of all of them they would go to Rome.
To avenge on those folk **Remus** the fair,
(Whom **Romulus** his brother in Rome had slain
Very many years before), for all that folk still lived there.

    The kings did everything just as they themselves decreed:
They assembled their full army on Frankish territory;   *Invasion*
When all the muster was complete, then at once they marched,   *of*
For there were so many men, and so innumerable,   *Rome*
That on no field anywhere could it all be held at once.   2620

They passed over Great Saint Bernard with all their huge army,
Then they passed, true it is, what is called Mount Senis;
They took all Turin and Ivrea and all the cities of Lombardy,
Vercelli and Pavia, and Cremona, Milan, Placentia and Bologna;
They crossed the water of Taro, and then crossed over Bardun;*
Tuscany they had completely won; in Salermo they slew many
      thousand men;*
So they were approaching Rome – found it too long till they might
      come –
And the Roman citizens were in total consternation,
For to them had come harsh tidings from Belin the king.
All legal recorders who resided there in Rome,   2630
And all the powerful men who were prominent in Rome,
Had elected two earls in that self-same year
Who were to guard that land and guide those who lived there,
And lead out their army wherever there was need,
And as for the names of both, these I will tell you:
The first was called **Gabius**, and the second **Prosenna**;
These same earls were valiant, courageous and accomplished,
And all the citizens of Rome acted on their resolutions.

    These earls came to Rome, to the men who were responsible,*
And asked what they advised in such a time of need,   2640
Whether they should summon forces for fighting against Belin,
Or should with him have conference and then request his peace.
There were in Rome men who were wise in opinion,
Who planned to betray Belin by their practised tricks;
They took as their counsel, in their secret conclave,
That they would not fight, nor lead out their forces,
'But we will sue for peace and love we will establish;
We'll place in their hands all these Roman lands,
And honour them in the land as a man should his leader,
Give them gold and silver, all this land to them deliver,   2650
Give to them treasure which they will keep,
Our children as hostages, if that's what they want,
The son of each baron who lives in this borough:
They shall be chosen; they must be of high station,
Children most pretty, as hostages four plus twenty.
These kings are strong and they come from distant lands;
They have as many followers as were never yet in but one force;
The kings are both young, and boldly ambitious:
As soon as they hear such words, they'll want to do this,   2660

They could hardly demand more without making us beg for mercy.
And if we can so well succeed that to this plan they will accede,
And will quit our country and go off to their own coasts,
Then we shall at once begin to do our own will;
For it is better we should lose our own beloved children,
Than that we adopt a course which makes us all corpses,
With all of Rome city burned down to cinders,
And all of the territory which to Rome is tributory
Being all ravaged, when it now stands so rich.
For if it's willed by Tervagant, our god here in this land,   2670
By this means we'll trick them and afterwards we'll break them,
So that never in one piece will they get back to their home.'
    Then said those in the hall: 'This is the opinion of us all!'
Those earls got themselves ready in very [rich] finery,
And took with them knights (as many as seemed right),
And they mounted their fine horses covered with splendid cloth;
Each man took in his hand a goblet of red gold.
For four complete days forwards they marched,
Until they came to the area where Belin was with his army,
And Brennes his brother, both of them together.   2680
Of the nobles they were asking where were the kings,
And were directed to the places where the kings' pavilions were;
They set off speedily so they should come there presently,
And were most amazed at all that assembly,
And where they had been taken from, those they saw there.
They spotted King Belin as he stepped out of his tent
And so they dismounted and dutifully on [knees]†
In front of the king they fell to the ground,
[And these words they spoke, with much intelligence]:†   2688a
'Lord, your compassion, for you are overlord and king.   *Truce*
We give to you Rome, and the whole realm,   2690
And all the territories which are tributory to Rome,
And all the treasuries which we have hoarded up,
And as much wealth as your warriors care to have,
And oaths we shall swear to you that we shall not betray you
Upon our god, Dagon by name, who is mighty in his fame.
We shall become your men, and magnify your honour,
With all our might, by day and by night,
And we shall assign, from out of this realm,
Twenty-four youngsters, the children of noblemen:
They shall be chosen; they shall be of high station.   2700

We shall from this government meet your requirement,
And wherever you decree, for you have the dominion.
And to offer such terms we have been sent here,
And we crave your mercy, now and for eternity.'
　The king stood quite still as the traitors spoke this evil;
He reckoned it was really truth which they had been reporting,
Yet they had designs quite other: to kill King Belin and his brother.
When the silence broke, it was good things that he spoke:
'It is good which you promise me; if you will perform it,
The better things will be for you.   2710
As to this agreement, I will accept it,
And you shall be my vassals, and view me as your leader,
And hold your lands in freedom, and we shall then be friends.
In one week from today bring me here straightaway
Gold and great treasure, gifts and your children,
And here before me have come the highest men in Rome,
To swear to me oaths, (it will go easier with them),
And now they shall become my men, and magnify my honour.
And unless you will, all of you I shall kill;
But now homewards quickly ride; see, I await you on this hillside.
If it's truth you speak, then come back in one full week;   2721
And if your speech is wrong, then remain in Rome,
And I'll come to you there, and bring you sorrow and care.'
　These traitors started riding homewards to Rome,
And got ready their gifts and gathered hostages,
And on the day they brought them to Belin the king,
And with respect he received them and in return gave friendship;
They handed over hostages and took from him vassalage,
And with this compact between them he marched back again,
While the traitors at once turned back to Rome.   2730
Belin and Brennes, both of them together,
Came to the conclusion by collaboration
That they would lead the men right through Lombardy,
And go off to Germany and conquer its nobility.
The German people of their coming were very well aware*
And gathered together to them powerful armed men,
From all of those lands which the emperor had in hand.
　Meanwhile the Roman men could clearly see then
That Belin and Brennes had both gone again.
They made ready riders, two thousand and rugged,   2740
And swiftly in great haste sent them in pursuit.

They sent off alongside another band of riders,
Ten thousand knightly men, all of them well known,
So that they should arrive there first to aid the emperor,
Who was intending battle against King Belin.
And this Roman troop came riding up behind them,
Intending they should meet where the mountains were most steep,
Sending them in single file through narrow defiles,
There to kill Lord Belin, and his brother with him.
They ignored their hostages and that peace which they had
    asked for, 2750
The oaths and the truce, and for that they had much torment.
Belin and his brother were both well aware
Of the coming of this treachery towards them from Rome city,
But felt more anxiety about the Roman emperor.
Then they took decision about their situation,
That Brennes and his men should march back again
To fight with the Roman force and fell them if they could,
While Belin, over the mountains bent with his mighty strength,
Should fight against the emperor and the German army,
Should put all to trial in fight, and maybe conquer them by might,
And whichever of the brothers should have first overcome, 2761
Must come back at once to give aid to the other.
    The men who came from Burgundy marched back with Brennes,
From France too, and Poitou: they vowed to him and promised faith,
From Maine then and from Touraine they truly gave service,
From Normandy and Flanders, freely they followed him,
And from Lorraine they brought their loyal strength,
And the men of Gascony who would not agree on peace,
And men from many nations now marched along with Brennes
Towards the Romans' men who were coming behind them; 2770
Brennes and his forces advanced towards them.
As soon as they saw Brennes changing course to meet them,
Then the Roman force sought refuge in flight,
And our men went after them and many men fell there,
And very many fled away and took flight to Rome,
With Brennes the powerful in steady pursuit,
With his stalwart men, marching towards Rome.
    And Belin the noble king was now in Germany,
He had more forces than enough, great and immeasurable:
Britons and Welsh, Scots there and Danes; 2780
King Godlac was present, good at every need.

When those men heard tell, the ten thousand knights,
Who had arrived from Rome to the emperor's aid,
That Brennes the powerful was marching on Rome,
And of their men some were slain and some of them were scattered,
Then they came to the conclusion that from there they would ride
Right back to Rome before Brennes could come there.
The news came to Belin about Brennes his brother,
How he had acted and all he had achieved,
Another messenger arrived then who at once informed him   2790
That two thousand knights who were in the German fight
Intended to go back at once, marching to Rome,
And it looked from their proceedings as if they would proceed by
     night.
Belin was most intelligent, alertness accompanied him:
Already many Germans he'd cut down with the sword's edge,
And many he led unharmed along with him and bound;
He had two clever men whom in the fight he'd won,
Who knew the land's laws and the speech of those who lived there;
King Belin spoke to them and said to them as follows:
'Listen, you knights, to what I shall make known to you: 2800
Both of you am holding in my [strong] bonds;[†]
If you two will follow instructions, then I shall free [you both][†],
Dress you in resplendent clothes, and will make you rich,   *Defeat*
I'll fetch you along with me, and become the friend of both,   *of the*
If, knowing this country, you will conduct me   *Germans*
Right to the route, which you two know full well,
Where this Roman army intends to ride forth,
And we shall fall on them and shall fight with them,
Fell all our foes and then move forwards after Brennes,
Travelling circumspectly and surrounding Rome.   2810
And this I entreat you, that we may all escape.'
   The knights were very thoughtful and very quick-thinking,
And played their part in everything which Belin was requiring,
And marked out their route: toward Great Saint Bernard Pass they
     marched,
Into a massive valley alongside the mountain,
Where the enemy would come out, then some men would be fated.
Belin was by the hillside, exceedingly silent,
And moving past there came those who were men of Rome.
Belin pounced on them, in front and behind them:
The knights were quite weaponless when tragedy struck them,   2820

73

They thought they weren't in danger when Belin descended on them;
Not a single knight they took alive, but all of them they slaughtered,
For Belin had no knight at all who was not a good champion,
And not a single herdsman who did not fight like a gentleman,
And not a single shepherd boy who did not rage as he struck blows.
The fight began at midnight, and it [lasted] until daylight.[†]
And then all the day long they went over the mountains
Killing all those others who that night had crept away.
In the morning Belin had them blow brass trumpets,
And summoned his army, gave instruction at once   2830
To ride along that very way that to Rome directly lay,
After his brother Brennes who was in front of them.
Brennes heard the message and held back for his brother,
Onwards they were both bound until they reached Rome borough.
That borough they besieged with their army of nations,[*]
And the folk within the town valiantly fought back.

   Belin and Brennes laid siege about the place,   *Siege of*
And the inhabitants shot at them with sharp spears,   *Rome*
And often sent hot molten lead pouring on their heads,
And beams and stones and blazing arrows: 2840
Very well they warded off attack on the city walls of Rome.
In spite of all the artifice those outside were aware of,
And of all the fighting which their forces expended,
In no way at all could they win Rome's city wall,
But they were losing many thousands of their own good men,
And so pulled back from the wall – weary were their spirits.
The king[s] considered carefully what could be their remedy,[*†]
And said just between themselves: 'Summon at once then
The twenty-four child hostages whom we hold as pledges,
And put up a gallows-tree and on it they shall tumble,   2850
And so we get our own back on our enemies,
For we shall go against them now in the way they'll find most
   ghastly.'
The struts were set up and they hauled up the hostages,
Hanging them there in front of their parents.
Most distressed the fathers were when they saw their children
   hanging,
They cried out with their voices and confirmed it with oaths
That in return for this things should turn out much more terribly,
So that not for death nor for life would they ever accept peace,

For those were the most powerful and the most noble,
And the most influential of the inhabitants of Rome   2860
Who before their very eyes beheld there and gazed
At their children being hanged upon the high timbers.
    The earls had now gone very far away from there,
(Those who should protect them, Gabius and Prosenna),
Into Lombardy, into that land,   2864a
Looking for people who were [to fight with] them†
To assist their own men against Belin and Brenne.
    A man then came running from the two earls,
Who brought secret writing into the Roman city,
Telling them truthfully the earls were on their way,
In that same night and with ten thousand knights,   2870
And with unmeasured forces of men who marched on foot,
Who would come to be their help and kill King Belin,
And Brennes his brother, both of them together:
'If you will believe me, as soon as it is evening
Send out the knights and begin then to fight;
Before it is midnight (I tell you this is true and right)
There will arrive with their men both Gabius and Prosenna,
Who will avenge you honourably against all your enemies.'
As soon as the day was gone those gates they opened,
Letting out the knights and beginning intense fights.   2880
So they fought all night until it was daylight;
Then there came hastening innumerable hosts,
Gabius and Prosenna with many marching men
All out of Lombardy, whose way led straight to Brenne,
And he fought against them furiously hard,
And Belin rushed towards him, to the Roman force,
And they made fierce onslaught: the fight was immense;
Disaster was abounding, the Britons were falling,
Belin and Brennes both had bad wounds,
And the Roman men were roaring this at them: 2890
'What do you want here, worthless things, and your British king?
Did you think, with your games, that Rome you would tame?
Did you think that by fighting you would fell our people,
And so become rich yourselves, and control all of Rome?
You shall drink your own blood: disaster shall be yours.
You were the butchers of our babes, for that you shall be smashed,
And our good men shall fell you in a way you shall find ghastly!'
    Belin and Brennes both went from the fighting*

Into a great ditch which they had had dug
So that their ranks could very well take refuge in it.   2900
In it they spoke, in it they consulted,
Just for a little while, it lasted less than walking a mile,
And this is what they said between the two of them:
'If we go from here like this, they will all be after us,
And if it should so happen that we come hobbling home,
We would ourselves be very sore and be reproached for evermore.
But let us go for them with swords: they shall all be quite destroyed,
So let us avenge [valiantly] our kindred and friends,†
For it is more dear to us to fall here in glory
Than to depart safely from here but to disgrace our friends.'   2910
     While they were saying this and speaking these words
The people of the country thought that Belin was going away,
And said to one another within the walls of Rome:
Now they will go from here, they won't fight any more!'
     But Belin and his brother, their thoughts were quite other.
They sent out of Rome knights who were venturesome,
Four thousand of them, to a fine castle,
To keep control on Belin and his brother Brennes,
[Who were supposed to be ahead of them], and boldly attack,†
And the other Romans would be riding in their rear   2920
'And we'll kill them between us and so avenge our wrongs!'†
     The knights were on their route, far outside Rome;
Then instructed Belin and his brother Brennes:
'Alight from your steeds and stand on your feet,
And cut down your spears which are long and make them short and
          strong,
Scrape from your shields all the sharp and narrow ends,*
And we in your van will either live or lie dead,
And let every good man make himself brave,
For this is where beggars will all become rich!
Blow your brass trumpets, bring together your forces,   2930
And let us compose from our companions fifty cohorts,
And in each contingent one valiant commander
Who can make them bold and get their lines to hold,
And work towards the walls from each of the sides;
In haste let us move on, so we can have it all well done.'
     They blew their brass trumpets so the Romans had to hear it,
And they marched out there, valiant warriors.
When those inside Rome saw Belin and his brother,

76

They shouted out aloud among all those who lived there:
'Now our foes are in flight, now we shall go to them and
    fight!'   2940
With the men in front out went Prosenna,
And Gabius came after with fifty hundred knights,
With all their weapons which were very weighty;
The others were speedy, their weapons were quite light.
They clashed together and they fought like fiends.
Those of Rome were all of them riders,
The others on foot, and flung themselves at them,
Killing all their steeds: their strength was all the less.
Gabius they killed, Prosenna they captured,
And did what they wanted with those men of Rome.   2950
All they struck down who stood up against them;
They broke down Rome's walls on every side,
And inside they came and the borough they conquered;   *Conquest*
They had then won Rome, that city rich and handsome,   *of*
And there they found much gold, and unmeasured treasure;   *Rome*
They undid the locks, and pulled out the rings,
The black pall and purple which was worked in Apulia,
And all the precious gems which were of many species;
Many a beggar there at once became rich!
In those seven nights were dreams fulfilled for every knight,   2960
In silver and in gold, in abundance from the land.
    There were orders from the kings for the doing of fine things:
The building of the halls, the repairing of the walls
Which had been torn apart with the terrible fight.
They had someone climb up high to call out to the people
That the kings would speak to them and settle peace terms with them:
No man was to be so wild as from another to shed blood,
Nor covet his possessions unless he were glad to give them,
'And all of the fugitives who have fled from Rome
Who are willing to return, desiring this king's peace,   2970
And become this king's men, as we have just announced,
Then let them come in amity and live their lives in the city,
And have the same law code as in their ancestors' days stood.
And Belin our high king delivers it to Brennes,
Who will remain here and be your emperor,
While he himself will lead his men and will take leave of you,
And from here he is bound for the shores of Britain.'
    Very great was the weeping when Belin went from there,

But they were soon solaced by the treasury of Rome.
Brennes remained behind as king of Lombardy,   2980
And Belin made his way back to this land.
He had throughout his castles royal works commissioned,
Repairing all the halls, and strengthening the walls,
Building living quarters and heightening the keeps,
And so this lovely land he ruled with regal honour,
While Brennes ruled Rome for fully fifteen years;
Then passed away Brennes – the Roman folk rejoiced at this!
They themselves took their land and held it in their own hand,
The city and their serenity, since Brennes was dead.
And Belin in this land made laws which were strong,   2990
And laws which were very good, which all his lifetime stood.
   Belin went to Wales and made there a borough,
Outstanding he made it upon the water of Usk,
And from that same flood the king found the name for it:
To the king it was special, and Kaer-Uske he called it,   *Caerleon*
And since then it's been called **Caerleon**, and now I'll tell you the
    reason. *
When many years had passed, after Belin's passing, *
[The men of Rome heard of the death of Belin]†
And said between themselves: 'He once did us great harm;
Now that king is buried, let's get our revenge on the Britons!
Into that land we'll go and bring there sorrow, care and woe.'   3000
They began to send here, from the Roman area,
Four raiding parties which we term armies,
And which in those same days were known as 'legions';
There were in each legion these many land champions:
Six thousand, six hundred and sixty men.
These travelled by water; they were well aware of warfare,
And in this land they brought grief to all those who lived here,
Yet always in the finish they themselves were fine,
And every single winter they went to ground in Wales:
They won the fort of Kaer Uske and into that they went,   3010
Until there came in passage more of their people,
And because of those legions they called Kaer Uske 'Kaer Liun';
Then there came another nation who called it Caerleon.
Now I have told you how things have gone with Caerleon of
    Glamorgan, *
Let us return to Belin, to that most blessed king,
When he had made this borough and had named it Kaer Uske:

When the borough was fine and strong, then he made a move from
    there;
He went right down to London, to the town which he loved well,
And embarked there on a tower, the strongest in all the town,
And with much ingenuity a gate beneath it made   3020
Which people then called 'Belinsgate',*
And now and evermore the name remains there.
    King Belin lived here in greatest bliss,
And all those who lived here loved him very much.
In his days there was so much food that it could not be measured,
And people through their drunkenness perished in their thousands.
The king lived a long time; when he drew towards his end
And died there in London, all who lived there were distressed,
They grieved for their very lives at the king's demise.
They went to his treasure-hoard and took from it much gold,*   3030
And fashioned a tomb out of gold and out of gemstones;
In it they placed the king who had been their own lord Belin,
And placed him up on high, topmost in the tower
So that they could behold him far and wide throughout the land;
This they did in their great love because he was their own dear lord.
So departed King Belin; then came his son Gurguint.
    Gurguint Bertruc was his son's name: most noble was   GURGUINT
    the man,
A very politic man this one, who with prudence ruled his kingdom;†
He loved concord and conciliation [and evil things he shunned],†
As his father had before, he kept as good peace as the best,   3040
Except that the Danish men downright refused
Ever to send any more on to Britain's shore
Of gold and good treasure and due tribute from the land.
Gurguint considered carefully what could be the remedy:
His messengers he sent wide throughout his land:
He summoned his folk and made ready his forces,
Immeasurably great, with unnumbered men.
    Aboard his ships he went and steered from the land,
Over the salt stream: splendid he found it!
On the second day he arrived in Denmark:*   3050
He went up on land, just as he wanted;
He demanded tribute from that land which had been in his father's
    hand,
Which King Godlac gave him with very good will.
Then King Godlac's son said, in a grim speech of anger:

'If my father acted freely, I shall not follow suit,
So let him get out of my land, if he wants to live.'
    This [enraged] Gurguint, who was the King of Britain:[†]
'Where are my leaders? Where are my servitors?
Where are my champions, and my courageous men?
Run now, and ride now, all this land burn now,   3060
And all men you can get close to see that you slaughter,
Their children and their wives chuck into the water,
And break down their walls and burn down their halls,
Assail all their towers, and set fire to their bowers,
Then they must understand that I am king of Britain's land,
And they are bound to pay me tribute, as they did to King Belin.'
    Away marched that army, as the king instructed.
They inflicted many sufferings with their superior strength.
The king of the land, with an enormous troop
Came against Gurguint, with his greath strength.   3070
Most destructive was their fighting, and Gurguint slew the Danish
      king,
And all his Danish force he felled to the earth.
They moved on to the boroughs, where all showed obedience,
And so he governed all, the good and the bad:
They became his men and oaths they swore to him,
And handed over to him three hundred chosen hostages,
And as much good property as King Godlac had promised
When Belin set him free, with all his fellow men,
And Gurguint then went off, back to this land.
    As he went on his way by the area of the Orkneys   3080
He found on the sea-flood thirty good ships afloat,[*]   *The Irish*
And the ships were [fully loaded] with weaponed men and women,[†]
With many kinds of weapons, all very fine.
All this seemed quite amazing to Gurguint, who was king,
What all these ships were which he found floating there.
He sent a message to them, instructing them to say
Where they were from, and what they had come for,
And if with him they wished to speak and request the king's peace.
Then gave his answer he who of all was leader:
'With him we will speak, and request his peace.'   3090
    Altogether they came and took their peace without delay.
Then spoke **Pantolaus**, with Gurguint he spoke like this:
We are sea-weary men, by adverse weather driven;
I am called Pantolaus, and you have lordship over us.

We have arrived in your land, and your laws we all approve:
You may wield control over us according to your will.
From Spain I was driven out, and all my doughty people.
So very much we have been seeking, beside this sea's rim,
A land which looks likely to us, in which we could live.
We simply cannot find it, not for anything,   3100
A land for us to live in, to which we could lead the way.
We have endured much hardship, much hunger and much thirst,
Very much queasiness, very many winds, upon this wild water.
Now we beg your mercy: no more can we such things endure;
If it should be your will, and you should wish to do this,
Then give us some plot within your kingdom;
We shall be your men, and do honour to your majesty,
And then we shall [laud] you for the rest of our lives.'†
    To this replied Gurguint, who was Britain's king:
'Not quite so shall I act, but your homage I accept,   3110
And now I shall send you into a land,
Since I don't know who you are, nor where you come from,
Yet you shall have pilots and from here you'll proceed,
And I shall lend to you, from my land's people,
Forty hundred knights, who are very good in fights;
To you they shall that land deliver, where you are to live,
And they shall promote your laws and so direct your people.'
Into Ireland Gurguint those people then sent,
Where never yet had man been living since Noah's flood ran over it,
And onwards Gurguint went, into this land,   3120
And Pantolaus dwelt over there, good man among the best,
And had himself called king, and his wife queen,
And he promoted strong laws to restrain his people.
    Because on the sea they had experienced sorrows
For seven whole years they had travelled astray,
Their clothes were all tattered and very badly they were clad,
Naked they were, and nothing at all cared
If anyone should see those limbs they carried [between their thighs].†
    And so they laid down their laws, and long indeed they lasted,
And Gurguint in this land lived in delight,   3130
And he maintained perfect peace all the time his life lasted.
In Caerleon he died: all who lived here were distressed.
One son he had, a brave man: **Guencelin** he was called; GUENCELIN
When his father died he ruled this whole land, and all those who
        dwelt here.

81

Absolutely and in all things this was a pure man and good king;
He led a very good life; he had a good wife,
Marcie people called her, far and wide she is acclaimed:
Now and evermore there is a record of her here.
    That queen learned a clever skill: she was well taught in books;
She had learned her lessons with a heart-felt love;   3140
Concerning her wisdom the word spread widely   *Laws of*
That she was very wise in the wisdom of this world.   *Marcie*
Then she made the law: it was laid down for all who lived here;
[When] this law was formulated, [to the land in writing it was
    promulgated];[†]
The Britons called the laws after their lady:
In truth without debate the law was called 'Marciane';
Then afterwards, later by many hundred winters,
Came **Alfred** the king, known as England's darling,
Who wrote the laws in English, where they had been in British,
And changed their name in his days, and called them 'Mercian
    laws',[*]   3150
But still, I tell you above all things: the first to make them wasn't
    Alfred the king,
But those were made by the queen whom people called Marcie,
And Alfred put them into English; and very true this is.
This wise queen had, by her king in this world,
Just one little son, who was named **Sillius**;
No more children she had, and at this the queen was sad.
When this child Sillius was no more than just seven years
His father had died and deserted his men.
His mother took the kingdom, and with consideration
    ruled,   MARCIE
And trained her son well, always by her side.   3160
    When the boy was so old that on horseback he was bold,
Then she made him king: his people were content.
He was a very good man, and quietly he would have lived,   SILLIUS
But he had not lived out half his life when he reached his death-time.
He left two sons, who both took their father's virtues;[*]
The elder was called **Rummarus**, the younger was called **Damus**.
For a while Rummarus was king, and then Damus took
    over.   DAMUS
This Damus in his days made choice of a mistress,[*]
And he had by that woman a very self-willed son,
By the name of **Morpidus**, strongest of all men   MORPIDUS

82

In power and in sinews, of all this same people.   3171
This man acquired this kingdom because of his great courage;
He was a knight most strong, courageous, generous, huge and long;
He would in all things have been good, had he not been highly
    moody:
The moment he got annoyed with anyone, in that spot he would slay
    him,
No matter how strong the knight, at once he killed him outright,
Were it right, were it wrong, in that spot he struck him down,
Yet the moment he was calm he did everything he was asked.
But this was a great fault in such a fine man,
That through his anger his intellect was impaired.   3180
    At that same time there came the Duke of Moray
Into this land to the harm of those who lived here;
He travelled down the sea-coast and committed many crimes,
Creating much butchery, and brutal he was in fight.
From the sea his way lay forward into Northumberland;
There he began to build a castle which was very strong,
And all around him in that land he seized into his own hand.
    Morpidus the fierce was infuriated by him,
And sent throughout this country and summoned his army,
And came to that duke all in bright daylight.   3190
There was many a good Briton and many a busy champion;
They fought against the duke all the day long.
When it was far into the afternoon the duke by the king was
    overcome;
He turned to flee; the king followed after him:
There he killed the duke and all his dependents;
Before the daylight went, dead were they all,
Through a very fierce fight which was wholly right,
And all those he found in the morning in the land
He either had them slain with fire or had them flayed alive.
By their own mouths they swore it, those who had seen it,   3200
That Morpidus with his own hands through his enormous strength
Slaughtered seven hundred and struck them down with weapons.
He had a ditch constructed which was long and very deep,*
And had all that carrion cast into it.
Then for some while his land in safety he could rule,
In peace and in plenty and with freedom in the people.
    Meanwhile there came tidings of a strange kind in the land,   *The*
Which soon was made known to Morpidus the king: *Sea-Monster*

There had come from the sea a beast very strange,*
From the region of Ireland on route towards here,   3210
And by the sea's rim it rushed out upon people;
Often in one day it made one hundred die,
And then the wicked murdering beast would go back to the sea,
And when it returned again, with rage it would meet them.
So it turned inland and tormented those people,
Inhabitants it terrified and towns it laid waste;
The people sped away on every side.
    The king heard tell of this and was troubled in his heart;
The king was going to the place – to his own grief –,
In that creature's direction: and there he came by death;   3220
When he came as far south as the fiend was living,
Then he ordered all his household to go to a borough,
And ordered them to be waiting there, and alone he would go riding.
When he went off he was wielding weapons:
These were a sharp sword and a quiver full of arrows,
A bow which was very strong and a spear which was very long,
At his saddle an axe, on the other side a short sword,
And off he went towards that haunt
Where he had heard tell that the fiend was living;
So far he travelled until he had found it,   3230
And he sent flying at it very sharp arrows;
All the arrows on it he spent as ever closer to it he went,
Galloping on his steed as if he was going mad.
When his arrows were all shot, then his bow was broken in bits,
And he gripped his spear so strong where he'd stuck it in the ground,
And ran upon the beast and plunged it in its throat,
So the beast fell back and the shaft all smashed;
But the beast stood up and rushed upon the steed,
And bit his breast right through, bones and all, and sinews,
And the lungs and the liver fell out on the earth.   3240
So the king drew his sword, ready to his hand,
And he struck the beast at once right upon its skull,
So the sword sank in deep and the hilt broke in his hand;
Now the beast set wide its jowls and bore down upon the king,
And bit him in the midriff, in half; and that was the end of the fight.
So the king perished because he was too bold,
Since a man is very stupid if he takes upon himself
More than he can cope with: he will tumble all the quicker,
For recklessness is very rash, and sends its lord rushing,

And again and again it will toss him to the ground.   3250
   The people were very sad about the king's disaster,
Although they were delighted at the death of the beast.
The king had had five sons by his lovely queen;
The eldest was called **Gorbonian** and there went a gracious man;
Argal they called another, Gorbonian's own brother,
The third was **Elidur**, the fourth **Ingenes**, the fifth was **Peredur**.
   The eldest brother, Gobonian, became king in this   GORBONIAN
     land:
He was very honest and very well behaved,
Ingenious and just and most generous with food.
In peace he held this land, and by his own demand,   3260
With great fidelity, as long as his fame lasted,
And kept himself under control until he came to his life's end.
In London he [lay dead]: those who lived here grieved.[†]
   After him came another, Argal his brother,   ARGAL
He was born next to him, and he was then chosen king.
This was the most depraved man who ever ruled the kingdom:
Injustice was dear to him and justice was distasteful;
Whatever man had riches he reduced to a pauper,
His good men he hated, and the wicked he raised high,
All his assemblies were all about avarice,   3270
He collected together a very great treasure,
And constantly thought about evil, and his actions followed suit;
That's how Argal led his life, from youth till time of death.
Then together came the rich men, who were high and mighty,
And held their hustings in a high state of anger.
They shook hands on an agreement, which they fully held,
That they would above all things banish Argal, the king,
And out they did drive him, a good distance from this land,
And took then the other, Elidur his brother: ELIDUR
This was the third, and they accepted him with concord,   3280
And made him the king. This knight was courageous,
And each man in speech he addressed as was most fit:
With the good he was supportive and was stern with the stupid.
   Argal had been driven out, and despair was in his heart:
He travelled far through many lands, making trial of those who lived
     there,
He begged many a king, and many a commander,
Many a rich leader, many a bold servitor,
He begged all the people where he passed by

85

That they should give him help, in his greatest need,
By force or ingenuity to regain his country.   3290
He could not find a single man to grant him the favour,
Who would give any assistance for his advancement here,
And they would not promise anything to provide him help.
    And then King Argal was abject in his mood,
Grieving in his spirit because of his great hurt;
Argal considered carefully what might be his remedy:
That he would travel back and try out his brother,[†]
And whether he might find any mercy from his men.[†]
    It was about five years since he fled from these shores,
Since he had set up all these sorrows for himself;   3300
He had himself disguised and departed for this land,
Towards his own acquaintance he made himself unknown,
Nor did any man know him at all who had ever seen him before.
He made enquiry of these inhabitants for their royal lord,
And they directed him to the king, out hunting, in encampment,
With his household retinue, in the wood of Kalatere.
The king he encountered and agreeably gave greeting:
'Lord King,' said Argal, 'may you be fit and well!
You are my brother Elidur: may you be ever happy!
I dare not make it known, because of this country's men,   3310
That here I once was king, lest they should recognise me,
But I entreat your mercy, both now and evermore.'
Then King Elidur announced: 'I am happy that you're here.'
He came over to his brother and affectionately kissed him.
King Elidur's eyes there were streaming with tears
As with great compassion he was kind to his brother,
And had him conducted, with gentle concern,
Into a castle which was known as Dumbarton,
And had him well bathed and bedded in comfort
And secretly he was guarded and his name was concealed.   3320
Who ever heard the record, in conversation or account,[*]
That ever any brother should do that for another
Which King Elidur did for Argal?
    The king affected illness, as if it were a fact,
And lay in his bedroom, sombrely in bed.
He sent out a summons throughout all his kingdom,
Asking all lords who held his lands on him to attend.
In words and in writing he made them well aware
That he could no longer live here upon this earth,

But from them [he]'d like advice, because of his imminent demise,[†]
That they should direct him where best his body would lie.   3331
   The news was known throughout this land, and so those knights
     convened,
In the borough of the king for a great husting.
The king and his brother were in one bedroom,
Where they had fully eaten and then had taken drink.
The king went to bed, while his brother hid,
And with him his most loyal men whom he knew in life,
Forty good knights, with coats of mail supplied,
With swords and with shields, as if they should have to fight.
The king lay in his bed, as if he could not live;   3340
Into the borough he sent instruction, through his best official,
Ordering his doughty people to make more silent discourse,
Because his head ached so badly that he could not bear
Listening to the mounting noise of so many people.
   The king set guards upon his doors so that no man might
     enter,
No living creature at all inside the castle-precinct,
Unless the king by his messengers had already sent for him.
   The king rose from his bed; on his back his byrny he fastened,
And took into his hand a battle-axe most stout,
And called into the bedroom Argal his own brother,   3350
And taking their messenger, sent him to the city,
To fetch the man of highest standing, who must come now to the
     king.
As soon as he came in the room, the king took hold of him,
And grew annoyed with him, as if about to hang him,
While he was surrounded by knights, looking most fierce,
As if with their own hands they'd like to hack him down.
   Then said King Elidur: 'Now I'm going to kill you,
Unless you keep quiet and do everything I want.'
The lord then replied: 'I'll do it with delight.'
'Here and now become my brother's man if you want to have your
     life!   3360
This is King Argal who from this land was made an exile
And who has come here now and shall become your king.'
The lord in utter silence did all the king required,
And the king had him secluded then in a secret chamber,
And so made a knight run to fetch another lord,
And there each behaved just as the other had.

In this way King Elidur acted with all those earls, *Elidur*
With this one, and that one until clear all were won. *restores*
Then he did one thing other: he then took his brother *Argal*
With great celebration, and conducted him to York, 3370
Where all of these people together had processed.
In the presence of his people he picked up his kingly crown
And placed it on his brother's head and raised him to the throne.
For ever afterwards Argal became the most admirable of all kings:
He abandoned wickedness, embracing all goodness,
And became so gentle, to young as to elderly,
And with all men certainly the king dealt most justly.
This land was stabilised and stood in this way
For ten full years, and then the king grew infirm.
Sick like this the king lay for three weeks and a day, 3380
And of this could not be cured, and so King Argal was dead.
      Then all those liegemen came travelling together
And took back Elidur, and restored his regal status,
Raised him to the throne with great rejoicing,
And for a season power resided in himself,
And Elidur was the most elevated of all of his people.
      I[ng]enes and Peredur could see that Elidur*
Had once again become liege-lord over this our land.
They summoned many people from many different kinds of men,
And led their army far and wide throughout all this country. 3390
Together came Elidur, Ingenes and Peredur,
And bitterly they fought and felled each others' knights.
Then in the fight Elidur was put to flight,
And his brothers went after him with all of their powers; *Elidur*
Ingenes and Peredur seized King Elidur, *Deposed*
And led him to London; distressed were his liegemen.
In a very strong tower they imprisoned King Elidur.
For many a year and many a day there in that tower the true king lay,
While his brothers made a circuit right round this country.
I[ng]enes had half this land, right up to the Humber: 3400
All this south end did he hold in his hand;
And Peredur had the north parts, all from Humber upwards,
And then later on he owned it altogether,
For Ingenes did not live above seven years.
Then Peredur took this land and placed it all in his own hand,
And then he became really bad and a burden to his people.
Then came sudden death and struck him to the ground:

So evilly he lived his life that the Devil came to fetch him.*

    Then assembled all who lived here and set off for London,

And took out Elidur, where he was lying in the tower,   3410

And did there an unusual thing: for the third time they made him
    king!

Then he became as good a king as a fine day is long: *Elidur*

All people he did right by, and this land was then ruled   *Restored*
    properly:

In happiness his liegemen lived here in joy,

And when he had to depart this life he had a lovely death.

    Then came the son of his brother, Gorbonian,

Who was the eldest of the five brothers;

This boy was called **Lador**, he was king of this land,*   LADOR

But Lador only lived a very little while;

After him came **Morgan**, the son of Argal,   MORGAN

One year he ruled the people and then he passed away;   3421

Anmaunus was the name of the other, and he was   ANMAUNUS
    Morgan's brother:

These were [one] man's sons, these [here] were kings.††

This same Anmaunus ruled this kingdom like this:

So that not one lord in all this land would not gladly have killed him
    with his hand,

And all his people he hated, and all of them he humiliated;

To all men he was hostile; it was the Evil One who loved him,

While his own household hated him to death.

Nevertheless in the end the folk of this land

Drove him out and exiled him a great distance from this area;   3430

Because he was so hostile they drove him from this area,

With sorrow and with soreness: he never came here any more.

Together came the highest earls who were in this land,

And chose themselves a king from a knight who was courageous;

He was In[g]enes' son, from Peredur's kindred come,†   IWALLO

Iwallo was the name of the king: he was good at everything.

Well did he emulate the deeds of his elders;

In all good manners the man was endowed:

He had good qualities and his country fared the better,

But a hateful disaster was it that he could not last: 3440

No longer than seven years was he able to live here,

Dead was King Iwallo: from his people he departed.

    Then a king ruled here who was known as **Rime**,   RIME

An offspring of Peredur, the brother of Elidur;

Then came **Goronces**, the son of Elidur; GORONCES
Then there was **Catalus** – his father was called Goronces – CATALUS
And then came **Coillus** – his brother was called Catulus; COILLUS
Then followed King **Porex**; he was of that same family; POREX
Then came **Cherin**, who was connected with Porex, CHERIN
But Cherin lived long in this very land, 3450
While the other six kings who had preceded in the land
Were not living here above eight years;
But long lived here Cherin; much did he drink of mead and wine,
And all of his forces were abandoned to drinking,[†]
And he lost all his dignity because of his wine-toping,
And never did any good to others nor got his people any wealth.
But there befell strange things concerning this king:
In this way he lived here for very many years,
And never did any invader ever this land enter,
But this land was at peace and well filled with plenty. 3460
Then came that day when dead the king lay;
Now he had three sons by his most high queen,
The eldest was called **Fulgenius**, next **Aldus** and
  Andragus, FULGENIUS
Yet very little time did these same men live; etc
Each of them for a spell was king in this land,
But within four years they were all dead here.
The youngest of the brothers, he was the best,
Andragus was his name, and one son he had:
Urrian the child's name, who became this country's king: URRIAN
One year he lived, and then death he suffered. 3470
  After King Urrian, there was **Eliud**, his cousin, ELIUD
Then came **Cledaus**, **Doten** and **Gurgguincius**: etc
These three kings ruled this country
One after the other, until they were all dead,
But nothing did they do here, either good or evil.
  Then came **Merian**, a most attractive man; MERIAN
Hounds and hawks he had in huge numbers,
So that every day he was diverted by his beasts.
But he was such a handsome man that women doted on him,
And of this he was aware, but he wasn't flattered, 3480
But he loved his queen, always, all his life.
Then there was **Bledon** his son, a king of bounteous fame; BLEDON
He had goods in plenty and shared them with his good men,
There has never since been any king so generous in everything.

Then his son was next king, **Cap** he was called;   CAP
And after Cap, **Oein**: for every evil he would yearn;   OEIN
Then came **Sillius**, who was Oein's son,   *etc*
And then after that came a king called **Bladgabreat**: BLADGABREAT
Since this world was begun no man knew so much of song,
On the harp and the psaltery, the fiddle and the [organ],   3490
The tympanum and lyre; musicians he would favour;
He knew all the songs and the music of each land,
Of him there were many legends among this world's inhabitants,
Such that all mankind who heard the stories of him
Said that he was the master of every musical skill;
This king was always sociable and loved all kinds of sport,
And like this he led his life, the whole time that it lasted.

    Then his brother became king, **Arkinaus** he was   ARKINAUS
      called,
He ruled it seven years, in peace he was dwelling here;
Then his son was king, who lived in wickedness,   3500
Aldolf they called the king; his actions were evil: ALDOLF
There was no good woman in the land whom he did not desire
(If she was at all pretty) to have her as his piece,
Even if she were an earl's wife, he deprived her of all her honour;
Both young women and aged he brought to disgrace;
For this vile habit those who lived here loathed him
To death absolutely; even for that he would not abandon it.

    Then came **Redion**, and he ruled this nation   REDION
For six months and seven nights; then he fell dead outright! *etc*
Then **Redert** his brother, for even less time than his brother; 3510
Then came someone who lived well: he was called **Famul-penicel**;
In his time he was so wealthy that he was like no one else;
Then came a king, he was called **Pir**, whose head of hair was like gold
    wire,   PIR
So that all people felt amazement where so lovely a man came from.
After him came **Capor**, who was king in the nation;   CAPOR
After him came **Eligille**, who held this land most   ELIGILLE
    peaceably:
This was a very wise man, and in all things very fine;
In joy he lived here for twenty-five years;
Then the king was his son **Heli** for years which totalled forty: HELI
Sometimes he maintained peace; sometimes he was opposed: 3520
He was a very intrepid person, and he engendered three agile sons:
Lud was the first one's name (he was a very intrepid man),

The middle one, **Cassibellaunus**, the youngest was called **Nennius**.
After King Heli, Lud his son ruled this land very long;   LUD
He was a very intrepid king, and of infinite courage,
And he was powerful, for he admired good policy;
He travelled round all this kingdom, and each borough he made
    strong;
Castles were built by Lud the king, and London he loved above
    everything:
While King Lud controlled this land, London was still called
    Troynovant,
And of forts in it there was no sign except the tower built by King
    Belin,
(As earlier this book recounts in this narration);   3531
King Lud had the wall laid down around the whole of London town,
Which has still lasted up to now and will do a long time yet; *London*
He had all the halls erected, very spacious in all respects,
And ordered every rich man to divide his wealth in two,[*]
And taking up the one half, to make himself a high dwelling.
Meanwhile all the wicked men he removed outside the walls,
And elevated the borough and made it most attractive;
He set aside the town's name and named it after himself,
Calling it 'Kaer Lud'; and had it everywhere announced[*]   3540
That he did it for the reason that many a man thereafter,
When the king would be dead, would judge of his deeds.
Later there came aliens here, entering this nation,
And they named the town 'Lundin', in their own language;
Then came Saxon men, and 'London' they called it:
The name has lasted long in all this land;
Then came the Normans, with their nasty malice,
And named it as 'Lundres' (those living here they harmed).[*]
   So has all this land fared, with aliens landing
Who have conquered this land and in their turn been driven
    away,   3550
And others again would gain it, who were foreign people,
And would refashion the old names according to their whim[†]
Of the good old boroughs, and change their names around,
So that there's not one borough, in this land of Britain,
Which still has the old name which it was first established with.
   Then things changed in the land so that this king met his end:
King Lud was dead and in London he was laid;
There came lords of great estate who laid the king beside a gate

Which is still called, true it is, 'Port Lud' in British,
But then came the English to rule the state, and they have called it
    '**Ludgate**',*
And so for very long it has remained with that name.   3561
Then there were two children, the sons of Lud the king,
The elder was called **Androgeus**, the second **Te[nnanci]us**;†
These children were little when their father died,
There came their father's brother, Cassibellaunus,
And himself became king and supervised the children,
And lovingly he tended them, for love of his brother.
    This Cassibellaunus was this land's king;   CASSIBELLAUNUS
The liegemen all loved him because his laws were good;
He imposed splendid customs upon this country,   3570
And was a very good king, and a good knight at everything.
    The children grew up quickly until they could rule territory,
The king gave to them two good earldoms:
Androgeus he liked better, so he gave London to him,
And along with it gave him all Kent, wanting to give pleasure,
And ordered Tennancius to take command of Cornwall,
And freely these two brothers held both these earldoms,
Except that they acknowledged the king as their leader,
Since he was their lord, as of all those who lived here.
While they were in agreement, and their men in accord,   3580
To this land all proceeded well: in peace they held it;
But then they became angry and things became worse,
So that the Roman race came to this nation
And imposed a tribute on this land, both silver and gold,
When never before in their lives had they dared to land here,
To require the king of this land to send tribute to Rome.
    So it happened at that date, as we in truth can now relate,*
That **Julius Caesar** advanced with an enormous army   *Caesar*
From Rome into France: the foe was enraged.
All territories he won which his eye glanced upon: 3590
He designed to acquire, by force and by guile,
All middle-earth's land and hold the world in his hand.*
But he couldn't do it, bring all the world under foot,
Yet three parts he did win of worldly dominion:
Fifty-five kingdoms' land he drew into his own hand,
Not counting his kingdom which came already with Rome.
He was a courageous conqueror, known through all middle-earth,*
And the wisest of men within worldly domains.

He constructed the calendar which appoints the months and the year;
He decreed many decisions which are still extant in Rome city.   3600
Alas that such a man of skill should ever have to go to [Hell]![†]
   Julius set off from Rome with men of great fame.
Lombardy he traversed, and the Great Saint Bernard Pass as well,
He conquered Lorraine, Gascony and Poitou,
Normandy and Brittany, Louvain and Germany;
After he'd won Gascony he turned back into Burgundy,
Advanced into Flanders and formed his fleet of ships.
Then on one occasion
When the day was light and the sun was very bright,
Caesar rode across Flanders' lands and looked at the sea from the
     strand:
The weather being very mild, he could make out this land,   3611
And Julius asked of his attendants its name, and spoke like this:
'What is that island there my eyes can just detect,
Lying far across the sea waters? It looks very fine to me.'
A man who knew responded, speaking to the ruler:
'It's an extensive island, supplied with all resources,
Which Brutus first laid claim to, [after the flood;[†]
There are fish, there are water-fowl], there are brave men
     around,[†]   3617a
And Britain is the name of the land which you behold.'
   Then spoke Julius Caesar, who was wise and well aware:
'I know quite well who Brutus was, because my books inform
     me: 3620
We all come from one common tribe, as the records tell us,
Our ancestors were in Troy, where they endured torment;
In the great fighting many thousands there were fated:
When they were conquered they coursed far and wide,
And travelled seeking land upon which they could live.
That's where Brutus settled and all his life he lived on it.
From him there came kings of amazing courageousness:
Belinus and Brennes, who both conquered Rome;
They destroyed Rome, that city so noble;
They took from Roman lands much silver and gold,   3630
They ordered their hostages to be hanged, and [our] residents to be
     ruined.[†]
   'So acted Belin and his brother, but now there is another:
I am called Julius Caesar and at this my heart is sore,
That my ancestors should be so shamed before I could yet be born.[*]

But now I will send into that land,
To learn from the best of them if they will bow to me,
And if they will send to me tribute from their land,
For if they are willing to seek peace, then I shall not attack them.
Find me two wise men who know the art of speaking,
[And] entrust to them at once a missive [well] composed,†   3640
Greeting well Cassibellaunus, who is king of Britain.'
    This is how the writing ran, which well conveyed the message:
'I am Julius Caesar who from Rome have come here;*
If you are willing to seek peace, then I shall not attack you,
And so hurry up and send me tribute from your land,
You yourself become my man, and treat me as your master,
Since everything is all my own which my eyes fall upon.'
    Cassibellaunus saw that writing, and was enraged about it;
He was amazingly annoyed because the message was offensive.
He composed a reply with considerable rancour   3650
And quite without greeting, and sent it to Caesar the king.
The reply came to the kaiser; on it these words were inscribed:
'Surprising does it seem to us, Caesar, you who are so wise and so
       aware,
That you should intend to be overlord of all men alive in the world.
You have come from Rome – your words are very stern – ;
You demand tribute from our land, but you won't be bragging of it:
You yourself are very grasping, your men are all too greedy,
You plan to seize into your hand all this middle-earth's land.
We are on an island, and at the world's end it stands,
Which Brutus acquired and on which we reside,   3660
And freely we hold it against all kings of the world,
And we will never send to you tribute from our land.
Now if you were as wise as I used to think you were,
Then you would understand that we're in our own land
As free and as clear at home as your people are in Rome,
For our ancestors from Troy fled and from one race we are
       descended:
Your ancestors and ours at Troy were confederates.
If you would believe me: unless you will leave us,
You shall from the Britons much bad luck obtain,
You and your companions, if ever you come here;   3670
Our ancestors, after all, were kings in this land,
And Belin and Brennes, both of them together,
They conquered Rome with regular power,

And by right that is ours which you are reigning over,
And therefore you ought to pay me tribute from your land:
You're holding it illegally, so you must have your penalty
For wanting to be my master: so you must bow to me!'*
    Caesar looked at this writing and gazed at it with wrath;
He was enraged in his feelings, and tossed it to his feet:
'Where are you, my knights who are valiant in fight?*   3680
Have my ships made ready, for now we must depart,
And we shall bend our course directly for Britain,
And capture there this land's king, and burn him alive and kicking,
And reduce all their land now into our own hand!'
    Sixty ships they made there, immeasurably mighty,
These being all new, strong and steering very true,
And of smaller ships there were so many that no man could make the
    tally.
There arrived for them good weather, wonderfully fine:
They set off from the sea-strand towards this our land;
They turned in to seek haven in the river Thames   3690
Where the Thames and the sea encounter each other.   *Caesar's*
    At once the news came to the king of this land,   *First*
And he had it proclaimed widely throughout all this people   *Invasion*
That Caesar had come here and where he had made landfall.
Cassibellaunus the king was aware of everything:
He knew well they had come over: he had seized the port of Dover,*
And there with his army lay the King of this country;
To that place came news which grieved him sore: the coming of Julius
    Caesar.
Many were the champions who were with Cassibellaunus,
And he had a chancellor, the wisest man in all this area: 3700
Belan he was called, gold rings he donated;
He was a knight most able to advise a king.
Under the king he held this land, and those who lived here hearkened
    to him.
The king raised up his brother's sons, both of them together:
The elder was called **Androgeus**, the younger one **Tennancius**;
These both stood before him, warriors most bold.
Nennius was the king's brother, and he had no other;
He went forward out of Canterbury with his brave forces.
Androgeus from London, with the Kentish lieges.
Tennancius from Cornwall: his champions were courageous.   3710
Aeridius the king, he brought his Scotsmen,

And **Britael** came in their need, the King of North Wales,
And **Gwaertaaet** the moody man, with the South Welshmen;
There came from Galloway **Aessel** the good;
There came from Moray many sharp spears.
From all of these peoples there came men in their need
To Cassibellaunus, the king of this land,
And all these liege-knights lent the king advice
That he by fighting should preserve his own freedom,
And by shaking their hands he gave sign he was bound   3720
To fight against Caesar who asked for land-tribute here.
    Forward they marched and his forces moved fast;
To the sea they went and Caesar there they met.
Of their [arrival well aware was Julius Caesar]:[†]
He called out to his knights: 'Make yourselves ready to fight,
For now with his army has come Cassibellaunus!'
    They locked in fight together with their long spears,
With axes, with swords, with sharp pointed halberds:
With hardihood they hacked; helmets rang out there;
Ferociously they fought; heads went falling.   3730
And Caesar the kaiser surpassed all in courage:
His long sword out he drew and many men with it he slew;
He laboured in that fight till he was lathered with sweat;
He slew those who were near him without any companion;
He did tremendous harm there: he slew there a full hundred
Of very brave men, that enemy with his brand.
    This was seen by Androgeus who called his [uncle], Nennius,[*†]
And both of the earls together banded forces,   *Nennius's*
With very many folk, and together they stood fast.   *Combat*
They spotted Julius Caesar fighting like a wild boar,   3740
And to him they hastened, fighting with hostility,
And many of their enemies they felled to the ground.
Then in the fight Nennius spotted Caesar Julius,
And he rushed across to him, raging with his sword:
He struck him on his helmet and the sword sank in it.
Amazing it seemed to many a knight
That he dared to get right close, since the kaiser was so famous.
Julius Caesar said not a word but he drew out his sword,
And Nennius he struck then too, upon his helmet so
That the helmet could not hold, and his head was bleeding.   3750
Yet he did not blanch at all for he was a knight without equal,
And Julius, without drawing breath, stood with blade uplifted,[†]

And Nennius lifted up his shield, so shielding himself;
Down Julius struck, and in the shield the sword stuck,
Julius gave it a twist but the sword lodged fast:
Julius held the sword, and Nennius the shield,
And so they went on tugging but the sword he could not drag out.
    Androgeus observed how things were with Caesar and Nennius,
And to them he hastened, to give [Nennius] assistance.[†]
Then Caesar noted this fact, and was greatly distressed,   3760
And he abandoned the brand and had nothing in his hand,
And then with ferocity turned round to flee.
    Nennius moved into the field and he turned round his shield,
Drew out the blade: then the earl was very brave:
Many Roman men with the sword he brought down;
Of many a man he was the bane, and many a one he shamed.
Everything he struck with the sword at once separated,
Everything it touched upon, whether it were flesh or bone:
From that sword's wounds those men fell to the ground.
    All day lasted the fight till the coming of dark night.   3770
Julius the commander, with all the Roman army,
Slipped off from the fight in the dark of night;
To harbour they crept, upon the sea's edge,
Leaving behind them twenty hundred knighted men
Lying beneath their shields, slain throughout the field.
Caesar went to his bed: his men were filled with dread;
He was guarded in the night by thirty hundred knights
With helmets and with byrnies and with swords of steel.
Julius Caesar was alert and was most aware;
He saw his huge losses and of even greater he felt fear: 3780
He got up about midnight and summoned all his knights,
And told them they were going to leave and from this land would flee,
Moving forwards into Flanders, and there they would be stationed,
Until he saw the chance came for him to sail back here again.
To their ships in flight they fared at once by night;
They had very fair weather and made their way to Flanders.
    In the morning at daylight the king with his doughty knights
Got ready his forces and advanced to the fight:
By then the Roman forces had fled from their land
So that they found not even one of all Caesar's men.   3790
Then indeed the British rejoiced in all their being:
Great was the celebration which they made, you may be certain,
Yet straight away after they became very sorry,

And Cassibellaunus the king was sorry more than anything,
For Nennius his brother found no cure to get better
From his head-wound, struck by Julius Caesar's hand;
Not by any skill of doctors could he safeguard his life;
There was no further advice and so came Nennius's demise,
And Nennius was laid at the north gate in London.
The king took a stone of marble and with gold had it
    concealed,*   3800
With gold and with gems, and there he laid his brother in:
With magnificence the Britons buried Nennius.
   Now you can hear the strangest words: the king took that very
    sword
Which Nennius his brother won from Julius Caesar,
And laid it by his brother, whose actual bane it was.
That forged steel blade was very long and it was very broad,
On [the hilt] were engraved many kinds of letter staves†   3807/8
Saying that in Rome the sword was called 'The Yellow Death';
That was how the sword was titled because of its great might;   3810
With it the kaiser threatened every country's army,
For there was never any man who ever might be born
Who, if he from that self-same sword had had but a single blow,
And if he from his body should lose a single drop of blood,
Would not instantly be dead, however doughty he might be.
   Julius with his forces was encamped in Flanders.
Word arrived in France of how he had fared,
And how with his army he was ejected from this country,
And then the men of France were most delighted at this chance,
Since they had dislike for Julius and were delighted at his
    disgrace,
Each Frenchman who had mettle had taken his own counsel   3821
And said to his companion: 'May that man never prosper
Who now and evermore ever bows to Caesar,
Whom the Britons have defeated and have driven from their land.
Never shall we honour him nor obey him as our overlord,
But against him shall we rather our freedom gain with fight;
For we shall be no tamer than the tribe of Britons are,
Who have driven him out and have slain all his knights.'
   Julius heard men say that the French talked in this way,
And that they spoke with threats and in proud boasts.   3830
He went into France with his enormous force
As if he did not know that they wished him harm,

And sent through all France for his free men, *Caesar's*
Who were to come to him as to their lord they must do. *Bribery*
All of them came to him, and all of them kissed him,
And all of them greeted him and hid their dissent.
Julius was very wise, and aware in his mind;
He had much gold brought in and a great heap of treasure;
First he gave to the highest, whose rank to his own was
    nearest:
Gifts really rich from his own red gold; 3840
He gave to every knight gifts shining bright.
With these gifts he overcame them, so that the best were won,
And freely gave him promises in order to be prosperous.
Then those men were his allies who had been his worst
    enemies.
Where is there a man who may not be bought off with money,
And through the love of property lay aside his enmity,
Make a full friendship even though he had been out of favour?
    Now announced Caesar (he was wise and most aware): *
'Hear me, my Frenchmen, my own free knights,
I wish to send to Rome, to my own men so noble, 3850
For them to send me outright five hundred knights,
For now I wish to go again into the land of Britain,
And you must go with me there in very mighty force,
And that land shall I win, which for you will work out well:
For your much increased worth there, you shall have wealth;
All your exiled men with my approval shall come back again,
For gifts I shall donate and the destitute make fortunate:
Freemen you shall all become and my friendship you shall
    have.'
    Then replied the retinue by raising their voices:
'With you we will live and with you we will lie dead, 3860
And for you we will gain glory by strength and by strategy,
And with you we will be bound, with our brave force,
Over the sea to Britain, to King Cassibellaunus,
And against him we shall fight, and avenge all your knights,
And conquer all that land, and place it in your hand!'
    But a lot more must be won before all this was done,
And all of them were contrite before it could come true.
    When Caesar had done this and dealt out his treasure,
And had also earned friendship for all of his fees,
Then he went to Boulogne, where it suited him best. 3870

He ordered them to build a tower, its beauty was a wonder: *   *Caesar's*
The tower was massive and high, and the sea was quite   *Tower*
    close by;
The kaiser gave it a name, and 'Otheres' was what he called it;
In that tower so strong the kaiser remained for long:
For thirteen full months Julius remained in Otheres,
And in it he had them store all his gold and great treasure.
There was never any castle which was so constructed,
With such great skill, as was the tower of Otheres.
There in its base might sixty hundred men be placed,
And yet the tower's top a man might cover with his cape.   3880
When the tower was quite completed, then Caesar felt less anxious;
He went into France and established his officers:
Everywhere he set up governors, powerful and great,
Who imposed a land-tax and with that income were to journey
Each and every year, to the tower of Otheres.
    Then he had fashioned – they were fantastically huge –
Six hundred ships, and set them in harbour.
When this work was completed, and all that was needed,
Then the kaiser announced that he would travel to Britain,
Onwards, by his very life: he would not let them get away with
    it!   3890
Six hundred ships, all good, he launched on the sea-flood,   *Second*
And no one knew the tally of the ships that sailed behind   *Invasion*
    them,
And directly they travelled into the Thames.
Now decided Julius Caesar – but this time he was unaware! –
He decided to advance up along the Thames,
To row so far along that he would come to London,
And there he would go ashore and attack the Britons,
And acquire all this land for his own hand.
But his luck did not hold like this: he lost it very quickly,
For sea-faring men said to the Britons   3900
That the emperor Julius was coming up the Thames like this,
Was moving on to London and would fight with those who lived
    here,
So the British were aware, and thought up a wise plan,
And took long stakes which were stout and very straight, *
And were shod with stout iron tips, and they stuck these in Thames
    stream;
There were five thousand of them firmly in the river bed,

With their upper ends hooded with cast-iron bands,
Holding out against them inside the harbour;
And so there these stood concealed by the flood.
    Then appeared Julius Caesar and of this he was not aware!   3910
The wind drove them swiftly along and the steersmen gave song;
The weather was as they wanted it, they were hoping to progress
    well;
They were speeding towards harbour when the ships suddenly
    halted:
The ships' bellies split; the water rushed in;
The sails were torn to shreds, the men drowned and dead,
And the Roman people rushed back across the waves.
The ships that drove to disaster numbered a hundred and fifty;
Afterwards came Julius Caesar (in his heart he felt despair):
They pushed out their luff and laid course for land,
And those who came after at once were alerted,   3920
And these had better luck so that most of them got to land.
They set up their tents far and wide across the grass-bents,
Deeply mourning all their friends who had been drowned.
    Then Cassibellaunus the king new for a fact
That Julius the commander was in London with his army.
Then Cassibellaunus the king uttered a lament:
'Alack, brother Nennius, I do not have you here alive, *
And your sword, the Yellow Death, which you won yourself in
    combat,
And here fit and by my side I do not see you ride!
On the other wing Androchius and his brother Tennancius –   3930
Then safely we'd move forward and fight against the kaiser;
Forwards we'd advance and fell all his adherents.'
    Cassibellaunus the Britons' king was a good knight above all
    things:
He assembled a huge army and advanced towards the kaiser,
And like this addressed his followers and with affection spoke:
'Consider now, you brave knights, how to claim your rights;
Consider now King Belin, and Brennes his brother,
How they gained Rome with their regal army,
And won all the realms which are tributory to Rome,
And in this way they mastered it for very many years,   3940
And so they subjected it during their lifetimes.
And I declare to you, knights: Rome is yours by right,
Which now is held by Julius Caesar who has twice come over here:

Over there he holds your heritage, yet here too he wants to exile you!
He hates you so excessively that he wants to drive you away.
If you lose this land, everywhere people will loathe you.
But turn now to business, for we are all bold Britons:
Caesar is in our land, and is lodged here by the sea strand.
Bravely let's advance on him and show him greatest enmity,
And let us master the emperor and all his Roman masses,   3950
And rescue our land from the Roman people!'
The army answered at once: 'Let us go quickly,
For Julius is fated, and all his folk of Rome!'
    Onward they hurried, hastening with speed,
Until they had come to where was camped the folk of Rome,
And they rushed upon them with rigorous force.
Ferociously they fought and the Romans were falling:
The army of Caesar was sinking to the earth,
Not in tens, not in twenties but in twenty thousands.
So they fought all day (many there were fated)   3960
Until it drew to night, and Caesar could no longer fight.
Caesar was very sad then and considered a plan
That he would, in the night, flee away with his knights.
Of his losses Julius Caesar was very well aware:
He had them sound his trumpets and summon his troops,
And got them to call out loudly and everywhere proclaim
That they should come to their billets and prepare their effects,
And polish up their weapons: tomorrow they would proceed to
        battle.
    This was heard by the spies there who were on the sidelines:
Immediately they came to Cassibellaunus,   3970
And said to him that Caesar was still going to stay there,
And tomorrow he would fight with all of his knights,
And fell all the Britons, unless he himself was fated,
Since this was being called out, and proclaimed all through his army.
But oh! alas and alack! that Cassibellaunus saw no trick,
But thought he was doing well when he wasn't doing so at all.
He pulled over to one side, and then set up shelter,
And all of that night there was preparation by his knights
Of their spear-shafts and their shields: the soldiers were misled,
For Julius Caesar, of his trouble well aware,   3980
About the hour of midnight gave warning to his knights,*
And to ship they dashed and departed without delay.
They had very good weather and were moving with the waves;

They were ferrying in their ships both dead men and the living,
Many a sorrowful stalwart wounded severely,
Many a dead knight from Caesar's bodyguard.
So they floated on the tide to the tower of Otheres.
There remained Julius Caesar, feeling very sad and sore.
 In the morning when it was daylight it was clear outright,
And declared to the king, to Cassibellaunus,   3990
How Julius the emperor from this land had departed,
And how he had flitted, fleeing with the tide,
So that nothing remained there of all the Roman people.
Then the king was saddened and said this, lamenting:
'Alas, alas for wrong advice! Many a man you bring to his demise.
Alas that I wasn't already aware that Julius wanted to be away!
Most truly spoke the sombre man who recounted this saying:
"Seldom do you get things done if you go round believing
  everyone".
So much did I think that the tale was the truth
Which was told me last night by a man deceitful and [craven],† 4000
That Caesar wanted now, today, to win himself Britain,
Or lie here from sword-blades battered to pieces,
And all his companions who came with him here.
You see, this same was said just to deceive me.
Alas, alas the day that like this he's gone away!
But all the same, I am content that ever to our life's extent
We can occupy this land before he comes back to attack us,
For now he can remember [our] reprisals here for ever,†
Since there lie in this year ten thousand of his men here,
Not counting all his splendid ships, sunk in the sea depths. 4010
But greatly I thank my gods for glory I have gained here
In twice routing the emperor with all his Roman [army],†
And now I'll go to London, the city I love so much,
And there I'll make devotions to my divinities,
And bountifully honour them because of all their blessings.'
The king had trumpets sounded and summoned all his army,
And released them all to return to their homes – and retainers were to
  be happy –
To groom well their horses and get ready their garments,
And three weeks from that day to make their way to London,
With wives and with children to cheer and rejoice,   4020
Earls and leaders, knights and servers,
And all the free people of proud Britain's land.

They agreed on the date, and to London they came,   *Victory*
With such regal splendour as if this had been Rome   *Celebrations*
The king began the ceremony with every kind of duty,
According to the heathen rites which were current in those times.
There were standing in the temple ten thousand men
Who were the most choice in all of Britain,
In front of the idol which they thought illustrious,
Apollin it was called: they accounted it the high creator.   4030
Each brave man held in his hand a torch all ablaze,
Each bold man was also embellished with gold.
On his head majestically the king wore his kingly crown.
In front of that altar an impressive fire was kindled;
The king threw riches in it, and all his noblest men with him,
Then they offered there the finest of treasures,
And he thanked his god Apollin who had granted him great honour.
   When the service was done, the time for feasting came.
About this I will tell you some surprising stories:
There were in the king's kitchen two hundred cooks,   4040
And no one could have counted all the many porters.
There were slaughtered for the feast twelve thousand prime beef
    beasts,
And thirty hundred harts, and just as many hinds,
And as to species of bird, of these none has known or heard,
And all the wealth and all the gold there was throughout the king's land
Was all assembled there for the food service.
This was never truly told, since the start of the world,
That there were in one spot such gifts all stored up,
Nor such a giving and receiving of such rich things.
   Cheerful was the day and light and the sun was very bright,   4050
All of the soldiers were well supplied with beer,*
And the distinguished men drank deep of wine.
They ferried to the fields their spears and their shields;
Some were racing horses and some were running races,*
And some of them were playing — when a sudden problem came.
Some were playing at board games and some were racing their horse
    teams.
   There were two men there, and proud were the pair:
The one had **Herigal** as his name, and **Evelin** the other;
Herigal was the king's relation (that was trouble on that occasion);
An adventurous knight was Evelin whose uncle was   4060
    Androgeus.*

These two knights were in process of skirmishing with shields:
At first it was a diversion, but then a dispute arose,
And Herigal struck Evelin very hard upon the chin;*
They began quarrelling and to them knights came riding;
In rage Evelin took his staff and with it gave a rebuff,
And struck Herigal on the ribs so that the staff broke in the midst.
Then Herigal declared: 'Evelin, that's just too much!
You have struck me on the back, but severely I shall get my own back.
Seeing your staff's now broken, a battering's coming your way!'
   Evelin was terribly sorry that his luck had turned like this: 4070
His opponent wanted him dead – a very tough plight he found this –
And he thought very carefully what might be the remedy;
He had nothing in his hand save a little shield.
He saw a courteous man standing on the sideline,
Who to that place came to see the knightly games;
The young man in his hand was holding a steel brand;
Evelin grabbed the sword, with ungracious expression,
And drew it from the sheath, and his anguish was eased.
He rushed up to Herigal and struck him really hard
So that his nose [and his lips] fell down, [cut right off].*   4080
Once again he took a swipe and he struck off his hand,
A third blow he gave him and straight in half shaved him.
The end of the game was that Herigal lay slain,
And Evelin made a getaway, the sword still in his hand,
He encountered no man brave enough to dare to seize and take him
    off;
All the people he deserted and to Androgeus's home he dashed.
   This the king heard: it was made known to him at once
How it had all happened and how Herigal lay murdered.
The king took three aldermen and sent them to Androgeus,
Ordering him to bring his kinsman to the king,   4090
To undergo the royal sentence for his murderous offence,
And if he refused then he would be outlawed.
The response from Androgeus addressed the king like this:
'Him I refuse to bring, no, not for anything,
For Evelin to be destroyed, either beheaded or hanged.*
But I have free land, which is freeholder I have in hand,
And I have my own [army], so high am I beneath the king.†
If here there is a knight who of Evelin demands right,
Let him come to my court and there he shall have it,
And I declare to you the truth, no other plan is any use.'   4100

This was at once made known to Cassibellaunus, *Civil*
And the king flew into a fury as if he had grown frenzied, *War*
And these very words he uttered, did Cassibellaunus:
'Out of my eyesight, Androgeus and his associates,
And if anywhere I can catch him, on that spot he'll be dispatched!'
Androgeus instantly took off with all his cavalry,
And at once he led the way out of London city
And journeyed to Kent, to his [own] castle,[†]
And fortified it well with food and with weapons,
While the king took London and the land into his own hand, 4110
And then pressed forward into Kent with an enormous army,
With fire and with [fighting] he savagely razed the region.[†]
    Androgeus took two knights and sent them to the king,
And the knights spoke to him like this: 'O king, Androgeus wants a
    truce;
Androgeus is your own man, all your wishes he'll see done,
If you will only make a truce and let him treat with you for peace,
And leave off all your burning of his land you're burning up.
Remember he was Lud's son: from your brother he's descended,
And his father owned all that land which now lies in your own hands,
And he reckons it would be well done, if you make
    reconciliation, 4120
But he refuses to surrender Evelin to you in terror
So that you can do one of two things, either slay or even hang him.'
    When the king heard this said he was very enraged,
And the king spoke thus, did Cassibellaunus:
'Where are you, my champions,
My own doughty men? Avenge me now, on Androgeus!
His land I shall consume, I shall be his killer!'
This was told to Androgeus, and he answered it thus:
'It once was reported in a really true remark
That many a man does much harm without intending to, 4130
And so I needs must now in dire necessity;
The man who puts up with people wanting to kill him, that's who I
    call really crazy,
As long as he can through any feat defend himself on the battle-field.
Any knight is bound to commit a crime to avoid undergoing a worse
    one,
And as sure as I shall ever bear shield and bear spear, I shall write to
    the emperor,
And greeting Julius Caesar, I shall complain to him of my grievance,

And request that he give me heed, for now I am in great need.'
  Androgeus the noble knight composed a letter which was written
    right,
And took a good messenger and sent him to Otheres,
To Julius the kaiser and all his Roman army,   4140
And like this the letter ran, and like this properly began:
'Greetings to you and your army, imperial Julius!   *Letter*
You are called Julius Caesar, it's to you I complain of my   *to*
    grievance,   *Caesar*
I, Androgeus, your own man; nor is there any treason done,
For the message which I send, by my own life I will uphold:
Should you refuse to believe that it is other than a lie,
Then I will give you proof through my glorious god,
Through my lord, Apollin, whom I love deep in my heart,
For often it has befallen, in very many peoples,
That after fierce hatred the highest men have loved each
    other,   4150
And after much public disgrace they have divulged a deep respect.
Twice you have been conquered, and your men we have captured, *
And driven you from Britain here with fighting most severe;
Among us you have left behind many thousand fighters.
This was not through our king's action, not through Cassibellaunus,
But it was through my own self, and through my splendid people,
For I was leading with me the local force from London
And also all the Kentish men – these champions were splendid then –
Which wasn't counting many a Briton who was bold in battle.
Now that we have conquered you, and killed your people and
    captured them,
Now Cassibellaunus and his men have become so mighty   4161
That by contest he wants to send me out of Britain's land,
Exile me from those living there, far off from this land.
All my land they have laid waste for me, London they have snatched
    from me,
And myself they intend to kill, and all my champions as well.
  If you wish to hear this missive, it will show where I am guilty:
When you had slipped away from us, on that last occasion,
The king was then so blithe as he had never been in his life,
Although on the other hand he was sorry because he hadn't known of
    your journey;
Nevertheless he announced, in front of all his army,   4170
"Now Julius has run away, and twice he has been routed:

Twice he came to Britain, and bad experiences were his lot.
Now we need never more see him again come here,
For here lie his best knights, slain in our fight.
Now let us for their deaths be quite delighted.
All of my Britons must, with very bold pride,
Leave home for London, and there let us worship
Our great lord Apollin and all our gods with him,
For the great glory which now I have gained."
So all those who lived in Britain left home for London,   4180
The knights and the lords, with their wives and children,
And with all the dignity in which they were dominant.
 So when we came to London, we began to celebrate
Our lord Apollin, and all our gods with him.
Since the start of the world it has nowhere been told
That anywhere there was so much food provided for one feast,
Nor so much good drink dealt out to people.
Great was the rejoicing; then they went to recreation:
Some on foot, with fine garments,
Some on horse, handsomely clad.   4190
There were present two soldiers, who took up their shields,
Advanced beneath their targes and skirmished with strength.
One of them was my sister's son, Evelin is his name,
The other Herigal, high in the court household,
From the king's close family he comes, he was his half-sister's son,
He was for the king the dearest of all his doughty men.
Herigal struck Evelin very hard upon the chin,
And Evelin grew angry and began to defend himself;
On his side he struck Herigal, and the blow made him very sore,
And Herigal then said, and with his own lips he swore,   4200
That Evelin that very day must endure his death;
Evelin was very scared, since he was threatened with death,
And struck at Herigal's shield and his staff split in two;
Often had Evelin been mad, but never till then were things so bad:
He shielded himself with his shield, having nothing else to hand,
And Herigal kept pressing him with overpowering strength,
Evelin saw a young man, standing on there beside him,
Carrying in his right hand a good steel brand;
Evelin rushed up to him, and grabbed it roughly.
In a hurry that sword he drew and Herigal he slew.   4210
 The news came to the king, to Cassibellaunus,
That Herigal was dead and Evelin away had fled;

To me he sent a message, minus every greeting,
Ordering me to bring him my own nephew Evelin,
To bring him to him speedily to suffer his court's decree,
Since he'd do to him one of two things, either killing or hanging,
And if I refused cooperation I must flee from his dominion,
And if he could catch me he would hang or dispatch me.
I craved the king's peace and with him wanted a truce,
To do right by him in my own court because I was his senior
    count,   4220
But deliver to him Evelin to destruction, that would I never,
And so he drove me out at once from his court.
He has taken London from me, and my knights he's killed,
Nevertheless I have a household of two hundred and fifty,
And still I have in my control twenty good strongholds,
And I myself reside in Kent with my courageous soldiers,
And still with hostile intent the king refuses me settlement.
    'Now you've heard my grievance, Julius Caesar, your grace,
All my words are true, as this writing had told you.
In this letter I have set down that I wish to become your man,   4230
And have you as head over me, and as my high lord,
On condition you help me in considerable need,
And rescue me from the king, from Cassibellaunus.
These words I will make good to you, by my own glorious god,
This I will prove as true, as I in writing tell it.
So come in haste to Britain: the land I turn over to you;
Because of me you left it, because of me you'll have it.'
    This letter was read to Julius, sent to him by Androgeus,
And then gave answer Julius the kaiser:
'I will not believe him, by the oaths of all nations,   4240
Unless he sends to me at once his lovely son, Conan,
And thirty other hostages he sends me to Otheres,
Who are all well chosen and born in high station.
If he will agree to this, I will accept his offer,
And come across and help him with a heavy force.'
    These words sent Julius in writing to Androgeus;   *Third*
Androgeus straightaway at once sent his son Conan,   *Invasion*
And thirty other hostages he sent to him at Otheres,
And Julius the lucky then set off upon the sea:
With all his forces he sailed fast towards Britain.   4250
The moment it was dawning he arrived at Dover;
Androgeus heard word of it and at once he went there,

And these words spoke Androgeus: 'Welcome to you, Julius!
You are very dear to me; this land I deliver to you.'
They spoke together privately and proposed a mutual pact.
   Meanwhile the king, Cassibellaunus,
All through his kingdom had assembled a strong force.
To London he would bend his steps and besiege [the] castle†
Which Androgeus the strong held still in his hand.
When the army was all massed, there came a man riding   4260
And at once he called out to Cassibellaunus:
'Good health to you, O King; I bring some tidings
Of the Roman people whom you passionately detest.
They are all in Dover, your most deadly foes,
And to there has gone Androgeus to parley with Julius.
These words are sober truth which I am saying to you,
So devise a course of action by which you could defend your people!'
   This indeed sobered King Cassibellaunus,
And at once at his bidding the bugles were blown;
He made known to his knights the tidings, newly arrived,   4270
That Julius the kaiser with his Roman army
Had right there and then arrived and at Dover entered port.
Then spoke the king, Cassibellaunus:
'London we must abandon and advance at once to Dover,
Gather our forces and let us go quickly!'
   Forward marched the king with unnumbered forces,
Straight towards Dover; but no good did such behaviour!
This heard Julius Caesar, who was wise and most aware,
That that way in haste was coming Cassibellaunus.
Then Julius rejoiced at this good piece of news: 4280
He marched out of Dover, by the seashore moreover,
Into a large secret valley where he slyly hid his troops,
And Androgeus entered it at the other end,
Into a wilderness, in a huge forest,
And like this spoke Androgeus, to his troops saying this:
'No knight is to be so brainless, no warrior so thoughtless,
As ever to utter a sound further than his spear's tip,
Nor from companions ride, for in company we shall slide
Speedily together and slaughter our foes.
If there is here any soldier listening who can seize the king,   4290
Let him capture him unharmed and not give him any wound,
(Because he is my lord and kindred I will not kill him);
But all his followers we shall fell to the ground,

III

And think about battle and not about booty;
Fell the proud fighters and leave the booty lying!'
   In the same way Julius directed his dear knights;
Julius had as supporters thirty hundred riders,
Knights of the choicest, courageous champions,
And Androgeus had as supporters ten thousand riders.
As they lay there silently discussing their policy   4300
Along came riding King Cassibellaunus,   *Ambush*
With innumerable forces, with innumerable folk,
And came in between then – that's how he came to grief!
Julius was in front of him, Androgeus behind him,
But Androgeus was first alerted and out of the wood he went,
And all the men he was leading loudly were screaming,
Blowing their bugles and emboldening their brave men,
And advancing upon them on every quarter.
   Of this heard the king, Cassibellaunus,
He could hear the great uproar and the huge din,   4310
And commanded outright: 'To your weapons, you knights!'
Sad at heart, the king was sure that this must be Caesar,
But Caesar, by his plot, ahead of them was quiet,
And could easily hear the noise from Androgeus's force,
And Julius was quite ready, on the point of rushing out,
But Cassibellaunus the king of this knew not a thing,
But he armed all his knights and prepared them for fight.
Before they were half prepared Androgeus appeared,
Flying upon them with ferocious strength.
The knights who were girt proceeded to fight,   4320
And Androgeus set upon them with outstanding strength.
At the first onslaught he felled from that force
Four thousand men – and that force was reduced.
When folk started fleeing, there came Caesar advancing,
Straight against their vanguard and so set upon them.
From those people he slew many and far from few!
   So fled the Britons' king, Cassibellaunus:
Often had he been sad, but never till then were things so bad:
Julius was in front of him, Androgeus behind him,
And on every side they sought him to his peril.   4330
The king had a plan, had Cassibellaunus:
He saw at his side a steep hanging wood;
At one edge of the wood, there did he enter,
And many of his forces fled with the king

And climbed up the hill with deep care in spirit.
   All the same, up there thronged full fifteen thousand.
The mountain was very high, overgrown with hazels,
[That grew very thickly, upon every side];[†]   4337a
The hill was enclosed with great clumps of stone.
They began to fell the wood and lay it in front of them,
Along with stumps and with stones and with steel points;   4340
So they began to defend themselves against their adversaries.
The king converted the hill into a strong castle:
In the space of a single night the stronghold was finished,
For there laboured workers and there laboured lords,
And the king with his own hands, Cassibellaunus,
Laboured very hard to defend his life.
   When the fort was set up, they [were] all [little] better[†]
[Since] Julius Caesar surrounded them there.[†]
On the hill was the king, Cassibellaunus,
And there he suffered dreadful torment, for they had neither wine nor
     refreshment;[†]
For three days and three nights not one thing ate any knight;   4351
They were in a very bad way, for the king had led them all astray
In refusing any settlement with Androgeus, his relative,
And therefore he was on the hill, with hunger tormented.
He was in a very bad way and couldn't think of any remedy
Since he did not know of any place which could provide him aid;
All day he saw before him placed his bitter enemies through choice:
Julius the kaiser and all the Roman army,
With all the Roman populace to the king's disadvantage,
And all day they called out to Cassibellaunus: 4360
'Now you must quake for all your former acts;
You were really delighted, driving us into the ground
With your fighting, and felling our relations;
Now your reckoning has come: you'll be reduced to death
By hunger and by hatred, and by great disgrace.
   Miserable was the king, was Cassibellaunus,
And he adopted a policy in his great necessity:
He took a wise knight and sent him off straight,
Out to the people who were his opponents,
To salute Androgeus with peaceful-sounding speech.   4370
He bad him recognise that he was his relative,
And the more so in his need, because he was his brother's son:
'For I haven't behaved so badly to you that I deserve to die for it!

It's really not at all right if ever any good knight
Were to kill without deserving his own dear kindred.
In this dire need now you must aid me,
Reconcile me with the emperor and with the Roman army,
And then I shall have words with you, and make peace such as suits
    you:
Together we shall live, together we shall lie.
Think of my plight: reconcile me with the Roman people!   4380
After all, if I perish here, you'll be the first to suffer,
For those who hasten my death now will be even more hated.'
    Then answered Androgeus, and to the knight he spoke like this:
'How long ago did it come about, in the kingdom of this world,
That my uncle's mighty arrogance should have turned so meek,
And that such a rash man should recognise what's right?
Five days have not yet fully passed by
Since he [wanted] to drive me out, deprive me of my life!†
For this he exerted all his might, he snatched away all that was mine,
And everything that I held dear he found amazingly
    distasteful.   4390
The king acted foolishly in behaving so high-handedly:
He was fighting against Caesar, the Roman emperor,
And twice he conquered him, and slew his folk and captured them,
But the king didn't do it all alone, but with all our cooperation!
I was there in the fight, along with all my knights,   *Appeasement*
And really hard pressed on plenty of occasions.
But if it had not been for myself, and all my good knights,
Our king would have been captured and his Britons all been killed.
But we in front of the king fought very fiercely,
And we drove out the emperor with his Roman army.   4400
The king did not do it all alone, but with our cooperation!
    'And when we had achieved all this and received much glory,
Then the king's spirit grew very proud, [as if he had driven him out!]
Since things have come to this pass, now my uncle's changed his
    voice,
With meek-sounding words he is begging my mercy;
Because his mad rage is cooled his words are now good.
Well, now I'll change my mood: for wrong I shall do good,
And I'll lighten his sorrow and reconcile him with Caesar
Before the end comes of this day, if I may help him in some way.'
    Androgeus, as good as his word, went barefoot and
    unshod,   4410

And all his best knights who were with him in the fight
Went over to the kaiser to where he was in his army,
And fell at his feet there fully to the ground.
With humility spoke thus the true knight Androgeus:
'Lord Caesar, your mercy, now and for eternity!
I crave an audience, I beg for clemency and peace:
My uncle took to flight; you conquered him in fight;
He's encamped upon this hill and craves life-truce, if you will;
After all, you've overcome King Cassibellaunus,
And most of his people you've felled to the ground,   4420
And the king and all his land you've acquired for your own hand.
Now give him his life-truce, and give him an audience.
Once he was a free king; [now let him be your underling!];[†]
Now you've had your revenge on him let him become your own man,
Each year to you let him send the tribute from Britain's land,
Much treasure and much property: the mastery is yours.'
   This was heard by Caesar: of this speech he was aware,
But he held himself aloof, and he would not hear,
Made out that he was wildly angered by the words which he was
      hearing.
Androgeus was wise and aware: to the emperor he went
      nearer   4430
And with grand expressions the emperor he greeted,
And like this spoke Androgeus: 'Hear me, over here, Julius!
Now do not be annoyed with me: my arrangement with you is
      completed,
And everything I promised you, in the presence of knights from both
      our sides.
I promised you all of Britain's land, and to place it in your hand,
And now I have done so, and it has all been accepted by you,
But never did I promise you to slaughter my uncle, Cassibellaunus.
With no justice can I destroy him, for I'm his relation and his retainer.
Nor must he ever death endure while I can bring him rescue.
Oh, but give my uncle his life-truce, and let him and you be
      reconciled;
He will become your liegeman, will as hostage give you his
      son,   4441
And each year to you he will send three thousand pound,
And this oath to you I'll swear upon my very sword.
If you will not observe this, then worse shall befall you,
And never with your army shall you leave Britain safely!'

This terrified the kaiser, and his Roman army:
More precious to him than all his provinces, than all his silver, than
    all his gold
Would be the safety of Otheres, inside his good fortress,
For then in much anxiety was Julius the kaiser,
Thinking that Androgeus was about to betray him.   4450
Julius was wise and aware, as he demonstrated there,
And this said Julius to the earl Androgeus:
'Androgeus my dear man, everything you want I'll see done:
I shall act on your policy because you helped me when most
    necessary,
And I've never found a truer man between here and the Lateran!'
    At once this was made known to Cassibellaunus,
Who then rejoiced much more than ever in his life before.
Out went the king, went Cassibellaunus,
Down from the hill, rejoicing in spirit,
But there Julius did well, winning great approval: *   4460
He had the king fed, he had him well clothed,
He even had him bathed, before he came to meet him.
When all was completed, then they came together.
They formulated peace terms, faithfully preserved;   *Truce*
They ratified their pact in front of their people:
Cassibellaunus became Julius's own man,
Each year he was to send three thousand pound.
Sworn oaths then they made which were never betrayed:
As true men they made them and in the same way held to them.
But all the same, Julius was the first man who ever plunged this land
    in serfdom
Since Noah and his sons out of the ark had come.   4471
    When all this was completed the armies separated,
And with his company the kaiser remained here all that winter,
In friendship and in peace and with prodigious pleasure.
Towards the summer time they went over seas,
Taking with them Androgeus, the dearest follower of Julius,
And Androgeus was master of all he wanted most:
From here as far as Rome stretched Androgeus's dominion,
And he never returned here, nor did any of his retainers.
    Nor did he survive for more than seven years, *   4480
Cassibellaunus, who was king of this land;
When his ending day came in York did he die.
[Before the king's death] his queen herself [died];†

The king was quite childless and the Britons were cheerless.
   To the Duke of Cornwall, Tennancius, came the news *
That his uncle was deceased and his dignity declined,
And his brother Androgeus had gone overseas with Julius,
And many of his relations had removed with him too.
Tennancius pondered carefully how he might proceed:
How he might bring things on so that he should have this
     kingdom   4490
Which King Lud his father had ruled for so long.
Tennancius took his spokesman and sent him into Britain,
To request them to reverence him, so things would go right for them,
To raise him to be their king, entirely without contest,
To invest him with all the land which his father Lud had had in hand,
And he would love them all as long as he lived.
And if they would do this, then he would have it,
Otherwise by battle he would beat them to the ground.
   The Britons travelled to London, to an important hustings,
Where the best plan, they decided, was to do what Tennancius
     wanted.
They sent for him then and raised him to the throne.   4501
There was in Britain great joy and bliss.   TENNANCIUS
For twenty-two winters he was ruler in this land,
Then came that very day when dead the king lay;
In London he lies: sad were those who lived here.
This king had one son, **Cymbeline** was his name;
He had voyaged with his uncle far off to Rome.
Augustus Caesar made him a knight, as was all very right,
For by then was Julius dead and his powers had departed,
Nor had they left a single one of Androgeus's relations   4510
Who could maintain fight and contest as Cymbeline could,
Who was defending the Roman nation against alien races.
   Of this heard the Britons who were then very busy,
How Cymbeline the brave dwelt within Rome,
Who was Tennancius's son and from King Lud's line come.
Two knights they chose and sent them off to Rome,
And these informed Cymbeline that his father was deceased,
And requested that he secretly depart from that country;
There was no long delay before he came here straightaway,
And the Britons welcomed him and raised him to be king.   4520
   In Cymbeline's days, when he was king in Britain,   CYMBELINE
There came in this middle-earth the son of a maiden

Who was born in Bethlehem of the best of all bright maids;
He is called Jesus Christ through the Holy Spirit,   *Christ's*
The joy of all the worlds and judge over angels;   *Birth*
He is the Father in Heaven and the Saviour of men;
He is the Son on Earth of the holy maiden,
And third, the Holy Spirit is united with him too;
Fully the spirit he imparts to those who are dear to him,
Just as he did to Peter, who was a humble fisher,   4530
Making him among mankind the highest of all men.
   Cymbeline the British king was a good man in everything,
And he lived here for twenty-two whole years;
In his days there lived a man here in this land;
Amazing things accompanied him; he was called **Taliesin;** *
They regarded him as a wizard because of his wise skills,
And they believed everything that Taliesin said to them:
He told them many tremendous things and all of it they found true;
Every year he told them what was coming to them.
The king sent to fetch him twelve wise knights,   4540
Who ordered him to come to the king and that he must do no other
    thing,
And at once they brought him before the people's king.
From the moment of their meeting the king gave him fair greeting:
'As I use my head and chin, you are welcome Taliesin!,
And dearer to me is your health than a thousand pounds of
    wealth!'
   Then responded Taliesin and said this to Cymbeline:
'I hope my health and goods may grow, if all of that you'll well
    bestow!'
This amused Cymbeline, who said this to Taliesin:
'To this land there have come mysterious doctrines,
From the land of Jerusalem of what has happened in
    Bethlehem;   4550
A little child has been born there in that land;
Great and powerful is the terror: there are tokens in the planets,
In the moon and in the sun, and awe among the race of men.
This is all widely known, and to me these letters came.
So I'd like to learn from you (after all, my friend, I like you),
What these portents proclaim, and to what things they proceed,
For of this the folk of every land are fearsomely afraid.'
   Then answered Taliesin and said this to Cymbeline:
'It was long ago prophesied: the predictions are now proved

That a child should come to earth, the most elect of all by
     birth,   4560
And he should be called the Saviour, and would help all his comrades,
Releasing his beloved friends from loathsome bonds of sin,
Out of hell bringing Adam, Noah and Abraham,
Sadoc and Samuel and Simeon the aged,
Joseph and Benjamin and all his brothers with him,
Joel and Elisha, Asor and Nason,
Isaac and his brother and very many others,
Many hundred thousand who have been thrust into hell,
And for such great need he has come to that people.'
These words spoke Taliesin and all of them were true.   4570
When this true information had been told to the king
Then the news was made known throughout the king's nation;
The Britons paid attention and did not let it be forgotten.

    Cymbeline was a good king and peaceable above all things,
And all the Roman people very dearly loved him;
And if the king had desired to be disobedient to them
He could have held back their tribute which Julius took from here,
Yet all the time, while he lived, he lovingly paid it to them.
After there came to him the tidings of Christ, God's own child,
The king did not live more than a mere ten years;   4580
Then the king gave up his life and even yet in York he lies.
He left here behind two sons, **Wither** and **Arviragus**:
Wither was the elder, and Arviragus the younger,   WITHER
But the king bequeathed to Wither the whole of his kingdom,
And after his father's days he made decrees and dealt with men.
He was a very good knight and had held his own in many fights,
But he was very stern and severe with the people;
He refused, despite the edict, any more to be Rome's subject,
And would no tribute to them send away from this our land,
But where he found a man who'd come out to these shores from Rome
He had his head chopped off: let him be deprived of life!   4591
And so he got ready for them his grimmest of games.

    There was a kaiser in Rome, **Claudius** they called him,
Who heard these tidings about Wither the king,
What disgrace he had done him and still more had promised.
The kaiser grew enraged (the Evil One was in his heart),
And swore by his spine that for this Wither must atone.
He proceeded to send to all within Rome's bounds,
Ordering all who were fierce and who were full of good advice,

All his haughty men, the hustings to attend.   4600
And together they came in the city of Rome.
They mustered their armies far and wide through the country:
With punishing force out of Rome they advanced;
So long did they travel that they came to this land,
Claudius Caesar and his whole Roman army;
At Portchester they came to land, stepping upon the
    sea-strand,   *Claudius's*
And with their folk besieged Portchester, very fast and   *Invasion*
    very fiercely.
They got men to dig ditches, enormously deep ones,
And all around it, everywhere, he built a stone wall there.
Till then Portchester had been a borough best among those seen,
But with the storming wind these had all become unsteady: 4611
With fire and with fighting they were felled by Claudius Caesar.
    The news came to Wither, who was the King of the Britons here,
That there had come to this land Claudius the strong.
The king assembled an army far and wide through all his country,
And Arviragus his brother assembled another,
And they marched towards the sea with a marvellous crowd,
Until they came up with their soldiers to Claudius Caesar.
Ferociously they fought; fated men fell there,
And Earl Arviragus with power gave aid to his brother.   4620
    Claudius had a mighty man who was called **Hamun**;
For the emperor he planned strategy for all the Roman army;
Hamun considered Wither and how he withstood them,
And how maliciously in fight he was slaughtering Rome's knights,
And felled at his feet all those whom he could meet;
Hamun considered carefully what should be his policy,
How he might best kill the Britons' King Wither.
Hamun strode through the corpses turning over the slain,
And found there a knight who had been slain outright;
He stripped off his byrny, took his gold-covered shield,   4630
He leapt on his own steed and to one side began to ride
Where he spotted King Wither with his hostile deeds on field;
Hamun the cavalier struck his own companions there,
And bestirred himself most actively as if he were a Briton;
King Wither considered he must be his companion,
Yet he had come there solely for the sake of treachery.
Hamun galloped upwards and another time went downwards:
When he saw a man who was Roman he rushed down upon him;

He spoke nothing but British as if he were a Briton.[*]

For so long did he ride that he arrived at the king's side.   4640

And in front of the king he began to fight like one born as his man,

And slew his own confederates (double treachery to perpetrate).

The king trusted him completely because he fought so bravely,

And thought it true and right that he was surely his own knight.

The king went riding straight to one side from the fight:

He was so very overheated that his byrny ran with sweat;

He let his byrny slide down from his back behind,

Hamun struck off towards him with his sturdy strength:

With his spear he was so brave that the king's breast in he stove:

King Wither he struck dead (there was great treachery

    indeed!)   4650

And then fled rapidly to his own Roman folk,

Announced to his emperor what he'd done with his spear.

    Then Arviragus saw that his brother had been   ARVIRAGUS

    slaughtered,

And in great haste he went rushing up towards the dead king,

Seized hold of his mount and all his equipment,

And bestirred himself in combat as if he were the king:

Almost all the Britons there thought that he was Wither;

They rushed the Roman forces and these took refuge in flight;

They slew there outright Claudius's knights:

A full nine thousand they laid to the ground.   4660

    Claudius Caesar had had sufficient of the combat;

His folk fled into their ships and set off from the land,

Forwards over the waves the foes were ferried;

Five thousand they left behind, up on the land,

Who could not reach the ships so as not to be killed or captured

And amazingly fast away they rode toward an extensive wood;

Arviragus went after them with twenty thousand knights:

They killed, they captured, with their hands they disembowelled.

Through the wood Hamun fled right down to the sea's edge,

He galloped to a harbour, hoping to take ship: 4670

The tide had gone out, the ships were all grounded,

And while he was pushing out the ships, Arviragus caught up with

    him;

Hamun had no more supporters than just thirty riders,

All of whom Arviragus slew; with horses Hamun in pieces he drew.

Because of his brother's death he was deeply depressed,

But on the other hand he was glad that his foes were all dead.

[Where Hamun in pieces was torn, there he founded a
    town]; 4676a
Because of Hamun's death he called it Hamtun: *
Now and for evermore the name remains there.
So now you know from what play derived the name we know today;
In this way many times do nick-names arise, 4680
And often from a little thing which lasts a long time,
For no other entertainment will be so firmly tenacious.
    When Hamun and his comrades were all of them dead
Arviragus was most glad [and did all that he was asked];† 4683a
But straightaway afterwards a sorrow came upon him.
He and his knights from there direct and straight
To Winchester went; at once disaster came:
They thought then for sure that they were secure.
Claudius the kaiser with all his Roman army
Went over the sea and all of them were safe;
They'd not been gone one night when the wind turned round
    quite 4690
Right towards the strand, directly to this land;
Claudius turned back: he had weather as he wished,
Swiftly, in no time, at Portchester they arrived.
Up then went the kaiser with all his Roman army,
Fully weaponed all, they went up to the wall,
To it all advanced on foot, and very frisky they felt:
Over the wall they climbed, and inside they thronged;
The people they all slaughtered, the goods they then seized;
All the splendid borough they burned down to dust.
So Portchester was razed and never since has it arisen 4700
So as to be once more just as it was before.
    Claudius the kaiser with an amazing army
Marched towards Winchester and besieged the borough closely.
There inside it there was Arviragus, intolerably oppressed,
And a great part of his race, of the British nation. *
Distressed was King Arviragus, and to his knights he spoke like this:
'Tell me now, good men, great and mighty champions, *Siege*
Will you now support me with your superior strength *of*
So I can retain my own reputation?' *Winchester*
Then answered the honourable knights: 4710
'We shall never leave you, not for life, not for death!'
On they put their war gear and leapt upon their horses;
The knights there were very intrepid: they raised the gates of the city,

They made their shield-wall – the warriors were undaunted –*
And now all the knights were ready for the fight;
Then were summoned all the old men, who in fighting would advise
     them,
On one flank they rode and spoke of right tactics;
They selected two knights and sent them to the kaiser,
To ask whether he wanted truce, or did he want no peace?
Before there came a greater loss he could make the choice.   4720
    Then responded Claudius and to the knights he spoke like this:
'Most useful is the man who makes a peace treaty!
I am a man rich enough, all Rome is my realm,
And within my hands lie all the lands
Which Julius the emperor before me obtained,
And subject to my decrees, to Rome they all defer.
Except that this same kingdom refuses to acknowledge me,
Nor will the people of this land regard me as their lord.
It seems to me a great dishonour: in my heart I feel much anger,
If Rome is to lose out, while I am alive,   4730
On her great reputation which my ancestors gained for her.
Not for any greed, not for any great avarice,
Did I come to this land to do battle strongly,
Not for any feud but only to obtain my dues,
And these I will regain or I shall rest among the slain.
    But, knights, you two have come here from your King Arviragus:
Pass quickly back again to your people's king,
Tell him the truth, which comes to his knowledge by mouth,
That if he agrees to under go the oath and to hold me as his lord,
If he agrees to do me homage, it will be the better for him;   4740
If to me he will but send what are my dues out of his land
Then will I honour him with highest respect.
And tell him most truly this: I'll give him my daughter, **Genuis**,
In kinship and peace, that we two may live better.
And if he refuses to do this, he shall receive worse things:
We two shall clash together and by battle shall decide it,
Make wretched slaughter, and then things will be worse.'
    The knights returned promptly to the people's king,
Conveyed to him true comment on Claudius the kaiser.
The king saw he was compelled and moved to his council,   4750
And with deep respect he returned the [message]†
That he, for his kingdom would be a vassal of Rome,
And then do him great honour and as queen would take his daughter.

Together then they came and were reconciled without delay,
And afterwards they all went into Winchester.   *Truce*
There were in this land the most happy songs.
They were living in Winchester for twenty-one whole weeks,
And sent to Rome, a fact it is, for the young girl Genuis.
 The girl, safe and sound, arrived in this land,
And Claudius the kaiser gave her to this king.   4760
Still in records it is seen that here she was a queen,
That it was King Arviragus who had as queen this Genuis.
These matters being done, Claudius had sent to Rome.
Meanwhile journeyed Claudius along with King Arviragus
Into Orkney, and beleaguered all that land,
[And] much land round about it: they acquired all of it;
Thirty-two islands they seized into their own hands;
They established a firm peace and went off to Winchester.
 From Rome had come by this the lovely young girl, Genuis,
In safety with her escort of sixty mounted men.   4770
The maiden once wedded, the king took her to bed.
 Great was the bliss there then was in Britain,
With King Arviragus and the emperor Claudius.
Then our people were more blithe than ever yet in all their lives:
In all their great bliss they erected a borough,
In a very lovely place up along the Severn;
When the town was all completed with considerable strength,
It was given by Arviragus to the emperor Claudius, *
With the land all around it, large tracts, and not a little.
He ordered a name which might be suitable to be settled upon it,
For the way the King Arviragus took as his queen Genuis;   4781
There the king gave it to Claudius, to the Roman kaiser.
Claudius the great gave it the name 'Kaerclou',
Yet it was not long that the name was allowed to stand,
But in Claudius's honour so was the name first called.
 Now when first Claudius came into this land he found a fine
  woman:
She was clever, she was wise too, and a virgin it is true.
Claudius's knights had won her in the fight
Inside Portchester, and they held her most securely,
And donated her to Claudius: he found this most delectable,   4790
And he took charge of her and away with him he led her,
And loved the woman with very loving care.
The woman conceived a child by Claudius the bold,

And when the child was born Claudius was happy for it.
When the time had now arrived that the babe must be baptised
According to the heathen rites which prevailed then at that time,
A name upon him they bestowed and **Gloi** the child was called.
This child grew and flourished and many folk him reverenced,
And Claudius bestowed on him the borough which he owned,
And settled it with knights who were excellent in fight,   4800
Ordering them to guard it well, and give it the name 'Gloichester';
All for love of his own son whom he loved very dearly,
Who later was to win the Welsh lands entirely by his own hands,
And of these he was the ruler and duke for many years;
This child was brought up within Gloucester's walls.
    When these things were done, Claudius went back to Rome,
And took the child's mother, for queen had he no other.
When Claudius came to Rome, news came to him very soon
That there had come travelling into that territory
A most mysterious man who from Antioch had come: 4810
Peter was his name, and he performed there many [miracles];†
He travelled right across that land and turned it all to God's own
      hand.
    Gone from this place was Claudius: it was governed by Arviragus
And by Genuis his queen, a most accomplished lady.
It was perceived by this land's king that he was not harmed by
      anything,*
And so he lived on here in bliss for twenty years.
During that time there came tidings, to Arviragus who was king;
No other help could be applied; in Rome Claudius had died.
Deeply grieved the king, and so also did the queen,
So did all the best men who were living then in Britain.   4820
By that time it came about that Gloi was a good knight;
When those tidings had arrived in the land,
Concerning Claudius Caesar and how everything had happened,
Then announced King Arviragus, and with his chief men spoke like
      this:
'As I ever hope for favour I refuse for ever more,
In spite of any edict to Rome to be subject
Never again shall I send them tribute from my land.
But if they come here voyaging, this people conquering,
Here they're going to suffer the sharpest of all sorrows,
And procure no other goods but pour out here their own heart's
      blood.

All of their wives shall at once become widows!'   4831
    So declared the king (even though it did not happen)
Where he sat with his beverage upon his kingly bench.
But quite otherwise it was to be within just two winters,
For the Roman people sent a message to this nation
And ordered them to send their tribute from this land,
And in rage King Arviragus gave answer to them,
Ordered them with great anger out of his eye-sight,
To take flight from this land before they were fated;
Back they made their way into Roman country.   4840
    In that very year **Vespasian** was emperor:
This message he disliked; it made him quite incensed.
He called to his council all the Roman people,
Declaring by his life that he would go to Britain's land,
To claim his proper rights which Claudius previously possessed,
And if they refused to treat for peace he would fight them no less,
And all the people of Rome advised him the same.
    Vespasian marched away until he reached France,
Which was all his own as yet, as with eye he surveyed it.
He led the king of the land, who acknowledged him as lord,   4850
Off with himself in hand away towards this land;
To the sea he was bound and ships there he found
Which for him were sent from home when he was still in Rome.
He awaited good weather: wind came from the west,
He embarked at Wissant and at Dover planned to land.[*]   *Vespasian's*
Arviragus was aware of this and proudly marched ahead   *Invasion*
     to meet him,
And drove him out with armed strength back into the sea-stream.
Along with him Vespasian had very able seamen,
Who cast out their luff and laid course on the current,[*]
Alongside the sea coast they sailed very swiftly.   4860
Going full speed in no time at Totnes they arrived,
Drew the ships up on the land and walked up on the sand.
They took their missiles and arms and ahead began marching;
In convoy they rode fast until they came to Exeter,
With the good idea of slipping secretly into the town,
But the townsfolk were wary and well did they keep watch,
And firmly closed their gates and got in readiness for fight.
And the borough they buttressed as well as the best.
For seven whole days Vespasian and his soldiers
Encamped outside Exeter and very closely besieged them.   4870

Arviragus heard this, that he had arrived like this;
He took the whole army from all Britain's country,
And at once made his way down towards Cornwall,
Into the town of Exeter which was the more secure:
Arviragus was within with the British men,
Vespasian was out, besieging the borough round about.
In the morning when day dawned they unbarred the doors;
Knights girded themselves in good and fine arms;
Brass trumpets were blowing, horns began sounding,
They handled their shafts and their gold-adorned shields.   4880
So rode out together the really brave Britons,
All thirty thousand: a greater threat for that.
Coming out against them was Caesar Vespasian:
Together they flew and bitterly fought,
With hardihood hacking — helmets were resounding —
Strongly they slashed with the edge of steel blades.
All that day the fight lasted between men of the greatest,
Until the dark night divided their protracted fight.
On both sides in heaps lay knights hacked in pieces:
There was grief of the greatest at the gates of Exeter!   4890
    This the queen beheld — Genuis she was called —*
She was deeply distressed, her heart filled with horror,
And called to her husband, who was dear to her heart,
To King Arviragus. The queen addressed him like this: *Genuis*
'My lord, take very careful thought: you are a man of   *Intervenes*
    great virtue,
You have great fidelity, faith of rock-firmness,
And these are the things which must befit every king,
Every man, great or mean who to avoid punishment would be clean:
Consider your own promises, which you yourself pronounced,
Towards Claudius my father, who was your acknowledged
    friend,   4900
And who did you the honour of giving me to you as wife;
And you are most beloved by me, being my king and husband.
My relations are outside here, and your relations are inside here.
If you break your promises and destroy my relatives,
The truth I have told you: against your son will be your feud;
And if my family should rise and bring your fortunes in decline
And you yourself and all your folk should fall to the ground,
If you and yours should be dead, then with my son I'll be at feud.
Better far would be a truce than such a loss of peace.

And think too of the pact before, how to my father you swore   4910
To release every year as long as you have life
The tribute due to Rome from your own kingdom.
And your life is still lasting (may it do so for long yet!),
Therefore you must perform what you had already promised.'
    All the knights at the court supported the queen.
The King and all his knights stayed awake all night,
All night they conferred on what would be their best counsel;
Nor could they find any guidance which seemed to them at all as good
As seemed to them the truthful counsel of their queen.
In the morning when the day dawned the doughty warriors got ready;
In company they advanced as if they intended fighting.   4921
Up came the queen and rode in between them;
First she made the peace, and then with them she had speech:
She confirmed reconciliation and called together knights:
Those who once were great foes she transformed into friends,
And the king promised them that he would keep his compact,
And he fulfilled this for the length of his life.
So they were reconciled, and so they were reunited.
Then was this Britain blessed with rejoicing,
And Vespasian and his supporters all that winter stayed here;   4930
From borough to borough they travelled in bliss.
As soon as summer came they travelled back to Rome.
Britain was blithe all the length of this king's life.
    Now this king Arviragus had a son who was called
    Maurus;   MAURUS
He was sent to Rome and put to learn in school;
There he was so well directed he was both scholar and strong knight.
A message for him came there, sent out from this land here,
That no help could be applied for the king his father had died,
And at once he must come to his own kingdom.
So was the message written, and immediately he did it: 4940
To this land he came and received the kingdom.
Very wealthy was Arviragus and much wealthier Maurus;
In this land he kept truce; in this land he kept peace:
Here was joy, here was food, and here was most of every good.
    In this very way things stood when there came over the   *The*
      sea-flood   *Picts*
A king who was called **Rodric**, before all others quite unique;
He came out from Scythia, land unlike any other;
He brought with him the Picts, people of enormous might.

Since Rodric first grew to man and knew how to do wrong,
He always travelled on the sea's flood and did evil, never
    good; 4950
Many hundred towns he had made totally bare.
He travelled by the sea-coast straight into Scotland;
That land he laid waste with anguish of the greatest;
Through the land he rode, ravaging and harming.[*]
So came these tidings to Maurus the king,
Of how King Rodric was doing all this ruinous ravaging.
At once he sent an errand through all this kingdom's land,
Instructing every single man who would accord him honour
To come in full armour to attend his muster.
    These men were all summoned, and the king marched, 4960
Hastening into Scotland, and King Rodric he found.
They fought very furiously, and the Picts fell there,
And there Rodric was killed, and then with horses drawn in pieces.
There Maurus the king did a most marvellous thing:
Upon that same spot where Rodric he dispatched,
At once he had raised up a quite amazing stone,
And on it had engraved in very strange runic staves
How he killed Rodric and with horses how he drew him to pieces,
And how all the Picts he had conquered with fights.
Up he set the stone – there it still stands, 4970
So it will do for as long as the world will stand.
A name was selected for it by the king, who called the stone
    'Westmering';
A great tract of land which lies around it there
The king took into his hands and called it 'Westmorland';[*]
So now you've heard the true tale of whom it takes its name from.
    When the Picts were conquered in the fight[*]
And Rodric was dead and his companions condemned,
There fled into byways about fifteen hundred,
Who were the finest men who had been in the fight;
They had as their commander a considerably well born man. 4980
These men wished to conceal themselves and run off aside
And slip out of the land to save their own lives.
It was noticed by three earls who in the fighting had been bold
In which direction those forces were making their flight.
The earls then gave them chase with all their good knights,
Drove them into a high wood where they endured much hardship;
This wonderfully fine wood stood in the middle of a forest,

And neither forwards nor backwards could anyone there escape,
But all of them they seized and yet not one of them they killed;
Firmly they tied them up and took them to the king,   4990
So that the king with them should deal: either to hang them or
    to kill.
As soon as the king spoke with them they begged for his pity,
Eagerly they proposed to him, appealed to his compassion,
That he accept them as his slaves, and they were willing to serve him,
And to him they would be loyal all their lives long.
    Everything the king did, just as they had begged,
And placed in their hands a great deal of land
All around Caithness where they did their commerce.
The land was very good, but since the time of the Flood
It was uncultivated by any land cultivation,   5000
Nor had there ever dwelt on it any form of living person.
At once they began to plough: the land was most productive;
They dug and they sowed, they reaped and they mowed;
Within just three years they adopted twelve partners,
Who set off without delay so that to this land they came;
The Britons they saluted with well selected words,
Bidding them be happy and all enjoy good health:
'We are seeking from you gifts which are most splendid:
That you give us women whom we may take as wives;
Then we shall be able to keep love for your land's people.'   5010
When the Britons heard this they behaved haughtily,
Ordering them to clear off and keep out of their land,
For they refused to allow them the things which they asked for.
    The Picts were rebuffed, and on their way they went off,
Home to their families and informed them of their news.
They took their message-bearer and sent to Ireland from there,
To the king of that land who was called **Gille Caor**,
And requested him to send women to them from his land.
And the king allowed them everything they asked for.
Through those same women who were there a long time   5020
Those people started speaking in Irish speech,
And ever since, those customs remain in that country,
As they are there now, and will be evermore.
    Meanwhile Maurus the king kept good peace in his land:
As long as he lived his people were contented;
Then came that same day when dead the king lay.
Then forward stepped the king's son, **Coil** was his name: COIL

This man was fierce, this man was strong, this man was firm of
    purpose.
This man knew all decrees which were passed in Rome's city,
But he did not live long, to his people's great loss,   5030
But all the time he lived he kept his land in bliss.
There was born to King Coil, who was Britain's ruler,
A most beloved son, **Luces** he was called;[*]   LUCES
He was the best man who ever ruled the kingdom,
Since to the land of Britain had come Brutus who obtained it.
Luces was a royal offspring, Luces was well raised,
And he was very famous and by the Britons favoured;
Many a good thing was known by Luces who was king:
There was no man beneath the sky who had more mastery;
Through this same noble man this land received Christendom, 5040
If any one would like to listen how it first befell
Then this book will tell him, in truthful words,
How King Luces first came to the love of Christ.
    Some excellent men came here from Rome,[*]
They came to the king and told him the tidings
Of all the [teaching] which was done by St Peter in Rome,[†]
And the kind of martyrdom Peter had there undergone,   *Christianity*
As had the other saints who were seated high with God.   *Arrives*
Then Luces the king longed very deeply
That he might know more about Christ the lord.   5050
There were then in Rome some most excellent men,
And the pope there was a holy man: **Eleutherius** was his name.
King Luces selected those men special to him,
Sent them to the Pope and gave him fulsome greeting,
And asked him in God's name that he graciously allow this,
To send him straight away some man who was holy,
Since the king wished to act well by receiving Christ's gospel,
To live in virtue and to love his Lord,
He, and all his people who were inhabitants of this isle.
    Then to Eleutherius this message seemed most joyous: 5060
There was no man then alive who could have been quite so blithe
As the holy man was when he heard of this news.
The Pope had two bishops who loved God's own precepts;
He sent them here to this country: the bishops began their journey,
Until God's messengers came into this our land,
To Luces the monarch and to all his warriors.
Then spoke **Dunian** and the other bishop, **Fagan**,

Preaching the king a homily to which he hearkened closely;
Before the homily was finished the king wanted to be Christian,
And all the knights of his retinue earnestly desired it.   5070
The king received baptism and all his good men with him,
And all of his Britons who wished to obey him;
And those who would not be baptised, these the king had destroyed.
   When this was all completed, in another way they acted:
Both of the bishops travelled right through Britain
To all those temples which the heathen had constructed;
They had all the vestments there thrown out at the door,
The walls they washed down as well as was ever done,
And took all the statues, which were called 'Mahun',
And had them all dragged out, either by hand or by foot,   5080
And had them all swallowed by flames in black smoking fires.
When this was all completed, in another way they acted:
They advanced immediately through the power of God Almighty
From place to place, really pushing themselves,
And sanctified all the temples in the name of the Saviour.
When that was all completed, in another way they acted:
They then appointed bishops to direct the people,
And over them archbishops to correct the clergy.
Churches [they] had erected, many and everywhere;†
Placing priests in them as would be appropriate.   5090
When all this was completed, in another way they acted:
Then arrived King Luces and to them land assigned,
And placed them under God's peace and in freehold put all
      churches,*
And those laws are still in many places just as Luces first applied
      them,
But all the same, they have since then been very much diminished,
Horribly debased through detrimental tricks,
But then again restored, for so designed the Lord.
   When all these things were completed, then to Rome the bishops
      retreated,
And left in this land those people in God's hand,
With Luces their lord, whom they loved with all their hearts.   5100
So things went on here for very many a year.
Luces, monarch in the land, lived for very long,*
For forty-two years' extent in the greatest content:
Here was food, here was drink, as men in joy would sing;
Here were boundless exploits among this excellent race.

So they were proceeding and forgot all too speedily
The teaching of the noble man, the good bishop Dunian,
And his fellow-priest Fagan, while they were in this land.
In peace above all things lived Luces the king;
Then came that same day when dead the king lay.   5110
Dear to him was calm advice; in Gloucester came his demise,
And there the noble Britons buried their king.
By then the world had so far moved on since our Lord was born
A full hundred and sixty years when the king sank to the
     grave.   '*160 A.D.*'
   When King Luces was dead a most grave danger prevailed:
He did not leave here either a sister or a brother,
No queen nor any kindred who might keep his possessions.
To Rome came the tidings of Luces the king,
How the king here was dead and in the land there was no head.
They made up an army and sent it to this country;   5120
Severus was their commander (he was born a Roman):   *Severus*
The army was very strong; they came then to this land.*   *Invades*
Severus proposed that very soon he'd have control of this kingdom,
But the British, keeping busy, frequently provoked him,
And frequently fought with him in many kinds of ways.
Severus thought carefully what could be the remedy:
Among his retinue he made peace and did away with injustice,
So that no one should get so maddened, of sense so deprived,
That in his retinue he'd break peace (on pain of loss of limb or life),
About any kind of grudge that came to his knowledge.   5130
It was spotted by the British, despite their being busy,
That Severus among his troops enjoyed perfect peace,
While among themselves there were unnumbered sorrows.
Some British stepped in convoy, seven thousand of them,
And had speech with Severus and desired truce from his army,
And he granted them this, and gave them splendid gifts.
In this way Severus's army was surprisingly strengthened;
All those who'd been superior he then made inferior,
And great love maintained for all who sought his favour.
   He journeyed to London and there they took him in then;   5140
He went right through this kingdom and took it into his own hand,
And all the time ahead of him fled those who were his enemies;
So severely did he harry them that they fled over the Humber:
They fled away straight until they came to the Picts,
Who took them all in and adopted them as allies.

They appointed a noble knight as their own commander by right:
A handsome and fine knight who was known as **Fulgenes**;
He was to lead them and he was to guide them.
One area of Scotland Fulgenes took into his hand;
This area was dear to him: it was called Deira.   5150
Southwards from Scotland Severus then went back,
And led his legions into London town.
And from out of Scotland Fulgenes made much slaughter;
He darted into Britain with great, disastrous raids:
Goods he took, men he slew; he did harm enough,
And so he behaved a long time, back up in Scotland.

    Severus got to hear of this (away in Rome he was Caesar,   *The*
And from there to here all the lands stood in his own hand);   *Severine*
The emperor sent his summons through many different lands,   *Wall*
Ordered to be sent to him so very many workmen   5160
That he ordered them to dig a dyke which was amazingly deep,
Massive and very strong, all alongside Scotland;
From sea to sea ran that dyke: it was all others quite unlike;
On top he made a timber wall, one amazingly ingenious,*
And then he set knights to guard it day and night
So that over it came no Pict whatever, and nor did any other man
      ever,
Unless he wanted to sue for peace, to seek speech with the Caesar,
And then live here afterwards along with Caesar Severus.

    The news came to Fulgenes that this earthwork was finished,
That he could not enter this land, neither by day nor night.   5170
Then he could think of no plot that seemed to him any good;
He called together all his soldiers to come to the hustings,
To give their king advice in his great plight;
They advised him to march right back into Scythia:
He came there speedily and was ceremonially received.*
He spoke to the Picts and gave them great prospects
That they gathered in that country a huge naval army
And travelled by the sea strands as far as this land.
He marched right to York – the Britons found it remarkable –
And at once besieged the town with very brute force;   5180
He then made people aware, by word and by writing,
– All those of his friends who were here in this land –
That they must do well and come to him all:
He would bestow on them wealth and would honour their worth,
And all through his life he would dearly love them.

This was heard by the Britons and it made them emboldened
To turn away from Severus the emperor of the Romans.
Many thousand Britons came to Fulgenes,
Who received them regally and promised great riches.
News reached Severus of Fulgenes's acting like this,   5190
And he summoned an army of folk from this country,
And dashed towards York on his own destruction.
When he arrived in York there was Fulgenes confronting him:
They proceeded to fight then, bitterly and fiercely;
On both sides there fell unnumbered forces.
There Severus was slain and a full toll of his Romans;
Fulgenes was wounded with astounding severity,
So that on the third day he died a painful death.
Of Severus's death the Britons made decision,*
And said among themselves, those who had authority: 5200
'Severus was a good knight, and he ruled us most rightly
While we were willing to adhere to him, before we turned to
        Fulgenes;
Because their luck was bad, both of them are dead!
So let's take Severus's corpse and bring it into York,
And there we shall see it buried with very great blessing,
And yield up the great force which once he gave us.'
All of these actions were done as they appointed.
    Severus left here two sons: like this their names were   BASIAN
        pronounced:
The elder was called **Basian**, the younger was called **Gezan**;
Both of them were brothers, but not of a single mother;   5210
Basian's mother came from the land of Britain,
And Gezan's mother came from the Roman men.
The British took up Basian and promised him this kingdom,
And the Roman men as king had appointed Gezan.
The Britons were busy, and Basian they loved,
While the Roman men very much loved Gezan.
Relations between these brothers were blasted by much conflict;
They each took their armies and came to pitched battle,
And there this King Basian killed his brother Gezan,
And the Roman forces fled from this island,   5220
But many men were felled there in that terrific fight.
In this land there was a young man, under King Basian,
Carrais he was called by name, a most remarkable man;
His father was a feeble knight, but the son was very firm,

And the most active man then alive in Britain.
Not for any living person had he the slightest concern;
He was aggrieved above everything that Basian was the Britons' king.
  Now Basian was a peaceful king, and Carrais found this far from
    pleasing.
Then at this same time on the sea-coast there had arrived
Outlaws, in fact, in sixty ships, to be exact.   5230
Carrais devised for himself an ingenious scheme
Whereby he would soon be travelling to Rome.
Off, without tarrying, he travelled to Rome,
And spoke with the emperor and with the Roman army,
And this was what Carrais then said (he was a traitor, indeed):
'All hail to you, **Cyrian,** I bring greetings from King Basian,*
Who'd like to make you aware, both in words and in writing,
That he can no longer send you tribute from the Britons' land,
For twice he has attempted to send it with an embassy,
But they came on outlaws while at sea, who killed all the
    embassy,   5240
And robbed all the treasury which was intended as your money.
The outlaws are so strong, by water and by land,
That no one can travel over the sea without very great anxiety.
  'But if it would please you to listen to my reasons,
And hand over to me your permits, and send me twelve good ships,
And give me your safe-conduct, under your protection,
Then I will to take to sea and all those outlaws I'll destroy
And I'll send you your tribute from the land of Brutus,
For I am a knight's son, and with a wide net of relations:
My father by the seaside has a splendid castle,   5250
And knights who are many and men in great plenty,
And close to me they'll all draw to kill off the outlaws,
And so by my own hand I'll guard your income and your land.'
  This was heard by Cyrian, the speech of that seditious man,
Who conceded everything that he craved from him:
Letters he handed him, weapons he delivered him,
And then off he sent him towards this our land.
And so off went Carrais, until he came to France,
Always unfolding his letters, as he moved forward,
And telling everyone about what he'd obtained in Rome,   5260
And the people flocked to him at every point.
  Carrais came to the sea with a surprising force:
He had as supporters five hundred riders,

And many foot soldiers he had, quite beyond measure;
All the ships along the coast he seized for his own use;
He set off on the sea: the waves sped him along,
And soon he arrived here in Britain's land,
And at once began ravaging the land of Basian, its king!
Carrais took his couriers, and dispatched them round this country, [*]
Asking every young man unwilling to work a hand's turn,   5270
And every single outlaw who had abandoned his own land,
And every knight's son who was keen to show his strength,
And every wicked man who wanted to get his hands on goods:
To him they must come for gold and great treasure.
This was made known fantastically far away,
And these ruffian outcasts assembled their rabble troops;
The[re] came to meet Carrais thirty thousand of these, [†]
And they marched along by the sea shore;
They pillaged, they plundered, they left nothing behind;
They captured the castles, they slaughtered the Britons: 5280
They burned to death many of the noble British;
They went north, they went east, laying all that land waste;
They marched into Scotland where they caused devastation,
And back again to this land, destroying those who lived here.
    He took a man of business and dispatched him to the British,
To say to them these words which Carrais was sending them:
'Carrais the strong, secure in his encampment,
Sends here in secret, giving greetings to the Britons:
You are magnificent men, and I wish to make peace with you,
And offer you your freedom and uphold your friendship,   5290
If you in your kindness will only make me king.'
And the Britons retorted (for they were really noble men)
Saying that above all things they would not betray their king;
Never for any living man to betray King Basian,
And back these words came to Carrais the strong.
Carrais thought carefully what could be his strategy:
By means of two clever knights he sent message to the Picts.
    The Picts had their territory next to King Basian;
To them came the message from Carrais the strong,
Who made them great promises of worldly possessions.   5300
The Picts were men of evil who'd abandoned all things noble;
They all swore outright and made a compact firm and tight
That they would betray King Basian in fight.
This word came to Carrais: then he was glad indeed at this;

At once he took his courier and sent him to the king,
Telling him outright that against him he would fight,
Unless he would clear off, and so vacate the kingdom.
Then declared King Basian: 'I should rather die before then!'*
In less than seven nights they assembled for the fight,
Before the borough of York: the fight was bitterly stark.
When they should have fought hardest, then all the Picts turned
    round and fled,
And they left King Basian entirely alone,   5312
And Carrais thrust at him and with his spear pierced him.
The British they slaughtered; many hundreds they captured.
Then all of this land lay in Carrais's own hand.
Then he took all the Picts and sent them to the Scots,
And gave them great tracts of land all within Scotland,
And their descendents have lived there ever since for ever more.

   This news came to Rome after that, very soon,
Of what Carrais had done, and King Basian he'd slain.   5320
They summoned two armies from the Roman territories,
And appointed two commanders who were most commendable:
Allec was the name of one, a wise and a strong man,
The other's name went like this: **Livius Gallus**.
They travelled from Rome and to this land they came,
To the point where they came upon Carrais the king;
Carrais they dispatched, his knights they captured,
And the Romans in this way made inroads on the country,
And Allec seized into his hand much of this land.   ALLEC
But still there were British, many in the by-ways,   5330
Who held castles which were strong, and boroughs broad and long;
They sent in great haste travelling south into Cornwall
Men for **Asclepidiot**, who in Cornwall was the duke;
He arrived hurrying and they raised him as their king.
Then the British summoned their splendid leaders
And ordered all the knights to come to the king,
And every single eager man to earn his reputation.
They summoned their army by threatening sheer disgrace for
    absence.

   By then King Allec had moved down to London,
And the King of the British at once bent his steps after.   5340
It happened on a holy day when people held ceremonies,
And Allec the King was there in some temple,
Inside London city, with his Roman lords.

Then there came to the king the noise of much shouting:
Those who lived inside London were all astir there.
Allec leaped out, his weapon he grabbed hold of,
And all his Roman lords who were then in London,
And they came out of the borough, and could see there before them,
Could see on all sides, and strange it seemed to them
Who could have sent there all those forces of men.   5350
The British advanced on them with bitter battle-onslaughts:
Allec they killed and many folk they captured,
And some swiftly rushed back inside the borough,
Among them the leader Livius, who fled into London,
Had the gates barricaded and himself went on the walls
As the British proceeded to ride around the borough,
And that borough they besieged in the best way that could be.
    King Asclepidiot, who as a knight was very good,   ASCLEPIDIOT
Sent off his messages up into Scotland,
Into Morayshire to seek forces of men,   5360
And also into West Wales to seek the Welsh British,
And also he swiftly sent men south to Cornwall,
Telling each man in the land there who on his chin could grow a
    beard,
Upon pain of loss of limb and life to travel up to London.
Within a single week they were all assembled:
They attacked the walls with wonderful vigour,
While Livius Gallus made a stout defence.
The British in the end broke down the walls,
And got themselves within them, and then the borough had been
    won.
And Livius Gallus got himself to a castle,   5370
And into it he rushed with all his Roman followers,
And the King of the Britons came behind him to the castle
And made all the British men mount upon it there.
Then Livius Gallus could see his help was very weak;
He leaned over the wall and loudly began shouting
To Asclepidiot the king: 'You're terribly brave;
I'd like to confer with you and crave the grant of life from you,
If you would allow me to travel off in peace towards Rome,
And with me my people, those who are still alive;
And I will swear to you upon my very sword   5380
That I shall never more come back again here.'
    Asclepidiot heard that; these words seemed good to him,

So he granted everything which Gallus there was asking.
Out from the castle they poured and oaths to him they swore,
So they proceeded to travel off out of the land.
Then the king of Scotland came marching to the hosts,
And encountered Gallus and all his good men.
At once **Columban** called out (he was the Scottish king):
'Where are you, my good men from out of Galloway?
Where are you, my own men, from out of Moray?   5390
Where are you, my Scots all? Stand firm beside me;
Here we shall well avenge our dearest allies,
And our most utter enemies we'll fell to the earth.
If King Asclepidiot (a knight who is very good)
Has been speaking with them and given them the grant of life,
Then I wasn't there, nor any of my companions,
And so we shall not keep the truce – after all, they killed our friends
          too!'
Between them they stretched out their long javelins,
And with utmost hostility they felled the Roman force,
And Gallus they took and they struck off his head,   5400
And tossed him into a brook which flowed past where they stood,
And all the dead they ferried into that brook
Where Gallus at the bottom of the same brook was buried.
And so was this nation cleansed of the Roman race,
And the Britons bequeathed a name to the brook:
Because Gallus was slain beside it, they said it should be called 'Galli',
And in the English books it is termed 'Walbrook';*
Now I have recounted to you how it had come by that name,
For now and evermore that is the name there.
     Then Asclepidiot was king, a knight who was very good;   5410
For ten whole years among the Britons he was living here,
And then his end arrived, and it was wickedly contrived
That he so very early had to depart from this life's days:
Because he was very law-abiding, all the Britons loved him.
In Gloucester there was an earl who came of noble stock:
He was the highest born man who was living here in Britain,
Coel was his name, noblest of all the British;   COEL
He came from the race of Gloi, who once had owned Gloucester.*
As it happened, with their utmost might they engaged in fighting:
As Earl Coel in the battle stood he felled King Asclepidiot; 5420
During this disturbance there came distress for this country,
As the emperor **Diocletian** to this land now sent **Maximien**;

He arrived here marching with an enormous army;
When he came ashore he encountered Coel,
Who in combat had by victory just become the king himself.
Coel and Maximien conferred very courteously,
And established a friendship which they made firm with oaths.
Then announced Maximien: 'My brother Diocletian
Has put into my own hands all of those lands
Which I shall be traversing between Saint Bernard Pass and Scotland,
To destroy each community which loves Christianity.'   5431
   Then Coel was wretched (he was now the king in Britain,
And had secured a peace treaty by performing oaths);
Coel remained silent and Maximien's way was violent:
Every Christian man he had beheaded,
And those willing to abjure their faith he set a special mark on;
In this way acted this Maximien: he martyred Saint Alban,
And Saint Julian, and Saint Aaron, and two hermits at Caerleon;
There was no bishop and no cleric and no knight however stalwart
(Unless he gave up Christendom) who was not sent straight to
     destruction.
When this was all done, off marched Maximien,   5441
And Coel stayed behind, the king within Britain.
   This king had a daughter; to him she was most dear,
And the whole of his kingdom he placed in that young girl's hand,
For he had no other child who could become king in this land.
This girl was called **Helena**; later she was Queen
In the district of Jerusalem, to the joy of all the people.
This girl was well instructed: from books she knew much informa-
     tion,
And lived in this land with her father who was strong.
After this, quite soon, the word came to Rome   5450
That Coel had killed Asclepidiot the king.
Then the Roman people were cheerful in their feelings,
Because by that man in his day many of their folk were slain.
Nonetheless, never did Maximien go back to Rome again;
So Diocletian selected a leader most accomplished,
And the most rigorous man then living within Rome,
Who had laid many lands beneath his conquering hand;
There was no man in those days who dared make himself a nuisance.
The emperor sent him here into this land,
Into our country, with an enormous army;   5460
Custance was the earl's name, the noblest of all knights.

Coel heard the news that Custance had come; *Custance*
He was really terrified for his very life. *Invades*
He took without delay six knights who were discerning:
To Custance they were sent to welcome him to the land,
Saying he wished himself to speak to him, to see if he'd make a treaty.
And Custance sent to fetch him: he must come with twelve knights.*
Together they came; together they conferred.
These were the words of King Coel: 'Custance, now hear me well:
I assure you before everything that I slew Asclepidiot the
     king 5470
Who, through his wicked beliefs, had killed lots of your relatives,
And by force wished to keep from you this country's tribute,
And great shame he did to you and died a fitting death the sooner;
For I was one of the most exalted who swore obedience to you,
That we should send to Rome this country's tribute.
These oaths the king broke; that's why he's now dead –
But let's abandon our fighting and we two seek what's right,
And I will be submissive and submit to you as leader,
And be most respectful and hold you as my ruler,
And each year send to you the tribute from Britain.' 5480
    Then responded Custance, a powerful man and very brave:
'Coel, you're a sensible man and there's common sense in you.
Now be a king of merit and be you a lord of men,
And I shall accord to you everything you asked for,
And with full honour I shall accept your homage,
For it was true homage and good when you slew Asclepidiot.'
With great ceremonial they were reconciled;
With great tranquillity they remained in the town.
But it was only a short time before there came another style:
In all not even forty days had completely passed 5490
Before this King Coel lay sick in his pavilion:
His head ached severely; the king was most incredibly ill;
For a whole week and one day very ill the king lay;
It gripped him under the ribs: it would not be long that he lived,
So he summoned to him his powerful barons,*
So that they could advise him in such desperate plight
How he could arrange things for Helena his daughter.
When they had said everything this was the ultimate plan,
That he should give Helen to Custance as his queen,
And all his royal lands he should place in Custance's hands; 5500
And Coel acted like that, he who was king within Britain.

Then there could be no more assistance: King Coel was now
    deceased,
And Custance had married Helen as his queen.[*]
She was the wisest woman who was ever living in Britain.
    Custance then took his queen: there was a baby born to them;
From the child's birth it was clear that he was divinely chosen;
At this all who lived in Britain were in a state of bliss.
They held an assembly of prosperous people
Who devised for the child an appropriate name;
They loved his little form, and gave him his father's name: 5510
Custance was the king's name and **Constantine** the child's,
Who was dear to the hearts of all the British [people].
His mother Helena was this country's queen.
    The child grew and flourished, with God's favour cherished,
The Britons all deferred to him and he had great affection for them:
They were his mother's kinsmen since she came of British stock,
While Custance his father had been raised in Rome.
All the child set his eyes on fell in adoration.[*]
When the child had been raised until twelve years of age,
No man alive in this country had a spirit so hardy;   5520
When Constantine was annoyed no one dared to seek audience,
But when he was happy he was all tranquillity;
Dearly did he love each knight who liked to choose the right,
And his British relatives very much respected him,
And his Roman relatives gave him really good advice.
When the child was just thirteen his father grew quite infirm:
Then came the ultimate plight: Custance the king had expired,
And the Britons took that child: of him they made themselves a king,
And Constantine the young king with much wisdom ruled this land,
As if he were of age and among kings the most courageous.   5530
    Now there was at that time an emperor in Rome
Who was known as **Maxence**: he was the Devil's favourite;
He was the most accursed man who was then alive,
All Rome he destroyed with his terrific offences;
All of its noblemen he hated to death,
And all of the humble folk he treated most harmfully.
There were many in Rome, men of power and fame,
Who left the population and fled from the land[*]
Through the shame and the dishonour inflicted on them by the
    emperor,
And they came to this land, to Constantine the king,   5540

Complaining to him of their injuries and of their times of sorrow,
And of the huge dishonour and of the great damage
Which Maxence had inflicted on them and so driven them from their
    land,
For they knew of no king to whom they could appeal
As they could to King Constantine because of their blood ties;
Eagerly they appealed to him that he should advise them*
How they could claim redress for their repression
From Maxence himself who had brought down their honour.
So long did they entreat for aid that he accorded them aid:
That he would make a raid with revengeful force,   5550
Onwards towards Rome, and would win the realm,
And avenge them on Maxence, who had ruined his relations.

    So King Constantine the good gathered an army,
Innumerable people from many a tribe.
The king set off riding towards the Roman people,
Until he came to Rome with his revenging force.
The king was a very good knight, and he prepared for fight,
And he killed Maxence: there was great rejoicing.
Then the Roman people were contented in their country,
And so Constantine the king became emperor in Rome,   5560
And there too was Helena the holy queen and her three uncles.
The eldest was called **Leonin**, then **Trahern** and **Marin**;
These earls were men supreme; to them Constantine gave Rome,
To guide all the race, to regulate the nation.

    And the lady Helena, the most holy queen,
Went to Jerusalem with a splendid retinue
And spoke with the elders of the Jews who were fearless,
And to them she promised very great possessions,
If they would conduct her where she could find the Cross   5569
Upon which Christ our Lord from sin released all this
    world.   *Invention*
So the Jews sought for it and to the queen donated it;   *of*
Then she was more delighted than she'd ever been before in *the Cross*
    life,
And beside it for many years she went on living there,
While her uncle, Leonin, remained in Rome with Constantine;
Among the brothers he was eldest, and of them in wisdom he was
    best,
The senators of Rome selected a woman whom they gave him,
From the highest station among Rome's population.

So the woman was wedded and Leonin took her to his bed;
He did what is the custom, and engendered on her a son.
When the boy was born, they devised for him a noble name,   5580
Straightway they named him outright Maximien the great,
And Constantine the king dearly loved the child.
    As things so fared over there, the worse did they fare here;
There was within the Welsh lands a duke who was very strong, *
Octaves he was called and he came of noble stock;
He laid claim to Britain as his own inheritance,
With all that the sea encompasses. Octaves was most brazen:
He took a great army and he went right through this country;
First he killed the leaders, then he enslaved the freemen,
He debased the bailiffs; not a single one was left;   5590
All this royal land Octaves seized in his own hand.
    This news came to Constantine, in Rome where he remained,
Of how Octaves had behaved, had slaughtered his folk and hanged
      them.
Constantine was sorry, and saddened in his heart,
Because he could by no means come, could not reach this kingdom,
Seeing he had all of Rome's lands lying in his own hands,
And his mother, Helena, had been sending after him.
So he took his mother's uncle Trahern, and taught him how to rule,
And delivered this land to him, if he could but win it,
For Constantine himself never came back here again.   5600
Yet he took men and money and to Trahern these   TRAHERN
      conveyed,
With a very large army, he sent him to this country,
And since he was uncle to his mother, if Octaves he could slaughter,
If he could really get that done, then he himself might take the throne.
Trahern set off then on his way to this land,
With an army among the greatest he came to Portchester.
The Britons were very bold and their gates fast shut they held,
And Trahern fought against them: after three days they asked for
      peace,
And then Trahern entered and so Portchester was conquered;
And from there he went on directly to Winchester,   5610
And Octaves had got there first and had gone into the city.
    Together they clashed: they fought and they killed, *
So that there could be no slaughter in any battle that was greater.
[Trahern] saw his tremendous loss and he took another course, †
And went travelling by night until he reached the very sea;

Before the Britons could get word, his troops were all aboard,
And off they went sailing up into Scotland,
And [all Scotland he] won into his own command,[†]
And he crossed over the Humber with very heavy forces,
And in this land of Britain laid waste the boroughs.   5620
    The news came to Octaves who was king of the country,
And he with his people pressed to that place fast;
Together they clashed, and fought there at once.
Now it happened that Trahern had very many people there:
The Scots and the Picts and the Roman lands' knights;
Trahern fought against Octaves and very quickly overcame him;
The Scots raised an enormous cry and Octaves's folk took to flight,
And the Roman battalions slaughtered the British.
Then Octaves, very sobered, set off to the sea:
By the sea sands he found ships to his hand;   5630
Aboard ship he went and to Norway he sped;
He had left, from his fighting, only thirty-one knights;
All the others had been taken, and Trahern's men they'd become,
And fifteen thousand lay there slain and had departed their life's days.
    There was in Norway's parts a king whose name was **Compert**:[*]
Octaves had speech with him and humbly asked for peace from him,
And told him how Trahern had driven him out, to his harm:
'And if you will assist me with your enormous army
So that I can get back to my own kingdom,
Then I shall love you, and regard you as my lord,   5640
In friendship and peace as long as I am living,
And after my death, I designate to you my people.'
So replied Compert, who was king of that part:
'You must for this year remain with me here,
And secretly send out into Britain's lands,
In word and in writing through men who will interpret them,
And send off your messengers to those who are your best friends,
Promising silver and gold, much property and land,
If any man could entice King Trahern to his death,
By poison drink, or sorcery, or the bite of steel,   5650
Or by any magic skill sap him of his strength,
Then you could go back again, and your troubles would be less,
And in that case I'll conduct you back and reappoint you king.'
    Octaves carried out all Compert's plan,
Sent out his messengers into this land,
By that same scheme which King Compert had shown him.

Trahern was king most contentedly in Britain,
And as for Octaves, about *him* he had no worries,
No more than if he'd not been born or had been lost at sea.
Trahern was in London, pleased among his people,   5660
For seven whole nights pleased among his knights.
    There was an earl in Kent, **Aldolf** by name;[*]
To the king he was opposed because of Octaves's feud;
Often he visited the king and heard of new things:
Merchants tying goods in bundles [said where] the king was going to
        travel.[†]
Aldolf went ahead with four hundred knights,
And wonderfully well weaponed, fell upon him from a wood;
He found King Trahern and stabbed him with a spear,
And set his huge army fleeing in panic,
With Aldolf after them in pursuit, and many people there he   5670
        slew;
And then he travelled into Kent, into a massive castle,
And sent off in great haste for King Octaves,
And he came at once into this kingdom.
As their king he was accepted; all seemed to him then well
        accomplished.   OCTAVES
They travelled round the land and they killed all the Romans,
The humble and the great, they killed them all alike;
Wherever he could detect [any] he did not leave a single one.[†]
And for twenty-two years after he went on living here,
In peace and in plenty, with the friendship of the British.
    Then when he was an old man a sickness on him came: 5680
The sickness held him hard, but for a long time he endured;
The king thought carefully what should be his policy.
To whom he should hand over the whole of his kingdom,
And all his loyal people, after his lifetime.
By cart he went to London and arranged his hustings,[*]
The earls all came there, great and well favoured,
And all the wise men who were living in Britain.
When the king had stated his position he asked them for direction:
To whom could be bequeath all his kingly realm,
For he had no son who his land might govern,   5690
No child except his daughter, who was so dear to him,
And to her he wanted to bequeath all his kingly realm,
And give to her as lord the noblest man in this land.
Some advised him instantly to give her to Earl **Conan**:[*]

He was wise and powerful; on him he might bestow her.
Others there were who refused this to hear.
    In Cornwall there was a good earl who was known as **Cradoc**;
He stood up on the hustings and spoke like this to the king:
'Listen to me, Octaves; listen to me, royal lord:
'I haven't heard any good views being put to you so far.   5700
If you make over to Conan all of your kingdom,
The news will quickly go off into Rome;
For Helena now is Jerusalem's queen,*
And King Constantine, and all his knights with him;
And dead is the great Leonin and his brother Marin,
And Maximien the young knight in Rome conducts great fights,
And Trahern in this land by a spear was stabbed,
And every day within Rome Maximien the most noble
Has very much rebellion from **Gracien** and **Valantin**,
So that Constantine the king cares about us just nothing;   5710
And in this way we're deprived of Britain's supporters.
    'Unless you bestow sensibly your noble realm,
The race of the Romans will come to this nation
And destroy us by battle and beat down our allies,
And cause us dissention and deprive us of independence.
When once you are deceased we shall never be free of miseries.
But send off to Rome for Maximien the well-known:
He's a very gallant man and was the son of Leonin;
Helena's uncle was his father, his origin is noble,
So give him to your daughter who to you is very dear   5720
And make him the king and your daughter the queen.
Then shall our lives be in peace and in quiet,
And for all of our lives we'll be guarding our people
With honour and with happiness, with great common sense.'
    Then Conan stood up and went in front of the king;
He was extremely enraged, because this speech didn't please him;
He contradicted Cradoc as if he would have liked to kill him,
But Cradoc wasn't bothered by all the things Earl Conan said,
Seeing all the hustings which were held before the king
Approved Cradoc's diplomacy, for they saw it was necessity.   5730
Then announced Octaves, lord of all Britain:
'Congratulations Cradoc!*
For this you shall acquire a great deal of honour.
Lend me your son **Maurice**, who's a very clever man,
To go as I need him to the Roman people,

To fetch Maximien, the powerful and courageous,
In order that he come with speed, while I am still alive,
And I will bequeath to him all of my kingdom,
And my daughter, **Orien**, to have as his queen,
And to Maurice I shall make over my recompense: 5740
I shall give him Northumberland, here, by my own hand:
This I bestow on him from out of my kingdom,
On condition he bring me Maximien the gracious.'

   Just as the king desired so Maurice performed for him: *Maurice*
He set off directly with three knights who were wise,   *in*
Until he came to Rome, to Maximien.   *Rome*
There was great disturbance; in all that land there was no peace,
But with disturbance there was much strife with Gracien and with
     Valantin.
They did Maximien immeasurable harm:
Of much land [he] had [been] deprived before the young man
     Maurice there arrived;†
As soon as Maximien saw him he turned to him at once,   5751
And welcomed him courteously with gracious words,
Who most sensibly led him to consultation,
And spoke like this, with outstanding grace:
'Listen, Maximien, you come of noble stock:
You are Helena's uncle's son; of most high kindred have you come.
Before I set off for here, and it was not long before,
Octaves who is our king in London held his hustings.
The husting was very good; it was the councillors' special moot.
Ill-health and being aged have made the king enfeebled.   5760
There were many good knights and the king asked their advice
As to whom he might bequeath his daughter and his realm,
And all his doughty men after his demise.
   'Three earls, there and then, selected Count Conan,
So that all of Britain into his hands should be given,
With the lovely Orien, the king's daughter, as his queen.
Kent is the name of the earldom of Conan,
And my father is Earl of Cornwall, a considerable lord,
Who is called Cradoc: he comes from your family;
And I am called Maurice, the eldest of his children.   5770
When they then and there had thus selected Conan
My father then leaped up as if he were a lion,
And opposed the choice in the presence of our king.
There was a great deal of din: men there were clamouring,

And my father called for silence and then like this spoke:
"There was a time when Helena was Custance's queen;
Helena had an uncle who was highborn in this land:
He was called Leonin: he travelled off with Constantine;
Trahern was his brother and Marin was the other.
In this land Trahern was slain by treachery: 5780
Conan's father was his killer, which was the gravest crime,
For King Trahern believed that they were good friends.
Listen well, Britons, standing here about me:
Leonin had just a single son who is living now in Rome;
Maximien he is called, of that noble stock.
Let us send to Rome, and tell him to come soon,
And let us in our hustings raise him up as king,
And the lovely Orien let us entrust to him as queen.
Only then can we live in sober calm and peace." '
   'That was how my father Cradoc in the people's presence
      spoke.   5790
Then answered the king: to him it would be pleasing,
And to all his bold men who inhabit Britain;
But Conan was much enraged because the choice did not please him.
So now call to council your good councillors and people,
And tell me here an answer for now tomorrow I'll depart.'
   At these words Maximien was quite delighted then;
He summoned his councillors and went into conclave:
The decision was soon issued, just as Maurice had requested:
Maximien departed soon in secrecy from Rome,
Within just seven nights with all of his own knights.   5800
The inhabitants of Rome thought he intended, for their harm,
To go off for fighting against Valantin and Gracien,
So afraid were they always of Maximien and his army;
But instead at once they went away towards this land,
And so he made landfall and went into London:
Fine things did he bring for Octaves the king, *
And the king gave to him his daughter as queen.
   So then Maximien was king: to the British it seemed   MAXIMIEN
      well done,
But Earl Conan in anger went off to the Scotsmen,
And many Scots supported him and started to build a city;   5810
There was not in all that area then another town so fair;
When the city was all completed and copiously fortified,
He settled a name on it, taken from his own:

Again and again he would ride right through, and he called it
    Conisborough: *
Now and for all time the name remains the same.
    Conan led his army into the north country:
He hated Maximien; for that suffered many a man.
The wise men in this land who loved well those who lived here
Arranged for a hustings between Conan and the king:
There they were reconciled and there they were reunited,   5820
And established in this land a peace outstanding among the best,
And at once the king promised to make him a powerful man,
Which he did subsequently; for that many a man suffered.
In peace he remained here for fully five years.
    By then Maximien had fortune without measure,
For he had not sent the tribute from this land out to Rome.
When the five years had all gone, then announced Maximien
That he would travel over sea to fight against the Frenchmen,
And if there he could succeed, towards Rome he would ride,
To avenge his injuries on Gracien and on Valantin,   5830
Who had done him many wrongs when they were in Rome.
Maximien spoke in this way because he was too merry, *
For this land was very good and he had it all beneath his foot,
And he had no awe of anything since the death of King Octaves.
    Maximien summoned an amazingly strong army:
The king had courageous men and fortune without measure:
Onward he began to journey out from this country;
Onward he began proceeding, out from this people;
He made himself a deal of pain, he never did see this land again!
Over the sea he went, and came safely to land,   5840
In a very rich country which was called Armorica;
The ships ran up onto the land; the men went up on the strand.
They began to build a castle, outstanding among the best;
They rode around the country, and were affecting there much
    grandeur,
They found plenty of plunder, and took it to their army,
And also they seized women, wonderfully many,
And did all that they wanted right through Armorica.
    This news came to **Humbald** who was the lord within that land,
How King Maximien was ruining his realm.   *Invasion of*
Humbald sent his messengers over all the lands   *Brittany*
Wherever he had any friend who was willing to help him,   5851
And thought he would be able to drive them from his land.

They came in full daylight into a severe fight:
The British overcame them, and they slew Humbald,
And fifteen thousand were slain there and deprived of their life's days.
When this fight was over, then Maximien moved
Back into shelter, so he could rest himself.
In the morning when the day came, the doughty men got ready:
They went to the great town which is known as Nantes, *
They could not find inside it a single human being   5860
Willing to withstand them and defend the city:
Everyone had fled away and from the land escaped,
Except a few odd women who were there within it.
The city fell to Maximien who placed his men as garrison.
    Then called out Maximien there to Earl Conan:
'Conan, you're a good knight, well did you sustain my fight,
And a great reward I shall now make over to you,
Because you had all Britain in your own possession:
If I were not king, you would be king there,
And to the Earl Cradoc, who is of my own kin,   5870
Even yet it may fall, much against your will.
But now look at these rivers and at these lovely lands,
These valuable woodlands, and all these fine wild beasts,
This is a lovely land in which to be alive!
This land is called Armorica, and this I'm giving to you,
And much more besides this, if only I can seize it:
You shall be king of this, and own this kingdom.
Out of it I shall drive all I find alive,
The young and the aged, out of this same land,
And whoever here I can catch on the spot he'll be dispatched: 5880
And I shall send off to **Athionard**, who is my personal justiciar:
He is an earl most trusty, to his promise always ready,
For I have properly entrusted to him Britain for protection,
And to me he must send into this same land
Weaponed men and women wise in many craft skills,
Knights and landholders and all their supporters:
Sixty hundred knights who are excellent in fight,
Ten hundred landholders, seven thousand supporters,
Seven thousand citizens, sound in their possessions,
Thirty thousand women, who are well endowed.   5890
When these folk have all arrived here and have taken their
        assignments,
Then all this lovely land will be placed in British hands,

So give them a name after your own people:
Call it "Little Britain";'
Now and for all time the name remains the same,
And this is how Armorica's name was thrown aside
So that never any more will it be reinstated.
  Conan received this gift and became the king's good friend;
With greatest honour and respect, and well did they preserve it,
And then the king sent off a message to this land,   5900
Ordering Athionard, who was protecting Britain's land,
Very swiftly to send him those people from Britain,
And folk from each profession he must assign to different ships,
And among the women not a single weaponed male,
Except the actual mariners who had to lead them there.
  All these plans proceeded as the king had instructed,
And Conan kept to them to his utmost powers,
While the king advanced forwards into France,
And conquered all that kingdom and placed it all in his own hand,
And from there he led his men into Lorraine,   5910
And all that land he conquered, as he did Louvaine as well;
So he led his men down into Lombardy,
And all that land he conquered; it was here that Cradoc died.*
Then sorrow in plenty overwhelmed his son Maurice:
There could be no other remedy: Maurice himself expired.
  Off to Rome went Maximien, against Valantin and against Gracien:
In fight he captured the latter, and was sued for peace by the former.
They were courteous knights: the king clapped them in irons,
And immediately after he appropriated all Rome.
The message reached Conan of the success of Maximien,   5920
And that Cradoc had died out in Lombardy,
And also his son Maurice, out of overwhelming sorrow.
Then the earl Conan took one very wise man,
And sent him to this country, to Athionard the mighty,
Who was the very busy Regent of this land of Britain.
A letter was brought to Athionard about the deaths of his brother,
Cradoc the famous, and his dear son Maurice;
Now Cradoc in this world had no brother save Athionard,
And he at once seized in his hand all of Cradoc's former land.
  Then the Frenchmen discovered that Maximien was in
    Rome,   5930
And that Cradoc was dead: then the French devised a plot
That away they would drive Earl Conan the brave,

Out of the land which Maximien had put into his hand,
Which lies beside France and which is called Brittany;
But Conan did not seek for peace, and fiercely fought against them,
And constructed well his castles, secure and founded fast.
And by all his men he was well liked, those who came out from this
    land,
For he'd received all those knights whom Maximien had promised
    him,
And also the rulers, the servants and landholders,
And all of the townsmen who were promised by Maximien;   5940
He had only a few women, not more than fifteen hundred,
For women refused to leave, to go away of from our land here,*
Except when the Earl Athionard, who was the highest in this land,
Would give them his assurance that their time would be well spent.
    Now Athionard had one daughter who was very dear to   *Ursula*
    him:
She had the highest reputation of all the maidens in this land;
This woman was most blessed: her name was **Ursula**.
Conan sent to this land, to the earl Athionard,
Requesting he should give him his daughter as his queen.
Athionard gave his answer – may he have honour for it –:   5950
'All praise go to Conan for so desiring my own daughter!
From now in only seven nights I shall send her to him by my knights,
And all those women he was given by my own lord, Maximien;
That way she's to be led if she wants to go on living,
Otherwise I'll have them all killed and suspended by the nipples!'*
Then prepared Athionard, this land's appointed guardian,
His own daughter, Ursula, who was a very holy woman,
Intending to send her over the sea-streams,
Into the land of Brittany to Conan the mighty.
News came to the women all throughout this Britain   5960
That Ursula was to be sent away to that land;
To her there came many: enough and beyond counting,
Who wished to travel with her off to King Conan;
Very many travelled to her, more than she had need of.
    When the day arrived which Athionard had contrived
For the young girl Ursula to set off on her journey,
Then she had as escort a count of twenty-seven ships –
All of them were [stationed] in the Port of London;†
Still within the Thames they hauled up their sails;
A fair wind they had with them and weather of the best,   5970

And they sailed onwards until they reached open sea;
Then after a short while more they could no longer see the shore.
Then arose a wind against them, on the opposing side;[*]　　*Storm*
Blackest thunder-clouds grew dark beneath the sun:
Hail and rain were stirred up – those who saw it felt sheer terror –
The waves there were racing as flames when towns are burning;
Shipboards smashed there; the women started wailing;
The ships which ran in front, twelve of them were sunk,
The others were all dispersed and were swept along by the surge;
None of the pilots there could ever know how to cope with
　　　　that:　　　　　　　　　　　　　　　　　　　　　5980
That man has never yet been born, not the most superb from any
　　　land,
Who would be a man stout enough, or sufficiently hard-hearted,
If he could have heard this wail and this terrifying scream,
With crying out in shrillest voice on all the saints there are,
Whose heart would not have felt some grief for the countless sorrows.
Since this world was established and into human hands was set
Never did any worse misfortune come to any women.
Some of the ships fled on, running before the storm,
A good fifteen of them; and in one was [Ursula].^{*†}
The sea was marvellously maddened and horrifyingly
　　　angered;　　　　　　　　　　　　　　　　　　　5990
And those ships [went wandering] over the wild sea,[†]
Always northwards straight, for three days and three nights.
　　There were two warlords travelling who came out of Norway,
Melga and **Wanis**: they were very bold indeed,
From Denmark and from Norway they were proscribed as outlaws
And they travelled by the sea-coasts far and wide without restraint.
They could see well by the massing clouds the nature of the weather;
They drew off to an island where they could lie under the leeside.
Wanis came from Hungary where he had wrought havoc;
Melga came from Scythia, where he had stirred up much
　　　uproar,　　　　　　　　　　　　　　　　　　　　6000
So that he could not linger in that land any longer,
And was exiled from Norway, where they had endured a fight;
So at sea they had been travelling for a good seven years,
And now were lying up at the island, and watching that severe storm.
They saw the ships, one by one, sometimes more, sometimes none,
Then there were four, then there were five; weird it seemed to them in
　　　the world alive!

What these wretched ships could be that were roaming over the sea.
    The wind began abating, and the weather then grew mild,
And Wanis could see the ships wandering over the sea,
And he spoke there in this way to Melga his mate: 6010
'Off now right away, us two, and after them quick!
With fifteen good ships let's be getting after them,
With the best of our knights who are good in the fight,
And leave all our other ships guarding our harbour,
Because this is some rich king, deprived of support,
Who'd intended with his people to proceed to some country,
And this wind and this rough weather have thrust him off his course,
Until his very life's a misery. Now let's [get] to him quickly,†
And if it is the will of Apollin, that much beloved god of mine,
That we're able in fight to conquer him and his knights,   6020
If they're not of our faith we shall deprive him of life,
And that way we get our hands on their silver and their gold,
Cart them off to where we stay, and boast about our gains!'
    Forwards drove upon the flood fifteen ships which were good,
The strongest there were in those days, and loaded with outlaws,
And instantly overtook five ships, all filled with women.
It seemed to them most odd, what this could be about,
And they hailed them with a shout: but there was no answer,
Since all of the women had been overcome by death.
Over to them they moved and those five ships they seized,   6030
And further they advanced and nine ships they captured,
And they then with all those fourteen ships went forward to the land.
Since this world was established it has nowhere been published
In song or in story, nor could any one report it,
That there were any women so wretchedly tormented,
Nor so pitifully upon the sea seduced.
Melga took [Ursula], who was to have been a queen,†
And disgrace he proffered her by leading her to bed.
When the heathen wretch on her had slaked his lust
He gave her to his crewmen straight, to have her as a whore.   6040
But some of them they sold, for silver and for gold,
And many and beyond number there they put to slaughter,
And some of them they drowned, deep in the sea,
And some of them abandoned God and adopted heathen practice.
And so they were seduced, in most pitiable state.
    Melga and Wanis heard reported most certainly
That this land of Britain was bereft of her knights

Because very many were led away to Armorica by Conan,
And Maximien led off to Rome many who were specially good;
Thus was this kingdom depleted in its numbers.   6050
Melga and Wanis went off into Scotland:
They rode through the land ravaging and burning;
The property they seized; the people they slaughtered,
And so they went towards us here, over the Humber.
Horrors they inflicted, and impoverished the land.
The Britons heard of this and were most distressed about it.
They took a messenger at once and sent him off to Rome:
They sent greetings to Maximien and told him about Melga,
And about Wanis his mate and what they'd done to this state,
And begged him for advice otherwise they would all perish.   6060
    Maximien was distressed on hearing news like this,
And at once released from fetters Gracien the gracious; *
The moment he approached him, like this he addressed him:
'Gracien, become my man, and see afterwards how well you've done,
For I intend to send you off into Britain,
All of that royal land I shall place into your hand,
And you shall be my justiciar, as was the earl Athionard,
And if you want to act well, I will make you a rich man,
If you drive out of my nation the alien invaders.'
Then Gracien responded with placating expressions: 6070
'I shall act entirely according to your wishes,
Shall go wherever you want, and regard you as my lord.'
The oaths then were sworn – and yet again they were broken.
    Maximien the kaiser summoned a most enormous army,
And selected from the mightiest ten thousand knights,
And appointed Gracien commander of men.
And so they began to travel off to this land;
And here he fought, true it is, with Melga and with Wanis,
It came to a good outcome when he conquered them in combat,
And drove them across the sea bounds out into Ireland,   6080
And then marched right on through this land where best of all he
    liked it.
And Emperor Maximien in Rome was the highest man,
And held Valantin securely enclosed within a castle.
    Now Gracien and Valantin in Rome had many relatives
Who noticed that one brother was parted from the other.
Their messenger they sent into the land of Apulia,
And they sent off to Gradie, the duke of Lombardy,

And into Germany, to great and noble people,
And into many lands which lay all around there,
And asked that from their countries they should all assemble armies,
And on a set day very soon should come to surround Rome,   6091
And avenge, upon Maximien, both Valantin and Gracien.
About this knew just nothing Maximien the rich king,
But he went on living in Rome in rich magnificence.

    After a little interim there the armies came,   *Roman*
All around Rome rode seven kings;   *Uprising*
They smashed down Rome's wall and marched in everywhere;*
The city of Rome they seized, and Maximien they slew,
And pulled out Valantin and all his fellows with him
From the strong castle, and made him their kaiser,   6100
And took their messengers and sent off to this land,
Sending Gracien word of what had happened there,
And Gracien at once took possession right away of this kingdom:*
This kingdom was held by Gracien when it had been owned by
    Maximien,
While Valantin of Rome owned all the realm.
So through just such a plot came Maximien's death,
And Gracien was king here, as was well known   GRACIEN
    everywhere.
Within a single year (the time was not any longer)
King Gracien became the most depraved of men:
He totally destroyed this land, its inhabitants he hated,   6110
The rich folk he destroyed, the humble he drove to exile;
The powerful lords lacked courage to bring against him any
    challenge,
But all of them fled from him and all of them deserted him.
    There were in East Anglia some freemen of good family,*
Two of them, brothers, and twin-born they were:
The one was called **Ethelbald**, the other one was **Alfwald**;
They could see in many places how the king this land defaced.
Those freemen thought out carefully what might be their policy,
And spoke very secretly of how they wished to kill the king,
And sent into East Anglia, far and wide throughout that land,   6120
And assembled in that area seven hundred freemen,
Announcing that above all things they wanted to seek out the king,
And beg him for mercy, through merciful God,
That he should, by his might, rule them with right.
But Alfwald and his brother really thought quite other:

They marched very cautiously, with captivating manner,
And each carried in his hand a cudgel which was stout,
And on their sides they all had hanging knives which were very long,
Under their breast-covers, to protect them from troubles.
And so they marched forth, all of them in safety,   6130
And after just one mile they took rest for a while,
And to every single courtier they gave a courteous greeting,
And graciously above all things enquired as to where was the king,
And the courtiers directed them to where they might discover him,
Where he was within a wood, in a wild place there,
Hunting for a boar – for which he suffered very sorely!
    The freemen went into the wood and warily took cover,
All except for two of them, who both worked their way toward the
        king,
And came upon the king with the dogs there at the baiting,
And they started calling out to him at the top of their voices: 6140
'Come this way, my lord the king, we want to tell you a wonderful
        thing,
About a particular boar which is about these parts,
Under one of the cliff-slopes where he's selected his lair.
We have never in all of our lives ever heard tell of such a swine.
If you would just ride that way, there he's waiting for you!'
The king was very glad at this, and was on his way there speedily,
And the two freemen were in front of him, both of them together:
The two men leaping out surprised him; as the king they recognised
        him,   *Gracien's*
And hurled him to the ground, and hacked him quite to pieces. *Death*
And that was how Gracien the king went out on his hunting.   6150
    Soon it was everywhere being said that the wicked king was dead;
Then there were in Britain very many joys!
But very soon after that sorrows came their way.
Then every single freeman behaved as boldly as an earl,
And all the soldiery as if they were sons of kings.
This news spread almost everywhere of how the former king had
        fared;
Sea-voyaging men came forth into Ireland,
And found there most certainly Melga and Wanis,
And told them the tidings concerning all this land,
How all things were faring and how the peasants had no
        cares,   6160
And had placed all this kingdom in the freemen's hands.

Then they rejoiced, be sure of this, did Melga and Wanis,
And said that they wanted to go towards this land.
With an enormous army they came into this country;
They had taken in from Jutland outlaws who were strong,
From Norway and from Denmark men who were very tough,
And, out of Ireland, **Gillomaur** the strong;
From the Scots they had some, all the highest-ranking,
And, out of Galloway, good men and courageous.
And so they started marching out to Northumberland: 6170
Possessions they seized, people they slaughtered,
Castles they erected and took ownership of the area;
All the towns they captured, and all things they came near to.
    Then the British realised there was disaster in the land;
They could not think of any remedy and assumed they would all die.
They took messengers very soon and sent them off to Rome,
And requested their assistance, then and for all time:
If they would aid them in their extreme need,
Then all of their lives they would be submissive to them,
And maintain their love for them, if only they would aid
        them.   6180
This message was sent out, in a very [secret] missive,[†]
And the letter was read over among the men of Rome.
    Then spoke up very soon the wisest men of Rome:
'They have hardly deserved that we should go to deliver them,
For Gracien they slaughtered and his men they destroyed;
But nevertheless we'll send them forces from this country,
Out of this country just one single small army.'
Out they sent from Rome some soldiers most fine;
Twenty-five hundred came riding to London
And summoned all the army of Britain's own country,   6190
And marched forth with certainty to Melga and Wanis,   *Relief*
And they fought against them and slaughtered their forces,   *from*
And those two in cowardly wise ran off into the woods,   *Rome*
And left their forces to be slain, their innumerable host,
While they themselves slipped away off to [the north of] Scotland,[†]
With **Febus** coming after them with his Roman knights.[*]
But they were not able for anything to discover Melga,
And speedily began to dig the very deepest ditch,
And on top of it, right along, a very strong stone wall,
Along the sea-side by the boundary of Scotland,   6200
Where outlaws were always accustomed to come into our land,

And then they organised themselves to guard the ditch with
  armed men.
  When the ditch and the wall were ready then the Britons had no
    anxiety;
They started returning to the city of London,
And Febus of Rome ordered that hustings be held soon.
Many prominent men came, promptly to the hustings:
Many a knight, many an earl, many a landholder, many a freeman,
Many a rich citizen, expecting soon to be contented,
Who were depressed in their hearts before the day had ended.
Febus the fine knight had his forces sumoned outright,   6210
That they should come to the hustings with all of their throng,
With their horses in their quarters being tended well by ostlers,
Who were to make the horses just as prepared as if they were to go
    from there.
And all the people did all this, as it was ordered by Febus,
And so they started moving on the way to their hustings.
  When the people had all arrived and each had taken up his place,
Then within London city the order came to listen.
Up then stood Febus, the noble knight, who said this:*   *Febus's*
'Listen to me now, you Britons who stand here at my sides,   *Farewell*
I have to announce to you the actual words of Rome.   6221
You sent us a summons into our homeland
For the grief done you (no doubt of this) by Melga and by Wanis,
And I with my army have come to this country,
And all of your foes I have felled to the ground,
And driven from your country Melga without his army.
Now [you] can for many years be living here without a care[†]
About that self-same army which is slaughtered in your country.
[But] you have often made us angry and for this in Rome you're
    hated,[†]
For frequently you've withheld from us the tribute from this land,
And also [you] committed crime, such as slaying your King
    Gracien,[†]   6230
And you keep on promising to observe your treaties,
And always in the end of it you weaken in your hold.
We have, in our love for you, lost many of our people:
A whole hundred thousand knights have perished in this land
Since the time when Julius Caesar first arrived here.
But as we hope for grace we shall have no more of this!
But we shall very soon be on our way to Rome,

And hand to you this royal land: now hold it in your own hands!
And may you now have joy of it,
For we shall never any more come back to you here!   6240
    'We have received from this land a good many thousand pounds
Which we requested from you here, but it was paid for very dear.
We have often travelled here with trouble and with care;
But now you can act properly: get yourselves some weapons quickly,
And defend yourselves against the alien tribes;
After all, your ancestors, were they not noble characters?
From here to Rome, all that land, lay within their own hands,
And all the land they ever saw, instantly they conquered it:
They conquered all of it with their stout weapons.
Do but construct in your own land castles which are strong,   6250
And defend your nation against the alien tribes,
And live here fit and well; and now farewell all of you!'
    When these words had been [declamed] there was a crisis here:[†]
There was never any man born, not in any borough,
Who could ever announce in any kind of account
The enormous sadness which had settled on the people.
There were in London unlovely gestures:
There was weeping, there was screaming, and immeasurable
        remorse.
    Then the Roman people rode out towards their ships,
And abandoned the Britons here in this land,   6260
In their immeasurable remorse. They did not know any remedy.
This message most certainly reached Melga and Wanis:
They had an army of uncountable forces,
And they began advancing into Northumberland;
All that land they overran, and slaughtered and burned,
And so they advanced until they arrived at the wall
Which the Roman people there had erected.
There were Britons there within, with very many men,
And Melga was outside, and was eagerly deciding
How he could contrive it so he could get inside it.   6270
They made a rush on the wall, the unruly leaders,[*]
Assembled all the army from many types of area:
The ditch was very wide and deep, and the force leaped at it,
While the British were in readiness and the wall defended;
These shot in, those shot out: soldiers were falling.
Arrows went flying over the wall, all around and over all,
As thickly were they clustered as if they were hailstones,

So the Britons, through those arrows could not attend to fighting,
But down from the wall they went running all,
And stampeded in flight frightfully quickly,   6280
And the others broke down the wall and got inside, right over it all,
And went in pursuit and slaughtered them hugely;
There was a great disaster: fifty-two hundred did they slaughter
Only from the actual British, without counting up the Scots,
And without those Danishmen who were left there in the ditch.
That's how this kingdom was flourishing in the hands of the British!
The British had been knights elect,
But now they were all very abandoned,
They can never get high[er] without having much help†
From men of other peoples, for they themselves are quite
        unable.   6290
    So fared with certainty Melga and Wanis.
Then the Britons sent to Rome from London at once,
Begging them come quickly and act as they'd been accustomed,
So they might rescue this land and take it all in their hands,
For they would allow it to them better than they would to the aliens.
Then like this they gave answer: 'We will never travel back there,
To endure that labour and that strife against that heathen tribe,
For he is God's own adversary, the one who is called
        Wanis,   *Renounced*
And Melga is his confrere: we will never come back there!   *by*
This is the finish: we will not travel there;   *Rome*
In a different quarter we have more than we can deal with.'   6301
There was no other answer than that, and the embassy started back.
When they returned, the Britons from Rome,
Telling those tidings which the Roman people gave them,
Then the folk of London were tramelled with sorrows.
    There was then an archbishop, who was a holy man and good, *
And to God very close: **Guencelin** he was called.
He sent his messengers throughout all Britain,
Seeking for all the clerics who knew the teaching of God;
All the men in holy orders hastily came to him,   6310
And they very soon came into London.
Like this went Guencelin's address: 'May we have with us God's
        peace!'
Now in Latin it goes like this: it's actually 'Pax vobis',
And they answered him promptly too: 'Et cum spiritu tuo'.
Then he began a homily and spoke of God most eloquently.

The archbishop's throne in those days was at St Paul's,
And for very many years the archbishops were there,
But after when St Augustine came it was transferred to Canterbury.
   Now announced Guencelin, who was a saintly man:
'Listen now, gentlemen, to what we declare: 6320
[See now] this heathen man, who is known as Melga,†
And Wanis and their army have brought [woe] to this our country,†
And will this our Christian faith quite destroy and disrupt.
Now if I will have your leave, I shall lay course onward,
And travel across the sea to some great high king,
And request that high king that he help us above all things.
And if I may succeed in speaking to such a king,
Then shall I most gladly come back here again;
Otherwise no more at all shall I ever come back here.
And do you pray for me upon your bare knees,   6330
And so I bid you good day; I'll come back if I may.'
Then the people were sorry and saddened in spirit;
The British never in their lives had experienced such griefs.
   Off went Guencelin and his clerics with him,
Right on towards the sea, where it seemed to suit them;
There they found ships and quickly went in,
And very soon across the sea they came
Right into Brittany (at this they were very happy)
Which that King Maximien gave to the Earl Conan,
But dead by now was Maximien, so too was King Conan,   6340
But his son was called **Aldroein** who had come from Conan's line:
All of Brittany's land he held within his hand,
(Armorica once they called the land, but that name was speedily lost);
There the king was A[l]dro[ei]n, under him many high barons.†
   Guencelin came towards the king, and well he had him received
      there;
The archbishop fell at the king's feet, and prayed him to think upon
      God:
'My lord the king, Aldroein, may God many times be gracious to
      you!*   *Guencelin's*
Remember you were Conan's son: out of Britain you   *Appeal*
      have entirely come.
I have come to speak with you and to crave of your favour life itself.
Into our land there have come a couple of heathen men,   6350
Melga and Wanis: much wrong they're doing to us.
They have taken from our land all the northern end,

And we are very much afraid lest they will now take more;
And yet more evil they think to do: to bring down Christianity,
And convert all to heathendom, both the high and the low.
Because your father took from Britain all of her strong knights,
And because Maximien the handsome many thousands took to
    Rome,
And because those now lie slain whom they left us in our days,
In this way is Britain's area quite depleted of its people.
Messages we sent to Rome, begging them to come,   6360
But they have merely sent us word, through the men we sent them,
That we must do the best we can for no more will they come,
But instructed us to gain such assistance as we can.
And they have pronounced us quits, now and for all time!
  'But that's all very well as far as it goes, for we remain beggars,
    Goodness knows!
There was a time when the British were the best men in the land,
Everything they embarked on, all of it they won.
Now they are defeated: either slain and captured
Or gone away with Maximien and with your father Conan,   6369
So there [is] hardly left even one you could really see any worth
    in.†
But you are of our race, from us you've no disgrace;
Help us! for you're able, otherwise we're in huge trouble!'
  So pleaded the archbishop that King Aldroein well understood.
The king began severely sighing; from him tears started falling:
His eyes were streaming so much that his courtiers could see it.
Then the king gave his answer, and spoke like this there with
    Guencelin:
'Yes I want to help you, with as much strength as I have:
I shall deliver to you two thousand knights,
Who shall be the best who are living within Brittany,
And **Constantine** my brother (of his like I know no other);   6380
As wide as shines this daylight I do not know a better knight,
Nor do I know in this world's reaches a knight who is his equal!
Make him the ruler over all Britain's area.'
Then summoned Aldroein the king his dear brother, Constantine,
And he immediately delivered to him those knights.
Off marched Constantine, and the archbishop with him;
And the king himself would well have gone, but was anxious about
    the Frankish men.

To these islands journeyed Constantine the gracious,   *Constantine's*
And his army quite secure all at Totnes came ashore.   *Arrival*
There arrived the brave man: extremely well was he
    endowed!   6390
And with him two thousand knights; the like no king has owned.
Onward they went marching into London city
And sent for the knights throughout all that kingdom,
And every single brave man, that in great haste they must come then.
This was heard by the British where they were living down in pits*
In the earth, and in tree trunks they were hiding out like badgers,
In wood and in wilderness, in heathland and in ferns,
So that practically nobody could ever find a Briton,
Unless they were in a castle or in a town enclosed securely.

   When they heard of this word that Constantine was in the land,
There emerged from the mountains many thousand men;   6401
They came springing out of woodlands as if they were wild beasts:
There went loping off to London many hundred thousand,
On streets and through forests all men forwards went marching,
And the brave women dressed in weaponed men's clothing,
And off they all went towards the great army.
When Constantine observed all these folk coming to him,
Then he was more blithe than he'd been ever in his life.

   Off they went on their way for two whole nights and a day,
Until they came, most certainly, on Melga and Wanis.   6410
Together they rushed on them with fiercest rigour:
Fought there with fury; the fated then fell there.
Before the day was quite over slain were Wanis and Melga,
And Picts quite enough and Scots without number,
Danish and Norwegian, men of Galloway and Ireland.
All the time that there was daylight still this slaughter lasted;
When it came to evening-time then called out Earl Constantine,
Asking for route planners to run ahead towards the rivers,
And sprightly men towards the sea, so that there they could spy out
    for them.
One really should have seen that sport, how the ladies all marched
    forward,
Right through woods and right through fields, over hills and over
    dales;
Wherever they detected a single man escaping   6422
Who had been with Melga, with the heathen king,
The women then laughed loudly and ripped him all to pieces,

Praying for his soul – that salvation never neared it!
So the British women were the death of many thousands,
And so they rid this kingdom of Wanis and of Melga,
And Constantine the brave marched to Silchester,
And there held his hustings for all his British feoffs.*

    All of the British were bound for the meeting,   6430
And adopted Prince Constantine and made him king of the Britons.
Great was the rejoicing there was among mankind,   CONSTANTINE
And afterwards they gave him a wife, a wondrously fair one,
Born of the highest, of the best of all among the British.*
From this high-born wife King Constantine had
Among this very people three little sons;
The first son very nearly had his own father's name:
The king's name was Constantine, and **Constance** was the child's
    name.
    When this child had grown till he was old enough for riding,
Then his father had him made a monk, through the bad advice of
    men,
And the child was a monk, enclosed in Winchester.   6441
After him was born another, who was the middle brother:
He was called **Aurelius**, and his surname was **Ambrosius**;
Then last of all was born a child who was specially chosen:
He was known as **Uther**: his honour was excellent;
He was the youngest brother but he lived longer than the others.
Archbishop Guencelin who was most good in serving God,
Took charge of these two children in his love for the king,
But alas that their own father was not able to live longer,
For he maintained good laws all the time he was alive,   6450
But he was not king here for more than twelve years.
Then came the death of the king: now listen through what scheming.
    He had in his house a Pict, a courteous knight and very valiant;*
He travelled with the king and with all his courtiers,
In no other manner than exactly like his brother.
And so he became very mighty, all his companions were not like this;
Then he decided to betray King Constantine the great.
He came in the king's presence and he fell upon his knees,
And this is how that traitor told lies before his lord:
'My lord king, come right now, and speak with your knight
    Cadal,   6460
And I shall instruct you in secret information
Such as you never before on earth have ever heard.'

So up stood King Constantine and off he went outside with him,
But alas that they knew nothing of it, Constantine's knights!
They went such a long while onwards that they came into an orchard;
There the traitor then said: 'Lord, here we are, the two of us.'
The traitor sat down, as if to hold secret council,
And bent towards the king as one does for whispering;
A really long knife he grabbed and with this the king he stabbed,
Down into the heart; and he himself slipped off.   6470
Dead there the king lay while the traitor fled away.
The word came to the court of how the king's life was cut short;
There was tremendous sorrow and it spread among the people.
   Then did the British start thinking very hard;
They had no idea of anything they could do about a king
For the king's two sons were both of them little:
Ambrosius hardly knew how to ride a horse,*
And Uther his brother was still suckled by his mother,
And Constance the eldest was away in Winchester:
A monk's habit he had on, like those of his community.   6480
Then all those living in this nation came up to London,
To their hustings, and to take advice about a king,
Which way they could act, and how they might tackle it,
And which of these children they could have as their king.
Then the people selected Aurelius Ambrosius
To have as a king over them all.
   This was heard by **Vortigern**, a wily man and wary.
Among the earls he was standing and earnestly he opposed it,
And this he told them (though it was not true):
'I shall now advise you, my advice is the best: 6490
Wait for a fortnight, and let's come back here straight,
And then I will tell you, with very true words,
What with your eyes you shall behold, and your time you'll well
      bestow.
This same thing we shall await, and to our homes meanwhile ride,
And keep peace and keep quiet with freedom in the land.'
   That assembly all did as Vortigern decreed,
And he himself went off as if going to his lands,
And then turned, right on to the way that down to Winchester lay.
A half share of the Welsh lands did Vortigern have in his hands;
Forty good knights he had in his retinue.   6500
He went off to Winchester where he would find Constance
And spoke with the abbot who was in charge of the convent

168

Where Constance was a monk, he who was the King of Britain's son.
He went into the monastery mouthing humble words;
He said that he wanted to have speech with Constance.
This the abbot granted him and led him to the parlour.
   In this way spoke Vortigern with the monk then and there:
'Constance, listen to my advice, for your father is now dead.*
There is Ambrosius your brother, and Uther is the other.
Now all the [elders], the most outstanding in the land,†   6510
Have selected Aurelius, whose surname is Ambrosius
If they can, above everything, they wish to make him king,
And Uther your brother is still suckled by his mother.
   But I have opposed them, and intend to refuse it,
For I have been justiciar of all of Britain's area,
And I'm a powerful earl, different from my fellows,
And a half share of the Welsh lands do I have in my hands;
I have more alone than the others all told.
I have come to you, for you are the dearest of men to me;
If you will swear me oaths, I will strip you of these clothes;   6520
If you will increase my land, and put your affairs into my hand,
And make me your justiciar, over all of Britain's area,
And on my veto do everything you do.
If you give me your hand on it that I shall be in charge,
I will above all things make you Britain's king!'
   This monk sat very quietly; the words worked with his own wishes.
Then the child-monk answered with much eagerness:
'Blessings on you, Vortigern, that you have come here.
If ever yet comes that day on which I may be king,
All my affairs and all my land I shall deliver in your hand,   6530
And everything you wish to do, my men shall undertake it.
And I shall swear you oaths that I shall perform this.'
So spoke the monk: he grieved very much
How it all could have been that he was a monk,
For to him black clothes were amazingly loathsome.
   Vortigern was wily and wary, (that he revealed everywhere):
He took up a cape from off one of his knights;
He put it on the monk and led him out of that place;
At once he took a servant and put the black clothes on him,
And went on whispering with the servant as if he were the
      monk.   6540
Monks were going upstairs, monks were going downstairs,
They saw as they went by the servant in monk's habit:

His hood was pulled right down as if covering his tonsure;
It was the thought of every other that this one was their brother
Who was sitting there so soberly, there in the parlour,
In broad daylight among all the knights.
 They came to their abbot and greeted him in God's name:
'Benedicite, my lord; we have come to see you to have word,
For it seems very odd to us, what Vortigern is up to,
There in our parlour where he is conversing: 6550
All this whole day no monk is allowed to go in there,
Except Constance alone, and the whole set of knights.
We are deeply anxious that they're guiding him astray.'
Then the abbot answered 'On the contrary! They're guiding him to
 good:
Telling him to remain in orders because now his father's dead.'
 Vortigern remained there while Constance rode away. *Constance*
Vortigern got up and strode out of the monastery, *escapes*
And all of his knights marched out straight.
Monks ran in there at once, expecting to find Constance:
Then they saw the clothes lying, there beside the wall; 6560
And each to his neighbour grieved for their brother.
The abbot leaped on horseback and galloped after Vortigern,
And soon managed to overtake Earl Vortigern.
This is what the abbot said to Vortigern as he rode:
'Tell me, you insane knight: why are you committing such a crime?
You are abducting from us our brother; leave him and take the other,
Take the child Ambrosius, and make him into a king,
And do not anger Saint Benedict: don't do him any wrong.'
 Vortigern could hear this (he was wily and very wary),
He turned straight back again, and took hold of the abbot, 6570
And swore by his two hands that he was going to hang him
Unless he would promise him that he would very swiftly
Unconsecrate Constance, the king's son in this land,
And in such great need as this was he must be king of this nation.
The abbot dared not do other than to unconsecrate his brother,
And the child put into the abbot's hands the gift of twenty
 ploughlands, *
And then they journeyed onwards up into London.
 Vortigern the most high forbade all his courtiers
Ever to tell any man what they were holding in their command.†
In London Vortigern was staying until came that agreed-on
 day 6580

When to the hustings were to come the knights from this our land.[†]
On the day they arrived, many and uncountable:
They held council, they conferred, those courageous soldiers,
Deciding that they would have Ambrose and elect him king,
For Uther was too little: for some time he'd have to suckle,
And the eldest of them, Constance, was an enclosed religious,
And no, not for anything would they make a monk a king.
    This was heard by Vortigern, who was wily and most wary,
And to his feet he leaped, as a lion springs.
(Among the British none at all knew what Vortigern had
      been up to: 6590
In a room he had secreted Constance the beloved,
Well-bathed and dressed and then by twelve knights guarded).
The following spoke Vortigern (in manuvering he was wily):
'Listen to me, princelings, while I speak to you of kings.
I have been in Winchester and there I was successful;
I spoke there to the Abbot, who is a holy man and good,
And told him of the crisis which has come upon this nation
With Constantine's death (about that he was distressed)
And with Constance, only a child, whom he had been holding,
And I begged him for God's sake the monk's hood from the child to
      take,
Since in this great need he ought to be king in the nation,   6601
And the abbot held his chapter and did everything I asked him,
And right here I have his monks, who are good men and gracious,
Who are bound to give evidence before you in audience.
Look now: here is that same child! Let us make a king of him:
I've got the crown here, which we need for the purpose.
Anyone who protests at this must pay the penalty!'
    Vortigern was very strong — the highest man in Britain's land;
There was no one else at all as high with courage to abjure his
      speech;
The archbishop in that very week departed from this world;   6610
There remained no bishop who on his way did not shuffle,
No monk, nor any abbot who on his way did not ride off,
For they dared not in the name of God commit there such a sacrilege
As to take an oblate monk and make him into Britain's king.
This noted Vortigern (of evil he was well aware!):
Up did he stand, picked the crown up in his hand,
And placed it upon Constance (which delighted him).
There was no man present to perform the Christian ceremony,

Who could impart the blessing upon the new king,
But Vortigern alone did it entirely for them all: 6620
The start was unfitting and so was the ending:
He abandoned holy orders and for that he endured sorrows.

    So the king was Constance, with Vortigern as his justiciar;
Constance put his royal lands all into Vortigern's own hands,
And with all those lands he did just what he wanted.
Then noticed Vortigern (of evil he was all too well aware!)
That Constance the king about his own land knew nothing,
For he had never learned any lessons at all
Except in his monastery of a monk's duties.
Vortigern noticed this (the Devil was very close to him);   6630
Often he thought deeply of what might be his policy,
How by his lying he could mollify the king.

    Now you can hear how this traitor prepared:
The best men of Britain now all lay dead,
And the king's brothers were as yet both quite little,
And Guencelin the archbishop before this had died,
And this very land's own king of its laws knew not a thing.
Vortigern observed this and he approached the king
With most submissive speech his overlord he greeted:
'May you prosper, Constance, ruler of Britain!   6640
I have approached you this closely because of great necessity:
Because of information which has just come to the land
Concerning the gravest danger. Now you must have power;
Now you must have weapons to defend your nation.
Merchants from other lands have come here, as it is customary;
To me they have brought the tax on their imports,
And they have been telling me (its truth they have vouched for)
That the king of Norway decided recently to come here,*
And the King of the Danishmen will make request for Danes,
And the King of Russia for the most rigorous of knights,   6650
And the King of Jutland, with a very strong army,
And the King of Frisia (which sets me shivering).

    'Most serious is this news which has arrived here on these shores:
It makes me deeply anxious because I can't think of any solutions,
Unless with our authority we were to send for knights
Who are good and strong and who are familiar with the land,
And invest your castles with courageous men;
In this way your realm might be guarded from the aliens,
And your honour be upheld by superior strength,

For there is no kingdom, however wide, however long,   6660
Which cannot rapidly be seized if there are too few soldiers.'
   Then responded the king (about his own land he knew nothing):
'Vortigern, you are justiciar over all of Britain's area,
And you are to govern it according to your wishes.
Send out for knights who are valiant in fight,
And take into your hand all my castles and my land,
And fulfil all your desires, for I shall remain silent,
Save for one single thing: I want to be called king.'
Then smiled Vortigern (he was of evil much aware);
He was never so blithe before this in his life.   6670
Vortigern took his leave and off began to move,
And so he [traversed all Britain's area;
All castles and] all the land he set in his own hands,†
And men's homage he took always wherever he came,
And [then] took his messengers and sent them to Scotland,†
And summoned the Picts, the very best of all knights:
Three hundred came to him, and he wished to do well by them,
And to him those knights came after that very soon.
   Like this spoke the treacherous fellow: 'Sirs, you are welcome!*
I have in my hand all this royal dominion;   6680
With me you are to march, for much I shall love you,
And I shall conduct you into our king's presence:
You shall have silver and gold, the best horses in this land,
Clothes and lovely women; I'll do everything you want!
You shall be very dear to me, for the British I find despicable.
Publicly and privately I'll [fulfil your desires],*
If you in this land will regard me as lord.'
Then declared straight each one of these knights:
'We shall completely fulfil all that you will.'
And then they proceeded to Constance the king.   6690
   Towards the king went Vortigern (of evil he was well aware),
And told him of his deeds, how he had proceeded:
'And here I've brought the Picts, who are to become royal knights,
And all of your castles I have very well appointed,
And these foreign knights in our defence shall fight.'
Everything the king believed, as Vortigern intended,
But alas that the king of his thoughts knew nothing,
Nor of his treachery, which he did afterwards and quickly.
   Those knights in the retinue were highly respected;
For fully two years with the king they lived there,   6700

173

And Vortigern the justiciar over all of them was ruler,
He kept on saying the British were no more use than rubbish,
But he said that the Picts were very good knights.
Constantly the British were deprived of goods,
While the Picts commanded everything they wanted:
They had drink, they had food, and they had great fun as well;
Vortigern gave to them everything they wanted,
And he was as dear to them as their own life,
So they were all saying, in the place where they were dining,
That Vortigern rightly deserved to rule this nation,   6710
In absolutely everything, better than three similar kings.
Vortigern gave these characters a great deal of treasure.
    Now it happened one fine day, as in his house Vortigern stayed,
He took his two attendant knights and sent after the Picts,
Instructing them 'come here', for they were all to dine there.
To him came those knights, to his house straightaway;
He tempted them by talking as they sat there at the table;
He had them served with draughts of many kinds of liquor:
They swilled and they sang and the day slipped away.
When they were so drunk that their legs folded under them   6720
Then announced Vortigern what he'd been thinking long before:
'Now listen to me, knights: I am going to tell you straight
About my very great troubles; I've been most mournful about them.
The king entrusted this land to me as his own justiciar;
You are in this life to me the dearest of all men,
But I have no fine things to give out to my knights,
For this king owns all this land, and he is young, moreover strong,
And I have to give him everything I take from off his land,
And if I ruin things of his I must suffer the rule of law,
And my own income I have spent, for I like to give you
      pleasure.   6730
    And now I've got to go from here, far off to some king,
To serve him peaceably and with him obtain property;
I cannot, for fear of great disgrace, retain here this dwelling-place,
But off I've got to go, off to foreign places,
And if the day ever comes when I can gain some goods,
If I can succeed in this so well that you come to the land where I have
      gone,
Then I shall protect you well with the greatest honour;
And so now I wish you good day: tonight I will have to go away;
It is very much uncertain whether you'll see me ever again.'

These knights did not know what the traitor was thinking.   6740
Vortigern was disloyal, for in this he betrayed his lord,
And the knights took as truth what the traitor was saying.
Vortigern told his servants to saddle his horses,
And nominated twelve men to travel with himself.
On horseback they mounted as if leaving the country.
It was noted by the Picts, those completely drunken knights,
That Vortigern was about to leave; at this they felt very much grief.
They went to take counsel, they went to confer;
They all mourned for their very lives, so very much was their love for
     Vortigern,
And like this spoke the Picts, those drunken knights: 6750
'What shall we do now for advice? Who will now advise us?
Who is going to feed us? Who is going to clothe us?
Who at the court is going to be our lord?
Now Vortigern has gone away we must all scurry off.
No, not for anything will we have a monk as king!
But very well we will do; right away to him let's go,
Secretly and quietly and do everything we want;
Into his bedroom, and drink up his beer,
And when we have drunk, let's make a loud din,
And some must go to the door, stand with swords in front
     of it,   6760
And some straight seize the king and his knights,
And strike off the heads – and we ourselves 'll be having court.
And get quickly overtaken our lord Vortigern,
And then above all things have him as king.
Then can we live the way we find most likeable.'
    Off went the knights to the king in person straight;
In marched they all, right through the hall,
Into the king's bedroom, where he sat by the brazier.
There was no one there who spoke except **Gille Callaet**;
Like this to the king he spoke – he intended to betray him: 6770
'Listen to me now, land-king, it's not lies to you I'm telling.
In your retinue we've been greatly respected
Because of your steward, who has governed all this land.
He has fed us very well, he has clothed us very well.
And the truth is, I can tell you, we dined with him today just now,
But we bitterly regret that we had nothing there to drink,
And now that we are in your bedroom, give us some draughts of your
     good beer.

Then the king replied to them: 'That shall be your least concern,
For you shall certainly have liquor for as long as you would like to.'
They were served with their drinks, and they started to get
     noisy.   6780
Then announced Gille Callaet (at the door he stood alert):
'Where are you, you knights? Stir yourselves now, straight!'
And the king they then grabbed and off his head they   *Constance's*
     slashed,   *Murder*
And every one of his knights they killed there outright,
And got hold of a messenger and sent him towards London,*
So that he should gallop quickly in Vortigern's wake,
For him to come back quicky and take over the kingdom,
For he must know above all things that slain was Constance the king.
    This message reached Vortigern (a traitor in deep secrecy);
In this way he instructed the messenger to ride right back,   6790
And told them to 'guard safely all our reputations,
So that not a single one of them must go out of that area:
But all be waiting for me until my arrival,
And then I shall divide this land among us all.'
Off went that messenger and Vortigern at once took another
And sent all over London, to hustings summoning them,
Rapidly and very soon they were all to come.
    All the citizens had come there, very confident they were,
And then spoke up Vortigern (a traitor in deep secrecy),
Without pause he was weeping and painfully sighing,   6800
But it was all from his mind and not from his heart.
Then the citizens asked him, very confident they were:
'O Lord Vortigern, what is causing you distress?
You are not a woman to be so sadly weeping.'
Then responded Vortigern (a traitor in deep secrecy):
'I shall to you reveal a too pitiful tale,
Of absolute disaster which has settled on this land.
In this country I have been the steward of your king,
And have been his confidant and loved him as my life,
But he would not in the end [begin to understand,†
Nor in his actions act by my advice]†   6810a
He favoured the Picts, those alien knights,
But to us he did no good, nowhere gave a kind reception,
But to them he was gentle all of their lives.
I could not get from the king any king of recompense:
I spent my own means as long as they lasted,

And then I took leave to go to my lands,
And when I'd collected my taxes to come back to the court.
When it was noticed by the Picts that the king had no knights,
Nor even any kinsman who would do anything to prevent them,
They forced an entry into the king's bedroom.   6820
I'm telling you the truth of the thing: they have actually killed the
    king!
And they intend to bring downfall on this kingdom and us all,
And they want without delaying to make a Pict the king.
But I was his steward, and I shall avenge my lord,
And let every brave man aid me to do that.
On will I put my armour, and straightway I shall travel.'
    There marched out of London knights numbering three hundred:
They rode and they ran, off with Vortigern.
Until they were approaching where the Picts were [stationed];[†]
And he took one of his knights and sent him to the Picts.   6830
To inform them he was coming, if they wished to entertain him.
The Picts showed enthusiasm for their own coming doom,
And put on their best gear – they had there neither shield nor spear.
Vortigern, most forthright, weaponed all his knights,
And there came the Picts, bringing the head of the king.
    When Vortigern saw this head he collapsed nearly to the ground,
As if suffering deep emotion, the most of all those men;
With his looks he was lying, for his heart was rejoicing.
Then announced Vortigern (who was a traitor in deep secrecy):
'Let every brave man with his sword lay into them,   6840
And avenge well on this earth the disaster of our lord.'
They did not capture any living, but each one of them they killed,
And went into the house inside Winchester
And slaughtered their servants and their attendants,
Their cooks and their boys – all they deprived of their life-days.
    In this way spread the tidings of Constance the king,
And worldly-wise men had charge of the other children:
Because of their concern about Vortigern they took Ambrose and
    Uther
And carried them abroad into Little Britain.
And graciously entrusted them to **Budiz** the king,   6850
Who as graciously received them: he was their relative and friend,
And with very great pleasure he supervised the children,
And so for very many years they lived with him there.
    In this land Vortigern was elevated to the throne;   VORTIGERN

All the stalwart British were within his power;
For twenty-five years he was king here.
He was crazy, he was wild, he was fierce and he was bold,*
In everything he had his desire — except for the Picts who were never
    quiet,
But constantly they entered all across the northern end,
And laid hold on this kingdom with uncountable horrors,   6860
And more than avenged their kindred here whom Vortigern killed.
   Meanwhile there came tidings into this land
That Aurelius (called Ambrosius) had been made a knight,
And so too was Uther: a good knight and very prudent,
And they wished to come to this land leading an army strong in
    numbers.
This was a remark which was frequently repeated;
The messages kept coming to Vortigern the king.
At this he often felt ashamed and his feelings were enraged
For men were saying almost everywhere: 'Here come Ambrosius and
    Uther,
And they wish to avenge Constance, [who was] king in this
    land.†   6870
Their course can be no other: they wish to avenge their brother,
And to kill Vortigern and him to dust and ashes burn;
So all of this land they will set in their own hand.'
So went the gossip every day of all who walked along the ways.
   Vortigern thought carefully of what could be his remedy,
And decided to send messages into other lands,
For knights from foreign places who might be his defence,
And intended to be wary against Ambrosius and Uther.
   Meanwhile there came tidings to Vortigern the king
That across the sea had come some very strange men,   6880
Up into the Thames they had come ashore:*
Three ships fine and good had arrived on the flood,
Three hundred knights, to all appearances kings,
Not counting the mariners who were below the decks there.
These were the most handsome men who ever came here,
But they were heathens, the more harm it was!
Vortigern sent to them and asked them their intentions,
Was it peace they were seeking and his friendship requesting?
Wisely they responded as they well knew how,
And said that they wanted to speak to the king,   6890
And lovingly revere him and regard him as their leader,

And so they started moving off to meet the king.
At that time King Vortigern was in Canterbury,
Where he and his court were holding high council;
There these knights arrived before the people's king:
As soon as they encountered him politely they saluted him,
Saying that they wished to serve him in this land,
If he were willing to support them and give them fair treatment.
  Then Vortigern responded (of every evil he was aware):
'For the whole of my life, as long as I've lived,   6900
By day or by night never have I yet seen such knights.
At your coming I'm delighted, and with me you must remain,
And your wishes I'll comply with, by my living life!
But from you I wish to learn, as you are true and worthy,
What knights you may be, and from what place you have come,
And whether you'll be as true, when vows are old, as new?'
Then answered the other, who was the eldest brother:
'Listen to me now, my lord king, and I shall inform you*
What knights we are and where it is we say we come from.
I am called **Hengest**, **Horsa** here's my brother;   6910
We come from Germany, most glorious of all lands,   *Hengest*
From that same area which is called Angle.   *and Horsa*
There are in our land very strange proceedings:
After every fifteen years the people are assembled,
All our national tribes, and they cast their lots:
He upon whom it falls must travel from the land;
Five are allowed to stay; the sixth must set off
Out of the country, into strange regions;
However popular he is, he must depart,
For the population there is huge, higher than they can control: 6920
A woman produces children as wild creatures do;
Every single year she'll have a baby there.
The [lot] fell on us so that we had to leave;†
We could not be left out, not for life or for death,
Not ever for any thing, for fear of the people's king.
So [things go on] there and therefore we are here,†
To seek beneath the [heavens] for land and a good lord.†
Now you have heard, my lord the king, the truth about us in all
      details.'
  Then answered Vortigern (of each evil he was aware):
'I believe you, sir, that you tell me the truth all right.   6930
And what are your beliefs which you believe in?

And your beloved god, to whom you all bow?'
Then replied Hengest, of all knights the fairest,
There is not in this kingdom's land a knight so tall nor yet so strong:
'We have powerful gods whom we love in our heart, *
In whom we have hope and whom we serve with our strength.
The first is called Phoebus and the second is Saturn;
The third is called Woden, who is a wealth-giving god;
The fourth is called Jupiter, of everything he is aware;
The fifth is called Mercury, who is the highest over us;   6940
The sixth is called Apollin, who is a god most splendid;
The seventh is called Tervagant, a high god in our land.
In addition we have a lady who is most high and mighty;
High she is and holy – courtiers love her for this:
She is called Frea; well does she direct them.
But before all our dear gods, whom we are bound to obey,
Woden had the highest rule in our elders' days:
To them he was dear, just as much as their life;
He was their ruler and they treated him with respect;
The fourth day in the week [we] give him for his worship.†   6950
To the Thunder [we] give Thursday, because he can give [us] aid. *
Frea [our] lady, [we] give to her Friday;
Saturn [we] give Saturday, to the sun [we] give Sunday;
To the Moon [we] give Monday, and to Tidea [we] g[i]ve Tuesday.'†
So spoke Hengest, of all knights the handsomest.
    Then responded Vortigern (of every evil he was aware):
'Knights, you are dear to me, but this report to me is dismal!
Your [beliefs] are iniquitous: you do not believe in Christ,†
But you believe in the Devil, whom God himself has damned;
Your gods are just worthless; in hell they lie lowest.   6960
But nevertheless I shall maintain you in my command,
For in the north are the Picts, very valiant knights,
Who often lead into my lands their forces which are very strong,
And often badly disgrace me, and this makes me enraged.
And if you will avenge me, and obtain their heads for me,
Then I'll give you land, much silver and gold.'
Then answered Hengest, of all knights the fairest:
'If it is the will of Saturnus, it shall all happen thus,
And of Woden our lord, in whom we believe.'
    Hengest took his leave, and to his ships did proceed.   6970
There were many knights who were strong: they dragged their ships
        up on the land.

Off went the soldiers to Vortigern the king.
At their head went Hengest, and of all men Horsa closest to him,
Then the men of Germany who were noble in their actions,
And afterwards they sent to him their splendid Saxon knights,[*]
Hengest's relatives [of his ancestors'] race.[*†]
Making much bravado they all marched into the hall:
Better were garbed and better were fed
Hengest's servers than Vortigern's landholders.
Then Vortigern's retinue were treated as ridiculous;　　　　　6980
The British were saddened by such an appearance.
　　It was not very long before there came to the king
Five sons of knights who had travelled with speed;
They reported to the king some recent tidings:
'Now rightaway the Picts have arrived:
They are riding through your land, and ravaging and burning,
And all the northern area they've laid flat to the ground.[†]
You must decide about this or we shall all be dead.'
The king thought carefully what might be his policy:
He sent to their lodgings for all of his soldiers.　　　　　　6990
There came Hengest, there came Horsa, there came many a man most
　　　　brave;
There came the Saxon men, who were Hengest's kinsmen,
And the German knights, who are excellent in fight.
This observed King Vortigern: happy was he then and there.
　　The Picts followed their custom: this side of the Humber they'd
　　　　come,
And King Vortigern of their coming was fully aware.
They clashed together and slew many there;
There was very strong fighting, combat most severe.
The Picts were well accustomed to conquering Vortigern,
And thought they would then also – but then it turned out quite
　　　　another way,
For it was a saving factor that our men had Hengest there,[*]　　7001
With those knights so strong who came out of Saxony,
And the bold men of Germany who came this way with Horsa.
Very many Picts they slaughtered in that fight.
Furiously they fought: the fated there fell.
When the third hour had come the Picts were overcome,
And swiftly away they fled, on every side away they sped,
And all the day they were in flight, many and uncountable.
　　King Vortigern went to his pavilion,

And always very close to him were Horsa and Hengest.   7010
Hengest was favoured by the king: to him he gave Lindsey,
And he gave to Horsa plenty of treasures,
And all their knights he treated all right.
And for a good space things stood on the same footing:
The Picts were too scared to come into the land,
There were no pillagers nor outlaws who were not swiftly executed,
And Hengest most handsomely was serving the king.
     Then it happened at one time when the king was very happy,
On a festival day, among his men of first rank,
Hengest was thinking carefully what should be his policy,   7020
For with the king he wanted to hold a secret conclave.
He went and stood before the king and gave him courteous
          greeting;
The king at once stood up, and seated him beside himself.
They drank and they grew merry: they were full of enjoyment.
Then said Hengest to the king: 'Lord, are you listening?
I want to give you news in very secret whispers;
If you wish to listen well to what you learn from me,
And will not be enraged at what I impart.'
The response of the king was: let Hengest have his wish.
     Then announced Hengest, of all knights the fairest: 7030
Lord, I have for many a day enhanced your dignity,
And been your loyal man in your luxurious court,
And in every fight the most superior knight,
And often I've been hearing anxious whisperings
Among your retainers: they really hate you deeply,
To the very death, if they dared to reveal it.
Often they speak very softly, and in whispers they discuss
Two young men living a long way from here;
One of them is called Uther, the other Ambrosius;
There was a third called Constance who was king in this
          [country],[†]   7040
And here he was murdered by treasonable practices;
Now will come the others and avenge their brother,
And totally burn up your land and slaughter those who live here,
And yourself and your bodyguard they'll drive out of the land,
And this is what your men are saying as they sit together,
Seeing the two brothers are [both] born of a king,[†]
From Aldroien's race, these nobles of Brittany.
In this way your doughty men silently condemn you.

But I will give you advice for your great problem,
That you acquire knights who are valiant in fight,   7050
And deliver to me a castle or a royal borough
In which I may reside for the whole of my life;
Because of you I'm hated: for that I expect death.
If I go wherever I may go, I am never free from stress,
Unless I am securely lying enclosed within a castle.
If you will do this for me, I shall accept it with affection,
And I shall speedily send for my wife:
She is a Saxon woman, well endowed with wisdom,
And for **Rowena**, who is my daughter, and very dear to me she is.
When I have my wife, and my close relations,   7060
And I am within your land fully established,
Then all the better will I serve you, if you allow me this.'
    Then replied Vortigern (of each evil he was aware):
'Take knights and swiftly, and send for your wife,
And for your children, the young and the older,
And for your relations: receive them with elation:
When they have come to you, you shall have wealth,
To feed them in luxury and splendidly clothe them.
But I shall not deliver you either castle or borough,
For I should be reviled within my own kingdom,   7070
Since you retain the heathen customs which were current in your
        elders' times,
And we uphold Christ's ways and will for ever do so all our days.'
Then again spoke Hengest, of all knights the handsomest:
'My lord, I will perform your will, in this and in all things,
And make all my actions accord with your advice.
Now I will speedily send for my wife,
And for my daughter, so dear to me she is,
And for bold men, the best from my race,
And you give me as much land to remain for ever in my hands
As a single bull's hide will in each direction cover,   7080
Far from every castle, in the middle of a field.
Then no one can accuse you, the humble nor the aristocrats,
That ever any high town to a heathen man you've given.'
The king granted to him just what Hengest craved.
    Hengest took his leave and off he proceeded,
And sent a message for his wife to his own land,
And he himself went through this land searching for a wide field,
On which he could extend fully his splendid hide.*

He came upon an area in a lovely plain;
He had obtained a hide suited to his need   7090
From a wild bull, and it was wonderfully strong.
He had a clever man who was well trained in skills,   *The Bull's*
Who took up this hide, laid it out on a board,   *Hide*
And sharpened his knives, preparing to slice;
From the hide he cut a thong, very narrow and very long;
This thong was not very wide, only like a thread of twine.
When all the thong was slit, it was wonderfully long;
Hengest stretched it round a huge tract of land.
He began to excavate a very deep ditch,
On top of it a stone wall, which was strong over all.   7100
He erected a town, a great one and glorious;
When the town was quite complete he assigned it a name:
He called it, now note this, Kaer Carrai in British,
And the English knights called it 'Thong-chester';
Now and for all time the name remains the same,
And not from any other exploit did the town carry that name,
Until the Danish men arrived, and drove out the Britons,
They applied a third name there, and Long-castle they called it,
And from all these men, the town had these three names.†
   Meanwhile Hengest's wife came here, travelling with her
      ships;   7110
She had as her escort fifteen hundred riders,
And with her came, to be specific, eighteen enormous ships,
There arrived in them many of Hengest's own kindred,
And Rowena his daughter, very dear to him she was.
It was after a short while that there came the actual time
When the city was completed among the very best;
Hengest came to the king and offered him hospitality,
Saying that he had a place prepared ready to receive him,
Inviting him to come to it, where he would graciously be welcome,
And the king granted him what Hengest wanted.   7120
   Then arrived the time for the king to proceed,
With the most esteemed men from all of his court.
Off he started travelling until he reached the town;
He gazed at the walls, up and down and all round,
And he liked very much everything he looked at.
He went into the hall, and all his men with him;
Fanfares were sounding; entertainments they were announcing.
The trestle-boards were spread, and knights sat down at them:*

They ate and they drank; there was joyful din in town.
    When the courtiers had eaten, even better luck befell them: 7130
Hengest went into the chamber where lodged fair Rowena.
He had her attired with excessive pride: *Rowena*
Every garment which she had on was extremely finely made,
They were among the best, embroidered with gold thread.
She carried in her hand a bowl made of gold,
Filled up with wine which was exquisitely good.
High-born men escorted her to hall,
In the presence of the king, she the fairest of all things.
Rowena went down on her knees and called out to the king,
And said for the first time in the land of the English: 7140
'Lord king, wassail! I am delighted at your coming.'*
The king heard this but did not know what she was saying.
King Vortigern asked his knights at once
What were those phrases which the maiden uttered.
Then replied **Keredic**, a knight who was most gifted
He was the best interpreter who [ever] came here:[†]
'Listen to me now, lord king, and I shall explain to you
What Rowena is saying, the loveliest of women.
It is a custom, in the Saxons' land
Wherever any band of men is revelling in drink,   7150
That a friend should say to a friend with sweet, gracious expression:
"Dear friend, wassail"; the other replies: "Drink hail".
The one who holds the bowl, he drinks it all up;
A second full goblet is brought there and is offered to his companion;
When that goblet arrives, then they kiss three times.
These are the pleasing customs within Saxony,
And in Germany they are considered noble.'
This was heard by Vortigern (of each evil he was aware),
And spoke this in British (he did not know any English):
'Maiden Rowena, then drink happily!'   7160
The girl drank up the wine and had some more poured in,
And had it offered to the king, and three times she kissed him,
And through that same race those customs came to this land:
"Wassail and drink hail"; many a man is glad about that!
    Rowena the lovely sat beside the king;
The king looked at her with desire; he was deeply in love with her:
Again and again he kissed her; again and again he embraced her,
All his feelings and his powers were bent on that girl:
The Devil was very close there (in [such] sport he is rampant);[†]

The Devil never does anyone good: he disturbed the king's emotions.
Sadly he yearned to have the maiden as his wife,   7171
It was a very heinous thing that the Christian king
Was in love with the heathen girl to his nation's harm.
To the king the girl was just as dear as his own life was;
He asked Hengest his tenant to give him that girl-child.
Hengest found this a good idea, to do as the king urged him;
He gave him Rowena, a very lovely woman.
The king found it [agreeable]: he made her his queen,†
All according to the laws they had in heathen days;
There was no Christian rite where the king took that maid,   7180
No priest and no bishop nor was God's book taken in their hands,
But in the heathen ritual he her wedded and he brought her to his bed.
As a virgin he took her, and the morning-gift he bestowed on her;*
When he had disgraced himself with her, he gave her London and
         Kent.
   The king had three sons, who were very courteous men:
The eldest was called **Vortimer**, then **Passent** and **Katiger**.
Garengan was the earl who'd owned Kent a long time,
As had his father before him, and then he through his descent;
When he most expected to retain his land,
Then Hengest had got it in his own hands;   7190
Strange it seemed to the knight what the king intended.
The king loved the heathens, and punished the Christians;
The heathens had all this land to govern under their own hand,
And the three sons of the king often suffered sorrow and care.
Their mother was then dead, for which reason they had less guidance;
Their mother was a very good woman who led a very Christian life,
But their stepmother was heathen, the daughter of Hengest.
   It did not take long, just a short while,
Before the king gave a really huge banquet;
He invited the heathens to it: he thought to act for the very
         best.   7200
To it came landholders, knights and landworkers,
But all who were literate avoided the banquet,
Because the heathen men had highest rank at the court,
And the Christian courtiers were accounted menials.
Then the heathens were happy because the king loved them so much.
Hengest thought carefully about his diplomacy:
He came to the king with a salutation,
And drank to the king.

Then like this spoke Hengest, the handsomest of all the knights
Who in those days were living under heathen laws: 7210
'Listen to me, my lord the king: you are my beloved above all things:
You have my daughter, who is so dear to me,
And I am to you in people's eyes as if I were your father.
Listen to my instructions: they shall prove attractive to you,
For I wish supremely to assist you to decide.
Your court hate you because of me, and are hostile to me because of
    you,
And those who hate you are kings, earls and leaders:
They advance into your land as a very large invasion.
If you wish to get your own back, with increased dignity,
And do your opponents harm, then send for my son **Octa**,   7220
And for yet one other, **Ebissa** his sworn-brother:
These are the boldest men who ever led an armed band,
And in the northern parts give them some of your lands.
They are magnificent in might and strong in every fight;
They will give defence to your land well among the best;
Then all your life you might wear away in full delight,
With hawks and with hounds enjoying courtly games;
You need never feel anxiety about foreign nations.'
    Then answered King Vortigern (of each evil he was wary):
'Send your messengers out into Saxony   7230
To fetch your son Octa and to fetch more of your friends.
Have him fully instructed to send out his missives
For all of the knights who are valiant in fight
Through all the Saxon nation, that they come to me in my great need,
And even if he brings a thousand, to me they are all welcome.'
This was heard by Hengest, of all knights the handsomest:
Then he was more blithe than ever in his life;
Hengest sent his messengers out into Saxony,
And ordered here Octa and his sworn-brother Ebissa,
And all of their relations whom they could obtain,   7240
And all of the knights whom they could acquire.
    Octa sent messages all through three kingdoms,
Bidding each and every brave man to come to him in haste
If he wanted to get lands, or get silver or get gold.
They arrived at the court as hailstones come tumbling,
To be more specific: in three hundred ships.
They set off with Octa, thirty thousand and yet more,
Bold men and courageous; and Ebissa his companion

Came voyaging after with countless supporters,
And the ships he led, precisely, were a hundred and fifty.   7250
After these came sliding five, and then five,
In sixes, in sevens, in tens and in elevens,
And so they came slipping towards this our land,
Heathen war-lords to the court of the king,
Until this land was so full of the foreign people
That there was no man so wise nor so quick-witted
That he could distinguish between the heathens and the Christians,
For the heathen were so rife, and were so rapidly arriving.
    When the British realised that there was trouble in the land,
They were most distressed about it and gloomy in their
              hearts,   7260
And they went to the king, the noblest in this land,
And addressed him as follows, in sorrowful tones:
'Listen to us now, lord king, from our people's council:
You because of us are the bold king in this Britain,
And you have brought upon yourself danger and much sinfulness,
Have brought in heathen people: it will still bring you harm,
And you abandon God's laws for these foreign people
And refuse to honour our Lord God for these heathen knights,
And we wish to request you for the sake of God's blessing
That you will relinquish them and drive them from your land.   7270
Or else, if you're not able to, we'll make a great confrontation,
And drive them from the land or fell them to the ground,
Or else we ourselves dead will lie there slaughtered,
And let the heathen hordes have control of the kingdom,
Enjoy it in comfort, if they can conquer it;
And if they are all heathen, and you are a Christian,
It won't be for very long that they keep you as king,
Unless you in your days will adopt heathen ways,
And abandon God Most High, and love their false idols.
Then you will be destroyed in the kingdom of this world   7280
And your wretched soul will sink down to Hell,
And you will have paid for the love of your bride.'
    Then responded Vortigern (of each evil he was aware):
'I will not relinquish them, by my living life!
For here has Hengest come: he is my father and I his son,
And I have as my beloved his daughter Rowena,
Whom I have wedded and taken to my bed,
And then I sent for Octa and for more of his companions;

188

So how could I, for shame, shun them so quickly,
Drive from the land my own friends so dear?'   7290
Then the British answered, bent down by sorrows:
'Never any more will we obey your instructions,
Nor come to your court here, nor regard you as king,
Rather, we will hate, with our utmost powers,
All your heathen friends, and with harm treat them.
We pray for our assistance from Christ who is God's son!'
   Off went the earls, off went the warriors,
Off went the bishops, and the book-learned clerics,
Off went the landholders, off went the landworkers,
All the people of Britain, till they came to London.   7300
There was many a noble Briton there at the hustings,
And the king's three sons; there all of them had come:
There was Vortimer, and Passent and Katiger
And very many others who came with the brothers,
And all people came there to the city who loved Christianity;
All the powerful people consulted together,
And took the king's eldest son (to the hustings he had come),
And with many songs of praise they raised him to the throne.
And so was Vortimer the Christian king there,   VORTIMER
And Vortigern his father followed the heathen;   7310
[It all came about as the decision had been made.]†   7310a
   Vortimer the young king had great courage above all things:
He sent word to Hengest and to Horsa his brother
That unless they would hastily travel from his kingdom
He would do them great evil: both blind them and hang them,
And his own father he wished to destroy,
And all the heathen race with most heavy force.
To which replied Hengest, of all knights the handsomest,
'Here we intend to remain, both winter and summer,
To ride and to run alongside King Vortigern,
And all those who side with Vortimer, they shall receive much sorrow
    and care!'
This was heard by Vortimer (he was wise and really aware)   7321
And summoned all his forces throughout all this nation,
Saying all the Christian folk were to come to court.
   Vortimer the young king in London held his hustings:
The king instructed each man who loved the Christian faith
That they must have hatred for the heathen race,
Whose heads they must bring to Vortimer the king,

Twelve pennies to receive as reward for [their] good deed.†
Vortimer the young advanced out of London,
And Passent his brother and Katiger the other;   7330
To them had come word that Hengest was at [Epi]ford,*
Upon that river which people call Derwent.
    There assembled together sixty thousand soldiers,
On one side was Vortimer, Passent and Katiger,
And all people living here who bore love for Our Lord;
On the other side were warriors with Vortigern the king:
Hengest and his brother and many thousand others.
Together they clashed and with force they attacked;
There fell to the ground thirty-two hundred
Of Hengest's men, and Horsa was badly wounded: 7340
Katiger had come there and with his spear had run him through,
And Horsa instantly there badly wounded Katiger,
And Hengest began to flee with all his soldiery,
And Vortigern the king fled off like the wind;
They fled onwards into Kent, and after them went Vortimer;
Upon the sea's edge, there Hengest suffered anguish:
There they made a stand, and fought for very long;
Five thousand there were slain and deprived of their life's days
On Vortigern's side, from the heathen tribes.
    Hengest thought carefully what might be his remedy: 7350
He saw on the side there a very splendid harbour:
Many a ship good there floated on the sea-flood.
They spotted on their right hand a very pretty island:
This is called Thanet: to get to it they moved smartly;
There those Saxon men took to the sea
And instantly started going out to the island,
And the British after them with many kinds of craft,
And driving across to them from every direction
With ships and with boats. They started striking and shooting.
Often had Hengest been sad and never till then were things so
        bad: 7360
Unless he took another course, he was going to get killed.
He took a spear shaft which was long and very strong,
And fixed on the tip a finely-made mantle,
And called to the Britons and asked them to wait:
With them he wanted speech and craved the king's peace,
And in peace to send Vortigern to land,
To make agreement with him that he must get away,

To prevent further shame done to the Saxons' land.
    The British went ashore, to Vortimer their king,
And Hengest spoke to Vortigern of very secret matters.   7370
Vortigern went up on land carrying a rod in his hand;
While they were discussing peace, the Saxons leaped aboard,
And dragged high their sails right up to the top,
Travelling with the weather upon the wild sea,
And leaving in this land their wives and their children,
And Vortigern the king, who loved them above all things.
With much grief of heart did Hengest turn to depart:
So long they journeyed until in Saxony they arrived.
    Then within Britain were the British very bold:
They took upon themselves great spirit and did everything they felt
      was needed,
And Vortimer the young was a valiant man above all things,   7381
And Vortigern his father went faring all through Britain,
But there was no man so feeble who did not pour scorn on him,
And so he went wandering for fully five winters,
And his son Vortimer, great king, was dwelling here,
And all the native people loved him very greatly:
He was gentle with every child and taught the folk God's law,
Taught the old and the young how they must keep their Christian
      faith.
Letters he had sent to Rome to the glorious Pope,
Who was called Saint **Romanus**; all Christendom he made   7390
      rejoice.
He selected two bishops, holy men were they both:
Germanus and **Lupus**, of Auxerre and of Troyes;   *Saint Germanus*
They travelled away from Rome until they hither came.
Then more blithe was Vortimer than he had ever yet been here.
He and all his knights made their way direct,
Walking barefoot, going to meet the bishops,
And with great happiness lips there did kiss.
    Now you can hear about King Vortimer,
How he spoke to Saint Germanus of how their coming made him
      glad:
'Listen to me, my lords, your graces: I am king of all this race;   7400
My name is Vortimer, this is my brother Katiger;
Vortigern was our father's name: evil doctrines make him foul.
He has brought into this land heathen people,
But we have driven them in exile as our sworn enemies,

And with weapons struck down many thousands of them,
And sent them over the sea-streams so they never succeed in coming
    back,
And in the land we shall love God our Lord,
God's people we shall comfort, and in friendship keep them,
And also be supportive to those who till the land;
Churches we shall erect and heathendom reject.   7410
Let each good man have his rights if these God will grant,
And each slave and each foreign captive will be set free;
And here I donate into your hand quite freely all church land,
And I donate to every widow her lord's legacy,
[And each man will love the other as if they were brothers],[†]   7414a
And so we shall in our own days bring down low Hengest's laws,
And himself and his heathendom which he has brought here,
[Who] deceived my father with his treacherous wiles:[†]
Through his daughter Rowena he miscounselled my father,
And my father proceeded most wickedly by renouncing his Christen-
    dom:
The heathen religion he loved far too much;   7420
These we shall avoid as long as we live.'
    Then replied St Germanus (at such words he rejoiced):
'I give thanks to my lord who created the day's light
That he sends such mercy down to mankind.'
    The bishops travelled round this land and placed it all within God's
    hand,
And Christianity they established and to it folk directed,
And then after this, quite soon, they went off back to Rome,
Informing the Pope there, who was called Romanus,
How they had been acting here, establishing Christianity.
And so for a time things remained the same.   7430
    Let us pick up again at Vortigern (of all kings may he be most
    wretched!);
He loved Rowena of the heathen race,
Daughter of Hengest: she seemed to him so soft.
Rowena thought carefully what should be her policy,
How she could avenge her father and the deaths of her friends.
She kept on sending messages to Vortimer the king;
She sent to him precious things of many different kinds,
Of silver and of gold; the best of any land;
She begged for his mercy that she might go on living here,
With his father, Vortigern, and follow his instructions.   7440

The king at his father's plea granted what she pleaded,
Save that she must behave well and embrace Christianity;
Everything the king requested, all she conceded,
But alas that Vortimer of her intent was not aware!
Alas that the good king of her intent knew nothing!
That he did not know the treachery plotted by the evil woman.
   It happened at one time that she adopted a plan
[That she would travel to meet King Vortimer;†   7447a
To act on his advice] in all her needs,
And to ask what time she could act well by receiving Christianity.
She set off riding, to Vortimer the king;   7450
When she had met him, courteously she greeted him:
'Good health to you, my lord the king, the Britons' own darling!
I have come here to you: I wish to take the Christian faith,
On whichever day that you yourself decide.'
   Then Vortimer the king was happy above all things:
He thought it was truth that the she-devil spoke.
Brass trumpets were blowing; there was bliss in the court.
They brought out the water before the king's presence;
They set up the trestles in greatest delight.
When the king had eaten, then the lords' sevitors took food: 7460
In the hall they were drinking, harps were resounding.
The deceitful Rowena went over to a wine-tun;
There was stored inside it the king's most precious wine.
She took in her hand a goblet of red gold,
And she began to pour the drinks at the king's high table.
When she saw her time, she filled her cup with wine,
And in the presence of all the company she went up to the king,
And like this the deceitful woman gave him salutation:
'Lord, king, wassail; I am celebrating with you!'
   Now listen how much treachery came from that wicked
      woman,   7470
How she set about it there, her betrayal of King Vortimer.
The king cheerfully received her for what was to be his doom;
Vortimer spoke British, Rowena spoke in Saxon;
The king found it most amusing: her speech set him laughing.
Hear now how she was going on, [this] deceitful woman:†
In her bosom she carried, underneath her breasts,
A flask all of gold, filled up with poison,
And the wicked Rowena drank deep in the bowl
Until it was half drained, on the king's direction;

While the king was laughing, she slipped out the flask,   7480
Set the bowl up to her chin and tipped the poison in the wine,
And then handed the cup over to the king.
The king drank up all the wine and the poison in it.
   The day went past; all the court was rejoicing,
For Vortimer the good king of the treachery knew nothing,
Since he saw there Rowena holding the bowl
And drinking half of the same wine which she had poured into it.
When it came to night time then came the parting of the court
    knights,
And the evil Rowena went to her apartment,
And all her own knights accompanied her straight.   7490
Then she ordered her servants and also the attendants
That they should speedily get their horses saddled,
And they should most silently steal out of the township
And travel right through the night to Thongchester directly,
And there most securely enclose themselves in a castle,
And lie to Vortigern that his son was going to besiege him;
And Vortigern the traitorous king believed in the lying.
   Now Vortimer his son realised he'd taken poison;
Nor could any medicine give him any relief at all.
He took many messengers and sent them round his country,   7500
And ordered all his knights to come over to him straightaway.
By the time the folk came the king was gravely stricken.
Then the king begged their favour and like this addressed them all:
'Of all knights may things be best for those of you who serve a king:
There is now no other course except my imminent decease.
Here I bequeath you my land, all my silver and all my gold,
And my entire treasury: your reputation's thus enhanced;
And do you directly send out for knights,
And give them silver and gold and yourselves hold all your land,
And avenge yourselves if you can on every Saxon man,   7510
For as soon as I have departed, Hengest will make great trouble for
    you.
So take up my corpse and lay it in a chest,
And convey me to the sea-shore where Saxon men will come to land.
As soon as they know that I am there they will go away again;
Neither dead nor alive do they dare to await me!'
In the middle of this discourse the good king collapsed and died.
There was weeping, there was wailing and gestures of grief.
They took the king's corpse and carried it to London

And beside Billingsgate with ceremony buried him,
And in no way did they carry him to where the king had
    ordered.   7520
So lived Vortimer, and so he died there.
    Then the Britons declined into a disastrous plan:
They at once took Vortigern and proferred him this   VORTIGERN
    kingdom.
Really pitiful there was everything now that Vortigern was again
    king.
Vortigern took his messenger and sent message to the Saxons,
Saluting well Hengest, of all knights the fairest,
Telling him speedily to come to this land,
And with him he should bring here a full hundred riders,
'For know this above all things, of the death of Vortimer the king,
And in safety here you may come, for dead is Vortimer my
    son.   7530
There is no need for you to bring a large troop along
In case our Britons get angry again
So that once more sorrows slip in between you.'
    Hengest summoned a force from many different places,
Until he had, to be specific, seven hundred ships,
And each ship he supplied with three hundred knights.
In the Thames at London Hengest came to land.
The news came very quickly to Vortigern the king
That Hengest was in harbour with seven hundred ships;
Often Vortigern had been sad, but not till then were things so
    bad,
And the British were saddened and gloomy in spirit;   7541
They did not know where in the world was a remedy to suit them.
Hengest of evil was well aware (and that he well showed there):
At once he took his messengers and sent them to the king,
And greeted King Vortigern with very courteous words,
And said that he had come, as a father should to his son,
In harmony and concord he'd like to live contented;
Peace he would love, injustice he would avoid;
Peace he would have, peace he would hold to,
And all the people of this land he would surely love,   7550
And Vortigern the king he would love above everything.
But he had brought into this land, from the Saxon people,
Seven hundred ships with heathen folk,
Who are the bravest of all men who live beneath the sun:

'And I wish', said Hengest, 'to conduct them to the king,
On an appointed day, in the presence of his courtiers,
And the king is to arise, and from those knights select
Two hundred knights to conduct to his fights,
Who shall protect the king honourably above all things,
And then are the others to return to their country,   7560
Peacefully and happily going back to Saxon lands,
And I will remain with the best of all men,
Namely Vortigern the king, whom I love above all things.'
The word came to the Britons of what Hengest had promised them:
Then they were delighted because of his fine words,
And arranged the peace and arranged the truce for a specific time
When the king on a certain day wished to review his troops.

    This was heard by Hengest, of all knights the handsomest;
Then was he more blithe than he'd been ever in his life
As he intended to betray the king and his realm.   7570
Here Hengest became the most depraved of knights,
As is every man who betrays the one who freely pays him.
Who would expect, in all this world's extent,
That Hengest thought to trick the king who had taken his daughter?
Yet there was never any man who could not be overcome by treason.
They took an appointed day when all the troops must come
Together in truce, and in friendship too,
On a lovely meadow which lay beside Amesbury.
Then the place was Ealing, now it's known as **Stonehenge.**[*]
There Hengest the traitor both in word and in writing   7580
Let the king know that he was coming,
With his body-guard, in the king's honour,
But he would not bring in his force more than three hundred knights,
The very wisest men whom he could find,
And the king should bring just as many of his brave supporters,
Who should be the very wisest of all who lived in Britain,
In their best clothing, quite without weapons,
So that they should not come to grief through trusting in the
    weapons.
Like this they proposed it, and then again they broke it,
For Hengest the traitor, like this he taught his men: 7590
That each should take a long knife and lay it beside his leg,
Inside his hose, where [he could] hide it.[†]
    When they came together, Saxons and British,
Then said Hengest, of all knights the most deceitful:

'Health to you, my lord king, each to you is your *The British*
    subject, *Massacre*
If any of your men at all has any war-gear round here,
Let him send it in amity far away from us,
And let us be joyful and treat now of truce,
Now we may in peacefulness live out our lives.'
So the malicious man there deceived the British.   7600
Then answered Vortigern (this time he was too unaware!)
'If any knight here is so mad as to have weapons at his side,
He must forfeit his hand through his own blade,
Unless at once he sends it far away from here.'
They sent their weapons right away; then they had nothing in their
    hands.
    Knights were walking up the field, knights were walking down the
    field,
Each chatting to the other as if he were his brother.
When the British were mingling with the Saxons,
Then shouted Hengest, of all knights the most deceitful:
'Take up your saxes, my lucky warriors,*   7610
And busily bestir yourselves, don't spare any one of them!'
    The British there were noble but they did not know the speech at
    all,
Or what the Saxon men were saying among themselves.
They drew out the saxes in every direction:
They struck on the right side, they struck on the left side,
In front and behind they laid them to the ground;
Everyone they slew whom they came near to;
Of the king's men [instantly] there fell†
Four hundred and five; the king's very life was grief.
Then Hengest seized him in his grim clutches,   7620
And by his mantle dragged him until the strings broke,
And the Saxons set upon him, wanting to kill the king,
And Hengest was defending him, and would not permit it,
But he held on to him very fast all the time the fight lasted.
    There many a fine Briton was deprived of his life:
Some fled hurriedly across the broad field,
And defended themselves with stones, for weapons had they none.
There was a very hard fight: there fell many a good knight.
    There had come from Salisbury a bold peasant fellow;
A huge powerful club he carried on his back.   7630
Then there was a valiant earl who was called **Aldolf**

A knight of the best: he was lord of Gloucester;
He went leaping to the peasant just like a lion,
And snatched away his club which he carried on his back;
Every single one he struck upon the instant died;
In front and behind he laid them to the ground,
Fifty-three there he slew and then towards [his] steed drew off;[†]
He leaped up on horseback and rode off in a hurry;
He galloped to Gloucester, and locked the gates most securely,
And immediately straight after had his knights get themselves
    armed,   7640
And all over the land they were to take what they found:
They took cattle, they took corn, and everything they found alive,
And brought them to the borough with the greatest pleasure.
The gates they barred firmly and guarded them well.

    Let us leave things standing like that and let's speak of the king:
Saxons leaped towards him and wanted to destroy the king.
Hengest called out straight 'Stop now, my knights!
You are not to harm him: he's had much trouble on our account,
And he has as his queen my daughter who's so lovely;
But all his fortified places he is to donate us   7650
If he wishes to enjoy his life, or otherwise he's doomed to misery.'

    Then Vortigern was firmly tied up,
Most massive fetters they attached to his feet;
He was not allowed to touch food, nor to speak to any friend,
Before he had sworn to them, upon a relic specially chosen,
That all of his kingly land he would deliver into their hands,
Boroughs and castles and all his [pavilions];[†]
And he did all of it, as it was determined.
And Hengest took into his hands all this glorious kingdom,
And dealt out to his people a great part of this land.   7660
He gave to an earl all Kent where near London it extends;
He gave his steward Essex,
And to his butler he gave Middlesex there.
The knights received all this and for a while they kept it.

    Meanwhile Vortigern travelled all round this land,
Delivering to Hengest his splendid boroughs,
And Hengest forthwith placed in them his knights.
All this time many lesser folk were located in South-sex,
And in Middlesex very many of the race,
And in East-sex their highest-born youth;   7670
Food they would fetch, everything they found;

They violated women and by them God's laws were broken.
They did in the land just what they wanted.
　　The British could see there was disaster in the land,
And how the Saxon men had slipped in beside them.
The Britons devised a name for the land because of the Saxon men's
　　　　disgrace,
And for the treachery which they had performed:
Because it was with knives that they had deprived them of life,
They called all that area East-'sax' and West-'sax',
And the third one Middle-'sax'.　　　　　　　　　　　　　7680
Vortigern the king had given to them all this land,
Till he had left in his hand not a single turf of land,
And he himself, Vortigern, fled across the Severn,
Deep into Welsh country, and there did he remain,
And his troop with him, which had become depleted,
And yet he had in hoard a very great treasure.
He got his men to ride very far and wide,
And made them summon to him some of every kind of man,
Whoever was willing to seek his property from patronage.
　　This the Britons heard; this the Scotsmen heard:　　　7690
To him then they came after that very soon,
From every direction, that way they came riding,
Many a nobleman's son, keen for gold and great treasure.
When he had together sixty thousand men,
Then he assembled the great who well knew how to judge:
'Good men, instruct me by your advice, for I am in very great need,
Where in the wilderness I might build a castle
Where I might live inside safe with my men,
And hold it against Hengest with powerful strength,
Until I might the better reconquer boroughs,　　　　　　7700
Avenge me on my enemies who have felled my friends,
And all who my kingdom's land have snatched out of my hand,
And so have exiled me, being fully my foes.'
　　Then responded a wise man who well knew good advice:
'Listen to me now, lord king, I'll show you a good thing:
On the mountain of Reir, as I would advise,*
Do you raise up the castle with strongest stone walls,
For there you could dwell and live with delight.
And still you have in your hands much silver and gold
To maintain your attendants who must give you aid:　　　7710
And so you in your lifetime might live the very best life.'

Then answered the king: 'Have it announced in all haste,
Throughout my great retinue that I intend to go
To the mountain of Reir, there to raise a castle.'
Off marched the king and the army with him;
When they came there they began a ditch at once:
Horns there were blowing, machines there were hacking, *
Lime they started burning, through the terrain running,
And all West Wales land they set in Vortigern's hand;
They took everything which they came close to.   7720
When the ditch was dug and completely deepened
They began the wall, on the ditch all way round,
And lime and stone they laid together;
Of amazing machines there were twenty five hundred.
   By day they laid the wall; by night the whole thing fell;
In the morning they repaired it; at night it fell in ruins.
For one whole week in this way [the work] busied them: †
Each day they repaired it; and each night it fell in ruins.
   This upset the king: he was gloomy above all things,
Also all the army was hideously afraid,   7730
For all the time they were watching for when Hengest would come on
      them.
The king was most anxious and sent for advisers,
For worldly-wise men who knew of wisdom,
And asked them to cast lots, and try incantations,
To find out the truth with their divinations,
What it could derive from, that the wall which was so firm
Could never stay upright for the whole of a night.
These worldly-wise men divided in two groups:
Some of them went to the woodland, some of them to the cross-ways;
They proceeded to cast lots with their divinations;   7740
For three whole nights their spells they recited:
They could not any way discover by any means whatever
What it could derive from, that the wall which was so firm
Every night fell to rubble and the king lost his labour.
But there was just one wise-man and he was called **Joram**;
He said that he had discovered (but it sounded like fiction)
He said if any one found in whatever land,
Any little boy who had never had a father,
And opened his breast and took some of his blood,
And mixed it with the lime, and laid the wall with that,   7750
Then would it stand for all the world long.

The message reached the king about all that lying,
And he believed it, although it was lies.
At once he took his messengers and sent them throughout that land:
Each as far as he for fear of death on any roadway dared to go,
Who in every township must listen to the gossip,
Of where they might discover some mention of such a child.
　　These knights travelled off far and wide round the land;
Two of them walked on a way which due westwards lay,
Which led directly in to what now is Caermarthen.　　　　　　　7760
Right outside the borough, on the broad roadway,
All the boys of the town were playing a great game;
These knights were very tired and were feeling most despondent,
And sat down beside the play, and were watching these boys.
After a little while they started quarrelling,
Which has always been the rule where there are children playing!
One of them punched the other and the [blows] landed on him;†
Then towards **Merlin** Dinabus got really cross,　　　　　　　*Merlin*
And **Dinabus** who was punched started shouting this:
'Merlin, accursed man, why have you done this to me?　　　　　7770
You've treated me most disgracefully and for that you are going to
　　　pay.
I am actually a king's son, and you come from just nothing.
You ought not in any place to have a freeman's house,
Seeing that was all the story, that your mother was a whore
And she didn't even know the guy who got her pregnant with you;
Nor did you among human beings ever have a father!
And here in our district you bring us to disgrace.
Among us you've sprung up, and you're not any man's son.
And for all that this very day you are going to die!'
　　There on the sidelines those knights were listening;　　　　7780
They stood up and walked closer and felt compelled to [listen]†
To this mysterious story which they were hearing from the boy.
There was in Caermarthen a provost known as **Eli**;
The knights at great speed came to the provost,
And addressed him like this, with most ready lips:
'Here we've just arrived, Vortigern's knights,
And here we have discovered a certain young lad
Who is called Merlin; we have no idea of his family.
Get hold of him quickly and send him to the king,
If you want to stay alive and keep all your limbs!　　　　　　7790
And his mother with him, who gave birth to this male child;

If you will do this the king will receive them,
And if you pay no attention, you'll be exiled for it,
And this town will be burned down and the people all condemned.
　To which responded Eli, the provost of Caermarthen:
'I am well aware that all this land stands within Vortigern's hand,
And we are all his men: the greater is his honour,
And we shall do this gladly and perform his wish.'
　Off went the provost with townsmen in company,
And discovered Merlin and his play-fellows with him.　　　　7800
Merlin they arrested and his companions laughed;
When Merlin was led off Dinabus was exultant,
Thinking he was being led off to have his limbs removed,
But quite another fate awaited before it was all finished.
Now Merlin's mother had been strangely beautiful;
In a noble monastery she was a professed nun.
To the place went Eli, the provost of Caermarthen,
And took with him the lady from where she was enclosed
And off he went, running, to King Vortigern,
And a crowd of folk with him, leading the nun and Merlin.　　7810
　At once it was announced to King Vortigern's face
That there had come Eli, bringing with him the lady,
And Merlin her son with her there had come.
Then by his life was Vortigern blithe,
And received the lady with many gracious glances,
While Merlin he entrusted to twelve loyal knights,
Who were true to the king and whose role was to guard him.
　Then asked King Vortigern as with the nun he conversed there:
'My good lady, tell me (good fortune shall be yours)
Where were you born? What kind of parents did you have?'　　7820
Then the nun responded and her father she named:
'A third part of all this land lay in my father's hand;
Of the land he was king, famed this was far and wide;
He was called **Conan**, lord of many knights.'
Then the king replied, as if she were his close relation:
'Lady, do you tell me (good fortune shall be yours):
Here is Merlin, your son: who begot him on you?
Who among the folk was regarded as his father?'
Then she hung her head, bent it down to her breast;
She sat very quiet beside the king, and for a little while she mused.
　After a time she spoke, and communed with the king:　　　7831
'King, I shall tell you, a most amazing story:

My father, Conan the king, loved me above everything.
In those days I had a marvellously lovely figure.
When I had advanced to fifteen years old,
I was living in the private rooms, in my own apartment,
My girl attendants with me, all really lovely.
When on my bed I was asleep in my soft slumbers,
Then came before me the loveliest thing that ever was born,
As if it were a huge knight, all in gold clothing.   7840
This I would see in a dream; each night in my sleep
This thing would glide before me and would glisten with gold;
Often it kissed me, often it cuddled me,
Often it approached and came very close to me.
   'In the end when I faced myself this seemed to me most odd:
I couldn't bear my food, couldn't recognise my body;
It seemed to me most odd what it could all mean.
Then in the end I realised I was going to have a baby.
When my time came, this boy here I had.
I don't know in the world what his father was,   7850
Nor who engendered him in this world's kingdom,
Nor whether it was a monster, or on God's behalf appointed.
Look, as I pray for mercy I don't know any more
To tell you about my son, how he has come into this world.'
The nun bowed down her head and arranged her [veil].[†]
   The king thought carefully what might be his policy,
And called good counsellors to him for counsel,
And they advised him with the best advice
That he should send for **Magan**, who was an unusual man:
He was a learned scholar and was skilled in many crafts,   7860
He knew how to advise well, he knew how to lead far,
He knew of the art which rules in the heavens,
He knew how to recite every kind of incantation.
Magan came to the court where the king resided
And greeted the king with most gracious words:
'May you be healthy and fit, Vortigern the king!
I have come to you: show me what your wish is.'
Then the king replied, revealing all to the scholar
Of how the nun had spoken, and asked him there for advice;
From beginning to end, everything he told him.   7870
Then Magan announced: 'I know all about this.
There live in the heavens many kinds of beings
Which are to remain there until Doomsday comes on us.

Some of them are admirable and some of them do evil.
Among them is a very large type which comes down among humans;
These are termed, to be precise, *incubi demones*;
They don't commit much wrong, but they make fun of people;
Many a man in dreams often they harass,
And many a pretty woman by their art at once gets pregnant,
And many a good man's child by their magic they beguile.   7880
That's how Merlin was begotten and born of his mother,
And that's how it all goes on,' said the scholar, Magan.
    Then Merlin spoke to the king in person:
'King, your men have captured me and I have come to you,
And I want to know what you intend,
And for what reason I've been brought to the king.'
Then the king explained, speaking very clearly,
'Merlin, you have come to this place; you are not any man's son;
You are requesting what you'll find repugnant:
You want to know what's going on: now you shall hear it!   7890
    'I have begun a fort with tremendous efforts
Which have very much consumed all of my great treasure;
Five thousand men are at work on it.
I have lime and stone, in the country there's none better,
Nor in our land are there any workmen as good.
All that they lay in a day, and it's the truth I can say,
Before morning the next day, all of it's down,
Each stone away from the next, thrown down flat on the ground.
Now my wise men and my wizards are all of them saying
That if I take your blood out of your breast,   7900
For making my wall, and mix it in with my lime,
Then it will stand all the world long.
Now you know everything that's going to happen to you.'
    All this Merlin heard, and was furious in mood,
And spoke these words in spite of his wrath:
'The very God himself, who is leader of good men
Would not have your castle stand because of my heart's blood,
Nor your stone wall standing firm and still.
For all your wise men are outright deceivers:
They pronounce lies in front of you yourself;   7910
This you'll discover in this same day's duration.
Now **Joram** has said this (he is openly my enemy);
The information makes me laugh: I was born to be his destroyer.
Get Joram your wise man to come into your presence,

And all his confederates, right here and now,
Who announced all that lying in front of the king.
And if I shall tell you in my own true words
All about your wall and why it keeps on falling,
And so declare truthfully that their tales must be lies,
Then give me their heads, if I improve your works!'   7920
    Then the king announced, speaking very clearly,
'As my hand may help me, I'll have this agreement with you!'
To the king was brought Joram the wise one
And seven of his confederates (all were doomed to die).
Merlin grew angry and spoke very grimly:
'Say to me now, you traitor, Joram, loathsome in my sight,
Why this wall keeps falling down to ground-level;†
Say to me why it falls out that the wall tumbles.
What can be found in the base of the moat?'
Joram was silent: he could not explain it.   7930
Then Merlin spoke these words: 'King, keep your promise!
Have this ditch dug out seven feet deeper.
They will uncover there a stone, amazingly lovely,
It is massive and pretty for people to look at.'
    The ditch was dug out seven feet deeper
And at once they found, right away, the stone.
Then Merlin spoke these words: 'King, keep your promise!
Say to me now, Joram, most hateful of men to me,
And announce to this king what kind of things
Have taken up their station underneath this stone here.'   7940
Joram was silent; he could not explain it.
    Then Merlin made a strange remark: 'There is a pool under here;
Take away this stone and you'll find the pool at once.'
They took away the stone in the king's presence at once,
And they found the pool there. Then Merlin spoke:
'Ask Joram for me (he is openly my enemy),
After a certain space to tell you of the abyss:
What inhabits that pool there, in winter and summer?'
The king enquired of Joram, but he knew nothing about it.
    Then once more Merlin spoke the words: 'King, keep your
       promise!   7950
Have this water drawn off, and drain it away;
There are living in its depths two powerful dragons:
One is on the north side, the other on the south side;
One of them is milk-white, unlike any other being,

205

The other one is red as blood, the boldest of serpents.
In the middle of each night they begin to fight,
[And because of their fighting] your building works fell:†
The earth started to tremble and your wall to totter;
Through marvels like these your wall has collapsed;
It occurred in this flood and not because of my blood!'   7960
    This water was all drawn off; the king's men were relieved;
Great was the rejoicing in the presence of the king –
Yet straightaway afterwards they were saddened again:
Before the day came to an end they heard the tidings.
When the water was all drawn off, and the pit was empty,
Then these two dragons came out, and made a terrific din,
Fighting ferociously down in the ditch;
Never was seen by any knight a more loathsome fight:
There flew from their mouths fiery flames.
The monarch surveyed their monstrous appearance;   7970
Then he was wondering what in this very world
This could be the sign of, as he looked there in the depths,
And how Merlin knew of it when no other man could know.
First the white one was on top and then it was underneath,
And the red dragon had wounded it to death,
And each one went to its hole, and no man born saw them ever
    after.
So proceeded this thing which King Vortigern was watching,
And all those who were with him much admired Merlin,
While the king hated Joram, and had his head removed,
And those of his seven friends who were there with him.   7980
    To his tent went the king, and with him he led Merlin,
And said to him with much love: 'Merlin, you are welcome!
And I shall give to you everything which you desire
Here from these my lands, of silver and of gold.'
(He thought that through Merlin all that land he would win,
But things went quite otherwise before the day's end came).
    This question asked the king of his dear friend Merlin:
'Say to me now, Merlin, most beloved of all my men,
What do the dragons signify which were making all that din?
And the stone and the pool and that terrifying fight?   7990
Tell me if you please, what all this signifies;
And afterwards you must advise me how I must conduct myself,
And how I may regain the kingdom that is mine
From Hengest, my wife's father, who has most gravely harmed me.'

Then Merlin replied to the king who addressed him:
'King, you are unwise, and your plans are silly!
You enquire about the dragons which were making all the din,
And what their fight signifies and their ferocious attacks.
They signify kings who are still to come,
And their fights and their behaviour and their doomed folk.   8000
But if you were as wise a man and as clever in thinking
As to have asked me about your many troubles,
Of your own great anxiety which is coming upon you,
Then I would tell you about your own troubles.'
    Then said Vortigern the king: 'Dearest friend, Merlin,
Tell me about the things which are destined to come to me.'
'Gladly' replied Merlin in very bold tones,
'I will inform you, but you will always regret it!
King, see to yourself! Trouble is to be your lot
From Constantine's family: his child you got murdered.   8010
Constance you had killed, who was king in this land:
You arranged for your Picts to betray him horribly,
And for that you will suffer the greatest of disasters.
Since you drew upon you the alien people,
The Saxons to this land, you shall therefore be disgraced.
    'Now out of Brittany the barons have arrived,
That is, Aurelius and Uther, and now you are aware of this.
They are coming tomorrow, certain it is, into this land at Totnes,
I inform you specifically, with seven hundred ships;
Even now on the sea they are sailing swiftly!   8020
You have done great evil to them and now you must take harshness
    from them;
On both sides you're faced by those who plot your downfall:
Your opponents ahead of you and your enemies in your rear!
But fly, fly, on your way, and protect your life!
Yet fly wherever you may fly, after you they'll quickly hie:
Ambrosius Aurelius will first of all have this kingdom;
But through a drink of deadly poison he shall suffer death;
And then shall Uther Pendragon inherit this kingdom;
But your own descendants will with venom destroy him,
Yet before enduring death he will make an outcry.   8030
Uther shall have the one son: out of Cornwall he shall come.
That will be a wild boar bearing bristles of steel;
The boar will burn down the loftiest boroughs;
All of the traitors he will demolish by sheer terror;

All your powerful descendants with torments he'll destroy.
He shall be a very valiant man and of noble virtue.
From here as far as Rome this same man will rule.
He shall fell to the ground all of his foes.
I have spoken true things to you, but no softer do they strike you;
But flee with all your forces: your foes are coming to you at your
      court.'†

Then ceased the speech of Merlin the sage,   8041
And the king had men blow thirteen brass trumpets,
And went off with his forces furiously fast.
After this things went apace but a single night's space
Before the brothers came, both of them together,
To the sea shore, true it was, at Dartmouth near Totnes.
The news came to the British, who were truly glad at this.
They rushed out of the woodlands, and from the wilderness,
Here sixty and there sixty, and there seven hundred,
Here thirty and there thirty and there many thousand.   8050
When they all assembled very good did it seem to them.

The brothers to this country brought a countless army,
And before them came all these bravest Britons,
An uncountable force which [covered] all the plain,†
Those who once were dispersed, desperate in the woodlands
Because of the great terror and because of the great trouble,
And because of the great misery which Hengest had made for them,
After he had murdered all their chieftains with those long knives
And with sword blades had sliced through the sturdy landholders.
The Britons set up their hustings; with great common sense   8060
They settled on Aurelius (the elder brother) at once   AURELIUS
In the highest hustings, where they raised him up as   AMBROSIUS
    king.
Then were the British all filled with happiness,
Happy at heart were those who had been grieving.
Then this information came to King Vortigern,
That Aurelius was chosen and raised to the throne.

Then Vortigern was wretched (and later even worse);
Vortigern went off, far away to a castle:
Ganarew it was called, high on a hilltop;
Cloard was the hill's name and Hergin the district's,   8070
Right beside the Wye, which is a lovely river.
Vortigern's men captured all that they came close to:
They seized weapons and provisions of many different types,

To the castle they carried as much as they cared to,
Until they had enough (though it helped but little).
    Aurelius and Uther were aware of Vortigern,
Where he was, up on Cloard, enclosed in the castle.
They had brass trumpets blown, to bring together their army,
An uncountable host from many different countries.
They marched upon Ganarew where Vortigern lay: 8080
There was a king outside; there was a king inside!
Knights there were fighting with furious onslaughts;
Every single good man got himself ready.
When they could see that they had not yet conquered
Then off to the woodlands went a wonderfully big force:
They felled the wood right down and dragged it to the castle
And filled in all the ditch, which was wonderfully deep.
With fire they ignited everywhere inside
And called out to Vortigern: 'Now you'll be nice and warm in there!
That's for killing Constance who was king here in this land,   8090
And then Constantine, his son; now Aurelius has come,
And Uther, his brother, who will bring you to destruction!'
The wind wafted the fire so that wonderfully it burned:
The castle started burning, the chambers were consumed;
The halls all fell in, fast collapsing to earth.
Not a single knight there could get control of the fire;
The fire spread right through it all and burned house and burned wall,
And also King Vortigern, inside he began to burn,   *Vortigern's*
And it consumed everything alive that was there inside.   *Death*
And so in great anguish Vortigern was finished.   8100
    Then in Aurelius's hand stood the whole of the land.
There was an honourable earl, **Aldolf** he was called;
He came from Gloucester, the cleverest of knights.
For all the land Aurelius made him his justiciar.
Aurelius by then and Uther his brother
Had felled all their foes and because of it were happier.
This was heard by Hengest, of all knights the strongest,
And then he was terrified, tremendously greatly.
He hustled his hosts and hastened to Scotland,
And Aurelius the king marched after him hurrying.   8110
Now Hengest thought he would flee, with all his host of men,
Should he be attacked, off into Scotland,
So that with ingenuity he could escape from there,
In case he could not make a stand against Aurelius in that land.

209

Aurelius marched forth and led his men due north,
With his full strength for one full week's length.
The British were the bravest and advanced over the forest;
By then Aurelius had an enormous army;
He found there waste land, people all slaughtered,
Churches fire-gutted, Britons burned to death.   8120
Then declared King Aurelius, the darling of the Britons:
'If I'm to survive so that back again I ride,
If it is willed by Our Lord who made the daylight with his word
That I may in safety obtain what is my heritage,
Then churches I shall raise, and the true God I will praise;
I will to each knight give what is his right,
And to every single man, both to the old and young,
I shall be kindly,
If God will grant me to regain my own country.'
    To Hengest came the tidings of Aurelius the king,   8130
[That he was bringing a force of innumerable folk];†   8130a
Then spoke Hengest, of all knights the falsest:
'Hearken now, my men! honour now is granted you;
Here comes Aurelius, and his brother Uther also;
They're bringing very many troops, but all of them are doomed,
For the king is stupid, and so are his knights,
And a mere boy is his brother – the one just like the other!
In consequence the British will be much less courageous:
When the head is pretty feeble, the [forces] will abate,†
So hold well in your memories what I'm about to mention:
Better are fifty of our men than a whole five hundred of them,   8140
And that on many occasions they have had to find out
Ever since they landed to test out the people,
For tales are widely told of our retaliation,
That we are stalwarts, elite among the best.
Against them we shall stand and drive them from our land,
And rule over the realm just as we wish to.'
Thus the bold Hengest, of all knights the handsomest,
Emboldened his forces as they stood on the field.
Yet quite otherwise it came about before a week was out.
    On then sped the tidings to Aurelius the king   8150
Of where Hengest was lodged, up high on the mount.
Aurelius had supporters, thirty thousand riders,
Very bold Britons who uttered their vows,
And also he had Welshmen, wonderfully many.

He insisted his knights, by day and by night,
Should always be weaponed as if going off to war,
For always he was anxious about the heathen hordes.
Then to Hengest came news that Aurelius was close:
He marshalled his army and marched out against him;
   When Aurelius was aware that Hengest was going to come
      there   8160
He moved into a field and was well weaponed behind shield;
He took with him straight ten thousand knights
Who were the best born and most select from his force,
And positioned them in the field, on foot behind their shields;
Ten thousand Welshmen he sent off to the woodland;
Ten thousand Scots he sent out on the flanks
To encounter the heathen on tracks and on paved street.
He himself took his earls and his excellent warriors,
And the most loyal men whom he had in his land,
And he formed up his shield-wall like a winter-hoary wood;   8170
Five thousand were on horseback, all these people to protect.
   Then shouted Aldolf, who was Earl of Gloucester:
'If the Lord should grant it me, he who governs every outcome,
That I'm allowed to be alive when Hengest comes here riding
(Who has so long remained here in this our land, ʹ
And betrayed my friends and loved ones with his long saxon knives,
Close beside Amesbury, to an atrocious death),
If however, from that earl I might win myself the glory
Then I could utter my own true declaration
That God himself had granted good things to me –   8180
If I could fell all my foes to the ground at once
And avenge my dear kinsfolk whom they have laid down low!'
Scarcely was this speech spoken to the end
When they saw Hengest advancing over the down
With an enormous force of men; furiously they advanced.
   Together they came, and [fiercely] they struck;[†]
There the stern men rushed straight together:
Helmets were resounding, knights there were falling,
Steel struck against bone, destruction there was rife,
Down the roads went gushing rivulets of blood;   8190
The fields were fallow coloured and the grass all faded.
   When Hengest saw that his help was failing
He dashed from the fight and fled to the sides,
And after him his people pressed on very fast;

The Christians coming in pursuit pounded them with blows,
And called upon Christ the son of God to give them assistance,
And the heathen people also called out loudly:
'Our own god, Tervagant, why do you fail us this time?'
When Hengest saw the heathens were surrounded
And the Christian men came down upon them   8200
Then Hengest fled on and on until he came to Conisborough;
Into the city he went seeking its security,
And King Aurelius went after him at once,
Calling to his people in a loud bellow:
'Keep on running, on, now, on: it is northward Hengest's gone!'
And after him they turned until they came to the town.
   Then Hengest and his son watched all the army coming after them.
Then declared Hengest (of all men the angriest!):
'I refuse to fly any more, now instead I want to fight,
And my son Octa, and his sworn brother Ebissa,   8210
And all my army of men. Now draw your weapons,
And let's march against them and make havoc-raids,
And if we don't fell those men, then it's we who're fated,
Laid out on the field and bereft of our friends.'
   Hengest moved out into the [field], left behind all his tents,†
And formed up his shield-wall entirely from his heathen men.
Then Aurelius the king arrived, and many thousands with him,
And began a second fight there which was frighteningly strong:
Many a great blow was dealt there in that combat.
There the Christian men were all but overcome.   8220
Then arrived galloping the five thousand riders
Whom Aurelius had there to fight men from horseback:
They struck at the heathen so they hurtled downwards;
There was a very stiff fight, most severe battle-ardour.
Into the fight came the Earl Aldolf of Gloucester
And discovered Hengest, of all knights the wickedest,
Where he was fighting fiercely and felling down Christians.
Aldolf drew his good sword and on Hengest he smote,
And Hengest threw his shield in front of him, or else his life would
         have been lost,
And Aldolf struck into the shield so that it split in two,   8230
And Hengest leaped upon him as if he were a lion
And struck at Aldolf's helmet so it fell into two pieces.
Then they hacked with their swords – the swipes were very savage:
Sparks sprang from the steel over and over again.

After quite a time Aldolf jumped down to the ground
And caught sight of **Gorlois**, and he was brave, most certain this is;
He was the earl of Cornwall and he was famous far and wide;
Then the warrior Aldolf because of that was much bolder,
And heaving high his sword let it come slashing down,
Until it struck Hengest's hand and made him drop his blade.   8240
Instantly he grabbed him with a grim expression
By the coif on the cuirass, which was covering his head,*
And by his own sheer brute force smashed him right down,
And then bounced him up again as if he wanted to break him up;
With his arms he encircled him and off then he led him.
   Now Hengest had been captured through Aldolf's skill in action.
Then announced Aldolf who was Earl of Gloucester:
'Hengest, you're not as jolly as you were by Amesbury,
Where you drew those saxon-swords and struck down the Britons!
With the grossest treachery you killed my kinsfolk.   8250
Now you must pay out compensation and your own friends shall
     perish,
And with gruesome torments you will go off from this world!'
Hengest walked silently: he could see no help at all;
Aldolf was leading him to his sovereign lord,
And greeted his liege lord with most loyal words:
'All hail to you, Aurelius, of most exalted rank!
I am bringing here before you the destroyer of your kinsfolk,
Hengest the heathen who has perpetrated harm for us.†
God has indeed allowed me to get him in my grip!
Now to you I'm going to give him, for you are dearest to me of all
     men,
So let the children of your courtiers play games with this
     pet dog,   8261
Shoot at him with arrows and put a stop to his race quickly!'
   Then the king made reply with a clear and eager voice:
'Blessings on you, Aldolf, best and noblest of earls!
I love you like my own life: you shall be a leader of this people!'
Here Hengest was seized and there Hengest was tied up;
There, by then, was Hengest of all knights the saddest!
   This fight was then concluded and the heathen folk had fled;
Then Octa noticed that his father was in trouble,
And with Ebissa his sworn brother joined forces together   8270
And fled inside York city amid every misery,
And got ready the walls and demolished the halls.

Certain of the heathen went off to the woodland
Where the foot-soldiers laid them flat on the ground.
    Then Aurelius the king was well content above all things.
He went into Conisborough with his household guard
And gave thanks to God for all such prowess.
For three days and three nights the king stayed there all right,
To doctor all the wounds of his most dear knights,
And to bathe in that borough all their weary bones.   8280
When the third day had come, and they had said the hour of nones
Then the king had trumpets blown and brought his earls together
So that they might come to hustings to Aurelius the king.
    When they had assembled the king asked them at once
What they would advise him, those who were his associates,
As to what kind of torture should form Hengest's execution,
And how he might best avenge his own dearest friends
Who beside Amesbury lay buried in the ground.
    Then up stood **Aldadus**, and he addressed the king like this
(He was good and in God's favour and was a holy bishop   8290
And was Earl Aldolf's brother – he hadn't any other):
'My lord king, listen to me now, to what I shall relate to you:
I shall pronounce to you the sentence on how he is to be struck down.
Because for us who live here of men he is most loathsome,
And has slaughtered our kinsmen and deprived them of their days of
        life,
And he is a heathen hound, so he must go down to hell:
There let him sink because of his treachery.
Lord King, hearken to me, to what I want to tell you:
There was a king in Jerusalem, Saul was his name,
[And] in the heathen territory a king of great power,†   8300
Agag he was called, and Jerusalem he hated,
He was King of the Amalekites (to him the Evil One was close);
All the time he hated Jerusalem to its greatest harm;
Never would he give them any peace but always he opposed them:
He burned them, he killed them, he gave them many sorrows.
    'It happened at one time that the sun began to shine
And Agag the king was sitting on his high throne,
And his doomed blood was stirred and put him in mind of marching.
He called to his knights right away and straight:
"Swiftly on your steeds, and off we shall ride!   8310
We shall burn and we shall kill all around Jerusalem!"
Off went the king and a huge army with him:

Through the land they started running and the towns they were
    burning.
This was noticed by those men who were living in Jerusalem,
Who then went against them, knights and serving men,
And fought against the king and by fighting overcame him,
And all his folk they slaughtered and King Agag they captured,
And so they conducted him up to King Saul.
And then Saul the king was more glad then anything;
The king asked his advisers about his course of action,   8320
Which would be the best thing: either execute or hang him.
    Up then leaped Samuel, a prophet of Israel;
He was a very holy man, high in the Lord's favour:
No one in those days knew such a high man under God's law.
Samuel took King Agag captive to the market-place
And had him tied up very tightly to a strong stake which was there,
And took in his right hand a valuable brand,
And like this he called out to him, did Samuel the good man:
"You're known as Agag the king, but now you are sorrowing;
Now you must take your recompense for ruining Jerusalem,   8330
For having so greatly damaged this dear and noble city,
And slaughtering many a good man and depriving him of life-days.
As I await God's mercy you will not do this any more!"
Samuel raised the sword and struck down with it hard,
And cut in half the king in the market-place of Jerusalem,
And he scattered the pieces far and wide over the streets.
That's how Samuel acted and so you ought to treat Hengest.'
    This was heard by Aldolf, who was Earl of Gloucester;
He leaped towards Hengest as if he were a lion.
And grabbed him by the hair, and after him he dragged him,   8340
And led him all around, and right round Conisborough,
And outside the city he had him tied securely.
Aldolf drew his sword and struck off Hengest's head,   *Hengest's*
And the king took his corpse straight, as he was so brave   *Execution*
    a knight,
And placed him in the earth after the heathen practice,
And prayed for the soul (that no salvation should come to it!).
    And now Aurelius the king had men summon a hustings,
And had brass trumpets blown to bring together his force.
Marvellous was the crowd of folk, and they marched direct to York,
And there they besieged within it Octa and his men.   8350
The king got men to dig a ditch all around outside York city,

So that no one there at all could either come out or go in.
This Octa perceived and it caused him much grief,
And his heathen horde which he had in the city.
They gathered to consider what they ought to do;
And this said Octa, to his close friend Ebissa:
'Now I have decided what I'm going to do:
I and my own knights will now outright
In oure bare breeches go out of this borough,
And wind round my neck a length of linked chains,   8360
And come to the king, his mercy begging.
Otherwise we'll all perish, if we don't follow this advice.'
   They all acted like this, just as Octa advised:
In deep concern, knights took off their clothes,
And out of the city went lords sick at heart,
All by twos together, twenty hundred of them.
   The noblest of kings, Aurelius, observed all of this:
He thought those naked knights a very strange sight.
Together came the army encamped about the country
And watched Octa coming, who was Hengest's son.   8370
He carried in his hand a long piece of chain;
He came up to the king in the presence of his soldiers;
He fell to the ground at the feet of the king,
And these words were spoken by Octa who was Hengest's son:
'Be merciful, my lord king, through the mild God himself,
For the love of God almighty, have mercy on my knights:
For all of our paganism has become paltry,
Our laws and our nation, since we're loathed by the Lord.
For we are failed all this time by Tervagant and Apollin,
By Woden and by Mercury, by Jupiter and Saturn,   8380
By Venus and Dido, by Frea and Mamilo,
And our beliefs are now loathsome to us,
But we want to believe in your beloved Lord,
For all the creed we've followed fails us all the time.
We are seeking for your grace, now and for all ages.
If you will make peace with me and will make a treaty with me,
We will be allied with you and become your loyal men,
Love your own people and preserve your laws.
If this you refuse, then do what you wish,
Whatever you want to do, whether execute or hang us!'   8390
   The king was compassionate and remained quiet;
He looked to his right hand, he looked to his left hand,

216

To see which of the wise men wished to speak first.
All of them were silent and spoke not a sound;
There was no man so great who dared declare one word,
And Octa went on lying at the feet of the king,
With all of his knights lying behind him.
Then the good bishop Aldadus spoke up and said this:
'It has always been and for ever will be, and is now required of us
[That whoever] asks for mercy, mercy [he] must have;††   8400
He deserves mercy who begs for it deservingly.
And you yourself, lord king, are the leader of the nation:
Give your favour to Octa and his companions as well,
If they wish with true belief to receive the Christian faith;
For it may still come to pass in some country or other
That they may dutifully honour the Lord God.
Now all this kingdom stands entirely in your hands:
Donate them a location which you find convenient,
And take from them hostages such as you'd request,
And have them held firm in fetters of iron;   8410
Supply the hostages with clothes and food, supply them every
      comfort, every need,
And then you may well retain this race within your land;
And let them cultivate the land and live by their produce.
   If it subsequently happens shortly afterwards
That they fail after a time to keep to the truce,
And grow lax in their labour and grow disloyal to you,
I'll now stipulate the sentence which at that stage you could give:
Get them run over by really savage riders,
And so have them destroyed, killed and also hanged.
This judgement I give you: may the just Lord give ear!'   8420
Then the king answered in keen and eager tones:
'I shall act exactly as you have made assessment!'
Then the king spoke like this: 'Get up now, Octa,
You are to act most virtuously by taking Christianity.'
   Then they baptised Octa and his bodyguard also
And all of his knights in that very place outright;
They selected their hostages and handed them to the king:
Fifty-three children they entrusted to the king,
And the king sent them straight in the direction of Scotland;
They swore solemn oaths that they would not betray him.   8430
The king gave into their hands sixty full hides of land,
And on this they lived for the length of many years.

The king was in York: a noble life he found it;
He took his couriers and sent them round his country
Ordering his bishops, his men of book-learning,
His earls and his landed men to come there to meet him,
To Aurelius the king, to a very great hustings.
In a very short time together they came:
The king greeted his people with most pleasing words:
He welcomed his earls, he welcomed his warriors,   8440
And all the bishops and the men of book-learning:
'I will declare to you quite undeniably
Why I have sent for you and for what purpose.
Here I present to each knight his property and his rights,
And to every single earl and to every single warrior;
What he may obtain, let him use that with pleasure.
And each man, on his own life, I command to love the peace;
I order you to design and to build up the churches,
To let the bells ring for God's praise to be sung,
For us with all our powers to honour our dear Lord.   8450
With all of his ability let each keep peace and amity!
See to cultivating land, now it all lies in my hand.'
    When this speech was uttered, they all liked this instruction.
The king gave them leave to go away from there:
Each journeyed homewards in the way he thought best.
For seven nights entirely the king stayed there quietly.
And then he took the long way down towards London,
To cheer all the citizens who had so often been concerned.
He had them strengthen the walls, he had them [erect] many halls,†
And put right all the earthworks which had formerly been
        broken,   8460
And he restored the law-code to them which existed in their elders'
        days.
There he appointed governors to control the people,
And from there he went directly to Winchester,
And there too he had constructed [halls and fine churches]†
Until he found it very pleasant there; then he moved on to Amesbury,
To the burial ground of his most beloved friends,
Whom Hengest with his knives had annihilated there.
He made enquiry there at once for masons skilled in carving stone,
And for every good artist skilled in working with the adze.
He intended to construct there a uniquely fine creation   8470
Which was to last for ever, as long as men shall live.

There was in Caerleon a bishop called **Tremorion**;
He was a very wise man among the kingdoms of the world;
He was with the king, up there in the forest,
And there Tremorion, God's servant, spoke to the king like this:
'Now listen to me, Aurelius, to what I want to teach you,
And I will pronounce to you the best possible advice;
If you will approve of it, in turn it will appeal to you.
We have a prophet who is called Merlin:
If any one could discover him up on this high forest,   8480
And bring him in your presence by any manner of means,
If you were willing to submit to his wishes,
He would impart to you excellent secrets
Of how you might make this building sturdy and strong,
So that it could endure as long as men exist.'
Then the king replied (these words made him rejoice):
'Tremorion, dear friend, to this I shall attend.'
  The king sent his couriers over all his kingdom's area,
Asking every single man to enquire after Merlin,
And if anyone could find him, to bring him to the king;   8490
He would give him land, and both silver and gold,
And in this wide world he would perform his wish.
The messengers started riding, very far, and widely:
Some of them went due northwards and some of them went
  southwards,
Some of them went due east and some of them went due west;
Some went straightway along until they came to Alaban[*]
(That is a spring which lies in Welsh lands);
That spring he loved and often in it bathed himself;
There the knights found him as he sat on its rim;
The moment they met him, politely did they greet him,   8500
And like this, very forthright, spoke to him those two knights:
'Health to you, Merlin, of all men the wisest!
Through us to you come greetings from one who is a good king:
Aurelius he is called, the most excellent of all kings;
All this great land stands in King Aurelius's hands.
Politely he requests that to him you should proceed,
And he will give you land, both silver and gold,
If in this state business you're willing to advise the king.'
Merlin gave an answer which depressed the knights there:
'I care nothing for his land, his silver nor his gold,   8510
Nor his clothes nor his horses: I myself have quite enough.'

Then he sat still for a very long space;
    Those knights were afraid that he would fly from them;
When at last his words broke they were good things which he spoke:
'You two are a pair of knights who have come here, directly:
Yesterday before nones I knew that you would come,
And if I had not wished it, you never could have found me.
You bring me greetings from Aurelius the king:
I knew his nature before he came ashore,
And I knew the other, Uther his brother: 8520
I knew both of them, before they were even born,
Even though neither of them had I ever set eyes on.
But disaster, O disaster, that destiny is such
That the people's liege is not to live long.
Yet now I will accompany you and be your companion:
To the king I will proceed and perform all his wishes.'
    Off travelled Merlin and those knights with him
So long till they came to their liege and king;
This piece of good tidings came to the king:
Till then never in his life was the king so blithe   8530
For the coming of any man at all who ever came to him.
    Off to get his steed, and out the king rode,
And all his knights with him to give welcome to Merlin.
The king met up with him and splendidly greeted him:
He caught him in arms, he kissed him,
He called him his close friend;
Great was the rejoicing among the assembled retinue
All for Merlin's coming (who was the son of no man):
Alas that in the world there was no wise man
Who ever knew here whose son he could be   8540
(Except the Lord alone, whose knowledge is total).
The king led Merlin who was favoured off to his chamber:
He began at once to request with courteous expression
That he should make him understand about the world's circuit,
And about all the years which were still to come here,
For it was his earnest wish that he should know of this.
    Merlin answered then, and to the king he said this:
'O Aurelius the king, you ask me an unusual thing;
See to it that no more do you any such thing utter!
For [of baleful effect] is the spirit here within my breast,[†]   8550
And if among men I were to make any boasting
As entertainment, as an attraction, with amusing words,

My spirit will be roused and become silent,
And deprive me of my brains and stop up my wise words:
Then I would be dumb upon every decision.
But stop this kind of thing,' said Merlin to the king,
'For whenever there comes trouble to any nation at all,
And people with humility wish to approach me,
If I by my own intent may remain silent,
Then I can pronounce on how things will come to pass.   8560
But I will advise you about your most pressing problem,
And tell you right here what you have in your heart:
There is a field beside Amesbury which is broad and very pretty,
Where by the knife your kin were deprived of life:
There was many a bold Briton betrayed to his death,
And you're intending to grace that place with great honour,
With marvellous buildings as memorial to the dead,
Which there will stand to the world's end.
But you haven't got a single man who knows anything about it,
Who could construct a building which would never collapse.   8570
But I shall instruct you in this difficulty,
For I know a structure surrounded with mystery,
And this structure stands within Ireland:
It is a most marvellous thing.
Its construction is of stone, apart from this one there is none:
As wide as the world's realm is, no other one resembles it.
When people are unwell, they journey to the stone,
And they wash the stone, and with that water bathe their bones.
Within a little while they're completely whole.   8580
But the stones are massive and immensely huge,
For there is no man ever born, in any borough whatever,
Who could by sheer strength bring the stones from there.'
      Then replied the king: 'Merlin, you are saying strange things!
If no man ever born could bring them home from there,
Nor by any power could take them from their place,
How could I bring them away from there then?'
Then responded Merlin to the king speaking to him:
'O but yes, yes, my lord king! Long ago it was recorded
That cunning is better than any brute force,*   8590
For with cunning one can achieve what force cannot compass.
But summon your army and advance to that country,
And be sure to take with you a force of good people,
And I shall go with you (this will enhance your honour).

Before you depart homewards you shall have your desire,
And you shall bring that structure with you to this land,
And so you shall convey it over to the cemetery,
And honour the location where your friends lie buried,
And you yourself are going to find rest for your bones in it:
When your life ends, there you shall rest.'   8600
    So spoke Merlin there, and afterwards sat silent,
Just as if he was going to depart from the world.
The king had him conducted into a handsome chamber,
There to be lodged in the way he liked.
    Aurelius the king had men announce a hustings
From all the lands which lay within his hands,
Asking counsel for himself in such case as this,
And they advised him sensibly, his senior nobles,
That he should follow the course which Merlin had proposed.
But they refused to lead the king out of this land: 8610
Instead they chose as leader Uther the good man,
And fifteen thousand knights, all with fine weapons,
Very brave Britons who were bound in that direction.
    When this force was all ready then they began to journey,
With all the best ships which were stationed by the sea,
And travelled so long that they came to Ireland,   *Invasion*
And those nights most valiant took harbour there and anchored.   *of*
They went up on the sea strand and gazed around at Ireland.   *Ireland*
Then Merlin spoke and made speech with these words:
'Do you see now, bold men, that massive hill,   8620
The hill so very high that it comes close to the sky?
That is that amazing thing, which there is called "The Giants' Ring",
A thing quite unlike any other; it came from Africa.
Pitch all your tents across all these fields;
Here we shall rest for three whole days' space;
On the fourth day from here we shall depart,
And make towards that mount: there is what we want.
But first we must bathe ourselves and bring together our bold men,
Get our weapons ready for we shall really need them.'
So things were left, and there lay the army.   8630
    Then a king who was very strong owned all of Ireland:
He was called **Gillomaurus**, and great lord he was of men.
To him came the tidings that the Britons were on his land.
He had men summon his army through all Ireland's country,
And he began uttering threats that he would drive them out.

When the news came through of what the Britons were there to do,
Of how they came just for one thing, to fetch away the Stone Ring,
Then Gillomaurus gave vent to much mockery and scorn,
And said that they must be allies in stupidity,
Those who had travelled there across the broad sea   8640
Seeking there for stones as if in their own land were none!
And he swore by St Brendan: 'They'll not be taking one stone,*
But for those stones they'll be getting the greatest of all troubles:
Their blood will come gushing out of their guts,
And that will larn 'em for looking for stones!
And then I'll be going off into Britain,
And tellin' King Aurelius I'll be fightin' for me stones,
And unless the king keeps quiet and does just what I want,
Then I'll be making a stand by fighting in his land,
Make waste places for him and many wildernesses   8650
And plenty of widows: their partners will all die!'
    So the foolish king played around with words,
But it turned out quite differently from what he expected.
His forces were ready, fell in and marched forwards,
So far, till they came to the British encampment.
Together they clashed and boldly attacked,
And fought very fiercely: the fated fell there.
The Irish were quite bare; the British wore their mail-coats:
The Irishmen fell, and covered all the fields,
And the king Gillomaur set off to flee from there,   8660
And fled away straight with twenty of his knights
Into a vast forest, quite bereft of honour:
His Irish folk had all been felled with steel.
So the king was ruined and his boasting at an end,
And so he went to the woods and left his folk falling.
    The British gazed round at the dead strewn over the ground:
Seven thousand lay there deprived of their life.
Across the fields the British advanced towards their tents,
And fittingly they saw to all their fine weapons,
And there they took rest as Merlin had instructed.   8670
On the fourth day they prepared to march forward,
Proceeded to the hill: they were all weaponed well.
    There stood that weird structure, massive and very strong.
Knights were striding up, knights were striding down,
Knights were going all around and earnestly observing:
They saw there on the land the amazing structure stand.

There were a thousand soldiers with weapons well supplied,
And all the others, in fact, were closely guarding their ships.
Then Merlin made a speech and spoke to the knights:
'You, knights, are strong: these stones are great and long;　　8680
You have to go close to them and get a keen grasp on them;
You must stoutly twine them with strong sail-ropes;
Shove then and heave with very heavy force
Trees huge and long which are very strong,
And go up to one stone, all you who are clever
And come down on it with strength, to see if you can stir it.'†
Merlin knew quite well how things would work out.
The knights stepped over to it with a great show of strength:
They sweated and struggled but had no success
In managing to shift even one single stone.　　8690

　　Merlin looked at Uther, who was the king's brother,
And these were the words of Merlin the wise man:
'Uther, now pull back and call your knights to you,
And all stand around and watch very closely,
And be very quiet and keep very still,
Until I say to you directly how we're going to begin.'
Uther drew right back, and beckoned his knights
So he left behind no-one close up to the stone,
Just as far as a man might toss a small stone,
And Merlin went around and examined it closely;　　8700
Three times he went round the ring, inside it and outside it,
And was moving his lips like a man saying prayers;
This Merlin went on doing there until he called to Uther:
'Uther, come quickly, and bring your knights with you,
And get hold of all the stones: you're not to leave a single one,
For now you can lift them like balls made of feathers†
And so by this expedient you can carry them aboard.'

　　Just as Merlin instructed these stones were extracted,
And they stowed them on their ships and sailed off, in fact,
And so proceeded to travel over to this land,　　8710
And conveyed them to a field which is amazingly wide:
Wide it is and very pretty, close to Amesbury,
Where Hengest betrayed the British with his Saxon knives.
Merlin began to erect them as they had stood earlier,
In a way no one besides him could have coped with or contrived,
Nor was there before that any man so clever born yet
As those stones to arrange and that structure to raise.

That news came to the king in the north region   *Stonehenge*
Of Merlin's behaviour and of Uther his brother:
That they had safely come back to this land,   8720
And that that structure was complete and was standing upright.
Within the king's breast was a marvellous bliss,
And he had the hustings called as far and wide as his land spread,
So that all his people very merrily might come to Amesbury,
All his noble people, on the Whitsunday.

   To the place came Aurelius the king and all his folk with him;
There on the Whitsunday he called an assembly,
As I intend to describe to you in the story of this book:
Upon the plain there pavilions were pitched,
Over that broad field were nine thousand tents.   8730
All the Whitsunday on the field the king stayed,
[Wearing his crown there high upon his head]:†   8731a
He called for the spot called Stonehenge now to be consecrated.
Quiet for full three days did the king stay;
On the third day he gave high honour to his nobles:†
He appointed two bishops, both extremely good;
St **Dubricius** to Caerleon and to York went St **Samson**;
Both of them were holy and close to high God;
On the fourth day the doughty folk departed.

   And so for some time things stood like this.
Now there was still one wicked man, **Passent**, son of Vortigern; 8740
This same Passent had gone into Wales,   *Passent's*
And there at this same time he had become an outlaw,   *Rebellion*
Though he dared not long remain there because of Aurelius and
      Uther,
But he got ships which were good and travelled on the sea-flood;
Into Germany he journeyed with five hundred men,
And there he won many followers and made up a war-fleet,
And travelled for so long that he came to this land,
Into the Humber; there he did much harm.
But not for long did he dare to remain in that area:
The king was marching that way and Passent fled away,   8750
Along the sea-coast for so long that he came to Ireland;
There he at once found the king of that land:
His heart was very sore when he greeted King Gillomaur:
'Good health to you, Gillomaur, great chieftain of warriors!
To you I have come: I was Vortigern's son.
Of Britain was my father king: he loved you above all things,

And if on this occasion to go there you'd yourself be my companion,
The two of us would so arrange it that my father we'd well avenge,
And we'd well avenge your folk whom Uther killed here,
And your magic stone-work which they dragged away;   8760
And also I heard it said, as I travelled on the sea,
That King Aurelius has become very sick,
And lies within Winchester where he's bedridden;
You can trust me totally for this is absolutely true!'
Passent and Gillomaur made their agreement there;
Oaths they swore there, many and uncountable
That all of this land they two would place in their own hands;
The oaths indeed were deeply sworn, but then again they were
    broken.

    The king gathered his army far and wide through all his country;
To the sea coast went Gillomaur and Passent,   8770
Into the ships they slid and off they let them glide;
Off they went speedily until they came to Menevia,
Which was at that time a flourishing town
Which now, to be specific, people call St David's.
There they took harbour in the greatest happiness:
Ships ran up on the strand: knights went up on the land.
Then said Passent (towards Gillomaur he went):
'Speak to me, King Gillomaur, now that we have come here:
Now I'm placing in your hands a half share of this kingdom,
For from Winchester there has come to me a certain knight's
    son   8780
And he tells me news of this kind: that Aurelius is going to die;
The disease lies under his ribs in such a way he can't live.
Here we two shall well avenge our associates and kinsmen,
Win for ourselves his dwellings, as will be best for us!'

    To the king that word came, inside Winchester,
That Passent and Gillomaur with an army had come over here.
The king called Uther, who was his dear brother:
'Uther, call up the army over all this country,
And march to our enemies and drive them from the country:
Either you must make them flee or you must fell them;   8790
I would go as well if I were not so ill,
But if I get better I'll come after you at once.'
Everything did Uther as the king said to him there;
And Passent at Saint David's was causing great distress,
And also King Gillomaur – much distress he made there.

They ran right through Britain, ravaging and burning,
While Uther in this country was gathering his army,
And it took a long time before he could move ahead,
And Passent set in his own hand all of the West Welsh land.
 Then it happened one day (his troops were very cheerful)   8800
That **Appas** there came faring (the fiends must have fetched him!)
And spoke to Passent like this: 'Come over here to us!
I will relate to you some really pleasant news.
I've just been in Winchester among your worst enemies
Where the king lies sickly and in a very sorry mood.
What will I get for it if I go that way riding
And give you the comfort of making him a corpse?'
As he went towards Appas, Passent's response was:
'I promise you today one hundred pounds (and I have got it)
If you give me the comfort of making him a corpse!"   8810
They made many promises to perform this treachery.
Appas went off in private to hatch out this plot;
He was a heathen person of Saxon derivation.
He put a monk's habit on and shaved his crown on top,
He took with him two supporters and then he set off
And went at once directly into Winchester,
Looking just like a holy man – the heathen devil!
 He went to the borough gate where the king lay in a bedroom
And greeted the porter by commending him to God   *Aurelius's*
And asked him in a hurry to go in to the king   *Death*
And to tell him in truth that Uther his brother   8821
Had sent to him there a splendid physician,
The very best doctor living in any land,
Who knew how to release every sick man from disease.
So this vile man lied to the people's very king,
For Uther had left and gone off with his forces,
Never had Uther set eyes upon him still less sent him there,
Yet the king thought it must be the truth and believed him well
   enough.
And who would have guessed that he was a traitor,
Since he was wearing chain-mail next to his bare skin,   8830
On top of that he had a horrible hairshirt
And then a monk's cowl made out of black cloth;
He had blackened his torso as if it were grimed with coal.
He knelt before the king; his words were very gentle:
'May you recover health, Aurelius, most excellent of kings!

I was sent here by Uther, who is your own brother,
And entirely for the love of God I have come here to you,
Because I'm going to heal you and make you quite healthy
For the love of Christ, God's son (I don't care about reward,
Nor payment in land, nor in silver or gold,   8840
But for each sick one I do this for the love of my good Lord).'
     The king heard all this and it consoled him very much;
But where is there ever any man upon this earth of ours
Who would have guessed that he was a traitor?
He took his glass bottle at once and the king urinated in it;
A short time after that he took the glass bottle in hand
And held it up for inspection by all the king's knights,
And the heathen man Appas at once remarked thus:
'If you would believe me before tomorrow evening
This king will be completely well, recovered, if he wills it.'   8850
Then all those in the bedroom were blissfully happy.
     Appas went off into a private room to hatch out that plot,
And used for it a poison which is called scamony,
And came out straightaway among the chamber-knights†
And to the king he gave a dose of a good deal of cinnamon,
And ginger and licorice he handed over generously;
They all received that offering and he took them all in;
This con-man fell upon his knees before the nation's king
And in this way to him he spoke: 'My lord, now you must take
A dose of this liquor which will bring you health and vigour.'   8860
And the king drank it down: and there he drank in the poison;
As soon as he had drunk the doctor laid him down.
Appas gave these instructions to the knights in attendance:
'Now cover the king well so he works up a sweating.
Above all else, I'm telling you, our king will be quite well,
And I'll go to my lodging to discuss it with my men,
And around midnight I shall come right back,
With some other medication which will be pleasant for him.'
Off went the traitor; the king lay in slumber;
Appas went to his lodging and spoke to his men   8870
In very secret whsipers; then stole out of town.
     When it was midnight then the attendant knights
Sent six of their men to Appas's lodging;
They expected to find him and to lead him to the king.
But then he had fled (the fiends had ferried him off!).
The men came back again to where the king was staying,

228

And announced in the chamber Appas's departure.
Then could be seen copious grief:
Knights were falling down and longing for their deaths.
There was much lamenting, much heart-felt groaning;   8880
There was pitiful talking, there were men screaming!
They leaped over to the bed, and the king was [un]covered:†
He was still lying there asleep and in a terrific sweat;
With tears streaming down them, the knights awoke the king,
And they called to him with very soft voices:
'How are you, my lord? How is your [affliction]?†
Now our doctor has departed without your permission!
He's slipped out of court and he's left us like idiots.'
    The king gave them a reply: 'I am completely swollen,
And there is no other help for it: soon now I shall be dead.   8890
And I'm asking you right now, you knights who are my own,
That you greet Uther, who is my own brother,
And invite him to hold my land in his control:
May God himself above all things let him be a good king!
And urge him to have courage and everywhere aright judge,
Be to the weak a father, to the destitute a consoler;
Then may he hold the land under control.
And now when I am dead today, all decide to act one way:
Let me arrive after my journey right there at Stonehenge;
There lie many of my kinsfolk, killed by the Saxons;   8900
And send off for bishops and men of book-learning;
My gold and my silver distribute for my soul,
And lay me in the east end right inside Stonehenge.'
There was no other help for it: there the king was dead,
And his men did exactly as the king had decreed.
    Of all this quite unaware, in the land of Wales was Uther;
Not by any cleverness could he know a thing about this,
But however he had with him the prophet known as Merlin.
He returned to meet the army which had come to the country.
Uther was camped in Wales, in a wilderness,   8910
And was marching forward fast to fight against Passent.
Then in the evening time the moon began to shine
Almost just as brightly as if it were sunlight.
Then they saw from afar a very strange star: *The Comet*
It was broad, it was huge, it was quite immense:
From it came rays horrifyingly gleaming:
That star is called in Latin a 'comet'.

There came from the star a most grim-looking ray;
At the end of the ray there was a fine dragon,
And from the dragon's mouth came many rays spouting,   8920
But two of these were vast, quite unlike the others:
One drew towards France, the other towards Ireland;
The ray which drew towards France gave a bright enough radiance:
The uncanny symbol was seen above the Great Saint Bernard Pass;
The ray which stretched westwards was composed of seven beams.
This was seen by Uther: what it meant he'd no idea.
He felt sad at heart and strangely afraid,
And so was all that great assembly who were in the army.

    Uther called Merlin, and asked him to come to him,
And in this way spoke to him in very soft accents: 8930
'Merlin, Merlin, my dear friend, find it out yourself,
And tell us about this symbol which we have just seen,
For I do not know in all the world what will turn up from it;
Unless you direct us we shall have to ride back!'

    Merlin sat silent for a long space of time,
As if in a dream he were deeply disturbed;
They would say, those who witnessed it with their own eyesight,
That he kept on wriggling just as if he were a worm!
In the end he started waking, and then he started quaking,
And Merlin the prophet uttered these words: 8940
'O wretched time, O wretched time in this world's realm:
Great is the sorrow which has settled on the land!
Where are you, Uther? Sit in front of me now, here,
And I shall tell you of very many sorrows.
Dead is Aurelius, most excellent of kings!
So is the other, Constance your brother
Whom Vortigern betrayed with all his treachery.
Now Vortigern's descendant has destroyed Aurelius;
Now you alone remain out of all your family;
But don't hope for any ideas from those who are lying dead,   8950
But think of yourself: good fortune is granted you,
For seldom does he not succeed who takes thought for himself;
You are to be a good king and the lord of great men!
If just at midnight you arm all your knights,
So that in the morning light we may arrive all right
In front of St David's, there's where you'll fight;
Before you go from there you shall make a slaughter:
Both of them you'll slay there, Passent and Gillomaur,

And many thousands of the men who have come here with them.
That sign from the star which we could see so far,   8960
True it is, Uther my dear, it signified your brother's death.
   'In front of the star was that dragon, quite surpassing every snake;
That portent was on your account: that was you, Uther, yourself;
You are to have this land: your power will be great and strong.
Likewise the tokens are uncanny which came from the dragon's
      mouth;
Two beams went out, marvellously bright:
The first went far south out over France;
This is a powerful son who from your body is to come,
Who is to conquer by combat many a kingdom,
And eventually he shall rule many a people.   8970
The other beam which stretched to the west, marvellously bright,
That will be a daughter who will be very dear to you.
The beams then separated into seven lovely rays:
These are seven lovely sons who from your daughter are to come,
Who will amass many royal lands into their own hands:
They will be very strong, both at sea and on land.
Now that you have heard from me things which will help you
Speedily forthright advance to your fight!'
And Merlin started dozing as if about to sleep.
   Up rose Uther, now informed and aware,   8980
And ordered his knights 'to horse' right away,
And ordered them with speed to gallop to Menevia,
And to prepare all their effects: they were going to fight.
In the leading troop he put knights who were well proved:
Seven thousand knights, brave men and valiant;
In the mid-section knights who were attentive,
Another seven thousand splendid soldiers;
He had as rear-guard very brave knights,
Eighteen thousand very brave warriors,
And so many thousands were the foot soldiers   8990
That not with any numbers could one count them up.
   Off they went apace until they came to St David's.
There Gillomaur spotted the arrival of Uther,
And ordered his knights to their weapons then, straight,
And they fell to with speed and they all grabbed their knives,
And it was off with their breeches (odd was their appearance!)
And they grasped in their hands their very long spears,
They hung across their shoulders enormous battle-axes.

231

Then Gillomaur the king said a most amazing thing:
'Here comes Uther, Aurelius's brother;   9000
He wants to sue for peace from me and not to fight against me.
The leading men are his servants: let us march against them,
You need not bother overmuch if you kill those wretches,
For if Uther son of Constantine wants to become my vassal,
And restore to Passent his father's realm,
Then I'll make a truce and allow him to live,
And lead him in shining fetters to my own territory.'
    The king spoke like this, whereas things turned out worse!
There Uther's knights were at the town in a trice:
They set fire to the town and were quickly fighting;   9010
With swords they rushed and struck them, and the Irish were all
    naked!
When the Irishmen perceived there was battle-ardour with the
    British,
They fought very fiercely, but nonetheless they all fell dead.
They challenged their king: 'Where are you, good for nothing?
Why won't you come this way, you're leaving us to be destroyed,
And your crony Passent, he can see us collapsing;
Come to our aid with full assistance!'
Gillomaur heard this and it caused him much distress;
With his Irish knights he entered the fight,
And Passent went ahead with him: both of them were fated!   9020
When Uther perceived that Gillomaur had arrived
He rode over to him and struck him in the side
So that the spear penetrated and pierced to the heart;   *Gillomaur's*
Hastily he turned around and overtook Passent,   *Death*
And these words were uttered by Uther the lucky:
'Passent, this is where you pause: here comes Uther on his horse!'
He struck him on his crown so that he fell down
And plunged the sword down his gullet – which wasn't to his
    palate! –
So that the point of the sword stuck into the earth.
Then observed Uther: 'Passent, you stop there!   9030
So you've laid claim to Britain now as all your own: *Passent's*
As much is allowed you as the bit you're lying dead on!   *Death*
Here you must remain, you and Gillomaur your friend,
Get the best from Britain, for now I'm bestowing it on you both,
So that you two for many a year with us can stay right here,
And you'll never need to worry about your food supply!'

Those were Uther's words and he rode afterwards
Driving those Irishmen over stream and over fen,
And slaughtered all the force which with Passent came ashore.
Some dashed to the sea and leapt aboard ship: 9040
What with weather, what with water, there they came to grief.
That was how they got on there, Passent and Gillomaur.

   Now this fight was done and Uther came back home,
And straightaway went into Winchester.
On a broad paved street he chanced to meet
Three knights and their squires coming towards him.
As soon as they met him politely they greeted him:
'All health to you, Uther, these honours are your own;
Dead is Aurelius, most excellent of kings,
And he has placed in your hand all his royal land;   9050
He wished you every joy and to remember his soul!'
Then Uther cried extremely copiously.

   Uther went directly into Winchester:
There stood before him, outside the city
All of the citizens with very sad expressions;
As soon as they saw him like this they addressed him:
'Uther, be gracious now and in all ages!
Our king we have lost; at this we are distressed;
You were his brother and he did not have another,
Nor did he have a son who the king might become.   9060
But do you take the king's crown: it comes as your inheritance,
And we wish to help you and have you as our lord,
With our weapons and possessions and with all our might.'

   Uther listened to this: he was wise and well aware   UTHER
That there was no other course since his brother was now dead;
He received the crown, which became him really well,
And so with much honour he was made the king,
And maintained good laws and loved all his people.

   At the time he was made king and was choosing his ministers
Merlin departed (he had no idea where he'd gone to,   9070
Nor in all the world's bounds what became of him).
The king was very sombre and so were all his soldiers,
And all his courtiers for this reason were depressed.
The king had people ride very far and wide:
He proffered gold and great wealth to each wayfaring man,
To whomsoever could find Merlin in the land,
And he added much of value – but he heard nothing of him.

Then Uther was pondering on what Merlin had been saying
On the armed expedition into Welsh land
Where they saw the dragon ummatched by every snake,   9080
And he thought of its significance, as Merlin instructed him.
The king was very dismal and felt very depressed,
For he'd never lost a dearer man since he'd been alive,
Never any other, not Aurelius his brother.
    The King had two images fashioned, two golden dragons,
All for love of Merlin, so much did he want him to come.
When the dragons were completed, the first was his companion,
Wherever in the country he would lead his army;
It was his army ensign in every single event;
The second he gave generously to the town of Winchester,   9090
To the bishop's throne which is situated there;
He gave his good spear in addition, so people could carry the dragon
When in procession the relics were borne round.
The Britons observed these dragons which in this way were
      constructed:
Ever after they called Uther, who bore the dragon as his ensign,
By the surname they attached, which was Uther Pendragon;
Pendragon in British is 'Dragonhead' in English.[*]
    Now Uther was a good king, but of Merlin he [heard] nothing;[†]
This news came to Octa where he lived in the north,
And Ebissa his blood-brother, and **Osa** was another;   9100
These Aurelius had sent there and established in his peace,
Placing into their hands sixty hides of his land.
Octa heard exactly how it had all occurred,
About Aurelius's death and about Uther's kingdom.
Octa called to him the closest members of his family;
They discussed between them their former deeds,
Saying, by their lives, they'd leave off Christianity;
They held their hustings and became heathen.
Then from Hengest's kinsfolk there came together
Six thousand five hundred men who were heathen.   9110
    The news was known at once and announced around the land
That Octa son of Hengest had become a heathen,
And all of those very people whom Aurelius had pardoned.
Octa sent his messengers into Welsh territory
After the Irish who had run away from Uther,
And after the Germans who had just managed to escape,
Who had fled into the forests while Passent was being killed,

And hid themselves just anywhere while Gillomaur was being killed.
From the woods these people skulked and off to Scotland slunk;
More and more kept coming, moving towards Octa;   9120
When they had all got together there were thirty thousand of them,
(Not counting the women) of Hengest's kinsmen.
    They took their forces and proceeded to advance,
And seized into their hands all beyond Northumberland,
And the men who lived there; where they started marching
The host was extraordinary, and it went straight to York,
And on every side the city was surrounded,
And they besieged the borough, those heathen men,
And took into their hands all from there into Scotland;
All they set eyes on they treated as their own.   9130
    But Uther's own knights who were in the castle
Defended the town from within so that they could not get in;
Never was it heard of anywhere that a small band did as well as there.
The moment that Uther of these things was made aware
He summoned a strong force through all his kingdom
And very hurriedly he marched towards York city;
He marched at once and direct to where Octa was camped.
Octa and his host hastened towards them,
And they flung together with very fierce strength:
Hardily they hacked; helmets resounded;   9140
Fields grew fallow-hued with the blood of fated men,
And the heathen souls sank down to hell.
When the day's end came it had been so badly arranged
That the heathen hordes had the upper hand
And with outstanding force overwhelmed the British
And drove them to a mountain which was immensely huge;
And Uther with his men withdrew to the mountain,
Having lost in the fight his beloved knights,
At least seven hundred: his [numbers] were the less![†]
    Uther was up the mountain which was known as Dinian;   9150
And the mountain was overgrown with a glorious wood.
The king was inside it with very many men
And day and night Octa besieged him, with his heathen men,
Besieged him all around; the Britons were in trouble!
It distressed King Uther that he wasn't aware earlier
That he did not have for his land a better understanding.
They frequently consulted about this special need,
As to how they could overcome Octa who was Hengest's son.

There was an earl named **Gorlois**, a great man indeed he was,
He was an accomplished knight, a retainer of Uther's,   9160
Earl of Cornwall, known far and wide,
A most intelligent man, in all ways most able.
Uther said to him, in a sombre mood,
'I salute you, Gorlois, good leader of men!
You are my own man, and very much to you I'll grant:
You are an accomplished knight and a man of intellect;
All of my men I put in your judgement,
All these who are my men I submit to your command,
And we shall do exactly what you shall decide.'
Then King Uther Pendragon hung his head right down,
And stood completely silent and asked Gorlois his intention.   9170
    Then Gorlois answered him – indeed most deferentially –:
'Tell me, Uther Pendragon, why do you hold your head right down?
You know God by himself is better than we are altogether?
To whomever he decides, he can distribute glory;
Let us promise him by our lives that in him we [will believe],†
And let us consider all our misdeeds;
Let each man right now be absolved of all his sins,
Let each man absolve the other, as if he were his brother,
And let every good knight take upon himself great penance,
And we shall promise God to make atonement for our sins;   9180
And then just at midnight we'll get ready to fight!
These heathen hounds think we're totally bound;
Octa son of Hengest thinks he's got us all trapped:
They're lying on the fields here under their tent covering;
They being very weary, their weapons they've done carrying,
Now they're going to doze a bit and then fall fast asleep.
They're not worried a bit that we're going to attack 'em!
Exactly at midnight we shall move straight
In total silence down from this hill;
Let no knight be so mad as to utter a word,   9190
Nor any man whatever to blow his horn here.
But we shall step towards them as if we were stealing:
Before they are aware of it we shall annihilate them;
Up to them we shall creep and tell them some secrets!
And let every valiant man stoutly set on them,
And so from this land we shall drive this alien band,
And by our Lord's might we shall reclaim our rights.'
    The whole army acted just as Gorlois had instructed;

Every man scrupulously made his confession,
Promising to do good and to abandon evil.   9200
Exactly at midnight the knights armed themselves
And in front of all descended Uther Pendragon,
And all his knights, in total silence,
And out upon the fields they struck among the tents,
And slaughtered the heathen with the utmost strength:
Their flaxen locks streaming, they fled down the fields;
For the men it was detestable: they were dragging their intestines;
In complete weakness they fell to the ground.
There at once was captured Octa son of Hengest,
His blood-brother Ebissa and his partner **Osa**.   9210
The king had them fastened with strong iron fetters,
And entrusted them to sixty knights who were expert fighters,
To hold them fast upon the open fields.
And he himself pushed on, producing a huge clamour,
And Gorlois the courteous from the other quarter,
And all their knights, ever right ahead,
Striking right down all they came near to.
Some crept towards the wood on their bare knees:
By the next morning they were most miserable people.
Octa was tied up and taken to London,   9220
So were Ebissa and Osa; they had never been so sad!
      This fight was finished and the king marched off
Into Northumberland in greatest triumph,
And then towards Scotland and set it all in his own hand.
He made truce, he made peace that each man might proceed by
From one land to another land, even carrying gold in his hand.
With his peace he did such things as never before could any king
Since the very time that the Britons travelled here.
      And then after a time he went back to London:
He was there at Easter with his excellent men.*   9230
There was rejoicing in London town at Uther Pendragon!
He sent his messengers throughout all his kingdom:
He asked prominent men, he asked peasant folk,
He asked bishops, he asked book-learned men
That they should come to London, to Uther the king,
Into London town, to Uther Pendragon.
Swiftly the noblemen came up to London:
They brought wife, they brought child, as King Uther commanded.
With great devotion the king heard the Mass,

And Gorlois, Earl of Cornwall and with him many knights: 9240
There was great rejoicing in the town with Uther Pendragon.
When the Mass was sung, to the hall they thronged:
Brass trumpets were blown, the trestle-tables laid;
All the company ate and drank, and were all making merry.
    There sat King Uther upon his high throne;*
Facing him was Gorlois – indeed the knight was courteous –
The Earl of Cornwall with his gracious wife.
When the nobles were seated, all at their meal,
The king sent a server to **Igerne** the gracious,
The wife of Earl Gorlois, the most courtly of women.   9250
He kept on gazing at her, flashing glances with his eyes,
Kept on sending over attendants to her table,   *Uther*
Kept on grinning at her, giving her special looks;   *in love*
And she looked at him affectionately (but I couldn't say whether she
    loved him).
The king wasn't clever or quick-witted enough
To be able to conceal his intentions from his courtiers.
The king kept up [this game] so long that Gorlois got annoyed,†
And was really enraged with the king about his wife.
    The earl and his knights stood up straightaway,
And those most affronted knights swept off with the wife.   9260
King Uther saw this and was upset about it,
And taking twelve wise knights to himself, straight
He sent after Gorlois, great leader of men,
And ordered him to come with haste to the king,
And give the king due reverence and admit publicly his fault
In disgracing the king by departing from his feasting,
He and his knights, without any right,
Just because the king was merry with him and was drinking to his
    wife;
And if he refused to come back to acknowledge his guilt,
The king would be after him with all his full force,   9270
Seizing all his land and his silver and his gold.
    Gorlois, great lord of men, got all this message
And delivered his reply, the most furious of earls:
'No, so help me the Lord, who made the daylight by his word!*
Never will I come back again nor sue for peace with him,
Nor shall he ever in his life disgrace me with my wife.
Just you tell King Uther he can find me at Tintagel:
If he'd like to ride that way, there I'll be waiting for him,

And there I'll give him a hard game, and very much public shame.'
Off went the earl, anger in his heart;   9280
He was enraged against the king, amazingly greatly,
And threatened Uther the king and all his lords with him,
But then he didn't know what was to come soon after.
   The earl went at once down into Cornwall:
There he had two castles securely enclosed;   *Gorlois's*
These castles were excellent, acquired from his ancestors: *Rebellion*
He sent off to Tintagel his beloved who was amiable,
Igerne by name, most gracious of women,
And enclosed her securely inside the castle.
Igerne was sorry, and saddened at heart   9290
That for her sake so many men would come to destruction.
The earl sent messengers over all Britain's land,
Bidding every worthy man to make his way to him,
For gold and for silver and for other good gifts,
So that they very quickly should come to Tintagel;
And his own knights came straightaway.
When they were assembled, those splendid soldiers,
Then he had fully fifteen thousand of them,
And very securely they shut fast Tintagel.
   Tintagel stands right upon the sea-strand   9300
And is firmly enclosed by the sea-cliffs
So that it cannot be taken by any kind of men,
Unless perhaps hunger in there were to enter.
The earl marched from there with seven thousand warriors
And went to another castle, and fortified it firmly,
Leaving his wife inside Tintagel with ten thousand men,
Since there was no task for the knights by day or by night
Except for some to guard the castle gate and the rest without care to
     lie and sleep,
And the earl maintained the other and with him was his own brother.
   Uther, that king most sturdy, came to hear of this,   9310
That his earl Gorlois had gathered his own force
And intended to make war with most extreme rage.
The king summoned his army through all this country
And through all the lands which he held in his command:
Peoples of many types travelled there together
And arrived in London, to the sovereign.
Out from London town went Uther Pendragon:
He and his knights went on straightaway

For so long a way that they came right into Cornwall,
And across that river they travelled which is called Tamar,   9320
Right up to the castle where they knew Gorlois was.

    With the greatest loathing for him they laid siege to the castle,
Often rushing upon them there with rigorous force;
United they dashed in: men fell there in death.
For seven whole nights the king with his knights
Lay in siege round the castle; his men there were stressed.
Against the earl he was not able to gain any advantage,
And for all those seven nights lasted that peculiar fight.
When King Uther realised that he had no success in this
He kept on musing thoughtfully what should be his policy,   9330
Since he loved Igerne every bit as much as his own life,
While Gorlois for him in all the land was the man he loathed most,
And in every way he was oppressed with grief in the kingdom of this
    world
Because he could not be entitled to have his way at all.

    There was with the king an old man who was most useful;
He was a very rich subject and was sound in each decision;
His name was **Ulfin** (there was much common sense in him).
The king stuck out his chin and stared hard at Ulfin
(He was very distressed, his mind was disturbed);
Then Uther Pendragon addressed Ulfin the knight: 9340
Ulfin, give me some advice, or I shall very quickly die;
I'm in such a state of deep desire that I simply can't exist
For the lovely Igerne. Now keep these words secret,
For, Ulfin my dear man, your splendid instructions,
Aloud and in silence I shall now observe.'

    Then responded Ulfin to the king speaking to him:
'What I hear now is surprising for a king to say!
You're in love with Igerne and this is how you keep it dark!
The woman is too dear to you and her husband too detested;
You've been burning up his lands and making him a beggar,   9350
And threatening to kill him and destroy all of his kinsfolk.
Now do you think all that oppression will win over Igerne?
If it does then she acts differently from every other woman,
Finding love's sweetness in the midst of utter terror!
But if you love Igerne then you ought to keep it secret,
And straightaway send to her some silver and some gold,
And artfully love her with amorous promises.
Even then it's quite debateable whether you could get her,

Because Igerne is well behaved, a very loyal woman,
So was her mother and more of her family.   9360
It's the truth I'm telling you, dearest of all kings,
You must go about it another way if you want to win her over.
    'Now yesterday there came to me a very virtuous hermit
Who swore by his chin that he knew where Merlin
Each and every night seeks rest beneath the skies,
And he'd often spoken with him and had told him stories.
So if we could coax Merlin into being in our scheme,
Then you would be able to get everything you want.'
    Then Uther Pendragon's mood was much calmer,
And he gave a ready answer: 'Ulfin, you've spoken well!   9370
I shall give into your hands thirty ploughs' worth of land*
If you get hold of Merlin and do just what I want.'
Ulfin went right through that army and sought through all the host,
And after a time that hermit he did find,
And in a hurry he brought him to the king,
Who would give him in hand seven ploughs of land
If only he could bring Merlin to the king.
    The hermit began to roam in the west region,
Into a wilderness, to a vast forest
Where he had been living for very many winters,   9380
And very often Merlin made his way in.
As soon as the hermit got in, then he encountered Merlin,
Standing under a tree, in strong anticipation.
He saw the hermit coming, which for some time had been his custom;
He ran towards him in greeting: they were both pleased to meet;
They hugged and they kissed and they chatted like friends.
Then Merlin remarked (he was really perceptive):
'Now tell me, my dear friend, why you didn't want to tell me
Not for any kind of thing, that you were going to the king!
But anyway I knew at once the moment that I missed you   9390
That you had come to Uther the king,
And what the king was saying to you, and offering you his lands
On condition you should bring me to Uther the king,
And Ulfin, who had sought you, to the king had brought you.
And Uther Pendragon, straightway at once,
Placed into his hands thirty ploughs' worth of lands,
And into your own hands seven ploughs' worth of lands.
    'So, Uther is passionate about the lovely Igerne,
Amazingly fiercely and for Gorlois's wife;

But for as long as for ever it will happen never   9400
That her he should win – except by my scheme –
For no woman is truer in the kingdom of this world.
Nevertheless he's going to have the beautiful Igerne,   *Merlin's*
And on her he'll beget one who'll be active far and wide;   *Prophecy*
He shall beget upon her a most remarkable man;
For as long as will be for ever, death will come to him never;
All the time that this world stands, his reputation will endure,
And within Rome itself he shall rule the leaders.
All who live in Britain shall bow down to him;
Of him shall poets sing their splendid praises: 9410
From his own breast noble bards shall partake;
Great warriors shall upon his blood be drunk;
From his eyes shall fly glowing coals of fire,
Each finger on his hand a sharp sword of steel;
Ahead of him shall fall stone-constructed walls;
Warriors will tremble, battle-ensigns will fall;†
In this way for a long time he shall march across lands,
Conquer those who live there and impose his own laws.
These are the tokens of the son who will come from Uther Pendragon
And from Lady Igerne. This prophecy is very secret   9420
Since as yet it's known by neither Igerne nor Uther
That from Uther Pendragon shall arise such a son,
Since as yet he's unbegotten who will arouse all the nations.
   'But my lord,' exclaimed Merlin, 'now it is your desire
That I shall hasten forth to the host of the king;
Your word I will listen to, and now I shall depart,
And for love of you I will travel, to Uther Pendragon,
So that you shall have the land which he placed in your hands.'
As they conversed like this the hermit began weeping;
Affectionately he kissed him; there they separated.   9430
Merlin travelled due south: he knew the land well enough;
Directly he hastened to the host of the king.
The moment Uther saw him, he moved over towards him,
And like this spoke Uther Pendragon: 'Merlin, you are welcome!
Here I place within your hands all the government of my lands,
And so that you may guide me in my pressing need.'
   Uther declared to him all he desired,
And how for him in all the nation Igerne was the dearest woman,
And Gorlois her husband the most detested of men –
'And unless I have your advice, very soon you'll see me dead   9440

[So desperately am I yearning for the wife of Earl Gorlois!']† 9440a
Then Merlin responded: 'Get Ulfin to come now,
And make him possessor of those thirty ploughlands,
And give to the hermit just what you promised.
But I don't want to own land, nor [silver, nor gold],†
Seeing that for giving good advice I'm quite the wealthiest man!
And if I wanted to own property my skills would grow the weaker.
    'But everything you want will turn out for you well,
For I know the kind of medicine, which you will find most pleasant,
So that all your [appearance] will become just like the earl's,†
Your voice, your gestures in the midst of that company, 9450
Your horse and your clothing; and just like that you'll ride off.
When Igerne is to see you, her reactions will be good.
She lies in Tintagel, securely locked in;
There is no knight however noble, elect of any nation,
Who by force could unbar the gates of Tintagel,
Unless they could be burst by hunger and by thirst.
This is the truth which I wish to tell you:
In all respects you'll appear as if you were the earl,
And I will be in precise detail like the man **Britael**
Who is a very stern knight and is the earl's steward; 9460
Jordan is his chamberlain (he's a very splendid man):
Instantly I'll transform Ulfin to be the same as Jordan;
So you'll be the lord, I'll be Britael your steward,
And Ulfin, Jordan your chamberlain; and this very night we're going
    in:
You are to go as I instruct, wherever I shall direct.
During this very night a full fifty knights
With their spears and their shields must surround your pavilions,
So that no living man can come anywhere near there,
And should any man at all come there, he must be instantly beheaded,
For those knights shall say (those splendid men of yours) 9470
That you have had blood-letting and are resting in your bed.'
    These things were immediately arranged just like this;
Off went the king: no one knew a thing,
And there went along with him Ulfin and Merlin;
They took the direct way that down to Tintagel lay.
They approached the castle gate and called out like acquaintances:
'Undo the bars on this gate: the earl's arrived here,
Gorlois the lord and Britael his steward,
And Jordan the chamberlain; all night we've been travelling!'

243

The porter proclaimed it all around and knights ran up on the
    battlements
And exchanged words with Gorlois, and identified him for
    sure.   9481
The knights were very prompt and opened up the castle gate,
And allowed him to come inside (they were not at all concerned that
    time:
They thought they were quite certain to have a celebration).
    So then by his magic they had Merlin inside there,
And in their command [were holding] no less than Uther himself, the
    king,[†]
And were conducting there with him his loyal servant, Ulfin!
This news travelled quickly indoors to the lady,
That her husband had come, and with him his three men.[†]
Out came Igerne, out to meet the 'earl',   9490
Speaking these words, with loving expression:
'Welcome, my lord, whom I love best of men,
And welcome Jordan, and Britael, you are too.
Did you escape from the king without any harm?'
Then Uther spoke with confidence (just as if he were Gorlois):
'Enormous is the throng which is with Uther Pendragon,
And I have in the night stolen away from the fight
Because I was longing for you: of all women I love you best!
Move into the bedroom and have my bed made up,
And I shall take my rest for this whole night's space,   9500
And all day tomorrow, so I can entertain my men.'
Igerne moved to the bedroom and had a bed made for him:
That most regal bed with royal cloth was spread.
The king looked at it closely and got into his bed,
And Igerne lay down beside Uther Pendragon!
    Now Igerne was confident that his man was Gorlois,
From no kind of hint of anything did she recognise Uther the king.
The king turned to her as man is bound to do to his mate,
And had his own way with the dearest of women,
And on her he begot a remarkable man   9510
Most courageous of all kings who ever came to men,
And **Arthur** he was known as, here on this earth.
Igerne had no idea who was lying in her arms;
All the time she was confident that this man was the earl Gorlois.
    There was no longer time than the arrival of daybreak
When all at once and rightly the knights there realised

That the king had travelled off away from his troops.
Then the knights declared (though it was not at all the case)*
That the king had fled away, quite prostrated by panic
(But they were all lying when they said that of the king); 9520
On this they held much discussion about Uther Pendragon.
Then the earls remarked, and the men of highest rank:
'Now that Gorlois is aware how everything goes here,
That our king has departed and has deserted his host,
He will instantly arm his infantry,
And out he'll come to fight and fell us to the ground,
Making huge slaughter with his savage leaders;
Then it would be better for us if we never had been born!
But let us blow brass trumpets and bring our host together,
And **Cador** the courageous shall carry the king's standard, 9530
Raising high the dragon at the head of this detachment,
And march to the castle with our courageous men;
And the Earl Aldolf shall be our commander,
And we shall obey him as if he were the king;
And so we shall rightly against Gorlois fight;
And should he wish to speak with us and request this king's peace,
Establish a settlement with true and sober oaths,
Then we may with full honour make our way from here;
Then our inferiors can't make any reproaches
That out of rank terror we ran away from here.' 9540
All the inhabitants approved of this notion.
 Brass trumpets they blew, brought the host together,
Up they raised the dragon, unique among all standards.
There many a strong fellow slung his shield over his shoulder,
Many a brave captain; and marched to the castle.
Gorlois was inside, with his brave men:
He had brass trumpets blown and brought his host together:
Leaping on steeds, the knights began riding.
The knights were very alert and sallied forth from the gate.
They encountered at once; steadfastly they struck: 9550
Fated men fell, sank down on the field:
There was much bloodshed, a bad time for the folk;
In the fighting, true it is, someone slew the earl Gorlois. *Gorlois's*
Then his men started fleeing and the others were pursuing; *Death*
They came to the castle and inside it they pushed:
Soon there came inside it both the two armies.
There they continued the fight as long as there was light;

Before the daylight had dispersed the castle was quite conquered.
No slave there so mean who was not an excellent leader.
    Swiftly came those tidings into Tintagel,   9560
Straight into the castle which Uther was in,
That he was slain, true it was, the earl, their lord Gorlois,
And all his men at arms, and his castle captured.
This was heard by the king as he lay there love-making,
And he leapt from the bedroom as if he had been a lion.
Then declared King Uther (of this information quite aware):
'Silence, silence now, you knights in the hall!
Here I am, no doubt of it, your own lord, Gorlois,
And Jordan my chamberlain and Britael my steward.
Myself and these two knights slipped off from the fight,   9570
And we made our way here and have not been killed there!
But now I shall hasten and assemble my host,
And myself and all my knights entirely by night
Shall march to a town and meet Uther Pendragon,
And unless he speaks of atonement I will avenge myself with honour.
And you will block up this castle extremely securely,
And encourage Igerne not to be too anxious;
Now I'm going off straightaway, so I bid you all goodnight!'
    In front of him went Merlin and the lord Ulfin,
And Uther Pendragon next, out of Tintagel fortress;   9580
They kept on going all night, until it was broad daylight,
When he came to the place where his army was stationed.
Merlin had by then replaced, in every detail, the king's face,
And then the knights recognised their own king and lord.
There many a fine Briton was filled with relief!
Then there was in Britain rejoicing in plenty:
Horns were sounding, musicians' songs resounding,
Glad knights, each and every one dressed in all his finery.
There for three days the king continued his stay,
And on the fourth day to Tintagel he marched.   9590
He sent into the castle his especially good lords,
To salute Igerne, the most noble of women,
And send her as a token what in bed they had spoken.
He ordered her to surrender the castle with speed:
No other course could be adopted, since her husband now was dead.
Igerne was still assuming that it was the case
That the dead earl had come to visit his household,
And would have believed that it must be a lie

That this king, Uther, could ever have come there.
    Knights went to take counsel, knights went to commune;   9600
They decided that they would not hold the castle any longer,
So letting their drawbridge down, they surrendered to Uther
    Pendragon.
Then all this royal land once more stood in Uther's hand.
    There Uther the king took Igerne as queen;
Igerne was pregnant by Uther the king,
All through Merlin's magic, before they were married.
The time arrived when it was destined that **Arthur** should
    be born.   *Arthur's*
The moment he came on earth, fairies received him:*   *Birth*
They enchanted the child with a very strong spell:
They gave him the power to be the greatest of all soldiers;   9610
They gave him a second thing: that he would be a noble king;
They gave him a third thing: that he should live long.
They gave to him, the royal heir, the most excellent gifts:
That he was the most generous of all living men.
These the elves bestowed on him, and so the child throve.
    After Arthur there was born the gracious lady –
She was called **Anna**, the graceful young girl –
And afterwards she married **Lot**, the ruler of Lothian;
In the land of Lothian she was the liegemen's lady.
    Long years lived Uther with great happiness here,   9620
In great peace, in great quiet, liberal in his kingdom.
When he was an old man, then a disease came upon him;
The disease knocked him down: sick lay Uther Pendragon;
In this sickness he lay here for fully seven years.
Then the British became very badly depraved:†
They frequently committed crimes, fearing no reprisals.
    All this time in London, lying fettered in prison
Was Octa son of Hengest who had been captured in York,
And his companion Ebissa and the other one was Osa.
They were guarded by twelve knights both by day and by
    night,   9630
Who were thoroughly bored with lolling round in London!
Octa heard information about the king's illness,
And chatted to the warders who were supposed to watch him:
'Pay attention now, you knights, to what I want to announce:
We are lying here in London, firmly trussed in prison,
And for many a long day now you've been in command of us;

It would be better for us by far to be living in Saxony,
Surrounded with great riches, than wretched like this here.
And if you were to change sides, and to do what I want,
I would give you land, much silver and much gold,   9640
So that, rich for ever more, you'd be rulers in that land,
And live out your lives as you'd most of all like to,
Seeing you can't expect to get good gifts out of your King Uther,
Since any minute now he'll be dead and his troops quite deserted;
Then you won't have either the one thing or the other.
But you work it out, you good chaps, and direct your charity at us,
And bear in mind what you'd prefer if you were lying bound like this,
When you could live in comfort in your own country.'
   Again and again did Octa talk like this with those knights.
Knights started discussing; knights started deciding: 9650
To Octa they said softly: 'We'll do just what you want!'
They swore solemn oaths that they would not betray them.   *Octa's*
Then there came a night when the wind was blowing right;   *Rebellion*
Off went the knights in the middle of the night,
Leading out Octa and Ebissa and Osa;
Along the Thames they took their way out on to the sea,
Off they sailed into Saxon lands.
Their kinsfolk came to meet them in enormous crowds;
They progressed throughout that people where they most preferred:
They were donated lands, they were given silver and gold.   9660
Octa thought carefully what could be his policy;
He intended to come here and avenge his father's wounds.
They acquired an army of innumerable folk
And travelled to the sea with tremendous menace:
[Off they set immediately] till they arrived in Scotland.†
At once they got quickly to land and they attacked it with fire!
The Saxons were cruel: they slaughtered the Scots,
With fire they destroyed three thousand farmsteads;
Many Scots they slaughtered, quite beyond reckoning.
   These bad tidings came to Uther the king: 9670
Uther grieved terribly and was dreadfully depressed
And sent into Lothian for his beloved friends,
And greeted Lot, his son-in-law, wishing him all health,
And instructing him to take in hand all his royal lands,
His knights and his freemen and freely to govern them,
And lead them in an army as the laws stood for the country,
And he instructed his beloved knights to be loyal to Lot,

With gestures of affection, as if he were the nation's king.
Because Lot was a very good knight, and had conducted many a fight,
And was very generous to every single man,   9680
He handed him the regency of this entire country.

    Octa caused much warfare and Lot fought him often,
And often he gained the advantage and often he lost it;
The British were high-spirited and excessively haughty,
And were quite without respect because of the king's age,
And behaved most contemptuously to the earl Lot,
And all his instructions they performed most inadequately,
Were all in two minds – they had more trouble for that reason!
This was soon reported to the sick monarch,
That his great men despised Lot totally.   9690

    Now I shall recount to you, in this same chronicle,
How King Uther then organised himself.
He said that he would himself travel to his army,
And with his own eyes observe who was doing well there.
There he had constructed a fine horse-litter,
And had forces summoned for defence throughout all his kingdom,
So that each man on pain of death must come to him at once,
To avenge the king's disgrace, or pay with lives and with limbs:
'And should there be any man who will not swiftly come,
I shall as swiftly execute him: either behead him or hang him!' 9700
All of them immediately came to the court:
There they did not remain, not the fat ones nor the thin.
The king straightaway took all of his knights,
And journeyed at once to the town of Verulam.

    Uther Pendragon surrounded Verulamium town;
Octa was inside it with all of his men.
In those days Verulamium was a very regal domain:
There St **Alban** was martyred and deprived of his life's days,
After which the town was laid waste and many people slain.
Uther was outside and Octa was inside;   9710
Uther's army advanced to the walls.
The proud men angrily made an assault:
Not one stone of the walls could they make fall,
And with no amount of force could they damage the wall:
Very pleased with himself was Hengest's son Octa
When he saw the British backing off from the walls,
And mournfully returning to their own tents.
Then Octa remarked to his companion Ebissa:

'Uther the crippled man came here to Verulam,
And wants a battle with us here lying on his stretcher!   9720
He's intending to use his crutches to give us a fatal thrust!
But tomorrow when it's daylight, the troops must all arise
And open up our fortress gates: we'll get a hold on all those great
    men;
We're not going to lurk in here just because of one lame man!
Out we shall gallop mounted on our noble steeds
And rush upon Uther and rout all his retainers:
All those who've ridden this way are all of them fated!
And then let's seize the cripple and shove him in our fetters
And keep the pathetic thing until he perishes,
And that's how his handicapped limbs will get healed,   9730
And his arthritic bones: with agonising rods of steel!'†
That was Octa's conversation with his comrade Ebissa,
But it all turned out quite other than what they expected.
   In the morning when the dawn came they unfastened the doors;
Up rose Octa, Ebissa and Osa
And ordered their knights to get ready to fight,
To undo their broad gates and unbar the fortress.
Octa rode out and after him went a great crowd;
With his valiant warriors he encountered disaster!
Uther had realised Octa was coming towards them,   9740
Intending to fell his force to the ground.
Then shouted Uther with a vigorous voice there:
'Where are you British, my brave commanders?
Now has arrived that very day when the Lord may give us aid;
Octa shall discover that for threatening to fetter me!
Remember now your ancestors, how good they were at fighting;
Remember the reputation which I have handed on to you:
Don't you ever let these heathens have use of your homes,
These same rabid dogs get control of your lands;
And to the Lord I shall pray who made the light of day   9750
And to all of the saints who are seated high in heaven
That on this field of battle [I] may have their succour.†
Now march speedily to them; the Lord give [us] his support,†
The all-powerful God give protection to my men!'
   Knights began riding, spears began gliding,
Broad spears were breaking, shields were splitting,
Helmets were shattering, soldiers collapsing.
The British were bold and active in the battle,

While the heathen hounds were falling to the ground:
There were killed Octa, Ebissa and Osa!   9760
Seventeen thousand there tumbled into hell;
Many escaped from there towards the north area.
All during daylight Uther's own knights
Killed and captured all they came near;
When it was evening the battle was all won.   *Victory*
 Then the men in the army sang with full force,
And these were the words of their joyful songs:
'Here comes Uther Pendragon,*
To Verulam he's come;   9768
He's been a-dubbing new knights:
Sir Octa, Sir Ebissa
And old Sir Osa too.   9769
He's cuffed them pretty soundly
To show they've joined the Order,   9770
To give men tales of them to tell
Among their tribe at home,   9771
And give men songs of them to sing
Throughout all Saxony.'   9772
 Then Uther was happy and greatly relieved,
And addressed his troops, whom he held in much esteem,
And Uther the aged uttered these words:
'The Saxon men considered me merely contemptible,
They mocked at my infirmity with their scornful words
Because I was carried here on a horse-litter,
And said that I was dead and my troops were in a trance;
Yet now a great miracle is manifested in this realm 9780
When this dead king has now killed off the living,
And has set some fleeing off on the wind.
Now this has occurred by the will of the Lord.'
 The Saxon men fled exceedingly fast,
Those who from the sides had escaped from the fight;
Off they went striding away into Scotland,
And chose as their king **Colgrim** the handsome; *Colgrim*
He was Hengest's kinsman and dearest of men to him, *the*
And Octa had loved him all the time he was alive.   *Leader*
Those Saxon men were severely disheartened,   9790
And strode off together straight into Scotland,†
And Colgrim the handsome they appointed as king,
And assembled an army far and wide around the country,

And said they were going, through their hostile arts
In Winchester town to kill Uther Pendragon.
O tragedy, that things like this should ever happen!
    Now the Saxon men said, in their secret consultations:
'Let us take six knights, clever men and agile,   *Saxon*
Cunning as spies, and let's send them to court.   *Conspiracy*
Make them move along in the guise of almsmen,   9800
And stay at the court with the great king,
And every single day travel through all the assembly,
And go to get the royal dole, as if they were infirm, *
And listen very keenly among those unfortunates
To learn if by a trick one might, by daytime or by night
Within Winchester town get at Uther Pendragon,
And with murderous intent kill that same king.'
(Then would all their wishes be entirely achieved,
And they would be unconcerned about Constantine's kin).
    Now off went the knights, all in broad daylight,   9810
In the clothing of almsmen (most accursed knights)
To the king's court: there they caused havoc;
They went to the dole as if they were not hale,
And listened eagerly for news of the king's illness:
How someone might contrive to bring about the king's death.
Then they met a certain knight coming from the king direct,
A relation of Uther's and his favourite retainer.
These traitors, as they were sitting all along the street,
Called out to the knight with kindly expressions:
'Lord, we are feeble men in the kingdom of this world;   9820
A while ago we were accounted great men in this country
Until the Saxon men displaced us to the depths
And deprived us of everything, taking from us our property.
Now we're reciting prayers for Uther our king;
For this each day in just one meal we have food in exchange:
Not at all do meat or fish come into our begging-dish, †
Nor any kind of liquor except for gulps of water,
Nothing but water drinks: that's why we're so thin.'
    The knight heard this lament and straight back he went,
And came to the king, as he lay in his bedroom,   9830
And said to the king: 'Good health to you, my lord!
Outside here are sitting six men similar in bearing,
All of them are companions and all are dressed in hessian.
Formerly they were, in the kingdom of this world,

Virtuous leaders, with goods well endowed;
Now to the depths the Saxon men have sent them
So that in this world they are reckoned worthless,
They can't get hold of any food except just for bread
Nor of any liquor except for gulps of water;
That's how they lead their lives within your own land,   9840
And they're praying their prayers that God will let you live long.'
Then said King Uther: 'Get them to come in here;
I want to clothe them, I want to feed them,
For the love of my Lord all the time I'm alive.'
There came into the bedroom those traitorous men;
The king had them clothed, the king had them fed,
And at night he would lay each of them in his bed;
And each for his part paid eager attention
To how they might kill the king with foul murder.
But not at all, not for anything could they kill Uther the king   9850
Nor by any scheming could succeed in getting at him.
    Then it happened at one time when the rain was pouring down,
That a doctor who was there called out from the bedroom
To one of the attendant knights and told him straightaway
To run to the well which was just outside the hall
And set there a good serving-man to protect it from the rain:
'Since the king can't endure any draught in the world
Except cold well water, in which he takes pleasure:
It's the finest of drinks for the disease that he has.'
Immediately those six knights heard that conversation: 9860
They were prompt in doing harm, and went out then in the dark
Straight to the well and there they did their harm.
They instantly drew out six shining phials
Brimful of poison, the most bitter of all liquids:
Six entire phials they poured into the well;
Then immediately all the well was affected by the poison.
Then the traitors were most blithe that they were alive
And off they went away: they did not dare to remain there.
    Then right away arrived two attendant knights
Carrying in their hands two goblets of gold.   9870
They approached the well; their goblets they filled
And went back again at once to where King Uther was,
Straight into the bedroom where he lay on his bed:
'Greetings to you, Uther! Now we have come here
And have brought for you what you have been asking for:

Cold well water; take it and enjoy it!'
Up got the sick king and sat on his bed,
And drank some of the water; at once he started sweating,
His heart beat grew weaker, his face grew ever blacker,[*]
His belly started swelling: the king was really dying!   9880
There could be no help for it: there King Uther lay dead,   *Uther's*
And everybody died if they had drunk from that water.   *Death*

    When the courtiers saw the tragic state of the king,
And of the king's attendants who had been destroyed by the poison,
Then out to the well ran those nights who were nimble
And blocked up the well with strenuous labour,
With earth and with stones they made a steep mound.

    Then the household detachment took the dead king's body –
A tremendous procession – and carried him out,
Stern-minded men, into Stonehenge,   9890
And there it was they buried him, beside his dear brother:
Side by side together both of them lie there.

    Then all together came those who were highest in the land,
Leaders and warriors and educated men,
They all came to London to a very crowded hustings.
The powerful leaders adopted as their policy[*]
That they would send messengers over the sea
Into Brittany for the best of all the youth
That there was in those days in the kingdom of this world,
Arthur he was called, the best of all knights,   9900
And announce that he must come at once to his own kingdom,
Because Uther now had died just like Aurelius before him,
And Uther Pendragon had no other son
Who after his own days could govern the British,
Could rule them with honour and take the kingdom over,
Since there were still in this land some Saxons left behind:
Colgrim the courageous and many thousand confederates
Who often brought vile injuries to our own British men.

    Speedily the British selected three bishops
And seven mounted men mighty in wisdom;   9910
Off they began to move right into Brittany
And very swiftly to Arthur they came:
'Good health to you, Arthur, most noble of knights!
Uther sent you greeting when about to depart
And requested that in Britain you should yourself
Hold to the just laws and help your own people

And defend [your own] kingdom as a good king should do,[†]
Put to flight your enemies and drive them from the land,
And to God's gentle son he prayed, to come to your aid
That you might succeed and receive the land from God,   9920
For dead is Uther Pendragon and you are Arthur, his son,
And dead is the other, Aurelius his brother.'
    So they finished talking, and Arthur sat without speaking:
One moment he was pallid, and in colour very blanched,
Next moment he was red and his emotions much aroused.
When at last his words broke, they were good things which he spoke,
Up he spoke like this, piously, that noble knight Arthur:
'Lord Christ, God's own son, now come to our aid,
So that all my whole life I may keep the laws of God.'
Arthur was fifteen years old when this message he was told   9930
And all those years were well employed for he had grown up very
    well.
    Arthur immediately summoned his knights
And ordered every single man to collect up his weapons
And get their horses saddled in most extreme haste,
For he intended to be on his way to this other Britain.
To the sea proceeded splendid leaders
At St Michael's Mount with a very massive army:
The sea sent them up on to that shore; at Southampton they came
    ashore.
Arthur the great began to ride off,
Directly to Silchester which seemed to him best.   9940
There the British troops were boldly assembled;
Great was the celebration when Arthur came to the city:
There was the blast of trumpets, and very triumphant men.
There Arthur the young was raised to the throne.   ARTHUR
    When Arthur was made king – now hear a strange thing:
He was generous with food to every man alive,
A knight of the very best, of amazing courage;
To the young he was a father, to the old folk a consoler,
And he was with the foolish amazingly strict;
Wrong he found really disgusting and justice always dear;   9950
Each of his cupbearers and chamber attendants
And all of his footmen carried gold in their hands,
On their backs and on their bed they had cloth of fine weave;
Every single cook he had was also a splendid champion,
Every single knight's squire was also a bold fighter.

The king kept all his court in the greatest content,
And with such qualities he surpassed all kings:
In vigorous strength and in great wealth,
And such was his character that all people knew of it.
Now Arthur was a good king, and his courtiers loved him,   9960
What concerned his kingdom was widely known all round.

The king held in London a very crowded hustings;
To it were invited all his feudal knights,
The great men and the humble, to honour the king.
When they had all come, an immense throng,
Up stood King Arthur the noblest of kings,
And had brought before him the most special relics;
To these did the king kneel some three times:
His warriors could not guess what he would decree.
Arthur held up his right hand: there he swore on oath   9970
That never in his life, not at any man's direction,   *Coronation*
Would the Saxons be contented in the land of Britain,   *Oath*
Would not be honoured with land nor enjoy any favours,
But he would expel them because they were his enemies,
Slew Uther Pendragon who was Constantine's son,
As they had done the other, Aurelius his brother,
For which in his land they were more loathed than all people.

Arthur straightaway took his wise knights:
Like it or loathe it, they must all swear the oath
That they would remain for ever loyally with Arthur   9980
And avenge King Uther who the Saxons had killed here.
Arthur sent written messages far and wide throughout his land
To seek out all the knights whom he might acquire,
So that at once to the king they might come,
And he would in his land with affection maintain them,
Supplying them with land, with silver and with gold.

Off the king went with an immense force of men;
He led amazing numbers and advanced direct to York;
There he lay for one night; in the morning he went right on
To where he knew were Colgrim and his confederates with
    him.   9990
Since Octa had been slain and deprived of his life's days
(He who was Hengest's son, who out of Saxony had come)
Colgrim was the leading man who came out of Saxon lands *Campaign*
Following Hengest and Horsa his brother   *Against*
And Octa and Osa and their companion Ebissa.   *Colgrim*

Colgrim held jurisdiction in those days over the Saxons,
He led them and he guided them with stern authority:
Many were the supporters who were marching with Colgrim.
    Colgrim heard the tidings about Arthur the king,
How he was coming towards him and wished to do him harm. 10000
Colgrim thought carefully what might be his policy,
And assembled his army all through the north country.
To there proceeded in unity all the Scottish people:
Picts then and Saxons joined forces together,
And men of many origins accompanied Colgrim.
Onward he was marching with an immense contingent
To oppose Arthur, most admirable king;
He proposed to kill the king within his own land
And fell all his followers, thrown to the ground,
And set all this kingdom in his own hands, 10010
Felling Arthur the young right to the ground.
    Off then went Colgrim and his army with him,
And went with his army till he reached a stretch of water;
The water is called the Douglas, the destroyer of people.
There Arthur encountered him, ready with his forces;
At a broad ford the forces engaged:
Their vigorous champions strongly attacked,
Those fated fell there, thrown to the ground;
There was very much bloodshed, misery was rife;
Spear-shafts shattered; soldiers fell down there. 10020
Arthur noticed that; his mind was disconcerted;
Arthur thought carefully what could be his policy,
And withdrew to the rear into a more open field;
His enemies assumed he was about to escape:
That delighted Colgrim and all his army with him!*
They assumed that Arthur must be filled with cowardice
And rushed over the water as if they were raging mad.
    When Arthur noticed that Colgrim had come very close to him
And that they were both of them on one side of the water,
Arthur noblest of kings announced these words: 10030
'Do you see, my Britons, right here beside us,
Our avowed enemies (may Christ exterminate them!)
Colgrim the savage, out of Saxon lands?
In this land his kindred slaughtered our ancestors,
But now the day's arrived which the Almighty has appointed
When he must forfeit his life and his friends will all be lost,

Or we ourselves must die: we cannot see him left alive.
The men of the Saxons are to suffer sorrow,
And we're to revenge honourably the dear men of our retinue.'
    Arthur caught up his shield, covering his breast,   10040
And began rampaging like the rime-grey wolf,[†]
When it comes loping from the snow-laden woodlands
Intending to savage such creatures as it fancies.
Then Arthur called out to his beloved knights:
'Forward and quickly, my valiant warriors,
All of us together at them! We shall all have victory
And they will heel over like the high wood
When the wild wind weighs into it with force!'
There flew across the fields thirty thousand shields
And struck into Colgrim's knights so that the earth
    reverberated;   10050
Broad spears smashed; shields were clattering;
The Saxon men fell, thrown to the ground.
Colgrim was watching this: he was distressed about it,
He the most able man to come out of Saxon lands.
    Colgrim began to flee, fast and furiously,
And his steed carried him with superb power
Over the deep water, and protected him from death.
The Saxons started sinking: disaster was their lot.
Arthur turned his spear's point against them and stopped them
    getting to the ford:
There the Saxons drowned, at least seven thousand;   10060
Some started floundering as the wild crane does
In the moorland fens when its flighting is impaired[*]
And the speeding hawks are bearing down upon it,
Hounds in the reedbeds pounce on the wretched bird;
Then nothing does it any good, neither land nor water:
Hawks are striking at it, dogs are biting at it;
Then the regal bird has reached its death hour.[†]
    Over the fields Colgrim fled with speed
Until to York he came, riding most remarkably;
He dashed into the city and firmly shut the gates: 10070
Inside there with him he had ten thousand men,
They were splendid citizens who were on his side.
Arthur came in pursuit with thirty thousand men
And marched direct to York with a record band of troops,
And besieged Colgrim who defended it against him.

Seven nights before this had gone marching southwards
Baldulf the great, the brother of Colgrim,   *Baldulf*
Encamped beside the sea's edge waiting for **Childric**.
Now Childric at that time was an emperor in firm command
Within Germany – which land he inherited as his own.   10080
Then Baldulf heard as he was camped beside the sea
That Arthur had Colgrim trapped inside York city.
Baldulf had assembled seven thousand men,
Very brave warriors who were camped by the sea.
They came to a decision that they'd ride back again,
Abandoning Childric, and march back towards York,
And fight against Arthur and annihilate his troops.
Baldulf swore in his rage that he'd put Arthur in his grave,
And be lord of all this realm with his brother Colgrim;
Baldulf would not wait for the emperor Childric   10090
But there and then he set forth and betook himself due north
From one day to the next with ever more determined troops
Until he came into a wood in a waste area,
A full seven miles from Arthur's forces.
With seven thousand knights, he had intended in the night
To ride down upon Arthur before the king was aware
And lay low his people and put Arthur to death.
    But it all turned out quite other than he had expected,
For Baldulf had in his bodyguard a certain British knight,
A kinsman of Arthur's who was known as **Maurin**.   10100
Maurin slipped away to the woods on the sly,
Through woodland and through fields till he came to Arthur's tents,
And straightaway said this to Arthur the king:
'Greetings to you Arthur, most admirable of kings!
I have arrived here: I'm one of your relatives,
And Baldulf has arrived here with a troop of tough soldiers,
And this very night intends to kill you and your knights
To avenge his brother who has lost all his vigour.
But God is to prevent him by means of his great powers!
So now send out **Cador**, who is the earl of Cornwall,   10110
And with him some fine knights, good and brave fighters,
A full seven hundred of the better leaders,
And those I shall instruct, and those I shall direct,
As to how to kill Baldulf just as if he were a wolf.'
    Off went Cador and all of those knights
Until they came near the spot where Baldulf lay under canvas.[*]

They made an assault on them from every side:
They killed and they captured all whom they came close to;
Those killed there amounted to nine hundred all counted.
    Baldulf had slipped away to save his own life   10120
And fled through the wild places with furious speed,
Having reluctantly left his own loyal men,
And fled so far northwards that he advanced forwards
To where Arthur lay on the uplands with his vast army
All around York city: that king was most amazing.
Colgrim was inside, with his Saxon men:
Baldulf thought carefully about what should be his policy,
By what kind of trick he could get inside quick,
Into the borough, to Colgrim his brother,
Who of all men alive was to him most beloved.   10130
Down to his bare skin Baldulf had himself stripped
Of the beard on his chin; he made himself a spectacle:
He had half his head shorn, and took a harp in his hand –
[He'd learned to play the harp well during his childhood]† – 10133a
And with his harp he made his way to the king's army
And there began to play and sing and provide much entertainment:
People kept on hitting him hard with sappy sticks;
People kept on cuffing him the way they do an idiot;
Everyone who met him contemptuously treated him
So that no one had any notion of Baldulf's true position,   10140
Thinking he was a mere idiot who had just come into court.
So long did he go up this way, so long did he go down that way
That those who were inside the town eventually got wind of it
That this was really Baldulf, brother of Colgrim.
They threw out a rope which Baldulf firmly grasped
And hauled Baldulf up until he heaved himself inside:
By a device of that kind did Baldulf get inside.
    Then rejoiced Colgrim and all his knights with him
And severely started menacing Arthur the king.
Arthur was close beside and could see all this mockery   10150
And he worked himself up into an amazing rage
And instantly ordered all his splendid folk to arm:
He intended to conquer the city by force.
Just as Arthur was about to make assault on the walls
There arrived on horseback the aristocrat **Patrick**,
A nobleman from Scotland, very well set up in lands,
Who started to call out at once to the king:

'Greetings to you, Arthur, most admired of Britons!
I wish to announce to you a fresh piece of news,
Concerning emperor Childric, the powerful and frantic,   10160
The strong and also brave: he is in Scotland,
Has anchored in a harbour and is burning down the homes
And controls all our land under his own cruel hand;
He has a force which is notable, made up of all the power of Rome;
He declares in his boasting when his bowl is filled with wine
That not in any place do you dare await his onslaughts,
Not on field nor in the woodland nor in any [place] at all,[†]
And if you were to wait for him, he would put fetters on you,
Slaughter your people and possess your land.'
   Often Arthur had been sad, but not till then were things so bad,
And he withdrew to the rear at one side of the city,   10171
Calling his knights to emergency council:
Warriors and leaders and the holy bishops,
Requesting them to advise him how he might, in his realm,
Maintain his dignity with his force of men
And fight against Childric the powerful and strong
Who intended to march that way to give aid to Colgrim.
The Britons there beside him then gave him this answer:
'Let's travel straight to London, and let him march right behind,
And if he comes riding past he'll have to take his
     punishment: 10180
He himself and his army are destined to be doomed.'
   Arthur wholly approved of what his people advised him:
He set off travelling until he came to London;
Colgrim was in York and was there expecting Childric:
Childric proceeded to advance through northern parts
And seized into his hands a great deal of land:
The entire Scottish region he gave to one of his retainers
And the whole of Northumberland he placed in his brother's hands;
Galloway and Orkney he gave to an earl of his;
He himself took the land from the Humber down to
     London;   10190
He did not intend to show to Arthur any clemency whatever
Unless Arthur, Uther's son, were willing to become his vassal.
   Arthur was in London with all the British leaders;
He summoned his army throughout all this country:
Every single man who bore him good will
Must rapidly and at once come up to London.

Then all the land of England was filled with misery:
Here there was weeping and lamenting and immeasurable grief,
Much hunger and distress at the gate of each and every man.
    Arthur sent across the sea two excellent knights   10200
To **Howel** his cousin, dearest to him of all creatures,
A knight among the best, who commanded Brittany,
Asking him to come over here at once,
To come to the country to help his kindred people,
As Childric had in his hands a great deal of this land   *Childric*
And Colgrim and Baldulf had become his allies
And intended to drive King Arthur out of his native land,
Depriving him of his birthright and of his noble realm:
Then all his family would be tainted with the terror of his disgrace,
Their reputation lost in the realm of this world;   10210
Then it would be better if the king had not been born at all.
    Howel, highest man in Brittany heard all of this,
And proceeded at once to call up his best knights,
And ordered them to horse in very great haste,
To travel to France to the other free knights
And say to them that they must come very soon and quickly
To Saint Michael's Mount with very many forces,
(All those who wanted silver and gold
And wanted to win honour in the kingdom of this world).
To Poitou he sent off his excellent soldiers,   10220
And some towards Flanders furiously quickly,
And two there went off into Touraine,
And sent into Gascony knights who were also good,
Motioning them in force towards St Michael's Mount,
And promising them splendid gifts before they went to sea
So that they would the readier relinquish their own land
And with Howel the gracious come across to this land
To give aid to Arthur, most admirable of kings.
    Thirteen days had gone by since the dispatch had reached there
When they surged towards the sea as hail does from the sky;   10230
Two hundred ships were there, very well captained:
They were all filled with people and put out to sea:
The wind and the weather stayed just as they wanted
And at Southampton they sailed into land.
Up from the ships leaped enraged soldiers
Carrying ashore their helmets and corslets:
With spears and with shields they covered all the fields.

Many a bold Briton was present; there was boasting uttered:
They swore with great boasts, by their own very lives
That they themselves would treat Childric known as great,   10240
The [aggressive] emperor with much injury there,[†]
And if he refused to flee away and be off to Germany
And wished instead on land in a fight to make his stand,
And with his bold warriors wait here for their [harm];[†]
Here they would have to leave what they liked the most:
Their heads and their hands and their gleaming helms,
And in that way they would on land be lost to all their friends;
The vile heathen hounds would hurtle into hell.

   Arthur was in London, most admirable of kings,
And heard being spoken most assured speeches   10250
That Howel the mighty had come to this land,   *Howel*
To Southampton directly with thirty thousand knights   *Arrives*
And with countless folk who were followers of the king.
Arthur turned towards him with tremendous joy,
With an enormous crowd of men towards his own cousin.
Together they came (there was delight in the court):
They kissed and embraced and spoke with affection,
And immediately assembled their knights right away.

   And so there were combined two excellent armies:
Howel was to command thirty thousand knights,   10260
While Arthur had in his land forty thousand in hand.
Directly they travelled towards the north district,
Towards Lincoln where Emperor Childric held siege,
But so far he had not been able to take it
Since there were inside it seven thousand good men,
Brave men they were, all day and all night.

   With his army Arthur advanced upon the town,
And Arthur urged his men sternly that all day and all night[†]
They must travel silently as if they were going stealing,
Travel across the country and relinquish loud noise: 10270
Their horns and their bugles must all be abandoned.
Arthur took a knight who was a good man and brave in fight
And sent him into Lincoln, to his well-loved men,
And as a certainty he must say volubly
That Arthur was coming, most admirable of kings
Exactly at midnight and with him many a good knight: –
'And you inside here, at that time must be alert
That when you hear the uproar, then the gates you must unbar,

And dash out of the city and destroy your enemies,
And hit out at Childric, the strong and the mighty,   10280
And then we shall larn 'em some good British yarns!'
   It was exactly midnight: from due south the moon was shining;
Arthur with his army swept down upon the city:
The men were just as silent as if they were going stealing;
They strode on till they could see a full view of Lincoln,
When Arthur the courageous like this began to call:
'Where are you, my knights, my champions in battle?
Can you see the tents where Childric lodges in the fields,
With Colgrim and Baldulf with all their brute force,
The people from Germany who have brought us tragedy,   10290
And the men from Saxony who promise us calamity,
Who have eliminated utterly the noblest in my family,
Constance and Constantine and Uther who was my father,
And Aurelius Ambrosius who was my father's brother,
And many thousand men of my own exalted kin?
Let us march over to them and lay them to the earth
And avenge honourably our family and realm.
And now each and every good knight all together ride on straight!'
   Arthur started riding, the army was stampeding
As if the whole earth were eaten up with flames;†   10300
In among Childric's tents they swooped down in the fields,
And the man who was the first there to start the battle cry
Was Arthur the great warrior, the son of King Uther,
Who shouted loudly and with courage, as comes best from a king:
'Now may Mary aid us, the meek mother of our God,
And I am praying to her Son that he be our assistance!'
   At these very words they took aim with their spears,
Stabbing and striking all those they came close to,
And knights from the city strode out towards them.
If they fled back to the city, there they would perish,   10310
If they fled to the woodland they would be destroyed there:†
Let them go where they could, they would still be attacked.†
It's not recorded in a book that there was ever any fight
Within this realm of Britain where destruction was so rife,
For they were the most wretched of all races who have come here!
There was a deal of bloodshed: there was destruction among men;
Death there was rife and the earth was resounding.
Childric the emperor had a single castle there
On the plain of Lincoln – he was lying up inside it –

Which was recently constructed and really well defended,   10320
And in there also with him were Baldulf and Colgrim,
Who saw that their army was undergoing huge fatalities,
And right away at once it was on with the mail-coats
And they fled from the castle, bereft of all their courage,
And fled right away at once to the wood of Calidon. *
They had as their companions seven thousand riders,
And behind them they left slain and deprived of their life's days
A full forty thousand who were felled to the ground:
Men who came from Germany all of them damned in misery,
And all the Saxon men levelled to the ground.   10330
    Then Arthur was aware, the most admirable of kings,
That Childric had fled, into Caledonia he'd sped,
And Colgrim and Baldulf, both had made off with him,
Into the high wood, into the high hurst.
And Arthur went on their track with sixty thousand knights:
The soldiers of Britain surrounded all the wood,
And on one side they felled it for a seven mile extent,
One tree on another, and 'truly' they worked fast! *
On the other side he laid siege to it with his levied army
For three days and three nights: it put them in tremendous plight.
    Then Colgrim realised as he was holed up in it   10341
(Who was there without food, in sharp hunger and distress)
That not for them nor their horses was there any help at all.
And in this way Colgrim called to the emperor:
'Tell me, my lord Childric, in words which are truthful,
Can there be any reason why we are lurking here like this?
Why don't we sally forth and summon up our armies,
And start up the fighting against Arthur and his knights?
It's better for us to be laid out on the land but with our honour
Than like this in here to perish with hunger.   10350
It's tormenting us terribly and our men are held in contempt;
Or else let's send straight out to him, and seek a truce from Arthur,
And plead for his mercy and pass hostages to him
And create an alliance with the noble king.'
    Childric was listening as he sheltered in the fort,
And he gave his reply in a really sad voice:
'If Baldulf your own brother wants this and agrees,
And more of our confederates who are here with us inside,
That we should sue for peace from Arthur and set up a treaty with
        him,

Then just as you want, that's what I'll do,   10360
Since in the realm this Arthur is reckoned a most noble man,
Beloved among his followers and a man of royal stock;
Entirely from kings he comes: he was King Uther's son,
And often it does come to pass in many kinds of peoples,
Where valiant knights embark on fierce fight,
That what they win at first they will lose again at last;
And for us right here and now it's turning out like that,
But if only we can live, then for us things will improve.'
    There can an instant and forthright response from the knights:
'We all approve of this proposal, for you have put it well.'   10370
They selected twelve knights and sent them off straight
To where he was in his pavilion by the edges of the wood.
One of them began to shout at once in a sturdy voice:
'Lord Arthur, your safe-conduct: with you we wish to speak!
Childric, styled the emperor, has sent us over here,
As did Colgrim and Baldulf, both of them together;
Now and for all eternity they request your clemency:
They will become your vassals and your renown they will advance,
And they will hand over to you hostages in plenty,
And regard you as their lord, as you will like most of all,   10380
If only they may leave and go from here alive
Into their own land and take there the loathed report;
For here we have experienced many kinds of evils:
At Lincoln we left behind our most beloved kinsmen,
Sixty thousand men who are lying there slain,
And if it might be the wish of your heart
That we across the sea may travel under sail,
Then never any more shall we come back here,
For here we have lost for good our own loved relations;
As long as will be for ever here shall we come back never!'   10390
    Then Arthur laughed, and with a loud voice:
'May thanks be given to God who governs all decisions
That Childric the strong has had sufficient of my land!
He divided up my land among all his doughty knights,
Me myself he had planned to drive from my native land,
To regard me as a wretch and to retain all my realm,
And to have destroyed all my family and condemned all my folk.†
But things have turned out for him as they do with the fox:
When he is most brazen, up in the forest,
And has his freedom for playing and has fowls a-plenty,   10400

In his wild sport he climbs and he seeks out the crags;
Out in the wild places he excavates dens:
Let him roam wherever he wishes, he never has any distress,
And thinks he is in valour the finest of all creatures,
When towards him up the mountains here come men climbing,
With horns and with hounds, and with hallooing voices;
There hunters are yelling; there foxhounds are belling,
Driving the fox on across dales and over downland:
He dashes to the highwood and seeks out his den;
At the nearest point he presses down into the hole.   10410
Then the bold fox is quite bereft of bliss,
And men are digging down to him upon every side;
Then he there becomes the saddest who of all beasts was the proudest.
   'That's how it was with Childric, the powerful and mighty:
All my kingdom he intended to get into his clutches,
But now I have driven him to the very edge of death,
Which of the two I decide to do, to behead or hang him.
Now I decide to give him peace and allow him speech with me;
I shall neither behead nor hang him but will accede to his request:
I wish to take hostages from his highest-ranking men,   10420
Horses and their weapons, before they go from here,
And so they are to travel like wretches to their ships,
To sail across the sea to their splendid land,
And dwell there dutifully within their realm,
And announce the tidings of Arthur the king,
Of how I have set them free for my father's soul's sake,
And from my own generosity have dealt gently with the wretches.'
   In this affair King Arthur was short of all good judgement,
There was no man who was quite so rash as to dare to put him right;
This he regretted bitterly a very short time after.   10430
Childric came from under cover to Arthur who was king,
And he became his vassal there with each one of his knights.
Fully twenty-four hostages Childric handed over there:
They were all selected specially and born in the nobility.
They gave up their horses and their fine mail-coats,
Their spears and their shields and the long swords of theirs:
Everything they had there they then left behind;
They started their journey till they came to the sea
Where their fine ships were standing by the sea.
   They had the wind they wanted, and very pleasant
      weather: 10440

267

They pushed out from the shore ships massive and long;
They all left behind the land and laid course along the waves
Until they could not see any sight of land at all.
The water was still, which suited their will;
They set their sails gliding right alongside,
Plank against plank; people spoke to one another,
Deciding that they wanted to come back to this land
And avenge with honour their own loved relations,
And lay waste King Arthur's land and kill those who lived here,
And conquer the castles and do acts of wild delight.　　　　10450
So they travelled on the sea for such a long time
That they arrived midway between England and Normandy;
They went about on their luff and laid course towards land,*
Till they came (no doubt of this) to Dartmouth reach at
　　　Totnes;
In the very greatest joy they jumped down ashore.　　　*Childric's*
　　As soon as they came to land they slaughtered the people:　*Return*
They put to flight the peasants who were ploughing the soil;
They hanged all the knights who had command of the lands;
All the dutiful wives they stabbed to death with knives,
All the young girls they gang-raped to death,　　　　10460
And the men of learning they laid out on hot coals;
All the serving-men at court they killed by clubbing them;
They demolished the castles, they laid waste the land,
They burned down the churches; there was distress in the land!
The babies at the breast they drowned in the waters;
The livestock which they seized they slaughtered completely,
To their quarters dragged it and stewed it up and roasted it;
Everything they grabbed which they could get close to.
All day long they were singing about Arthur the great king,
Claiming they had won for themselves homes　　　　10470
Which were going to be their holdings in their own control,
And there they would be staying in winter and in summer,
And if Arthur had such courage that he wanted to come
To fight against Childric the powerful and mighty,
'[We]'ll make a bridge, really fine, from the bits of his spine†
And pick out all the bones from the admirable king,
And join them together with links of gold chain,
And lay them in the hall doorway which each man has to go through
In tribute to Childric, the mighty and the rich!'
　　All this was just how they played, to King Arthur's disgrace,　10480

But all happened quite another way very shortly after:
Their boasts and their games turned into their own shame,
As it does almost everywhere when a man behaves like that.
The emperor Childric conquered everything he looked at:
He took Somerset, and he took Dorset,
And all Devonshire's people he entirely destroyed,
And he treated Wiltshire with the utmost wickedness;
He seized all the lands down to the sea sands;
Then ultimately he ordered men to start blowing
Horns and brass trumpets, and his host to assemble, 10490
And he wanted to be off and completely besiege Bath,
And also to blockade Bristol round about the coastline;
Such was their boasting before they came to Bath.

 To Bath came the emperor and besieged the castle there,
And the men inside it with valour proceeded
To mount upon the stone walls, well supplied with weapons,
And they defended the place against the mighty Childric.
There encamped the emperor and Colgrim his companion,
And Baldulf his brother and very many others.

 Arthur was in the north, and knew nothing of this; 10500
He travelled all through Scotland and set it all into his own hand:
Orkney and Galloway, the Isle of Man and Moray,
And all of the territories which were their tributaries.
Arthur assumed that it was a certain thing
That Childric had laid course back to his own land,
And that never again would he ever come back here.

 Then to Arthur the king there came the tidings
That Childric the emperor had come to the country
And in the south region was wreaking great chaos.
Then Arthur announced (most admired of kings): 10510
'I am deeply sorry that I spared my enemy,
That in the hilltop wood I did not [kill him off] with hunger,[†]
Or did not slice him right up with slashes from my sword!
Now this is how he pays me back for my good deed!
But so help me the Lord who made the light of day
For this he shall endure the most extreme of all agonies,
Harshest contests; I shall be his killer,
And both Colgrim and Baldulf I myself shall kill,
And all of their supporters shall suffer death.
If the Ruler of heaven wishes to grant this, 10520
I shall honourably avenge all his evil deeds;

If the life in my breast is able to last in me,
And if he who created moon and sun is willing to grant me this,
Then Childric will never cheat me again!'
    Now the call went from Arthur, the most admired of kings:
'Where are you, my knights, brave men and valiant?
To horse, to horse, worthy warriors,
And swiftly towards Bath we shall now be on our way.
Get men to erect really high gibbets
And bring here the hostages in front of our knights,   10530
And they shall be hanged there upon the high trees.'
    There he had executed all twenty-four children,
From the German race, of very noble families.
Then came the tidings to Arthur the king
That his cousin Howel was sick (and this news made him sad)
Lodged in Dumbarton by the Clyde; and there then he had to leave
    him.
With exceeding haste he started making off
Until beside Bath he moved on to a plain,   *Siege*
And there he dismounted, and all of his knights,   *of Bath*
And on with their mail-coats, those stern men of war,   10540
And he divided his forces into five sections.
    When he had stationed them all and all were surveyed
Then he put on his mail-coat fashioned from steel mesh*
Which an elvish smith had made with his excellent skill:
It was called **Wygar**, which **Wiseman** had smithied.
His thighs he covered up with cuisses of steel;
Caliburn his sword he strapped by his side –
It was made in Avalon and endowed with magic powers;
His helmet he set on his head, high and made of steel:
On it was many a gem and it was all bound with gold –   10550
It had once belonged to the noble King Uther –
It was known as **Goosewhite**, among all others quite unique.
He hung about his neck a shield which was precious:
Its name in British was entitled **Pridwen**;
Inside it was engraved with red gold stencilling
A most precious image of the mother of our Lord;
In his hand he took his spear which bore the name of **Ron**.
When he had donned all his armour, then he leaped on his charger;
Then the bystanders were able to behold
The most handsome knight who ever led forth host: 10560
Never did any man see a more splendid knight

Than was this Arthur who was most aristocratic.
  Then Arthur called out in a loud voice:
'Look here now, ahead of us, those heathen hounds
Who slaughtered our ancestors with their evil tricks,
And who for us in the land are the most loathsome of all things.
Now let us charge towards them and fiercely set upon them
And avenge with acclaim our race and our realm,
And avenge the great disgrace by which they have debased us
When over the billows they came to Dartmouth sound.   10570
And they are all utterly forsworn and they are all utterly cast down:
They are all doomed, with the Lord's divine aid.
Now let us hasten forward in combined formation
Every bit as gently as if we had no harsh intentions,
And when we come up to them, I myself will start:
Among the very foremost I shall begin the fighting.
Now we shall ride and across the land we'll glide
And no man for his very life must move at all loudly,
But travel with all speed. Now the Lord give us support!'
  Then Arthur the great man set off at a gallop,   10580
Headed over the plain and was making for Bath.
The tidings came to Childric, the powerful and mighty,
That Arthur with his forces was coming all prepared for fight.
Childric and his bold men leaped upon their horses,
Firmly grasped their weapons, knowing Arthur was their enemy.
Arthur, most admired king, noticed this thing;
He noticed one heathen earl making straight for him
With seven hundred knights all prepared for fight,
The earl himself advancing in front of his contingent;
And Arthur himself was riding at the head of all his army.   10590
Arthur the resolute took Ron in his hand,
He steadied the sturdy shaft, that stout-hearted king,
He set his horse galloping so that the earth resounded,
And raised his shield before his breast: the king was enraged!
He struck the earl Borel straight through the chest
So that his heart was split; and the king called out at once:
'The first one is fated! Now may the Lord afford us aid,
And the heavenly Queen who gave birth to the Lord.'
  Arthur, most admired of kings, called out again:
'Now at them, now at them! the first deed was well done!'   10600
The British set upon them as must be done with scoundrels:
They gave savage slashes with axes and with swords.

From Childric's men there fell fully two thousand,
While Arthur did not lose a single one of his!
There the Saxon men were the most abject of people,
And the men of Germany the most mournful of all nations.
Arthur with his sword sent many to their doom:
Everything he struck with it was instantly done for.
The king was every bit as enraged as the wild boar is
When among the oakmast he meets many [pigs].[†]   10610
    Childric was aware of this and began to turn away,
And he set off across the Avon to find safety for himself,
And Arthur leaped into pursuit just like a lion
And flushed them into the water: many there were fated;
To the depths sank there two thousand five hundred,
And all the River Avon was spanned with a bridge of steel.
Childric fled across the water with fifteen hundred knights,
Intending to slip off and pass across the sea.
Arthur spotted Colgrim climbing to the mountains,
Making a break towards the hills which look down on Bath,   10620
And Baldulf made off after him, with seven thousand knights,
Supposing that up in the hills they could make a noble stand,
Defend themselves with weapons and wound Arthur's force.
    Then Arthur noted, that most admired king,
Where Colgrim offered resistance and made his stand too;
Then the king called out, loudly and with courage:
'My bold-hearted warriors, march to the hills!
For yesterday Colgrim was of all men most courageous,
Now he's just like the goat holding guard on its hill:
High on the hillside it fights with its horns;   10630
Then the wild wolf comes, on its way up towards them;
Even though the wolf's alone, without any pack,
If there were in one pen a full five hundred goats,
The wolf would get to them and would bite them all.
In just that way today I shall quite destroy Colgrim:
I'm the wolf and he's the goat: that guy is going to be doomed!'
    Once again Arthur called out, most admired of kings:
'Yesterday Baldulf was of all knights the boldest;
Now he's standing on the hill and staring at the Avon,
Sees lying in the stream fishes made of steel,   10640
They're girded with swords but their swimming is all spoiled;
Their scales are fluttering like shields adorned with gold;
Their spines are floating just as if they were spears.[†]

These are remarkable sights to see in this land:
Such beasts on the hill, such fish in the spring;
Yesterday the emperor was the most audacious monarch,
Now he's become a hunter and horns are his accompaniment,
He's dashing over the broad plain and his dogs are barking;
There beside Bath he has abandoned his hunting:
He's in flight from his own quarry, so we'll be the ones to kill it
And so bring to nothing those brazen boasts of his,   10651
And in this way we'll regain true rights of ownership.'
   And with those very words which the king was speaking
He raised high his shield in front of his chest,
Grasped his long spear and set spurs to his horse;
Almost as fast as a bird in its flight
There went following the king twenty-five thousand,
Of valiant men in wild rage, armed with their weapons.
They made towards the mountains with very mighty force
And into Colgrim they struck with most savage whacks.   10660
And Colgrim took them on and felled the British to the ground,
Fully five hundred in the first onrush.
This Arthur noted, that most admired king,
And marvellously and mightily he became maddened,
And in this way started shouting Arthur the great man:
'Where are you, my British, my bold and brave soldiers?
Here ahead of us are standing all our noted enemies!
Good warriors of mine, let us grind them to the ground!'
   Arthur grasped his sword in his right and he struck a Saxon knight,
And the sword (it was so splendid) sliced till at his teeth it ended!
And then he struck another who was the first knight's
     brother   10671
So his helm and the head with it fell upon the ground;
At once he gave a third blow and he cut one knight in two.
Then the British men were strongly emboldened
And imposed upon the Saxons some most severe contusions[†]
With their spears which were long and with their swords which were
     strong.
There the Saxons fell in their last fatal hour,
In hundreds upon hundreds they fell in heaps upon the ground,
In thousands upon thousands they went on falling on the ground.
   Then spotted Colgrim that Arthur was coming to him: 10680
Because of all the corpses Colgrim couldn't slip aside;
Baldulf was fighting there right beside his brother.

Then Arthur called out in challenging tones:
'Here I come, Colgrim! we two are reaching for this country
And now we're going to share this land in a way you'll find least
    pleasing!'
After these words which the king was uttering
He lifted high his broad sword and heavily struck down
Striking Colgrim on the helmet and carving down the centre,
And through the coif on his mail-coat, till it stuck in
    the man's chest,   *Colgrim and*
And he reached out to Baldulf with his right hand   *Baldulf*
And swiped his head right off together with his helmet.   *Die*
    Then noble King Arthur gave a great laugh,   10692
And began to recite these words of rejoicing:
'Lie there now, Colgrim: you certainly climbed high,
And your brother Baldulf who is lying by your side,
Now's the time I invest all this realm in your possession,
The dales and the downland and all my doughty men!
You climbed up this hill marvellously high
As if you were on your way to heaven; now you've got to go to hell;
There you will recognise a good many of your tribe.   10700
Give my regards to Hengest who was the most handsome knight,
Ebissa and Octa and from your tribe lots more,
And ask them to stay there all winter and all summer;
Then in this land we shall live in joy,
And pray for your souls – that they will never have salvation! –
And your bones shall lie here, right beside Bath.'
    Arthur the king called Cador the courageous
(He was the Earl of Cornwall and a most courageous knight):
'Listen to me, Cador, you come from my own family;
Childric has now run off and has gone away from here;   10710
He thinks that he'll be safe to come travelling back again.†
But take from my forces five thousand men,
And travel directly, by day and by night,
Until you arrive at the sea in advance of Childric,
And everything you can conquer, enjoy that with pleasure,
And if you manage to kill the emperor with the greatest cruelty,†
I'll give you as reward all of Dorsetshire.'
    As soon as the noble king had spoken these words
Cador sprang to horse as a spark does from the fire;
A full seven thousand accompanied the earl.   10720
Cador the courageous and many of his kindred

Went across the wolds and over the wild places,
Over dales and over downlands over deep waters;
Cador knew the way which towards his own lands lay:
Westwards he went, this is the case, right on to Totnes,
By day and by night; he got there directly,
So that Childric never discovered the least detail of his coming.
Cador came to his country in advance of Childric
And had all folk in the area marshalled in front of him,
Vigorous peasants with enormous clubs   10730
With spears and great cudgels collected for that very purpose,
And he put every single one of them into the ships' bilges,
Ordered them to keep well hidden so that Childric wasn't aware of
    them,
And when his men arrived and were trying to climb in
They were to grab their cudgels and vigorously thump them,
And with their staves and with their spears to slaughter Childric's
    adherents.
    The peasants did exactly as Cador had instructed:
Off to the ships went the peasants in grim fury;
In each of the ships there were a hundred and fifty,
And Cador the courageous moved towards a high wood   10740
Five miles from the spot where the ships were stationed,
And hid his men as he desired in the utmost silence.
    Childric came soon after marching on the plain,
Intending to rush to the ships and run away from the land.
As soon as Earl Cador, a man of courage, could clearly see
That Childric was on the plain between him and the peasants
Then Cador called out in a clear voice:
'Where are you, my knights, my good, valiant fighters?
Remember what Arthur, our admirable king
Commanded us at Bath before we left the company!   10750
Now see Childric flying, trying to flee from the land
And making for Germany where his ancestors lie
Where he'll collect up an army and come back here again
And invade our interior, intending to avenge that Colgrim
And Baldulf his brother, who lie dead beside Bath.
But may he never survive to see that hour! He will not if we have the
    power!'
Upon concluding that speech the great earl had spoken
In a mood of harsh anger he rode at their head;
The valiant soldiers strode out of the wood-shaw

And went after Childric, the powerful and mighty.   10760
Childric's knights looked back behind them:
Saw battle standards proceeding across the plain,
And five thousand shields gliding across the fields.
Then Childric became most distressed in his emotions,
And the mighty emperor ventured these words:
'This is King Arthur and he wants to eliminate us all!
Let's run off now quickly and rush into the ships
And get away from here by water and not bother about where we go
        to!'
    When the emperor Childric had uttered these remarks
He set off in flight fearfully quickly   10770
With Cador the courageous coming after him at once.
Childric and his knights came to their ships straightaway
Intending to shove off those sturdy ships from land.
The peasants were hiding, with their cudgels, inside them:
They raised up their cudgels and brought them down hard;
By their clubs many knights there were instantly slain,
And stabbed by their pitchforks and pinned to the ground.
Cador and his knights attacked them from behind.
    Then Childric realised they were facing disaster
When all his great force fell in heaps on the ground!   10780
Now he spotted to one side a very lofty hill;
That river flows beneath it which is termed the Teign
And the hill is called Teignwick: that's the way Childric fled*
As quickly as he could manage with twenty-four knight companions.
Cador was aware how things were going there,
That the emperor was in flight and heading for the heights
And Cador went after him with as much speed as he could,
And gained on him steadily and caught up with him.
Then announced Cador, the most courageous earl,
'Wait, Childric, wait; I want to give you Teignwick!'   10790
Cador raised his sword and struck and killed Childric.   *Childric's*
Many who were fleeing made for the water: *Death*
In the waters of the Teign there they met their end:
Cador killed everyone whom he found alive,
And some crawled into the woodland and he destroyed all these
        there.
    When Cador had conquered all of them and had seized all that land
        as well
He imposed a very firm peace which remained a long time after:

Even were a man wearing gold rings upon his arms
No man whatever would dare to treat another man with
    wrong.   10799
   Arthur had travelled on out into Scotland   *Scottish*
For Howel lay firmly enclosed in Dumbarton beside   *Campaign*
    Clyde:
The Scots had besieged him through their base deception,
And if Arthur had not come very soon Howel would have been
    captured
And all his people slain and deprived of their life's days.
But Arthur arrived speedily with superior strength
And the Scots started fleeing far from that area
Off into Moray with much man-power.
And Cador came to Scotland where he found Arthur:
Arthur and Cador marched into Dumbarton
And there discovered Howel with great joy, in health: 10810
From all his former sickness he had now recovered;
Great was the rejoicing held in the fortress.
   The Scots were in Moray and intended to remain there,
And with their brazen words they uttered their boasts,
Claiming that they wanted to take charge of the realm
And await Arthur there with their bold force,
Since never would Arthur ever dare, for his life's sake, to come there!
Arthur, quite devoid of fear, then came to hear
Of what the Scots had been saying in their words of scorn.
Then announced Arthur, most admired of kings: 10820
'Where are you, Howel, highest of my kindred,
And Cador the courageous, you who come from Cornwall?
Have brass trumpets blown and assemble our forces:
Exactly at midnight we shall march off directly
Towards Moray, there to prove our honour;
If the Lord who made the light of day should so desire it
We shall be telling them some mournful stories,
Bring down their boasting and themselves be killing.'
   Exactly at midnight Arthur arose directly:
Horns began blowing with resounding noise,   10830
Knights began getting up and speaking words of anger.
With great manpower onwards into Moray,
Thirteen thousand men [forced] their way onwards:[†]
In the first company, men especially courageous;
Then came Cador, the earl of Cornwall,

With seventeen thousand splendid combatants:
Then came Howel with his champions, to fight well
With twenty-one thousand most outstanding champions:
Then came Arthur, most admired of kings,
With twenty-seven thousand, striding after them.   10840
Shields there were gleaming as the dawn light began.
    News came to the Scots where they were now living
That King Arthur was coming towards their own land,
Fantastically quickly with an enormous force.
Then those were in most terror who before had been most bold
And took off in flight amazingly fast
Into that water where there are very many marvels.
    This is an uncanny mere set upon middle earth,   *Loch*
With marshland and reeds and the water is very broad,   *Lomond*
With fish and with water fowl, with fiendish creatures!   10850
The water cannot be measured; vast sea-monsters swim round
        within it;
There are elvish creatures playing in the terrible pool;
There are sixty islands stretching down the long water:
On each of the islands is a rock both high and strong
Where eagles make their nests and other huge birds;
The eagles have a certain custom in the reign of every king
Whenever any invading force comes flocking to the country:
Then all of the birds fly far up into the air,
Many hundred thousands of them and create a huge contention;
Then the people know without doubt that a great trial is to come to
        them
From some kind of people who propose to visit that land.   10861
For two or three days this sign occurs in this way
Until unknown men journey to that land.
There is still one more marvel to mention concerning that water:
There flow [into] that mere on many a side†
From dales and from downlands and from deep valleys
Sixty different streams, all gathered together,
Yet out of that mere no man has ever found one
Which flows outwards there, except at one end
A normal sized brook which discharges from the mere   10870
And trickles very tranquilly down to the sea.
    The Scots were scattered and in much distress
Over the many mountains situated in the water;
Arthur commandeered ships and proceeded towards them

And slew them without number, many and in plenty,
And many thousands there had died for total lack of bread.
Arthur the admirable was on the east side;
Howel the good was in the south part
And Cador the courageous was on guard in the north,
And his lesser people he placed on the west side; 10880
Then all the Scots seemed very foolish men,
Lurking there among the crags entirely encircled;
Of these, sixty thousand came to a sad end.

By then the king of Ireland had arrived in the harbour,
Twelve miles from where Arthur was encamped with his force,
Having come to help the Scots to bring down Howel.
Arthur, most admired king, came to hear of this,
And took his one main force and hastened there with speed,
And found King Gillomaur who had come ashore just there:
Arthur fought against him and refused him any truce, 10890
And felled the Irish men with great fierceness to the ground,
And with twelve ships Gillomaur took flight from the shore
And travelled to Ireland with very great trouble,
While Arthur on the land slew all whom he found,
And then returned to the lake where he had left his kinsman, *
Howel the courteous, highest-ranking in Britain
(Not counting Arthur, most noble of kings).
Arthur met Howel where he was stationed by the harbour,
Beside the broad loch where he had been waiting;
Then the men in the army were extremely happy 10900
About Arthur's arrival and his noble achievements.

There Arthur remained for two days and two nights;
The Scots were lying on the crags, many thousands of them dead,
Perishing with hunger – the most abject of peoples.
On the third day the dawn brought in good weather,
There came approaching the army all those who bore the tonsure,
And three intelligent bishops well instructed in the Bible,
And many priests and monks who could not be counted,
Canons were coming there, many most distinguished men,
With all of the relics most respected in the land, 10910
And they all craved peace with Arthur, and his compassion.

To that place came the women who were living in that land:
They were carrying in their arms their unfortunate children;
They were crying in Arthur's presence amazingly bitterly,
And tossing their lovely tresses down to the earth,

279

Cutting off their locks and laying them down there
At the king's feet in front of all of his soldiers,
[Dragging] their nails down their faces and leaving them bleeding;[†]
They were nearly all of them practically naked.
In great distress they started calling out to King Arthur,   10920
And some of them spoke like this in their [affliction]:[†]
'King, we are upon this earth the most abject of all people!
We beg for your compassion, for the sake of God's care.
In this country you have slaughtered our own compatriots
With hunger and distress and with many kinds of harm,
With weapons and with water and with many misfortunes,
Have made our children fatherless, bereft of every comfort.
You are a Christian man: we ourselves are Christian too;
The Saxon men are merely heathen hounds:
They came to this land and these folk here they killed;   10930
If we gave them allegiance it was to avoid trouble,
For we had no man at all who might reconcile us with them.
They caused us great disaster, and you are doing just the same:
The heathen men hate us and the Christians give us grief;
What will become of us?' cried the women to the king.
'Give us back those men still living lying on the crags there,
And if you show compassion to those human creatures
Then your honour will be greater, both now and hereafter!
Lord Arthur, our king, loosen our fetters;
All this land you have captured and all this people overcome: 10940
We lie beneath your feet; with you lies our entire release.'
    All this heard Arthur, most admired of kings,
This weeping and this lamenting and untold desolations.
Then he gave it consideration, and he felt compassion;
As he deliberated he found he could do as they asked:
He gave them life, he gave them limb and their own lands to manage.[*]
He had brass trumpets blown and summoned the Scots
And down from their crags they came to the ships;
From each and every side they sidled towards land:
They were very badly harmed by the sharp pangs of hunger.   10950
Oaths they then swore that they would never be traitors,
And then they handed over hostages to the king,
And all of them immediately became the king's men,
And then they hurried off; the hosts separated there,
Each man to the area where he had his homestead,
And Arthur established a peace there, good among the best.

'Where are you, my cousin Howel, the man I love the most?
Are you looking at this enormous mere where the Scots have been so
    harmed?
Can you see these lofty trees, can you see the eagles soaring?
Within this vast fen there are fish beyond counting: 10960
Are you looking at the islands which are lying in the water?'
The whole vista seemed to Howel uncannily strange,
And standing by the surging water he was extremely surprised,
And like this responded Howel of noble rank:
'Since I was born a male child lying at my mother's breast
I have never seen in any land such surprising things
As before me right now with my eyes I behold.'
    The Britons were exceedingly surprised and amazed.
Then Arthur called out, most admired of kings:
'Howel, my own cousin, the man I love the most,   10970
Listen to my words, about a most famous marvel
Which to you I will recount by my own true account:
At this mere's end where this water leaves
Is a little tiny pool which people wonder at:
It is in its length sixty-four handbreadths,*
Measured in its width it is twenty-five feet;
It is but five feet deep; it was dug out by elves;
It possesses four corners and there are four kinds of fish in it,
And each fish is in its area, where it finds its species,
Nor can any reach the others except for those which match its type;
No man was ever created who was in any skill so far
    advanced,   10981
No matter how long he might live, who might ever understand
What it is that stops one fish from floating off to the others
Since there is nothing between except just pure water.'
    Then Arthur, most admired king, once again continued:
'Howel, at the limit of this land, close to the sea shore,*
Is a loch extremely vast; its waters are unpleasant,
And when the sea is surging as if madly raging
And spills over into the loch in huge quantities,
Even so there is no more water added in the mere;   10990
But when the sea gushes out, and the earth shines with moisture,
And it's gone back in, into its former gulf,
Then the mere swells up and the waves grow dusky,
Waves are spilling out there, enormously huge ones,
Flowing out on the land so people instantly get fearful;

If any man comes by there not knowing anything about it,
To see the strange sight beside the sea-shore,
If he turns his face towards the mere there,
No matter how low born he is, he'll be very well protected,
The water will slip by him and the man will stay there
    gently,   11000
According to his desire he remains there very quiet,
So he's not any way damaged by the action of the water.'
    Then remarked Howel, high-ranking in Britain:
'Now I hear described wonderful accounts,
And wonderful is the Lord who established it all!'
Then called out Arthur, most admired of kings:
'Blow all my horns with resounding echo,
And announce to my knights that I shall travel straightaway.'
Brass trumpets were blowing, horns there were sounding:
There was acclamation in the army beside the active king   11010
For each was reassured and was marching to his region,
And the king made proclamation, by their pure existence,*
That no man in the world should become so insane,
Nor any soldier so stupid as to break his truce,
And if any man did this, he must endure the punishment.
    After these words the army advanced:
Men there were singing unfamiliar songs†
About this King Arthur and about his warriors,
And they said in their songs that while this world lasted
There would never again be such a king as Arthur was in
    everything,   11020
No other king nor kaiser in any country whatever.
    Arthur went off to York with an amazingly large force
And stayed there for six weeks in supreme delight;
The walls of the city were broken down and crumbling
Where Childric had burned them up, with the halls, completely.
Then the king summoned a famous priest called **Piram**;
He was a very wise man and very well versed in books:
'Piram, you are my own priest, so the easier will you find things.'*
The king took a true cross relic, potent and authentic,
And [placed] it in Piram's hand and with it extensive tracts of land,†
And the archbishop's crozier he handed to Piram there;   11031
Piram had been a good priest; now he was an archbishop.
Then he was instructed by Arthur, most admired of kings,
That he should erect churches and restore the ritual

And protect God's people and in fairness instruct them;
And he ordered all the knights to give just decisions,
And the tillers of the soil to betake themselves to toil,
And every single man to greet every other; *
And whichever man acted worse than the king had given orders,
He would have him hurried off to burn at the stake,   11040
Or if he were of lowly birth then he must hang for it. †
    Then once more called Arthur, most admired of kings,
Instructing that each man who had forfeited his land
No matter what the penalty which had driven him away,
He should now return, rapidly and soon,
Whether great or mean, and have his own again,
Unless he were so ill disposed as to be traitor to his lord, *
Or a perjurer against his lord – such a man the king condemned.
    Three brothers arrived there, who were of royal descent,
Lot, Angel and **Urien**, a splendid trio of men! *   11050
These three chieftains came towards the king there,
And went down upon their knees in the emperor's presence:
'All health to you, Arthur, most admired of kings!
And your warriors with you: may they ever flourish!
We are three brothers, from kings we're descended;
All our rightful land has gone out of our hands
For the heathen men have made us most abject,
And laid waste for us Lothian, Scotland and Moray, *
And we beg you, for the love of God, that you give us assistance
And for your own reputation that you be gentle with us.   11060
Give us back our rightful land and we shall always love you,
Regard you as our lord in every manner a subject should.'
    Arthur, most admired of kings, was listening to this,
To how these three knights made a courteous request,
He felt pity in his heart and he proceeded to speak,
And these words were said by the most supreme of kings:
'Urien, become my man: you're to return again to Moray;
In it you shall be called the king of that land,
And be exalted in my army with those who owe you allegiance.
And in Angel's hand I place all of Scotland now at once: 11070
Take it now into your hand and be king of all that land;
From the father to the son, down the line my men you'll all become.
And you, Lot, my beloved friend, may God be gracious to you,
You have my sister as your wife: you will fare the better for it!
I am giving you Lothian, which is a lovely country,

And I will add to it lands which are excellent
Alongside the Humber, worth a hundred pounds,
For my father Uther, in the time that he was king here
Had great love for his daughter who shared his very thoughts, *
And she is my sister, and she has two sons herself,   11080
Who in this land are to me the most beloved of children!'
In this way King Arthur spoke; **Gawain** was then a little child,
And so was the other, **Modred**, his brother –
That Modred was born was a pity: he was cause of much tragedy! *
    Arthur went to London and his liegemen with him;
In his own land he held a very great assembly
And reinstated all the laws which were in statute in his forebears'
     days,
All the good laws formerly extant here;
He established peace and plenty and all liberties.
Then he went to Cornwall to Cador's own kingdom.   11090
Here he encountered a girl unsurpassed in beauty:
This young girl's mother came from the Roman people,
A relation of Cador's, who gave that girl in wardship to him,
And he took her in tenderly and delicately fed her;
Her family was noble from among the Roman people;
Not in any country was there any girl so courtly
In her speech and her behaviour, nor of such gracious manners.
She was called **Guinevere**, most gracious of women;
Arthur took her as his wife, and loved her very dearly;
This maiden did he wed, and he took her to his bed.   11100
    Arthur was there in Cornwall throughout all that winter,
And all for the love of Guinevere, whom he loved most of women.
When the winter was over, and quickly it was summer,
Arthur considered carefully his next activity,   *International*
That his good people should not lie in idleness.   *Reputation*
He marched off to Exeter at the midsummer festival
And there held an assembly of the aristocrats,
Announcing that he intended to go to Ireland,
To transfer all that kingdom into his own hand,
Unless its king, **Gillomaur**, came first and very soon to him   11110
And spoke to him graciously and requested Arthur's mercy,
Then he would lay waste his land and handle him harshly
With fire and with steel play a very strict game there,
And slaughter the inhabitants who wished to oppose him.
In response to the words which the king had been speaking

The assembled folk answered the king very fairly:
'Lord king, keep your promise, we are all prepared*
To march and to ride everywhere as you require!'
    Many bold Britons there looked like the angry bear:
They had lowering brows and battle-fury in their brains;   11120
Off to their quarters marched the knights and their squires,
Rocked their mail-coats free of rust and burnished their helmets,*
Rubbed down their precious horses with pieces of linen,
Horses well-shorn and shod: a superb cavalry turn-out!
Some trimmed horn, some trimmed bone and some prepared steel
    arrows,
Some made leather thongs, fine and very strong,
Some prepared spears and got ready the shields.†
    Arthur sent a summons throughout all his kingdom
That every good knight should come to him straight
And every fine man should come straightway at once,   11130
And each man who would not take part would have his private parts
    removed,
But whoever came willingly, he would become rich.
Seven nights after Easter, when men had finished fasting,
Then to the ships straightaway came all of the knights:
The wind stayed on their side and sped them to Ireland.   *(i) Conquest*
Arthur went on land and harried those who lived there: *of Ireland*
He slaughtered many people and plundered cattle in great numbers
But kept on pressing every man to respect church property.
    The message came to the king who was overlord in the land
Of the arrival there of Arthur who was wreaking untold
    harm there;   11140
He summoned all his people throughout all his kingdom,
And his Irish forces marched forward to the fight
As opponents of Arthur the admirable king.
Arthur and his knights armed themselves straight
And marched forth against them, an enormous force.
Arthur's followers were all protected with armour;
The Irish men were almost entirely naked,
With spears and battle-axes and with very sharp knives.
Arthur's men sent flying countless feathered arrows,
And massacred the Irish, sending many of them tumbling: 11150
They were unable to endure in any way whatever,
But fled away fast in very many thousands,
And Gillomaur the king fled, taking himself off,

With Arthur coming after him. He captured the king,
And so had within his hands the king of that land.
  Arthur the mighty went to set up headquarters;
In his mind he felt all the more relieved that Gillomaur was so close
    by.
Arthur, most admired of kings, was now displaying
In the presence of his people plentiful friendship:
He had the king well dressed in every kind of splendour,   11160
Who even sat beside Arthur, alongside him even ate,
With Arthur he drank wine, which he did not think so fine,
Nonetheless when he perceived that Arthur was delighted,
Then exclaimed Gillomaur (in his heart he felt most sore):
'Lord Arthur, be reconciled! don't mutilate or murder me!
Your vassal I'll become and deliver to you my three sons
(My own beloved sons) to perform all your desire.
I'll do something still more, if you wish to show me favour:
I will deliver to you some very high-born hostages,
Some sixty children of very powerful noblemen.   11170
I'll do something still more, if you wish to show me favour:
Seven thousand pounds every year from my own land
I will send off to your land, with sixty marks in gold.
I'll do something still more if you will show me favour:
All of the horses with all of their trappings,
The hawks and the hounds and my finest treasures
I shall place into your hands from all of my lands;
And when all this is completed I shall take a sacred relic
From Saint Columkille who performed God's own will, *
And the head of Saint Brendan which God himself made
    sacred,   11180
And the right foot of Saint Bridget, most holy and effective,
And plenty of sacred relics which have come here from Rome,
And I'll swear to you in truth that I shall never betray you,
But instead I shall love you and regard you as my lord,
And regard you as the high king and myself as your mere underling.'
  Arthur was listening, most admired king,
And he began laughing with a loud bellow,
And gave him an answer with most gracious words:
'Cheer up, now, Gillomaur, don't let your feelings be so sore,
Since you have been sensible, things will turn out well
    for you,   11190
For people who are intelligent merit sympathetic treatment;

You shall not suffer any more, because of your common sense:
You have offered me a lot; for that you shall be better off!
On this spot, outright, in the presence of all my knights,
Let there be restored to you the larger part of that half measure
Of gold and of treasury; but you must become my vassal,
And send half that tribute each year into my country.
Half of the horses, and half of the trappings,
Half of the hawks and half of the hounds
Which you were offering me, I will leave to you,   11200
But the children I will take with me who come from your nobility,
Those whom they love best of all – then I can trust them the better!
And so you'll remain in your self respect,
In your own kingdom, in your rightful inheritance:
To you I shall give this so that no king shall do wrong to you
Without atoning for it on his bare back!'
So spoke Arthur, most admired of kings.
     Then he had within his hand the whole region of Ireland
And its king who had become his man and had bestowed his three
          sons on him.
     Then Arthur spoke out to his own superb knights: 11210
'Let's go off to Iceland and take it into our own hands!'
The army advanced there and came quickly to Iceland: *Conquest*
Alcus the king was called, chieftain of that area,   *of*
He listened to the tidings of Arthur the king,   *Iceland*
And acted like a wise man and went towards him at once,
At once and straightaway with sixteen knights in envoy,
Carrying in his hand a massive bar of gold.
As soon as he saw Arthur he bowed down upon his knees
And the terrified king uttered these words to him:
'Welcome, Sir Arthur, welcome my lord!   11220
Here I place within your hands the whole region of Iceland:
You are to be my high king, and I shall be your underling;
I shall owe you such obedience as one ought his overlord,
And your vassal I'll become and deliver to you my beloved son
Whose name is **Esscol**, and you are to do him the honour
Of dubbing him as knight in your own retinue;
His mother, whom I married, is daughter of the King of Russia.
And also, every year, I shall give you money:
Seven thousand pounds in silver and in gold,
And for every proposal I'll be ready at your need.   11230
This I shall now swear to you upon my own sword here:

The sacred relic in its hilt is the highest in this land;
Whether I like it or I don't, I shall never be your betrayer!'
    Arthur heard all this, most admired of kings,
(Arthur was agreeable where he got what he was after,
And savage as a man possessed with his opponents)
Arthur heard the placating words from the king of the people,
All that he requested, all this he granted:
Hostages and oaths and all that he promised.
    Then a message was reported with reliable words   11240
To the King of Orkney who was extremely brave –
He was called **Gonwais**, a heathen champion –
That King Arthur intended to come to his land:
With a vast navy he was hurrying to his nation.
Gonwais marched to meet him with his wise leaders
And delivered into Arthur's hands all of Orkney land,
And thirty-two islands which are part of it,
And did homage to him with the greatest reverence,
And he made him a promise in the presence of his courtiers
That each year he would furnish a full sixty ships: 11250
At his own expense he would convey them to London
Loaded, to be specific, with splendid sea-fish.
And this covenant he confirmed and hostages he found,
And firm oaths he swore that he would never be a traitor,
And then he took leave, and began to travel away:
'Lord, I bid you a very good day; I shall come whenever I may,
For you are my lord, and most beloved of all kings.'
    When Arthur had completed this, he wished to accept still more:
He instructed his good scribes and sent off to Jutland,
With greetings to King **Doldanim**, with orders to come at once to
      him,
And to become his own liegeman and to bring to him his
      two sons: 11261
'And if you should refuse to do what I propose
Then I shall send you all of sixteen thousand
Brave battle warriors to your grave disadvantage;
They will lay your land waste and slaughter your people,
And dispose of that land as seems most suitable to them,
And fetter you yourself and bring you here to me!'
    The king heard this threat coming from the emperor,
And instantly seized his own splendid garments,
His hawks and his hounds and his fine horses,   11270

Much silver and much gold and his two sons in his hands,
And off he went marching to Arthur the great king
And Doldanim the good made this declaration:
'All health to you, Arthur, most admired of kings,
Here I'm bringing the two, both of these here are my sons:
Their mother is a king's offspring; she is my own queen,
I won her in my plundering in the land of Russia;   11278
I deliver to you my beloved sons; I myself will become your own
       man,[†]   11277
And I shall send tribute from my own land
Every single year as items of tribute:[†]   11280
I shall send to you in London seven thousand pounds' worth;
This I shall swear: that I shall never be a traitor,
But rather I shall become your vassal: this will enhance your honour;
You shall I never betray, not to the very last day!'
   Arthur selected messengers and sent off to Wendland,[*]
To **Rumareth** the king, with instructions to inform him with speed
That he had within his grasp both Britain and Scotland,
Jutland and Ireland, Orkney and Iceland;
He directed Rumareth to come and bring him his eldest son,
And if he refused to, he'd drive him from his lands,   11290
And if he could catch him he would execute or hang him,
And destroy all his land and condemn all his liegemen.
   The message came to Rumareth, the rich king of Wendland;
He too was very frightened as the others had been earlier:
Most unwelcome were the tidings from Arthur the king!
Nonetheless King Rumareth listened to advice:
He took his eldest son and twelve excellent earls
And went off to Arthur the admirable king,
And went down at his feet and decorously greeted him:
'All health to you, Arthur, most admired of Britons!   11300
I am called Rumareth, I am the king of Wendland;
I have heard a good deal described concerning your courage,
And that you're famous far and wide, king of greatest valour!
You have in many lands conquered realms by your own hands;
There is no king of any land who could ever you withstand,
Neither king nor kaiser, in no combat whatever;
In every project you begin you act according to your whim.
Here I have come to you and have brought you my eldest son;
Here I place within your hands my own self, my royal lands,
And my own beloved son, and my liegemen every one,   11310

My wife, my jewelled garments and all my joys together,
On condition you secure me against your savage attacks;
And do you now be my high king and I shall be your underling,
And deliver into your hands five hundred pounds of gold;
Such gifts I shall find for you every single year.'
    Arthur granted everything which the king requested,
And then he held secret council with his best leaders
And declared that he wanted to return to this land
And to see Guinevere the most gracious queen.
He had brass trumpets blown to summon his host   11320
And off to ship they marched, soldiers marvellously pleased.
The wind blew as they wished, the weather was as they wanted,
They were all delighted at it; they landed up at Grimsby.
    The nobles of this land heard of this at once,
And to the queen came tidings of Arthur the king,
That he had come safe and sound with his men in good spirits.
    Then here in Britain there was great celebration:
There were songs sung to fiddles and harping as well,
Pipes and brass trumpets merrily played there;
Poets sang in praise of Arthur the king   11330
And of the great reputation which he had earned for himself.
People came to his court from many different countries;
In every direction the people were contented.
Everything that Arthur gazed at paid homage to him:
The rich and the poor, as thick as hail falling;
The most wretched of the Britons was greatly enriched.
    On this topic one may read concerning King Arthur
That for twelve years after this he went on living here
In peace and in plenty, in total tranquillity:
No man contended with him, nor did he create any contests,   11340
Nor could any man whatever imagine any pleasures
In any other country in more measure than in this,
Nor could any man experience half as much enjoyment
As there was with Arthur and with his folk here.
    I can describe how things turned out, amazing though it's bound to
      seem:
It happened one Christmas day, when Arthur was lodged in
      London,   *Yuletide*
People had come to him from each of his dependencies: *Fight*
From Britain's land, from Scotland, from Ireland and from Iceland
And from all the other lands which Arthur held in hand,

290

All the greatest leaders with their horses and their squires: 11350
There were seven sons of kings with seven hundred knights who'd
    come,
Not counting the courtiers paying service to Arthur.
Each of them was feeling proudly exultant,
Giving out that he himself was better than his fellows;
The folk came from many realms: there was much rivalry,
Since if one would count himself so high, the second would much
    higher.
    Then the brass trumpets were blown and the trestle-tables covered:
Fine golden bowls were carried out to the hall floor,
And with them soft towels, all made of white silk;*
Then Arthur sat down, and beside him Queen Guinevere,   11360
Then all the earls were seated, and after them the barons,
Then next the knights, as they were assigned;
The nobly connected then brought in the food,
Exactly in decorum, first to the knights,
Then to the foot soldiers and then to the squires,
Then to the baggage-men, right down the tables.
    The company became aroused: blows were freely given;
First they started throwing loaves, as long as there were some left,
And then the silver goblets which were filled with wine,
And after that, clutching palms quickly caught up throats!   11370
    Then a young man jumped forward who'd come there from
    Wendland;
He'd been given to Arthur to be held as hostage;
He was the son of Rumareth who was king of the Wends;
In this way the knight spoke there to Arthur the king:*
'Lord Arthur, be off quickly, into your bedroom,
And your queen with you, and your close relations,
And we'll decide this conflict between these foreign combatants!'
Having spoken these words he leaped up to the trestle-boards
Where carving knives were lying in front of the lord king:
Three knives he caught up and with one quickly struck   11380
Into the neck of the knight who first began that very fight
So that down to the hall floor his head went crashing;
Fast he slew another, this same fighter's brother:
Before the swords came out he had finished off seven.
There was a huge fight there: every man struck the other;
There was enormous blood-shed, consternation in the court!
    Then the king emerged from out of his chamber;

With him a hundred courtiers, with helmets and with corslets,
Each carrying in his right hand a broadsword of bright steel.
Then shouted Arthur, most admired of kings: 11390
'Sit down, sit down at once, all of you, or you will lose your lives!
Anyone who refuses to will be condemned to death.
Seize and bring me the actual man who first started this fight,
Clap a noose around his neck and drag him to the marshes,
And fling him in a deep bog and there let him lie,
And seize all his closest relatives whom you can discover,
And strike off their heads with your broad swords;
From the women you can discover among his closest relations
Carve off the noses and let their beauty be destroyed; *
In that way I'll quite obliterate the tribe from which he
          came,   11400
And if ever any more I subsequently hear
That any of my courtiers, whether great or humble,
From this same slaughter should [seek] revenge after, †
Then no compensation from gold or treasure will atone,
Neither strong steed nor war gear, to buy him off from death
Or from being drawn apart by horses, which is the punishment for
          traitors.
Bring here the sacred relics and I shall swear upon them,
As shall all you knights who were present at this fight,
You earls and barons, that you will never break it.'
    The first to swear was Arthur, most admired of kings,   11410
Then the earls took the oath, and then the barons took the oath,
Then the landholders took the oath, then the servitors took the oath,
That they would never again instigate a brawl.
The dead were all taken up and carried to their resting-place,
And then brass trumpets were blown with very rousing sound:
Whether they liked it or loathed it, each one took water and a cloth, *
And then, reconciled, they sat down at the table,
All in awe of Arthur, most admired of kings.
Cup-bearers were jostling, minstrels were singing,
Harps gave out joyful sounds: courtiers were jubilant.   11420
For a whole week like this the court was employed.
    Next, it says in the story, the king went to Cornwall;
There a man came quickly to him who was a skilled craftsman,
And he encountered the king and gave courteous greeting:
'All health to you, Arthur, most admired of kings!
I am your own vassal; many a land I have traversed;

I know a marvellous number of the skills of woodworking.
I heard tell beyond the sea such novel tidings
About your own knights who at your table started fighting
At the midwinter feast; many fell there.   11430
In their mighty arrogance they were acting games of murder,
And because of their high connexions each must sit near top-table.
But I shall make for you a most suitable table   *The*
Where sixteen hundred and more can easily be seated,   *Round*
Each in turn all round so that no one gets left out,   *Table*
No inclusion and exclusion, just one man opposite another.
When you want to ride you can carry it alongside,
And set it up wherever you want, according to your fancy,
And you need never again be afraid in all the wide world
That ever any proud knight would at your table start a fight,   11440
Since the important there must be equal with the simple.'
     Timber was obtained and the table was begun:
In the space of four weeks the work was completed.
On a certain festival the court was assembled,
And Arthur himself turned quickly to the table,
And ordered all his knights to the table straightaway.
When all those knights were seated at their food
Then each was chatting to the other just as if he were his brother;
They were all seated around it and none was excluded;
Every single kind of knight was very well placed there;   11450
Each was seated equally, the important and the simple,
And no one there could boast about a different kind of toast
Than the drink of his companions who were sitting at the table.
     This was the very table which the Britons boast about,
And they tell many kinds of fiction about Arthur who was king,
But so does every man who has great love for another:
If he loves that man too much then he is bound to lie,
And in his fine praise he'll say more than he deserves;
However bad a man he is, his friend will back him up still;
On the other hand if should arise in the community,   11460
On any occasion between two individuals,
Lies will be invented about the one who isn't liked:
Even if he were the best man who ever ate bread at table
The man who found him hateful would invent some vices for him:
It's not all true, it's not all false which poets are proclaiming,
But this is true fact about Arthur the king:
There has never been a king so valiant in everything;

It's found as fact in the annals just as it actually was,
From the start to the end, concerning Arthur the king,
No more and no less, just as his deeds were recorded,   11470
But the Britons loved him greatly and often lie about him
And recount many thing about Arthur the king
Which never really happened in the whole of this world!
A man can say enough, if he just tells the truth,
Of outstanding things about Arthur the king.

    Arthur was then very great, his court very glorious,
So that no knight was valued nor his actions reckoned valiant,
– Not in Wales, nor in England, in Scotland nor in Ireland,
In Normandy nor in France, in Flanders nor in Denmark,
Nor in any land whatever which lies on this side of the
        Alps –   11480
No knight (as I said) would be thought good, nor his deeds reckoned
        bold
Unless, concerning Arthur and his outstanding court –
His weapons and his garments and also his war-mounts –
He was able to tell in song, about Arthur the young
And about his knightly courtiers and about their great prowess,
And about their magnificence and how well it suited them;
Then he would be welcome anywhere in this world's span,
Wherever he might come to, even if he were in Rome.

    All those who heard the stories told about Arthur
Found accounts of the good king very extraordinary;   11490
And so it had been prophesied before he was even born,
So the famous prophet Merlin had foretold about him,
Saying that a king would come from Uther Pendragon
Such that minstrels should make a board for food from the king's
        own breast*
And at it would be seated really splendid poets,
Who would eat their fill before they fared away;
And they would draw draughts of wine from the king's tongue
And be drinking and delighting by day and by night;
This sport was to endure for them as long as this world lasts.

    In addition Merlin stated that more was to come: 11500
That everything he looked at was to bow down at his feet;
In addition Merlin stated a marvel which was greater:
That there would be immoderate sorrow at this king's departure,*
And as to this king's end – no Briton would believe it,
Unless one means the final death at the last great Judgment

When our Lord God is to judge all the nations;
Otherwise we can't determine as to Arthur's death
Because he himself said to his splendid Britons,
Down south in Cornwall where Gawain had been killed[*]
And he himself was badly wounded, grievously severely,   11510
That he was to voyage into Avalon,
Into the island, to **Argante** the gracious,[*]
Because with health-giving lotions she would heal his wounds,
And when he was entirely healed he would instantly come to them.
The Britons believ[e] this: that he will come like this,[†]
And they are always looking for his coming to his land,
Just as he promised them before he went away.
　　In this world Arthur was a wise king and powerful,
A good man and peaceful; his subjects all adored him.
He possessed knights both proud and exalted in spirit   11520
Who reported to the king of remarkable things;
In this way the courtiers called upon the high king;
'Lord Arthur, let us voyage to the realm of France
And reduce all that land into your own hand,
Put to flight all the French and fell their monarch,
Get control of all the castles and put British guards in them,
And rule over their realm with robust force.'
　　Arthur then responded, most admired of kings: *International*
'I shall perform your wishes, but first I wish to go to   *Reputation*
　　　Norway,
And with me I wish to take Lot, who is my brother-in-law: 11530
He is the father of Gawain whom I love so dearly,
For there has come from Norway some new
　　　information   *(ii) Conquests*
That King **Sichelin** is dead there, his courtiers deserted,   *in*
And he has biqueathed all his kingdom already to Lot   *Scandinavia*
　　　here,
For the king's entirely lacking either sons or daughters,
And Lot is his sister's son: for that reason he's preferred.
So as a new king in Norway I intend to invest him,
And well I shall instruct him to direct his people well.
And when I have done this, I shall afterwards come home,
And prepare my forces and voyage across to France,   11540
And if the king opposes me, refusing to sue for peace,
Then I shall fight against him and fell him to the ground!'
　　Arthur had horns blown and also brass trumpets

And had his very bold Britons mustered at the seaside;
Fine ships he possessed beside the sea waves:
Fifteen hundred of them hastened from the land
And went winging across the sea as if they could fly,
And turned towards Norway with terrific force. *Conquest*
As soon as they arrived they went into harbour, *in*
With their full power they stepped on the realm's shore. *Norway*
Arthur sent his messengers far throughout that country 11551
Ordering them to come at once and take Lot as their king,
And if they refused to he would slaughter them all!
    Then the Norwegian earls took their ambassadors
And sent them to the king with request that he depart:
'And if you refuse to return you will have sorrow and misery,
For as long as is for ever it will not happen ever
That we shall choose as king a man who is a foreigner;
For if Sichelin has departed there are others here as talented
Whom we can by our own decision choose to be king, 11560
And this is a fact and there is no other!
Either take yourselves off now and go straight back home,
Or in one week from today we'll give you a great battle!'
    Next the Norwegian earls came to the conclusion
That they would have a king who came from their own race,
For all the words of Sichelin they reckoned were stupid.
'And as long as shall be for ever this shall happen never!
But we shall take **Riculf**, a rich and powerful earl
And elect him as our king: this we find agreeable,
And shall summon our army throughout all this country 11570
And advance towards Arthur and rout him in battle
And we shall get Lot running and rout him from the land,
Or else by fighting we'll cause him to fall.'
    They elected Riculf who was an earl of Norway,
And raised him to the throne (though not by right of succession)
And summoned their army through all Norway's country:
And Arthur for his part began to march through that land;
He traversed that land; its towns he burned down,
A good deal did he plunder, many people did he slaughter,
And Riculf started riding towards Arthur right away: 11580
Together they clashed and battle commenced;
The Britons turned towards them; there was trouble in full;
They snatched from the scabbard swords of great length;
Heads flew on the battlefield; faces were blanched;

Man against man set shaft into breast;
Byrnies were broken; the British were busy;
Shields bristled with shafts; soldiers were falling,
And all through the daylight lasted this great fight.
If they shifted east, if they shifted west, the Norwegians got the worst;
If they shifted south, if they shifted north: the Norwegians were
    falling.
The British were bold: the Norwegians were killed.   11591
Of the Norwegians there fell twenty-five thousand,
And King Riculf was killed there and deprived of his life-days;
Few were left on their feet from the folk who had lived there;
Those whose wretched lives remained to them begged for Arthur's
    mercy.
   Arthur gazed at Lot whom he loved very much
And Arthur the great man began to call to him:
'Lot, come over here to me: you are my dear kinsman;
Herewith I bestow all this kingdom upon you;
You are to hold it of me and have me as your guardian.'   11600
   Now Lot's eldest son, Gawain, had come there from Rome
From the court of the Pope who was called **Sulpicius**,
Who long had been training him and who dubbed him as knight;
Things were very well ordained that Gawain was created
Because Gawain was most high-minded, and excelled in every virtue:
He was generous with food and a knight among the best.
All Arthur's courtiers were greatly enlivened
By the coming to court of Gawain the courageous,
And by his father Lot, who had been elected a king.
Then Arthur spoke with him, bidding him to keep a binding
    truce,   11610
And bidding him to love those of his people who stayed peaceful,
And to eliminate entirely those who would not keep the peace.
   Then Arthur, most admired of kings, cried out again:
'Where are you, my Britons? now get marching at once!
At the sea's edge prepare my good ships!'
The knights did exactly as Arthur commanded:
When the ships were ready, Arthur set off for the sea,
Taking with him his knights, his Norwegian leaders,
And his bold British men; and he launched off on the waves,
And the undaunted king came into Denmark.   11620
He had his tents erected: out across the fields they spread;
Brass trumpets he had blown, his arrival to make known.

Now there was then in Denmark a very mighty king,   *Denmark*
Aescil he was called, chieftain of the Danes;   *Invaded*
He could see that Arthur conquered everything he wanted;
King Aescil thought carefully what might be his policy:
He could see that by power he could not hope to prevail
Against Arthur's force in any combat at all.

He sent his good wishes to Arthur the king,   11630
Some hounds and some hawks and some very good horses,
Silver and red gold, with really [prudent] words.†
And Aescil the famous did one thing further:
He sent to the most excellent in Arthur's entourage,
Asking them to intercede for him with the noble King
So that he could become his vassal and give up his son as a hostage
And send him every year a certain tribute from his land,
A boat solidly filled from gunwale to bilge
With gold and great treasure and with gorgeous garments,
And then he would swear that he would never be a traitor.   11640

News came to Arthur, most admired of kings,
That Aescil, the Danish king, wished to become his underling
Without any fighting – he and all his knights.
Then Arthur the great was in very good spirits,
And answered like this, with unassuming words:
'Good luck to the man who with very good sense
Gains peace and goodwill and lasting friendship for himself;
When he can see how he'll be bound by sheer force
On the verge of losing all of his beloved realm,
Then with forethought he may loosen the fetters he so
    loathes.'   11650

Arthur told the king to come and to bring his eldest son,
And the King of Denmark did so at once:
He quickly fulfilled what Arthur had willed;
They came to a conference and were accorded.
Then Arthur cried again, that most admired of kings:
'Now I wish to go to France with my enormous force:
I desire to have from Norway nine thousand knights,
And out of Denmark I shall conduct nine thousand of the country-
    men,
And from the Orkneys eleven hundred,
And out of Moray three thousand men,   11660
And out of Galloway five thousand of the people,
And out of Ireland eleven thousand.

And out of Britain from my own bold knights
There shall throng past me thirty thousand,
And from Jutland I shall lead ten thousand of the people,
And out of Friesland five thousand men,
And from Brittany Howel the brave,
And with such folk I shall invade France.
And as I trust in God's grace still more shall I promise:
That from all of the lands which lie within my hands   11670
I shall order out every worthy man who knows how to wield his
        weapons,
As he wants to live, and to retain his limbs,
That he must come with me to fight against **Frollo**
Who is the King of France — he must meet his fate —;
In Rome city he was born and comes of a Roman clan.'

 Arthur moved forwards till he came to Flanders; *International*
He conquered that land and settled it with his men,   *Reputation*
And then he turned from there towards [Boulogne][†]
And took [all of] Boulogne's lands into his own hands[†]
And then he took the route which led towards France.[*] 11680
Then he issued his instructions to all in his service:
Wherever they advanced they were not to take plunder
Unless [they] were able in strict fairness to obtain it,[†]
By fair exchange in the king's entourage.

 Frollo heard information where he was, in France, *(iii) France*
Of Arthur's success and all his attainments   *Invaded*
And how he won everything which he had looked at,
And everything he set his eyes on gave allegiance to him.
Then was King Frollo horribly frightened!
In that same age when this was occurring   11690
All the land of France was known as Gaul,
And from Rome into France had Frollo advanced,
And every year he was to send tribute from that land
Ten hundred pounds' worth in silver and in gold.
Now as chieftain of France Frollo received information
Of the country-wide chaos Arthur caused in the land.
He sent messengers at once quickly towards Rome,
And urged the Roman people to make right consultations
About how many thousand knights they wanted to send there.
So that with ease he might against Arthur fight,   11700
And send Arthur the strong flying from the land.

 Knights began riding out of Roman territory,

Twenty-five thousand of them advanced upon France.
Frollo heard of this in his enormous force,
That the Roman forces were riding to his country;
Frollo and his folk advanced then to meet them,
And they came together, men of courage and valour,
An immeasurable army from all parts of the earth.

    This news came to Arthur, most admired of kings,
Who summoned his army and moved off towards them.   11710
There has never yet been a king alive on this earth
Who ever in the world before commanded such an army,
For from all of the kingdoms which Arthur had in his control
He led off with him all the bravest men,
Until he had no idea at all how many thousand there were.

    As soon as Arthur and Frollo had encountered in combat
Fiercely they attacked all those whom they met.
Knights of great strength grasped spears of great length
And rushed at each other with furious force.
All through that day there were very many blows;   11720
Folk fell to the ground in their fated final moments;
Grieving soldiers sought a couch in the grass;
Helmets were ringing, warriors howling;
Shields were shattered, soldiers were slumping.
Arthur, most admired of kings, called out then:
'Where are you, my Britons, my very bold fighters?
The day is drawing on, and this army is defying us;
Let us send flying to them sufficient sharp spears,
And teach them to ride the road back towards Rome!'

    After those words which Arthur was speaking   11730
He sprang forward on his steed as a spark does from the fire;
Following him there were fifty thousand men,
Hardened battle-champions hurried to the fight,
Struck down on Frollo where he was in the throng
And forced him to flee with many of his folk.
There Arthur slaughtered countless numbers of folk.
Then Frollo the great fled into Paris
And barred up the gates in very deep gloom,
And these words he spoke, in sorrowing mood:
'I wish very much that I had never been born!'   11740
Inside Paris then there were pathetic tales indeed,
Gestures of despair; citizens shivered in terror;
The walls they were repairing, the gates fortifying,

Food they were seizing, everything they got hold of;
From every quarter to the city they hurried;
All those who held with Frollo travelled there fast.
Arthur, most admired of kings, heard this,
That Frollo was hiding in Paris with an enormous force,
Declaring he intended to resist Arthur.

    Arthur went to Paris, quite unfaint-hearted, 11750
And surrounded the walls and erected his tents;
Round it on four sides he lay for four weeks and a day.
The people who were inside there were absolutely terrified;
The city was packed with people inside it
Who quickly ate the food which had been collected.
When the full run of four weeks had passed by since Arthur stationed
        himself there
There was in the city immeasurable sadness
Among the wretched people who were lying there starving:
There was weeping, there was wailing and tremendous distress.
They cried out to Frollo and begged him to come to terms, 11760
To become Arthur's vassal and enjoy his favour,
And hold the kingdom now from Arthur the courageous,
And not permit the abject folk to perish quite from hunger.

    Then Frollo replied – he had a fine spirit!
'No, so help me God, who controls all destinies!
Never shall I become his man, nor he become my liege lord;
I myself shall fight; on God's side lies the right!'
Once more exclaimed Frollo, a fine man in spirit:
'No, so help me the Lord who made the light of day!
Never shall I at all beg Arthur for mercy, 11770
But I intend to fight without any single knight,
Body against body, in the presence of my people,
Hand against hand, with that King Arthur.
Whichever of us two will prove the weaker, straight he'll be the lesser,
Whichever of us two is able to survive, by his friends he'll be more
        celebrated.
And whichever of us two can get the better of the other,
Is to have all the other's lands delivered into his own hands.

    'This I shall request, if Arthur wishes to grant it,
And this I shall swear upon my own sword,
And I shall find hostages, the sons of three kings, 11780
To prove that I shall surely keep to this promise
And will not renege on it, by my very life;

Because I prefer to lie dead before my own people
Than to see them on the ground perishing from hunger.
After all, we have destroyed our knights in the fighting,
Full fifty thousand soldiers are fallen
And many a good housewife has been made a grieving widow,
Many a child fatherless and bereft of comfort,
And now these folk are fearfully harmed by sheer hunger.
Therefore it is better that just between us two   11790
We deal and dispose of this kingdom by fight;
May the better man have it and enjoy possessing it!'
    Frollo took twelve knights straight after speaking these thoughts
And sent them with speed to Arthur the king,
And enquired if he wished to accept this agreement
And through his own hands to lay claim to the kingdom;
Or to reject it to his own people's ruin;
And if he obtained it, let him possess it with power.
    The message came to Arthur, most admired of kings,
Who had never been so blithe before in his life: 11800
He was pleased by the tidings from Frollo their king,
And Arthur the lucky made this declaration:
'King Frollo of France has spoken most aptly:
It is better that the two of us decide for this realm
Than that our stalwart lords should be slaughtered there.
I approve of this arrangement in my people's assembly,
To do what he proposes on an appointed day;
This is to be tomorrow, in front of both sets of men,
When we shall each of us fight the other, and may the less plucky man
    fall!
And whichever of us two retreats and wants to give up this fight,
Let him in each land be cursed as a coward.   11811
Then songs can be sung of such a king as that
Who gave his solemn promise and then forsook his knighthood!'
    Frollo king of France heard this reported,
That Arthur wished to fight in person without any other knights.
Frollo was a strong man and stern in his emotions, *
And he had made his promise in the presence of his whole household
And he could not without great disgrace bring shame upon himself
By going back on the bold bragging he had uttered in the city.
When he said what he said, he had certainly believed   11820
That Arthur would decline it and would not accept the challenge,
For if Frollo had known, as the king within France,

That Arthur would allow him what he had asked for,
He would not have been so bold for a ship full of gold!
But just the same, Frollo was a very brave fighter,
A tall knight and a strong man and full of great spirit,
And he said he would keep to the day they'd agreed,
'On the island which is encompassed by water:
The island lies – be sure of this – within the city of Paris;
There I will in fight determine my own rights,   11830
With a shield, and in the garb of knight.
Tomorrow now will be the day; let it go to him who win may!'
　So came the tidings to Arthur the king
That Frollo was willing to contest France by fighting;
He had never been so blithe before in his life,
And started to laugh in a really loud voice,
And these were the words of Arthur the brave:
'Now I know that Frollo is willing to fight with me,*
Tomorrow at daylight, as he himself determined,
Upon the island which water has surrounded,   11840
For it befits a king that his word can be relied on.
Have the brass trumpets blown and bid my men assemble,
So that every good man may tonight be keeping vigil
And praying to our Lord, who controls the lot of all,
That he may protect me against Frollo the furious,
And with his right hand may preserve me from shame.
And if I succeed in winning this kingdom to my own command,
Then every single poor man will be provided for,
And I shall perform Almighty God's will.
Now may he give me assistance who can do all things well;   11850
May the high, heavenly King support me with his aid,
For I intend to love him as long as I have life!'
　All through the long night there were hymns by candle-light:
Devoutly clerics were intoning holy psalms to God.
When daylight came next morning the attendants started stirring;
Arthur the mighty took his weapons in his hands;
He threw on his back a most precious mantle,
A shirt of soft linen and a tunic made of velvet,
A very choice mail-coat of interlocking steel;
On his head he set an excellent helmet,   11860
By his side he buckled his sword Caliburn;
His legs he protected with mail leggings of steel,
And fastened on his feet very fine spurs.

303

Equipped in this way the king leapt on his steed;
Then he was passed a really splendid shield
Which was made entirely of elephant ivory.
Then he was handed a stout ash shaft
At the end of which was a very fine spearhead
Forged in Caermarthen by a smith whose name was Griffin;
This had belonged to Uther, the previous king here.   11870
   When the fierce man was armed, he prepared to move off.
Then anyone who had been about would have observed
The regal champion riding off vigorously:
Since this world's creation it has been nowhere narrated
That any man so handsome ever moved on horseback
As was King Arthur, son of King Uther.
   There rode behind the king brave army commanders,
Forty hundred of them in the first contingent,
Noble army leaders arrayed all in steel,
Bravest Britons, ready with their weapons;   11880
After them hastened fully fifty hundred
Whom Gawain headed: a champion who was deadly.
Afterwards there surged out sixty thousand men,
Very brave Britons bringing up the rearguard.
   King Angel was there; Lot was there and Urien,
And Urien's son was there, whose name was **Ywain**;
Kay was there and Bedevere, supervising the army there;
Howel was present, leading man in Brittany;
Cador was there too, most courageous in the throng;
From Ireland there came Gillomaur the mighty;   11890
King Gonwais was present, Orkney's favourite;
Doldamin the brave was there, who'd come from Jutland,
[And Rumaret the strong who'd come from Wendland];†   11892a
King Aescil was there, Denmark's favourite.
Of folk on foot there were so many thousand men
That no man in this world's region has ever been so clever
In any number system as to total up the thousands,
Unless he naturally had the wisdom of the Lord,
Or unless he had within him the same brain as Merlin.
   Arthur moved forward with innumerable folk   11899
Until he came completely inside Paris city,   *The*
On the west bank of the river, with his vast company.   *Fight with*
On the east bank stood Frollo with a huge force too,   *Frollo*
Ready for the fight in front of all his knights.

304

Arthur took charge of a good boat and embarked in it
With his shield and his steed and all his war-gear
And he shoved that sturdy boat off from the shore
And strode up on the island, leading his steed in hand.
His men who brought him there by the king's order
There on the waves left the boat, freely floating.

 Frollo got into his boat — this king was regretting   11910
That he'd ever had the idea of fighting with Arthur;
He crossed to the isle with his splendid armour,
Up on to the isle he stepped, dragging his steed after;
The men who brought him there by the king's order
There on the waves left the boat, swiftly floating,
And the two kings remained there alone.

 Then people who had been about would have observed
Folk on the banks who were fearsomely afraid;
They scrambled up on halls, they scrambled up on walls,
They scrambled up on bowers, they scrambled up on towers   11920
So they could see the contest between the two kings.
Arthur's men prayed, with very much devotion,
To the good God and to his holy mother
That their own lord might have victory there;
And the others likewise prayed for their king.

 Arthur set foot in stirrup and leaped on his charger,*
And Frollo in his war-gear leapt on his steed,
The one at his own end upon that island,
And the other at his end in that island.
Those royal knights brandished their spears   11930
And reined in their steeds; they were experienced knights.
The man could not be found in any land whatever
Who had sufficient foresight to be able to foretell
Which one of the two kings would lie there defeated,
For both of them were brave knights, worthy men and valiant,
Men powerful in vigour and of very mighty strength.
They spurred on their steeds and were riding to make impact,
Furiously galloping, sending sparks flying after them:
Arthur struck Frollo with furious force
High up on his shield;   11940
And the trusty steed jumped out in mid stream.
Arthur's sword came out: destruction was in its point!
And he pitched into Frollo where he was, there in the water:
Very soon their contest might have come to a finish!

But Frollo gripped in his hand his lengthy spear,
And made a counter-attack on Arthur as he came at him,[†]
And struck the brave steed right in the breast
So that the spear went right in and Arthur tumbled off.
    Then a roar arose which the earth again re-echoed:
The skies were resounding with the people's shouting.   11950
The Britons there were on the point of crossing the water
But Arthur started up at once unharmed in full strength,
And gripped his good shield decorated with gold,
And against Frollo, with expressions of hostility;
He flung over his chest his fine, broad shield.
And Frollo flung himself at him in a fierce attack
And lifting his sword up struck it down hard
And smashed into Arthur's shield – it fell on to the field;
His helmet on his head and his battle-coif of mail
Suddenly failed on the front of his head   11960
And he received a wound which was four inches long;
It did not pain him badly because it was not too big,
But the blood spurted down all over his chest.
Arthur was deeply enraged in his feelings
And his sword Caliburn he swung with full strength
And struck Frollo right on his helmet so that it split in two,
Sliced through the mail-coif till it stopped at his breast.
Then Frollo fell on the earth of the field:
On that grass bed he gave up his spirit.
The Britons rejoiced with a roar of acclaim   11970
And the (other) folk fled exceedingly fast.
    Arthur the mighty came to the shore,
And the most admired of kings shouted out like this:
'Where are you, Gawain, my favourite man?[*]
Order all these Roman citizens to leave here in peace:
Let each man have his home, as God permits him.
Command each man to keep the peace, on pain of life and limb,
And I shall confirm it just a week from today.
Order these people then to travel together
And come to me in person; they shall prosper because of it.   11980
They are to give to me homage with due honour,
And I shall maintain them within my control
And impose on the land very just laws,
For now the Roman law code must fall in abeyance,
Which formerly applied here in the reign of Frollo

Who lies slain on the island and deprived of his life's days.
After this very soon his kinsfolk in Rome
Shall be hearing tidings from Arthur the king,
For with them I wish to speak and Rome's walls I shall break
And remind them how King Belin there led his Britons in,   11990
And conquered all the lands which belong to Rome.'
    Arthur turned to the gate in the front of the city;
Discerning men arrived, who directed the city,
And allowed Arthur in with all of his men,
Delivered to him the halls, delivered to him the castles,
Delivered to him (most surely) the whole city of Paris.
There was much rejoicing among the British forces!
    That day arrived in the city which Arthur had appointed
And all the male inhabitants came, and became his vassals.
Arthur took his army and divided it in two,   12000
And handed over half of it into Howel's charge,
And instructed him to go at once with that great army,
With the British men, territories to win.
Howel then acted just as Arthur had instructed:
He conquered Berry and all the lands near by,
Anjou and Touraine, Auvergne and Gascony   *Conquest*
And all of the ports which belong to those parts.   *of France*
    The Duke who ruled Poitou bore the name **Guitard**:
He refused to obey Howel and remained always opposed to him,
Refused to seek a truce; but Howel fought against him;   12010
Frequently he felled men, frequently he made them flee:
Howel devastated all that land and destroyed the people.
It was obvious to Guitard, who was overlord in Poitou,
That all those who lived there were being lost to him;
He made peace with Howel, along with all his followers,
And became the vassal of the valiant King Arthur.
Arthur was gracious to him, loved him very greatly,
And allowed him to retain his lands because he did him homage.
And so Howel had made a handsome beginning!
    Arthur governed France by a generous arrangement: 12020
Taking his army he traversed all that country;
To Burgundy he travelled and brought it under his control,
And then he laid his course into Lorraine
And all of its lands he took into his own hands.
All that Arthur set his eyes on gave allegiance to him,
And he returned after this home again to Paris.

When Arthur had established France by a sound truce,
Ratified and reconciled so the country could relax,
Then he directed the veteran knights whom he'd retained for a long
    time
To come before the king and to receive their reward,   12030
Because for many years now they had been his partners;
To some he gave lands and to some silver and gold,
To some he gave castles, to some men he gave clothes;
He bade them depart in joy, atone for their wrongdoing,
And forbade them to bear weapons now that age had come upon
    them,
And told them in this life to have great love for God
So that at its finish He would surely give them paradise,
Which they might enjoy with the angels in delight.
All the veteran knights travelled off to their lands,
While the young remained with their beloved king.   12040
    For all of nine years Arthur remained there:
Nine years liberally he held France in his control.
And then no longer afterwards did he rule that land,
But all the time that kingdom remained in Arthur's hands
Remarkable things occurred in the region:
Many a haughty man Arthur made humble
And many an arrogant man he brought underfoot.
    It happened one Easter when men had finished fasting
That Arthur on Easter Day had assembled his nobles,
All the greatest people who belonged to France   12050
And to all the territories tributary to her.
There he confirmed his knights in all their own rights:
To each he gave such property as he had deserved.
    In this way spoke Arthur, most admired of kings:
'Kay, look in this direction! You are to be my   *Governorships*
    seneschal;
Here I donate you Anjou because you've acted well,
And all the privileges which appertain to it.
Kneel to me, Bedivere: you are my senior butler here:
As long as I'm alive I shall have love for you;
Here I give you Neustria, neighbour to my own realm.'   12060
(In those days Neustria was what is now called Normandy);
That same couple of earls were Arthur's favoured men
In council and in consultation on every occasion.
Then once again said Arthur, most admired of kings:

'Come here, **Howeldin**, you're my subject and my kin,
You take Boulogne and possess it with pleasure.
Draw nearer, **Borel**, you're a wise knight and sensible:
Here I donate to you Le Mans with much respect:
Possess it with pleasure because you've acted well.'
So did King Arthur deal out his illustrious lands,   12070
According to their deeds because he deemed them worthy.
Then there were happy tales in King Arthur's halls:
There was harping and singing and pleasures all the time.
     When Easter was over and April went from homes
And grass was growing everywhere and water was calm   *The*
And men told each other that May had arrived,   *Crown-Wearing*
Arthur took his splendid folk and travelled to the sea
And assembled his ships which excelled among the best
And journeyed to this country and came ashore in London;
He came ashore in London to the joy of those who lived
          here: 12080
Everyone who set their eyes on him was full of delight
And at once started singing about Arthur the king
And about the splendid triumphs which he had achieved.
There father kissed son and wished the boy welcome,
Daughter her mother and brother another,
Sister kissed sister (their feelings were more tender).
In many hundred places there stood by the wayside
People who were asking about many kinds of things,
And knights who were informing them about their achievements
And bragging a good deal about great acquisitions.   12090
No man could describe, however dextrous his style,
One half of the happiness there was among the British.
Each man moved as he required freely in this kingdom,
From one town to the next with considerable ease,
And so for a short time things stayed just like this:
There was content among the British while their brave king was
          there.
     When Easter had gone and summer came to the land
Arthur consulted with his chief councillors
About how in Caerleon he'd wear his crown ceremonially
And upon Whitsunday his people there he'd summon.   12100
     At that particular time it was the general opinion
That there was not in any land a city as lovely,
Nor as widely renowned as Caerleon-upon-Usk,

Except for the noble city which is called Rome.
Even so with the king there was many a man in the land
Who declared the city of Caerleon more resplendent than Rome,
And said that the Usk was the sweetest of all rivers.
There were extensive meadows all around the city;
There were fish, there were birds, and it was very beautiful;
There was timber and wild animals in wonderful profusion;   12110
There was all the pleasure any man could imagine,
Yet never since Arthur's visit has the town ever flourished,
Nor is it ever going to between now and Doomsday.
Some books declare as certainty that the city was bewitched,*
And it is very obvious that this is quite likely.
   In that city stood two very glorious minsters:
One dedicated to Saint Aaron – it had many relics in it –
The other to Saint Julian the Martyr, who is favoured by the Lord.
There were most devout nuns, many of them noblewomen;
The bishop's chair was at Saint Aaron; there was many a
     good man.   12120
Canons were there, who were known far and wide;
There was many a good scholar, well-steeped in learning:
They were most advanced in the skills of surveying the heavens,
Of looking at the stars, both the near ones and the far;
This art is labelled 'Astronomy'.
Frequently they told the king about very many things:
They informed him in words what would happen to him here.
   Such was the city of Caerleon: there was great wealth in it,
There was much excitement around the active king.
The king took his messengers and sent them through his
     country   12130
Ordering the earls to come, ordering the barons,
Ordering the kings to come, and also the warlords,
Ordering the bishops to come, ordering the knights to come,
Ordering all the freemen who were in the land at all:
On their very lives, ordered them to be at Caerleon on Whitsunday.
   Knights began riding very great distances,
Riding towards Caerleon from many kinds of lands.
On Whitsunday there arrived King Angel,
King of Scotland with his splendid folk;
Many was the handsome man who accompanied that king.   12140
From Moray King Urien and his handsome son Ywain;
Stater king of South Wales and **Cadwathlan** king of North Wales,

Cador, Earl of Cornwall, whom the king was fond of;
Morvith of Gloucester, **Maurin** of Winchester,*
Gurguint, Earl of Hereford, and **Beof**, Earl of Oxford;
Gursal the brave from Bath came riding there;
Urgent of Chester, **Jonathas** of Dorchester,
Arnold of Salisbury, and **Kinmarc** of Canterbury,
Balien of Silchester, **Wigein** of Leicester,
Argal, earl of Warwick, with outstanding followers;   12150
Dunwale, son of **Apries**, and **Kegein**, son of **Elauth**,*
Kineus who was **Coitt's** son, and **Cradoc** son of **Catell**;
Aedlin, son of **Cledauke**, **Grimarc**, son of **Kinmark**,
Run Margoitt, and **Netan Clofard**, **Kincar** and **Aikan**,
Kerin Neton and **Peredur**, **Madoc**, **Traher** and **Elidur**:
All of these were Arthur's admirable earls,
And the highest born and worthiest leaders in all this land,
Except for the barons who ate at Arthur's table.
    No one could identify or name all those people.
There were three archbishops within this nation: 12160
In London, and at York, and St **Dubric** in Caerleon,
Who was a very holy man, accomplished in everything.
In London stood the archbishop's see which later moved to
        Canterbury,
After the English won this island for themselves.
    It would be quite impossible to count the folk at Caerleon:
Gillomaur the king was there, favourite of the Irish,
Malverus, King of Iceland, King Doldanim of Jutland,*
King **Kailin** of Frisia, Aescil king of Denmark;
Lot was there, the courageous, who was King in Norway,
And Gonwais King of Orkney, beloved of the outlaws,   12170
The man of fury came, the earl of Boulogne:
Laeyer was his name and his men came with him;
From Flanders the earl Howeldin, from Chartres the earl Gerin:
These two conducted with them all the men of France;
Twelve fierce earls came, who were ruling men in France:
Including Guitard, earl of Poitou, Kay the earl of Anjou,
Bedevere, earl of Normandy (the land was then called Neustria),
From Le Mans came the earl Borel, from Brittany the earl Howel –
Earl Howel was a grand man and gorgeous was his apparel,
And all those folk from France were clothed very finely,   12180
All armed appropriately with horses in good condition.
There were in addition fifteen bishops.

There was no knight and no squire, nor leader one would admire,
From the ports of Spain to the towns of Almaigne
Who had not arrived there if he had been invited,
All out of their respect for Arthur's noble rank.
    When all this assembly had arrived, each king with his retainers,
Then anyone who had been about could have beheld
Many an unknown man who had made his way to the city,
And many kinds of new things around Arthur the king: 12190
There were many unusual clothes, there were many stern knights;
There the lodgings were luxuriously adorned,*
There the quarters were forcefully appropriated;
On the fields there were many thousand tents,
And huge supplies of bacon and oats and [wheat];†
No one could make an estimate of the wine and of the ale there;
Hay was supplied, and grass and good things in quantities.
    When these people were assembled with the splendid king,
Then Whitsunday arrived as the Lord had appointed it;
Then the bishops all came in the presence of their king,   12200
And the three archbishops, into Arthur's presence,
And took up the royal crown which was right and proper for him
And placed it upon his head amid great celebration,
And so they conducted him wholly under God's direction;
Saint Dubricius walked in front – he was Christ's elect –
The archbishop of London walked at his right side,
And by his left side the archbishop of York,
Fifteen bishops preceding, selected from many places,
All of them there were vested in very resplendent copes
Which were embroidered all over with bright-burnished
     gold.   12210
    Four kings walked there ahead of the kaiser,
Bearing aloft in their hands four swords made of gold;
The first, a very valiant man, was named as follows:
This was Cador the king, Arthur's protégé,
The second, carrying sword in hand, came from Scotland,
Then the King of North Wales, and the King of South Wales,
And so they conducted the king to the cathedral.
The bishops were entoning as they conveyed the people's king;
Brass trumpets were blowing, the bells there were ringing,
Knights came riding past, ladies came gliding past.   12220
Truly it has been declared and proved to be a fact
That nobody has ever before seen among mortal men here

Half such exalted pomp in any convocation
As there was with Arthur of noble lineage.
   Into church proceeded Arthur the magnificent.
Archbishop Dubricius, to whom the Lord was gracious,
(He was the Papal Legate and in parliament a prelate)
Sang the holy Mass in the presence of the king.
There accompanied the queen most attractive women,
The wives of all the prominent men living in the country,   12230
And the daughters of the great men had come to the Queen,
Just as the Queen had instructed, on pain of her full censure.
   In the south transept of the church sat King Arthur in person
While on the north side sat Guinevere the Queen.
There came in ahead of her four eminent queens,
Each wearing on her left hand a ring of red gold,*
And with three snow-white doves sitting on her shoulders;
Now these four queens were the consorts of those four knights
Who were carrying in their hands the four golden swords
In front of Arthur, the most admired of kings.   12240
Many little girls were there with the lovely queen,
There were many gorgeous robes on those handsome people;
There was also much rivalry among so many nations,
For each thought themselves to be better than the others.
   Many knights at once arrived at the church,*
Some to pick a fight, some to see the king,
Some to stand and stare at the outstanding women.
There were songs of rejoicing which lasted a long time:
I reckon if it lasted seven long years
Then those who were there would still be wanting more.   12250
When the Mass was over they crowded out of church:
The king with his attendants went to the feast
Among his great retinue: there was revelry in the court!
   The Queen on the other side went to her seating;
She had an amazing number of her own attendant women.
   When the King was seated with his followers at the feast,
To the King came Saint Dubricius, his Bishop who was so virtuous,
Who removed from his head his high royal crown:
– Because the gold was so heavy the king was disinclined to wear it –
And placed on the King's head a much lighter crown,   12260
And then he put a similar one on the Queen as well:
These were the customary ways in Troy, in their ancestors' days,
From whom the Britons in their great renown were all descended:

All the men who could bear weapons were seated at their feasts
Apart in one place; they reckoned this good manners;
And likewise the women had their location.
    When the King was seated with all his courtiers at the feast,
The earls and the barons at the King's high table,
The Seneschal stepped forward; this was Kay,
Most exalted knight in all the land after the King,   12270
In the whole crowd of those at Arthur's court;
Kay instructed those attending on him, many men of high standing –
There were a thousand brave knights, of extremely high fame,
Who waited on the King, and on his bodyguard.
Each knight wore crimson cloth and ornaments of gold
And on all their fingers were clusters of gold rings:[†]
These men carried the food courses from the kitchen to the king.
    On the other side was Bedevere, the chief Butler to the King;
With him were the sons of earls, born of noble lineage,
And the sons of the highest-ranking knights who had arrived there,
And the sons of seven kings who were serving with him.   12281
Bedevere walked ahead with a golden mazer,
After him a thousand more thronged towards the courtiers
With every kind of beverage which one could imagine;
And the Queen on her side, most gracious lady,
Had a thousand men in attendance, noble men and prominent,
To serve the Queen and those who were with her.[†]
    No person in existence, however great his prominence,
Learned man or layman, living in any nation,
Could ever know how to describe in any kind of archive   12290
One half of the magnificence there was in Caerleon,
In the silver, and the gold, and resplendent clothes
On the men of noble status who were present in the Court,
In the horses and the fine hawks, in hounds for the hunt,
And in the rich garments which there were on the courtiers;
And of all the peoples who were living in the world there,
The people of this land were accounted most attractive,[*]
And the women also most lovely in complexion
And most splendidly dressed and most accomplished of all.
For they had all promised one thing, by their very persons,   12300
That they would all wear outfits in one colour scheme:
Some wore white, some wore red, and some wore vivid green,
And every kind of homespun tweed they found most disagreeable,
And each discourtesy they reckoned unworthy.

The country of England then enjoyed its greatest fame,
And the inhabitants were also most esteemed by the king.
The upper-class women who were living in this land
Had all declared, in their undisputed words,
That in the whole of this nation none would take a husband,
Not one single knight, however noble his rank,   12310
Unless he had been tested three times in combat,
And given proof of his valour and made trial of himself.
In confidence then he might seek himself a bride.
Because of these high standards the knights were valorous,
And the women most virtuous and better provided for.

   In Britain during those days were many delights.
When the King had feasted, with all his company,   *Sports*
Then the very brave warriors turned out from the town,
All the kings and their commanders,
All the bishops and all the clerics,   12320
All the earls and all the barons,
All the leaders, all the servers,
In their best clothes went down the fields.
Some began horse-racing, some began foot-racing,*
Some began vaulting, some began shooting,
Some were wrestling and holding competitions;
Some on the tilting field were dodging behind shields;
Some were hurling balls far across the fields –
A multitude of sports they were playing at there,
And whoever managed to win the first prize in his sport   12330
Was escorted with singing in front of the king,
And for his victory in sport the king gave him good prizes.

   All the queens had come to that place,
And all the ladies were leaning over the walls
To watch the contestants and the people playing.
These games and competitions continued for three days;*
Then on the fourth day the King made a speech,
And awarded his fine knights all their just deserts:
He gave silver, he gave gold, he gave horses, he gave lands,
Castles and suits of clothes: he made his men contented;   12340
There was many a bold Briton before Arthur's throne.

   Now novel tidings came to the King:*
Arthur the great king was sitting at a table;   *Roman*
In front of him were sitting kings, and many war-leaders,   *Campaign*
Bishops and clerics and very valiant knights.

There arrived in the hall some amazing information:
There arrived twelve valiant lords clothed in rich cloth,*
Exalted war-leaders, great men in their armour,
Each holding in his hand a massive gold ring,
And round the head of each man a golden band was
    encircled.   12350
They advanced together, two by two in pairs,
Each by the hand clasping his partner,
And paced across the hall floor into Arthur's presence,
Until eventually they arrived before the throne of King Arthur.
    They saluted Arthur immediately with deferential   *(i) Challenge*
    words:
'Good health to you, King Arthur, beloved of the Britons,
And good health to your attendants and all your gracious people.
We are twelve knights who have come here with a purpose,
Powerful and important: we are from Rome.
We have come to this place from our emperor   12360
Who is called **Lucius**; he commands the Roman people.
He instructed us to come here to Arthur the king,
And commands us to greet you with his grim message,
Saying that he is amazed to an extreme degree
Where on this globe you discovered such conceit
As to dare to decline any order from Rome
Or to level your gaze at the face of our forebears,
And who it was dared to teach you to turn so assertive
That you dare to threaten the issuer of decrees,
Lucius the emperor, most supreme of all men living.   12370
You have control of all your kingdom under your own rule
And you refuse to pay homage to the kaiser for your land,
For that same land which Julius had in his hands,
When in days gone by he conquered it by fighting.
And you have been holding it under your control;
With your bold knights you deprive us of our rights!
But tell us, Arthur, quickly, and send reply to Rome –
We shall bear your message to Lucius our emperor –
If you will acknowledge that he is the king over you,
And if you will become his subject and acknowledge him   12380
    as lord,
And make amends to the kaiser for Frollo the king
Whom you wrongfully did put to death in Paris,
And now you're holding all his lands, unjustly, in your own hands.

316

If within the next twelve weeks you turn to just ways
And are willing to submit to all Rome's jurisdiction,
Then you might continue living with your countrymen.
And if you refuse to do this, you will receive much worse:
The kaiser will come here, as a king does to what is his own,
– A king most courageous – and seize you by force,
Lead you fettered in triumph before the people of Rome;   12380
Then you'll have to endure what previously you scorned!'
   As these words were said the Britons leapt from the table:
All Arthur's court there was considerably enraged
And swore a mighty oath by our Almighty Lord
That all those who brought this message must be put to death,
To be drawn apart by horses was the death they must endure.
The deeply roused Britons rushed there to them,
Latched on to their hair and laid them out on the ground;
There the Roman men would have been wretchedly maltreated
If Arthur had not leapt across as if he were a lion   12400
And as the wisest of the Britons spoken these words:
'Stop it, stop at once! Let these knights live!
Here in my own court they are not to come to any harm!
They have ridden here from the territory of Rome
As Lucius who is their lord had given them instruction:
Each man must travel where his lord tells him to go;
No man ought to condemn a messenger to death,
Unless he has behaved so wickedly as to be traitor to his lord.
But now, sit down quietly, you knights in this hall,
And I shall make my own decision in this extremity   12410
What message they are to take back to Lucius the emperor.'
   Those warriors on their benches then all sat down,
And the disturbance died away in the presence of the king.
Then Arthur arose, the most admired of kings,
And he summoned to him seven sons of kings, *
The earls and the barons and the bravest soldiers,
And all the most intelligent of the country's inhabitants;
They went into a structure which was firmly secured,
And old fort made of stone: stout men had fashioned it.
There his wise counsellors began to hold council   12420
As to what answer he would give to Lucius the emperor.
When all the barons had been seated on benches,
Then all within the hall went utterly silent:
So great was their awe of the glorious king

That no one there dared to speak in case the king would punish them.
   Then Cador stood up there, the most senior earl present,
And uttered these words in the great king's presence:
'I give thanks to my Lord, who made the light of day,
That I have lived to see this day which has dawned in the court,
And these same tidings which have now come before our
      king,   12430
So that we need not any longer lie lolling around here!
For idleness is hateful in every nation,
For idleness makes a man lose all his manhood!
Idleness makes a knight abandon all his duties,
Idleness encourages many wicked actions;
Idleness brings to grief many thousand men;
In an easy life few men make great achievements;
For ages we've been lying quiet: it's diminished our renown.
But now I give thanks to the Lord who made the light of day
That the Roman people have turned out so aggressive,   12440
And are making boasts about coming to our boroughs
And tying up our king and carrying him to Rome.
But if what is being said is true, as some men are telling,
That the Roman people have turned out so aggressive,
And are so hardheaded and so full of hatred
That they now want to come into our country,
Then we shall draw up for them some dire messages:
Their savagery shall turn out to be their own sorrow.
Well, I've never for very long liked peace in my land:
Peace gets us so tramelled we're practically in torpor.'   12450
   Gawain, who was Arthur's nephew, was listening to this,
And grew very annoyed with Cador for making known these words,
And Gawain the good answered in this way:
'Cador, you may be a great man, but your advice is not much good!
Peace is good, and quiet is good when people agree to it freely,
And God himself created it through his own divinity,
For peace makes a good man perform actions which are good;
Because things go better for each man, the land is the happier.'
   Arthur was listening to these earls disputing,
And the noble man spoke like this to his angry men: 12460
'Sit down, all of you, straightaway, my knights,
And each, on pain of death, hear my decree!'
Everyone in the hall sat completely silent;
Then the bold king spoke to his great people:

318

'My earls, my barons, my bold battle-leaders,
My valiant men, my beloved friends,
Through you I have won, beneath the path of the sun,
Gains which make me a great man and ferocious with my foes:
I have gold and great treasure, I am a ruler of good men;
Alone I did not conquer; no, we did it all together!   12470
To many a fight I've led you, and always [you] arranged things well†
So that many kings' realms are under my control;
You are good knights, valiant, courageous;
This I have put to proof in very many lands!'
     Arthur, most admired of kings, then continued speaking;
'Now you have heard, you highest of my leaders,
What the Roman men between them have all been arranging,
And what message they have sent us here into our own land,
In writing and by word of mouth and with much venom;
Now we must consider how we can defend,   12480
As right demands, our nation and our own reputation
Against this powerful race, against this Roman people,
And send them a reply in our regal words,
How with true wisdom we can send our note to Rome
And demand of the emperor for what reason he despises us,
For what reason he is treating us with threats and with scorn.
I am severely angered and extremely ashamed
That he reproaches us for losses which in past days we incurred:
They say that Julius Caesar won by combat on the field;
In battle and by force men commit great injustice,   12490
For Caesar attacked Britain simply by brute strength
And against him the Britons could not defend their land,
But with force of arms [he] went at once, and took from them all their
     lands,†
And immediately after, they all became his subjects;
Some of our race they had slaughtered and some had torn apart with
     horses,*
Some they led in chains out of this our land,
And they conquered this land unjustly by transgression,
And, as if by right, they now demand tribute from this land!
We can just as easily, if we agree to it,
Make just claim on them through our King Belinus,   12500
And through Brennus, his brother, the Duke of Burgundy:
These were our ancestors from whom we are descended;
These men besieged Rome and conquered all the realm,

And in front of mighty Rome they hanged their hostages,
And after that they took the entire land and placed it in their own
    hands;
And so we ought by right to ride away to Rome!
   'Now I'll speak no more of Belin and say no more of Brennus,
But discuss the emperor, Constantine the mighty:
He was the son of Helena, from British stock descended;
He conquered Rome and ruled over the realm.   12510
   'Let's set aside Constantine, who gained himself all Rome that
    time,
And speak about Maximian who was a very strong man:
He was the king of Britain who conquered all France;
Maximian the strong took charge of all Rome,
And he conquered Germany with tremendously great power,
And everything from Romagna in Italy to Normandy.
   'And these were my ancestors, my esteemed predecessors,
And they owned all the territories which were tributary to Rome,
And through such example, I ought to possess Rome.
They want me to hand over tribute from my lands,   12520
I'm going to do the same, if I get the chance, to Rome!
I desire to rule all Rome at my own discretion!
And he wants to bind me up securely here in Britain,
And slaughter my British with his assaults in battle.
But if it's granted by the Almighty, who created days and nights here,
He must bitterly atone for all his brazen boasts,
And his Roman people will perish because of it,
And I shall be savage where he now holds sway.
   'All stay quiet now; I want to announce my intention –
No one is going to act otherwise, but it will so be performed!   12530
He wants it all, I want it all, which we two both have;
Let the one who can win it with ease have it now and always!
And now we shall discover who God will favour with it!'
   So spoke the bold man who had the Britons in his command,
Who was Arthur the king, the Britons' own darling!
His champions were seated: to his speeches they listened;
Some of them sat silent a long space of time;
Some of them whispered many words secretly between them:
Some of them found it really fine; for some of them it troubled the
    mind.
   When for a long time they'd been listening to the king,   12540
Then spoke Howel the gracious, greatest of Brittany,

And uttered his speeches in the stern king's presence:
'Lord king, hear me out, as I have now done you!*
You have spoken the sober truth, and may salvation be yours!
Long ago was announced what we are now to determine,
In former years what is now found here:
Sibyl spoke of it – her statements were true,*
And she set it down in a book to be a guide for people –
That three kings would come from the land of the Britons
Who were to conquer Rome and the entire realm,   12550
And all the lands which lie adjacent to it;
The first of these was Belinus, who was a British king;
The second was Constantine, who was king here in Britain;
You are to be the third who is to possess Rome,
And if you want to begin this you're going to win it,
And I will assist in it with my utmost ability:
I'll send across the sea to my own splendid soldiers.
To my brave men of Brittany, and we'll then fare much better;
I shall give notice to all the noblemen of Brittany,
Throughout all my lands, on pain of losing life and limb,   12560
That they must at once be ready to march with you to Rome;
I shall place all my land in pledge for silver coin,
And all the property of my lands, for silver and for gold,
And so we'll march to Rome and slay the emperor Lucius,
And restore your own rights. I'll convey you ten thousand knights.'
    So ran the speech of Howel, the highest man in Brittany.
When Howel had spoken what seemed to him appropriate,
Then spoke Angel the king, Scotland's own darling,
As he stood upon a bench, with both of his brothers,
Namely Urien and Lot, two very able men.   12570
This was how King Angel spoke, to Arthur the courageous:
'My lord Arthur, I declare to you with true observations
That to those same things Howel has spoken none shall take any
        exception,
But we shall perform it by our very lives!
And, mighty lord Arthur, listen to me for a space:
Call to give you counsel your powerful earls
And all the greatest men there are in your court
And invite them to tell you in their truthful declaration
What they will do to aid you to destroy your enemies.
I shall convey you the knights of my people,   12580
Three thousand warriors, all selected for their worth,

Ten thousand men on foot, most efficient fighters,
And let us march on Rome and conquer the realm.
Very deeply may we be ashamed and very greatly angered
That they should send messengers seeking tribute from our land,
But, so help us the Lord who made the light of day,
They shall atone for this with their very lives,
For when we have Rome and all of that realm,
We shall take the territories which are tributaries to it:
Apulia and Germany, Lombardy and Brittany,   12590
France next and Normandy' (it was then called Neustria),
'And so we shall moderate their unmitigated pride!'
    When this king had spoken then all of them responded:
'Disgraced be the very man who refuses his assistance
With goods and with weapons and with all his strength of arms!'
    So all at Arthur's court were strongly aroused there:
Knights were incensed until they trembled with fury.
When Arthur had listened to the clamour of his courtiers,
He called out sharply (the King was really angry):
'Sit down quietly, you knights in this assembly!   12600
And I shall describe to you what I intend to do:
I shall have my missives prepared and carefully composed,
And send the emperor heart-sorrow and a fine supply of grief,
And I shall march immediately down upon Rome;
I shall not carry tribute there, but instead I'll bind the emperor,
And after that I will hang him, and I'll lay waste all that land
And put all the knights to death who have opposed me in the
        fighting.'
    Arthur took hold of his document with its defiant declaration
And handed it to the men who had brought him the message,
And then he had them robed in ultimate splendour,*   12610
In the most superior robes he had in his chamber,
And ordered them to leave at once for Lucius in Rome,
And he would come after them as fast as he was able.
These twelve went on their way towards their own land;
[There were not in any land] in such silver and such gold†
Knights so well robed, nor in all respects so well treated
[As] Arthur treated these, [for all] the words they brought!†
These twelve knights voyaged till they arrived in Rome:
They saluted their emperor, their sovereign lord:
'All health to you, Lucius, you are our high master!   12620
We have been with the stern man, with Arthur the king;

We have brought you in writing very proud words;
Arthur is the boldest man whom we have ever gazed on,
And he has supreme power, and his soldiers are brave;
Every mere [serving-boy] acts like a knight there;†
Every mere squire acts like a mighty warrior there;
There the knights act as if they were kings.
Food comes forth abundantly and men are very confident,
And the women the most lovely of those now alive,
And Arthur himself, the valiant, is above all the most
reslendent   12630
   Through us he sends word to you that he intends to come to this
      land;
He refuses to bring tribute, but in person wants to fetter you,
And then he wants to hang you, and lay waste all this land,
And Germany, and Lombardy, Burgundy and France, and also
      Normandy,
And just as he slew Frollo, his foe, so will he do us all,
And possess himself solely of everything we own.
He will conduct here kings, earls and commanders;
And we hold here in our hands the documents he sends
Which spell out to you what he will do when he invades us here!'
   When the message was delivered the kaiser was a desperate
      man,   12640
And all the Romans were excited by a most extreme rage;
They kept on conferring, they kept on consulting,
Before they could agree what action they should take,
But all the same, eventually they found a solution
By means of the senators who conduct the senate:
They advised the kaiser that he should write closed letters*
And send out his summons through many kings' realms,
And command them to come quickly, all of them to Rome,
Out of every single land which bore [him] allegiance,†
And all those who were keen to gain land or goods by
      fighting.   12650
People soon arrived in the city of Rome,
No one had ever assembled so many there before.
They declared they'd decided to cross by Great St Bernard Pass
And to make an assault upon Arthur wherever they came upon him,
Killing Arthur in battle or hanging him, and annihilating his army;
And appropriate for the emperor the realms of King Arthur.
   The first king who arrived there was a very courageous man,

Epistrod, king of Greece; also **Ethion**, duke of Boeotia;[*]
With a great fighting-force came **Irtac**, king of Turkey;
Pandras, king of Egypt, from Crete King **Hippolytus**,   12660
From Syria, King **Evander**, from Phrygia Duke **Teucer**,
Maeptisas from Babylon, from Spain the emperor **Meodras**,
From Media King **Boccus**, from Lybia King **Sextorius**,
From Bithynia **Polydeuces**, from Ituria King **Sexes**,
Ofustesar, King of Africa — no king bore him resemblance —:
With him came many an African, from Ethiopia he brought the black
    men.
The Roman people themselves marched to the mustering,
Those who lived closest to mightiest Rome:
Marcus, Lucius and **Catullus, Cocta, Gaius** and **Metellius**:
These were the six who supervised the whole Senate.   12670
    When this force was assembled from many kinds of places
Then the kaiser had people count up all the army:
There were counted aright there a sum of eager fighters,
It came to four hundred thousand, the knights in that throng,
With their arms and their mounts, the equipment of a knight.
That man has never been born, not in any borough at all,
Who could have counted the masses who marched there on foot.
Before August the first they moved off on their march,[*]
Always directly on the path which lay towards St Bernard pass.
    Now for a time let us leave these forces,[*]   12680
And let us speak of Arthur, that most admired of kings:
When he had sought out his excellent soldiers
And each of them had gone home to where he had land
And the knights had come back again swiftly to the court
With arms well appointed to their utmost ability.
From Scotland, from Ireland, from Jutland, from Iceland,
From Norway, from Denmark, from Orkney, from the Isle of Man,
From those same lands there were a hundred thousand
Valiant champions in armour in the style of their own homelands:
These men were not knights nor in knightly guise attired   12690
But they were the most courageous men who have ever been
    acknowledged,
With massive battle-axes, with long two-edged swords.
From Normandy, from Anjou, from Brittany and Poitou,
From Flanders, from Boulogne, from Lorraine and from Louvain
There came one hundred thousand to the royal army,
Knights among the very best, fully tried under arms.

There came the Twelve Companions whom France was to obey,
They brought along with them twelve thousand knights;
And from this land of ours Arthur took in his charge
Fifty thousand valiant knights and brave men in the fight;   12700
Howel of Brittany from his native people
Led ten whole thousand, knights among the best.
The soldiers on foot, as they moved off,
No one knew how to count in any number system.
    Then Arthur gave command, that most admired of kings,
At an appointed time that the army should assemble
(On pain of losing life itself) at Barfleur harbour, *
And there he would muster his glorious troops.
He entrusted this land to a remarkable knight,
He was Gawain's brother – as regent there was no other; *   12710
Modred he was called, the most dishonourable man:
He never kept a promise to any man at all,
(He was related to Arthur, from his illustrious race)
Yet he was a knight supremely brave and he had tremendous spirit,
Arthur's sister's son. For the queen he harboured passion
(That was wicked behaviour; to his uncle he was a traitor!)
But it was all kept very quiet in the parliament and at court,
Because nobody realised this could be really going on,
But people assumed him honest, since Gawain was his brother,
And the most loyal of all the men who ever came to court;   12720
Because of Gawain, all the more was Modred popular with people,
And the valiant Arthur made him very satisfied:
He took his entire kingdom and placed it into Modred's hands,
With Guinevere his queen, most respected of the women
Who among this people have been living in the land;
Arthur donated everything he owned
To Modred and the Queen; this made them most contented.
It was a very bad thing that they were ever born:
They betrayed this country with unmeasured miseries,
And in the end the Evil One brought them to destruction   12730
In which they forfeited their lives and their souls
And have ever since been loathed in every single country,
So that nobody ever wanted to proffer a good prayer for their souls,
Because of the treason that man did to Arthur his uncle.
    All that Arthur had he made over to Modred,
His land and those who lived there, and his beloved Queen,
And then he took his army of very fine soldiers

And then marched immediately towards Southampton.
At once there came sailing across the wide sea
Innumerable ships to the king's people.   12740
The king dispatched the folk over all the long ships:
Thousands and thousands of them thronged to the ships:
Father wept for his son, sister for her brother,
Mother for her daughter, when the host departed.
They had very fine weather with a following fresh breeze:
Exceedingly excited were men to enter open sea;   *Roman Campaign*
They hauled up the anchors; the army started cheering;
Onwards the ships were surging, the minstrels were   *(ii) Departure*
     singing;
They hauled up the sails, they tautened the rigging;
With the most serene weather and the sea slumbering,   12750
Lulled by this calmness, Arthur fell asleep.

     As the king slept, he experienced a dream,   *Arthur's*
The dream itself was fearsome and it frightened the king;*   *Dream*
When the king awoke he was extremely disturbed
And began to moan in quite a loud voice.
There was no knight so venturesome in the whole of Christendom
Who dared enquire of the king about his condition
Before the king himself spoke, and conversed with his barons there,
And so Arthur stated, when he woke up from his sleep:
'Christ, my Lord and Master, controller of what comes to us,   12760
Guardian of this good world, comforter of men
By your gracious will, O commander of the angels,
Do you permit my vision to turn to my advantage!'
     Then Angel the king spoke, the beloved of the Scots,
'My Lord, describe to us your dream, and may our destiny be
     fortunate!'
'Gladly,' said the King, 'may good things come of it!
As I lay dozing, I drifted into sleep:
It seemed to me that in the sky a mysterious beast appeared,
In the clouds to the east, ugly in appearance,
With lightning and thunder, menacingly it advanced;   12770
There is no bear so hideous in any land on earth;
Then there came from the west, whisking through the clouds,
A dragon all burning which engulfed boroughs;†
With its fire it set alight all this land's realm:
It seemed to me as I stared that the very sea caught alight
With lightning and the fire which the dragon carried by.

326

This dragon and bear, both from opposite directions,
With intense speed were approaching each other,
They crashed into each other with furious impact:
Their eyes were flaring as if they were firebrands;   12780
Time and again the dragon was winning, and then again it was losing,
But all the same eventually it managed to fly up
And flew down instantly with a furious assault
And struck at the bear which then tumbled to the earth,
And there he killed the bear and tore it limb from limb.
When the battle was finished the dragon flew away.
This was the dream I had when I was lying there asleep!'
    The bishops listened to this, and men who'd learned from books;
Earls listened to it; barons listened to it;
Each from his understanding spoke intelligently: 12790
They interpreted this dream [as they thought appropriate];†
No knight there had the courage to interpret it unfavourably
Lest he would be made to lose those parts he specially loved!
    On they were speeding, eastwards and quickly:
They had a favourable wind and the most serene weather;
They had everything necessary; they came to land at Barfleur.
At Barfleur in Côtentin many men came pouring in
From all of the lands in which Arthur held command.
As soon as they were able they disembarked from the ships;
The King instructed his retainers to go and seek for shelter,   12800
And the King wished to relax before his men arrived.
    After just one single night there came to him a courteous knight
Who came to tell tidings to Arthur the king:
He said that a monster had made its way to the place
From the west side of Spain, a really bloody fiend,†   *The Giant*
And within Brittany it was actively doing harm: *of*
Along the coastlands it had devastated widely;   *Mont Saint Michel*
In what is now Mont Saint Michel it destroyed the land everywhere.†
'My lord king,' said the knight, 'I'll tell you truly right away:*
He has seized a relative of yours with hideous force,   12810
A lady of noble birth, Howel's precious daughter,
Elaine was her name, most exquisite of maidens;
He has dragged off to the mountain that most exquisite of maidens,
And this fiend for a full fortnight has held her captive in that plight;
We have no idea at all whether he has mated her;
The males whom he seizes he makes into his meals,
With cattle, sheep and horses, goats and pigs as well;

This whole land he'll bring to ruin unless you remove our grief,
The land and those who live here: we depend on your entirely!'
The knight continued speaking to the people's king: 12820
'My lord, can you see the mountain, and the enormous forest?
That's where the monster lives which is preying on the people.
We have tried to attack him a great many times,
From the sea and on the land: he has crushed his attackers,
Has sunk all our ships and drowned all the mariners,
Has laid lifeless those who were fighting him on land.
We've endured it all so long that now we leave him alone,
To do what he wants according to his fancy;
The knights in this district dare not fight him any more.'
    Arthur was listening, most admired of all kings;   12830
He called Earl Kay, his Seneschal and kinsman, over to him,
Bedivere he also called on, he was the king's butler.
He instructed them precisely to be all prepared at midnight,
With their full armour, to go adventuring with the King,
As long as no man in Christendom knew about their movements
Except for King Arthur and those two knights going with him,
And their six squires – fine men and courageous;
And the knight who told the king about it was to be their guide.
    Exactly at midnight when men were all asleep
Arthur made his way, most admired of all kings;   12840
Ahead of them rode their [local] knight, until it was daylight;[†]
Then they dismounted from their steeds and arranged their armour.
Not far away they could see a massive fire smoking
On top of a hillside surrounded by the sea-tides
And there was a second very high hill there, which the sea flowed up
    close to;
On the top of it they could see a fire which was large and very fierce.
The knights there were doubtful as to which way they should go
So the giant wouldn't be alerted to the king's arrival.
    Then Arthur the determined came to a decision
That they should move together very close to the first fire   12850
And if they found him there they should put him straight to death.
The King moved forward until he came close:
He couldn't find anything save a huge fire there, blazing.
Arthur walked round it, with his knights by his side
And they couldn't find anything on the hill which was living,
Only that huge fire and a great heap of bones,
At a guess they would estimate thirty cartloads' worth!

Then Arthur couldn't think of any useful plan,
And began to converse with his earl, Bedivere:
'Bedivere, go quickly down from this hill, 12860
Make your way across the deep water, wearing your full armour,
And being very cautious approach the other fire,
And walk all around it and look about attentively
To see if you discover any trace of the ogre.
And if you get wind of him in any way whatever,
Go down quietly till you come to the water,
And say to me speedily what it is you've seen;
And if it should happen that you get up to the fire
And the ogre gets wind of you and makes a lunge at you,
Then take up my good horn which is bound round with gold 12870
And blow it with all your strength as one must in emergency,
And fling yourself at the fiend and begin to fight him,
And we shall come rushing as quick as we can get there;
And if you find him there close beside the fire
And you can get back again without being noticed,
Then I utterly forbid you, as you value your own life,
To start any fighting whatsoever against the demon.'
     Bedivere attended to what his lord said to him:
He buckled on his weapons and made his way forward
And ascended the mountain, which is very lofty; 12880
He was carrying in his hands a very sturdy spear,
With a shield on his back all garnished with gold,†
High helmet on his head all made of steel,
His body encased in a fine gleaming corslet,
He bore by his side a blade made of steel,
And on he went striding, that sternly strong earl,
Until he soon came close beside the fire,
And underneath a tree he began to pause.
Then he heard sobbing, desperately strong,
Sobbing and wailing and miserable crying; 12890
Then the knight assumed that it must be the giant,
And he broke into a fury as if he were a wild boar,
And instantly forgot what his lord had said to him;*
He threw his shield before his breast, gripped his spear firmly
And rushed forward closer towards the great fire,
Expecting to discover the fearsome devil
So that he could fight it out and give proof of his prowess.
     What he found there was a noblewoman, her head all a-tremble,

329

A white-haired woman weeping in her anguish,
Cursing the bad luck that left her still alive   12900
And sitting by the fire with pitiful crying,
Sitting and staring, all the time, at a recent grave
And giving vent to her expression in a voice of misery:
'Alas, Elaine, alas dear girl!
Alas that I fed you, that I fostered you,
Alas that the death-demon has destroyed you like this here,
Alas that I was ever born: he has smashed my limbs as well!'
Then the woman looked around her to see if the giant was returning,
And saw Earl Bedivere who had arrived there;
Then the white-haired woman spoke, as she sat beside the
        fire:†   12910
'What are you, radiant creature? are you an angel or a warrior?*
Is your coating of feathers all fastened with gold?
If you come from Heaven you might go from here safely,
But if you are a mortal knight you'll be destitute immediately
Because now the monster's coming and he'll tear all your limbs apart;
Even if you wear steel all over he'll master you entirely.
    'He went into Brittany, to the noblest of all dwellings,
To the castle of Howel, the chieftain of Brittany:
He smashed all the gates and squeezed himself inside,
He grabbed the curtain wall and hurled it to the ground,   12920
He tossed down the chamber door and it shattered in five pieces;
He found inside the chamber the loveliest of all young women,
Elaine was her name, of most exalted lineage,
The daughter of Howel, chief man in Brittany,*
Relative of Arthur, of the royal line itself.
I was her foster-mother, and delicately reared her.
There the giant dragged the two of us away off with him
[And carried us, in a short time] the length of fifteen miles†
Into this wild desolate wood here to this very place;
A week ago this same day he did all this to us.   12930
As soon as he came here, he grabbed hold of that virgin,
He wanted to have intercourse with the innocent girl:
She wasn't any older than a mere fifteen years
And being a virgin she couldn't endure his intimacy:
The moment he laid her she lost her life immediately,
And here is where he buried her, that most gentle of all ladies,
Elaine, my own foster child, Howel's own daughter.
When he had finished doing that, he grabbed me the same way,

Threw me on the floor and laid me as well;
Now he has painfully broken all my bones,   12940
My limbs are all out of joint; my very life is joyless.
    'So, now I've told you how it was we were got here,
Fly from here fast in case he should find you,
Because if he comes in rage with his evil attacks
The man has not been born who could stand as your protector!'
    At these very words which the woman was saying
Bedivere began to reassure her with most respectful words:
'My dear madam, I am human, and a knight of some repute,
And I wish to declare to you the clear explanation
That no warrior has yet been born of any kind of woman   12950
Who could not with sheer strength be made to stoop down low.
And I honour you, old woman; your strength is very weak now,†
But now I bid you good day, and I'll be off on my way!'
    Down clambered Bedivere, back towards his liege lord
And told him about his concern and all of his adventure
And what the ancient woman had told him of the maiden,
And how every day the ogre raped the aged woman.
Then the three of them together held whispered consultation
Of how they could embark on the monster's destruction.
    Meanwhile the giant came striding, moving swiftly to his fireside:
He was carrying on his shoulders an enormous load   12961
Of twelve pigs together, all tied in a bundle
With very thick twine which was twisted together.
He tossed down the dead swine and squatted beside them,*
Stoking up his fire by piling on to it huge trees;
As he tore apart six pigs at the woman he kept grinning,
And after a few minutes he flung himself upon her,
But he had no expectation of what came from his copulation:†
He raked out his ashes and started grilling his rashers
And he gulped those six pigs down before he got up from
        his seat,   12970
All smothered in ashes – it was a quite disgusting dish!
And then he shuffled off and started to stretch†
And sank down beside the fire spreading out his limbs.
    Now let us leave the giant there and consider the king:
Arthur at the water's edge gripped his weapons in his hands,
With the brave earl, Sir Bedivere, both prudent and wary,
The third man being Kay, the king's steward and his kinsman.
Across the stream they came, resplendent in their armour

331

And went climbing up the hill as hard as they could
And finished up striding close alongside the fire   12980
Where the giant sprawled and slept as the woman sat and wept.
Arthur stepped back beside his companions,
Forbidding them on pain of losing both life and limb together
That neither of them should presume to proceed any further
Unless [they] should see that there was dire need.†
Bedivere halted there and Kay kept him company;
Arthur strode ahead, a warrior stern of spirit,
Until he came to the hearth where the demon lay unconscious.
Arthur was utterly devoid of all timidity –
This was quite apparent, amazing though it seems,   12990
For Arthur there and then could have easily hacked the ogre,
Struck down the demon as he lay there sound asleep;
Yet Arthur refused absolutely to attack him in his sleep,*
Lest at some future date he might hear himself reproved.
    Then at once Arthur called out, that most admired of kings:
'On your feet, you fiendish brute, and face your final moments!
Now we two shall hold debate on the death of my kinswoman!'
Before the king had finished saying all these words
The giant started up and seized his mighty club
Intending with the blow to pound Arthur all to pieces;   13000
But Arthur raised aloft his shield high above his helmet
And the giant struck it from above so it was entirely shattered
And Arthur swiftly struck at him a blow with his sword
Swiping off his chin along with all his jawbone,
And slipped behind a tree which was standing alongside,
And the giant's swift return blow did not hit him at all,
Instead he struck the tree so his club splintered to shreds,
And Arthur at once ran right round the tree,
And like this Arthur and the giant ran all around it three times.
Now the giant was very heavy, so Arthur ran much faster,   13010
And overtook the giant and raising his fine blade
Sliced him off at the thigh – and the giant collapsed,
And Arthur stood watching as the demon started speaking:
'Lord, lord, spare me now! Who is it I am fighting with?
I never guessed that any man in the great realm of this world
Could ever have so easily defeated me in battle
Unless it had been Arthur, the most admired of all the British,
And anyway I've never been all that afraid of Arthur.'
    Then to him spoke Arthur, most admired of kings:

'I'm King Arthur myself, favourite of the Britons!   13020
Tell me about your own tribe and where they are located,
And who it was in the world who were counted as your parents
And from which country you have sneaked in here,
And why with violent death you have murdered my kinswoman.'
Then the devil responded, lying helpless, gazing on:
'All this I shall do, and I'll be reconciled with you,
If you'll only let me live and get my limbs all healed.'
    Arthur lost his temper, in a total fury,
And called out for Bedivere, his brave champion:
'Move quickly, Bedivere, and chop his head off right here,   13030
And carry it away with you down from this mountain!'
Bedivere came quickly and chopped his head off neatly,
And so they went away from there down to their comrades.
[Then finally the king sat down] and had a chance to rest,†
And these were the words of the plucky Arthur:
'I have not fought a fight before within this fine country
(Except when I killed King **Riun** on the mountain of Ravinity).'*
    Then they walked onwards and came to the army;
When [they] saw that head they found it very strange,†
Wondering who beneath the heavens might lay claim to such
      a head.†   13040
Howel of Brittany came towards the king,
And the king told him all about the girl.
Then Howel was distressed and grieved deeply about it,
And took all his friends and found his way to the mountain
Where the girl from Brittany lay buried in the earth.
There he soon had erected a most elegant church,
Dedicated to Saint Mary, the mother of Our Lord,
And then he gave that hill a name before he went away,
And called it 'Elaine's Tumulus'; now they call it Mont Saint Michel.
    Then Arthur's army was assembled in their glory,   13050
From Ireland and from Scotland people had by then arrived.
Then the king gave the command to blow brass trumpets in the army,
And off marched from Brittany brave and active men,
All throughout Normandy (which then was known as Neustria),
Through all of France they marched, and folk flocked to join them,
They moved out from France and into Burgundy.
There his informers came and halted his companions,†
And made known to the king there in that country
That **Lucius** the emperor and all his Roman army

Were coming to that place, away from their terrain,   13060
Intending to forge ahead in towards France
And conquer it all, and then move on to this land here,
And slaughter all the Britons whom they found there still alive,
And lead Arthur the courageous in chains off to Rome.
   Then the bravest of all kings was furiously angry
And gave orders that his tents should be pitched across the plains,
And there he would encamp until he knew the facts
Of where he might with confidence intercept the kaiser;
Where the brave king was stationed was a river called the Aube.*
A cautious knight came riding to the king's encampment   13070
Who was very badly wounded and his army sadly battered:
The men who came from Rome had robbed him of all his land.
He revealed to the king unknown information
Where the emperor was in camp, with all his Roman force,
And where he might [encounter] him if he wanted to attack him†
Or to make a treaty with the men of Rome:
'But, sir Arthur,' said the knight, 'I shall declare to you outright
That [making peace] will do you more good than going to fight
    [against him],†
Because for every two of yours, they can count on twelve,
So many of them kings, so many of them commanders;   13080
There is not in any territory anyone who could inform you
Of the total of the folk who are following that king,
Excluding the Roman people from his own population
And excluding the peoples who from him seek peace.'
   When the reports were all recorded and Arthur had assessed them
Then the king called immediately for his closest knights
And they decided among themselves on constructing a fort
Next to the river which was known as the Aube.   *Roman*
In a most convenient spot it was speedily constructed: *Campaign*
Many men had a hand in it and in all haste it was complete;   13090
For if Arthur had misfortune when he came to fight,
Or his folk were to fall, or started to flee,
Then he intended to stand firm, in his strongly-built fort.
   Then he called to him two earls, dignified and wise,
Born in the aristocracy: the king held them in affection;
The first came from Chartres and was called Gerin: there was much
    common sense in him;
The second one was Beof of Oxford: far and wide spread that earl's
    fame;

In addition the king called Gawain, the kinsman he
    held most dear,   *(iii) Gawain's*
Because Gawain knew Latin, Gawain knew Celtic too: *Embassy*
He had been raised in Rome for very many years.   13100
The king took these three courteous knights and sent them off to the
    kaiser,
Ordering him to take his army and be off back to Rome
And never again into France lead any force whatever:
'And if you should go there leading in your own army,
You shall be captured and condemned to death!
For France is my own, and I won it fairly in fight,
And if you refuse to give up the idea of going there
Then let us prepare for battle and let the worse man perish!
And let's leave the poor people to live their lives in peace.
There was a time when Romans did conquer that nation,   13110
But since then they have lost that nation in battle,
And I conquered it in fight and by fighting will retain it!'
   Off went the knights, splendid warriors,
Namely Gerin and the gracious, Beof and Gawain the doughty,
Corsleted and helmeted on their lofty steeds,
Each one carried on his shoulder a very fine shield;
They held in their hands very strong spears.
Off they set on horseback, proud men from the host;
Many of those tried warriors who were staying with Arthur
Accompanied Gawain and requested him humbly   13120
To raise up some contention among the Roman people
'So that we can prove ourselves in the press of battle,[*]
For it's many years now since their threats arrived here,
And boasts they keep making that they are going to behead us.
Now it's a great disgrace to our race if it will all be put aside
Unless there can be some strife before we sign the truce:
Some spear-shafts shattered, mail-coats shredded,
Shields smashed to bits, soldiers hacked about,
Swords deeply plunged into crimson blood!'
   The earls forced their way through a vast tract of forest   13130
And marked out a course which lay across the mountains
Until they soon arrived at the Roman army:
Admirably armed and advancing on their horses.
There anyone who happened to be on the spot might see
Men by many thousands thronging from their tents
Just to get a glimpse of those three gallant knights,

And to gaze at their horses and to gaze at their equipment
And to listen to the tidings from Arthur the king.
And first of all, right away, they questioned the knights,
Asking if the king had sent them to the emperor   13140
To consult with the kaiser and plead for his peace.
But not for any conversation would those three noble earls
Pause and wait before they arrived on horseback
Before the door of the tent in which the emperor was.
    There they dismounted and handed over their horses
And so in full armour they entered the tent,*
Into the presence of the emperor, Lucius by name;
As he sat on his couch they announced their message to him:
Each spoke his piece as seemed appropriate to him,
Telling him to travel back to his country,   13150
And never in hostility ever visit France again.
All the time those three earls were announcing their message
The emperor went on sitting there just like a moron,*
And no response whatever did he return to these earls,
But he was listening intently, malevolence in his mind.
    Then Gawain was as outraged as an angry noble can be,
And this was the outburst of Gawain the brave:
'Lucius the great, you are the emperor of Rome;
We are the men of Arthur, most admired of the British:
He sends you his instructions without any greetings,   13160
Commanding you to go to Rome, the realm which is your own,
Leaving him to rule in France, which he conquered by fighting,
While you rule your realm and your Roman citizens.
In the past your ancestors made invasion in France,
In battle they acquired immeasurable goods;
And so for a time they lived there, and subsequently lost it:
Arthur won it in fair fight and now he wants to keep it;
He is our liege lord, we are his feudal knights:
He ordered us to tell the true facts to your person;
If you refuse to turn back, he will be your killer,   13170
And if you persist in not returning, but pursue your own purpose,
If your aim for that kingdom is to clutch it in your hands,
Then tomorrow is the very day: if you can catch it, keep it!'
    Then the emperor did reply, in a towering rage:
'I refuse to go back again, and I will conquer France;
My ancestors held it, and I intend to have it.
But if he's willing to be my vassal and acknowledge me as lord,

336

And pay me loyal allegiance and look up to me as leader,
Then I shall make a truce with him and all his trusty men,
And concede the regency of Britain, which Julius had at his
    command,
And many other countries, which Julius also had
    command of,   13181
Those realms which he controls to which he has no right at all;
And these he's going to lose unless he lets a peace be made.'
   Then answered Gawain who was Arthur's nephew
'Belinus and Brennes, both those two brothers*
Were rulers in Britain and by conquest won France,
And then they turned swiftly and took charge of Rome,
And there they stayed afterwards for very many years.
When all this was happening, Brennes was your emperor
And ruled the Roman people and all her tributaries.   13190
And so Rome is our inheritance, and you've got it in your grasp,
And we intend to get it or we'll die in the attempt,
Unless you're willing to admit that King Arthur is your liege,
And send him every year the tribute from your lands;
And if you go to him in peace, then you can live the easier!'
   Now there was sitting by the emperor a knight of his close family:
Quencelin was his name, an important man in Rome;
This knight responded, in the emperor's presence,
And like this he spoke (he was a most unlucky man):
'Knights, go back again and give this message to your king: 13200
[The British may be daring] but they're thought to be worth nothing†
Because for all that they keep bragging, their prowess is very small.'
He was about to say more when Gawain drew his sword
And struck him on the head – and so he split in half!
And Gawain with all speed made straight for his steed,
And all of them mounted with murderous expressions,
And Gawain the plucky spoke these words in parting:
'So help me the Lord himself who created the daylight
If anyone at all among you men is so courageous
As to come in pursuit of us, I shall cut him down: 13210
He shall be sliced in pieces by my broad-bladed sword!'
   After this very speech the emperor exclaimed:
'Stop them, stop them! They're all going to swing
High on the gallows, or else be drawn apart by horses!'
After this outburst coming from the emperor
The earls galloped off and set spurs to their steeds.   *The Pursuit*

337

In their hands they were brandishing very strong spears,
Carrying before their chests their wide covering shields.
Immediately in a rage earls started riding after
And all the time the emperor was shrieking aloud: 13220
'Seize them, kill them! They have disgraced us all!'
There anyone who happened to be on the spot might hear
The shouting of thousands of men of that nation:
'To arms, to arms here! Let's be getting after them;
Fetch our shields here: the scoundrels are escaping!'
Fully armed champions at once set off after them,
Six here, seven there, eight here and nine over there.
And meanwhile those earls were galloping madly
And every now and then they would have a look behind,
And all the time the Roman knights were coming after
      quickly,   13230
And one who galloped fastest was coming very close,
Shouting out all the time in a really savage way:
'Turn back, you knights, and defend yourselves by fighting!
You disgrace yourselves badly by wanting to sneak off!'
   Gawain understood the shouting from the Roman soldier*
And turning his steed, started riding over to him,
And ran him through with the spear so that he was spitted on it,
And drew the spear towards him: the fellow died at once,
And Gawain the courageous called out these words:
'Knight, you ride too quickly; you'd be better off in Rome!'   13240
The knight's name was **Marcel**, one of the nobility.
When Gawain noticed him collapsing to the ground
He instantly drew out his sword and struck off Marcel's head,
And Gawain the plucky expressed this opinion:
'Marcel, go to hell, and tell them your tittle-tattle,
And stay there a long spell with Quencelin your pal,
And hold secret meetings there: you'd've done best to stay in
      Rome;
And like this we'll teach you how to speak our British tongue!'
   Gerin saw how things were going, saw there the Roman lying,
And urged on his horse and encountered another one,   13250
And struck him through with his spear and gave expression to these
      words:
'Keep on riding, Roman, and roll down into Hell,
And so if God will aid us, we shall bring [you] down to earth;†
Threatening doesn't do much good unless there are some deeds too!'

338

Beof who was a brave man saw what his comrades had done,
And wheeled his horse round with terrific speed
And made for a knight with all the force he could find,
Striking him above the shield so his fine corslet collapsed
And so right through his neck; [he] died on the spot.[†]
And so this earl gave a shout of inspiration for his friends: 13260
'The British will pour scorn on us if we get away from here
Unless we get things going better before we go away!'
After that challenge which the earl had issued,
They all turned round immediately, tremendously fast,
Each drawing his sword swiftly, and each one slew his Roman,
And then they turned their horses and continued on their track,
With the troops of the Romans always riding behind them:
These kept on striking blows at them, kept on shouting names at
    them,
Kept on screaming out to them 'You are all going to perish!'
But they did not succeed at all in making even just one of them fall,
Nor in doing any harm to them in those hostile assaults;   13271
But every so often the earls wheeled around again,
And before the two sides parted, the Romans had come off the worse.
So they continued for fifteen whole miles
Until they came to a position below a splendid woodland
Close beside the fortress where Arthur was enclosed;
Three miles away from it there came thronging to the wood
A force of nine thousand whom Arthur had sent,
From the brave Bretons, who knew the land best:
They were anxious to get news of brave Gawain's progress,   13280
And of his companions, what had become of them,
Whether they were still alive [or] lying by the roadside.[†]
    These knights slipped through the woodland in utter silence
To the top of the hill, and gazed round expectantly.
They made all the horsemen dismount in the woodland
And prepared all their arms and all of their armour,
Except for a hundred men who were to keep watch
In case they could by any chance catch sight of anything.
Then they spotted in the distance on a spreading plain
Three knights galloping as fast as they could go;[*]   13290
After those three knights there were coming thirty;
Behind that thirty they could see three thousand;
Behind those were thronging another thirty thousand!
They were Roman soldiers, all arrayed in armour,

And the earls in front of them were galloping fast,
Exactly on the right road which led towards the wood
Where their companions were lying well concealed.
    The earls rode right into the woods, with the Romans in pursuit;
The British made a rush at them on their rested steeds
And struck them from the front, [felling] one hundred at
        once.[†]   13300
    Then the Roman forces thought that Arthur was arriving,
And they [fled] in frightful panic, with the British in pursuit[†]
Who slaughtered fifteen hundred of the Roman force.
Then there arrived to their assistance from their own armed force
Sixteen thousand soldiers whom Arthur had sent to them,
Very bold Britons clad in coats of mail.
There arrived on horseback an earl of great repute,
Petreius by name, a nobleman from Rome,
With six thousand warriors to give aid to the Romans,
Who with tremendous force hurled themselves at the British,   13310
Taking very few of them captive there, but killing very many.[†]
The British made for the wood, with the other men behind them,
And the British, now on foot, made a firm stand against them,
While the forces of the Romans fought from their horses,
And the British set upon them and slaughtered their [horses][†]
And seizing many captives dragged them into the woods.
Then Petreius grew enraged about his men getting the worst of it
And along with his forces he withdrew from the wood,
While the British rushed upon them and struck them from the rear.
    When the British, clear of the woodland, came out on the plain
The Romans resisted them, repulsing them fiercely.   13321
Then in earnest began the fighting: earls were falling, and many a fine
        knight:
In just one day fifteen thousand fell there,
Excellent men, before it was evening.
There a man might discover if he wanted to try his might,
Arm against arm, strong man against strong man,
Shield against shield; soldiers kept on falling.
The roadways were running with thick streams of blood;
Across the fields were scattered gold-adorned shields.
All the day long they kept on fighting strongly.   13330
Petreius on his side kept his people together,
With the result that very soon the British got the worst of it.
    The great earl of Oxford realised at once —

(Beof was his name, a noble British man)
That in no way whatever was it likely to happen
That the British could avoid a rout, unless they had direction.
Then the earl called together the excellent knights
From the very best men of all the British forces
And from the most stalwart of those still surviving,
And making his way out on the field, close up to their forces,   13340
(Much disturbed by deep emotion) he made a speech like this:
'Knights, now listen to me: may the Lord aid us!
We have come to this place and embarked on this battle
Without Arthur's advice, and yet he is our leader:
If things go well for us, we shall please him all the more,
And if things go badly for us, he will simply hate us.
But if you want my advice, then let's advance in high hopes!
We are three hundred knights, all warriors in helmets,
Valiant men and brave and of very highest rank.
Make known your nobility: we come from one nation!   13350
Ride in when I ride, and follow as I guide;
All of you charge on the knight that I choose;
Don't seize any chargers, nor any knightly armour,
Just let every brave knight strike always on target!'
     After the words addressed by the Earl of Oxford
To his comrades at his side, then he started to ride,
With just as much speed as the hound drives the deer,
With his comrades behind him with their utmost power;
Right through the thick of the fighting sped the band of knights,
Galloping their steeds, killing people as they went –   13360
Tragedy overtook those who were on their path ahead of them
Because they trampled everything on their horses and their chargers
And so they came close and captured Petreius:
Beof rode up to him and got his arms round him
And dragged him off his horse and knocked him to the ground
Knowing that his bold knights were right at his side;
The Britons struck out and dragged Petreius off
And the Roman army fought resolutely back
Till in the end no one recognised who it was they were fighting,
They were so coated with gore there was confusion in the combat!
     Then Gawain caught sight of them from his position in the battle:
With seven hundred knights he made his way in that
          direction,   13372
Killing everything in his path which he came across there

341

And at the gallop he grabbed Petreius on his good horse's back
And took Petreius off with him, though he was troubled by it,
Until they came into the woodland, where they were confident
That they could guard securely the leader of the Romans,
And then back out on to the field they went, and again began fighting.
    There was to be seen a great deal of distress:
Shields shattering, soldiers falling,   13380
Helmets caving in, great men perishing,
Blood on the fields and faces bloodless.
The British made an assault and the Roman forces fled:
The British struck them down and seized many alive,
And then by the day's end the Romans were in trouble [there].[†]
Men were firmly trussing the Roman champions,
Marching them to the woodlands in front of Gawain:
All night they were watched there by two thousand knights.
The next day, as dawn broke, the detachment started moving,
Onwards they marched to meet their liege lord,   13390
Bringing him such booty as he rejoiced to accept.
Then Arthur spoke as follows: 'Welcome to you, Petreius!
Now I'll give you a lesson in the Celtic language:
In the presence of the kaiser you boasted you would kill me,
Seize hold of all my castles, and my kingdom as well,
And much joy will you get from what you wanted to grab!
Certainly I'll give you my castle in Paris,
And there you will be living – but not in the style you'd like –
And nor will you ever get out of there again alive!'
    Arthur took the knights who had been captured there,   13400
And three hundred horsemen he also took at once,
All from one contingent,
Very brave knights and valiant men in fight
And told them next day to rise with determination
And fasten the Roman men with very strong chain fetters
And conduct Petreius to the city of Paris.
Four earls he detailed to escort them as they went:
Cador, Borel, Bedivere and **Richer**;
He told them to keep close so that they would be safe
And return immediately to their sovereign lord.   13410
This was all discussed; but it was soon discovered:
There were informers moving through the king's army[*]
And they heard rumours of an accurate report
Of where Arthur was dispatching the knights he held as captives,

342

And the spies very promptly made off into the night
And came very quickly to the Roman kaiser
And recited their entire report: how those four earls were to travel,
Conducting Petreius to the city of Paris,
And they outlined the complete route which conveyed them to Paris
And where they could be intercepted in a narrow deep
    ravine   13420
And relieved of their possession of the important man, Petreius,
And the four earls could be overcome and tied up securely.

    The emperor of Rome, Lucius, listened to all this
And leapt for his arms as if he were a lion,   *Roman*
Giving orders to ten thousand sturdy campaigners   *Campaign*
To arm and to mount and to move ahead with speed.
He summoned **Sextorius**, Duke of Turkey, King of Libya,
He sent for **Evander**, who from Babylon had come there,
He summoned the senators, **Bal Catel** and **Carrius**,
(All these were of royal blood, and all of them were
    excellent)   13430
To ride on the instant and rescue Petreius.

    As soon as it was evening they began advancing,
With twelve local people to act as their guides
Who were very cautious and knew the routes thoroughly.
As the Roman party rode out, their mail-coats were ringing,
Their helmet plumes tossing, high on their heads,
And shields at their shoulders: they were tough Roman soldiers.
They travelled all night, eagerly spurring   *(iv) The*
Until they reached the track which led towards Paris.   *Ambush*
They had got there first: the British hadn't come yet –   13440
O alas! courageous Cador knew nothing about this:
That the Roman forces had ridden in front of them there.
They arrived in a forest in a really pretty setting,
In a deep valley with no view on either side.
They made the arrangement to take up positions there.
There they lay in silence for just a little space,
And day began breaking and the wild creatures started waking.

    Then Arthur's men arrived, jogging down the road,
Along the very way where the other army lay.
They rode along singing: the soldiers were exultant.*   13450
Just the same, Cador was present, very clever and alert:
He and the good Earl Borel were riding abreast there
And leading between them five hundred knights

And moved on ahead then, fully armed soldiers;
Richer and Bedivere moved to their rear there
Conveying the knights whom they had taken captive,
Petreius and his comrades, who had been conquered.
    So they came riding right into the Romans,
And the Romans rushed upon them with really savage force,
Slashing at the British with very severe blows;[†]   13460
They broke the British line: disaster hit the men;
The woods began re-echoing; warriors were falling;
The British stood up to them, defended themselves stalwartly.
    Richer heard the turmoil, as did Bedivere the earl,
As their comrades up front were fighting it out;
They seized hold of Petreius and all of their captives
And with three hundred squires sent them into the woods,
While they themselves hastened towards their companions,
Striking at the Romans with redoubled strength:
Many blows were inflicted; many men there were
    slaughtered.   13470
Then Evander realised – the heathen king was very clever –
That their own folk were doing better and the British getting weaker
And, his most superior knights moving in unison,
Fell on the British as if about to devour them:
The British collapsed then and came off the worst.
They were slaughtering and capturing all they came near to;
The British were in trouble without King Arthur there:
They had too little support there in their supreme need.[†]
    There Borel was slain, deprived of life's days:
King Evander killed him, with his evil tricks,   13480
Along with three Britons who were noble men born.
There in the slaughter were three hundred of their supporters,
And many captured alive: they were chained up closely.
They knew of no useful plan; they all expected to perish,
But all the same they fought on as bravely as they could.
    Now there had gone out on reconnaissance from Arthur's army
The King of Poitou, a veteran of fame,[†]
Guitard he was called, and Gascony he ruled;
He had as his companions five hundred riders
And three hundred bowmen, valiant in battle,   13490
And seven hundred footmen eager to inflict great harm:
They had gone into the countryside to collect provisions,
Both fodder and food to carry back to the forces.

They heard all the clamour coming from the Romans
And abandoned their activity and advanced in that direction,
Stern-minded men, and speedy, they were not at all slow,
And so quickly they came up level with the fighting.
Guitard and his knights instantly and tightly
Gripped hold of their shields (they were very brave knights)
And all their archers too pressed ahead beside them,   13500
And the foot-soldiers moved ahead fast,
And all together they struck in a savage onslaught:
At the first onrush the Roman troops fell,
Fifteen hundred of them in heaps on the ground;
There Evander was killed, he who had been so cruel;
Catellus of Rome there forgot all his decrees;
Those who had been keeping stationary started off in flight.
The Romans turned their backs and took off and fled,
The British made off after them and attacked them savagely,
Taking so many captive, killing so many more there   13510
That the British force could not slaughter any more,
And the men of the Romans who were able to escape
Rushed away instantly off to the emperor
And gave him these tidings about Arthur the king,
Because they thought for a fact that it was Arthur who had come!
    The emperor and his force were terribly afraid.
When the Britons had been slaughtering to their own satisfaction
They turned back again then, boldly with their booty,
Returning to the place where the battle had occurred,
They buried the dead and carried off the living,   13520
And sent for Petreius whom they had previously captured
And for his companions who had been captured too,
And sent them all, no doubt of this, into the city of Paris,
Filling three castles with them, and firmly locked them in,
At Arthur's instructions, most admired of kings.
    All the British people felt affection for Arthur,*
All who lived in the land felt very much in awe of him,
As indeed did the emperor: Arthur made him feel most anxious!
And all the Roman people were afraid of King Arthur.
So what Merlin had prophesied was proved to be true,   13530
That Rome would [feel fear] because of King Arthur*
And the stone walls around it would tremble and fall;
This same symbol would signify Lucius the emperor,
And those of his senators who came with him from Rome,

345

And concerning the very manner in which they would collapse;
What Merlin in former years had said, they found it happen there,
As they had done already and did subsequently everywhere:
Before Arthur was born Merlin had predicted all of it!
  The emperor heard reports, accurately recorded,
Of how his men were captured and his soldiers also slain.   13540
Then in all his army there was uncontrolled sorrow:
Some were mourning their friends, some were cursing their foes,
Some were calling for weapons: they were all in confusion!
Then Lucius realised how bad his luck had become,
For every day he was losing people from his lands,
But the sorrow he felt most was the loss of his nobles.
He then became terrified to a tremendous degree,
And accepted advice and secret opinions
That he should go to Aust with all his armed forces:*
On past Langres he would travel – he was in terror of King Arthur!
Arthur had his informers in the army of the emperor   13551
Who quickly let him know which way he was to go.
Arthur very quickly had his army assembled,
Secretly by night, with his very best knights,
And off the king went with his splendid army.
He left Langres behind him lying on his right hand,
And marched in front on the road which Lucius was to march on.
When he came to a valley under a hillside
The most courageous of kings came to a halt;
By its correct title, the valley is called Sosie.   13560
There Arthur dismounted and commanded all his veterans
[With very great speed to (make ready) their weapons]†   13561a
And prepare themselves for fighting in the way that brave knights
     should,
So that when the Roman people came riding along there
They could take vengeance on them, as brave knights should also do.
All the young squires and the warriors who were unwell,
And very many thousands of the inferior ranks,
The king positioned on a hillside along with many standards: *Battle*
He did this as a trick intending to talk much of it,   *of*
As indeed happened subsequently, just a short time later.   *Saussy*
  Arthur took ten thousand of his noble knights,   13570
And sent them out to the right, well clad in their armour;
Another ten thousand he kept on his left side,
Ten thousand to the fore, and ten thousand to the rear;

With himself he retained just sixteen thousand;
He dispatched at a distance, in a wood nearby there,
Seventeen thousand superior knights,
Men with good war-gear, who were to guard the woodland
So they could all withdraw there if the need arose.
   There was in Gloucester city an earl among the best of them,
Morvith was his name, a man who was most brave: 13580
To him Arthur entrusted the wood and the detachment:
'And if it should happen, as immortal God may arrange,
That they are overwhelmed and start to make a run,
Then set off in pursuit, with all the strength you have,
And deprive of life at once all those you can overtake,
The fat ones and the thin, the rich ones and the poor,
For in no [nation] anywhere nor among any people[†]
Are there knights as excellent as those I have myself,
Knights as fierce, knights as fine,
Knights as strong there are not in any land: 13590
You are the most courageous knights in the whole of Christendom,
And I am the most powerful king after God himself!
Let us perform this action well. May God give us success!'
   The knights replied softly, out in the open air:
'We shall all do our best and we shall all make an effort;
May the knight who does not show his strength be ever counted
     craven!'
Then he sent out on both flanks all the foot-soldiers,
Then had the dragon banner raised, unique among standards
And entrusted it to a king who knew well how to hold on to it.
Angel, King of Scotland, held the first battalion in his command;[*]
Cador, the Earl of Cornwall held the next contingent;   13601
Beof, Earl of Oxford, he had one as well,
And Gerin, Earl of Chester held the fourth one himself;
Escil, the Danish King, controlled the forces which were on the
     downs;
Lot held another one: he was much loved by the king;
Howel of Brittany held yet another one,
And Gawain the courageous stood beside the king;
Kay who was the king's High Steward was in charge of one division,
The king's Butler, Bedivere, he had another;
Howeldin, Earl of Flanders, had a company under him;   13610
Guitard, King of the land of Gascony, had a great force;
Wigein, Earl of Leicester, and **Jonathan**, Earl of Dorchester,

These controlled two detachments which were on foot there;
Curselin, Earl of Chester, and the Earl of Bath, called **Urgein**,
Were both controlling the detachments which were on foot there
Which on the two flanks were to move forward to the battle;
In these two earls, who were valiant knights,
Arthur had confidence: they were trustworthy earls.

   When all the battalions were positioned as Arthur thought
      appropriate,
Then the King of Britain called over to him   13620
All his advisers, who made incisive decisions,
And Arthur said immediately to his admirable men:
'Now pay attention to me, my very dear friends:
You have made two attacks on the men of the Romans,
And twice they have been conquered and slaughtered and captured
Because with great injustice they coveted our land,
And, my heart is telling me, through our Lord on high,
Once again they shall be conquered, both slaughtered and captured.
You have conquered Norway, you have conquered Denmark,
Scotland and Ireland you've brought under your control,   13630
Normandy and France you have conquered in battle:
Thirty-three kingdoms I hold in my own possession
Which for me you have won in this world beneath the sun;
And these are the most accursed men of all men now alive,
A race of heathens – to God they are loathsome:
They abandon our Lord God and give allegiance to Mahound,
And the emperor Lucius has no concern for God at all;*
Heathen hounds he has as his companions,
God's antagonists; we shall overmaster them,
Fell them to the ground and ourselves stay safe and sound,   13640
By the goodwill of the Lord, who governs all actions!'†
   Then the earls who were there replied 'We are all ready
To live or to lie dead beside our beloved king!'
When the army was quite ready it was by then daylight.
Lucius turned off at Langres, with all his Roman liegemen;
He got his men to blow his fine golden trumpets
To summon his army: he wished to ride onwards
From Langres to Aust, as his direct route lay.
The troops of the Romans started riding off,
Until they had arrived one mile away from Arthur.   13650
Then the Roman forces heard really dire reports:
They could see all the valleys, all the downlands,

All the hillsides, quite covered with helmets,
With soaring battle-standards, supported by soldiers,
Sixty thousand of them, tossing in the wind,*
Shields were glinting, mail-coats shimmering,
Gold-coloured surcoats; soldiers looking very grim;
Steeds were prancing; the earth seemed to shudder.
   The kaiser saw the king striding along beside the wood edge;
Then Lucius remarked (and he was lord of all Rome),   13660
Addressing his men with echoing tones:
'What are those outlaws who are obstructing our road here?
Let's seize our arms and against them advance!
They must be destroyed; some must be flayed alive;
They have all got to die, to perish by dire torments!'
When these words were said, they all seized their weapons;
   When they were equipped with their splendid weapons,
Lucius the lord of Rome made a speech at once:
'Let's quickly up and at 'em; we're all bound to do well!'
There had travelled with him twenty-five kings,   13670
All heathen people, who held their lands from Rome,
Earls and dukes as well, from the eastern world:
'Masters,' Lucius spoke again, 'may Mahound show you his favour;
You are powerful rulers and yet subject to Rome;
Rome is mine by right, the most resplendent of all cities,
So I ought to be the greatest of all men who are alive.
You see here upon the field those who are our foes;
They intend to rule in dominance over our realm,
To treat us as menials and themselves be triumphant.
But we shall prevent them by forceful resistance,   13680
For our race was dominant over all mortal men
And conquered all the lands which they once looked upon,
And Julius the conqueror journeyed into Britain
And gained by his conquests very many kingdoms.
Now it's the ambition of our underlings to be over us as kings!
But they are going to pay for it on their naked backs!
They shall never again travel back to Britain!'
   As soon as he had spoken, the army started off;
By thousands together they thronged in a convoy:
Each king formed a platoon from his own people.   13690
When it was all positioned and the armies in place,
Then there were, if counted accurately, fully fifteen contingents!
Two kings in every section worked in co-operation;

Four earls and a duke formed a joint detachment,
And the emperor alone, along with ten thousand warriors.
When that host started marching the earth began resounding;
Trumpets were blowing to summon the forces;
Horns were re-echoing with uplifting tones:
Sixty thousand of them were blowing in unison;
From Arthur's companies responded even more   13700
Than sixty thousand soldiers blowing at the horn;
The very heavens echoed; the earth began to quake.
    Together they charged as if the sky would crash down:
First they sent flying over, tremendously fast,
Arrows as thick as the snow falling down;
Then they sent stone-balls crashing their way savagely;
After that spears were cracking, and shields were splitting,
Helmets were caving in, and great men falling;
Coats of mail were shattering, blood gushing out;
The fields were discoloured; their standards tottered;   13710
All through that wood went wandering wounded knights every-
        where,
Six thousand there were who were trampled by steeds;
Men lay expiring, blood was pouring [out] there;[†]
Bloody streams went tumbling along all the tracks;
There was turmoil in the host; the tragedy was immense.
According to what the writings say which wise men have composed
That was the third greatest conflict to occur in this world.
Then in the end no combatant knew
Whom he was supposed to strike and whom he ought to spare,
Since men could not recognise each other as there was too much
        blood.
    Then the battle moved ground from where they had been
        fighting   13721
And they began across a wider area to assault each other,
And began a new contest, bodies closely pressing;
The Roman soldiers were being roughly handled there!
Then three kings arrived there who came from heathen lands:
The first was Ethiopian, the second was an African,
The third came from Libya, which is a heathen land.
They entered the battle-line from the east end of it,
Breaking the shield-wall which the British were holding there,[*]
And instantly felled fifteen hundred men,   13730
Very brave fighters from King Arthur's forces;

350

Then at once the British turned their backs on the battle.
  Then there rode upon the scene two courageous earls,
Namely Bedivere and Kay, Arthur's butler and his cousin;
They saw their British soldiers being hacked down by blades
And those very fierce earls, growing furiously angry,
With ten thousand knights moved straight into the fighting,
Into the midst of the throng where it was thickest,
And struck down the Roman soldiers remorselessly,
Moving through the skirmish exactly as they wished.   13740
In this they were too daring, protecting themselves feebly:
O woe, alas, woe alas that they were not cautious then!
That they could not defend themselves against their opponents,
But they were too foolhardy and too presumptuous,
Fighting too strongly and going too far in
And moving too far apart in that far-spread fighting.
  Then the King of the Medes arrived, a massive and well built man,
A heathen warrior, who caused great harm there;
He led in his contingent thirty thousand horsemen
And was holding in his hand a very sturdy javelin: 13750
He stabbed with the javelin with his forceful strength,
And struck Earl Bedivere from the front on his chest,
Which shattered the mailcoat both behind and in front:
His chest was laid wide open: warm blood came gushing out.
Instantly Bedivere fell down, stark dead upon the ground.
There was anguish, grief in plenty;
Kay found Bedivere lying stretched out dead there
And wanted to carry away the corpse by himself
So he surrounded it with two thousand knights,
Fighting very fiercely and felling the Romans   13760
And slaughtering many hundreds of the Median men.
The fighting was extremely keen and they stayed there too long!
  Then there came passing by a most unpleasant king,
With sixty thousand superior men from his own lands;
It was Se[x]tor[ius] the valiant who came out from Libya;[†]
There the stalwart king started fighting against Kay
And wounded him severely in the savage contest
To death itself: the action was tragic!
Immediately his knights carried him out of the fighting:
With immense force they plunged through the press.   13770
King Arthur grieved bitterly when he heard the news.
  The great leader called **Ridwathelan** noticed this fact then —[*]

351

He was Bedivere's sister's son, descended from high-ranking
    Britons –
That with his sturdy javelin **Boccus** had stabbed Bedivere;
He was mortally dismayed [to see] his uncle's death[†]
For of all the men there he had loved him most;
He called for the best knights from his own kindred,
From those whom he loved the most and knew were living still:
Five hundred by the count hurried together.
Then spoke Ridwathelan, the nobleman of Britain: 13780
'Sirs, you come from my family: come over here to me
And let's avenge my uncle Bedivere, who was the best of our clan,
Whom Boccus has stabbed to death here with his stout spear;
Let's all rush together and beat down our enemies!'
Uttering those words, he galloped away
Instantly accompanied by his admirable comrades,
And spotted King Boccus in the centre of the combat
By his spear and his shield; many a king had he killed!
Ridwathelan drew his sword at once and struck a blow at him
And struck the king on the helm so that it split in half,   13790
And the coif underneath it too, and then it stopped at the teeth!
And the heathen king collapsed to the ground,
And his foul soul sank down into hell.
Then Ridwathelan spoke (he was revengeful in mood):
'Now Boccus you have paid for Bedivere's slaying,
And for all eternity your soul will keep the Devil company!'
After these words, as fast as the wind blows
He hurled himself into the fight like whirlwind over fields
When up on high it piles the dust from the earth;
In just that way Ridwathelan rushed upon his foes.   13800
Everything they came close to they slaughtered right there
For as long as they could wield their glorious weapons;
In all that great fight there were no better knights
For as long as the life in their breasts lasted within them.
King Boccus they had slaughtered, and a thousand of his warriors:
So Bedivere was avenged in truly fitting fashion!
    There was a valiant earl from a noble line[*]
Whose name was **Leir**; he was the lord of Boulogne;
In the battle he caught sight of an enemy approaching
Who was an emir: he was the governor of Babylon;   13810
He was felling many people flat upon the ground,
And the earl discerned that: it made him feel most distressed;

352

He pulled across his breast a very broad shield
And grasped in his hand a spear which was very strong,
And spurred on his horse with all the strength he had
And he hit the emir hard then with a penetrating blow
Underneath the breast-bone so that the corslet shattered
And the spear went right through him and came out behind
To the space of six full feet; the foe fell upon the ground.
The son of this emir soon spotted this;   13820
Gecron he was called; he gripped his spear at once
And struck the earl Leir sharply on the left side
And straight through the heart; the earl sank to the earth.
Gawain noticed that from where he was in the fight
And he grew extremely strongly enraged;
Howel, high ruler of Brittany, saw it as well
And he moved in that direction with fifteen hundred men,
Seasoned soldiers in battle they sped there with Howel,
And Gawain along with them, a very valiant-hearted man,
And he had as his followers two thousand five hundred   13830
Very brave Britons; then they began the battle.
    The Roman soldiers were being roughly handled there:
Howel was attacking them, Gawain was assaulting them;
There were hideous horrors: the heavens resounded;
The earth began to tremble; the very stones split;
Torrents of blood gushed from tormented people;
The carnage was tremendous. The British were exhausted.
Kinard, the earl of Striguil went away from King Howel*
And took with him **Labius**, **Rimarc** and **Boclovius**:
These were the men of greatest courage that any king
        commanded,   13840
These among mere mortals were earls strong and mighty;
In their magnificent spirit they refused to follow Howel the good
But by themselves they slaughtered everyone whom they came close
        to.
    A man who was important among the Roman forces
Saw Kinard the courageous killing their countrymen
And the knight dismounted from his precious steed
And seized in his hand a spear with tip of steel,
Which he plunged into blood, and then went to one side
Until he came in the end where stout Kinard was fighting:
He lifted Kinard's corslet and there struck the earl dead.   13850
All the Roman legions gave a loud cry then

And bearing down upon the Britons they broke up their ranks,
And their standards were flattened; folk slid to the ground;†
Shields split apart there; soldiers were falling;
There fell to the earth fifteen thousand men,
Very bold Britons; disaster was everywhere.
That contest was so severe it lasted a long time there.

    Gawain began proceeding through that prodigious carnage,
Summoning all his knights as he found them in the fighting.
Close by there came riding Howel the mighty: 13860
They combined the men they both had and began to march off in
    haste,
Riding up to the Roman folk in fierce raging anger,
And turning on them vigorously broke the French ranks,
And Gawain immediately there discovered
Lucius the emperor lurking under his shield†
And Gawain struck a blow at him with his sword made of steel,
And the emperor at him; it was a savage sport,†
Shield against shield – splinters flew about –
Sword against sword struck blow after blow:
Sparks sprang from the steel; the foes were mad with fury.   13870
There was a most vicious conflict: all the army was aroused;
The emperor was trying to destroy Gawain
So that on a later day he could boast about the deed,
But the British crowded in on him in terrific choler
While the Roman soldiers rescued their emperor
And they clashed together as if the skies were crashing down.

    All through the daylight they continued with that fight.
Then just a short time before the sun's decline
Arthur, most admired of kings, let out a cry:
'Now all of us at 'em, my valiant knights,   13880
And may God himself assist us to topple our enemies!'
When Arthur had spoken brass trumpets were blown:
Fifteen thousand men crowded there to blow
Horns and trumpets; the earth began to tremble
At the tremendous blast. Because of the huge threat†
The Romans turned round, away from the fighting,
Their standards fell flat, their great men expired;
Those who could took flight; the fated fell there;
There was massive slaughter: [massive grief, massive dread]†
No one could recount, [in annals or in oral tales]   13889a
How many hundred men were hacked to death there   13890

354

In the tremendous press, in the great slaughter.
   The emperor was slain in a very strange way,
So that no one knew afterwards how to give an explanation
In any country anywhere, of who killed the kaiser,
But when the fighting was all finished, and all the folk rejoicing
Someone found the emperor stabbed to death there by a spear.
Word came to Arthur as he sat in his tent
That the emperor was slain and deprived of his life's days.
Arthur had a tent pitched in the middle of a wide field
And had Emperor Lucius's body carried there on a bier,   13900
And there had him shrouded with a gold-embroidered pall,
Setting men to keep watch there for three entire days,
While he ordered the construction of a magnificent object,
A lengthy coffin, and had it all coated in gold,
And had the body placed in it of Lucius of Rome,
A very formidable man for all the length of his lifetime.
   Arthur did even more, that most exalted of all Britons:
He ordered a search made of all the nobility,
The kings and the earls and all the greatest soldiers,
Who had been slain in the battle and deprived of their lives' days;
He had them all buried with very great ceremony.   13911
All but three kings he got men to bear to Lucius the
      emperor,
And had biers fashioned which were rich and most resplendent,
And had them speedily send dispatches to Rome
And greet all the Roman citizens with really great derision,*
Saying that he was sending them this tribute from his lands
And that he would send them more salutations of this kind again,
If they were eager to gain King Arthur's gold,
'And very shortly afterwards [I]'ll be riding into Rome†
And first-hand news [I]'ll give [you] about the King of Britain,†
And repair the walls of Rome which long since have been ruined:
And so I shall overmaster the untamed men of Rome!'   13922
All this vaunting was done in vain, because it turned out quite
      otherwise;
Quite differently things went; he turned away from that people,
All through Modred his [kinsman] – that most wicked of all men!†
   In the great battle those knights lost to Arthur
Were twenty-five thousand men, hacked to pieces on the earth,
Very brave Britons, bereft of their lives.
Kay was very gravely wounded, grievously badly;

He was carried into Kinon and shortly afterwards he died.*   13930
There he was buried, just beside the castle,
In the hermitage. He was a splendid man!
Kay was the earl's name, and they called the castle Kinon;
Arthur had given him the town, and that's where he had his tomb,
And the name there was altered, taken from his own,
Because of Kay's death: Caen, Arthur called it,
And now and for all time so the name there will remain.*
After Bedivere was slain and deprived of his life's days
Arthur had him borne off to his castle Bayeux,
And there he was buried inside the borough limits: 13940
Just beyond the south gate he was placed in the earth.
Howeldin was ferried across the foam to Flanders,
And all his best knights were ferried directly,
Off to the earldoms from which they had come.
And all of their dead were laid in the earth:
In Thérouanne they are lying, every one of them.
The Earl Leir was led away into Boulogne.
    And Arthur subsequently stayed in a district,
In Burgundy it was, where it best pleased him.
He took control of all that land and commissioned all the
        castles,   13950
Announcing his intention of annexing that land.
And then he made a declaration that in the summer he'd decided
To travel down to Rome and take possession of all the realm,
And himself be the emperor where Lucius used to live;
And many of the Roman citizens wanted things to go that way,*
Because they were so terrified out of their very lives
That many had taken flight from there and abandoned their castles,
And many sent messages to Arthur the mighty,
And many sought audience, and entreated Arthur's favour,
But some there were who wanted to hold out against Arthur,   13960
To hold Rome against him and defend all the realm,
But all the same, so afraid were they of meeting misfortune,
That they could not in the name of Christ adopt a useful course of
        action.
Then came to pass what Merlin spoke of long before,
That the walls of Rome would fall down before Arthur;
This had already happened there in relation to the emperor
Who had fallen in the fighting with fifty thousand men:
That's when Rome with her power was pushed to the ground.

And so Arthur really expected to possess all of Rome,
And the most mighty of kings remained there in Burgundy.   13970
   Now there arrived at this time a bold man on horseback;[*]
News he was bringing for Arthur the king   *Arthur's*
From Modred, his sister's son: to Arthur he was welcome,   *Downfall*
For he thought that he was bringing very pleasant tidings.
Arthur lay there all that long night, talking with the young knight,
Who simply did not like to tell him the truth of what had happened.
The next day, as dawn broke, the household started moving,
And then Arthur got up, and, stretching his arms,
He stood up, and sat down again, as if he felt very sick.
Then a good knight questioned him: 'My Lord, how did you get on
    last night?'[*]
Arthur responded (his heart was very heavy):   13981
'Tonight as I was sleeping, where I was lying in my chamber,[*] *Dream*
There came to me a dream which has made me most depressed:
I dreamed someone had lifted me right on top of some hall
And I was sitting on the hall, astride, as if I was going riding;
All the lands which I possess, all of them I was surveying,
And Gawain sat in front of me, holding in his hands my sword.
Then Modred came marching there with a countless host of men,
Carrying in his hand a massive battle-axe.
He started to hew, with horrible force,   13990
And hacked down all the posts which were holding up the hall.
I saw Guinevere there as well, the woman I love best of all:
The whole roof of that enormous hall with her hands she was pulling
    down;
The hall started tottering, and I tumbled to the ground,
And broke my right arm, at which Modred said 'Take that!'
Down then fell the hall and Gawain fell as well,
Falling on the ground where both his arms were broken,
So with my left hand I clutched my beloved sword
And struck off Modred's head and it went rolling over the ground,
And I sliced the queen in pieces with my beloved sword,   14000
And after that I dropped her into a dingy pit.
And all my fine subjects set off in flight,
And what in Christendom became of them I had no idea,
Except that I was standing by myself in a vast plain,
And then I started roaming all around across the moors;
There I could see griffins and really gruesome birds.
   'Then a golden lioness came gliding over the downs,

As really lovely a beast as any Our Lord has made.
The lioness ran up to me and put her jaws around my waist, *
And off she set, moving away towards the sea,   14010
And I could see the waves, tossing in the sea;
And taking me with her, the lioness plunged into the water.
When we two were in the sea, the waves swept her away from me;
Then a fish came swimming by and ferried me ashore.
Then I was all wet and weary, [and I was sick with sorrow].†
And upon waking, I started quaking,
And then I started to shudder as if burning up with fire,
And so all night I've been preoccupied with my disturbing dream,
For I know of a certainty this is the end of my felicity,
And all the rest of my life I must suffer grief.   14020
O alas that I do not have here my queen with me, my Guinevere!'
    Then the knight responded: 'My Lord, you are mistaken; *
Dreams should never be interpreted as harbingers of sorrow!
You are the most mighty prince who has rule in any land,
And the most intelligent of all inhabitants on the earth.
If it should have happened – as may Our Lord not allow it –
That your sister's son, Lord Modred, your own queen might have
    wedded,
And all your royal domains might have annexed in his own name,
Those which you entrusted to him when you intended going to Rome,
And if he should have done all this by his treacherous deeds,   14030
Even then you might avenge yourself honourably with arms,
And once again possess your lands and rule over your people,
And destroy your enemies who wish you so much evil, †
And slay them, every one alive, so that there is none who survives!'
    Then Arthur answered him, most excellent of all kings:
'For as long as is for ever, I have no fear whatever,
That Modred who is my relative [the man whom I love best]†
Would betray all my trust, not for all of my realm,
Nor would Guinevere, my queen, weaken in her allegiance,
She will not begin to, for any man in the world!'   14040
Immediately after these words, the knight gave his answer:
'I am telling you the truth, dear king, for I am merely your underling:
Modred has done these things: he has adopted your queen,
And has placed in his own hands your lovely land;
He is king and she is queen; they don't expect your return,
For they don't believe it will be the case that you'll ever come back
    from Rome.

I am your loyal liegeman, and I did see this treason,
And so I have come to you in person to tell you the truth.
Let my head be as pledge of what I have told you,
The truth and no lie, about your beloved queen,   14050
And about Modred, your sister's son, and how he has snatched
    Britain from you.'
   Then everything went still in King Arthur's hall;
There was great unhappiness for the excellent king,
And because of it the British men were utterly depressed;
Then after a while came the sound of a voice;
All over could be heard the reactions of the British
As they started to discuss in many kinds of expression
How they wished to condemn Modred and the queen
And destroy all the population who had supported Modred.
Most courteous of all Britons, Arthur then called out aloud,   14060
'Sit down quietly, my knights in this assembly,
And then I shall tell you some very strange tales.
Now tomorrow when daylight is sent by our Lord to us,
I wish to be on my way towards entering Britain,
And there I shall kill Modred and burn the queen to death,*
And I shall destroy all of them who gave assent to the treason.
And here I shall leave behind my most beloved man,
Howel my dear kinsman, the highest in my family,
And half of my army I shall leave in this country,
To hold all this kingdom which I hold in my command;   14070
And when this matter is all done, then I shall go back to Rome,
And entrust my glorious kingdom to Gawain, who is my kinsman,
And then I shall fulfil my vow, upon my very life:
All of my foes will make a miserable end!'†
   Up stood Gawain then, who was Arthur's nephew
And uttered this speech (the earl was enraged):
'Almighty lord God, controller of our lot,
Protector of all this planet, why has it happened
That my brother Modred has devised this murderous plot?
But today I renounce him here, in front of this assembly,   14080
And I'll condemn him to death, with the Lord's consent;
I want to hang him myself, the highest of all criminals,
And following canon law I shall have the queen drawn apart by
    horses,
For I shall never have any happiness as long as they're alive
And until I have avenged my uncle in the most appropriate way!'

The Britons then answered him with very bold voices:
'All our weapons are prepared; so tomorrow we shall leave!'
    In the morning when daylight was sent by the Lord to them
Arthur began marching with his noble followers:
Half his army he left behind and half he led off with him: 14090
Off he went through that land until he came to Wissant;*
Rapidly he assembled ships, many and well supplied,
But for a whole fortnight the force had to stay there,
Awaiting the right weather, deprived of every wind.
    Now there was a wicked soldier in King Arthur's army
Who, as soon as he heard discussion about Modred's death,
Took his squire at once and sent him to this land,
With a warning to Guinevere of what had been happening,
And how Arthur was travelling with numerous troops,
And what he was proposing to do and exactly how he would
        act.   14100
The queen came to Modred, whom she loved best of all men
And told him the tidings of Arthur the king,
What he was proposing to do and exactly how he would act.
Modred took his messenger and sent off to Saxony
For **Childric** the second, who was a very powerful king,*
Inviting him to come to Britain: he could share it if he did so.
Modred asked Childric, the mighty and the powerful one,
To send messengers far to the four corners of Saxony
And ask all the knights whom they were able to acquire
That they should come quickly here to this kingdom,   14110
And he would give Childric a share of his realm –
Everything beyond the Humber – in return for helping him
To fight against his uncle, who was King Arthur.
Childric turned instantly in towards Britain.
    When Modred had stocked up his army with men
The full total of them came to sixty thousand,
Hardened battle-heroes who came from heathen races,
And who had come over here in order to harm Arthur
To give aid to Modred, most accursed of men.
When the army was assembled from every human race,   14120
When they were there in mass they made up a hundred thousand,
Heathens and Christians, all with 'King' Modred.
    Arthur waited at Wissant: a fortnight seemed too long to him,
While Modred knew everything which Arthur planned there:
Messengers came to him daily from King Arthur's court.

Then on one occasion heavy rain began to fall,
And then the wind began to shift: it was now blowing from the east,
And Arthur rushed aboard along with all his army,
Giving orders to the mariners to bring him in to Romney,*
Where he intended to gain entry into this country.   14130
But when he came to the haven, there was Modred facing him:
As the dawn was breaking, they started fighting;
And went on all that long day: many a man there lay dead.
Some were fighting on the land, and some down on the sands;
Some sent sharp spears flying from on board the ships.
    Gawain pressed ahead and was clearing a passage,
And very swiftly struck down eleven leaders there:
He struck down Childric's son, who with his father there had come.*
The sun went to rest; for men there was distress!
There Gawain was slain, and deprived of his life's days   14140
By some Saxon earl: may his soul suffer for it!
Arthur was dismayed and grieved deeply about it,
And the greatest of all Britons gave vent to these words:
'Now I have lost my own beloved liegemen!
I knew from my strange vision that sorrows would befall me:
Slain now is King Angel, who to me was very special,
And Gawain my own sister's son: I despair that I was ever born!
Up now, from the ships, my valiant soldiers, quick now!'
At these words there went to battle
Sixty thousand on the instant, very splendid men,   14150
And broke Modred's battle-line, and he himself was very nearly
    caught!
    Modred took to flight and his men followed suit:
They fled in full panic: even the fields were shaking!
The rocks were set [rumbling] by the streams of blood.†
That battle would have been quite finished, but the night came down
    too fast:
If the night had not come they would all have been killed!
The night came down between them out in hollows and on
    downland,
And Modred got so far that he arrived in London.
The citizens had heard how everything had gone†
And denied him entry, along with all his army.   14160
Then Modred made off from there towards Winchester
Where they took him in along with all his men,
And Arthur went in pursuit with all the power he had,

361

Until he came to Winchester with a very large force,
And encircled all the city, while Modred stayed inside it.
    When Modred realised that Arthur was so close to him
He kept on thinking frantically what could be his policy;
Then on that very night he ordered all his knights
Fully armed to make a sortie from that city,
Announcing that he wished, by means of battle, to resist.   14170
He promised to the citizens their full freedom for ever
On condition they would help him in his dire need.
When it was daybreak, all their strength was ready.
Arthur was watching it: the king was in a fury;
He had shrill trumpets sounded to summon men to battle.
Ordering all his leaders and his noble knights
To begin battle together and beat down his opponents,
And destroy the whole city and hang those citizens.
    They advanced to the attack and made a fierce assault;
Then Modred mused on what he might do,[*]   14180
And he did again there just as he'd done elsewhere:
It was the basest kind of treachery, since he always acted vilely:
He betrayed his own comrades outside Winchester,
And had fetched to his presence his favoured knights, on the instant,
And all his dearest favourites from his entire force,
And crept away from the conflict – may the Devil get him! –
And left those good people to perish there completely.
    All day they fought on: their lord was with them, they thought,
And must be alongside them in their extreme need.
Meanwhile he took the route which led into Southampton,   14190
And pressed on towards the port – that most accursed of men! –
And seized all the ships there which were of any use,
And all the steersmen he needed for the ships,
And the most evil king alive then sailed off to Cornwall!
    Meanwhile Arthur was forcibly setting siege to Winchester,
And all its inhabitants he executed: there was mourning in excess!
The young and the aged, all of them he slaughtered.
When the people were all dead, and the town entirely burned,
He had the walls absolutely dismantled then completely.
Then had come to pass there what Merlin once predicted: 14200
'You shall be wretched, Winchester, for the earth shall engulf you!'[*]
So spoke Merlin, the most trustworthy prophet.
    The Queen was lodged in York; she had never felt such horror;
This was Queen Guinevere: most unhappy of women.

She had the report, reliably expressed,
Of how often Modred had fled, and how Arthur had besieged him;
She hated the very time that she was still alive.
She stole out of York when it was dark
And made off towards Caerleon as fast as she could manage,
[Because she did not wish to see Arthur again for all the world
    around,   14209a
She came to Caerleon by night, with two of her knights],   14210
And she had her head covered with a holy veil,
And she was there as a nun: the most troubled of women.
No one knew about the queen, about where she had gone then, *
Not for many years afterwards was it known for sure
[How she had met her] death [and where she departed],†
Any more than if she herself had been plunged in the sea.

    Modred was in Cornwall and had summoned many knights;
To Ireland he sent off his messengers at great speed, *
To Saxony he sent off his messengers at great speed,
To Scotland he sent off his messengers at great speed: 14220
He ordered to come immediately all those who desired to have lands,
Or silver, or gold: either money or land;
In every respect he protected himself;
That's what any wise man does when necessity compels it.

    Arthur (the angriest of kings) heard about this,
That Modred was in Cornwall with a massive following of men
And intended to remain there till Arthur arrived.
Arthur sent out couriers throughout all his kingdom
Ordering all in the land still alive to attend
If they were fit for fighting and carrying arms,   14230
[Excluding any traitor who was loyal to Modred,   14230a
Those he refused to have, though they might well want to   14230b
    come];†
And whoever ignored what the king demanded
The king would burn alive upon the spot where he was standing!
There came flocking to the army a tremendous force,
On horseback and on foot, thick as hoarfrost falling.†

    Arthur went to Cornwall with his enormous army.
Modred heard of this and moved up against him
With an enormous host: many there were fated.
Upon the River Tamar they approached together: *   *Battle of*
The place is called Camelford – may that name last for   *Camelford*
    ever!

And at Camelford sixty thousand were assembled,   14240
And many thousand in addition; their leader was Modred.
   Then Arthur the powerful rode to the place
With an enormous host; however, it was doomed!
Upon the River Tamar they encountered each other,
Raised their battle-standards, rushed together there,
Drew their long swords, laid into helmets:
Sparks started out, spears were clattering,
Shields were shattering, shafts were splintering:
In all parts of that vast host all the men were engaged:
The River Tamar was in flood with a great tide of blood.   14250
No one in that battle could recognise any warrior,
Nor see who did less well, nor who better, so confused was the
      conflict,†
For each man struck forcibly, whether he was knight or squire.
   Modred was there slain and deprived of his life days,
[And all of his knights were slain] in the fight;†
There were slain all the sprightly
Courtiers of Arthur, the high [and the low],†
And all of the Britons of Arthur's Round Table,
And all those whom he fostered from numerous kingdoms.
And Arthur was badly wounded with a broad halberd;   14260
Fifteen appalling wounds he had on him:*
Into the very least of them two gloves could be thrust!
Then there were no more who survived the battle,
Out of two hundred thousand men who lay there hacked apart,
Save King Arthur alone, and of his knights just two.
   Arthur was mortally wounded, grievously badly;   *Arthur's*
To him there came a young lad who was from his clan,   *Death*
He was Cador the Earl of Cornwall's son;
The boy was called **Constantine**; the king loved him very much.
Arthur gazed up at him, as he lay there on the ground,   14270
And uttered these words with a sorrowing heart:
'Welcome, Constantine; you were Cador's son;
Here I bequeath to you all of my kingdom,
And guard well my Britons all the days of your life
And retain for them all the laws which have been extant in my days
And all the good laws which there were in Uther's days.
And I shall voyage to Avalon, to the fairest of all maidens,
To the Queen **Argante**, a very radiant elf,*
And she will make quite sound every one of my wounds,

Will make me completely whole with her health-giving
    potions.   14280
And then I shall come back to my own kingdom*
And dwell among the Britons with surpassing delight.'
   After these words there came gliding from the sea
What seemed a short boat, moving, propelled along by the tide
And in it were two women in remarkable attire,
Who took Arthur up at once and immediately carried him
And gently laid him down and began to move off.
And so it had happened, as Merlin said before:
That the grief would be incalculable at the passing of King Arthur.
The Britons even now believe that he is alive   14290
And living in Avalon with the fairest of the elf-folk,
And the Britons are still always looking for when Arthur comes
    returning.
The man has not been born of any favoured lady,
Who knows how to say any more about the truth concerning Arthur.
Yet once there was a prophet and his name was Merlin:
He spoke his predictions, and his sayings were the truth,
Of how an Arthur once again would come to aid the English.*
   So Constantine lived in this land and the British   CONSTANTINE
    loved him,
And very dear to them he was and they regarded him with honour.
Now Modred had had two sons, of great physical strength;   14300
They saw how things were going here for Arthur the emperor
And how their father had been slain and deprived of his life's days,
And how the British were oppressed by many kinds of disasters.
Then those same two brothers spoke to one another
And summoned all the knights who seemed to them most likely,
Who had fled far and wide away from the dire conflict,
And they summoned an army from all over the country,
Intending to slay Constantine and take from him all his lands.
   Constantine heard news of this: the king was enraged,
And sent out his messengers far and wide through his lands,   14310
Ordering his supporters to come and help the king.
Young men of spirit came marching to the muster:
Thirty thousand at once came crowding together
And the king on the spot dubbed them all knights.
The other knights arrived there who had been at the battle,
And then altogether he had sixty thousand of them.
Both of Modred's sons heard this being announced

And they decided together in secret discussions
That one of them would travel up to London town
And the other one would make his way down into
      Winchester, 14320
And there they would lie in wait until the king arrived
And they would do battle with him to their utmost strength.
But when it came to the push, quite otherwise it went!
    Constantine started marching on his way to London.
Those who were on guard in the city heard this announced;
They came together to assemble at their hustings
And decided together in their joint discussions
That they would all of them side with Constantine the king,
And desert Modred's son who was the cause of the misery.
Modred's son ran off and rushed into a monastery,* 14330
And Constantine came in pursuit and that was where he caught him:
With his sword the king sliced his head off at a single swipe.
And these were the king's words – his emotions were wrathful –:
'Lie there, you loathsome man; be the Devil's beloved;
Quickly kill everyone that you can find there,
All my opponents: see them hurled to the ground!'
    This execution was soon over, for many a man turned to it,
And Constantine, who was king in the land, then issued instruction
For his trumpets to be blown and his army brought together,
And he went on the direct way which led towards
      Winchester 14340
And was leading ahead with him the Britons of London.
And to Winchester they came and straightaway they went inside.
Melou noticed that (he was Modred's son)
And turned away from his friends and fled into a church,
And immediately fled right to the front of an altar.
Constantine drew out his sword and took his head off with one swipe
So that Saint Amphiball's altar was all bloody from it,
And he ordered the execution then of all of Melou's men.
    Then Constantine was king here of this realm of his kinsmen:
Then bliss began to reign in the land of Britain: 14350
There was peace here and plenty and laws of freedom for the folk,
And most properly they maintained those laws which had force in
      Arthur's days.
But all too little time did these same conditions last,
For he only lasted a mere four years: his mortal foes destroyed him,*
And his people bore his bier off to Stonehenge

And there they laid him down by his beloved ancestors.

Afterwards **Conan** was created the king here: [*]   CONAN
He was the most accursed man whom the sun here ever shone on!
He was Constantine's sister's son: he betrayed his uncle to his death
Because he was entitled to rule in this realm.   14360
By using poison Conan murdered the sons of his uncle;
He caused insurrection: his own people fought against him,
And he proceeded to seduce his own two sisters.
Each town in the land fell into utter scandal,
This entire nation was most severely disrupted.
For six years this sad state lasted in the land,
Then the king fell off his horse, his last fatal journey:
All the folk were relieved about his fatal injury!

  When things had all gone on like this, the next king was
    Vortiporus;
That was when the Saxon men came sailing to the country   14370
And caused harm and much destruction up beyond the
    Humber;   VORTIPORUS
They killed and they captured all that they came near to,
And the gracious Vortiporus summoned the troops
And marched down upon them and felled the Saxon men
And sent many thousands to the sea-bottom,
And so he scared them off and sent them from the land
So that never again in his days did they desire to come back here.
His days lasted just seven years, and after that he died.

  And then **Malgus** the fierce took over this realm;   MALGUS
He was the most handsome man, apart from Adam and
    Absolom,   14380
Who has ever been born (or so the books tell us!)
This man had his court filled entirely with brave knights,
All the simple squires seemed exactly like great leaders,
All his court attendants had the demeanour of good squires;
No man without true courtesy dared ever visit this king's court.
He won back all the lands which should be in his possession;
Then all this land of Britain was filled with sheer delight:
The blossoms were opening all over this kingdom;
The king was not concerned for money, but gave it all to his knights;
One could not devise any more fine delights   14390
Than there were with the king—save for just one bad thing:
He loved that same sin which is hateful to Our Lord
By which men avoided women and to a greater sin adhered:

The male loved the male; the female they found hateful,
So that many thousands emigrated from this land:
Really beautiful women went off to other nations,*
Thinking it a huge insult that men cared nothing for them.
In every kind of respect this was a good monarch,
Except for that sin which I have just mentioned.

    Then there came one of his relations who was called **Carric** CARRIC
And took on this kingdom and dwelt in it disastrously;   14401
A fine knight was Carric, but not a lucky man,
And that was because aliens damaged all his nation.
This king was a noble British man; scorn and derision were heaped on
    him;
He gave up the name Carric and called himself '**Kinerich**',*
And in many books even now his name is written like that.
People began to despise him; people began to detest him,
And to sing mocking songs about the much hated king.
Then war began over all this land,
And Saxon men quickly sailed to this country,   14410
Taking up their quarters close by, just beyond the Humber.
And the king began to wander far and wide through all the nation:
He was unpopular with everyone who ever set eyes on him.

    Now there was in Africa a really powerful king;*
He was an African, known as **Anster**;
He had a pair of sons, both of them keen knights:
Gurmund they called the elder and **Gerion** they called   *Gurmund*
    the younger.
The old king died: his days had run their course;
He bequeathed his splendid realm to his son Gurmund
But Gurmund despised it and refused to accept it,   14420
And had other ideas and gave it to his brother
Saying that he refused to possess any realm
Unless he had won it with weapons and with men,
But through combat he was willing to possess a kingdom,
And otherwise not at all: he would not have any.

    Gurmund was a champion prized for his strength,
And he was the strongest man whom anyone has ever seen.
He proceeded to send throughout all the lands:
Into Babylon, and into Macedonia,
Into Turkey, into Persia,   14430
Into Nubia, into Arabia,
And encouraged all the youngsters through all the heathen lands

To get for themselves suitable arms
And then he would instantly create them all knights,
And then would travel with them and make trial of where he could
With stalwart champions win himself a kingdom.
　　From many a kingdom there was movement towards Africa
Of many a great man's son, of many a heathen man;
These came to Gurmund, to the heathen chieftain.
When this force was assembled and the folk counted up,　　14440
Those very brave knights there were numbered off
As one hundred and sixty thousand, generously armed,
Excluding their archers who were to press ahead in the van,
And excluding the craftsmen who came to Gurmund.
Forwards they marched, an enormous host;
They went to the sea when they had the wind,
Those heathen warriors embarked in their ships.
Seventeen moved forward there who were the sons of kings;
Twenty-eight of them were offspring of earls.
Seven hundred ships sped away from the shore　　14450
In the first flotilla, not counting those that followed.
Forwards over the waves floated the vast fleet.
All of the islands which they found on their route
Came into subjection to Gurmund the king;
Many a king did he fight with, and all of them asked him for peace,
And he conquered all the countries on which he set his eyes,
And then in the end he came to Ireland
And he conquered the land completely and killed all the people
And was pronounced the king over that kingdom there,
After which he started moving across into this land;　　14460
They pulled the sail to the masthead and put in to Southampton.
　　Up beyond the Humber there lived those of Hengest's　　*Invasion*
　　　race,
In the north region, some six or so chieftains.
They heard the tidings of Gurmund the king:
They kept on musing thoughtfully what was to be their policy,
How they could by treason trick Carric of his kingdom
And kill every Briton through their evil arts.
The Saxon men sent messengers to Carric the king
Saying that they wished to make a treaty with him:
It would be more pleasant for them to obey Carric　　14470
Than it would Gurmund, the alien king,
If he would make peace with them and allow them to remain

369

And give them that land which once Vortigern the king
Had committed to Hengest when he took his dear daughter,
And if they were to send him tribute from that land
And regard him as High King, as Carric their darling;
And this they requested of him, with hostages to confirm it.
And Carric believed them, all their lying talk,
And agreed to this peace and appointed a day.
So Carric was quite deceived, entirely through their tricks   14480
And ever after Carric was known as Kinerich (Kingdom-rich):
With mocking expressions they scoffed at the king.
    Carric believed as truth the expressions of the Saxons;
During the discussions they had a message written
And sent it with their messengers to Gurmund the king,
And thus ran the words inscribed in the message:
'All health to you, Gurmund: all hale, O heathen king!*   *Saxon*
Health to your courtiers, health to your retainers!   *Deception*
We are men of Saxony, the most splendid of the race
Whom Hengest of Saxon lands brought here with him;   14490
We dwell within Britain, to the north of the Humber:
You are a heathen king, we are heathen warriors;
Carric is a Christian man: we loathe him for that;
And if you want this whole land, seizing it in your own hands,
Then we shall fight along with you with our utmost force
And destroy Carric and put his knights to flight,
And place all this kingdom into your own hand.
If you will grant us possession, we shall pay to you
Six thousand pounds in every passing year,
And we agree to become your vassals, to give you our sons as
      hostages.
And if it should be your will to make your way over here,   14501
To conclude this agreement and to confirm this speech,
Then we shall at all points incline to yourself,
And by sea and by land take you as our king.'
    Then Gurmund the fierce made incisive response:
'Prepare my ships without delay: I intend to travel away.'
They hauled up the sails and off they travelled:
They secured the long ropes and sailed over the waves,
And so they proceeded to Northumberland,
Conferred with the Saxon men, and made alliance with
      them,   14510
Swearing that they intended to keep the agreement.

When they were united, Gurmund and the Saxon men,
They then summoned in that country an enormous army,
And marched towards Carric, the king over this realm,
And kept on singing mockingly about 'Kinerich' the king.
Carric mustered his Britons and called them together,
And towards him came all there were in the land
In true necessity they knew no better course.

    Carric had a lot of followers and a massive army,
And came to combat repeatedly against King Gurmund,   14520
And kept on fighting him, never seeking peace from him,
And because they were mocking him he became a very fierce man,
And if he had had a host equivalent to Gurmund's,
Gurmund would soon have been slain, his folk deprived of life's days.
But all the time it ended with Gurmund's host increasing
And all the time it ended with Carric's forces falling.
Gurmund drove Carric all around this realm,
Until Carric securely enclosed himself in Cirencester,
And for many days before that he had had ferried there
All that he'd preserved of the corn from this land,   14530
And he fortified the walls exceedingly strongly.

    Gurmund got news of this and rode in that direction
And set a very tight siege outside Cirencester;
Gurmund took this kingdom totally into his own possession:
He burned down boroughs, consumed towns with fire,
He murdered British men: there was misery in the land;
He tortured the monks in many kinds of ways;
He allowed his supporters to use noblewomen as their whores;
All priests he executed; all the churches he demolished;
Scholars he slaughtered (all those whom he could find);   14540
And then every child [in water he had drowned];[†]
All of the knights he had hanged there outright.
This land was quite ruined in every kind of way.

    Such refugees as could fled wretchedly from the country,
Some to Wales, some to Cornwall,
Some into Neustria, (now known as Normandy);
Some fled overseas out into Brittany   *Celts*
And inhabited afterwards the land called Armorica,   *in Exile*
And some fled to Ireland in terror of Gurmund
And lived there in servitude as other men's slaves,   14550
These and all their descendants; and they never came back here again.
And so all these kingdoms were lost to the Britons.

Meanwhile Gurmund held siege very tightly outside Cirencester,
And Carric was inside there and many of his men.
Those who were alive then were in desperate straits!
   It happened one day when Gurmund with his attendants
(Heathen noblemen) were riding out hunting,
That a man there came riding up towards King Gurmund
Whose name was **Isemberd** (in France were his estates);
He was the son of **Louis**, the king of that nation: 14560
His father had exiled him from his entire kingdom
And he was not allowed to dwell in the whole of his dominion
So he fled to this land, to Gurmund the king;
He had as his comrades two thousand knights,
And he became Gurmund's vassal: he could not have acted worse,
For he deserted Christ himself and adopted the Devil,
And there abandoned Christianity and accepted heathen practice!
   And so the two of them marched with their much enlarged host
And besieged Cirencester from each side very tightly.
Frequently Carric's men made sorties from the town   14570
And charged upon Gurmund with savage assaults,
Killing several thousands of his supporters,
And sending them to hell: heathen hounds the lot!
   Carric was a very fine knight and continued fighting bravely,
And held Cirencester firmly with most supreme power
So that Gurmund was never able to cripple his forces
Until by a stratagem he betrayed them from within.
   Gurmund built fortresses all around Cirencester;
Three of these he committed to three heathen knights;
He himself controlled one, and Isembard another.   14580
Gurmund constructed a keep and in it built a chamber;*
In this he followed his rituals which men favoured in those times:
He kept in it his maumet which he thought of as his god.
   One day it happened, when Gurmund and his household
Were extremely merry and very drunk on wine,
That a heathen man arrived there (may he be cursed for this for ever!)
Asking information from Gurmund the king:
'Tell me, my lord Gurmund, a very great king you are!
How long are you going to dither here around this borough?
What will you give me if I give the borough to you,   14590
And everything that's in it, to do with as you like,
So that nothing is left out, but you shall have the lot?'
Gurmund gave his answer, the great heathen monarch:

'I shall give you an earldom, to possess in perpetuity,
On condition that you speedily deliver me the town!'
This compact was made instantly: few men knew about it;
Then this heathen knight stood up straightaway
And looked about for netting with a very narrow mesh,
And equipment for it, and drew it into very narrow strips;[†]
In front of it he poured around draff, and chaff, and oats.   14600
When he had set it up, sparrows flew down on to it,
And the first time he pulled it up he had caught a great number,
Which he collected from the ground, making sure they were
  unharmed,
So that all their wings were completely undamaged.   *Sparrows*
Then he looked about for nutshells and had the kernels all   *set Fire*
  removed,   *to*
And took pieces of tinder which were inserted in the shells *Cirencester*
And as the night was falling he applied a flame to the
  tinder
And to the sparrows' feet he firmly affixed the shells.
In that way he set free a great many sparrows:
The sparrows took flight and flew to their roosts   14610
All over the city, where they had their territory:
In the eaves they [crept], and on to the corn-stacks;[†]
As the fire grew hot, so the sparrows crept further in;
During the night the wind got up and stirred up the flames,
And in many different places the city was aflame,
On the east side, on the west side: the Britons there panicked;
When they sought safety by rushing into corners
They fire blazed up at once, in front and behind them!
 Gurmund got horns and brass trumpets blowing:
Fifteen thousand of them thrusting upwards at the blast.   14620
The British were burning; the British were running: [*]
They jumped from the walls and were then struck down, all.
It has not been reported, nor read of in books
That any folk so fine were ever made to perish
As Carric and his troops were; and he was King of Britain!
The borough burned all night; it was a tremendous fire;
The fighting quickly ended; the fire came down upon them,
And King Carric realised that he had been conquered; [*]
On his hands and his knees the king started crawling
As if he were feeble and fatally injured,   14630
And so very secretly he stole away from his troops

And went away westwards into the Welsh lands,
And went in this guise out of this land,
And no one ever knew where Carric had got to, *Carric*
Until at one time a knight came riding by *in Exile*
And reported to Gurmund the news about Carric:
That he was in Ireland gathering armed men
And intended to return here and battle it out,
But no one ever discovered where the threatened force got to.
    And so Cirencester and its surroundings were laid waste, 14640
And Gurmund came to be king of this entire GURMUND
    kingdom,
For then the town was taken by that sort of stratagem,
From sparrows carrying the flames, so that sparrows burned it up;
And for many years following the folk who lived around there
Called it 'Sparrowencester' in their own native speech,
And some people still do, to commemorate the old deeds.
And so this noble borough was pitifully destroyed,
And Gurmund was made king here in the land,
And Gurmund was a heathen man, and destroyed Christianity.
    When all this had been dealt with, there was much dismay and grief
    here:
Gurmund toppled monasteries and hanged all the monks, 14650
From knights he chopped the lips, from young girls the nipples;
Priests he blinded; all the peasantry he maimed:
Every man left alive he had castrated,
And this was his course of action, and so he destroyed this Christian
    land.
And then he went to London, to a great hustings:
To it proceeded all the Saxon people
Who were living in this land alongside King Gurmund
And they became his vassals, numerous and many,
Keeping their agreement he at once gave them all this
    land, 14660
To hold it in feoff from him, and have him as their king.
And the king instructed all those who loved him
That wherever they could find any Briton in this land
Such a man they should slay instantly or draw apart with horses,
Unless he were willing to live his life in slavery
And renounce God's Holy Mass and honour heathendom,
Then he might be allowed to live, a servant on this land.
    Right beside Almaigne is a land known as Angles;[*]

It was there they were born, those same who were selected,
To whom Gurmund in keeping handed over all this
    kingdom,   14670
As he had promised them if he should win it:
To them he fulfilled his entire promise;
They came out from 'Engles' and from that they took their name,
And so in fact they had themselves called, those folk who were
    'English',
And this land they called 'engle-land': after all, it was in their hands!
Since first the Britons had come travelling to this land
It had been known as 'Britain' and took its name from the Britons,
Until this race arrived, who deprived it of this name,
Along with many of the boroughs and many of the towns,
And many of the districts and many of the homes: 14680
They took away their names because of the Britons' shame,
And took over all this land and placed it all in their own hands,
Because Gurmund granted them all of it, and himself went back
    again.*
  So they came to London, to the huge hustings
And wanted to appoint a king for this kingly realm.
But then they could not agree at all on who should own this land,
And dispersed altogether then in very great anger
And appointed five kings all at once within this land,*
And each took from the other everything he could,
At one time in discord, and at another time in harmony,   14690
And so they went on living here for a hundred and five years,
While no Christianity ever came here or was acknowledged in this
    land,
And no bells were rung, and no masses sung,
No church there was ever consecrated, no child there was ever
    christened.
  Now there was once in Rome a Pope under God's laws,
Gregory he was called and God himself loved him.
Now on one occasion the pope wished to travel
In order to [further] some business of his;†
He came to a street which stretched towards Rome
And he saw there being led in chains some of the English
    nation,   14700
Three very fair men firmly secured;   *Conversion*
They were about to be sold, and the coins had been   *of England*
    counted.

Then the Pope at once questioned the comely young men,
As to where they were from, how they came to be there,
And on which distant shore they had been engendered.
Then one of them answered, a man who was most handsome,
'We are heathen men and we have been brought here
After being sold off, away from Angle-land,
And we beg you to baptise us if you would only set us free.'
So spoke the English men; they were nobly born.   14710
Then Gregory felt pity (God loved him much),
And this was the reply of the blessed Pope:
'Certainly you are Angles; in fact more like Angels!   *Gregory and*
Of all of the nations who dwell upon the earth,   *the 'Angels'*
Your race is the fairest of all mortal men.'
    The Pope enquired of them much information
About their laws and their lands and about this people's king;
And they gave him true answers to everything they knew of,
And he had them set free and brought baptism to them,
And then turned straight back once again towards Rome,   14720
He summoned a cardinal, selected from his people,
Augustine he was called, an admirable priest;
The Pope instructed him, in private audience:
'Augustine, you are to go, with pious intention,
Into England, to King **Ethelbert**,
And there preach God's gospel: you will succeed very well!
And I shall supply you with forty very fine priests.
Now tomorrow is the day when you must set off on your way!'
    Off went Augustine and his clerics with him;
He accepted willingly, and he made landfall here at Thanet, *   14730
And accordingly he went ashore and so entered Kent.
On he went to Canterbury, which he found most satisfactory,
Where he found King Ethelbert who was high king in that land.
To Ethelbert he told the tidings of the heavenly king himself;
He described to him the gospel and the king listened to him very well;
Well did he receive the teaching and straightaway desired
        Christianity:
So King Ethelbert was christened and all his household with him,
And at once began constructing a very beautiful church,
In the Holy Trinity's name: great grace he earned for this!
    Then Saint Augustine set forth, east and west and south and north,
And then all through England, converting it to God's
        command.   14741

Clerics he trained, churches he raised,
Sick men he healed, through the Saviour's power.
And so he drew southwards till he came to Dorchester*
Where he found the most wicked men who lived in the whole land:
He told them God's teaching and they treated him with scorn;
He taught them Christianity [and they grimaced at him];†
There stood Saint Augustine and his priests alongside him
Speaking of Christ the Son of God, as it had been their custom,
And there men approached them to their disadvantage   14750
By taking tails of sting-rays [to the dismay of many],
And hanging them on his cope on either side,
And then running away and pelting him with bones,
And then they yelled at him with horrifying taunts,
And so they dispatched him and drove him from that district.
Saint Augustine was annoyed with them and grew very angry;
He walked for five miles away from Dorchester
And came to a hilltop very high and beautiful,
Where he fell on his knees in prayer calling continually upon God
For Him to avenge him on the accursed people   14760
Who had dishonoured him with their harmful actions.
     Our Lord heard his voice reaching into heaven
And sent down his vengeance on the [wretched] people†
Who had hung sting-ray tails on to the clerics:
Those tails stuck on to them, and for this they can be derided;†
All that tribe were disgraced: they all had little
          muggles,*   *Englishmen's*
And in every household people called them 'mugglings',   *Tails*
And every gentleman says foul things about them,
And English gentlefolk in foreign countries
Because of that very deed go round with red faces,   14770
And many a good man's son when he is abroad,
Who never went anywhere near that place, is called by everyone
          'base'.*
     Augustine remained at the foot of a mountain,
And his priests with him too, who had come with him from Rome,
Calling to the Lord who made the light of day,
Penitent and saddened: they were bitterly ashamed
That that evil group of men should have disgraced them.
So because of that he wanted to return at once to Rome,
And complain to Saint Gregory, the holy apostle,
How the inhabitants of Dorchester thought fit to treat him.   14780

As soon as he was quite ready and about to go upon his way,
In that same night Our Lord came there to him,
Calling him by his own name – at that he greatly rejoiced:
'What are you thinking of, Augustine, what are you thinking of, my
    friend?
Do you want to go away so soon, back again to Rome?
You are not yet to leave, to hasten from the land.
You are very dear to me, and I intend to dwell with you,
And very readily will you come to the kingdom of heaven:
Heaven is all prepared for you; that way your soul is to travel!'
So spoke Our Lord with Augustine his knight.   14790
    When Augustine understood what Our Lord had been saying,
And when he looked at Our Lord, who made him this promise,
Our Lord rose to heaven and Augustine stayed on his knees,
Down on the soil, where he'd seen Our Lord standing;
Weeping, he called to the heavenly king,
Earnestly he begged Almighty God for mercy,
Before he fell completely prostrate upon the earth;
On that same spot where Our Lord had been standing
There he stuck his staff, he himself knelt beside it,
And preached his fellows a sermon, which greatly satisfied
    them.   14800
    When he had recounted the speech made by Our Lord,
Taking his staff in his hand, he was about to go to his lodging;
He pulled up the staff: water poured out behind it,
The loveliest fountain which flows upon earth;
Before that there was no town, no person living there.
Soon folk were flocking, gathering round the good Augustine,
And quite with his consent began arriving there
And beginning some building-works beside the glorious stream.
Many a man did the water heal; he called that place Cernel:
'Cerno, cernis': that's Latin, I tell you this;   14810
'Cerno' in English speech is 'I see' as we pronounce it;
'El' is a Hebrew word, and in fact it means 'God';
So he called the town 'Cernel': 'I see God completely'; *
As long as this world lasts, the name will remain there
As it is pronounced, after God's own discourse,
To commemorate the spot on which Our Lord stood,
And his angels with him, when he spoke to Augustine.
    Augustine travelled far across England's regions:
He baptised her kings and their chief warriors,

He baptised earls, he baptised barons,   14820
He baptised Englishmen, he baptised Saxon men,
And placed in God's hands all who were in the land.
Then he was very satisfied that he had sanctified the people.
    In the north of England the Britons had at their command
A large tract of the land and some very strong forts;
The British refused to submit to the English.
Among them was included a large contingent of monks.
Saint Augustine discovered within this same district
Seven bishops, no less, and all singing mass,
And a single archbishop, with his throne at Caerleon,   14830
And at Bangor was a monastery with huge numbers of monks:
Their abbot was called **Dionot**, who came of a great family;
He controlled, in seven daughter houses, sixteen hundred monks,
And even more besides; very brave monks they were,
And from true British stock; stern-minded men.
    Augustine sent letters to the seven bishops,
Instructing them to come with speed and speak with him in person,
And submit to him in obedience, and sing mass as his subordinates,
Because he had been put in possession of the primacy of this land:
He was entitled 'legate', and of this land he was the primate,   14840
And these things had been done by the Pope in Rome.
These bishops were resolute, and returned their response:
'Under the man called Augustine we are in no way subjected,
But in this land we are men superior in our power,
And have our jurisdiction from our own archbishop
Who is located in Caerleon: a fine cleric in his vocation,
Who received the pallium himself from Gregory the Pope,*
And with great dignity demeans himself in office.
    Now it shall never come to pass at all within this wide world's
        realm
That we shall ever submit ourselves to Augustine the
        stranger,   14850
For we are fully at variance with him, and with his fellows as well,
Since Augustine has travelled here, into this our land,
And has baptised the so-called king, prince of the men of Kent,   *Celts*
Known here as Ethelbert, high-born among the English,   *refuse*
And has encountered here those hounds of heathens   *Augustine*
Who came out of Saxony with Gurmund the king:
All those he is baptising and bringing those to God,
Who are holding onto our kingdom, most unjustly, in their hands.

We are all of us Christian and we come of Christian stock,
And our ancestors were also, for the last three hundred
  years.   14860
And these have newly come here and have now adopted Christianity,
And Augustine is baptising them and is bringing them to God,
And therefore we intend to hate him, and [to obey him we refuse]:†
Never in all our lives will we bring ourselves to like him!'
 Very swiftly the news of this reached Saint Augustine,
Of how the bishops were insulting him and what reply they were
  sending him,
And how the British clerics spoke of him in derision.
Then he was dispirited and most depressed in mood,
And went off with haste and hurried to the king,
Complaining to Ethelbert, King of the East Angles, 14870
Of how the British bishops were treating him with mockery,
And how they scorned utterly to consider him their superior.
The king was exceedingly annoyed about this matter,
And said that he was going to kill them in their country,
And he did so subsequently, quite soon after this.
 Down in Kent this Ethelbert was king in that district;
Now he had a kinsman who was called **Alfric**,
The most despicable of kings, out in Northumberland:
He devised many stratagems for killing off the bishops,
So that they would all be slain, and deprived of their life's
  days.   14880
The Britons there did not know at all that calamity was their lot.
 Ethelbert sent messengers right throughout his lands:
Alfric sent messengers right through Northumberland:
They summoned an army, a huge one, in the county,
Wanting to destroy the British quite, and put the priests to death.
They marched down to Leicester, and besieged the borough closely:*
Within it they knew that **Brochinal**, who was a British earl,
A knight among the best of them, was living, inside Leicester.
Brochinal came out, and got ready all his forces,
And moved them up to fight against Ethelbert's knights, 14890
And swiftly he was overcome, and all his British men were captured,
And so they started surging into Leicester city:
They slaughtered and they seized all whom they came close to,
Announcing their intention of next invading Wales,
And slaying all the British who were within its bounds.
 Alfric was living comfortably in the city of Leicester.

While things were like this, there came to King Alfric
Holy monks and hermits and Augustinian canons,[*]
Bishops and clerics and priests with God's tonsure,
Who fell at his feet and begged him for peace,   14900
And entreated him for the love of God to leave them alone in their
      land,
And they would intercede for him with the Most High King.
And this was the response of the most depraved king:
'Now listen here, all of you, to what I want to say:
Go out on the open field, with all your attendants,
And I'll send you word of what's going to happen;
Meanwhile my advisers will give me advice.'
Out went the monks, and also the mass-priests,
Out went the clerics, out went the canons,
All went outside, all those who had come there   14910
Desiring the king's peace, for the love of God himself.
Outside the city, on a spreading plain,
The party soon assembled; but disaster was to come to them!
      Alfric made a decision, though no one offered him advice:[*][†]
That he would fell the lot of them down to the ground!
He dispatched forthwith five hundred knights,
And along with them a full nine hundred bold men on foot
With enormous battle-axes, marched out on to the plain,
And [utterly] they slaughtered all those they got close to.[†]
They hacked to the ground fifteen hundred at once,   14920
And sixty-five more, most excellent men,   *Slaughter*
All of them scholars; there was panic among the people.   *of the*
News of this spread swiftly everywhere around.   *Clergy*
      There were in the land three men of good breeding,
And all the British immediately flocked to those men:
Baldric the brave, Earl down in Cornwall,
So the first was called, a great man in the land:
He ruled all Devonshire in his jurisdiction,
From where the River Exe goes down in to the sea —
The Britons ruled that land for a very long time,   14930
Until **Athelstan** the mighty, king of all this country,
Deprived them of all those territories and drove them over the Tamar,
And so never after that did they govern that kingdom.   *Loss of*
In North Wales lived a king, **Cadwan** the courageous;   *Devon*
From South Wales came **Margadud**, most handsome of men:
All the good land [they governed], over to the Severn,[†]

From the end near the mouth, where it runs into the sea.
In Malvern, near the Severn,
King Margadud dwelt, with very many folk,
And Athelstan, king of this land, advanced upon him,   14940
And pressed them so hard, and treated them so harshly,
That by force of arms he drove them out cross the Wye,
And took the land away from them which is lying there between
The Severn and the Wye: they have not controlled it since.
    Margadud and Baldric and Cadwan the bold
Mustered an army of numberless men,
And marched down upon Alfric, the Northumbrian king,
And fought with him vigorously and felled all his forces.
There very soon wounded, and most severely,
Was the King of Northumberland: the combat was immense;   14950
There Earl Baldric suddenly was hacked down by blades.
There in that battle fell ten thousand knights,
Very brave Britons, from the biting edge of steel,[†]
And seventeen thousand Angles and Saxons
Were cut to death by sword blades; the crowd of them was smaller![†]
Alfric made his way onward to Northumbria,
Very severely wounded; his followers were saddened.
    In this land they were coming to meet at the hustings,
Cadwan, that is, and Margadud, and their supporting men.
All the people of Britain began to move with them.   14960
They marched down to Leicester and captured the city;
Then they gave orders to come in haste to the hustings
All those who wished to live as part of this nation.
Angles came, and Saxons came:
They elected as their king there Cadwan the courageous;[*]   CADWAN
Everything he gazed at made him disgusted.
    By then in Northumbria the wounds sustained by Alfric
Had all been healed, but his health was much impaired
By the loss of his men and the fall of his people.
From the king's army Alfric would hear   14970
Frequent tidings of Cadwan the king,
Threats without number from the most hateful of men.
Alfric sent messengers off into Scotland,
And into the North lands, where he could find knights,
Seeking all the people who were able to come there,
And requested their help in his supreme need.
Cadwan gathered an army throughout all this country,

382

And all those of the Welsh lands came under his command.
And later he moved off towards Northumbria.
   Alfric heard of this and went out against him,   14980
Until between them there was nothing but a bare two miles;
The forces approached as if about to fight.
The earls could see, the barons could see,
The bishops could see, and the men of book-learning,
That if they engaged in fight and struck each other with weapons
Many a doomed soldier would fall there and die.
They considered repeatedly what should be their policy:
They arranged peace, arranged a truce for just one day's space;
They conferred among themselves and they held joint discussions,
Agreeing that all of them would reconcile the kings.   14990
   Both the two kings became reconciled there:
Reconciled and united, many times they embraced;
Again and again these kings lovingly embraced each other;
Each earl embraced another just as if he were his brother;
The squires joined in sport; there was relief among the leaders.
Alfric was to be the king in the land north of   ALFRIC
    the Humber,   *and*
And Cadwan was the good king in the part south of   CADWAN
    the Humber.
There was content in the armies of those valiant kings!*
It has never been recounted, not in legend nor in rhyme
That greater love could be found between two such kings,   15000
For everything that one had, this they both possessed:
The one held the other even dearer than a brother;
Both of them took wives, they met together many times;
At the wedding of these wives, they both went to bed at the same time,
Each turned in his love towards his own wife:
They begot two sons on their wives both at the one time;
Both on a single day in their turn they were born;
Together they were engendered, together they were nurtured.
   The children grew up and greatly they flourished;
Their parents were delighted.   15010
So as to confirm the love of their loving fathers*
They were taught together, they were trained together;
Both of them used to wear clothes which matched each other;
The children did exactly what their parents did before:
They maintained so much love it seemed miraculous to men.
And so they lived here for very many years,

Until those children had grown very big:
They could ride upon chargers, and they loved a knight's armour;
They gave proof of their strengths on many occasions;
They had powerful arms, they could break lengthy shafts,   15020
They could strike with the long swords which give severe blows.
Then their parents came, with the greatest pleasantness
And with great bliss, into Brittany
(That royal land then was still called Armorica);   CADATHLAN
Both the young men were there dubbed as knights.   *and*
Within a few years their fathers had died   EDWIN
And the two children were raised to the throne;
Each held his rightful territory as their fathers had before.
    At that time there was in Canterbury (when the town enjoyed
        prosperity)
An archbishop living who was a very good man.   15030
He forbad the two kings to assume the crown
Until he himself should come and place it on their heads.
The command was upheld on the archbishop's authority,
And so **Cadwathlan** had his lands on this side of the Humber
And **Edwin** everything beyond towards the northern limit.
As kings they were anointed, as kings they took the oath,
But the crown was forbidden in the name of Our Lord.
    Cadwathlan kept thinking (he was Cadwan's son);
He thought very carefully what should be his policy,
Now that both their fathers had already passed away.   15040
The peace had only lasted just the space of seven years.
Cadwathlan possessed a great many castles,
And the kingdom in Cadwathlan's hands was much more illustrious.
Cadwathlan set off towards London city;
He sent exellent men to find the Archbishop,*
And issued instructions that he should come straight to London.
When he came to London, the king was content;
On foot he advanced to meet the archbishop
Outside his hall door, with the words: 'You are welcome',
Looking at him with affection and calling him 'My lord'.   15050
He accorded Our Lord all judicial rights,
He spoke of fine learning and all about God's mercy;
His talk with the archbishop was very successful.
The king was [asking the archbishop], politely and frequently,†
That he should make him king within his rightful lands.
On an appointed day when the people were assembled

Cadwathlan was speedily crowned as the king.
Great was the rejoicing there was in the city.
Edwin knew nothing about these proceedings,
But as soon as he found out he was quite furious,   15060
And straightaway voiced his hostility: 'I am going to stir up strife,
And I am going to kill everyone whom I come across alive
Of Cadwathlan's followers: he's the falsest man there is!'
  He gathered an army of many thousand men,
Having [intended] to harry to the south of the Humber.[†]
The excellent knights consulted together,
All the wisest men who were living in the land:
They gave advice to King Edwin, who was their liege lord
That he should send his messengers to Cadwathlan the king,
Requesting him politely, as his beloved brother,   15070
And for the deep affection which their parents had enjoyed,
That to be king he should allow him, and to receive his crown,
And then he would return and go home to his people,
Back over the Humber, and there keep the peace,
And never come back any more; as long as he could be king,
Installed and supported with Almighty God's sanction,
And as long as he lived he would love Cadwathlan,
And be ready when he needed him in every land.
  Cadwathlan was listening (he was king in the south lands),
And he responded with regal expression: 15080
'Now I have heard here [the wisely worded
Request of King Edwin], who is my dear brother,[†]
I shall take some advice in this situation'
And after only a few days he would give him an answer,
Whether he would allow this, or would refuse it,
Depending on how his nobles would direct his decision.
The day was appointed, but little good it did.
When all this had been arranged, then they approached a ford,
The river was called Douglas which they moved towards;[*]
There occurred the meeting between the two kings.   15090
Edwin petitioned to his utmost ability
That Cadwathlan would permit him to wear his own crown,
And then he would love him for as long as he lived.
Nobles went into conclave to consult in this necessity:
Some advised for it, some to forbid it,
Some there supported it, some would not give assent.
  While wise knights had to arbitrate the course of the debate

The king dismounted from his steed, on the meadowland;
A desire for sleep came on him; the nobles were in council.
An attendant knight arrived, [and sat down right beside],[†]   15100
He was the king's sister's son and his name was **Brian**.
He loved his lord among men, so taking his head,
He laid it in his lap, and parted his hair.
The king fell asleep, and Brian began to weep:
The tears began dripping on the king's cheeks[*]
And the king awoke from his sleep: his cheeks were all wet!   *Brian's*
He felt all over his face, thinking it was bleeding,   *Tears*
And then looked at Brian, gazing wide-eyed,
Seeing the tears spurt from Brian's eyes:
Bitterly the warrior was crying over his king!   15110
Then the king called Cadwathlan asked him at once:
'What's the matter with you today? dear cousin, why are you crying?
People call you a tough man, have you started acting like a woman?
Tell me quickly what bad luck has come to you.'
Then Brian replied (he was an excellent knight):
'Now we can really weep, with expressions of despair,
Count ourselves trash where we used to be great.
Now you are going to undertake something never done before:
Two kings to be wielding crowns in one land!
Now we shall be weeping, we who used to be mighty,   15120
For respect has now collapsed, where there used to be rejoicing!'
    The king of the land, Cadwathlan, listened to this,
And he grew infuriated, frenzied with rage,
And at once sent a message across to King Edwin,
Commanding him quickly to go away from his realm,
'For never as long as I'm alive shall he possess a crown,
And if he wants to receive it, then I shall refuse it,
And I shall deprive him of his very life,
And seize all Northumberland into my own hands,
And control all his realm, and he'll be an outcast!'   15130
    These tidings were taken to Edwin the king,
And he grew infuriated, (extremely annoyed)
As a wild boar does[†]
When in the holt-wood he is baited by hounds,
And this answer was issued by that very angry king:
'So help me the Lord who created the daylight,
And by all the sacred relics which are found in Rome's city,
I shall possess a crown, and he is going to pay for this,

And for this he will endure the most excruciating agonies:
He shall have trackless wastes and many wildernesses, 15140
And very much heart-sorrow: his reputation will collapse!'
And so it later came to pass, quite a short time after.
  Each of them threatened the other savagely and thrust at him with
      words,
And like this they parted, each promising death.
Edwin was a warrior, and his men were warlike;
Cadwathlan was a splendid knight and he had tremendous spirit.
Edwin went across the Humber and Cadwathlan back to London;
The kings were very angry; then the war arose:
They rode and they ran, they ravaged and they burned,
They slaughtered and they captured all whom they came
      close to; 15150
Misery for the peasants who were living in the land!
  Cadwathlan was in London, and summoned his supporters:
Far and wide he sent a message through very many kingdoms:
He had [gathered] for his force fifty thousand men,[†]
Haughty battle-heroes, eager to do harm.
Edwin in the north wrote letters round at once
And sent them into Denmark,
To Galloway, and Scotland, all lands in Edwin's hands:
He summoned his army all through his territory
Until he had gathered sixty thousand men, 15160
Most courageous knights, madly keen in the fight.
Cadwathlan set out, marching from London,
On the way to Northumberland. He inflicted great harm;
He crossed over the Humber in very great haste,
And started laying waste the lands which were in Edwin's hands.
  At this Edwin the king, devoid of all cowardice,
Spoke with his knights without any delay:
'May the man who refuses to stir be ever reckoned craven!
Let's have the heart of a boar, the cunning of the raven,
Let us show the king that we are alive!' 15170
He had brass trumpets blown, to bring his army by summons,
Off he set on the march until he came to the part
Where King Cadwathlan was encamped in his tents.
Noble captains clashed together in an onslaught:
Long spears were breaking, shields were clashed in the hands,
High helmets were hacked, corslets were cracking:
Wretched soldiers were falling, saddles were emptied;

There was clamour in the throng: the earth was re-echoing;
The brooks were running with red blood;
Men fell in [heaps], their faces quite blanched.[†]   15180
The British line began to crack: there was chaos in the army.
　Like this they carried on for one complete day,
Right up to the evening; then fled Cadwathlan the king,
And Edwin pursued him to the utmost of his power.
All night Cadwathlan fled with his knights:
All he had left from his force was just five hundred knights.
They fled up to Scotland; they had sorrow on their hands!
And Edwin at once was after them with fifteen thousand men,
Very brave fighters: their vow was fulfilled;
Following their forces came folk in countless numbers.   15190
From one day to the next they were driving the king:
There is truth in the tale that they wanted to kill him!
　Cadwathlan fled to the sea, where he found ships;
At a very high price they managed to hire the ships,   *Cadwathlan*
And the ships proceeded off into Ireland   *in*
Where they made harbour; the ships arrived safely.   *Exile*
Ireland was ruled then by a very powerful king
Gille Patric was his name, a good king in his realm:[*]
He greeted Cadwathlan with courteous kisses
And gave him living-places all throughout Ireland.   15200
　So let us leave Cadwathlan and return to Edwin again.
Edwin was ruining those who lived here in this land:
He was burning towns, he was toppling castles;
In the land his army caused untold harm;
He brought under his own command all Cadwathlan's land.
　Then came some informers into this king's court,[*]
Reporting information about King Edwin –
(May they be accursed for this, in ever being born).
They were telling him tales about a young girl,
Who was Brian's gracious sister, the loveliest of ladies: 15210
She was lodged in Winchester, inside a stronghold,
So with his army Edwin made his way there;
As soon as he arrived there he seized her by force
And very capable knights carried her straight off to York.
To the bedchamber she was led, straight to the king's bed.
The king committed folly by raping that particular girl
Because the girl ever after was this very king's foe.
　There lived at the court a cleric who had come from Spain,

Pelluz was his name; he had very deep knowledge.
He knew many skills: when he gazed at the sky   15220
At the stars and at the sun, and across the broad sea
He obtained intuition [from] wind and [from] moon,[†]
From the fish where it [floated] and from the worms where they
      squirmed.[†]
   In Ireland Cadwathlan was gathering troops,
And moved to his ships with a massive force.
Pelluz from afar, by gazing at the stars,
Knew an army was coming down upon King Edwin;
So Pelluz advised him[†]
How to the best advantage he might protect this people.
Both by land and by ship Cadwathlan and his men   15230
Often started moving off to come into this land:
Each time Edwin was in front of them, denying them the harbour:
Because of Pelluz's warning they could not make landing.
Cadwathlan was despairing of his very life
That he had begun the treachery against his own sworn-brother
And out of it he himself had the greatest harm!
Cadwathlan called to him all his best knights
And announced that he wished to go off to Brittany
And there visit the king who was called **Solomon**:
It would make him feel much better because they were
      related: 15240
They came from one family, both those two kings,
Both of them were British, but they had quite lost their spirit.
   Cadwathlan came to ship, and sailed off on the waves,
And sailed along the waves feeling unhappy at heart;
They came to an island which lies beside Guernsey,[*]
And like it or not that's where they had to stop;
There they waited on the weather, for the wind was against them.
There the king next grew extremely unwell,
And had a dangerous fever: his good health had gone.
   When nine days had elapsed the king was very weak   15250
And desperately craved some venison to eat;
He called his cousin Brian and quickly informed him
That unless he had deer-meat at once he was bound to suffer death.
Brian had often been sad, but never till then were things so bad:
Brian took hounds and men experienced in hunting:
Over woods and over fields they sped very fast,
By no kind of stratagem could they catch any deer,

Neither hart nor hind could they anywhere find.
The king sent his messenger for Brian, who was taking too long.
Brian loved the king very much: his life was a misery.   15260
He thought over frequently what might be his strategy,   *Brian's*
And hit upon one solution which [turned out very well]:[†]   *Venison*
He grasped a knife for trimming nails, extremely sharp and well
        honed,
And shaved himself so closely that he took his own thigh:
In this extreme urgency he made a roast out of it!
He cooked it very quickly and took it to the king:
'May your health return, Cadwathlan, you who are my royal liege:[*]
Here I have brought you the most precious roast
Which ever on any board I have borne before a king;
Come here to me and eat some of it quick and it will restore your
        health.'
The king sat up in bed and his barons beheld him;   15271
He ate some of the roast and soon afterwards he recovered:
The king began sweating; the illness at once left him;
Within just five nights the king became completely fit,
And so the king never knew what he had partaken of.
The king became completely fit: his folk were delighted;
Wind came as they wanted it: they wound the sails up to the topmast;
The ships began moving, the minstrels were singing,
Both the sea and the sun were in a state of harmony,
The wind and the wide sea also both in concord;   15280
The flood ferried the ships, the poets were singing.
    He came ashore at Ridelet: there was rejoicing and singing,[*]
Between Dinon and the sea: the place can still be seen.
As soon as he arrived there he was courteously received:
The kings were contented in each others' company.
The king remained there, relaxing all the winter.
Afterwards came spring and the days started to lengthen:
There they started assembling a vast navy of ships;
Innumerable people disembarked on the shore.[†]
As Cadwathlan was doing this, Pelluz knew it right away,[*]   15290
By means of his magic arts residing in the elements,
And all this he found in the sky and on the ground;
By every possible means he always gave warning to King Edwin,
And fully informed him about the armed force and the ships.
    Cadwathlan was in Brittany together with King Solomon
Who was the son of his aunt and loved him very much;

And he heard it told, very many times,   *Magic*
That Pelluz the adroit who had his origin in Spain
Alerted King Edwin always by all means
To very many kinds of things which would be coming to him.   15300
Upon Cadwathlan the good there came a gloomy mood,
And he often spoke with Brian, who was his favourite man,
And they consulted together in secret communing,
Deciding that all the time Pelluz was to remain alive
Cadwathlan would not be able to come to this land
With any kind of [trick], without Edwin knowing of it.†
    Brian announced his departure: Brian was most anxious.
In his hands he carried, in silver and gold,
Treasures of many a kind in infinite numbers,
And took some stout trunks and put the valuables in them.   15310
He set out to sea and sailed on the waves;
He had on his voyage a supply of wine-tuns:
At sea and on land he had his wine sampled,
And in all respects behaved as if he were a merchant.
He embarked at Barfleur and left ship at Southampton:
There he had the wine drawn from his tuns
And courteously shared it out to all the company
Who were standing round him, both rich folk and poor,
And all who looked at him liked this merchant very much.
    After seven nights he spoke with his knights –*   15320
All behaved like his partners, as if they were merchants –
And they hired a cellar, with stout walls for a strong room,†
And they locked inside it all of their wine tuns,
And devised for their lord a different name:
They titled him '**Kinebord** the Spaniard'.
He announced that he wished to travel far and wide round this land
And find out where he would be able to market his wine freely.
Off he set by night with one of his knights:
Onwards he travelled, up into London
And immediately went close to Westminster,   15330
Asking for tidings of Edwin the king.
At once people told him what they found to be true:
That the king lived up in York with all of his men
In the greatest content; he had many attendants.
    Brian set out with just one companion:
Secretly he moved away, out of London city,
On the road which led to York, rage in his heart.

When he had travelled for seven whole nights　　　　　　　　*Brian's*
He then encountered a pilgrim, a pikestaff in his hand,　　　　*Disguise*
Coming in a hurry from the court of the king.　　　　　　　　15340
Brian enquired of him all his experiences;
The pilgrim told him all he wanted to know.
Brian exchanged with him all of his garments,
And each travelled off in the direction which suited him.
Brian found a smith who was talented in smithying,
And announced he was a pilgrim but he hadn't got a staff with him:
A couple of days earlier he had lost it in his lodgings.
They settled on the charge and the smith began to forge
A pikestaff, very long, very massive, and very strong:
The point was very sharp and the stick was very special.　　　　15350
He took the staff in his hand and walked across the land
Until soon he arrived at the king's palace.
Brian went walking up, Brian went walking down,
He was not able to hear any news of his sister.
And he did not dare enquire for fear of the king's men.
　　Then it happened one morning sent by Our Lord himself
That the king was feeding all those who were needy,
All of the desitute who dwelt in the city.
They had been given orders to come in haste to the castle:
In thousands upon thousands they started thronging in.　　　　15360
Brian went indoors with other down-and-out people:
His condition looked exactly as if he were a cripple;
All his clothes were in tatters (and yet he wasn't born to that!).
One of them shoved him this way, the other shoved him that way:
He really wasn't used to people acting like this;
He held his pikestaff by his side and sat down among the others.
The king began serving him, with all his warrior knights;
The queen and her ladies-in-waiting all carried out the drink.
　　And very soon after it then came to pass
That the young girl **Galarne** came walking that way:　　　　*Galarne*
She had a mazer-bowl in her hands in which she carried
　　　　drink.
　　　　　　　　　　　　　　　　　　　　　　　　　　15371
Then she saw Brian there, her own beloved brother,
Looking like a beggar man, although he was a noble.
As soon as the girl caught sight of him she moved in his direction,
Drawing from her fingers one of her rings,
And putting into his hand a ring of red gold;
And the virtuous maiden Galarne spoke in this way:

'Take this gold, you poor creature; God be gracious to you, *
And buy yourself clothes with it which can protect you from the
     cold.'
Then he knew for sure that his sister recognised him,   15380
And these were the words which the good Brian spoke:
'May the Lord who made the light of day reward you for this,
That you have given your gold to this lame man!'
The young girl concealed herself among the beggarfolk,
Between two [windows] the girl seated herself†
As she spoke to her brother; the better she felt for it,
And gave him information all about the king's courtiers,
Pointing out to him Pelluz, the scholar who came from Spain,
And he began to look closely at this man he hated most of all.
When they had spoken together they swiftly separated,   15390
Because neither of them wanted, for their equal weight of gold,
That the king should discover that they were together,
For they would both at once be put to death, by beheading or by
     hanging.
   All the folk had finished eating and had risen from their seats:
Drunken men were singing loudly: the folk there were rowdy.
Pelluz was nearby and had charge of the drinking-bowl;
Brian steered his course to him since he had caused him great
     anguish,
Taking his pikestaff in his hand he concealed it underneath his cape,
And made his way so far along that he came out behind him,
And in the midst of all the crush he stabbed him in the back   15400
So that he ran him right through and out beneath his breast.
And he made his escape, leaving his pike behind,
And slipped off among the crowd; and then he was safe,
And quickly went away, out of the king's court,
Always pressing on his way, as to the south it lay.
   When he came to the end of it, he arrived at Exeter,
Where he found without delay many of his knights,
Asking them eagerly about his liege lord.
And Brian then reported the welcome news to them,
Saying that Cadwathlan would be coming at once now   15410
With so great an army from so many kinds of country
That King Edwin would not dare to make any opposition
Nor in any town anywhere would be dare to wait for him.
Those in Devon heard this, and the men of Dorchester,
And the men of Cornwall: they were exuberant with joy.

Brian sent his messengers across the sea to Brittany,
Sending the king information, both verbal and written,
About all he had done, and that Pelluz now lay dead,
Requesting him with all speed to come to this country;
And the king did so, as fast as he was able.   15420
And Brian sent messengers into Southampton,*
And had all his precious treasures transported to him.†
At once all the soldiers who wanted to side with him
Came immediately over into Exeter,
And sternly-intentioned men by then controlled the borough.
Cadwathlan heard the news and the king was delighted,
And summoned an army over in Brittany,
Until he had obtained three hundred high-masted ships,
And he had all the tackle for them which they required.
And King Solomon sent out far and wide,   15430
And he began the journey, accompanied by his Bretons,
This was, to be specific, with two hundred ships,
To assist his kinsman, King Cadwathlan.

They had the weather they wanted, a wind of the very best:
They adjusted their luffs and hauled up their sails,*
Glided over the sea-stream, as seemed to them splendid.
Then they arrived at Totnes, both of the kings,
Solomon the good and Cadwathlan the courageous:
The inhabitants rejoiced over their sovereign king.

Now there was in the Eastlands a king who was called
  Penda:*   15440
At that time he administered those who lived under Mercian laws,
And he loved Edwin and Edwin loved him,   *Penda*
And he was always willing to give Edwin advice when needed,
And Penda heard it told in very true report
That Brian held Exeter closed securely from within,
So King Penda then sent far and wide around
And summoned an army and onwards he sped,
And marched down to Exeter with innumerable troops,
And very closely besieged the borough of Exeter.

Brian the stalwart with two hundred knights   15450
Was inside it there and defending the town.
As soon as the tidings had arrived in Totnes harbour
With Cadwathlan the king, of how Brian was besieged,
He got men to blow trumpets to muster his forces
And marched straight down the road which led towards Exeter,

Dividing his doughty knights into three parties;
And the king, in a passion, began to shout like this:
'Let every good knight set upon them straight, *
For we are good knights, with arms well supplied;
Let's rescue Brian, who has been my man from birth,   15460
For if they captured Brian they would certainly kill him,
And then they would hang him and destroy all his companions,
And us, right after that, with all the force they have.'
   They started riding, let their spears go gliding;
Broad clubs were cracking, shafts were splintering,
Gold-painted shields were very quickly spoiled;
There fell the knights, faces grew blanched there;
Strewn over the wide fields, fated men expired;
Blood ran down the pathways in very broad streams;
A nobleman there was not more honoured than a peasant.   15470
Fully seventeen thousand then were slaughtered there
Of the Mercian men who had come down there;
Then they lowered their bright battle-standards,
Quickly tossed away their shields: the earth was resounding.
These most dejected of all folk then took to flight,
And Cadwathlan after them as hard as he could,
And with his own hands he captured King Penda
(He was **Merwal's** father, grandfather to **Mildburg**). *
They took Penda captive and put him in fetters
Within Exeter's walls, and they kept close watch on him.   15480
   So mysteriously it befell in all the fighting
That Penda the king was not wounded by anything.
And Cadwathlan protected him well with every provision,
And most sumptuously was he fed, and sumptuously he went to bed.
When one week had gone by, Penda took aside a knight,
A most circumspect man who could speak very well,
And called him for advice and told him of his anxieties,
Earnestly begging him, for the love of Our Lord,
That he should converse with Cadwathlan, who was his own liege
    lord,
So that he would come to terms, through the Most High
    God,   15490
And he would do homage to him, and enhance his reputation,
By day and by night, he and all of his knights.
   The knight went away from him to Cadwathlan the king:
There did he meet him and courteously greet him,

And acted like an honest man (may he have honour for it,
For it is always by loyal men that loyalty is preserved):
'Good health to you, Cadwathlan, my own sovereign liege!*
The captive King Penda here to you has sent me,
And craves your compassion now and for evermore,
And he will do you homage and give you his son as hostage,   15500
And hold his kingdom from you and acknowledge you as overlord,
And in every country as you need him he'll be ready:
He will be your most special man in the face of every other man.'
   Then with most gracious expression his answer then gave
Cadwathlan the courageous, the king of the Southland:
'If Penda is willing to keep to what he promises me to do,
To deliver me his son, his gold and his great treasure,
And ever to be my true man, and never devise my harm,
And whether or not he likes it, never to betray me,
Then I would consider carefully such a contingency.'   15510
Then the good knight immediately responded most promptly:
'Look, as I hope for life eternal for him I shall stand bail,
I'll be one, and as supporters I'll have a hundred knights,
On pain of forfeiting all our lands, our silver and our gold.
And as I hope for God's pity, there is more that he wishes:
He has a lovely sister in the eastern quarter,
No more beautiful woman does the bright sun shine upon;
The King of France, **Louis**, desires her, true it is,
And as her morning-gift he will give her Le Mans,*
And have her as his Queen, that sweet young girl, **Helen**.   15520
And so I'm telling you honestly, as if I were your brother:
It's much better for you if you have her yourself:
Through her you might gain the goodwill of her race,
And gain the whole of your kingdom in your own control,
And live in the land and rule your own realm.'
   Then answered Cadwathlan, who was king in the land:
'It seems reason to me too, what you suggest to do,
If you could, by your Christian faith, enact for me this agreement,
Then I should give you in recompense all of Devonshire,
All for the love of Helen; have her come to me in haste!'   15530
   The knight went away with a very large retinue
To the castle of Dover, on the sea shore;
There he took charge of Helen, radiantly lovely,
And conducted her on her way into Winchester.
There was much rejoicing: the citizens were celebrating.

There Cadwathlan the king came to meet with them:
The maiden he wedded and took to his bed:
There was a rich wedding and boundless rejoicing.
　It happened one morning as the household started stirring,
When the king had confirmed his entire contract,　　　　　15540
That he took a large detachment and sent them for King Penda,
Where he was kept most secure in the castle in Exeter,
And, with great affection, instructed him to come up to London.
Penda came to London city: he was received with dignity
As Cadwathlan the courageous greeted him with affection,
And Penda became his vassal there: this enhanced his honour.
Then the inhabitants of London were the happiest of all people.
　Later it happened, not very long after,
That Cadwathlan went travelling far and wide in this land:
With all who revered him he made reconciliation;　　　　　15550
From all who rejected him he took their very lives,
And from all their dependants and all who'd held them dear;
And then in haste he journeyed on towards the Humber,
And was laying waste the territory with the greatest terrors.
　This news came to Edwin, and to all those who loved him:
They were in very great terror of Cadwathlan's terrorism;
Edwin took ambassadors and sent them off to Saxony; *
He dispatched men to Denmark, he dispatched them to Norway,
Into the Welsh lands, and into Scotland,
Into the Orkneys, and into Galloway,　　　　　　　　　15560
Off into Iceland, and into Friesland,
Away into Jutland where men were full of mettle:
He begged them to come at once, with well cared-for weapons,
To drive out the British who were too bent on doing harm,
And when by means of sword-blades he had hacked down the British,
He intended to put in these men's hands the whole of this kingdom,
With the reservation that he be called king of the land;
This land he wanted to divide among those troops entirely;
But all too little did he know what was to happen later!
　There came towards the land, towards Edwin the king,　　15570
By sea and by land many different kinds of people:
There came seven kings and six sons of kings,
Seventeen earls and sixty thousand warriors.
Never has he yet been born in any borough whatever
Who could by any means of reckoning count the other peoples;
It has never yet been said nor in books has it been read

That there had ever been before any army so great
Together in England for any king whatever.
    Edwin started marching with his enormous army,
And Cadwathlan went after him with innumerable folk.   15580
Where they took stand behind their shields the place is called
    Hatfield: *Battle of*
Edwin at his end pitched all his tents,   *Hatfield*
His banners and his boundaries and his bands of men, *
And Cadwathlan the courageous confronted him at once:
There the countless hosts came charging together:
They fought furiously: fated men fell there;
The brooks there were gushing with gigantic surges
Of deep crimson blood: the chaos was boundless.
Helmets were ringing, warriors were falling,   15590
Shields were shattering, soldiers were expiring –
In the first onrush fully fifty thousand
Very brave warriors; their boasting would be weaker!
    There in the army of Edwin were the most dejected of all men,
And Edwin instantly himself the most abject of kings:
There Edwin was slain, and both his two sons;   *Edwin*
The seven kings fell there and the six sons of kings,   *Killed*
His earls and his barons, his knights and his freemen,
The squire and the stable-lad were both in one condition;
They had no compassion, not of great nor of lesser men,   15600
But all the host was slaughtered, and deprived of their life's days.
From the fight fled just one man, who was Edwin's youngest son,
A most courteous young man, who was called **Osric**;
He had as his companions but two hundred knights.
These went into the woodlands and there they took refuge,
And burned Cadwathlan's lands and dealt evilly with him,
Killing his people in many kinds of ways.
    The news came to Cadwathlan, who was king in the country,
How Osric son of Edwin had adopted outlaw's habits.
Cadwathlan took a large troop and sent them off to the
    woods,   15610
Where they discovered Osric and did battle against him:
There they killed Osric and all his associates, *
And now King Cadwathlan was the most exultant of all warriors,
And Cadwathlan was now called King over the Angles;
Penda was an under-king as were more whom he found pleasing.
    Cadwathlan had killed, of the kin of Edwin,

All who were close relatives, excluding just one,
He was called **Oswald**; in the Lord's name he was bold: * [OSWALD]
He was from Edwin's family and a man he had loved much,
And he was the most high-ranking of Edwin's close relations.   15620
   Oswald took into his hands the whole assembly of Edwin's land:
The earls and the warriors all became his followers;
He was held to be the high King beyond the River Humber.
   Cadwathlan heard this, and spoke in this way to his earls:
'Let's now summon an army through all of my regions!
The moment I win back my land, the next moment Oswald has it,
But for this shall be decreed to him the most terrible of all torments:
For the sake of the kingdom I am going to kill him,
And fell to the ground all of his army,
And all those he comes from I intend to destroy,   15630
And that will teach him a lesson for taking over a kingdom!
I want to allay his mighty arrogance: he's the most abhorred of men
      for me!'
Cadwathlan summoned an army, a huge one, in this country,
And travelled towards the Humber, all prepared for battle.
Oswald the elect of the Most High God heard this,
And drew to him all the host which in his region he possessed
But at once renounced the battle (reluctantly though he did it),
And advanced ever onward;
And Cadwathlan pursued him but he could not overtake him.
Then Cadwathlan was afraid because he and the Scots
      were foes   15640
Since he had so severely injured those northern peoples,
And he took the decision, in such extreme need,
That he would go back, since there he had trouble,
And would hand over to Penda, who was his under-king,
His followers and forces, to put to flight from the place
Edwin's kinsman Oswald, and drive him from the land.
And as he had described, so Cadwathlan dispatched:
Back again he went into this land
And in the northern area he set up King Penda
To expel Oswald out of this land.   15650
   Oswald had heard that Cadwathlan had returned
And that Penda was staying there to drive him from the land.
Now in his plans this King Oswald acted very boldly,
And he set marching against him his enormous army,
Opposing that King Penda, to expel him from there.

Penda thought carefully how he could act treacherously:
He sent word to Oswald, to the northern king,
Proclaiming his wish to work towards peace
And in short time to confer with him and establish peace and amity,
And be reconciled and reunited just as if they were brothers,   15660
And travel from those limits to Cadwathlan the king,
And allow King Oswald to have his realm and his lands.
    The day and the place they appointed to establish the peace,
And very soon after this they came there together.
Oswald came there much beforehand (he was elect to God's own
        hand);
The place was called Heavenfield where Oswald placed his tents.
Swiftly he had raised a great and glorious cross,
And instructed all his forces to fall down on their knees
And to pray to Almighty God, through his great and gentle heart
That he would have mercy on them for all their misdeeds,   15670
And that if Penda should break the truce, Our Lord would avenge it.
    As these prayers were ending so there came Penda riding,
And these were the words of the most treacherous of all kings:
'Oswald, you are welcome; joy is granted to you:*
You have your entire kingdom, but take your silver and your gold,
Take one hundred hounds, take one hundred hawks,
Take one hundred chargers, take gold-embroidered garments,
And dispatch these as greetings to Cadwathlan the king.
And so with these you may establish peace and amity for yourself
        with him,
And I shall remain in your place, so that the love may flourish. 15680
And also I should like to say to you one separate secret counsel,
On how you might begin so that it will never be undone,
And so call to you two men, and let both of them be your true men,
And I'll call two to me as well, who will give good advice.'
    Then this falsest of all kings rode out on the field,
And Oswald rode out on the field: he had neither spear nor shield;
Penda drew out his sword and he struck and killed Oswald:
This was Saint Oswald who by murder was killed,
While Penda took to flight with all of his force.
This Oswald's own knights immediately caught sight of,   15690
And after them they set with all the strength they had:
They slew a great part of the people in the host,
And King Penda himself only just got away,
But all the same he rode off, this man who betrayed Saint Oswald.

Penda came to King Cadwathlan, here in this country
And described to the king exactly how he had behaved.
It was agreeable to the king, except for one single thing:
He repented very quickly of this piece of treachery.
    Now this Oswald who was killed by murder
Had one solitary brother, and there was no other: 15700
He was called **Oswy**, and he was very hardy;   [OSWY]
The warlords of the north appointed him as their king,
For they were deeply distressed because of their lord's death.
Oswy took into his hands all his brother's royal lands.
Oswy's uncle had two sons, who were exceedingly proud men,
And there were more of the family who were most ambitious:
They were extremely envious about the kingdom
And caused much dissention and often fought against him,
Intending to kill him so they could get his kingdom.
But Oswy was a stern knight, and this he demonstrated: 15710
All those who bore him ill-will he drove out of the kingdom;
With all haste he chased them out over the Humber
So that there was none remaining of those whom he hated,
And so they proceeded towards that King Penda,
Complaining to Penda about Oswy the king,
That he had driven them out from all their rightful land
And they requested Penda, the king of the East-lands
To give them assistance in annihilating Oswy,
And they would become his men and exalt his reputation,
If he would execute Oswy, by beheading or by hanging.   15720
Then Penda responded, the King of the East-lands:
'You get no support from me, since Oswy is my enemy*
Because I killed Oswald, the bravest of all kings,
And his brother Oswy is a fine knight, not cowardly in the least:
If he could catch me he would surely kill me!
But go to Cadwathlan, who is king in this land,
And if he's willing to send the men of his land,
Knights of good fame, coming from Cornwall,
And from the Welsh lands, along with silver and gold,
Then I shall instantly treat Oswy most harshly,   15730
Driving him from the land, to disgrace his people,
Or slay him with sword's edge, most hated of all families!'†
    The knights then proceeded to Cadwathlan the king:
To Cadwathlan they came with their false claims;
They recounted to the king all that they required.

It happened at one time, just at Whitsuntide,
That the king ordered all those in the land to come up to London.
All who desired his peace and wished for friendship with the king.
To the place came kings and also battle-leaders,
To the place came earls, to the place came barons,   15740
Bishops came along there, and men of book-learning;
The great and the humble: to London they all came,
People of all types who had true love for the king.
And during that period the king wore his crown.
There was much rejoicing with the valiant king,
For the king was very trustworthy and observed the truth closely.
    When all these people had come to one place,
Then up stood King Penda before King Cadwathlan,
And started talking like this with his false speeches:
'My lord, we have come, as you had commanded,   15750
All your native subjects, the English and the British,   *Penda's*
Earls and barons, knights too, and clerics,   *Plot*
And we who are your kings, who are your underlings.
But Oswy kept on saying he refuses ever to come,
Refuses to observe your edicts, but promises to do harm.
You are lacking in the mettle which Oswy possesses,
He is indeed contemptuous of visiting your court!
But if you would afford me, and grant me your leave,
And if you will assist me and entrust me with an army
And as much of your gold and treasure as seems to you
        good,   15760
I shall be off quickly and cross over the Humber
And there make Oswy the most abject of all kings:
In spite of all his power he shall not find the place
Where I shall not be able to put him into your hands,
Either alive or dead: this seems to me a good plot.
And if you refuse to do this, then you'll get the worst of it,
For Oswy is the kind of man who'll bring you disgrace.'
    Then Cadwathlan the courageous gave his reply:
'Penda, I'm telling you absolutely that Oswy's in some difficulty,
Or he's lying bedridden, restrained by some disease,   15770
Or else foreign nations have invaded his region,
For [I] can never [believe] that he would not come to me†
When I commanded all to come, in peace, in amity and love.
But Penda, go out of here right away; I shall, among my earls,
Hold my secret conclave and discover my conclusions

About whether I shall grant you the thing for which you're asking,
And I shall send for Oswy by my royal summons,
And order him in all haste to come to my realm.'
    Penda went outside there; an earl was his partner,
And Cadwathlan remained indoors, with very many men.   15780
Cadwathlan, king of the Angles spoke up like this: *Cadwathlan's*
'You who are in this meeting are all of you my men,   *Council*
And you have all heard what King Penda has been saying,
And how he wants to set about quite destroying King Oswy
If I wish to furnish him with my people for support,
And I want you to advise me about such an enterprise:
Whether I have Oswy removed or get him to come to me;
And if he neglects to come here in spite of my message
Then afterwards I'll get my army to humble him totally!'
    Then a Welsh king in the audience grew extremely
        annoyed: 15790
His title was King **Margadud**: may he be sorriest among men,
For he always threatened the English men with the greatest harm;
Like this spoke Margadud – in South Wales he was a duke –:
'Hear now, Cadwathlan, what I wish to make clear to you:
You have spoken of your intentions: but this is not a good plan.
It is a very long time since the British race came here,
And among them our ancestors, British aristocrats they were,
And the British people invaded this country,
And governed it a long time according to their wishes;
All the time it was in their hands it was known as 'Brutus's land'.
Now from that land we have nothing but the western edge.   15801
When the British had been inhabitants here for very many winters
Then the English men arrived with their evil artifices;
They were full of trickery and took over this land entirely,
And rapidly deceived their lord and all of his people
By giving their king in marriage a queen who was heathen
And came out of Saxony; to us this race is repulsive,
And by means of that queen they killed off our kin here.
And so the English race have retained the land which is our right,
So that never since then have we been able to get hold of it.   15810
King Penda is English, and so is Oswy; you know this.
You let those hounds perish together,
Each of them to eat the other, as a dog does his brother,
And let their little puppies roam about alongside them,
Each of them kill the other until there's none left alive,

And if Oswy comes out on top, and manages to win the battle,
We shall tear him to pieces and drag him down to the ground,
His land and those who live there, and his laws we'll demolish;
And if Penda comes off best, and manages to win the contest,
Penda is your own man anyway, with all his royal lands.   15820
So then you've got the English lands all within your own hands,
And your entire reputation; this is how you can conquer,
And live out your life as you would most like to.
You won't find anyone again who will dare to challenge you.'
    Then one man responded who was prominent at court:
'Now listen to me, Cadwathlan, listen to me a minute.
There is no better plan than Margadud has pronounced,
And if you won't do that, then you'll get the worst of it,
And so will all your people, the longer you delay the crisis.'
With this declaration delivered by the Briton   15830
Penda was called for and came into the tribunal
And Cadwathlan granted him everything he wanted.
Then Penda was delighted and very excited.
Penda and his knights got to horse without delay,
Sped off on their journey towards Northumberland,
And Oswy heard reports that Penda was pursuing him
And got his army ready and advanced towards Penda;
They commenced battle: they were both determined;
Furiously they fought, for they were bitter foes.
Vast numbers of fated men fell to the earth.   15840
Then in the late afternoon, when the sun began sinking
Oswy was slain and deprived of his life-days,*
And his son, and his uncle and some five of the earls;
There were nine whole thousand of the northern fighters
Slain on that day: the retinue was reduced,
And King Penda too was severely wounded there,
And from there away he went eastwards to his lands.
    Oswy had just one son, his name was **Osric**;
For a time he had been with Cadwathlan the king;
Fed in his court and affectionately fostered.   15850
Osric begged Cadwathlan, as a man must do of his lord,
That he might become his vassal and receive his father's land.
Cadwathlan granted him everything he craved:
He delivered into his hands all his father's royal land,   [OSRIC]
Ordering him to have it and to hold it with joy.
    Cadwathlan was a good king, in accordance with his nature.

404

He was king here for forty-seven years.
Then he went to London for the people's pleasure,
And he held a banquet with the inhabitants of London.
He kept on eating at some fish with immense appetite:* 15860
Before the fish was eaten up, the king was taken very ill;
For a week and a day in the throes of sickness the king lay;
There was no other help for it: the king afterwards died.
They buried him in London; the people were in mourning.
   Cadwathlan had a son; he was called **Cadwalader**:
He was Penda's sister's son: he came from kings on both sides.
This man succeeded to the realm after his father's time. CADWALADER
The man was very amiable: his subjects adored him;
He was a very good knight, and very stern in the fight,
But in his time there occurred disaster in the nation: 15870
First the corn failed throughout the whole realm;* *Famine*
After that it was extremely dear and all the people were dying
So that you might travel for seven whole nights
Without being able to find bread, no, not at any price,
In town or in country (people were to be pitied),
Nor any folk in country regions who were not desperately hungry.
   When that had long been continuing throughout all the country,
Another distress came very soon after it
In that a most virulent disease descended on the cattle:
A peasant driving his plough with a team of four fine oxen,* 15880
Would sometimes bring home only half of his oxen,
Another time brought home one, yet another brought not one.†
And so this endured a long while in the land.
Soon after this incalculable sorrows
Came to the people right through this kingdom:
Upon the [human] race a mortal sickness fell;†
Earls were dying, barons were dying,
Lords were dying, servants were dying,
The learned were dying, the lay-folk were dying,
The older folk were dying, the younger folk were dying, 15890
The women were dying, the weanlings were dying,*
So that not in any region could the folk in the country
Bury the dead. So quickly did they die
That often into the plague-pit where the dead man was being put
The living would expire on top of the dead.
And so it went on widely throughout the English nation
So that folk were fleeing the land in every district:

Many hundred towns were abandoned by inhabitants
So that few people could be found travelling through the land.
    The king of the country, Cadwalader, was distraught: 15900
He could not flee, for the disgrace of it; for the danger, could not stay.
All the same, he thought carefully how he might proceed:
He amassed all his treasures and his favourite men
And crossed south over the sea into Brittany,   *Cadwalader*
And there took up lodging with **Alain** the king,   *in Exile*
Who was the son of Solomon, that saintly king
Who had so loved Cadwathlan as long as his days lasted.
There Alain the king received King Cadwalader,
Providing for him in the land all that he wanted.
For eleven years the king remained there,   15910
And for eleven years the sorrows remained here,
Namely hunger and hardship (the people simply had no food),[†]
And the virulent disease which the human race endured,
So that people fled into the woods and were living in the caves,
They slept out in stone-quarries and lived [like] wild creatures:[†]
They lived off bark and wood, they lived off bulbs and weeds,
Off berries and off roots: there was nothing else to help them.
    When eleven years had almost elapsed
The sun began to shine and the rain began to rain,
The disease began to abate and men began emerging: 15920
From the woods they came and were living in villages;
They were speaking to each other and conversing together,
And they took up their messengers and sent them to Saxony,
Declaring to their kin how they had died from a disease
And what they had experienced for eleven years,
And how that illness had abated and how they were building villages,
And how they had productive land, plenty of gold and silver,
And asking them to come with speed, here to their rightful country,
For the Britons who used to be here were still living in exile
And dared not mingle at all among the English men,   15930
And anyway they'd no idea of the affairs of the English.
These were the messages they sent out to Saxon lands.
    The Saxon nobility listened to these messengers
And then fast towards the sea fifty thousand made off
Of men brave in battle, with shields and with byrnies,
With women and children; to this country they went.
In the first onrush came three hundred ships;
Then after that sailed here sixty in convoy:

In sixes and sevens, in tens and elevens,
In twelves and in twenties, in thirties and forties.   15940
With them came out of Saxony **Athelstan** the aristocrat;   ATHELSTAN
In London they crowned him, and appointed him as king.
On a concubine this man was begotten by King **Edward**;
This was the first English man who acquired the whole of England:
He was crowned and anointed: this entire land was his own,
And afterwards he lived here for the length of sixteen years.
    It happened in [former days] long [before] this time,[††]
That there was a noble man here who was known as **Ine**.
The king went to Rome, to the supreme pontiff,
And there he visited with pleasure the altar of Saint Peter,   15950
Taking there as a gift his own precious treasures.
He did still more then in respect for Saint Peter:
From every single house in which a householder was living
(If the wife he had wedded were in the same dwelling)
The King granted one penny to the House of St Peter;
Ine was the first man who initiated Peter's pence.
    When King Ine was dead and his laws had been put aside,
Then that silver tribute ceased for sixty-five years,
Until Athelstan arrived here in this land,
And had been living here for a full fifteen years.   15960
The king kissed [the Pope's] feet and saluted him respectfully[†]
And granted once again that tribute which King Ine had made before,
And so things have [stood] ever since in this land:[†]
The Lord knows how long these customs will continue.[*]
    These tidings came soon to Cadwalader the king,
Into Brittany where he was residing
With Alain the king, who came from the same clan:
He was given information about all of this nation:
How Athelstan had come travelling here out of Saxon lands
And how he had taken all Engle-land into his own hands,   15970
And how he appointed the law courts, and how he appointed his
        parliament,[*]
And how he established the shires, and created forests for deer,
And how he set up manor courts and how he divided counties in
        hundreds,
And the names of the villages in the Saxon language,
And how he was creating guilds, great ones and glorious,
And churches he was founding in the style of the Saxons,
And in Saxon he identified the names of the people;

And he was told about all the events of this land.

    Cadwalader was distressed that he was still alive:

He would have liked to be dead rather than to be alive;   15980

His emotions were sorrowful, his followers were sombre;

With his friends he would frequently discuss

How he might voyage, and regain his birthright,

And in what manner he might against Athelstan fight,

And win back his inheritance into his own possession

Which Athelstan, and his knights also were holding unjustly.

Some advised him to fight, some to make a truce

By which he could from Athelstan hold his lands, and be his vassal.

Under these circumstances he summoned an army

From all of the men whom he could procure,   15990

And assembled all the ships which were floating along the sea,

Intending with a show of strength to step upon this shore.

    When the army was ready and the ships all equipped,

A wind came from the south, the direction which suited them.

Then the king announced: 'Now aboard, and hurry!'

And the king went into church to perform his Christian duties

And there he heard mass sung by a celebrated priest.

They king remained on his knees, calling out to Christ,

And he prayed to Our Lord who governs our deeds

That from himself directly he would send him a sign,   16000

If this were agreeable to the Heavenly Judge,

As to whether he should advance or abandon the attempt.

As he was addressing God he fell into a trance,

And then he slept deeply, and gladness was granted him

From Our Lord himself who made this light of day.

    Then the king dreamed, as he slept on his knees   *Cadwalader's*

That there came in front of him a wondrously fair man   *Dream*

Who addressed these words to the King of the Britons:

'Awake now, Cadwalader; you are precious to Christ,*

And prepare for your voyage and pass swiftly to Rome;   16010

You will find there a pope, a priest among the very best,

Who will give you absolution for all your worldly actions

So that all your sins will drop away from you,

And you will become pure entirely by God's provision†

From all your misdeeds, through the might of Our Lord,

And then you will depart and go to the heavenly kingdom,

For never more may you own the Angles' land

But instead the men of Almaigne will be owners of England,

And never more may British men be its possessors
Until the time arrives, which was announced long ago,   16020
Which Merlin the prophet pronounced in his words.
Then the British shall soon turn towards Rome
And draw out all your bones from their marble tomb
And carry them rejoicing away with them again,
Enshrined in silver and gold, into Britain's land.
Then at once the British will become emboldened:
Everything they begin to do will happen as they wish:
Then within Britain bliss will be abundant,
With fruits and fine weather, exactly as men want.'
    When Cadwalader awoke this seemed to him miraculous: 16030
He was deeply over-awed, horribly afraid
And to what sort of thing would occur as it was betokened to him
      there.
Frequently he had consultation, frequently he took counsel,
And revealed this to the king who resided in that land
Who was known as Alain, Cadwalader's nearest kinsman.
The king sent his messengers through all his territory
And issued a summons for all the wise book-scholars
Relating to them the revelation of Cadwalader the king.
There they proceeded to counsel, there they proceeded to commune,
And advised him to proceed as God had revealed to him to act; 16040
So there he abandoned his ships and his supporters,
His way and his wishes; secretly he called upon
Yuni and **Ivor**: he held them both most dear;
Ivor was his step-son, and Yuni was his sister's son;
Both of them he loved, both of them he cherished;
They were both of them knights and very well equipped.
    Like this spoke Cadwalader, who was the King of Britain:
'Both Yuni and Ivor, you two are of my people:
Listen to my instruction; you shall not regret it ever!
From heaven there have come to me signs from most high
      God   16050
That I must journey to Rome, to the illustrious Pope.
The pope is called **Sergius**, who has charge of Peter's House;
Me and my wife he is to bless and to shrive,
And there we shall both live out the last of our days.
As long as is for ever, me again you shall see never;
But here to you two I am handing what I still hold of the Welsh lands,
So take this great army and travel to the land,

And rule it in delight as long as you can defend it,
And I entreat both the two of you, by the King of Heaven
That each of you two must love the other as if he were his brother,
Then have that land for ever more, to your own lives' end,　　16061
And possess it in joy, and all your progeny.

'Yuni, it has all been revealed to me, as you will now perceive
(For Merlin the wise declared this in words)
Concerning my departing and of my excessive grieving,
And Sibyl the sagacious set it down in book-form
That I am to fulfil all my Lord's will.
Let each now go his way; I bid all farewell and good day!'

Cadwalader hastened until he reached Rome,
Where he found **Sergius**, the saintly man who was Pope:　　16070
He absolved Cadwalader who had been the King of Britain.
The king had not lived there above four-and-a-half years[†]
When a sickness came upon him, as God wished things to happen;
Eleven days before May he passed away from this life
And sent his soul forth to the heavenly King.
His bones are securely encased in a golden coffin,
And there they shall still remain until the days have arrived
Which Merlin in days of yore determined with his words.

Let us now go again to Yuni, and to Ivor his sworn-brother:
They assembled an army far and wide throughout the
　　　country;　　16080
Forwards they journeyed fast, with five hundred ships:
It was not at all long before they came to the Welsh lands:
All the British had been scattered across crags and across cliffs,
Around churches and round monasteries, around woods and across
　　　mountains.
As soon as they were told that there had sailed into their land
With Ivor and Yuni ten times fifty
Ships which were brimful with very bold Britons,
From every region these Britons travelled to the Welsh lands,
And they loved their own laws and the customs of their nation,
And so they still live there, and they will do for ever more.　　16090
And the English kings hold sway in this land,
And the British having lost this land and those who live here,
Since then have never more been the kings here;
So far it hasn't come, that actual day, let future things be as they may.
Let come what must come: let God's will be done!

AMEN

410

NOTES

1 This self-introduction was probably written after Lawman had completed his translation of Wace's *Rome de Brut*. King Alfred prefaces his translation of Gregory's *Cura Pastoralis* with an account of the genesis of his translation. The standard modern study of medieval prefaces in Alastair Minnis, *The Medieval Theory of Authorship* (1984); see esp. Chap. 5. Lawman is using an informal version of the Aristotelian Preface, with its four divisions of *Causa efficiens* (i.e. the author [L 1–13]); *causa materialis* (source materials [L 15–23]); *causa formalis* (or: *forma tractandi, forma tractatus*: procedural method and arrangement [L 24–8]); *causa finalis* (aim of the writer and purpose of work [L 29–35]). Like the later Ranulph Higden (and, but ironically, Chaucer) he is a compiling historian by intention (in actual fact he seems to have used Wace almost exclusively), and gives his name partly in the later medieval spirit of self-assertion (no longer is the author the agent of divine authority) but chiefly, it seems, to serve the final cause: prayer for his soul and his family.

Wace in his preface merely introduces himself and the subject-matter: the kings of England. Wace does not tell us of his patron/recipient, Eleanor: this information comes from Lawman; and nor does Lawman tell us of his: only MS O tells us (3) that he lived 'with the good knight', or perhaps 'with' (*wid*) means 'near, close to, alongside'. The possible implication of this is discussed in the Introduction.

2–5 *Liefnoth*: MS C has *leouenaðes* (OE *Lēofnōð*); the name occurs at least eleven times in records, three of which are from Worcs. [H]; but MS O has *Leucais*, which D&W derive from *Lēofeca*, a hypocoristic (pet-name) form of *Lēofnōð*; it may simply be a scribal error. *Redstone* is a red sandstone cliff near the Severn, from which, after Lawman's time, a ferry ran to Wales. *Missal*: this is Hall's interpretation, followed by D&W, of MS *bock*; MS O has *bokes*, and B&W prefer to translate 'read books'. MS C has *boc* as pl. in line 24, but *bocken* in 11027, which itself is *on boke* in MS O; in 10907 *a boke* means either 'in the Bible' or 'in books'. It is not very likely that Lawman would have owned many books.

16–19 The three sources Lawman claims are: (i) Bede's *History of the English Church and People* in the Old English version made under King Alfred's sponsorship in the late 9thc. (ii) an unidentified book 'by St Albin and St Augustine' by which critics assume Lawman was referring to

Bede's original Latin version of his *History*: near the opening of this work Albin is mentioned (not as a saint: he was never canonised) and much of Book I deals with Augustine and the conversion; Albin was born over 100 years after Augustine's death, but he was Abbot of St Augustine's in Canterbury, and some form of scribal error may have occurred here. Eric Stanley ('Laȝamon's Antiquarian Sentiments' *MÆ* 38 (1969], 32–2) suggests that Lawman made a common identification of Albin with Alcuin and may have actually seen a book containing works by Alcuin and Augustine of Hippo (not the converter of England). (iii) Wace's *Roman de Brut*, a Norman-French translation of GoM in octosyllabic couplets, completed as Wace says in 1155. Lawman's main written source was in fact Wace.

42 Paris's surname, *Alexander*, not in Wace, may have come from Dares the Phrygian or Dictys the Cretan (M), authors regarded by medieval writers as contemporary with the Fall of Troy; Lawman does not mention either of these as his sources, yet he had apparently had access to books or oral information more extensive than the three sources he lists, which some critics believe he drew on quite extensively.

111 The foundation of *Alba Longa* (the manuscripts call it *Albe Lingoe/Lingwe*) is also given in Nennius and in Virgil, *Aeneid* v, 597 (M).

117 This allusion to an idol, invented by Wace and not found in GoM, was inspired by French vernacular tales of the twelfth century; in the French romances which developed soon after Wace, Saracens were regularly represented as worshipping an idol called *mahum*, (from Mahomet, Mohammed), the form used by Lawman here.

137 Geoffrey took this episode from Nennius, who has one magician, killed by Ascanius because of his prophecy.

167 Lawman seems to have muddled *Helenus* Priam's son and Helena wife of Menelaus (and Paris): both manuscripts have *Heleine/ Eleine*; the Otho scribe's a 'correction' of 'son' to 'daughter' is also mistaken. Wace's text makes it clear that Helenus son of Priam should be referred to; 'queen' is wrong. GoM borrowed from Virgil who says that Helenus reigned over Epirus after Pyrrhus's death (*Aeneid* iii, 295, 334) [M] for this part of his invented 'history', and added the detail that Pyrrhus kept him as a slave.

316 *Greek fire* was actually encountered by the crusaders in the Third Crusade (1189–92) but was known of before, and reference to it occurs (as *Graece igno*) in GoM; it is not in Wace [M], perhaps an indication that Lawman did consult GoM's Latin as well as the French of Wace. The author of *Ancrene Wisse* knew of it (and described how to extinguish it in Part VII, see G. Shepherd, ed., *Ancrene Wisse*, Parts 6 & 7 [1959], p. 27 and note); it was made of naphtha, pitch and sulphur and first used in England at the Siege of Nottingham in 1194.

376 *Brutus's speech*, with his instructions to Anacletus which include Brutus's directives for Anacletus's own speech, breaks off abruptly with an unexpected transition into the action which ensues when Anacletus has performed Brutus's supplied speech. One of two things has happened here: either Lawman has conflated Wace's version of Brutus's speech and

Anacletus's repetition of it, as Madden implies, or the scribe of an early MS, antecedent to both surviving manuscripts of Lawman's *Brut*, conflated the two speeches. The latter is more likely: in Wace Anacletus receives much briefer instructions, concluding with Brutus's declaration that he will ambush the guards Anacletus brings, to which he assents. If Lawman supplied Brutus with a fully anticipatory speech describing all the ensuing action, and then repeated this nearly verbatim, in a technique similar to Androgeus's retrospective account of the events at Cassibell-aune's festival, then it would be easy for a scribe to move by eye-skip from Brutus's plan to its execution, and in the process to omit several important details of the action: Brutus's placing of his troops in three places (four in Lawman), Anacletus's deception of the guards by simulating flight from prison, his claim that he left the king in the wood because he could not move in his heavy fetters, and his conducting of them into the ambush.

499–504 Lawman adds this conclusion to *Membricius's speech*, as he expanded Brutus's opening address at the hustings (L 434–45), and added Brutus's speech at L 414ff.; the addition of direct speech in 'formal', public addresses is characteristic of Lawman's version; it adds to the impression of group interaction in the narrative but does not characterise the speakers as individuals.

513ff Pandrasus is courteously treated in Geoffrey, rather more brusquely in Wace, and with threats here in Lawman, who makes him a pathetic and reluctant figure, not disposed to praise his captor as *gentilz hom e pruz* as he does in Wace (W 582), and he does not give gifts to Brutus's followers as in Wace (W 608).

547 *Ignogen* is also treated more sympathetically here than in Wace; in GoM she becomes very emotional at leaving her home and family (Thorpe, p. 64).

561 *Logice* has been conjectured to be Leucadia (Levkáš: Santa Maura) 'one of the larger Ionian islands (Blenner-Hassett) or, less likely, Lycia.

620ff This description of Britain, unlike those in lines L 1002ff (W 1209ff) and L 2404ff (W 2604ff), is not found in Wace.

639ff GoM took this voyage from Nennius's journey of the Scythians from Egypt to Spain, perhaps based on Orosius's *Historia*, and Wace and Lawman repeat it [M].

642f The *Lake of Silvius* is really 'the salt lake' in Geoffrey; Wace has *lac des Salins* (W 709); and the *Lake of Philisteus* is 'the altars of the Philistines' in GoM (Thorpe, p. 66) and Wace (710); Madden notes that they are found between Tripoli and Cyrene (III, 304). *Ruscikadan* (GoM *inter Russicadam*) is an ancient Roman city on the Algerian coast at the mouth of the River Lessaf (Blenner-Hassett). *Azare* may be part of the Atlas range in S. Algeria (B-H; M, III, 304–5).

652 *Malvan* is R. Muluya which flows into the Mediterranean, separating Algeria and Morocco [B-H, M].

660 Wace (729) does not say that the *Pillars of Hercules* were marble; Robert of Mannyng's translation of Wace makes them brass (Mg 1444).

663 Wace (733–64) makes more of these *mermaids*, likening their blandishments to the Devil's, but Lawman compensates by developing the nautical details (L 671–2), in which he frequently shows interest.

684 Both Virgil (*Aeneid* i,242) and Livy (Bk i, chap. 1) state that Antenor settled at the mouth of the Po and founded Padua [M].

714 The sources all have 200 knights [M]. Lawman mentions the number 200 as the total slain by Corineus (L 780), a detail he adds; this seems to indicate his method of translation: reading large sections of Wace and working freehand from blocks of copy, adding, occasionally condensing (as in Corineus's speech to Goffar, L 790ff) and modifying, sometimes recycling material discarded or adapted within the block. Another instance of this is his suppression of Wace's simile comparing Corineus to a lion in sheep flock, replaced by lines L 803–4, and its insertion at L 774–5, where the simile is changed to a wolf, anticipating the famous similes comparing Arthur to the wolf (L 10041ff, 10631ff). Wolves did not become extinct in England until the 16thc.

836 *Three thousand*: Wace has 12,000 but some manuscripts must have read *deus* (2) for *dous* (2) since Mannyng has *twey thousand* (Mg 1649).

838 *Scorn*: the original has *nithinges beard*, a term of severe opprobrium derived from Old Norse which also occurs in lines L 5338, and cf. L 15168.

850–51 Comparison of a hero with a *wild boar* is a commonplace in medieval romance, yet no extant English romance is as early as Lawman's *Brut*; this simile does not occur at this point in Wace [M], and nor does another such at 15132–4. Boars died out in the 17thc in England.

867 This derivation of *Tours* from Turnus occurs in GoM (Thorpe, p. 71) and in other early traditions (see Madden, III, p. 308). Such place-name etymologies in his source inspire Lawman to try many of his own to supplement the original.

895 Despite Madden's statement that Lawman means that *Dartmouth* is the port in the district of Totnes, Blenner-Hassett interprets this as 'at the mouth of the River Dart'; Totnes is, of course, some ten miles from the mouth of the R. Dart. Dartmouth was the port from which Chaucer's Shipman worked.

905 *Gogmagog . . . the chief*: the Middle English has *heihste* 'highest' which in Lawman usually means 'noblest, most important' but Madden points out that since here it refers to a giant it may also literally mean 'tallest' (III, 308). In GoM he is 12 cubits (*elbows*), in Mannyng 20 feet; Wace explains that he had been chosen as leader by the rest because of his *force e . . . grandur* (W 1071–2).

934ff–965 The fight with Gogmagog is heightened from Wace's account (W 1111–68), especially lines 942–45, with some exaggeration (only three of Corineus's ribs are broken in all the sources). In 934 'squared . . . shoulders' Wace has *se rembraça* 'turned back his sleeves'. The name *Gogmagog's leap* (L 965) occurs in GoM as *saltus Goegmagog* but not in Wace, an indication that if Lawman did not know GoM he must have known the same oral tradition. Camden and Drayton in the

16thc and 17thc associate it with Plymouth Hoe/Haw [M].

1012ff *The foundation of London*: Wace also presents this, with the addition in some MSS (and in Arnold's printed text) of a passage from GoM concerning Eli, High Priest of Jerusalem, which must have been missing in Lawman's MS of Wace. Similar omissions of references to world history in Lawman (and presumably his copy of Wace) occur at: L 1261 Samuel and Homer (GoM: Thorpe 78, W 1451–2); L 1281: Saul and Eurysthenes of Sparta (Thorpe, p. 78; W: Saul and Eristeus, 1469f in Arnold's ed.); L 1327 King David (GoM: Thorpe p. 79, W 1512–6); 1416 Solomon and Amos etc, (W 1621–6, a conflation of two such passages in GoM, Thorpe, p. 80). Wace and Lawman omit the quarrel between the brothers Lud and Nennius over the substitution of the name London for New Troy. Lawman expands the account of the by-laws of London (L 1039–46): as elsewhere in *The Brut* he shows a great interest in law.

1047f Neither Wace nor Lawman marks this off as the beginning of a new section: in some MSS of GoM this begins Book II (Thorpe, p. 75) but Wace (and perhaps Lawman) seems to have known a MS of GoM without book divisions.

1057 The tradition that Locrin's lands were in the south, from Totnes to Trent, is not in GoM or Wace (M); it occurs in other medieval historians.

1060 Lawman, who lived near the Welsh border, supplies this observation about the Welsh love of their wild land; Wace, on the other hand, mentions the Severn as the *northern* boundary but L adds more accurate geographical references, at L 1067–8. Lawman omits comment on Galoes' fame and power here, but adds his own comment on her beauty at the appropriate point (L 1357–9).

1070–71 The *seventeen years* of peace are Lawman's invention; GoM has 'a long time'. A similar addition at L 1259 adds 'nine days' to the fifteen years of Gwendoline's rule. Throughout the narrative, Lawman adds references to duration of time, to distance and to numbers of people; where numbers exist in the source he often increases them.

1096 The *Scottish Water* is the Firth of Forth (B–H); Wace himself has the English word Escoce *Watre* (W 1307) here.

1126 *Given her his pledge*: MS C says 'had taken her in handfast'; handfasting was an ancient betrothal ceremony, which survived till the 18thc in Scotland [M]. Madden assumes from this that Lawman knew the practice, although this use of the term does not prove that he knew the custom. Wace simply speaks of *covenant* and MS O 'had plighted troth with her'.

1156 Wace's Corineüs has the axe on his shoulders as he speaks, and Geoffrey makes him simply brandish the axe while speaking, as if going to attack; the dramatic gesture of smashing the rock Locrin is standing on is Lawman's own invention. He expands all this Astrild-Gwendoline episode, especially the fitting-out of the earth-house (L 1181–90): Geoffrey merely says that Locrinus had a cave dug out in New Troy in which he made love to her secretly (Thorpe, pp. 76–7) and Wace is even briefer.

1185 Lawman says 'golden pennies'; for many centuries the silver penny was the staple coin, the first gold coin being issued in 1257. It is unlikely that Lawman was writing as late as this: his allusion to gold pence is an exotic and romantic detail, something unlike ordinary experience.

1203 *Abren* is *Habren* in GoM: she is drowned in the *Severn* (*Habren* in Welsh, *Sabrina* in Latin (Thorpe, p. 77), and Welsh and English translators of GoM follow this, as does Mannyng, who is working from Wace (Mg 2146–10) but Wace equates the name Abren with *Avren*, i.e. *Avon*, which enters the sea at Christchurch in Dorset (formerly Hants.) (W, 1439–40; L 1254). This Dorset setting may have been suggested by the localisation of Locrin's death 'near the Stour' (Thorpe, p. 77): this was usually thought of as a tributary of the Severn (Tatlock, p. 29) but Caldwell suggested the Dorsetshire Stour (*MLN* 69 [1954], 327–9, cited in Thorpe) and Wace explicitly states that he means the Dorset Stour (W 1424–5), echoed by Lawman (L 1237–8); the Dorset Stour rises in N. Dorset and flows into the Avon at Christchurch. Stour is a common river name in the south of England; like many English river names, it is Celtic, meaning 'shining water' (Ekwall, *English River Names*, [Oxford, 2nd ed. 1968], p. 381).

Madden accounts for the transfer from Avon (now Dorset) to Severn through the occurrence of two other rivers Avon and Stour in Warwicks.: that Avon joins that Stour which joins the Severn (M, p. 314]. Other critics suspect the confusion operated in the reverse direction.

1257 Not in Wace [M]. It is a commonplace of romance tradition that travellers can transport money unmolested in the reign of an exemplary monarch, see *Havelok*, 45–50, ed. G. V. Smithers (OUP, 1987), and other instances cited by Madden, III p. 314. Bede has a hagiographic equivalent: in Edwin's time a woman could carry her new-born baby unmolested from one side of the country to another (a sorry indictment of his own times? *Historia*, II, 16).

1321 Wace (W 1506) specifies the lands of the Flemings and Germans here.

1333 *Adud* (MS O: *Aldud*) is *Alclud* in GoM and *Aclud* in Wace (W 1520) and is actually Dumbarton on the R. Clyde, OW *alt clud* 'rock on the Clyde'; Lawman's *-d-* is a misreading of *-cl-*. The Scots Gaelic name for the place is *Dun Bretan* 'fort of the Britons', i.e. Dumbarton (B-H), capital of Strathclyde.

1335 Wace explains that the 'foreign men' were the *Franceis* 'French' (W 1253) and Mannyng repeats this (Mg 2156). The passage on pronunciation is not in GoM. Lawman's form *Eoverwic* (Wace has *Evrewic*) is in fact (approximately) Anglo-Saxon, and the pronunciation ʒeorc, which he claims is recent, is attributed to the local inhabitants ('northern men'). Lawman is correcting and updating Wace but records (see M, III p. 315) do not indicate a date for this change of pronunciation (essentially a semi-vocalisation of [v] to [w] similar to that in *havek* › *haw(e)k* 'hawk' but which normally occurs before velar consonants and *l*

[Jaček Fisiak, *A Short Grammar of Middle English*, 1968, p. 61:4]). The sound-change itself is usually dated early 13thc, but this is not precise enough to give an exact date for Lawman's work. *York* is indeed a Celtic name, but its first recorded form, *Eburacum*, probably derives from the British word for 'yew tree' or just possibly from a proper name *Eburos*, a place-name type more common in Gaul (Margaret Gelling, *Signposts to the Past*,1978, p. 40); the Anglo-Saxon form *Eoforwic* is a rationalisation of British *Evorog*, the form in which 4thc Germanic mercenaries under the Romans would have encountered the original name, into the English elements 'boar-farm' (*ibid.*, p. 58).

1340 *Maidens' Castle* is not the place in Dorset but probably Edinburgh; in GoM it is *Castellum Puellarum* (Thorpe, p. 79).

1347ff The list of Ebrauc's children is found in GoM and Wace; *Brutus* should be 'Greenshield' (Lawman has not translated the cognomen), *Ricar* is 'Kincar', *Pardan* is Dardan, *Luor* is 'Ivor', and *Ruc* is 'Rud'; the daughters fare less well: *Ocidas* is (presumably) 'Oudas', *Radan* is 'Ragan', *Guenboden* is 'Guenlodoe', *Zangustel* is 'Tangustel', *Scadud* is 'Stadud', *Gaz* must be 'Gael', *Wladus* is 'Cladus' (Wace *Gladus*), *Bedra* is 'Edra', *Eangnes* is 'Angoes', *Scadiald* is 'Stadiald' and so *Echem* must be 'Chein'. There are obvious scribal errors in Lawman's forms (*c* for *t* for example) and one mindless error: Wace's *e Bodloan* 'and B.' becomes 'Ebedloan' and *e Angues* becomes 'Eangnes'. However, it is amazing that such exotic names should have survived 70 years of copying at all; some of them are recognisably Welsh, some (Gorgon) look like one of Geoffrey's jokes. Lawman follows Wace's order of names. In 1360 *Andor* is miscopied by scribe C as 'Another'.

1389ff Wace does not tell us of the perfection of *Carlisle* and it is just possible that Lawman knew the place. 'Shaftesbury' (*Scephtonia* in GoM) seems to be meant by Lawman's *Cestesburi* (Wace 1614 *Cestrebire*) and *Waladon* (GoM, Wace: *Paladur*) may be nearby Walton (B-H). The eagle which spoke there remains mysterious in GoM and Wace; only Lawman informs us that he foretold Ruhhudibras's death (L 1415) although 14thc writers interpolated a 'Prophecy of the Eagle'. Mannyng and Leland turn the bird into a man called Aquila [M] (Mg 2235 *Awhileon* in MS Petyt 511).

1421ff The description of *Bath* is expanded but seems confused: in GoM the fires which never go out turn into balls of stone (Thorpe, p. 80); L 1422–3 has an engine like a wooden beam to generate heat; this is not in sources and Madden suggests this account derives from local tradition.

1434 Wace's account of Bladud's flight (W 1645–54) does not refer to the altitude, the disruptive effects of the wind, or the broken strings.

1455 Wace adds the detail of the later decay of Leicester; Madden noted (Vol. I, p. xviii, Vol. III, pp. 319, 658) his opinion that Wace might be referring to its destruction by Henry II in 1173 on the rebellion of Robert, Third Earl of Leicester, (whose father Robert was justiciar from 1155–68 and twin brother of Waleran de Meulan, co-dedicatee of Geoffrey's *Historia Regum Britanniae* in some MSS), but this was after Wace's poem was finished; although it might have been the destruction

Lawman was aware of as he translated, Wace must have been referring to the damage inflicted by William the Conqueror, William Rufus, or Ivo de Grantmesnil under Henry I in 1101 (Arnold, *Roman de Brut*, p. 797).

1482 Wace, who gave his *Roman de Brut* to Eleanor of Aquitaine, is not responsible for this antifeminism; possibly it is meant to be a joke, which need not indicate that Lawman was writing for a male audience.

Lawman's treatment of the famous King Leir story is more dramatic than Wace's: his characters converse more; Leir's letter (L 1576–94) is not given verbatim in Wace; and the characterisation of Gornoille and Regau is more pointed in Lawman's version. On the other hand, both vernacular authors omit GoM's Leir's tasteless and tearful outburst on his crossing into France as he laments his former glories (Thorpe, p. 84), both placing Leir's lament before he goes to France, although Wace still has some of the rhetoric of Geoffrey, including the references to Fate and Fortune, whom Wace's Leir invests with the classic revolving wheel.

Lawman invites us to see Leir's daughters cleverly outmanoeuvring the old man with his decrepit intellect; he makes the most of the parallels and contrasts afforded by the three sisters, and H. C. Wyld and C. S. Lewis praised Lawman's sympathetic observation in the change in facial colour of Leir who turns white as a sheet in surprised anger (L 1533) and Cordoille who is red, as if from drinking, with supressed emotion when Leir seeks reconciliation (L 1762). Leir's faint (L 1535) is added by Lawman. However, this observation is external, and the inner psychology of the characters, which is so finely noted in Wace's Cordeille (W 185–97) is less marked in Lawman's Cordoille (who simply keeps her room in Lawman [L 1555]), and seems to be laughing at Leir (L 1521) where in Wace she is trying in jest to expose her sisters' sycophancy (W 1775). Conversely, Lawman's Leir is more plausible, and especially pathetic when he goes to France with only one attendant (L 1750), having already lost some in translation: Wace has 50, GoM 60 knights to the 40 in L 1635.

Lawman puts emphasis on the external circumstances, especially the court ceremonial at Cordoille and Aganippus's court: from the messenger's speech to the equipment Cordoille sends to assist Leir's recovery until he is fit to appear at Court and be acknowledged formally, as king, we are conscious of the public life of the court; Aganippus's generous gesture of self-deposition is formally announced from the battlements (L 1820ff). Aganappus's speech (L 1837–48) is entirely Lawman's own. All this episode, much expanded from Wace, owes its immediacy to Lawman, who heightens the Biblical overtones (latent in the sources) of the Prodigal's return, the Good Samaritan and Job's final state which surpassed his former one.

Lawman is confused: in L 1617 Leir gives all his land to his daughters; in 1624 their husbands conspire to take it from him; in Wace the division was to take place after Leir died [H]. Gornoille is married to Maglaune of Scotland (L 1640) but in 1546 she was promised to the Duke of Cornwall.

Shakespeare's source for *King Lear* was not, of course, Lawman but the 16thc chronicle play *King Leir* and Holinshed; Geoffrey Ashe believes that Shakespeare may have known GoM (BBC Radio 4 interview, April 1990).

1802 This resembles a proverb in the *Proverbs of Alfred*: 'for God may give good after evil [H].

1860 *As the book tells it*: if the book meant is Wace's and the allusion is to W 2050 it seems superfluous to call attention to a single line reference. The phrase is a commonplace in later Middle English romance, and often indicates a longer account in an original which is suppressed by the English redactor; GoM describes how Leir was buried in an underground chamber below the River Soar, downstream from Leicester and dedicated to Janus, on whose feast-day local artisans would begin here their first enterprise of the new year. It looks rather as if Lawman knew of this, judged it irrelevant but wished to signal his knowledge of the pagan allusion.

1865–74 Wace says that the nephews hated their aunt, but this implication that there was resentment at female rule is Lawman's own. Cunedagius's resentment at Morgan's behaviour ((L 1915–1917) is also Lawman's invention [M].

1930 *Margan* is Glamorgan (B-H); both Wace and GoM have the form Margan.

1935 Here for once Lawman has included some reference to universal history by locating British history by the founding of Rome, but he omits Wace's reference to Ezechiel and Isaiah and the prophecies of Emmanuel (W 2111–20).

1952 Lawman does not state that Lago was Gurgustius's nephew, Kinemark Sisillius's son [M]: Lawman's list of kings emphasises the pathetic brevity of their reigns, and because he omits Wace's relationships he heightens the sense of discontinuity.

2012 Iudon's death by drowning is not given in GoM and Wace; Madden notes a Welsh tradition that she was thrown alive in a sack into the Thames; several of Lawman's women are drowned, cf. Astrild and Abren (L 1245) and the companions of Ursula (L 6043).

2013–2018 These lines describing social anarchy are very similar to a passage in Wulfstan's *Sermo Lupi* in Old English, dating from 1014: 'nothing has prospered for a long time now at home or away, but there have been war and hunger, burning and bloodshed . . . we have had rapine and slaughter, plague and pestilence, murrain and disease, malice and hatred . . .' Two words are almost identical: *mon-qualm* in L resembles *orf-cwealm* ('murrain') in Wulfstan, and both have *hete* 'hatred'. In lines 15871–75 there is another passage reminiscent of prose antedating Lawman and still extant; there may well be other early 'borrowings' embedded in Lawman's *Brut*. The phrase 'hunger and hatred' is one of Lawman's favourites; Barron and Weinberg translate the second element 'heat' (note to 10199) but this is unlikely.

2036 The use of superlatives in description is typical of medieval romances; Madden points to the parallel with Havelok, who is the bravest (*Havelok*, 9) and most stalwart (*Hav* 25); Horn is fairer than all, and his friends are respectively the best and the worst (*King Horn*, lines 8, 27, 28).

2042ff As Madden notes, Dunwallo does not actually go to Wales in Wace's version. The terms *truce* and *treaty* in 2045 (*sæhte*, *sibbe* and *some* in the original) are ambiguous and seem to imply that Dunwallo is caught by a feigned truce [M] whereas Wace shows that they formed a confederation against him (W 2225: *contre lui*; *him* in 2044 properly refers to Rudac; Dunwallo's complaint at the 'treachery' (L 2057–8) is not in Wace.

2119-20 Wace does not declare that Dunwallo was a famous high king, although he does dwell on his being the first to wear a crown, and on his laws; Madden therefore assumes that 'books' must refer to some source other than Wace. It seems more likely that the plural (if not merely a hyperbole) refers to Wace and Geoffrey; if Lawman knew Geoffrey's Latin he would there have seen that Geoffrey claims Gildas as his authority (Thorpe, p. 89). With his interest in good laws, Lawman would infer from Wace's account of Dunwallo's laws that he must have been great, and Wace's claim that the English still used his law code (W 2306) implies that his fame continues. In fact this claim (from Geoffrey's account of Belinus [Thorpe, p. 94]) is fictitious, although popular with medieval Welsh writers; the law of sanctuary was, however, in the codes of Ine and Alfred [M]. Lawman's reference to the peasant at his plough (L 2126) is a distortion of the declaration that the peasant's plough should be inalienable in GoM (Thorpe, p. 89).

2139 Lawman omits the dedication of the temple to Concord in Wace (and GoM), but adds the exotic detail of the burial with gold, Madden suggests a gold shroud or coffin, but Lawman probably means grave goods; perhaps he had seen the contents of a pagan grave excavation. There is a similar addition of pagan ritual in the account of Cassibellaune's victory ceremonial (L 4034ff); like Chaucer and Gower over 150 years later, Lawman is fascinated by the pagan past.

2140 This is the beginning of Book III in some MSS of GoM [M].

2150 Mannyng here inserts his own animadversions on the incompatibility of north and south, which he has not taken from Wace.

2156ff This speech is over 60 lines in Wace (W 2341–2404) and is even more manipulative, but anonymously ascribed to one of the evil counsellors, as in GoM; Lawman's invention of the name Malgod (L 2198;? OFr *mal*- bad, evil) is interestingly like Malory's invented names for nameless knights in his OFr sources. Its second element resembles that of the Bigod family, who by marriage entered the ranks of the marcher lordships on the Welsh borders in 1245, some decades later than the date usually given to Lawman's *Brut*, (R. R. Davies, *Conquest, Coexistence and Change: Wales 1063–1415*, History of Wales, Vol. II [Oxford, 1987], p. 280). Roger Bigod was Earl of Norfolk, one of the fifteen earls in England at the time of Magna Carta; King John captured his chief castle, at Framlingham, in March 1216 during the Civil War.

2172 *Moray*, which gave its name to the Moray Firth, was part of the ancient Scottish kingdom of Fidach; it is a Celtic compound meaning 'settlement by the sea' (B-H); in GoM the leader is Cheulfus of the Moriani (Thorpe, p. 90).

2182 *Alfing* (*Ælfinge* in MS C) takes his name from a scribal error in Wace or his copy of GoM: Geoffrey calls him *Elsingius* (Thorpe, p. 90).

2211–2224 The only part of this passage which occurs in Wace is 2216–2219; like the name of the woman, Delgan, the expansiveness and emotive pathos of the passage is Lawman's, from Brennes's honeymoon exuberance to Godlac's swoon of shock on hearing of his beloved's marriage (L 2253); he adds the detail of Delgan's information that Brennes will leave in three nights, and her sad farewell (L 2250–2), the details of the fight at sea and Godlac's joyful recapture of Delgan, spoiled by the horrific storm (L 2276-97). Although Wace includes the storm and the two battles, at sea and in Kalatere, Wace's balanced style robs such violent episodes of the raw fury Lawman manages to convey; there is nothing in Wace like the waves running like towns burning (L 2285; cf L 5976).

Wace for his part has added reference to the letter which the Norwegian princess (L's Delgan) sends to her lover, but without giving its substance. In the sequel, with the capture of the shipwrecked lovers (L 2302–12) and Godlac's speech to the king (L 2315–2338) Lawman greatly expands the episode and adds pointing (the four hundred ships of Brennes in L 2343). Lawman's expansion seems to owe much to the diction and narrative mode of romance (e.g. 'sea-weary men'; 'dear one' (*leoue-mon*); the episode of the arrival on the coast and self-presentation before the ruler, which occurs in *Beowulf* as well as romances such as *King Horn*).

2363 Blenner-Hassett assumes that *Kalatere* is the flat lands, the carse of Falkirk in Scotland, from Falkirk to the Firth of Forth; he equates it with Celtic *Calathros*, 'hard promontory'; Madden derives from it the appellation 'Thane of *Cawdor*' and gives the modern name as Torwood. Kalatere is the place where Elidur meets his deposed brother (L 3306).

2370, 2387 One of Lawman's methods of making his narrative more concrete and eye-catching is to supply figures and increase Wace's numbers: Belin only kills 15,000 (W 2568); the £3,000 Godlac promises are Lawman's invention.

2400 Once again, Lawman shows interest in the law; this passage is in GoM with reference back to Dunvallo (Thorpe, p. 93) but Wace, having anticipated this (see note to 2119, above) omits it here. Lawman misses the real point of the road-building, which in GoM is to settle the disputed roads in order to establish the Molmutian law of sanctuary for travellers.

2411 *From outside Totnes*: GoM has 'from the Cornish sea'; Wace names Totnes but also says the road begins near Cornwall, from which Lawman cobbles the false location of Totnes in Cornwall. The 14thc historian Ranulf Higden copied GoM's statement and then supplied a correct route for the Fosse Way, including its termination in Lincoln. The second street is Ermine Street (L 2413) and there should have been *two* more, 'in a diagonal pattern' (Thorpe, p. 93) which were Watling Street and the Icknield Way [M]; Wace mentions four altogether (W 2627).

2435 Wace confused the sequence of events here by omitting GoM's account of how Brennius could not get support for his invasion in France; Wace describes Brennes's popularity and his requests for aid, which lead him to Burgundy, without explaining the refusals; Lawman complicates things further by making the King of France promise aid, and by adding Brittany to Seguine's possessions.

2450 Here Lawman's deployment of conversation does enable characterisation to develop: the narrator in Wace listed Brennes's accomplishments, as Lawman does (L 2443ff), but presenting him through Seguine's eyes and through Seguine's remarks to Brennes is an effective device. The courtly qualities of Wace's Brennes, his ability to hunt, hawk, and perform courtly amusements and speak *corteisment* and his *gent cors* ('noble physique') are repeated by Lawman (who adds harping, making Brennes resemble the romance hero Horn very closely indeed); it is significant that Lawman does match Wace's terms for courtliness in his use of *hende* (L 2443), which I translate 'gifted'.

2487–90 I have adopted the reading of MS O here, since C seems defective.

2491–544 Lawman adds considerably to his source and Tonwen's speech at 2540–43 is his invention. Madden thinks Wace's rendering more 'touching and natural', but Lawman alters Wace (Madden suggests it is a misunderstanding) so that Tonwen puts on a tattered garment before setting out, rather than ripping her clothing to the waist in front of two assembled armies in battle formation, which seems to me more decorous for a queen mother; instead, Lawman's queen pulls up her hem and reveals her knees and her bare feet rather than her shrivelled breasts: she dresses like a peasant, in other words, in a gesture of abject humility which is more touching than the histrionic gesture of GoM's heroine.

Geoffrey took this episode from Statius's *Thebaid*, modelling it on Jocasta's unsuccessful attempt to persuade the invading Polyneices to be reconciled with Etheocles (*Thebaid*, VII, 474–538; 481: *venit ante hostes pectore nudo*). H. C. Wyld (*RES*, 6 [1930]) praised Brennes's gesture of throwing his shield out on the field (2534) where in Wace he disarms and leaps from the field himself (W 2821). The celebration in Lawman's version (L 2532–50) and the ensuing hustings derive from six lines in Wace, a narrative statement that the war was over and parliament summoned.

2568–2614 The conquest of France and the killing of the four kings is much expanded from Wace's baldly factual statements (W 2842–64). The determination to avenge Romulus's killing of his twin Remus (not in Wace) is an especially nice touch coming from two brothers who have only a few lines earlier been about to attack each other. Wace, however, adds the itinerary over the Great St Bernard Pass, which Lawman copies, accurately except for 'Salome', which seems to be a corruption of *desaloee*, an epithet applied to the devastated Tuscany (W 2784).

2639–2730 The negotiations in the Senate and the deputation to Belin are simply reported in Wace, who uses the abbreviation formula 'why should I tell you a long story?' to speed the narrative (W 2884–2918) which is hardly longer than the three sentences in GoM (Thorpe, p. 97). Lawman's version adds the drama of the noble Belin sensing what we know to be true, that the Romans have no intention of maintaining the truce. Lawman adds the amount of the tribute and the names of the pagan gods.

2735–2836 In the German war and Roman ambush episode, Lawman's additions are strategic: he tells us that the Germans were prepared for war (L 2735–6) and that the Roman forces comprised two companies of two and ten thousand men, and adds Godlac and his Danes to the force with Belin (L 2781), and in place of Wace's peasant guides, adds the scene in which Belin bribes two captives to reveal the best spot for ambush. His main omission is his neglect of Wace's splendid description of the weather and visibililty for the midnight assault on the Romans: in the light of the full moon on a mild summer night the Romans see the ambushers' armour gleaming (W 2997–3007, which Wace may in his turn have taken from *Thebaid* II, 527–40). Wace does not praise Belin's troops, nor recount the following days's elimination of survivors in the mountains. The account in GoM (Thorpe, p. 98) explains that the Romans were without armour and not in formation.

2835 Wace lists the various siege engines used to hurl stones to break the walls of Rome (W 3035–8); he does not explain where the invading forces acquired them.

2847ff The hanging of the child hostages shocks the modern reader; even in GoM Brennius and Belinus first erect gallows and threaten to kill the hostages if the Romans do not surrender, before killing them when their parents renounce them (Thorpe, p. 98). The runner who arrives with a message is Lawman's invention; in Wace the besieged wait until they know reinforcements are due before sallying forth (W 3074–78) [M].

2898–2991 Wace considerably amplified the sparse narrative in GoM in which the two brothers narrowly avert defeat by rallying their men; Wace especially adds the taunts of the Romans, which Lawman then abbreviates, but there is nothing in Wace to match the brothers' parley in a trench, nor the pillaging of Rome's treasury (L 2955ff) and Belin's pronouncement to the citizens (L 2965ff). The stratagem with the shields comes from Wace, who means the long, pointed Norman shields which would have been too long to walk with, as would the cavalry lances. The 'fine things' (L 2962) done by Lawman's two brothers in rebuilding the city directly contrasts with the 'unheard-of savagery' of GoM (Thorpe, p. 99) and Wace (W 3157).

2996 *Caerleon-on-Usk* is a favoured locale in GoM, which he mentions 13 times: it is the seat of the archbishop of Wales at the conversion (Thorpe, p. 125) and location for Arthur's magnificent coronation; Madden objects to Wace and Lawman who put it in Glamorgan, averring that it was, in the 19thc, in Monmouthshire; the point is that Caerleon was the centre of the *Principality* of Glamorgan, and with the success of the Welsh in 1136, when Morgan ap Owein killed Richard Fitz Gilbert de Clare and was reinstated in the dignities of his grandfather, taking the title of king in the principality, the place was of some political significance (this information is derived from a paper given by John Gillingham to the London Medieval Society in 1990). In Domesday Book entries for Caerleon are made under both Herefordshire and Gloucestershire (Davies, *Conquest*, p. 7). Since 1975 Caerleon has been in Gwent.

2997 As usual, Lawman develops a scene out of the plain statement in Wace that the Britons occupied Rome long after Brennes died, and worked at remaining there.

3021 *Belyneszat* is the reading of MS O, while C has *Belʒæsʒate*; as Mannyng's version has it: '*Byllyngesgate* men calle it now' (Mg 3610); it seems to mean 'the gate of Billa's people' or 'of Billing' (= son of Billa) (B-H, citing Ekwall *DEPN* under other instances of Billing (Billingshurst Sx, etc.).

3030 Wace explains that Belin was cremated and placed in a golden vessel (W 3231–2).

3050–77 Lawman expands the Danish invasion from 9 lines in Wace, adding the detail that the Danish king is Godlac's son (L 3054) [M]. In 3057 I have adopted the reading of MS O: the C scribe confused a metathesised form *worþ* (wroth) with *word*.

3081–3120 GoM names these people *Basclenses* (Madden assumes this means the Basques), and he and Wace state that they had been travelling for one and a half years (L 3125: 7 years) before encountering Gurguint. The name of their king, Partholoim in Geoffrey, is a corruption of Nennius's Partholomus, who brought the Scots from Spain. Wace stresses the uninhabited state of Ireland, but the pathetic condition of the people is Lawman's addition, and the scribes seem to have suppressed some of the naked intensity of the description (L 3128: C omits 'thigh' and O corrupts 'limb' to 'lemman' = 'lover'.

3150 The identification of Mercian Law with Marcia is folk-etymology by GoM; Alfred was King of Wessex.

3165 The oddly named *Rummarus* in L and W is *Kinarius* in GoM (Thorpe, p. 101).

3168 GoM names the mistress as *Tanguesteaia*; Wace speaks only of 'bastardy'.

3203 Lawman invents this 'carnage pit'.

3209 Wace writes very emotionally about this *orible beste* (W 3421–1); in GoM it is apparently a female monster (Thorpe, 102); Wace stresses Morpidus's foolhardiness in venturing alone against it, but there was consolation in the death of the monster from its wounds (W 3461); Lawman's contribution is the list of weapons the rash king uses on the monster, and his focus of interest in the episode is Morpidus.

3321 Wace is more enthusiastic about Elidur's *pieté* (W 3523–4) and GoM dubs him *Pius*.

3408 GoM states that Peredur, once king, reigned benignly and moderately (Thorpe, p. 104) but Wace contrasts his bad life and end (W 3598) with the good life and end of Elidur (W 3610).

3418–9 *Lador's* brief life passed unnoted by Wace and GoM; perhaps he arose from a misreading of Wace: *out . . . l'enor* 'took office' (e.g. W 3611). Lawman supplies the single year of Morgan's reign and the 7 of Iwallo's (L 3441) and omits the 6 years of Enmaunus's.

3486 *Oein* has no evil reputation in GoM or Wace; the family relationships in 3485–7 are Lawman's additions [M].

3498 Arkinaus is Archmail in GoM and Archinal in Wace.

3508–16 Lawman invents the duration of Redion's and Redart's reigns. Famul-Penicel in GoM is Samul *and* Penessil (Thorpe, 105); the error is Wace's. Eligille should be son of Capor (GoM, Wace) and is Digueillius in GoM; Heli's (as in GoM) duration of reign and its experiences are not in Wace or GoM.

3535f, 3537 Lawman adds the information about the instructions to the rich and the expulsion of the wicked.

3540ff These observations about London's name are in GoM, who gives the second form as *Kaerlundein*; in Wace: *Londoin* (W 3764). *Troynovant* seems to be an invention of GoM; *London* is a Celtic name and seems to mean '(place) belonging to Londinos' (= 'the bold one') so recorded c AD 115 in Tacitus (Ekwall, *DEPN*).

3560 Ekwall derives Ludgate from OE *ludgeat* 'back-door, postern', from OE *lutan* 'to bend' = 'gate where one has to bow one's head to enter' (*Street Names of the City of London*, [Oxford, 1954], p. 91).

3587 This is the beginning of Book IV in GoM (Thorpe, 107). Wace alone locates these events 60 years before the Incarnation.

3592 The term 'middle-earth', employed in Middle English alliterative poetry until the end of the medieval period, was retained from Germanic mythology, in which the inhabited earth was situated at midpoint on the great Earth Tree, with Hel's region at the tree roots and Asgard, domain of the gods in the upper branches. Its revival by J. R. R. Tolkien makes it familiar again to many readers.

3597 Wace added an appraisal of Caesar's character and list of his conquests, to which Lawman, typically, appends the total of 55 realms, and also adds information on Caesar's creation of the calendar and Roman legal code; the cry of regret that such a man must go to hell (L 3601) occurs only in Lawman.

3534 Lawman's Cesar wishes to revenge the insult to his ancestors in Belinus's conquest of Rome, while Wace's cites the movement of Fortune's wheel (a favourite image in Wace) as an index of the shift in world powers: the Britons must make reparation (W 3887).

3643 Lawman invents this (intentionally ?) illogical letter from Cesar. He presents Caesar as an egotist, citing his name in formulaic rhymes which themselves indicate a point of view: *Cesar* rhymes with 'here', perhaps an echo of his famous 'veni, vidi, vici', with 'ware, wary', ironically in 3653, and with *sare*, 'sad, grievous' when he is out of luck. Wace seems most impressed by Caesar, applying to him the epithets of the romance hero (*forz, pruz*; his *chevalerie* is outstanding – perhaps an echo of Suetonius's account of his cloven-hoofed horse which he alone could tame? [*Twelve Caesars: Julius Caesar*, cap. 61]).

3677 In Wace the British declare that they are, and wish to remain, free (W 3924f, 3949, 3959); only Lawman's Cassibellaune asserts as a splendid climax the claim that Cesar should bow to *him*.

3680 Cesar's call for his knights is an addition by Lawman in a formula which he reserves for his great leaders; it is frequent in the Arthurian section. His anger is not recorded in GoM and Wace, but occurs in Nennius, together with the 60 ships (80 in Wace) [M]; Lawman must have had access to other records, or a glossed copy of GoM.

3696 'Dover' is Wace's translation of GoM *Dorobellum oppidum* [M], but GoM *Durobernia*, properly Canterbury, is also translated Dover in W 4564, L 4281. Caesar landed between Walmer Castle and Sandwich [M].

3737 *uncle*: MS C has 'father', but Androgeus's father was Lud.

3800f Nennius's pagan burial, like the Celebration Rite which Cassibellaune performs (L 4025–37) are additions by Lawman.

3848–65 Lawman invents the speeches in this appeasement of the French.

3871 The Tower of Odnea (GoM, Thorpe, 113), brought forward and enhanced by Wace from GoM's brief account after Caesar's second repulse, survives in the hamlet *Ordre* in the Parish of St Martin in Boulogne (B–H); Lawman adds the odd detail of its shape.

3904 Lawman adds details on the size and number of the stakes, which GoM must have taken from Caesar (*De Bello Gallico*, V, cap. 18) and perhaps Nennius. Bede stated that these stakes were still visible in his time, the early 8thc, *History of the English Church and People*, tr. Leo Sherley-Price, chap. 2, p. 40: 'cased in lead and thick as a man's thigh, fixed immovably in the river-bed'.

3927 Cassibellaune's stirring speech is not in the sources.

3981 Lawman omits Wace's romantic invention of Cesar's determination to enter ship after all his men, but adds, rather pointlessly, the episode in which Cassibellaune is falsely informed that Cesar is not leaving, with his and the narrator's consequent laments (L 3965–4015).

4051–2 The distinction between the men who drink beer and the officers who have wine is Lawman's; it contrasts with *King Horn* 1133, where both knights and squires drink beer.

4054ff Wace details the kinds of sports (jousting, fencing, casting the stone, wrestling and jumping) to which Lawman adds board-games, running and horse-racing.

4060 This is really a family quarrel, with disastrous consequences for the kingdom: *Evelin* is Androgeus's sister's son (L 4193), *Androgeus* is Cassibelaunus's brother Lud's son (cf. L 4118) and *Herigal* Cassibellaunus's half-sister's son (L 4195); Lawman adds these relationships via the sisters, always felt to be a poignantly close relationship (cf. *Battle of Maldon* 113–6, and L 13773, where Bedivere is avenged by his sister's son). Men married up the social scale in Europe and England, and therefore boys would be sent as squires to their mother's family rather than their father's, and find affinity and protection from the more powerful and wealthy side of the kinship group.

4063–4088; cf. 4197–4212 There are interesting discrepancies between the narrator's version of events and that which Androgeus gives in his letter: Androgeus emphasises that Evelin was defending himself, omits to say that the staff broke when he hit Herigal's ribs with it, claiming instead that it hit Herigal's shield, and totally omits Evelin's merciless butchery of Herigal by first mutilating his nose, chin and hand and then slicing him in half. Mannyng's version repeats the narrative verbatim in Androgeus's letter (Mg 4753ff and 4917ff), while Wace condenses the initial narrative. By accident or design, Lawman has enhanced the role of Androgeus as traitor by suggesting that he is economical with the truth as well, but somewhat redeemed by his request that Cassibellaune, his kin and lord, be taken unharmed (L 4290ff, Lawman's addition); only Lawman makes even Cesar afraid Androgeus will betray him (L 4449); it is only in L's version that Androgeus ends his days in wealth (L 4477).

4095 Lawman often wrote *oðer slæn oðer a-hon*: usually it seems to express a distinction between two kinds of judicial execution, perhaps between the beheading or judicial combat reserved for the nobility, and the hanging to which other criminals were relegated; occasionally it seems to mean 'kill in battle or hang if captured'.

4460 Lawman alone has Cesar allowing Cassibellaunus a wash, fresh clothing and a meal before the treaty is ratified.

4480 Lawman is ambiguous; GoM says that six (Wace seven) years after Cesar left *Cassivelaunus* died (Thorpe, 118); I have pointed the translation accordingly, but Lawman may mistakenly have intended to refer to Androgeus's early demise. Madden corrects the punctuation of his translation (III, 479) to give the same sense as my translation.

4485–05 Lawman builds up Tennancius from a 4-line entry in Wace [M].

4535 Wace supplies the reference to Taliesin, from Welsh or even Breton traditions [M]. Lawman amplifies, from the Gospels, Wace's much briefer prophecy of Christ.

4639 Lawman omits to say that Hamun (in GoM Hamo) had been brought up with British hostages (Thorpe, p. 120, W 4945). Lawman invents the incident where Wider is murdered when he takes off his corslet to get air (L 4646).

4677 Portchester is not devastated here in GoM but blockaded (IV, 12); Wace says this devastation happened later but after Hamo's death, not at the Roman landing (W 5011–2, contrast L 4611); L repeats the incident with slaughter and burning (L 4700).

4705–81 The narrative in Wace is conducted without dialogue here, and Wace simply records the reconciliation (W 5050), not mentioning the rejoicing. Wace includes Genuis's arrival, and her beauty (W 5064) which is omitted by Lawman, but not the statement in GoM that Arviragus was madly in love with her [Thorpe, 121].

4714 *shield-wall*: see 13728n.

4778ff The gift of the city to Claudius, the romantic tale of his lady-love, and how she was won in battle, are all Lawman's invention.

4815 GoM states that Claudius was still alive and had sent Vespasian to bring Arviragus to heel; Lawman assumes that Vespasian had succeeded Claudius as emperor (L 4841) and Madden thinks this is proof that Lawman did not read GoM.

4855 It was from Wissant (between Calais and Boulogne) that Julius Caesar had come to Britain but Lawman did not say this in L 3610. Wissant–Dover was the regular medieval channel crossing route [M].

4859 The *luff* was 'a spar holding out and down the windward tack of a square sail while going into the wind' (MED *lof* [4]); *wenden lof* (L 10455) is 'to change course'; the MED does not cite Lawman's use of *lof* with *strecchen* (here), nor the idiom *casten lof*.

4891–4926 This moving tale of Genuis's divided loyalties has the ingredients of an Old English tragic tale like that of Freawaru and Hildeburh in *Beowulf* (2022ff, 1114ff); women given in marriage as ratification of a truce must often have lost their own and marital families in any renewal of hostilities, but Lawman's women are usually romantic rather than tragic heroines. Lawman develops this episode from 8 lines in Wace (W 5135–42), who himself developed one sentence in GoM (Thorpe, 122).

4954 This line resembles 6052 and 6986, 8797, except for *hærmde*; since this final element may alter the alliterative structure to a vowel rhyme (with unstable initial *h* effectively permitting vowel alliteration) I have not translated this line on the pattern of the others (cf. also 8313).

4974 *Westmorland* is in fact 'the land of the *Westmoringas*'. i.e. 'west of the Yorkshire moors'; Lawman's form *-mære-* is either OE *mære* 'boundary' or *mere* 'sea'; GoM has *West marilanda* and Wace *Vestinaire* [B-H].

4976–5023 The details of the arrival of the Picts, including the Irish Gille Caor's name, are Lawman's invention.

5033 *Luces* is the Lucius of Bede I, 4. The other Luces, Arthur's enemy, I have translated in the form Lucius used by later writers in the Arthurian tradition, to make a distinction.

5044–5048 Lawman's reference to St Peter is not in Wace, nor is his claim that Lucius killed those who refused conversion (L 5073). The simple cleansing of the pagan temples in Wace inspires Lawman to some graphic detail (L 5077–81) which Lawman may have derived from Ælfric's *De Falsis Diis*.

5093–4 As usual, it is Lawman who adds the details about Church law.

5102 This is the opening of GoM Book V. Lawman misrecords the date of Lucius's death, given as AD 156 in GoM and Wace (W 5266). GoM presumably took the date from Bede, *History*, Bk I, cap. 4, which records Lucius's request to Eleutherus, but Bede's date refers to the succession of the Emperors Marcus Antoninus and Aurelius Commodus.

5122ff Wace simply describes how Severus enlarged his two legions by giving gifts to the British (W 5273–84) and so overcame opposition. At 5126–36 Lawman makes the British accept Severus voluntarily; in Wace he conquers them cruelly (W 5281–4).

5164 The word used by Wace is *palis* 'fence' and Lawman translates accurately as *shid(e)-wall* ' a wall made of planks or rampart made of piles'; Madden translates 'broad wall' in error. Hadrian's wall was begun in AD 122; it was constructed in two parts, the eastern section from Newcastle to the River Irthing (45 Roman miles) was of stone; the second section, the final third from R. Irthing to Bowness-on-Solway (31 Roman miles), was originally turf, perhaps for speed of erection with the threat of invasion. The stone section was 10 Roman feet (3m) thick and may have been 15 Roman feet (4.5m) high. The turf section was double this thickness and nearly as high (David J. Breeze, *The Northern Frontiers of Britain* (1982), p. 76f); it was made of clay, marsh earth as well as turves, on a foundation of turf, stone or subsoil (Paul Austen, *Current Archaeology*, 108, 1988, 18f). This turf was replaced by stone: the work was begun in Hadrian's lifetime and completed before the Antonine wall was built. Hadrian's wall was ruinous by the end of 2ndc AD. Neither Bede nor GoM apparently knew of the later Antonine Wall, built 139–142 and abandoned after 161 (Thorpe, 126) which was entirely a turf rampart, like the western section of 'Hadrian's Wall; although most Roman boundaries (like the boundary of Germania) were of wood, Hadrian's was not, still less the very substantial wall, repairing and replacing Hadrian's, which was built by Septimus Severus (196–211) when the previously abandoned Hadrianic wall was reinstated, after the northern uprising in AD 197, by being supplied with more forts, replacing the original mile-castles, and reconstructed with very hard white mortar. Archaeological evidence suggests that it was Hadrian's wall which had been badly built, not Severus's, and needed to be almost totally reconstructed, so that it was, in consequence, called Severus's Wall from late Roman times until the 19thc (*Current Archaeology*, 96, [1985], 16–19); Severus was badly served by Bede and his descendants.

5174 MS C spells 'Scythia' as *Cise*; in MS O it is *Scice* as in Wace 5322.

5199ff The deliberations about Severus's burial-place are not found in Wace and GoM.

5236 Carausius (Carrais) speaks to the Senate in GoM and Wace (W 5391) but his words are not cited; Lawman seems to have invented both the speech and the Emperor Cyrian [M]. Bede Bk I cap. 6 must have been Geoffrey's source for Carausius and Asclepiodotus.

5269–5303 Wace, whose Carrais ravages Europe prior to coming to Britain [M], and has an inferior personality (W 5431–2, as in GoM), does not present the Britons staunchly refusing to betray their King Basian, as Lawman does. In Wace Carais picks up the dregs of Europe's society but Lawman's (briefer) account of his ravages in Britain after gathering the idle youth is his own (L 5270).

5308 Basian's terse refusal, the location of the battle at York, and Carrais's killing of Basian with his own spear are all additions by Lawman.

5407 The Walbrook in London takes its name from the Walisc or 'Welsh', i.e. Britons, who must have been living there in early Saxon times. Interestingly, a large quantity of severed heads was discovered in this stream, and can be seen on display in the Museum of London.

5418, 5421–41 These details are in fact wrong: Coel is only a nobleman in Wace, and Gloucester should be Colchester (Thorpe, 131), and the killing of Asclepiodotus follows the martyrdoms in Wace, GoM; in Wace, it is not explicitly stated that Maximian was in Britain and personally responsible for the deaths of Alban etc., but GoM *does* (pace M) state that Maximianus came to Britain (Thorpe, p. 130).

5467–86 As usual, Lawman has developed a scene from a statement of narrative fact in GoM and Wace (W 5633–48).

5495–5501 Lawman invents the scene where Coel is advised to marry Helena to Custans: in GoM he seizes the crown and marries the beautiful daughter when Coel dies; in Wace he takes her as queen (5658) after Choel's death; in Bede (Bk I, cap. 8) Constantine is said to be Constantius's son by his *concubine*, Helena. Coel is the King Cole of Nursery rhyme fame.

5518–22 This character portrait (*notatio* in the medieval rhetoric of Geoffrey de Vinsauf) of Constantine is not in the sources, which mention only his love of justice and early maturity (W 5682–6).

5538 and 5563 In the sources Maxentius is deposed, not killed, and the three uncles are made senators, not controllers of Rome [M].

5546 Here, unusually, a brief speech in GoM does not appear in direct sp. in Wace and L.

5584 In GoM he is not Welsh but from the Gewissae, who were actually West Saxons, living near the Severn estuary (Bede, III, 7) [M].

5612 In the sources the battle-field is Maisure (W 5753), Maisuria GoM. Welsh sources have *Maes Urien* 'Urien's battle-field' [M].

5635ff The discussion between Compert and Octaves is Lawman's own.

5662 Earl Adolf is simply *uns cuens* 'a count' in W 5791.

5685–89 The sick king's journey in a cart, his summoning parliament to get advice about the succession, are Lawman's invention.

5694 Conan was Conan Meriadoc, Octaves's nephew [M].

5703ff As Madden notes, history goes wild in this addition by Lawman: Maximus the tyrant (the Maximianus of Nennius and GoM) came to power in AD 382, while Gratian and Valentinian became joint emperors in 374; Constantine, however, having become emperor in 306 had died in 337, while his mother, who lived to be eighty, had died in 326, so that neither could still be monarchs of Jerusalem in Octaves's days. Nevertheless, GoM does say that Maximianus was son of Constantine's uncle (Thorpe, p. 135).

5732 Octaves's speech proposing Maurice's journey is not in Wace.

5806 Wace and Lawman omit the fears of the British that Maximianus had come to conquer Britain, with L, but not W, applying the detail instead to the expectation in Rome that Maximien and Maurice would attack Valantin and Gracien (L 5801).

5814 Conan's building of Conisbrough/-borough is Lawman's invention; Hengist is captured there in the subsequent narrative. In fact it is in Yorkshire, not Scotland, and the name derives from OE *cyning* 'king' (with ON *konungr* substituted) rather than Conan (B-H).

5824 Like GoM, Lawman has five years here, but Wace has three (W 5887).

5832 In GoM Maximianus is an assertively aggressive and acquisitive king; Wace omits this, but Lawman's Maximien also delights in his power and so decides to attack France; the details of his journey, the building of the castle and the plundering (L 5835–47) are not in Wace.

5859 In GoM and W it is Rennes rather than Nantes (MS C *Nanstes*, in error) which is seized before Maximianus orders 100,000 men and women (in Thorpe, p. 141, and *pace* Madden) to go to Brittany. In Wace the city is taken *after* Maximien and Conan confer about the 'New Britain'. Lawman makes Maximien promise his justiciar Athionard's aid in sending people when he proposes the country for Conan's future command, suggesting that he had read ahead to W 5991 and picked up Dionot's (Athionard's) name before returning to give his version of Maximien's speech and following events; but he forgot, in introducing Athionard to Conan, that Athionard is Cradoc's younger brother, as Wace says when Maximien conquers France and Rome (W 5995), and L when Cradoc dies (L 5928).

5913 Cradoc's death in Lombardy, Maurice's death from grief, and Conan's message to Athionard are all invented by L, who has meanwhile omitted Maximien's adoption of Treves as his capital, a detail which GoM derived from Gildas (Thorpe, 141, n. 1). L also alters the fates of Valentin and Gracien: one is expelled, the other killed in W 5990.

5942 Lawman explains the discrepancy between Maximien's promise of women as well as men (L 5904: their virtue was to have been secured by isolation on the voyage) by the explanation that only 1500 women had been willing to go (L 5941–2).

5955 Athionard's brutal command brings women flocking (L 5962), but in W 6017–9 he is required to send girls from the gentry and the peasantry and complies with 11,000 and 60,000 respectively (W 6039/42).

5973 Lawman excels in storms (L 5976 occurred in the shipwreck of Godlac and Delgan [L 2285]). Wace views the storm from a distance – while at the same time reminding his reader that no one seeing it could have had so cruel a heart as to remain without pity – and in Lawman's version the situation is viewed in close-up: the ships' timbers crack, the steersmen cannot cope.

5989 Each writer stresses the women's plight in this episode: GoM, unlike his successors, says that the girls were unwilling to go anyway: some loved their homes and families too much and some preferred virginity to marriage (like Chaucer's Emelye in *The Knight's Tale*); his women suffer a comparatively painless fate: they are killed for refusing intercourse or are sold as slaves. Wace's girls are more melodramatic, tearing their hair, calling on parents, saints, and screaming; they are killed, sold, and 11,000 are slaughtered at Cologne, including Dionot's daughter Ursula (whom Conan had so long loved, but who was not named in GoM at this point). Lawman's account is less hagiographic: his girls are more stoic, and call on saints rather than parents, but their fate is ghastly, for they survive the storm only to be seduced, slaughtered or drowned in the sea; in this version, Ursula is forced to become Melga's whore, and some of the girls become heathen. The brilliant scene in which Melga and Wanis, riding out the storm, see the fifteen surviving ships, speculate, investigate, and casually rape the survivors is entirely Lawman's own (L 6003–45). MS C twice has *Oriene* (5989, 6037) but at 5957 *Ursele*, 5960 *Vrseine*.

6062 This Gracien is quite distinct from the emperor of the same name whom Maximien had captured in L 5916. In GoM this one is called Gracianus municeps, and the former emperor had been killed by Maximian (although Melga and Wanis are unaccountably said to be acting as pirates on the orders of Valentinianus and Gracianus (Thorpe, 142). Lawman has invented 6062–74.

6097 As in GoM, Maximien is killed in Rome in Lawman's version, although the detail is invented; Wace corrects this to Aquilea (W 6122), from Bede (I, cap. 9).

6103 This is where Book VI begins in GoM.

6114–6150 All GoM says is that Gracianus was killed by plebs; Wace adds the detail that they tore him apart like mastiffs (W 6138). Lawman's hilariously unhistorical account, located in East Anglia and with two churls with Saxon names, must have come from folklore (and presumably a very different king's death). Frankis ('English Sources', 70, n. 20) notes that in ASC s.a. 778 two versions of the entry have, respectively, an Æþelbald and an Ælfwald.

6196 Febus is not named in GoM and Wace; the wall Lawman mentions (6199–200) is apparently a coastal defence; in GoM it runs from one sea to the other, paralleling his previous account in Bk V. 2, where he described a turf wall. Bede himself knew two walls (Bk I, cap. 6), one built by Celts, from Abercorn to Old Kilpatrick, of turf, and inadequate, and the second on the lines of 'Severus's earthwork'. The final Legion sent to Britain was in Italy at the Battle of Pollentia in early AD 403 [M].

6218 In GoM Guithelinus, Archbishop of London, delivers a speech after the (reported) words of farewell from the Romans; in Wace it is simply a wise man from the Romans who speaks, and the British do not respond in words; Lawman follows, with expansion.

6271 There must be a vestige of true history here: the attacks on the wall, from GoM, via Wace, come from Bede, (I, cap. 12) who took it from the 6thc Celt Gildas [M].

6306 The conference of bishops and its deliberations are added to Wace's brief statement that Guencelins went by the advice of the bishops; Lawman also adds the explanation which Wace cannot supply (W 6328) that Canterbury became an archbishopric after Augustine's arrival (L 6318).

6347 In Wace Guencelins does not remind the king that he is Conan's son and that all the good men left Britain with Maximien and Conan; in fact, Aldroien is the 4th king from Conan (W 6336). GoM adds an authorial exclamation at Maximian's folly in leading away the best British fighters (Thorpe, 147). In GoM Aldroenus prevaricates before agreeing to send Constantine, and in both GoM and Wace the Archbishop greets Constantine with the Latin 'Christus vivat' antiphon.

6395–6405; 6420 The details of the British living in pits in the wilderness and the women dressing like men and attacking the enemy are Lawman's own. In Wace they simply come from woods and mountains and the 'evil folk' are conquered in two lines (W 6435–6).

6429 Constantine's parliament is held at Silchester in GoM; *Cirecestre*, in MS O and some MSS of Wace (cf. Madden's note) perhaps reflects the *l/r* interchange in Anglo-Norman spellings of English place-names, rather than an alternative location in Cirencester.

6434 Wace (6444), following GoM, says that the wife was of Roman, not British, blood.

6453–6464 Constantine is stabbed in a thicket in GoM, *en un vergier* W 6463, but the rest of the scene, and Cadal's name, are only in Lawman.

6477ff Marcie's son was not made king until he could ride (L 3161), and therefore Ambrosius is not qualified yet; in Wace both are said to be little, and still at nurse (W 6472–3) but in Lawman Uther is being fed by his mother's milk, uncommon in the upper classes in medieval times, although Malory's Arthur is fed by Kay's mother while Kay is put to nurse. The choice of Ambrosius (L 6485) deviates from GoM and Wace, where opinions are divided between Ambrosius and Uther. To the barons in Wace's version Vortigern's solution seems *orrible chose* (W 6497).

6508–6607 In Wace Vortigern simply proposes escape to the already ambitious Constanz and the escape is instantly effected; the scene in Lawman is superbly conceived: additional lines stress Vortigern's grandiose self-image (L 6514–19) and the boy's wistfulness at his monastic seclusion (L 6528–35). The trick whereby the boy is extracted and the monks duped is reminiscent of fabliau, and Lawman manages the sense of place and the shifts in point of view typical of fabliau with expert skill, (despite the anachronism in making these Benedictine monks [M]; Benedict of Nursia was born c480, over half a century after any events supposed to have happened shortly after the Romans left in AD 410).

6576 A ploughland was the area of land which one plough and ploughman could keep under cultivation, and thus a unit of land-measure.

6648ff Vortigern builds on the boy king's insecurity by suggesting that his kingdom is vulnerable from many sides: only Picts, Danes and Norwegians are mentioned in GoM and Wace; untypically, L has condensed this interchange from two speeches each from Vortigern and Constanz to one from Constans, with Vortigern's second speech abbreviated.

6679–6783 This duping of the Picts is much expanded from GoM and Wace: L's additions include the agreement between Vortigern and the Picts, their two-year stay at court, the deprivation of the Britons at their expense, the detail that Vortigern had his horses ready and pretended to leave after his 'farewell speech', which he delivered at a feast, and the rôle played by Gille Callaet – who is simply 'one of them' in Wace – and the imperious demand of the Picts for drink in Constans's bedchamber.

6785–845 Vortigern's manipulation of the London citizens, their exchanges, the pursuit of the unwary Picts and Vortigern's feigned tears in his speech and distress at seeing Constans's head (L 6836) are either derived from a source other than Wace or, more likely, inventions of Lawman; this occupies 8 lines in Wace (W 6661–68).

6857–8; 6875–8 The description of Vortigern's character and his secret intentions of calling over Ambrosius and Uther are not mentioned in the sources; although Wace shows Vortigern's anxieties about reprisals from both Picts and Bretons, he does not report the gossip.

6881 It is said that Hengist and Horsa landed in Thanet; Wace says at a port in Kent (W 6705) and GoM also alludes to 'certain parts of Kent' (Thorpe, 155). Three ships are mentioned in Bede (I, 15) and ASC s.a.449 (Laud MS.) and in GoM (VI, 10) and in Wace (W 6704).

6908ff Lawman varies the account here, in making Hengest come from Germany (*Alemainne*) rather than Saxony (W, GoM; Hall [*EME*] observes that they were Jutes); and declares that lots are cast every fifteen years (L 6914) rather than on men over fifteen years of age (W 6753; GoM: 'young men'). Vortigern's sudden enquiry about their god (L 6932) in GoM and W follows from Hengest's attribution of their arrival to Mercury's guidance (W 6765) [M].

6935ff GoM mentions Saturn, Jove, and Mercury who is known as Woden by Saxons, to which Wace adds Phoebus [M]; Lawman adds the 'pagan' gods of French romance, accredited to the Saracens: Apollin and Tervagant (he omits Mahomet); *Tervagant* is *Diana Trivia*, sister of Apollo in her three aspects of sky, underworld and earth. 'From the first century the Roman gods were identified with those of the Teutons and Celts and clerics such as Martin of Bracara (6thc Spanish) and Ælfric of Eynsham (end of 10thc) deprecating pagan practices do so too. Under this system Mercury = Woden, Jupiter = Th(un)or, Mars = Tiw, Venus = Frea' (Hall, *EME*).

6951ff GoM and Wace note that Wednesday is Woden's and Friday is given to Frea, and cite the English forms of the days (W 6785, 6792). Lawman expands by tracing 5 other days, omitting Wednesday. Hall (*EME*) notes that the Romans adopted from the Chaldeans the seven-day week allotted to heavenly bodies; they knew of it fully in the 1stc AD and it was in regular use by the third, after which it spread everywhere among the northern nations, who each substituted their own equivalent deities for the names of the days, 'Saturn alone proving intractable'. The northern invaders were apparently indeed already in possession of the system when they settled in England. *Tidea* (L, MSS C and O) must be an error in a common ancestor for *Tiwe*. Hengest's 'pious' farewell (L 6968–9) is not in Wace.

6975–7017 Hall (*EME*) suggests that *sent* in 6975 should read *siʒen him to* 'next the Saxon knights followed after them'. Wace does not say that the Saxons were better fed and clothed than the Britons, and he does not have the five noblemen's sons asking for assistance against the Picts.

Lawman also enhances the battle details (L 7005–10).

6976 *ancestors' race*: MS C reads *aldene* (O is absent) for which Hall's emendation (*EME*) *aldrene* has been adopted.

7001 *saving*: or 'secret' if *hele* means 'hidden' rather than OE *hǽlo* 'safety'.

7011 Lindsey: so Wace (W 6842) and GoM but Nennius says it was Thanet [M].

7031–83 In this discussion between Hengest and Vortigern, Lawman adds the sly allusion to the two boys (L 7037–48) and Hengest's wish to send for wife and daughter, to which L then makes Vortigern respond (L 7064–5). This points up the dramatic irony: in his fear of reprisals from one family, Vortigern invites another, equally dangerous to himself, into the country. Hall (*EME*) notes that *Androien* (L 7047) should be *Androgeus*, L's usual form.

7088 *splendid hide*: Skeat and Morris suggest that for MS C *feire hude* Lawman wrote *fere* 'bull's *hude*; MS O has *bole hude*.

7095 A similar tale of land 'covered by a bull's hide' is told in Saxo Grammaticus of Ivarr's foundation of London; both derive from Virgil, *Aeneid* i, 371 [Hall]. The names Kaer Carrai and Thongcastle (*Thwancastre*) are in GoM and Wace (W 6917/19) but 'Long castle' (*Lane castel* L 7108) is not in either, although the earlier edition of Wace contained this corrupt reading (as Hall and Madden note) and Lawman must have used a similarly corrupted MS. The traditional site for Hengest's castle is Tong, nr Milton, in Kent, but Camden in 1586 put it at Caster in Lincolnshire near Grimsby [Hall]. Blenner-Hassett has an irrelevant note on Lancaster on the Lune.

7128 *trestle-boards*: fixed tables were rare before the 16thc: in house and castle food was eaten on removable boards balanced on trestles which were covered in cloths for meals and stacked away after feasts; *were spread*: MS O has *lette* 'had' (spread) MS C *hetten* 'ordered to be (spread).

7141–57 Wace and Geoffrey both give Rowena's words and the correct response in 'Saxon'; 'wassail' means 'be hale'; Geoffrey took it from Nennius, without giving the interpreter's name; Wace found *Keredic* (W 6957) in Nennius, and L copies W [M]. The Old English occurs in *Beowulf* 407 as: *Wes hāl*; Lawman's forms *wæs hæil* are actually West Norse rather than Saxon (Hall (*EME*)].

7163–7164 Lawman's observation about English drinking habits (not in Wace here) reflects the poor image the French had of the English, also found in Nigel Wireker at the end of the 12thc: 'sine lege bibunt wesseil et dringail' and in Wace's account of the English on the night before Hastings: 'They cry "be blithe" and "wassail", and "let the cup come" and "drinchail", "drink after drink" and "drink to me, drink full, drink half and drink to thee"' [Hall (*EME*)].

7182 For Lawman it is scandalous that Vortigern has to dispense with the Church twice: at Constans's coronation (L 6620), and his own wedding; Wace is more scandalised by the shame and sin of Vortigern's loving a pagan (W 6993).

7183 The morning-gift in Germanic law was given by the husband to his new bride on consummation of the marriage to provide her with means of support in the form of land in the event of her widowhood. Kent was demanded by Hengest's people as a condition of the marriage in Wace and GoM, and London is not mentioned [M].

7195–7197 Another 'family' detail, not in Wace, who merely says the mother was dead.

7211ff The opening of this feast is lost in surviving MSS of Wace. Hengest is now handling Vortigern as the latter had handled Constans; there is a hint of this in the similar style Wace allocates to Vortigern's response (W 7051–2, cf. W 6595), a point L misses in his rendering although there is some parallelism (L 6665, cf. L 7230, added by L).

7221 Ebissa is simply the younger brother in GoM (Thorpe, 161) and cousin in Wace (W 7042). The sworn or blood-brotherhood was a specially close relationship, more intimate than that between siblings, which is found in medieval romance and Icelandic saga.

7263–7296 As usual, Lawman has supplied a debate where Wace merely states that the British asked Vortigern to send back all or most of the Germans, he refused, and they elected Vortimer.

7331 Lawman has conflated two battles: the battle at Epiford is distinct from and follows that on the Derwent in GoM, being the second of the four in which the Saxons are defeated; the other two Lawman has correctly: on the coast (L 7346) and on Thanet (L 7354). The Anglo-Saxon Chronicle records the 'Epiford' battle s.a. AD 455 as 'at Aylesford (where) Horsa was slain'; s.a. 457 is a battle at Crayford in Kent where the Britons are routed (which may be the battle at 'Derwent'), and under 465 is a battle at *Wippedesfleot* where 12 Welsh nobles are slain, and a British thane called Wipped; GoM and Wace have the battles in the order Nennius lists them. Then s.a. 473 the ASC records the total victory of Hengest and Æsc, with the British fleeing 'like fire': this is the point where GoM sends back the *defeated* Germans Vortigern's internal exile (L 7382) is not mentioned in Wace. *Epiford* occurs in GoM and Wace and is Nennius's Saxon equivalent (as *Episford*) of *Rit hergabail* 'ford of the great ambush'; *Epiford* is 'Eoppa's ford' or 'ford at the high place' [B-H].

7392 St Germanus's arrival is narrated immediately after Vortigern's marriage in GoM; L follows Wace's re-ordering. Germanus in fact came in AD 429 and c435–44, first with Lupus and secondly with Severus (Bede, I, 15, 21), Nennius referring only to the second visit. GoM conflates the two in mentioning Lupus of Troyes as Germanus's companion; Bede dates the arrival of Hengest and Horsa to 449 (I, cap. 15). Wace has put Germanus into Vortimer's reign (AD 464–68) under Pope Romanus (AD 897–98) [M]; he may have been misled by Bede's arrangement, which mentions Hengist and Horsa in I, 15 and Germanus and Lupus's arrival in I, 17.

7400–30 Vortimer's speech, his religious and legal reforms, and Germanus's reply are not in Wace.

7431 Lawman adopts the romance transition device 'Now let us turn to X . . .', cf. L 7645.

7434–7497 In GoM Renwein gets a servant to poison Vortimer (Thorpe, 162) and in Wace she simply has him poisoned. Le Saux shows that GoM's *Vita Merlini* states that Hengist's sister (*sic*) Renua gave poison to Vortimer (*Sources*, p. 113). Once again, with no prompting from his source, Lawman develops a scene where a woman plays a prominent (and here notorious) rôle. Madden thinks this is evidence that he had access to other traditions. He could have made this up, however, using the famous 'wassail, drinkhail' seduction scene and parodying it in this grotesque way. Rowena is the wicked step-mother of folk tale, who poisons her step-son with venom which she carries at her breast instead of mother's milk (L 7476).

7519 Lawman invents the burial-place at Billingsgate:; in GoM Vortimer ordered a brass pyramid, in Wace simply a long-lasting tomb (W 7175).

7574 The moralising is not in Wace, who does, however, follow GoM's dating of the appointed meeting to the Kalends of May (May Day), perhaps too learned for L's audience?

7579 The place is spelled *Ælenge* in MS C, *Elinge* in O, and Madden and Blenner-Hassett associate it with Allington, 4m from Amesbury and 5 from Stonehenge; not in GoM or Wace.

7610–11 This famous command is found in corrupt form in Nennius, GoM (as *nimet oure saxes*) and in Wace: *nem eure sexes*; *eoure* 'your' must be correct, and such a command would originally have been: *nimeð eowre seax*. The *sax* was a short sword, and it may be true that the Saxons took their name from this weapon but not, of course, from this incident (L 7679ff). The peasant who supplies the club is Lawman's invention: Eldol 'found' the club in GoM and Wace does not know who had brought it (W 7264). Lawman adds to this episode (as usual) the speeches of Hengest and Vortigern and the impression of a vast, ostensibly friendly crowd (L 7606–08).

7652ff Lawman enhances Vortigern's plight, making him unable to eat, and left without one turf of land (L 7682). Vortigern's council of prominent men (L 7695–7714) is not reported in direct speech in Wace; in GoM they are magicians, in W prominent men and sorcerers. The Mount of Reir (L 7706, Wace *munt d'Erir*, W 7328) is Mount Erith in GoM and may be Snowdon (Welsh *Eryri* [B-H]).

7717, 7724: *machine* (MS C *machunnes*, lacking in O): one of Lawman's rare French words and perhaps some form of excavation equipment using a bore or battering-ram.

7745–7882 Lawman's account of the discovery of Merlin shows a refinement of characterisation and a pointing up of situation compared with his sources. He supplies a name for the spokesmen of the counsellors, Joram (L 7745) and for the reeve Eli (L 7783), and supplies conversation for each where Wace merely alludes to their opinions; like GoM he tells us that the messengers looking for the boy without a father were weary and sat down outside Carmarthen to watch the boys at play (this is om in Wace). He adds the amused observation that boys at play always quarrel (L 7766) and Dinabuz' delight when Merlin is taken off by the authorities (L 7801–2). His handling of Merlin's mother is masterly: in GoM she speaks dispassionately, unlike a nun and certainly not like a woman mystified and disturbed by an unexplained pregnancy (Thorpe, 167–8). Wace adds mystery: the creature is *une chose*, repeated in Lawman ('thing') but it is Lawman who gives the girl a home, a devoted royal father and attendants, and tells us that she was only 15 at the time; his presentation of her discovery of her pregnancy from her symptoms (L 7845–8) is convincing, as is her modesty and embarrassment shown in her gestures (L 7829, cf. W 7412 and 7855).

7859 Magan, Maugantius in GoM, appears from nowhere (Tatlock) and may, with Dinabuz (L 7768) have come from a now lost written or oral tradition.

7883–8 Lawman's presentation of the clever boy Merlin is convincing: the shorter lines assigned to him (L 7906–20) give the impression of a child speaking, and Lawman adds the ill-feeling between Joram and Merlin as a motive for Joram's lies in 7753 (Wace merely said that the requirement of a fatherless boy's blood might be a lie [W 7348]). The beautiful stone (L 7933) is Lawman's, probably deriving from Merlin's statement in GoM and Wace that a pool, in which two dragons reside in hollow stones, underlies the castle foundations (W 7517–20). Lawman enhances the description of pool and ensuing dragon-fight.

7971ff At this point in GoM Book VII, the originally separate 'Prophecies of Merlin' begins. Wace declines to repeat these, since they are well known and he can't understand them (W 7535–42) and Lawman supplies the detail that first the White Dragon won, then the Red, and then the Red wounds the White to death. The battle, but not its outcome, prefaces Merlin's prophetic trance in GoM; L then moves, with Wace, to GoM VIII, cap. i; in W, Vortigern requests to know his own fate; L has a telling rôle-reversal in which the bastard child rebukes his monarch (L 7996ff) for not asking the right question. Mannyng completes the account of the dragons by declaring that the White kills the Red and then dies four days later in grief (Mg 8208); Mannyng's dragon-fight is not from Wace, and is very graphic.

8070 *Cloard* (GoM Cloartius) is Little Doward (Welsh, 'two hills') in former Monmouthshire, which Madden thinks gives Cloard by *d/cl* confusion in an early scribe in GoM. In Wace and GoM Aurelius calls upon Eldol of Gloucester (L Aldolf) to avenge Constantine and Constans upon Vortigern; L substitutes the mocking speech L 8089–92 and brings Aldolf back only in L 8102.

8132ff Hengest's speech, voicing sentiments ascribed to him in Wace, is Lawman's own.

8166 These Scots, not in Wace, are an error, since they were on Hengest's side (L 8109).

8198ff The prayers of the pagans, the battle-cry of Aurelius and Hengest's speech are not in Wace's version.

8242–8265 Eldulf grabs the nose-piece of his helmet in Wace (W 7812); the *coif* was a protective layer, usually also chain-mail, worn under the helmet, connecting with the cuirass ('coat of mail, byrny') by means of a neck-piece to protect the back of the neck. Aldolf's cry of derision in L 8248 is not in Wace. In Wace he has prayed to God for this chance to get Hengest and in GoM has requested it of Aurelius; L brings both ideas into Aldolf's speech in L 8256–62, which he has modified from Eldulf's general speech of triumph in Wace, adding Aurelius's reply; L 8261 is based on Eldulf's remark in Wace that the mad dog must be killed (W 7819). See also line 10689.

8281 The liturgical 'hours' of the Church were sung throughout the hours of daylight at intervals which varied according to the length of day, from prime at dawn to compline at dusk, with Matins (in a strict monastic régime) sung in the small hours. In high summer, nones would be about 3 p.m. in Lawman's latitude. However, Madden (III, 491) equates this expression with Danish/Swedish *non* 'midday meal', which is the interpretation given for this instance in MED, so that the line should perhaps read: 'When the third day had come and when they had dined'.

8345–6 The pagan rites (from Wace) in GoM included the building of a tumulus (Thorpe, 193); the prayer for no salvation is one of Lawman's own jokes.

8359 In GoM Octa and his men have chains round their necks and gravel on their heads, a gesture of humiliation similar to the ceremony of creating a serf, in which money was placed on the head and a rope round the neck. Neither GoM nor Wace mentions that the men were nearly naked and walked in pairs, nor that Octa lay prostrate before Aurelius (L 8396).

8378 This list resembles the gods named by Hengest, although Dido and Mamilo are odd. Wace and GoM do not have the promise of conversion (L 8383–4), nor is this made the condition of their reprieve as in L 8404. In Wace Eldaldus speaks of the mercy shown by the Jews to those of Gabaon rather than the terrible reprisals to be meted out in case of recidivism (L 8418–20).

8422ff, 8442ff, 8476ff, 8486ff These addresses by Aurelius and the advice of Tremorius are not given in direct speech in Wace. The effect, as with so many of Lawman's additions of direct speech, is an impression of rule by consultation and shared decision-making; Wace had already added much direct speech to the third person narrative of GoM with its occasional long and rather florid speeches, and Lawman takes the development much further. There is not much evidence that these speeches add significantly to characterisation.

8496 *Alaban* is an unidentified spring which Blenner-Hassett locates in the district of Eywas Harold in Herefordshire (Gwent); Wace has *A Labanes*; GoM has *Galabes . . . in natione Gewisseorum.*

8500–8739 This episode of the transfer of Stonehenge from Ireland shows Merlin in the same semi-comical, semi-admonitory light of Part I of Malory's *Le Morte Darthur*; despite Merlin's refusal to do party tricks (L 8548ff, also in GoM and Wace) laughter and misunderstanding figure several times in the narrative, as in the sources, but to this Lawman adds Merlin's intuitive knowledge of why he has been sent for (L 8515ff,

8562ff), his stout rebuke when offered reward (L 8510), his advice to the men to bathe and rest before removing the Giants' Ring (L 8625–29). L has rearranged material, leaving Merlin explaining to the soldiers, rather than to Aurelius earlier as in Wace that the stones were brought from Africa (L 8620) [M].

8590 As Hall notes, this was a medieval proverb.

8642–51 Gillomaur's scornful speech is not in Wace. *St Brendan* was an abbot, born in C. Kerry, c 486 and died c 578. Of him were written the 10thc *Voyages of St Brendan*. Gillomaur's speech abounds in assertive expressions: *ne scullen heo, ich wulle*, which, perhaps by coincidence, parallel modern Irish use of *will*, and I have therefore incorporated this idiom into the translation.

8658 The nakedness of the Irish is regarded by Tatlock (pp. 416–7) as evidence that Lawman had been to Ireland; Wace merely says that the Irish were not well armed nor used to combat (W 8113–4). The same remark occurs at L 9011, with no parallel in Wace; Madden notes that the Irish lacked armour as late as the 16thc and reckons they might have removed the trews for battle; the arms attributed to the Irish (L 11147–8), axes, spears and knives tally with contemporary records of the 12thc–15thc (M, III p. 367).

8680–8710 Lawman heightens this account of how Uther and his men could not move the stones, and extends Merlin's speeches (L 8680ff, 8693ff); the strange account of Merlin's magic incantations (L 8700–02) is in Wace, but not the claim that the stones are like feather-balls (L 8706–7), which in O reads 'feather-beds'. Recent geological evidence suggests that the bluestones at Stonehenge were not, as previously assumed, transported by human agency 4,000 years ago (considerably earlier than Merlin), but erratics from an iceflow 400,000 years ago moving from the Irish Sea across the Preseli Mountains; the sarcens came from within 25 miles of Stonehenge.

8736 St Dubricius was Bishop of Llandaff and died in AD 612; Samson, Bishop of Dol, had no connexion with York; he attended the Council of Paris in AD 557 [H].

8740–9099 *Passent's rebellion and Aurelius's death*: Lawman supplies Passent's speeches (L 8754–64, 8778–84), in the first of which he supplies the information of Aurelius's illness which follows their arrival in Wales in Wace, and Aurelius's words (L 8788ff). His handling of Appas's proposal reveals the man's cynicism: he will please Passent (*iqueme*) by killing Aurelius (*aquele*) in a clumsily punning *contrarium* lost in translation (L 8807). I the reward Appas is offered is a captaincy in the army in GoM, a thousand pounds in Wace (W 8243) and only one hundred in Lawman (8809); in GoM Eopa describes his plan elaborately to Passent; Lawman and Wace have him arriving in monk's habit but are silent about his medical knowledge and equipment until he begins his deception; only Lawman makes him address Aurelius and claim that he is acting out of love for God (L 8835–41) and ingratiate himself with the king's knights with his spices and issue instructions for the king's care (L 8864ff). The discovery of Appas's flight, the grief at the discovery of the mortally sick king, and his dying speech of benediction on Uther and burial directives (L 8889–8903) are all Lawman's invention; in GoM Aurelius dies in his sleep (Thorpe, 200). Uther's urgent whisper to Merlin on seeing the comet (L 8931–4) and Merlin's odd reaction, revolving like a worm, are not in Wace, who does, however, record Uther's grief at his brother's death (W 8321–3).

8853 *scamony*: a gum-resin from the roots of *convolvulus scammonia* which comes from Syria, used as a highly irritant purgative. It is noted in the *Anglo-Saxon Leechdom* of c1000. Madden points out that *scamony* is not really lethal (III, 365ff).

8948, 8979 Hall identifies Merlin's behaviour with the Welsh Awenyddion described by Giraldus Cambrensis c1194 in *Descriptio Cambriae*; the sleep resembles the shaman's cataleptic trance.

9000–07 Compare Gillomaur's previous boast and the narrator's comment, L 8642–53.

9028 This is another of Lawman's own jokes. All the battle exchanges and details are Lawman's: Wace merely reports that the British killed Passent and the Irish king.

9070ff Merlin's disappearance is not recorded in Wace; in GoM he plays no part after the entry into Tintagel.

9098 *Pendragon* probably means 'head (i.e. 'chief') Dragon' [M].

9106 Utherpendragon is the title now applied to Uther in Wace, but in GoM he has this name from his first mention, in babyhood (Thorpe, p. 151).

9100 *Osa* is *Eosa*, the name of Octa's companion in GoM from Bk VIII, cap. 6; *Ebissa*, the brother whom Nennius said came with Octa is mentioned in GoM VI, cap. 13 and not afterwards; Wace retains *Ebissa* until Aurelius dies and then substitutes *Eossa* although other versions of the Brut use *Eosa* for *Ebissa* throughout. Lawman, finding first *Ebissa* and then *Eosa* in Wace assumed two people were involved, and this error recurs, [M III. 367–8]; in subsequent instances L calls him *Ossa* but I have normalised all forms to *Osa*. B&W, following Tatlock, assume that Os(s)a and Ebissa are indeed two characters.

9150 Mount Dunien is Danien in Wace, Damen in GoM [M], and may be *Dinnand*, a boundary-stone in the hills N. of Danby parish, 30m. N.E. of York [B-H].

9163ff Uther does not appeal specifically to Gorlois in Wace, and he does not behave in the depressed manner of Uther in L 9169. In the account of the battle Wace has an extended simile modelled on several in GoM (but this one is not in GoM) of the lion scattering a flock of sheep. GoM likes pastoral imagery of this kind; Lawman several times refers to a hero in battle 'like a lion', a commonplace simile in later chivalric romance, but does not echo Wace here. However, this kind of simile in Wace (and GoM?) may have inspired Lawman to produce his own 'long-tailed similes' in the Arthurian section.

9230 Easter is his coronation day in Wace (8554), and one of several crown-bearing days in GoM.

9245ff This is the point where Malory's *Le Morte Darthur* begins;

Malory is able to suggest by opening 'in medias res' that there had been a long antipathy between Gorlois and Uther, whereas the complete context points up clearly not only Uther's ingratitude to Gorlois, who has been the means of rescuing the king and turning imminent defeat into victory, but also the grim parallel with Vortigern, who brought near disaster on his kingdom by falling in love with an unsuitable woman at a feast.

9250 Wace's praise of Ygerne is fuller: *Curteise esteir e bele e sage* (8575), as indeed his description of Gorlois had been: very dignified, wise and courteous (W 8466); Lawman confines himself to *hende* 'courteous' in L 9170 and 9246 for Gorlois.

9254 Lawman seems to hint at a response here from Ygerne, but he is simply translating Wace: 'Here Ygerne behaved so that she did not approve, did not contradict (W 8595–6). Her inscrutability is dropped when she laments the men who lose their lives for her sake (L 9290–1), and Ulfin declares that she, like her mother, is faithful (L 9359–60, not in Wace).

9274–79 Gorlois's angry outburst, his threats and pending fate (L 9283) are not in Wace.

9300 *Tintagel* 9320 *Tamar*: Tintagel, the site still visible as a 12thc castle built on a Romano-British settlement partly eroded by the sea on the North Cornish coast, is the setting for the Tristram legend. 'Tamar', MS O *Tambre*, MS C *Tambreis* should be the Rivel Camel which flows into the Bristol Channel: here Arthur is to fight his last battle against Modred, his life moving in an inexorable circle back to its beginning (L 14238); see note to 14238 on the form *Tambre*.

9329 Lawman omits Wace's statement that Gorlois was expecting support from Ireland, but has already added information that Uther had men from many lands (L 9315) and has added the numbers involved (L 9304/06), enhancing the impression that a serious insurrection has broken out over one man's lustful fancy. Uther's passion is restrained compared with the lyrical outpourings of Wace's Uther (W 8657–67: 'I cannot go, come, wake, sleep, rise, retire, drink or eat without remembering Ygerne').

9363–9432 Once again Merlin knows why he is being fetched, and makes this declaration the opportunity for a prophecy of Arthur in the style of GoM's *Prophecies of Merlin*, incorporating the famous allusion to the literature of Arthur in future times (L 9410–2), of which Lawman's work was one instance. Yet all this is an addition to Wace, in whose version, as in GoM, Merlin is already present in the army. Merlin's second refusal of payment (L 9444f) and his arrangements for guarding the king's tent (L 9466ff) are not in Wace [M], and Le Saux thinks that both are taken from the lesser-known third work by GoM, the *Vita Merlini*, from which in her opinion Lawman also drew the reference to Merlin's abode in the wilderness and his acquaintance with a hermit: in the *Vita* Merlin himself becomes a hermit (Le Saux, *Sources*, p. 114f.).

9371 *plough's worth*: see note 6576; this is a huge bribe.

9475–9507 The domestic details, servants, a porter, the lady of the castle greeting her husband and arranging the bed, are all Lawman's additions to this scene, as is his repeated assertion that Ygerne did not know 'who lay in her arms' (L 9506–7, 9513), and his later addition (L 9598–9) shows her stubbornly refusing to believe that the secret message Uther gave her in bed proved that her husband was not with her. As Rosemary Morris states (*Character of Arthur*, p. 28), Ygerne is raped, an innocent who suffers at the hands of men, as are so many of Lawman's women; when Uther leaves her in Wace, he kisses and embraces her (W 8783–4) but Lawman's Uther strides out masterfully leaving instructions that Ygerne is to be reassured (L 9577).

9518–40 Lawman's sense of situation is keen: the anxiety of the men whose general has disappeared is evident, as is their good martial training: they work out what to do. This is not in Wace, who, however, makes his Uther more devious, pretending that he left the siege because he feared treason (W 8767) and feigns anger at Gorlois's death (W 8800) [M].

9608–15 The 'elves' are Lawman's addition to Wace; Madden thinks they have been taken from French romance, into which they were adopted from the Norse tradition in which *norns* attend a child at birth. If Lawman were writing significantly after 1200, his inspiration could have been the tradition presented by works like *Ogier le Danois*, as Madden notes. An obvious influence could have been the prose *Lancelot du Lake*, in which Lancelot is cared for in infancy by the Lady of the Lake; if Lancelot was becoming a popular romance hero, ousting Arthur from the centre of narrative interest, at the time Lawman wrote, this could have been one of his strategies to reinstate the original hero of the Matter of Britain.

9620–9890 Lawman's version of Uther's final years differs from Wace's in the handling of Octa and the rebels: the suborning of the guards, reported in Wace, becomes a dramatised episode (L 9634–51) and the ensuing threat to the kingdom is given more prominence (L 9684–88) so that Uther's self-assertion, characterised by two challenging speeches added by L (L 9699–700 and 9743–54) is the more impressive. Octa's mockery is represented (L 9719–31) rather than simply echoed in Uther's own triumph (L 9776–83) as in Wace, which itself is heightened both by the religious note and by the additional song of triumph of the men, set off from the surrounding text by its more marked 'rhyme' (L 9768-72). The savage humour of Octa's vaunting (L 9728–31), matched by Uther's (L 9781), is Lawman's own. The plotting of Uther's murder (L 9810–76) is entirely Lawman's: Wace simply relates that spies lived in court until they found out that Uther drank from a fountain which they poisoned and fled (W 8964–89).

9707 As Wace and Lawman explain, Verulamium took the name St Albans from Alban's martyrdom there (c287 AD).

9768–72 I have laid out the half-lines of the B&L edition as single lines (and created an additional half-line from line 9769) to give some impression of a soldiers' marching-song.

9791–2 Lawman has just said this.

9795 *Winchester* is an error: Wace has Verolam and explains that the barons dissuaded Uther from pursuing the fleeing Saxons, and he retained only a small retinue (W 8939–50).

9803 Kings and great households distributed to the needy through their stewards the 'broken meats' from their feasts. It is at such a distribution of food that Brian is able to enter Edwin's palace (L 15357).

9879 Lawman's *blakien* can mean 'become pale' as well as 'grow black', but Wace here has 'changed colour and went black' (*teinst e nerci*). In L 9924 *blac* clearly means 'pale' and is glossed 'pale, wan pallid' in MED; for L 946 *blake* MED glosses under both *blak* 2(a) 'dark' and *blok* 1(b) ?livid.

9896–9981 Geoffrey's Book IX begins with the plea of Archbishop Dubricius of Caerleon for Arthur to be crowned, but neither he nor Wace claims that Arthur was in Brittany (where Aurelius and Uther had been kept safe in their childhood). The official greeting and Arthur's response (L 9913–22; 9928–9) are Lawman's additions and modelled on his handling of the emotional pointing in the Leir story (cf. L 1533, 1537; 1762, 1764).

9945ff GoM mentions Arthur's generosity, courage and innate goodness, Wace adds his qualities as knight and leader and love of glory; Lawman's additions emphasise the wealth of his household.

9962–10199 *The Coronation; Campaign against Colgrim and Baldulf*: Lawman's handling of this episode highlights Arthur's qualities of leadership and powers of decision: he consults and advises. The assembly in London and Arthur's oath are not in Wace (L 9962ff) [M], nor is his stratagem of simulating retreat (L 10023ff). The River Douglas (Celtic: 'dark stream') in 10014 rises near Wigan and joins the Ribble near its mouth (B-H).

This section and that following are noted for the similes, notably from the pastoral and natural world, which may imitate French romance, and also GoM's similes in the style of classical epic. These similes are as follows:

(i) Arthur likened to the wolf in winter snow (10041–2);
(ii) Arthur and his men advance like the high wood under a raging wind (10047–8);
(iii) Colgrim's defeated Saxons are like a crane in the marshes (10061–67);
(iv) Arthur likens Childric to the hunted fox (10398–413);
(v) Arthur is like the wild boar encountering other swine (10609–10)
(vi) Arthur likens Colgrim to the goat harassed by a wolf (10629–36);
(vii) Arthur describes how Baldulf sees steel fish in the Avon (10639–45);
(viii) Arthur likens Childric to a hunter whose hunt is abandoned (10647–50).

The seventh is not, of course, a simile but a metaphor: the 'fish' are drowned warriors in armour, a startling image because it is unexpected.

The images cluster in two sections of a 600–line textual area and may derive from a lost neo-epic on Arthur's conquest of the Saxons (presumably in French, if so), but may simply be original with Lawman, prompted by typical images of warriors as beasts of prey and routed warriors as sheep or goats, and large hosts resembling rain/hail/leaves falling; such images abound (obtrusively for the most part) in GoM. There is one slight blemish in that Baldulf is to be killed like a wolf (L 10114), the aggressor animal to which Arthur is elsewhere likened.

10025 *army*: Lawman here uses *ferde*, the OE word for the defending army, to refer to the invader Colgrim's forces; in the Cassibellaune episode he is, apparently, preserving the distinction between OE *here* 'hostile force' and *fyrd* 'levy of home or English troops'.

10062 MS O here reads *fliht* 'power of flight', while MS C has *floc* 'flock', which B&W prefer: 'his flock is scattered'; D&W prefer O: 'his power of flight is diminished', and Madden trans. 'his flight is impaired'. The crane is gregarious outside the breeding season, and although extremely rare now, was a regular winter-visitor 150 years ago, and presumably flocks were a familiar sight in medieval times.

10100, 10155 *Maurin* the British mercenary with the Saxons and Patrick the Scot who defects to Arthur are Lawman's inventions; their speeches, and the words of Arthur's Britons (L 10179–81) give depth to the presentation of Arthur: we see him as his men do and the demonstration of their loyalty and cooperation enhance his prestige as a good leader. The extent of his problem is stressed in L's addition in 10185–99.

10116 *under canvas*: *on comele* occurs several times in Lawman and nowhere else. Madden thought it meant 'tent', Brook suggests 'hiding-place', Hall 'assembly, expedition for hunting or war'; here MS O has *in teldes* 'in tents' and Wace *buschement*, but in 15173 Cadwathlan is not in hiding nor hunting as he attacks Northumberland, and 'encamped in tents' or 'on expedition' must be the meaning there.

10133ff A similar story is told of King Alfred, who is said to have entered the Danish camp disguised as a minstrel. B&W cite Tatlock, (*Legendary History*, p. 347) who claims that GoM used this account of Alfred in William of Malmesbury's *Gesta Regum*, completed 1125.

10160 *emperor*: Lawman treats Childric as if he were the Holy Roman Emperor, a title used by the head of the Western Empire, also styled Emperor (under the form Kaiser) of Germany or Almaigne. Richard of Cornwall, brother of Henry III, took this title in 1257 and was crowned 'King of the Romans' but never received the Imperial Diadem; this, however, was probably some four decades after Lawman completed his *Brut*.

10201–10799 *The Defeat of Childric*: This long section only occupies chapters 2–5 of GoM's Bk IX, but it is already extended in Wace by a rousing speech from Arthur (replacing the earlier speech of Dubricius in GoM), with some modification of the British losses and difficulties. This is considerably amplified by Lawman, (i) by supplying specific detail, such as the numbers of Howel's and Arthur's forces (L 10260f), the newly-built castle of Childric, and the countries from which Howel's men came (L 10220–23), the counties devastated by the Saxons (Wace names only three) and the districts Arthur conquers in Scotland, additional atrocities committed by Childric's men (L 10459–72), their threats to Arthur (L 10473–83), and by filling out the narrative, for example with the celebrations at the arrival of Howel (L 10254–7), the name of Arthur's first victim in battle (L 10595), the method of killing Childric's men at the boats (L 10734–78). (ii) by inserting additional narrative themes, such as the dispatching of a man to open Lincoln gates (L 10272–81). (iii) as usual, by supplying speeches (e.g. L 10287–98, 10345–54, 10357, 10370f, 10374–90, 10392–10427) and prayers (L 10305–6). (iv) by poetic heightening: the army moving like a fire advancing (10300), Childric like a trapped fox (10398ff), with the other images (above), Arthur riding as fast as a bird flies (L 10656), Cador leaps on horseback like a spark from fire (L 10719). (v) by developing a sense of place and perspective: Childric comes out of the tent to do homage to Arthur (10431); the weather at sea is glorious as the Saxons set off (10440–4).

From a plain, if important, narrative statement in Wace of Arthur's growing political control, the episode becomes a study in the interplay of personalities: Colgrim and Baldulf regret Arthur's sudden eminence, he overreacts to power and unwisely grants clemency, which no one dares speak against, until he is confronted by treason, when his self-disgust is transmuted to vengeance (L 10510–31). Typically, where GoM and Wace merely mention the killing of hostages (W 9261) Lawman's Arthur calls for gallows and we hear that 24 noble children are killed (L 10529–33), a reminiscence of Belinus's behaviour at Rome. Lawman completes the vengeance by making Arthur's foes die at his hands: Wace merely reports that Colgrim and Baldulf were killed (W 9358), and so lacks Arthur's mocking funeral oration: 'we pray that your souls never have bliss' (L 10694–706).

10201 In GoM Howel is said to be Arthur's nephew, his sister's son, but Arthur's sister Anna married Lot; Thorpe claims he was Aurelius's son, and so Arthur's first cousin (Thorpe, pp. 214, 216), but M. Blaess (*BBIAS*, 8 (1956), cited in B&W, suggests that the 'sister' intended might have been one of Igerne's children by Gorlois; Lawman resolves the problem by calling him 'kinsman'.

10325 *Calidon* is probably meant to be in Scotland (cf. Caledonia), but Mannyng claimed that it was in Lincolnshire in his 1338 *Chronicle*.

10338 Lawman puns on *treo* 'tree' and *treoliche* 'truly', but MS O removes the pun by reading *kenliche* 'bravely'.

10455 *luff*: see note 4859.

10543–60 The description of the arming of Arthur, a motif common to epic and romance, is similar in GoM and Wace, but Lawman adds the name of his helm, Goosewhite (10552) and perhaps of his byrny. Line 10545 is problematic: depending on whether the referent for *he* is *smið* or *burne*, *Wygar* could be the name of the smith or of the cuirass (but its meaning, 'battle-spear', makes this second unlikely); *Witeȝe* could be an

adj. referring to Wygar 'the skilful smith'. The line therefore may mean:
(a) 'he (the smith) was called Wigar, who made Witeȝe'; (b) 'he was
called Wygar the skilful smith'; (c) 'it was called Wygar which Witeȝe
made'; Brook and this translation interpret according to (c). Madden
suggests that a confused recollection of Wayland the Smith lies at the
back of line 10545, and D&W derive *Witeȝe* from *Widia*, son of
Wayland the smith, but not himself a smith. *Pridwen* 'blessed form' is
Arthur's boat in Welsh tradition, rather than his shield; the name may
refer to the image of the Virgin painted on the shield; in L 11866 we are
told that the shield was made of ivory. 'Ron' means 'spear'; in L 11869–
70 we are told that the spear was also once Uther's and was made in
Caermarthen by a smith called Griffin [M]. *Caliburn* (Excalibur), like
Ron and *Pridwen*, occurs in GoM.

10564–79 This is the only speech in the episode which is also in Wace
(W 9317–36), with Arthur's war-cry (L 10597–10600; W 9342–44). In
GoM the speech has preceded the arming and is backed up by the
Archbishop Dubricius; in Wace, once armed, the troops advance to meet
the Saxons on a hilltop (W 9301–14), omitted by Lawman who instead
has Childric and his men mounting as if for combat on level terrain
(L 10582–5).

10689 *coif*: see note to 8242.

10783 Teignwick (W 9393) is Wace's 'correction' of GoM 'Thanet',
not the obvious place to leave ships when fighting at Bath [M]. Blenner-
Hassett prefers identification with Kingsteignton, surmising that the old
name for *Teignmouth* might have been *Teignwick*. Cador's sense of
humour (L 10790), like his style of battle address (L 10748) is modelled
on his king's.

10798 Brook compares *Peterborough Chronicle* s.a. 1135 'no matter
who was carrying a freight of gold and silver, no one dared treat him
other than properly', and cf. 1257 and n.

10800–11102 *The Scottish campaign* is not structurally different
from Wace. Wace added the mothers and their plea to GoM's clerics.
This speech, with its moving rhetoric, is the only direct speech in this
section of Wace, apart from Arthur's presentation of the pond with its
Wordsworthian proportions and four species of fish and the sea-water
pool, with Howel's 2-line response. Lawman has developed the interac-
tion of Arthur and his nobles by supplying many more passages in direct
speech.

10848–52 GoM the three water-marvels derived from the work 'The
Marvels of Britain', attributed to Nennius [M], and the loch (*stagnum
Lumonoi* in GoM and Wace) is probably Loch Lomond, but this passage
is not in GoM or Wace and resembles, probably fortuitously, the lake in
Beowulf in which Grendel's mother lurked, along with dragons and
water-monsters. If Lawman took it from a written rather than an oral
source, this is likely to have been a homiletic work in the same tradition as
'Visio Pauli' (Blickling Homily 17), or 'St Michael's Mass', in the *Blickling
Homilies* (EETS OS (58), p. 209–11, or 'St Patrick's Purgatory' in the
South-English Legendary (EETS OS (87), pp. 331–53. The 'other-

worldly' and watery nature of the setting is perhaps a deliberate echo of the 'underworld' visit of Aeneas to Hades: GoM enhances Arthur's status by placing him in an 'uncanny' setting, as Virgil did Aeneas; Lawman's addition enhances the mystery.

10895–6 Lawman has drawn Howel and Cador more forcefully than Wace, who did not mention that Howel was left guarding the lake while Arthur dealt with Gillomaur: similarly, Lawman has Arthur calling on Howel and Cador (L 10821ff), and arranging for them to lead battalions (addition at L 10829–40). He has, however, confused the narrative by not stating at L 10841 that the Scots had taken refuge at Loch Lomond, *Lumonoi stagnum/estang* in GoM and Wace.

10946 *gave them limb*: i.e. did not remove hand, genitals or ears by maiming.

10975 It is supposed to be twenty feet by twenty feet and five feet deep (GoM, W 9543) and elves did not dig it in Wace's version [M].

10985 In GoM and Wace the phenomenon is in Wales near the Severn, and is probably meant to be the Severn bore; Lawman's account here is confusing: Madden suspects textual damage or corruption.

11012–5, 11028–35, 11038–41, 11047f Additions: Arthur's insistence on the truce being kept, and his arrangements for restoring religious observance and law and order mark him as a good king.

11050 *Angel* is really the Angusel of Arthurian romance, and of the sources [M].

11058 *Lothian* is *Leonæis* in MS C; *Leoneys* in O resembles the *Lyonesse* of Arthurian romance with which it is identical in form; the area is equivalent to modern West, Mid- and East Lothian (Haddington, Edinburgh and Linlithgow) [B-H].

11079 This line is an insoluble crux: MS C reads *wes his bæd ipohte* and MS O sophisticates to *þorh alle cunnes þinge*. Madden suggests that *bæd* is OE *beada* 'counsellor' and *ipohte* means 'reckoned'; Brook suggests 'in thought' for *ipohte*. B&W equate *bæd* with 'prayer' and translate 'remembered in his prayers'; as Lawman himself indicates in his preface, the offspring had the duty of praying for the souls of departed parents, rather than vice versa, especially as Anna must have outlived Uther (Arthur speaks of her as alive in 11080). One suspects that the original may have alluded to her demeanour or deportment (ME *ibere* or ME *tuhtlen* used of Andor in L 1360 and of Guinevere in 11097) but the text has been badly corrupted if so.

11084 This prophetic warning is not in Wace, who only mentions the young Gawain.

11090–112 Wace explains that Cador had had Guinevere cared for as his closest relative; he also explains that Arthur loved her very dearly, but they did not have a child; instead of this Lawman says that Arthur stayed in Cornwall all that winter for love of her.

11103–11343 *Arthur's International Repute*: (i) Conquest of the Far North.

In GoM this section has an internal coherence: Arthur, having already reduced Scotland before his marriage, conquers first Ireland then Iceland,

and takes homage of the rulers of Orkney and Jutland; after 12 years establishing a court of international fame, Arthur conquers Norway, Denmark, defeats Frollo of Gaul and over 9 years conquers all Gaul; he is then crowned, and sets off on the Roman campaign.

Wace extends this by introducing the Round Table, and firmly locating within the twelve years of peace all the 'aventures' of the Round Table (W 9797–9798): poets are not strictly accurate about these and he claims he is uncertain whether the audience knows of them; this addition effectively divides the conquest of N. Europe given in GoM in two in Wace and Lawman. Lawman extends Wace by developing Gillomaur's humbling (L 11154–11206; 4 lines only in Wace) and the homage of the kings of Iceland (11213–39; 2 lines in Wace) and Orkney, Jutland and Wendland (L 11240–11315; one line each in Wace, with general summary of fealty: W 9703–26). Lawman's principal addition here is the long account of the fight over precedence which led to the need for the table (L 11345–11420) and the manufacture of it (L 11422–45). Wace's remarks about the marvels of Arthur Lawman extends into a discussion of Celtic imagination (L 11471–5) and then L 11489–11517: Merlin's prophecy of his death and the British hope of his return.

Lawman has broken the sequence of the original narrative: the swift progression of conquests, with a 12-year peace between Northern and Southern European campaigns, becomes a sequence of episodes focussed on Arthur's relations with foreign nationals on their own territory and in his court. Wace mentioned the Round Table as an explanation of GoM's assertion that Arthur's cosmopolitan court set fashions for all Europe; Lawman presents this racial admix as a source of strife, and so has two allusions to the composition of court: one preceding and explaining the need for equality in seating (L 11347ff), the second after the Table has established the fame of the Court (L 11476–90).

11106 *Midsummer festival*: (MS C *mid festen*) originally the pagan festival of midsummer fire, taken under the auspices of the Church by being designated the Eve of St John the Baptist's Feast on June 24th.

11110 *Gillomaur*. He is the third king of Ireland of this name to appear in Lawman's *Brut*.

11117–8 There is no direct speech at all in this section in Wace, and all 12 speeches, long and short, in Lawman's version are his own.

11122 Chain-mail rusts very quickly (in one morning of fine rain, according to those who re-activate medieval tournaments today) and the standard method of removing rust was to place the cuirass in sand; perhaps the term 'rocked', used also in *Sir Gawain and the Green Knight*, 2018, indicates that the chain-mail was placed in a cylinder of sand and fine gravel which was rotated (MED, s.v. *rokken* v. 2 (c).

11179–81 *Columkille* or *Columba*, b. c521, d. Iona 597, preached first in Ireland and then in Scotland, where he evangelised the Picts. For *Brendan* see 8642n. *Bridget*, b. c450, d. 523, founded a religious community at Kildare, the first for women in Ireland. Like Columba, she was a popular saint in Scotland, Wales and Ireland, and all three of these saints are probably mentioned here becauase their relics had been discovered in the late 12thc.

11212 There is no semblance of historical truth in the conquest of Iceland, which GoM mentions but without naming a king; Iceland was not discovered until 9thc and never at any stage had kings.

11285 The Wends are not mentioned in GoM. Wendland is the term for the territories of the Slavic tribes near the W. Baltic; the Wends (Tacitus calls them the Venedi) are first recorded in the lower Danube but after AD 600 settled east of the Elbe in areas vacated by Germanic tribes; in the period into which Arthur is supposed to fit, they would not have been living near the Danes. Wulfstan described to King Alfred his visit to Weonodland in the famous addition to the Anglo-Saxon version of *Orosius* (Sweet's *Anglo-Saxon Reader*, 15th ed., pp. 20–2). In the 12thc there were two campaigns against the Wends, the first in 1147, just before Wace finished his *Roman de Brut*. Lawman seems to intend Wendland to mean the territory between Elbe and Vistula, but W. Sayers claims that Wace's *Wenelande* is not Wendland ('Rummaret de Wenelande: a geographical note to Wace's *Brut*', *Romance Philology*, 18 (1964), 46–53, cited in B&W, p. 220).

11359 Before eating, the medieval nobility washed their hands at table in bowls of scented rose-water and dried them on white napkins.

11375 Many readers find the fight at the Yule Feast uncourtly and primitive (in tone it resembles the Celtic feast narratives from which it may derive) but the noble Wendish prince deserves neither epithet as he saves the lord whose hostage he is and kills seven brawlers unaided. Madden thinks the account must be traditional.

11399 This 'barbaric' treatment of the women is to prevent their marrying (because they will be too hideous) and so begetting children to avenge their relatives. Hjalti in *Hrólfssaga kráka* bites off his mistress's nose because she contemplates taking another lover should he die.

11416 See 11359n.

11494–11499 The allusion to tales of Arthur as drink for minstrels composed from Arthur's tongue with his breast forming a table sounds like some of the vatinicia of GoM's Merlin: 'The Boar shall be extolled in the mouths of its peoples, and its deeds will be as meat and drink to those who tell tales' (Thorpe, p. 172); Lawman's Merlin made the prophecy at L 9410–12; Madden thinks that L may have known GoM's *Prophecies of Merlin* in an Anglo-Norman version, but Le Saux finds other evidence that Lawman knew GoM's *Historia* in its original Latin (*Sources*, p. 117).

11503 See 14279n.

11509 As Madden notes, Gawain did not die in Cornwall but at the first landing of Arthur, given correctly at L 14140.

11512 Argante is not known in other versions, where it is Arthur's half-sister Morgan who claims him at death, and Argante may be a corruption of Morgan; Le Saux would see a connexion with GoM *Vita Merlini*, lines 918–23, where Morgan, healer and magician, is chief of nine sisters on a blessed isle (*Sources*, p. 114); J. D. Bruce and Visser also found this connexion (ibid., p. 127); see L 14278.

11518–11675 *Arthur's International Repute* (ii) The Conquest of Scandinavia: Wace amplifies the Scandinavian conquest by developing the Danish campaign and by filling out names and details of governors of Gaul under Arthur. Lawman has again added direct speech where Wace has none (apart from one-and-a-half lines from the Parisians, W 9989–90) in this section, and the effect, as before, is to increase the impression of collaboration between Authur, who announces his intentions before implementing them, and his men, who request the invasion of France (L 11523–7) and are given orders to carry out (L 11614f). The Norwegians communicate with Arthur and each other (L 11556–73), and Frolle tries to assert his independence (L 11765–92): when these are inevitably destroyed by Arthur his prestige is correspondingly higher. Lawman considerably extends the fight with Frolle, adding verbal negotiations, the conventional arming of Arthur, details of the supporting British side (L 11877–98) and the arrangements for fighting on the island (L 11904–15).

11601–09 GoM says that at this time Gawain was 12 years old and was still at the Papal Court; in GoM and Wace Gawain does not join his father in Norway. This eulogy of Gawain (Lawman calls him Walwain) is not in Wace; by the time Lawman was writing, Gawain's reputation had diminished as Lancelot's was enhanced by Chrétien and the authors of the prose *Lancelot* and (if Lawman wrote as late as the fourth decade of the 13thc) the *Queste del Saint Graal* and *La Mort le Roi Artu*; here Lawman boosts the reputation of Gawain, who remained popular in England until the end of the Middle Ages.

11657–67 These numbers and nationalities of knights are not in Wace, who simply states he does not know how many thousand knights and archers Arthur took from Denmark (W 9892).

11676–12073 *Arthur's International Repute* (iii) The Conquest of France and Defeat of Frolle:

11680 This is Boulogne-sur-Mer, Pas-de-Calais [B-H], after which Arthur moves down into France.

11697–11706 There is no mention in GoM or Wace of troops being sent to Frolle from Rome.

11816–28; 11838–54 In GoM Frollo is said to rely on his huge size to win the contest, but neither he nor Wace says either that Frolle regretted his challenge, or that Arthur relied on God. The prayers at L 11922–5 are also an addition: Lawman here faces for the first time the problem of Christian knights attacking fellow Christians: his solution is reticence (11925). The anxiety about dying in battle (those who died in tournament were given extreme unction but refused burial in sanctified ground) appears in L 12029–39, much extended from Wace 10135–8, where the old knights are simply sent home, with no concern expressed for the souls of those whose life-work has been the killing of others (L 12036–7). Le Saux outlines the means by which Lawman focusses on Arthur and enhances his opponent Frollo, excluding the direct speech of the Parisian citizens and so converting the episode into a significant duel between Arthur and an opponent more worthy than Wace's Frolle (*Sources,*

p. 76–79).

11926–69 This contest is exciting even in GoM but Lawman's account improves on the sources by more clearly realising this as a fight on an island, with restricted room for manoeuvre (although Madden thinks that 11941–3 is a misunderstanding of Wace, whose Frolle is knocked a long way from his horse). By 1225 the joust, between a pair of contestants and more organised than the massed mêlée of the tournament which evolved in the early 12thc, had become popular on the continent (perhaps less so in England) and Lawman may be describing something he was essentially familiar with. Judicial combat, perhaps introduced by the Normans, was often held on an island in a moated area to ensure fair play.

11974ff This challenge by Arthur, forming a preliminary transition to the Roman Expedition, is not in Wace, who instead says that Arthur stayed a time in Paris settling peace (W 10103–4). Mannyng locates in these 9 years in France the adventures of the French prose romances which dominate 13thc Arthurian literature (Mg 10961–78); for the second time (cf. Mg 10580–614, on rhymed romances) Mannyng complains that there is little Arthurian material in English; he finished his book in 1338; most Middle English Arthurian romances seem to date from the 1390's and after.

12055ff. The apportioning of governorships to Kay, Bedivere, Howel(d)in and Borel is merely noted in Wace (W 10153–66); this is obviously not the Borel who was killed by Arthur in L 10595, an incident only found in Lawman, who is somewhat economical with names. He omits Ligier and Richier from Wace's account, but Richier appears in L 13208 in the Ambush, and then disappears from the action, and in L 12171–2 Laeyer (= Ligier ?) is said to be earl of Boulogne (but not of Flanders). Howeldin is Holdin in Wace (W 10163) and distinct from Hoel (L Howel), Arthur's cousin ('nephew' in GoM, W).

12074–12341 *The Crown-wearing of Caerleon*: This is the climax in GoM, and he lavishes detail on it. His Caerleon is the counterpart or even prototype of the Camelot of later romance tradition. Apart from the opening of the sequence, which resembles the 'seasons settings' of French romance, and later English romances like *Kyng Alysaunder* and *Sir Gawain and the Green Knight*, Lawman follows Wace closely. He is uninterested, however, in the family reunions and telling of news in W 10175–96 and reduces 20 lines to 7.

12112–4 No record survives of the 'bewitching' of Caerleon; Geoffrey refers to its site, now merely ancient 'walls' (Thorpe, 125) but says nothing of its collapse; its major troubles occurred in 1171, 1173, 1175, 1217 and 1231. Le Saux thinks this may be a reminiscence of GoM *Vita Merlini* 624–5 which says that Caerleon will fall into the Severn and lose its citizens for a long time, and notes Lawman's allusion to 'books' at this point (*Sources*, p. 112).

12144 In GoM and Wace *Maurin* (W *Mauron*) comes from Worcester (W: Guirecestre); *Gursal* is *Cursal de Cestre* and *Urgent* is '*Urgent de Bade*' in Wace; L has reversed the two names in W 10261. Arnald in

L 12150 is *Anaraud. Balien* (W: *Baluc*; GoM *Galluc*) is 'from Silchester' in MS C, 'Cirecestre' in MS O: both forms occur in the MSS of Wace; in the Bern MS of GoM he is 'Guintoniensis'. *Wigein* is *Jug(e)in* in GoM and Wace. The Earl of Oxford is *Boso* in GoM, *Bos* in Wace, and owes his name in Lawman to a scribal confusion (*f*/long *s*); since he is *Beofs* in MS O, *Beof* in MS C (in C 13602 he is *Bos*) it is difficult to know whether the error was Lawman's or that of the scribe of the MS which formed the common ancestor of the two extant; it looks as if Lawman or a scribe has assumed that this is a form of *Bevis*, hero of an Anglo-Norman romance, c1200, which was translated into Continental French shortly after this, and into Middle English c1300.

12151ff Lawman (or his source MS, or the scribes of CO and antecedent copies) has corrupted the names here; *Peridur* and *Elidur* (L 12155) are *Peredur map* ('son of') *Peridur* (W 10881–2; Thorpe, 227). GoM states that there were many others whose names would be too tedious to tell, and Madden that there are errors in Lawman's list which it would be superfluous to note, while Mannyng, after also corrupting a brief selection (and listing them as children) concludes that 'to rekene them alle hit ys but fable' (Mg 11120); many students feel the same indifference about the innumerable lists of knights in Malory (also often corrupted from the sources). In fact chivalry was a very serious matter in the middle ages, and identities, places of origin, and paternity were of vital importance, and romance (and pseudo-historical) writers echo this contemporary interest in their works. Geoffrey's apparent lack of concern is an instance of rhetorical *occultatio*: he has given a long list and another follows. Wace, very significantly, adds that these were knights of the Round Table (W 10285), an Order not mentioned in GoM, which is omitted here by Lawman.

12167 *Malverus* is *Malvasius* in GoM. In L 11231 the king of Iceland was *Alcus*. MS C *Doldanet* was *Doldanim* in L 11260; he is *Doldanied* in Wace. *Kailin* of Frisia (12168) is not in Wace. *Lot* (L 12169) is King of Norway (W 10308: *Norreis*), perhaps an error in ancestor of MSS C and O.

12192–97 Lawman is muddled and seems unaccountably bored; Wace explains clearly that the city was astir with people seeking lodgings, with pavilions being erected, horses being led and groomed, and fodder carried, and clothing being carried and arranged (W 10337–58). By contrast, he expands the details (and number) of the archbishops (L 12201–10 and 12218–23).

12236 The rings are an addition by Lawman, as also, with gold trimmings too, in L 12275–6.

12245–9 Lawman omits the details of the gorgeous clothing (L 12247: W 10407–16) and the glorious music (L 12248: W 10420–4).

12297–8 Wace says that even the poor peasants were more courteous and brave than knights of other kingdoms and so too the ladies (W 10499–502) and then speaks of the clothes of men and of women all in one matching ensemble (W 10503–10) which Lawman seems to apply to the women, for whom he suggests a male's opinion of appropriate colour schemes (L 12302).

12307–15 Wace does justice to the declaration in GoM that ladies would not give their love to any man who was not proved three times in battle (Thorpe, 229) by talking of *druerie*: a courteous lady is an *amie* (W 10512–3), but Lawman talks of seeking a bride (L 12313: *ʒirnen brude* could mean seek a lady but *chevalier* is rendered *lauerd* 'lord' in 12309, which suggests that Lawman was speaking of marriage.

12324ff These games may be compared with those at Cassibellaune's festival. GoM there spoke generally of sports: here he mentions shooting with bow and arrow, hurling javelin, putting the stone and dicing; Wace adds *bohorder*, (games of armed skill on horseback), fencing, jumping and wrestling, in addition to putting the stone and hurling the javelin, but omits shooting; on dicing and gambling he adds a lively account of its effects (W 10557–88, the authenticity of which Madden doubts since it is missing in 9 MSS). Lawman's list matches Wace's (if 'playing behind the shield' is *bohorder*), but adds running and restores shooting and adds what looks like a reference to football (12328). He omits Wace's list of court entertainers and musical instruments, and the account of dicing (W 10543–88).

12337 Most tournaments seem to have lasted 3 days, with a prize-giving at the end. Wace lists the prizes (W 10595–616); Lawman seems to have abbreviated this list (L 12339f). Wace omits the ecclesiastical preferments also handed out by Arthur in GoM.

12342–12750 *The Roman Campaign* (i) Challenge. This is the opening point of the early 15thc Alliterative *Morte Arthure*, itself probably based on Wace, most of which Malory re-worked as *The Tale of the Noble Kyng Arthur*.

In both GoM and Wace this section consists largely of long speeches and Lawman does not extend these, apart from one speech, that of the twelve ambassadors when they report to Luces (Lucius) on their return. Lawman has, however, increased the excitement by making Arthur's courtiers far more unruly than Wace's: three times he has to order them to sit down, and they are already maltreating the ambassadors before Arthur intervenes to remind his men of the international inviolability of messengers (L 12402–12) whereas in Wace he speaks up in time and curtails merely verbal abuse. As in the preceding section, there is some abridgement here, most notably of the stirring passage in Wace where the ships are being prepared for the Roman expedition and manoeuvred out of harbour (W 11190–238), which Lawman presents with emphasis not on the bustle of embarkation but on family farewells on the quayside and the movement of the ships into open sea in L 12743–50. Madden thinks Lawman did not know the vocabulary, but Mannyng did cope with some of the technical terms in the French (Mg 12053–12098).

12347ff These are old men in Wace, carrying olive branches, details which L omits as he adds a more factual description. They read aloud their letter from Lucius in the sources [M].

123415–19 In Wace Arthur takes his dukes and counts and goes to a huge tower nearby, and the conversation between Cador and Gawain takes place as they go up the steps. Wace adds Gawain's speech, and his Gawain speaks of the pleasures of love which peace makes possible; Lawman's Gawain is consistently presented in a more favourable light, and his comment on peace seems morally unexceptionable (L 12454–58), which leaves a faint and perhaps unintentional criticism of Arthur's speech advocating all-out war.

12495–505 Julius Caesar's atrocities are not noted here in Wace, and were not evident in Lawman's own account of the Roman invasion (L 3588–4471); there is little justification for Arthur's proposed attack on Rome. This double standard is very noticeable in GoM where Arthur declares that nothing seized by force is legally held, yet justifies his recent forceful annexation of Roman territory in France with the specious claim that the Romans did not turn up to defend it (Thorpe, 232–3)!

12543ff Lawman has shortened Howel's speech by cutting his appeal for immediate invasion; he similarly abbreviates Angusel's cries for vengeance on Rome (W 10958–11040; L 12572–92).

12547 Prophecies of various kinds (such as those of Merlin) were a distinct medieval literary kind; GoM alludes to the Sibylline Prophecies but it is not clear what, if anything, he knew of prophesying to the British controlling the Roman Empire. Brook says that the Sibylline Oracles were composed from 2nd century BC to the 3rd century AD in Alexandria by Jewish and Christian authors, comprising pseudo-prophetic pictures of Universal History. The term 'Sibyl' is used here simply to give weight to Howel's pronouncement.

12590–1 Brittany and Normandy, under control of the pro-Arthurian Howel and Bedivere respectively, cannot be envisaged as conquests and must be Lawman's errors.

12610–12; 12614–17 Wace does not mention the clothing supplied to the ambassadors.

12646 *closed letters*: MS C has *write runen*, which originally would have implied 'write in runic symbols'; I take it that the letters are to be private documents and have used the expression current in Lawman's time for this: *litterae clausae*, letters folded, sealed on the outside, and addressed to a single recipient.

12658ff Book X in GoM begins here. Lawman manages the oriental names better than the Roman: Maptisas should be Micipsa (GoM and Wace) and Ofustesar is Mustensar, while Ali Fatima of Spain has been replaced by Meodras. The Romans should number four: Marius Lepidus, Gaius Metellus Cocta (who has become three people and was already two in Wace), Quintus Milvius Catullus, and Quintus Carucius, who is omitted in W and L.

12658 Lawman's expression is 'harvest day' which probably means Lammas, August 1st; in GoM the date is the Kalends of August (1st) and in Wace 'the beginning of August'. Only three months have elapsed since the challenge was issued at Whitsun in Caerleon.

12674–702 The numbers are corrupted in GoM, Wace and Lawman and cannot be made to tally.

12680–1 Another transition device taken from romance narrative.

12707 Barfleur, La Manche, Brittany.

12710 This and the following allusion to Gawain (L 12719f) are not in Wace.

12751–13049 *The Roman Campaign* (ii): Arthur's Dream and the Giant of Mont Saint-Michel.

Once more, Lawman has developed a dramatic scene from the Dream of the Dragon and Bear which Wace simply reports, until Arthur's closing observation. He adopts a similar technique in the encounter with the giant, but there the old nurse utters a *planctus* (lament) in GoM, which Wace extends into a conversation. Lawman's handling of the terror of the giant's arrival at Howel's castle and his systematic destruction of the barricades (L 12919ff) has no counterpart in Wace.

12753–76 Arthur is not scared by his dream in Wace, nor are his attendants afraid to ask him about it, nor to interpret it unfavourably for fear of castration (L 12792): they believe it foretells what proves to be the conquest with the giant, Arthur thinks it presages the issue with the Emperor (W 11239–78). Arthur's prayer (12760–3) resembles Old English religious poetry (as does Gawain's in 14077–8).

12809–29 Arthur simply hears of the giant in Wace (W 11288) but Lawman's invention of a knight who reports its atrocities from his own experience heightens the emotional tension.

12893 This disobedience (not in Wace, whose Bedoer is not given instructions to leave the giant alone) resembles Bedivere's reluctance to throw Excalibur back into the Water in Malory, an episode which does not in fact occur in Lawman's account of Arthur's death.

12911–16 The old Nurse's momentary illusion of an angel, not in Wace, is convincing.

12924 In GoM and Wace the girl is Howel's *niece*, not daughter (W 11399).

12964ff The giant's leering at the old nurse and then raping her are only in Lawman's account; in Wace he is by the second fire on the other hill. He is not asleep in Wace but eating swine and his face is smeared in fat; in the Alliterative *Morte Arthure* he is eating babies and warming his privates, and in GoM he eats some of the swine raw while the rest cooks; the subject allowed for free imaginative play.

12993 Only Lawman makes Arthur show this British love of fair play by refusing to attack the giant asleep, but then he spoils it by beheading the giant when he surrenders (L 13030).

13037 GoM and Wace tell the story of Riun (GoM: Retho) who demanded Arthur's beard to add to those on his cloak; the poet of the Alliterative *Morte Arthur* confuses the accounts and attributes the hirsute collection to this nameless giant, (who is Dinabuc in Wace), and is copied by Malory, who has already recounted the correct version in Part I of *LMDA*. *Ravinity* (MS C, MS O *Rauin*) is *d'Araive* in Wace, *Aravius* (mons) in GoM; B-H assumes these are errors for *Mons Erir*, i.e. Snowdon.

13050–13399 *The Roman Campaign* (iii): Gawain's Embassy and the Pursuit.

The main narrative addition in Lawman is the wounded knight who gives craven counsel to Arthur (L 13070–84). The emperor's nephew *Quencelin* is *Quintillianus* in GoM and Wace.

13069 MS C has *Albe*, which is the Aube (as in MS O): it joins the Seine in Champagne.

13122–28 Here Lawman leaves the reported speech of Wace and moves into direct speech.

13146 To enter the royal presence without leaving arms outside was both a threat and an insult, cf. *Beowulf* 325, 333.

13153–4 The stupefaction of Lucius is Lawman's addition.

13184ff, 13235ff Lawman has enhanced Gawain's already prominent rôle in the episode by giving him this retort and a defiant speech after killing Quencelin, and making him the first rather than the third of the three ambassadors to kill a pursuer; he gives Gawain at this point both his own speech (L 13245ff, W 11833ff) and Guerin's (L 13240, W 11789ff). Significantly, however, he deletes the second of the men whom Gawain demolishes in the flight in Wace's version, a cousin of Marcel, whose arm he slices off. At L 13374 Gawain is credited with the capture of Petreius which Boso (until he fell off his horse) had almost managed unaided in Wace (W 10218).

13290–96 Lawman's command of perspective, with the soldiers scanning the plain below and seeing the dramatic pursuit we have been watching at close range is original, and masterly; it also reveals new details: the three thousand and then thirty thousand following. A further detail supplied by Lawman is the stirring in camp at dawn (L 13389).

13400–13968 *The Roman Campaign* (iv): Ambush of the Prisoners; The Battle of Saussy.

This is the most densely narrative section in GoM and forms the climax both to Arthur's career and the book as a whole. It is little altered in Wace, who also relishes the battles, although he tones down Arthur's rallying speech which decides the battle. Despite his censure by critics as savage and bloodthirsty Lawman is not deeply engaged by these two episodes: he adds very little, apart from the ironic greeting to Petreius (L 13392ff) and cuts the battle formation for the defence of the prisoners (W 12130ff) and the names of those Britons killed with Borel, whose death-throes he omits, leaves out Wace's description of Luces (W 12452ff), an admirable and more gracious character than Lawman's emperor at L 13645, and pares Arthur's decisive 'kill them all, I shall conquer or die' speech to two lines (L 13880f), which are as much prayer as battle-cry; Arthur's ensuing slaughter, 'like a raging lion', is cut.

13412, 13447, 13435f, 13450 Lawman develops a narrative framework by small touches like these: introduction of spies in Arthur's army, mention of animals stirring at dawn and the nodding of Roman plumes and singing of British men as they march to Paris; Arthur's men live in a recognisable environment.

13427–9 Comparison with the list of Roman allies at 12658ff shows discrepancies: *Sexstorius* (GoM: *Sertorius*) King of Libya is given Turkey as his duchy in MS C (Irtac was its king); Babylon's king was *Maeptisas* and *Evander* should be from Syria (GoM and Wace); *Catel* (now *Bal Catel* or *Catellus*) in GoM is *Vulteius Catellus* (but was previously *Milvius Catullus* in GoM X.i) and *Carrius* is *Quintus Carucius*. At 13690 Lawman and Wace omit the list of oriental commanders of the Roman divisions, thus losing symmetry but gaining coherence.

13526–32 Lawman's ideal king is one who is loved for his firmness and rigorous decisions.

13531 Lawman's *ifullen afure* could mean 'feel fear', or 'fall in flames' as in B&W 'be put to the torch', but if Madden's suggestion that it alludes to GoM VII, iii 'Timebit (Wright's edition of the Bern MS reads *Tremebit*) Romuleas domus ipsius saevitium' is right, then the former is the sense intended. Le Saux also thinks this indisputable evidence that L here used the *Prophetia Merlini* (*Sources*, p. 116). Madden adds a note (III, 509) declaring that he does not know the meaning of MS C; he corrects his printed text of MS O to *al forfare*, which has not been instated in B&L.

13549 In GoM Lucius makes for Autun in Burgundy (Wace: Hostum) to await reinforcements from the Emperor Leo, Lucius having been introduced as the *procurator* of the Roman people; in the battle of Saussy, however, GoM refers to Lucius as 'emperor' and by omitting the reference to Leo, Wace calls Luces 'l'empereur' throughout, as does Lawman. In contrast to GoM/Wace who have *Autun*, Lawman seems to locate the place at either Aouste (Ardennes) or Oust (Somme) [B-H]. Langres is in Upper Marne and *Sosie* (L 13560) is either the Val Suzon, Dijon, (W. Matthews, *Speculum*, 49 (1974), 680–6; H. E. Keller, *Speculum*, 49, 687–98) or high ground at Saussy (Tatlock, 102–3, and Thorpe, 127n 1).

13600–15 Lawman has confused the clear battle divisions of Wace (themselves clearer than the scribal confusion of GoM's version in CUL MS 1706 edited by Griscom and trans. Thorpe): the battle lines are in eight main divisions, with the king to the rear and the reserve detachment under Morvid behind him. Four front divisions are commanded by: Cador and Angusel (Angel); Gerin (who should be Earl of Chartres, not Chester) and Boso; Aschil and Lot; Hoel and Gawain; behind them in a second rank are: Kay and Bedivere; Holdin (Howeldin) and Guitard; Jugein and Jonathal; Cursalem and Urbennius (Cursalem [or Cursal] was Earl of Bath at 12146, and Urgent (so-called in L 12147, here Urgein) was Earl of Chester). These pairs command the left and right wings between them, but Lawman's *baften* implies that he thinks of the two commanders placed front and rear. He omits the archers.

13637 This is the justification for attacking a fellow Christian: he has no care for God anyway, and this is displayed in Lucins's doubly-directed address, to the Romans on the one hand and their pagan allies on the other (L 13662ff; 13673ff, the latter not in Wace).

13655 *tossing*: MS C has þrauwen, presumably from þrean 'afflict, throw awry'.

13729 The *shield-wall* was a 'hedge-formation' (*Battle of Maldon*, 102), a defensive wall of overlapping shields as in the Bayeux Tapestry

(Scragg, *Battle of Maldon*); this is distinct from the Roman *testudo* in which shields were also raised over the heads by those within a phalanx, to provide protection from arrows and javelins.

13741 The rashness of Kay and Bedivere, their presumption, the avenging of Bedivere by his sister's son, the dispatching of the heathen soul to Hell and the diction of lines 13802/04 are strongly reminiscent of the tone and diction of *The Battle of Maldon*; the only parallel in Wace is that Kay and Beduer are *trop talentif* (W 12611, cf. L 13741, 13744–6).

13772 (Ri(d)wathlan is Hirelgas in Wace; see 4060 n. above for the 'sister's son' motif. In Wace he chops Boccus's body in pieces, perhaps copied – and toned down – from Tydeus's behaviour in Statius's *Thebaid*.

13807–23 The passage of arms between Leir and the emir is expanded from Wace, and Gecron is Lawman's invention, but he omits the deaths of Balluc, Cursal and Urgent, the praise of the Bretons, and, surprisingly, shortens the encounter between Gawain and the emperor.

13838–56 The most famous Earl of Striguil or Pembroke was William Marshal, who acted as Regent in Henry III's minority and died in 1219 in his 80th year. His career was like that of a medieval knight, winning the Earldom of Pembroke and control of the realm by his own success in tournament and battle and as adviser of kings. His son William married a sister of King John. Kinard of Striguil is Kinmarc de Triguel in Wace: Lawman has altered the name to match a place he knows, and probably to compliment a man he admires. This may provide some clue to the dating of the *Brut*.

13915 The 'joke' is in poor taste and more laboured than in Wace.

13930, 13937 *Kinon* and *Caen*: Wace has Chinon (in Touraine) as Kay's burial-place, but some writers took it as Caen, as Lawman seems to in L 13936.

13955–68 The political implications of Arthur's conquest are not mentioned in Wace, nor the numbers of dead in the armies of the Romans (L 13967) and British (L 13927).

13971–14295 *The Downfall and Death of King Arthur.*
Only the outline of the sequence is present in Wace and GoM: Arthur returns without attacking Rome because of Modred's insurrection; Modred flees three/two times at Richborough/Romerel, and Winchester; Guinevere becomes a nun and Modred and Arthur are killed and Arthur goes to Avalon (Wace: where he may still live). Arthur's dream, the person of the messenger, the incensed reaction at court to the news, with Gawain's speech, Constantine's presence as Arthur lies wounded, the arrival of the boat with the two queens to take Arthur away are all either Lawman's invention or, as Madden prefers it, derived from another tradition. Le Saux thinks that the source was GoM *Vita Merlini*, or, less probably, the Welsh poems which were GoM's sources (*Sources*, pp. 113–4).

13982ff The courtier's question would probably be recognised by contemporaries as regal etiquette; B&S compare the question put to Hroþgar in *Beowulf* 1319–20.

13982ff Arthur's dream provides a negative counterbalance to his propitious dream on the outward journey. In the unrelated *La mort le roi Artu* he has two dreams, on consecutive nights: one of Gawain and another of the Wheel of Fortune, in which he is pushed to the ground by a beautiful lady (Fortune) and in falling breaks all his bones (*Death of King Arthur*, ed. and transl. James Cable (Harmondsworth, 1917), pp. 204–5); in the Alliterative *Morte Arthure* he dreams of the wheel of Fortune just before Craddok tells him of Mordred's rebellion, and in Malory he has two consecutive dreams, one of a chair on a wheel above a pit of black water full of serpents into which he falls, and a second of Gawain.

14009 MS C has the masculine *Leo* but the fem. pron. *hire* in the following line; if this is a lioness it may stand for Argante. This second part of the dream is especially effective because it suggests authentic emotional disturbance without the precise correspondence which makes many medieval *somnia* (dreams) seem merely contrived.

14022–51 The ingenious reply of the terrified messenger, Arthur's incredulity and the switch from the tentatively suggestive subjunctive mood (14026–31) to the inescapable facts of the perfect and present indicatives (14043–51) are superbly paced with mounting dramatic tension, matched by the ensuing silence (14052) and Arthur's reassertion of control, in exactly the words he used after the riot which occasioned the need for the Round Table (11390), and again after Lucins's letter was read (12409, 12461).

140651 Arthur's desire to execute Modred and Guinevere is not merely savage vindictiveness: both have committed treason and endangered the country. B&S state that burning at the stake (e.g. for petty reason) was a punishment for women; ripping apart by attaching limbs to unbroken horses (Gawain's judgement, L 14083) is a punishment often applied to romance traitors: Gawain is enacting the requirement for every noble to be judged by his peers, an already existing practice further enshrined in *Magna Carta*; as his brother, Gawain is exactly Modred's peer. Wace and Lawman omit here the authorial disclaimer of responsibility for narrating this treason with which GoM begins his Book XI.

14091 *Wissant*: see 4855 n. The fortnight's delay before Arthur gets a favourable wind is not in Wace, nor is the traitorous spy who informs on Arthur to Guinevere (L 14095–100). B&S note that medieval sailing ships could not go much to windward.

14105 This Childric is not necessarily the son of the Saxon emperor whom Cador killed (*pace* B&S and Emerson) in L 10791; in GoM he is Chelric, where the other was Cheldric in the Bern MS.

14129 MS C *Romerel*, MS O *Romelan* are *Romenel* in Wace 13079 (and in the same number of MSS: *Sandwiz*) and 'in Rupini portu' (Thorpe: Richborough) in GoM; Arnold points out that Richborough was silted up by the 12thc and the nearest port would be Sandwich. Recent archaeological excavation has shown that Romney Marsh held a large population in Roman and Saxon times, Saxon Old Romney having been a major port; Lawman might have been aware of its former importance.

14138–41 Neither Wace nor GoM tells us that Gawain killed Childric's son, nor that Saxons slew Gawain [M]. This account of the battle is closer to GoM than to Wace, who says that Modred's untrained soldiers fled at once [B&S].

14180–9, 14195–9 Lawman emphasises much more than Wace the tragic effects of Modred's disloyalty on his men: he has added the promise of franchise (L 14171) [B&S] and Arthur's destruction of Winchester [B&W].

14201 This quotation from the prophecies of Merlin is not in Wace; GoM, Book VII, 3, 4: 'Say to Winchester: "The earth shall swallow you."' Le Saux considers this clear evidence that Lawman knew the *Prophetia Merlini* (*Sources*, p. 117).

14213–6 Wace tells us that Guinevere was not seen or heard of again; Lawman's reference to her disappearance as if 'sunk' without trace does not seem to mean that she was executed by drowning, like Astrild, Abren and Iudon (L 1245, 2012). Emerson assumes that 14216 means 'or whether she had been (sunk) . . .'. The closest parallel in Lawman is 5659: Trahern has no more worries about Octaves than if he had not been born or had been 'lost in water' (at sea?): *oðer i watere for-loren*; allusion to water seems to be an idiom, simply meaning 'disappeared without trace', and there is not necessarily any implication that Lawman knew of a tradition in which Guinevere drowned.

14218–20 Wace emphasises that Modred's allies were pagans as well as Christian, and adds Norwegians and Danes (W 13226–8).

14238–9 The Tamar seems to be intended by MS C *Tanbre* (cf. L 9320 MS C *Tambreis*, MS O *Tambre*) but Camelford is on the R. Camel. GoM has *Camblan*, and the *Annales Cambriae* have *Camlann*; *Tamble/Tanbre* in some MSS of Wace are scribal errors of GoM [B-H]; Arnold prints *Camble* (W 13253). In Malory the last battle is near Salisbury – but also, unaccountably, near the sea.

14261–5 Wace says nothing of the wounds, nor of two survivors, although this is the number in the *Mort Artu* and in Malory, where they are Bedivere and Lucan.

14278, 14291 Only in Lawman is Arthur said to be living among elves; in several early traditions he is said to be with his sister Morgan, who is one of those in the boat in Malory's *LMDA*. Gerald of Wales says that she took Arthur's body to Avalon (*Speculum Ecclesiae*, c1216). *Avalon* is the Welsh *Afalxon* 'apples' or *Afallon* 'apple-trees' [B&S]. Lawman does not mention Glastonbury here, where in 1191 two bodies were found which were claimed to be Arthur and Guinevere [B&W]. The boat and its occupants are Lawman's addition; Malory is imprecise as to whether there are three or four ladies in the boat.

14281–82, 14290–7 GoM does not mention Arthur's return, but speaks of him as mortally wounded and taken to Avalon so that his wounds can be attended to, which Wace echoes (*Fud el cors nafrez mortelment*) but adds that the Britons await his return and he, Wace, will say no more than Merlin did: that his death would be doubtful (cf. GoM,

VII, 3: 'exitus eius dubius erit'), and people still doubt whether he is dead or alive. D&W note that in 1113 a French monk at Bodmin was reprimanded for denying that Arthur still lived. Lawman adds the promise from Arthur's own mouth of his return, and in L 14289 translates W 13286 *dutuse* as *care*, 'grief' (or, Emerson: 'trouble').

14297 *An Arthur*: Tatlock thinks this means Richard I's designated heir, the grandson of Henry II, Arthur of Brittany, who died in 1203 (*Legendary History*, 504–5), although Stanley (*N&Q*, 213 [1968] doubts that the English had the same hopes of that Arthur as the Bretons. O here reads *Bruttes*: 'aid to the British'.

14330–47 Lawman adds Constantine's curse, the name of the second brother, and reverses the two deaths, making the beheadings more melodramatic and bloody than in Wace.

14354 Constantine reigns four years in Lawman and GoM, three in Wace and is popular and effective; Wace merely says he was mourned; in GoM his early death is a punishment (for breaking Dunvallo's law of sanctuary, presumably).

14357ff Lawman adds to Wace: Conan's murder of his uncle (as in GoM) and the killing of his cousins by poison (Wace simply says he killed his uncle's two sons), the fact that he was Constantine's sister's son (compare Bedivere's nephew Ridwathlan and Cassibellaunus's Hirelgas for the true responsibilities of this relationship), his attack on his sisters and his death in a riding accident. In GoM he dies in his third regnal year, Wace after four and a bit years.

14396 Wace says Malgo was a sodomite, but not that the rest of his court were, and has nothing about the women emigrating in disgust; Wace puts more emphasis on Malgo's courtesy, Lawman on his court.

14405 This story of Carric's pseudonym is not in Wace, who says instead that Britain lost *her* name through him. He is consistently *Careticus* in GoM, *Caris* and *Certiz* in Wace.

14414ff Lawman develops Wace's additional matter to GoM by naming Gurmund's father and brother, adding the racial origins of the motley army and their numbers, but omits Wace's allusion to Merlin.

14487ff Lawman dramatises with direct speech the negotiations between the Saxons and Gurmund, inserts the passage where Carric does battle frequently against Gurmund (L 14516ff) and transposes after the start of the siege of Cirencester the outrages committed by Gurmund (L 14536–42) which he has toned down from W 13494–509. His Carric is a more determined and noble individual than Wace's: L 13570–77 has no counterpart in Wace, who instead has an account of siege warfare (W 13535–58).

14581–95 Gurmund's heathen rites and his conversation with the fellow heathen are not in Wace. This *maumet* is an idol; the word is a corruption of Mahomet and frequently found in Medieval romance (see L 117 and n.). Lawman gives more details of the use of sparrows to fire Cirencester, and also the punning nick-name *Sparewenchestre*; this is not in GoM, who instead utters a diatribe against 'you foolish' British whose civil war lost the realm of Britain (Thorpe, 264). Hall explains that

Gurmund is Guthrum, the Dane who besieged Cirencester in 879. A *chanson de geste* from the 11thc, entitled *Gormond et Isembart* recounts the death of these two at the hands of King Louis. Louis III defeated an army of Danes under a leader called Wurm in 881 and thus there has been conflation of two 9thc Danes, Guthrum and Wurm.

14621–4 These graphic and compassionate lines are not in Wace.

14628–31 Lawman invents this, since Wace says he does not know what became of him; Lawman turns this into 14634: he deserts his men just as Modred did his at Winchester.

14651–5; 14663–7 These atrocities are not in Wace, who talks of destruction of religious and secular buildings, (W 13624–33); Lawman reverts to the previous passage of Gurmund's cruelty in Wace (W 13478–87), which there preceded the siege of Cirencester.

14668ff This passage, following Wace, is inserted to account for the selection of the name England by a race hitherto referred to as 'Saxons' in both texts. It is not in GoM. 'English' does in fact derive from 'Angle' (with *i*-mutation of A to Æ) but Lawman (or his scribes) is troubled by the vowel distinction and so writes *Englen* in 14673 to account for 'English'. Mannyng adds a further legend about a *Briton* called Engle who contested the land (Mg 14789–838).

14683 Gurmund's departure is not mentioned in Wace, but Mannyng says he went off to win France because Arthur had done so (Mg 14769–70).

14693 This allusion to the silencing of bells and no masses being said is not in Wace and seems to reflect the circumstances in England during the 1208–16 Interdict; only the Cistercians were allowed to ring bells and say Mass.

14695–14923 *The Conversion of England and slaughter of the clergy.*

The famous story of Gregory and his pun 'non angli sed angeli' is not in GoM nor Wace; it is found in Bede's *Historia*, Book II, cap. 1. Bede explains that before he became Pope, Gregory saw fair-haired boys for sale in the market, wanted to go to England to convert the people but was prevented by the Roman people and so sent Augustine in AD 596. He and his companions were at first reluctant (contrast L 14730) and timid but were encouraged by a letter from Gregory, which Bede quotes (Book I, cap. 23). GoM and Wace pick up the account at the arrival of Augustine (Austin), at Thanet, with forty companions says Bede (cap. 25), and Wace (and Lawman) echo this, but it is not in GoM.

14730 He was invited to Canterbury by Ethelbert who had first confined him to Thanet (Bede, I, 25).

14744–14817 The story of Augustine's rejection by Dorchester and his encounter with God is not found in Bede or GoM; Wace is Lawman's source for the explanation of the old joke of the 'caudati angli', the account of the divine revelation, and the amazing false-etymology of Cerne Abbas.

14766 MSS C and O have *muggles/moggles*: Madden cites Fordun, *Scotichronicon*, mid-14thc, who uses the form *mughel*. MED also cites two uses of the word as a surname in 12thc and 13thc, but only has Lawman's use of *mugling*. The word seems to be connected with *mugil*, a mullet (fish) and suggests a meaning 'fish-like tail' for *muggle*.

14769–72 Wace, who came from Jersey, did not need to confess to embarrassment at this *soubriquet* of the English; Lawman's lines sound like the authentic experience of someone he knew, perhaps his patron's or the man's son? Mannyng says 'we are censured for having tails' (Mg 15212).

14772 *cued* is a pun on *cué* 'having a tail' and *qued* 'wicked, evil, sinful', but MED cites this instance only in the second sense, whereas Le Saux takes it only in the first (*Sources*, p. 5); it surely means both, but 'base' is the nearest I can get to the pun in modern English. Tatlock notes that Richard I's crusaders in Sicily in 1190 were taunted with having tails (*Legendary History*, pp. 506–7).

14813 Cernel as it appears in Domesday Book (Abbot's Cernel was Hardy's name for Cerne Abbas) is really derived from the River Cerne which, like the identically-derived R. Char, comes from the Celtic *carn*, 'cairn, heap of stones'. As Madden notes, it is 7.5 miles N.W. rather than 5 miles S of Dorchester. MS O and one MS of Wace read 'Rochester'; in 19thc there were local traditions in both Kent and in Dorset that locals carried Augustine's curse.

14847 Lawman says *cantel-cape*, which must mean the length of white woollen cloth sent or given by the Pope to his appointed bishops, which Bede and other medieval writers call the *pallium*; *cantel-capes* occurs in ASC s.a. 1070 (Peterborough Chronicle) but in the sense 'copes'.

14885ff Bede describes the ravaging of Britons and Scots by Ethelfrith (Lawman calls him Ælfric) and his defeat of King Aidan at Deganstan (AD 603) in I, 34. In II, 2, having described how the British bishops refused to accept Augustine as their primate, and refused to compromise over their differences by accepting the Catholic date for Easter, Bede says the British were warned by Augustine that the English would destroy them; after Augustine died in 604 Ethelfrith slaughtered the praying monks of Bangor, inadequately defended by Brocmail, *before* the battle of Chester (Old English *Legacestir*). Bede does not suggest that this act was a direct reprisal or that King Ethelbert connived at it: this is due to GoM. Ethelfrith was pagan.

14886 Lawman has *Leirchæstre* (W 13901 *Leircestre*; GoM *Legecestria*); it was Chester, 8 miles from Bangor [M]; see previous note.

14898–923 Wace says that the monks and hermits went to beg Elfrid for mercy (W 13094); he seized and beheaded 2,200 of them. Lawman forgets the situation and adds various other classes of cleric (L 14898f). The trick Alfric plays in L 14904–7 is not in Wace.

14965 The election of Cadvan/Cadwan as king begins Book XII in GoM.

15001–08 Lawman heightens the emotional element here by stressing the two kings' love and claiming that the boys were both conceived and born at the same time, and increases the 'romance' tone Wace added to

GoM, where Ethelfrid takes a mistress, and banishes his pregnant wife, who seeks refuge with Cadvan where she has her son. Edwin was actually the son of Ælle, not Ethelfrith.

15010–15 This 'inseparability motif' operates in several romances (e.g. *Floris and Blauncheflur, Amis and Amiloun*) but Lawman misleads by introducing it here: it belongs in a context where the two characters undergo separation/disagreement followed by reunion/reconciliation; Edwin and Cadwathlan (he forgets their names, all-important in romance, until 15035/8) are not reconciled and their later enmity is not explicitly set against their earlier love in any way; the reader is confused by this moral indirection which leaves the narrative shapeless and the inherent poignancy of the events unfocussed.

15045–58 The negotiation with the archbishop is not in Wace and must form some kind of instructive pointing to a contemporary event or concern, perhaps King John's poor relationship with the Church.

15089 The River Douglas near Wigan in Lancs.; see note 10014.

15105ff In GoM Cadwallo thinks it's raining; Lawman chooses blood as a more ominous liquid. The taunt that Brian is behaving like a woman is only in Lawman; Brian is a Celtic name well known in the Welsh marches (E. J. Dobson, *The Origins of Ancrene Wisse* (1976), p. 349).

15198ff Lawman supplies Gille Patric's name, as he has supplied the direct speech in the conflict of Edwin and Cadwathlan. Lawman may have taken the name *Gillapatric* (not mentioned here in GoM or Wace) from an Irish chief killed at Camlann in GoM XI, 2 [M].

15206 Lawman creates an episode out of a statement in GoM and four lines in Wace, in which Edwin seeks out and rapes Brian's sister; the reader's sympathy is aroused for the girl (who is never named in the sources) and his curiosity enhanced about the promised outcome.

15245 MS C has *Gernemuðe* which Madden interprets as Yarmouth; Wace has Gernerui; Guernsey is in GoM (Garnareia). Yarmouth may well be Yarmouth, Isle of Wight.

15267ff Wace hurries over this disgusting incident, has no direct speech, and discreetly says he does not know if Cadwathlan liked the food (W 14221); Lawman labours it less than GoM where the king finds this sweeter than any meat.

15282 *Ridelet* seems to be an error for *Kidalet* (W 14225–8), the ruins of which Wace says he had seen.

15290ff Lawman adds the detail of how Pelluz works his magic.

15320–51 Brian's merchant disguise, his conversation with the pilgrim, and his commissioning of the lethally spiked pilgrim-staff are invented by Lawman, again borrowing motifs from romance; in GoM he forges the staff himself and disguises himself as a beggar.

15378ff Galarne is more enterprising than her source models: in GoM she nearly faints, and in Wace she has to be told not to show she recognises him; there is no direct speech here in either GoM or Wace. Lawman shows great narrative skill in describing how they huddle inconspicuously among the beggars in a dark area away from the windows. The recognition by means of food-dole and drink (in W 14276 she is merely fetching a bowl of water for the queen) and gold-giving and a secret conversation are also romance motifs (cf. *King Horn*, 1139–1220, reversed gold-giving; Thomas's *Tristan* [Le Saux, *Sources*, p. 89]). But again the motifs fail to satisfy reader-expectation because these are siblings, not lovers, and because Galarne (as in GoM) does not manage to escape with Brian; in GoM she tries and guards prevent her, but Lawman omits this. In Wace Brian simply waits for Pelluz to reach him (W 14297f.), while in L 15399 he seeks him out like a romance hero.

15421–5 This fetching of the goods and men from Southampton, like the initial merchant disguise, is Lawman's invention.

15435 *Adjusted their luffs*: see 4859n. MS C reads *rihten loues*, MS O . . . *hire loues*.

15440 Penda was King of Mercia, not 'East Anglia'; he was a pagan (Bede, *Historia* II, 20).

15458–62 Cadwathlan's motive of rescuing Brian is not in Wace, nor his speech.

15478 Mildburga, daughter of Marwale, was foundress and first abbess of the Convent of Wenlock in Shropshire, where she died c680 [M]; Lawman has recognised the grandfather of a religious woman and adds mention of her family connexions. Wenlock is twenty miles from Areley Kings [B&S].

15497–15538 Wace merely recounts that Chadwalein married Peanda's sister (W 14388–90); there is no account of the knight's mediation or the fetching of Helen, who remains nameless. Nothing is said in GoM of Cadwallo's sin in marrying a pagan.

15519 See 7183n.

15557ff Edwin only calls on English kinglets (and the Orkneys) in GoM and Wace; these additional lands remind us of Arthur's conquests and allies; to what purpose is not clear.

15583–95 The disposition of the battle-field and the battle itself are not in Wace.

15612 Bede says that Edwin's son Osfrith died in the battle, and the other son Eanfrith was treacherously killed by Penda in Oswald's reign; Osric was son of Edwin's uncle and an apostate who died while besieging Cadwallo (III, 1); GoM simply states that Offric, Edwin's successor, was killed in battle by Cadwallo; Wace says he had rebelled (W 14429).

15618–94 Oswald was a canonised and popular saint of the Church; Bede's definitive account was echoed by Ælfric in his *Life of Oswald* and runs as follows: Edwin, a devout convert to Christianity for the last six years of his 17-year reign, died in battle against the rebel British King Cadwalla, who was supported by the Mercian Penda, at Hatfield near Doncaster in October 633, together with his son Osfrith; a second son Eadfrith was captured (II, 20). He was succeeded by his nephew Osric in Deira and Eanfrith son of Ethelfrith in Bernicia, but both apostasised and were killed by Cadwalla, Osric in 633 and in 634 Eanfrith, who visited him to negotiate peace, with a bodyguard of only twelve (III, 1). Oswald, who succeeded his brother Eanfrith, beat and killed Cadwalla at Denisesburn, which then became known as 'Heaven Field', after praying devoutly at a wooden cross before battle, (III, 1, 2). Oswald reconverted Bernicia with Aidan's guidance but was killed, by Penda, as Edwin had been, at Maserfeld in 642 (III, 3, 9).

GoM gives all insular history from the British viewpoint; Oswald on this count is not a sainted hero but an enemy, like Edwin. Geoffrey squares this with his clerical status by treating Oswald like any other Saxon, conquered by the great British hero, Cadwallo, but killed by an army led by Penda, a historical fact. Geoffrey has in so doing (a) given to Cadwalla the 17 years (and more) of rule which belong to Edwin; (b) ignored his actual death by making Penda conduct his army at Heavenfield. The fraud is obvious: Cadwallo is alleged to be angry when Penda loses at Heavenfield, so marches against Oswald, and *Penda* kills Oswald at 'Burne' – itself probably derived from *Denisesburn* (XII, 10). He also makes Cadwallo not Penda the victor at Hatfield (XII, 8) and confuses Edwin's sons and nephew. GoM's Cadwalla is formed on the W. Saxon *Coenwalh*, who married a sister of Penda (whom he repudiated, incurring reprisals from Penda [Bede, III, 7]) and had a son called Ceadwalla, whom GoM deliberately confounds with Cadwalader (XII, 14; contrast Bede, IV, 15), even ascribing to Cadwalader a death in Rome 12 days before May, which Bede recounts of Ceadwalla, who went to Rome in 688 and was baptised there at the time of Sergius I, 687–701 (Bede, V, 7) [M]; Yuni [L 16043, Yni, GoM XII, 18) seems to derive from Ine, son of the historical Ceadwalla [M].

Wace follows GoM, even to including Chadwalein's (= Cadwalla's) murders of women and children (GoM XII, 9, W 1441–2) which Bede found so repugnant (II, 20, III, 1); he does upgrade Oswald as 'a noble man of fine courage' (W 14437) but does not call him 'saint'.

Lawman follows GoM in the confusion between Eadfrith and Osric and the prolongation of Cadwalla's life beyond Heavenfield, but redirects the narrative focus to the English: Edwin's emotions are noted in L 15594–5; details of Cadwathlan's (Cadwalla's) atrocities are omitted at L 15707 and he repents of the betrayal of Oswald (15698); and Oswald is termed the chosen one of the Most High (15635), and given the title 'Saint' (L 15688);

15674–94 Oswald's death unarmed at Penda's hand is the story of a man betrayed through guileless trust, while negotiating a truce, which really belonged to his irreligious predecessor Osric, tricked by Penda. Strangely, Lawman omits the actual prayer at the cross included in GoM and Wace at L 15672: he (or a scribe) has disastrously conflated the two battles of Heavenfield and Maserfeld (L 15666), perhaps by eye-skip through the identity of the second element of the names.

15722–32 In Wace Penda merely says he dare not break peace without Chadwalein's consent [M] (W 14529ff).

15812–5 The sentiment is from Wace (and GoM, Thorpe, 279), the ferocious image of dog eat dog is Lawman's. This very observation that the opposing side were destroying themselves was made of the Welsh by the Norman administration in Shropshire in the early 12thc (*Welsh Brut*, s.a. 1111, cited in Davies, *Conquest, Coexistence & Change*, p. 72,

n. 30); GoM, as usual, reversed the common stricture against the Welsh. The important claim that Oswy is recruiting forces in Saxony (W 14555) is omitted by Lawman [M].

15842 Oswy in fact killed Penda, the reverse of Lawman's account, in 655 in the thirteenth year of his reign (Bede, *Historia*, III, 25) and subsequently converted Mercia to Christianity, ruling Mercia for three years before handing South Mercia to Penda's son Peada. In 664 Oswy presided at the Synod of Whitby where Catholic and Celtic Churches were reconciled (III, 25), and died in 670 after a reign of 28 years (III, 14). He was succeeded by his son Ecgfrith [M].

15860 Wace and GoM do not say that Cadwathlan died of eating fish [M]; Henry I, however, died after gorging on lampreys, as Henry of Huntingdon describes.

15871–6 This description of the devastation of famine seems to be modelled on the Peterborough Chronicle account for the year 1137 of the depredations in the Fenland region during the Civil War under Stephen and Matilda: 'When the wretched men had no more to give (in tax) they plundered and burnt all the villages, so that you could easily travel a whole day's journey without finding a man sitting in a village, or any land under cultivation. Then corn was dear, and meat, and cheese and butter, for there was none in the countryside. Wretched people died of starvation.' Cf. W 14665–8, which is similar in sense but less rhetorically pointed: 'you might be three days without finding any bread there or wheat or other food to buy'. The plague (L 15587) actually occurred: ('a sudden plague, which first decimated the southern parts of Britain and later . . . the Northumbrians, raged for a long time and brought widespread death . . . (and) was equally destructive in Ireland' [Bede, III, 27]; and ASC s.a. 664: 'a great pestilence' [M].

15880–95 Wace does not have cattle-murrain in his plagues, but has a similarly rhetorical if more effective passage on the human mortality (W 14677ff).

15908 Alain II, nephew of Salomon II (Wace: *niés*) came to the throne in 679 [H].

15961 Wace says that Edward the Elder, Athelstan's father, restored Peter's Pence; neither he nor his son went to Rome [H], although Athelstan's great-grandfather Æþelwulf did so in 855.

15964 Ine died in Rome in 727 after abdicating in 725, but Athelstan came to the throne in 924. Lawman seems to doubt whether Peter's Pence will continue, perhaps because of the Papal Interdict under John, or because it had been discontinued or misappropriated several times in the 12thc, and John had forbidden its collection in 1206.

15971ff Lawman omits Wace's linguistic notes on the Welsh, English and French equivalents of common words, presenting a more emotive account of the events at L 15970–7, and he expands Wace's addition of the (inaccurate) arrival of Athelstan instead. Lawman's version reads like the genuine reaction of a subject people to the alien master-race and may be an echo of the 11thc Anglo-Saxon reaction to the Norman invasion, which Lawman could have heard through oral tradition, or found recorded. The Normans changed the administrative system and (to a lesser extent than the Anglo-Saxons) the place-names: e.g. OE *Scrobbes-byrig* › *Srobbesbyrig* › *Sarobesbery* › *Salopesberie* (Shrewsbury). 15972, in particular, records the Norman forest law established by William the Bastard; there was no such law in Anglo-Saxon England until Cnut's laws (1027–34) [H]; pre-Conquest guilds were different from the Norman, being largely ecclesiastical; (ʒ*ilden*, which I translate 'guilds', following Madden and Hall, may well mean 'taxes' (cf. Peterborough Chronicle, s.a. 1137: *hi læiden gæildes on the tunes*': *mære* 'glorious' should then read *mare* 'huge'); 15976 may possibly record a change in architectural style, from Saxon to Romanesque, or revisions of monastic and episcopal government.

16009–29 The actual words of the angelic voice are not given in GoM and Wace.

16072 The four and a half years are not in Wace and may derive from a Welsh tradition [H].

16095 The poem closes with a proverb, which is used in tones of despair in one of the later MSS of *The Proverbs of Alfred* 504–5 and in the 1066 entry in the ASC, which Le Saux (*Sources*, p. 222) assumes is its usual connotation: this would imply that Lawman ended his poem on a note of bitterness; on the contrary, it sounds to me like relief at a completed task!

EMENDATIONS TO THE CALIGULA MS

This list records instances where the translation is based on a correction of the base manuscript, BL MS Cotton Caligula A.ix. The emendations are usually based on the corresponding reading of the other manuscript, BL MS Cotton Otho C.xiii but are occasionally conjectural. The readings of MS C and MS O are cited in the original spelling. The letters B&L after an entry indicate that this reading has been entered into the edited text of the Caligula MS in the EETS edition by Brook and Leslie; other letters record the emendations suggested by other editors and are explained in the list of Abbreviations. I have also included a number of alternative translations of lines or phrases. Line numbers are those of the translation, which correspond to the numbering of MS C allocated by Brook and Leslie; 'a' following the number indicates an additional line from MS O; these are often included in the B&L text of C in square brackets with this form of numbering; where B&L do not admit the lines I adopt the same system of numbering.

30 A half-line must have been omitted in the shared ancestor of both MSS [M].

87 Or: 'disturbed by anger' [M].

119 *she*: he C; om O. I assume the referent is Lavinia (117 *heo* [i]); but 117 *heo* (ii) may also be sg. 'she', the sg. vb. obscured by *-n* of NWorcs. 'nunnation'.

130 *grown handsome*: reading *feir and muchel* for *feir muche*; *mochel* O [M, III, 441].

192a From O; not in C.

383 *rocks*: *cleues* O; *lude* C; B&L emend C to *clude*.

422 *carnage*: *deade* O; *vær* C; B&L emend C to *wæl*.

503 *want*: *wælde* C; om O = *wædle* 'penury' [M, III, 449].

536 *lord and*: *Louerd and* O; om C.

558 Madden's alternative rendering 'which teemed with wild animals' is unlikely: ME *tēman* means 'to bring forth' (trans. and intrans.); the sense 'to abound, swarm' is not instanced before 16thc (OED, s.v. *teem* v[1], 3; the verb here is OED *teem* v[2], 2 (intr.) (of water) 'to pour, flow'.

568 *carrying . . . as much as ever they (wished)*: *ladden so moche so iwolden* O [B&L]; om C.

580 *things:* þincge O [B&L]; *kingen* C.

639 *currents:* reading *water* C, rather than *weder* O as M prefers [III, 450].

750 *the case:* soþ O; *sum* C.

771 *for shame:* *a-wæi* C; Madden suggests *awac* O 'wake up' is correct.

816 *easier:* eþere O [B&L]; *at* C.

834 *advanced:* toȝen [M; B&L]; *to* CO.

946 *blanched:* *blake* CO; glossed under both *blak* adj 2(a) 'dark, discoloured' and under *blok* 1 (b) ? 'livid' in MED. They might be pale with anger or purple through lack of breath; the contrast in 947 suggests 'pale' is the meaning here.

982 *special:* deore O [B&L]; *dema* C.

1047 *Brutus's:* *Brutus* O [B&L]; om C.

1360 *Andor:* cf. 1357, no. 28; *Annore* O; *Anoþer* C.

1362 *they . . . clothed:* *alle heo weren wel i-scrud* O; om C; Madden thinks that O also contains an error because its punctuation is faulty [III, 457].

1499 *second:* oþer O [M; B&L]; om C.

1502 *she:* ȝeo O; om C; Madden would read *Regau.*

    but . . . heart: *and noht mid heorte* O; om C.

1503 *me:* *me* B&L; *me alf* ('half so dear to me') O; om C.

1512 *(of ready truth) the strictest:* ȝær-witelest as compound B&L; Madden gl. ȝær 'well'; Hall interprets the compound as 'studious' here, 'sagacious' in its other occurrences in the *Brut.*

1525 *ruler of:* weldende O [M]; *velden* C.

1551 *anguished:* wo O [B&L]; *þa* C.

1578 *for:* *for* O [M]; om C (*þire wel-deda* presumably in dative case).

1631 *liked:* *was wel ipaid* O; *iherde* C 'heard of'; Madden would read *iwærþ.*

1740 *(as) one should a father:* *man his fader* O [M; H]; *monnes f.* C, which looks like an auditory error.

1775 *lodgings:* on *in* O, which however sophisticates the line; *burie* C, repeated from 1774; Hall suggests *huse;* this looks like an error in the shared ancestor, perhaps for [*nimen him rum in ricchen an inne*].

1781 *bed:* bed O [M; H]; *baid* C; M: 'influenced by following *baðie*'.

1792 *father's:* Hall's emendation *faderes* for *lauerdes* C; om O.

1803 *a noble:* Madden's emendation *are hæȝene* 'a high, noble' for *hare æȝene* 'their own' C; *one* O.

1818 *rings of bright gold:* ringes of golde O [M; B&L]; om C.

1329 Conjectural interpretation of an obscure line which Madden says is corrupt.

1874a *we . . . land:* conjecture; om CO.

    and . . . hand: *take hit þe children hond* O; om C.

1930a Line from MS O [B&L]; om C.

1956 *Kinemarck:* *Kinemarck* O; *King Mark* C.

1963 *envy and in ⟨hate⟩:* *in niþe and* O; *mid* C.

1974 *Siward:* O; *Sward* C.

2000 *six: six* O; *swic* C.

2051 *mob: heap* 'throng, crowd' O; *wæl* 'slaughter' C. Both scribes had difficulty with *wæl* in 422, but the scribe of MS C also often omits or glosses *heap*. Either might be right here.

2060 *us: we* O; *þe* altered to *ve* C.

2106 set on] *legge ʒam on* O; *slæn heom* C.

2124 *long: lange* O; *lond* C.

2215 *those who: þat* O; *he* C; *þe* B&L.

2279 *very soon after: sone þar after* O; om C.

2314 *the:* B&L emend to *þa; to* C; line om O.

2341 *things: þing* O [M; B&L]; *kinge* C.

2365 *groaning:* gl. 'dying' MED.

2375 *force: folke* O; *monnen* C, from preceding line.

2382 *he:* B&L supply *he; ich* O; om C.

2467–8 *then . . . dead/territory . . . hand:* second half of MS O 2467 appears as first half of 2468 in C, which omits 2468 *into . . . hand* O, and reads *duweðe* in 2468 for *cunde* 'inherited land' O.

2473 *how: hou* O; *an* C.

2475a From O; line om C.

2487 *but one mile lay between them: þar ʒam (bit-t . .e bote) . . . mile* O; *þere twa ferden* C. Both C and O look like scribal attempts at emendation of a corruption. The translation follows O for the second half of the line, but the usual rhyme in *Brut* for *næh*, which ends the first half-line in C, is *bæh* and the original may have read something like *þæt heo to þere oþere ferde bæh* 'that they reached the other armed force'.

2488 *their mother: hire mod . . .* O; *þa ælde quene* C.

2489 *(Belin) and Brenne: and Brenne* O; om C.

2496 *she was shown: me hire tehte* O; om C.

2500a *Line from MS* O; om C.

2524 *folk: folke* O; *mannen* C.

2588 *slaughter:* Madden's emendation *gumene wæl* 'destruction of men'; *cumene fæl* C; line om O.

2610 *people: þan leoden* [M; B&L] *þat londen* C; line om O.

2687 *(on) knees: a cnowe* O [B&L]; *on onden* C; Hall emends to *on [honden eo]den:* 'made their submission'.

2688a Line from MS O; om C.

2737 Reading *þa þe; þat þan* O; *þon* (keiser) C.

2801 *(my) strong: .onge* O; *mine* C.

2802 *you both: inc* supplied by B&L; *hit* C; O sophisticates.

2826 *laste: laste* O; om C; [M; B&L].

2847 *kings: kinges* O; *king* C; [M].

2865 *fight with: mid ʒam solde fihte* O; om C; *fulsten* conjectured by M and supplied in 2862–66 follows suggestion by Madden, Vol. III, p. 469.

2908 *valiantly: mid mansipe* O; om C.

2919 *who . . . ahead of them: þat solde heom bi fore beon* O; om C.

2921 *our (wrongs): ore* C; *houre* O; Madden says *ore* C is an error for *heore* and regards O *houre* as an error for *hire*, in which case this line is not direct speech, as I have translated it.

2997 From MS O; line om C.

3038 *this one:* þis *was* O [M]; *wes* þer C.

3039 *and . . . shunned: onselþ he sonede* O; *unstronge monnen he leoðede* C 'he hated evil men' [M]; see also 3537, and note.

3057 *enraged:* þo *was wroþ* O; Þat *word come to* C.

3082 *fully loaded: al grund-lade* O; þe *schipe wel a-fulled* C.

3108 *(shall) laud: lofuie wolleþ* O; *leofuen wið* C.

3128 *If anyone . . . between their thighs:* þoh *hire lemman sehe al* þat *were bi* þeʒe O; *wha heore leome sæʒe alle* þe *on heom weoren* C, O of *leome* added by interlining.

3144 *when:* þo MS O; om C.

to . . . promulgated: his writ to londe he was i-broht O; om C.

3263 *lay dead: lið* 'lies' C; *in Londone me hine leide* (second half-line), O.

3297–8 Madden suggests that these two lines should be translated: 'seek his brother, where he might find (mercy)'.

3330 *he: he* O; þe *king* C.

3387 *Ingenes: Ingenes* O; *Iuienes* C.

3423 *one man's: Argales* O; *mannes* C: O is probably correct; I have supplied 'one'.

here: ær C; om O.

3435 *Ingenes: Ingenes* O; *Inienes* C.

3454 Madden suggests (III, 473) that *duʒeðen* 'forces, powers' is an error for ʒuʒeðen 'youth'; Wace reads *joventé*; line om O.

3490 *organ: coriun* C; line om O; Wace 3701 has *chorum*. Madden connects this word with *coruth*, which he calls a 'wind instrument'; Ellis called it a 'trumpet'. The *chorus* (coruth, or crowd) was actually a bowed lyre; the lyre is mentioned in 3491, however, and I have assumed that the form *coriun* may have come from an original *chair*, later *choir*, a positive organ, between the great and the portative organ in size.

3552 *the old names:* þe *olde names* O; Þene *ælden nomen* C; Madden says that the C reading is an error for Þa *ælden nomen* (pl.); it might perhaps be an imitation of the OE þone *ealdan naman* (sg.).

3563 *Tennancius: Teunancius* O; *Temelcinus* C, added in a later hand, the margin has *Androgeus Tennancius*. In lines 3576 and 4485 the form of the name in C is *Tennancius*; O has *Teu(n)anciu[m]* and *Teunancius* respectively.

3601 *Hell: helle* O (M; B&L); *eælde* C.

3617 *after the flood: after* þan *flode* O; not in C.

3617a *There are fish . . . water-fowl:* þar *his fis* þar *fowel* O; om C.

there are . . . around B&L print þer *beoð duhtie men* C at the end of 3617; þar *beoþ men kene* ends 3617a in O.

3640 *And: And* O; *He* C.

well: wel O; *al* C.

3724 *arrival . . . Caesar: come was war Iulius Cesar* O [B&L]; om C.

3737 *uncle: heam* O; *fader* C.

3752 *without . . . breath:* noht ne na bræd C; mid þe seolue (b)reþ O;
B&L emend and print *nefde .na,* with punctus instead of usual punctus
elevatus. I conjecture *ne atmede* ('did not breathe').

3759 *Nennius:* .emnius O; monie C, minim error and *e/o* confusion
for *nenie* (Nennius).

3808 *on the hilt:* B&L print as two lines 3807 *þer-on weoren igrauen*
C and 3808 *æ ðere hilte wes igrauen,* but 3808 (only a half line) is
presumably a correction of the first half of 3807; I have translated 3808
as the first half of 3807 and omitted line 3808 from the numbering so as
to maintain identical numbering with B&L; neither line is present in O.

4000 *craven* onbold O; bald C; here as often elsewhere the prefix *un-*
may have pejorative rather than negative force (see 9625 below, and cf.
vnstronge, 'evil' line 3537, but in 8578 *un-hal* means 'unwell') and the
meaning would then be 'aggressive'.

4008 *our:* emending to *þat we him her imunten; þat we him
here a-sende* O; *þat he him her imunten* C.

4011 *army:* here O; loede C.

4080 *his nose . . . lips:* þe nose mid þe lippe ('limb'; ? read *lippe*) O; his
neb & his neose ('nose and . . . nose') C.

    fell . . . off: niðer ba heolden C 'both fell down'; boþe awei
    cutte O.

4097 *army:* om C, with blank left; line om O; B&L supply *hired*
'court', I assume *here* 'army'.

4108 *own:* owe O [M]; ane C.

4112 *fighting:* feht O; here C.

4258 *the (castle):* þane o; enne C.

4300 An alternative translation would be: 'As they lay there silently
awaiting their opportunity'.

4337a *þat swiþe þicke in euereche side* O; *swiþe* (in line 4338) C,
which otherwise lacks the line; there is corruption in both C, where a line
seems to have been omitted, and in O, where 4337a lacks a verb; I have
conjectured a verb *greowen* in 4337a, which might have caused eye-skip
from *greowen* in 4337a to 4338 if *greowen* or *bigreowen* ended line
4337a, as in 4337; in this case, the second half of 4337a must be wrong in
O, where the scansion and rhyme/alliteration are also poor. The error
may derive from the common ancestor of C and O, and scribes C and O
may have independently attempted to patch corrupt or unreadable copy.

4347 *were . . . little:* lut him wa. O; heom wes alles C.

4348 *since:* for O; & C.

4350 *torment:* burst C; þorst O, which may be correct.

4388 *wanted:* wolde O; nolde C.

4423 *now . . . underling:* from MS O; om C.

4483 *before . . died:* Her þe king were dead deaide (þe cwene) O;
[B&L]; not in C.

4676a From MS O; line om C.

4683a *and . . . asked:* and dude al þat me hine bad O; om C; the first
half of this line is printed at the end of 4683 in B&L.

4751 *message:* þe bode O; þas cnihtes C.

4811 *miracles*: *tockne* 'signs' O; *teonen* 'injuries' C.

5046 *teaching*: *lore* O; *fore* 'business, actions' C.

5089 *they*: *hii* O; *he* C.

5277 *there*: *þar* O; *heo* C.

5614 *Trahern*: *Traharn* O; *he* C.

5618 *all Scotland he*: *he al Scotland* O; [B&L]; om C.

5665 *said where*: *Chæpmen bunden* C; *þo seide me* O; I have conflated the two readings. C has *heore ware* 'their wares', O has *him ware* 'to him where'; it is likely that C is right with 'merchants' but that *bunden heore ware* (C) is a corruption suggested by the context and a spelling like O's *ware* for 'where'; Lawman's original may well have meant: 'Merchants told him where the king intended to travel then'.

5677 *any*: *eni* O; *hine* C.

5750 *he had been deprived*: *hii hadde hine binome* O; *heo hæfden binomen* C.

5968 *stationed*: *ifunde* O; *isunde* ('safe') C.

5988 *Ursula*: *Vrsele* O; [B&L]; *Oriene* C.

5991 *went wandering*: *walkede* O; om C; Madden suggests *weolcen*.

6018 *get (to him)*: *wende* O; om C; Madden says (III, 484) MS C is correct with *nu we him to*.

6037 *Ursula*: *Vrsele* O [B&L]; *Oriene* C.

6181 *secret*: *deorne* O; *deore* 'precious' C.

6195 *the north of*: *bi norþe* S. O; *biuoren* S. C.

6226 *you*: *we* CO: B&L emend to *ʒe*.

6228 *but*: *for* CO: I emend to *but*.

6230 *you*: *ʒe* O; [B&L]; *we* C.

6253 *declamed*: *iseid* O [B&L]; om C.

6289 *higher*: *hehere* O; *hæʒe* C.

6321 *see now*: *Lo* O; *þa* C.

6322 *woe*: om in both MSS; emendation supplied by B&L.

6344 *Aldroien*: *Aldroim* O; *Androgien* C; B&L.

6370 *is*: *nis* O [B&L]) *is* C; the idiom *wel neh nan* requires a neg. vb.

6510 *elders*: *ælde* C; *alle Bruttes* O; Madden suggests (III, 486) that *ældre* is correct.

6579 *in their command*: Madden reads *(hæfden) on anwolde* for MS C, as in O; the last two words have been om in B&L's edition.

6581 *from . . . land*: Madden reads of *þissen londe* for C, as in O: *londe*. has been om from B&L's edition.

6672–3 *traversed . . . castles and*: From MS O; om C.

6675 *then*: *suþþe* O; *swa* C.

6686 *fulfil . . . desires*: *don oure wille* O; B&L emend C to: *don eore wille*.

6810 *begin to understand*: *noht hit onder-stonde* O; *nænne ræd luuien* C. O presents a typical half-rhyme.

6810a Line from O, not in C but *ræd* is present in 6819 C.

6829 *stationed*: *wonede* O; *weoren* C.

6870 *who was*: *þat was* O; *þene* C.

6923 *lot*: *lot* O; *beoð* (= beod) 'offer' C.

6926 *things go on*: *hit fareþ* O; *we uerden* 'we travelled' C.

6927 *heavens*: *luste* C: Madden, B&L emend to *lufte*; om O.

6950–3 *we/our*: *we* O; *heo* C: emendations based on the abbreviated version of the passage in O, which uses first person pl. pronouns.

6954 *give*: ȝ*euen* C; om O.

6958 *beliefs*: *ileuen* C, interlined in later hand over *ilauerd*, struck out.

6976 *ancestors'*: *aldene* C: Madden emends to *aldrene*; om O.

6987 *they've*: *iuæld* C: supplying *habbeð*, as suggested by Madden, (III, 487); *falleþ* O.

7040 *country*: *lond* interlined in later hand, C; *þat þou dedest to deaþe* O.

7046 *both*: *beyne* added, later hand, C; line om O.

7109 *men*: *gomen* C: Madden translates 'event' (Errata, Vol. II) but 'gomen' could mean 'men', especially as Lawman is talking of three nations; line om O.

7146 *ever*: *euer* O; *ær* 'before' C.

7169 *such*: *soche* O; *ælche* C.

7178 *aggreeable*: *icweme* O [B&L]; om C.

7328 *their*: *his* CO.

7381 *young*: Madden says read ȝ*unge king* as in ȝ*onge king* O, but in the orig. the adj. may have been ȝ*inge*; cf. *King Horn* 129 ȝ*inge*: *tiþinge*.

7414a Line from MS O, with *hi* supplied; line om C.

7417 *who*: *þat* O; *&* C.

7447a–7448 *advice*: From MS O; om C.

7475 *this*: *þes* O; *þus* C.

7592 *he could hide*: *he hit habbe mihte* O [M. B&L]; *hit hit hæle* C.

7600 *deceived*: *biswac* O [M III, 488]; *bispac* C (wynn/*p* confusion).

7618 *instantly*: *sone* O [B&L]; om C.

7637 *his*: *his* O; *ane* C.

7657 *pavilions*: B&L emend MS C *coine lan* (altered from *coine lond*) to *comelan*; om O.

7727 *the work*: *þis worck* O; om C.

7767 *blows*: *dunt* O; *dudes* C; B&L emend to *duntes*.

7781 *listen*: *lust* O; ȝ*erden* (?= *Yherden*) C; Brook reads ȝ*ernden* and gl. 'made enquiries'.

7855 *veil*: *huȝe* C; om O; Brook gl. 'composed her features' (i.e. reading C as = *heue*; I read *huue*, *houve* 'headdress' (OE *hufe* 'head-covering').

7927 MED equates *folden to grunde* with *fellen* 'collapse' (cf. 13819 *feol to grunde*); in Lawman it is usually MED *folden* v. (2) 3(a) 'lay (someone) low'; (b) *folden to grounde* 'collapse, fall in battle; fell, kill'. Madden (III, 490) interprets *uolden* as adverbial = 'down to the ground'.

7957 *And . . . fighting*: from O [B&L]; om C.

8040 *court*: *hirede* C, altered to *herede*; O sophisticates. Madden, reading *hirede* trans. 'all together'.

8053 *covered*: *wræc* C: Madden suggests emendation to *wræh*

[B&L]; om O.

8130a From MS O; not in C.

8138 *forces . . . abate*: hælp C; *heop* O. A crux: Brook accepts *hælp* C and trans: 'when the head (i.e. king) is worthless he is unable to provide help for his subjects in their misfortunes'; Madden emends to *hæp* 'lot'; I read *heap* 'crowd, bulk, or strength'. MED s.v. *hep* gl. 'strength'. Madden cites Wace: 'Rien ne valt *li gent* que on amine/Qui a faible et fol chavetaine', (from MS Bibl. nationale fonds francais 1450, used as base MS by Le Roux Lincy) which would support the sense 'crowd of men', but Arnold prints (W 7693ff): 'Petit fait a criendre *compaigne*/Ki ad fieble e fol chevetaine/De malvaise gent senz seinnur/Ne deit l'um mie aveir poür', which cannot have been in Lawman's copy of Wace. *Heap* 'crowd' occurs several times in Lawman (e.g. 2051, 2948, 9149), usually with some scribal confusion, especially in C, and it seems likely that it is the right reading here.

8186 *fiercely*: *fastliche* O; *feondliche* C, prob. from prec. line.

8215 *field*: *feld* O; *wald* C (?= 'plain').

8258 *perpetrated*: reading *iuræmmed* [M; B&L] for *iuræinned* 'sought, asked' C; O sophisticates.

8300 *and*: *and* O; om C.

8400. *that whoever*: *þat wo* O; *þene we* C.

he: *he* O; *we* C.

8459 *erect*: *arere* O; *bulden* C.

8464 *halls . . . churches*: from MS O [B&L]; om C.

8550 *of . . . effect*: *bæli wis* C [M], printed *bæl iwis* in B&L; Hall emends *bælwes* 'of malignity'.

8686 *come down on*: trans. *cumeþ* C; Hall emends *scuueþ* 'push'.

8706 MS O reads *ase feþerbeddes*.

8731a From MS O; line om C.

8734 *gave high honour*: reading *heʒe wurþede* C, as in B&L; line om O: Madden reads (unconvincingly) *he ʒewurðede* 'he honoured' = *he iwurðede* while Hall emends to *hæʒe wurþede he*.

8854 *chamber-knights*: emending *burh-cnihtes* C to *bur-cnihtes*; *cnihtes* O.

8882 *uncovered*: *hedden* C; om O.

8886 *affliction*: *beonste* or *beoste* C, with marginal cross: emended *beorste* [M, B&L]; line om O.

9098 *heard*: *ne horde* O; *nefde* C.

9149 *numbers*: *heap* O; *hælp* C: Madden (III, 494) thinks the meaning here is 'hap, luck'; Brook says 'help, means of assistance' is possible, here; MED gl. this instance as 'strength, numbers'.

9175 *will believe*: *loueie wolleþ* 'will praise' O; *nulleð liʒe* 'will not lie' C.

9257 *this game*: *game* O [Brook]; *him* C.

9416 *battle-ensigns*: reading *heore mærken* C, *hire marke as here-merken* [Madden, III, 494].

9440a Line from MS O; om C.

9444 *silver . . . gold*: om CO [B&L, based on 9986, etc.]

9449 *appearance: cheres* O; *gareres* C [B&L].

9485 *were holding: heo Vðer* C; *Vther* O; B&L emend to *heolden*; Madden and B&W delete *heo*, but Madden adds 'or read *æc*'.

9489 *three: sic*, both MSS; in fact he has *two* men but the error is presumably either authorial or archetypal; it may be a confused attempt to echo the OE construction *he þreora sum* 'he with two companions'.

9625 *depraved: onbalded* O [B&L]; *balded* C: B&L read *ibalded* 'emboldened', but Madden gl. *vnstrong* as 'bad, wicked' in 3039 (see above) and 3537; and this seems to be a similar pejorative use of the prefix *un-*; see 4000 above. In 5223 *vnstrong* trans *de bas parage* (Wace) and *infimus* 'basest' (Bede).

9665 *off . . . immediately: forþ hii wende sone þat* O; om C.

9730 *agonising*: leaving *bitele* C 'sharp' [B&W] rather than emending to *bitere* [B&L].

9752 *ich* O [B&L]; om C.

9753 *us: vs* O; *eou* C.

9826 *not at all*: reading *na no fisc* as in Madden's text and B&W, rather than *ma no fisc* in B&L's text.

9917 *your own: þine* O; *þisne*.

10041 *rime-grey: rumie* C; *wode* O: Brook reads *rimie*, but B&L leave *runie*; Madden derives *rimie* from OE *hremig* 'wild', but MED gl 10041 with 774 as 'rimy', s.v. *rimie*; B&W read *runie* and gl 'savage'.

10051 *clattering*: or, 'shattering' ('burst'); D&W gl 'bristled', B&W 'clashed'.

10067 *death hour*: reading *on his fæie-sið* for *fæie on his siðe* C; *adrad in eche side* O.

10133a Line from O; om C.

10167 *place: stude* O [B&L]; *hude* C.

10199 *distress: hæte* C; *hate* O. Cf. 10342 *hete* C, *hate* O, 10925 *hete* C, *hate* O (and see 2017, 4365, 15912). In most instances at least the word seems to be OE *hete* 'malice', cf. OE *hetol* 'fierce', rather than OE *hætu* 'heat'; B&W suggest 'drought, thirst'.

10241 *bold: bolde* O [B&L]; om C.

10244 *harm: beorkes* C; om O; *barque* 'vessel' is not attested before 15thc; B&W interpret C as 'barking of dogs', i.e. antagonism, and Brook emends to *beornen* 'soldiers, men'; I emend to *beorstes* 'harm', gen. sg. after *abiden*.

10268 *urged . . . sternly: for-bæd* C; *forbed* O: Madden trans 'fore-ordered', unparelleled before 17thc *for-bode*; B&W suggest *for-bede* MED v 1 (c) 'restrain, control'; I read *for-* as prefix in intensive rather than adversative or temporal sense: 'command strongly' (see Jaček Fisiak, *A Short Grammar of Middle English* I, (1966), p. 114 (7).

10300 *for-bærnen* C; om O: Hall emends to *forwurþe* 'would perish' (as in 10310).

10311 *they . . . destroyed: me* 'one' *heom for-dude* O; *hi heom fordudenc.*

10312 *they . . . attacked: me hii* O; *heo heom* C; Hall reads *me heom* (passive; see 10311).

10352 *send straight*: following Hall's interpretation of *wið and wið* as = *wið þet* 'at the same time'.

10397 *all . . . folk*: reading *cun al* with Madden, Brook and B&W, rather than *cun ai* B&L.

10430 *he regretted*: Or: 'they suffered for' [Hall].

10475 *we*: *we* O; *heo* C.

10512 *kill . . . off*: *a-cwelled* O; *adefed* 'made deaf' C is emended [B&L, Brook] to *adrefed* 'driven off'; B&L suggest *adeded* 'deadened'; I read *aderfed* 'killed with want', cf. MED *derfen* v. (a) 'afflict, harass, torment', as in L 4354 *hunger him derfde*; but MED gl 10512 (unconvincingly) s.v. *adeven* 'subdue or annihilate' (‹O.E. *adȳfan* 'drown' or ‹*adēafian* 'deafen').

10610 *pigs*: *swyn* O [B&L]; om C.

10624 *floating*: reading *wleotweð* C as a sp for *fleoteð*, *u-* sp for voiced *f-* misinterpreted by scribe as *w-*?; Burrow suggests [*N&Q*, 225 (1980), 2–3] a derivation from *wlitigian* 'shine, gleam' (cited in B&W).

10711 *come . . . again*: *aȝen cumen liðen* C; *aȝein hider wende* O; B&W trans 'hoping to sail home in safety' (Madden: 'with safety again to come', noting *hider* O); but *aȝen* means 'back' and in 10753 Cador's anxiety, as he interprets Arthur's instruction, is that Childric will return: *and æft cumen hidere*.

10716 Taking *ufele* C as adv. 'harmfully, injuriously', as elsewhere in L, rather than adj agreeing with 'Childric', as in B&W.

10833 *forced*: *þreaste* O [M]; *wræsten* C.

10864 *flow into*: *falleþ in* 'flows into' O [M, D&W, B&W, suggested by Brook, not in B&L]; *walleþ* of 'flows from' C.

10918 *dragging*: *sette* O; om C.

10921 *affliction*: *on sið* C; om O; B&W interpret *sið* '(in) distress'; Madden suggests 'in affliction?' or 'on journey'; Lawman may have written *on site* 'in care, grief, trouble'.

11019 *singing*: *songen* O [M, B&L]; *suggen* C.

11030 *placed*: *bi-toc* ; [B&L]; om C.

11041 *lowly*: reading *læȝ* 'low' for *læd* 'odious' C; om O.

11127 *prepared*: *beouwden* C, altered to *beoveden* by interlining and crossing through, later hand; *beoude* O, line 11125: Brook follows C, B&L read *beoveden*; B&W suggest *bounen* 'get ready', but this is essentially identical in sense with *b(e)onneden* following.

11277 The line is displaced in C, not in O; I follow the emendation of B&W.

11280 *items . . . tribute*: *giueles* C; O sophisticates: emended by Madden to *gaueles*.

11403 *seek*: *are* C: read *arere* 'stir up' [B&L, Hall, B&W]; om O.

11515 *believe*: *ileueþ* O; *ilefde* C.

11632 *prudent*: *red-folle* O; *ræh-fulle* C: B&W read with C and trans 'brave'.

11678 *Boulogne*: *Boloyne* O [B&L]; om C.

11679 *all of*: *and al* O [B&L]; om C.

11892a Line from MS O; om C.

11946 *made a counter-attack*: *kept* C; *kepte* O: Madden corrects his trans 'observed' to 'intercepted'; B&W trans 'fended off' (MED *kepen* v 3b(b); in fact he seems to be attacking, see MED *kepen* v. 7. 'meet in resistance'; 18. 'assault'; MED gl 11946 (sense 17) 'await arrival of'.

12195 *wheat*: *wete* O; *water* C: B&W read with C.

12276 Madden would read *irinen* 'adorned' from OE *gehrinan* (III, 503), though his text, and that of B&W, reads *iriuen*; MED regards *iriuen* as an error for *irinen*.

12287 *those*: *þaie* O; *þan* C: B&L read *þai*, which means that the female attendants also serve the Queen, (but the 3 pers. pl. pron is usually *heo* or *hii* in L); presumably the maidens were also served by the 1000 serving-men, and therefore the pronoun should not be nom; B&W read *þan* with C, which they identify as the dative of the demonstrative pronoun *þat* (more usually *þe/þa* in pl), and remark that *þæninen* 'serve' takes the dative in L as in OE.

12471 *you*: *ȝe* O; *ȝet* C (?= *ȝit* 'the two of you', but Arthur is addressing all his men).

12493 *he*: *he* O; *heo* C, which reads *ah mid stre(n)ðe heo eoden an hond and bitahten him al heore lond* which Brook trans: 'but they resisted *him* with force and *yet* they had to hand over all their land to him'; B&W trans 'but they yielded to force and surrendered all their land to him'; O has *ac mid strenþe he* (Caesar) *ȝeode an hond and bi-nam ȝam hire lond*: Madden says (III, 504) that O is right, C scribe having in error taken *eoden an hond* in sense 'submit' and made pl subject.

12215 *there . . . land*: from MS O; om C.

12217 *as*: *ase* O; *þus* C. *for all*: *al for* C; om O.

12625 *knight*: *cnaue* O; *swein* C, by attraction to 12627.

12649 *him*: *he* 'which he loved' O; *heom* 'who loved them (?)' C.

12773 *which . . . boroughs*: from O; only *bur* and *suel* in C, the rest, written by second hand in margin, was trimmed 'by the rascally binder' [!, Madden, III, 505].

12790 *as . . . appropriate*: *ase heom best þoht* O; om C.

12805 *bloody*: *reordi* C; *loþliche* O: Angart (*Engl. Studies*, 36 (1955), 3) suggests *dreori*; B&W trans 'cruel'.

12808 *destroyed*: *he hit wasteþ* O; *þat lond ewelde* C: Madden emends *ewelde* to *awalt* as in 12016.

12841 *local*: *lod-cniht* CO: B&L emend to *lond-cniht*; B&W keep C and trans 'guide' [MED *lodes-man* n (b)].

12882 *garnished*: *irust* C [B&W] (? from OE *gehyrstan* 'adorn', with metathesis); Madden (III, 506) emends to *ibrusted*, found three times elsewhere in L; O is damaged: . . . *st*.

12910 *white-haired*: (ore) O; *here* C: presumably for *hore*.

12928 *and . . . time*: *and hire bar a lutel wile* O; om C: emended to *us bar*.

12952 *honour*: *hire* C; om O: Madden gl 'serve', B&W trans 'and so aid you', from MED *heren* v 6(a); I read *here*, MED *heren* (c) 'serve (God), hence 'revere' or (b) '? take your advice'.

12968 *copulation*: *wif-þing* C; *wisinge* O (?= wishing 'concupiscence'): B&W trans C as 'woman'; *wif-þing* must mean 'sexual congress' (cf. Madden, III, 505).

12972 *shuffled . . . stretch*: *ræmien . . . raxlede* C; *remi . . . leyde* O (sophisticates): it is not clear what happens here; M gl 'roar . . . stretch'; B&W have 'yawned and stretched'; MED gl *ræmien* s.v. *remen* 'stretch oneself, yawn' and gl *raxlien* similarly: (a) 'stretch, stretch arms; (c) 'exhale?, yawn' (PPl B V 391 [ed. Kane and Donaldson] *raxed and [remed]* has *rored* in 13 MSS (MED *ramen* 'cry, shout'): the two verbs *remen* and *ramen* must have been often confused; the giant may have been stretching and yawning or roaring or any combination of these; since he has just been eating and is now getting sleepy, he may be belching rather than yawning.

12985 *they*: *hii* O; *he* C.

13034 *then . . . down*: *þo sat þe king adun* O [B&L]; om C.

13039 *they*: *þo hii* O; *þa he* C.

13040 *lay claim to*: *were ikenned* O; *hafed ikenned* 'had engendered' C.

13057 *halted*: *heolden* C; O sophisticates: B&W trans 'and joined his company'; Madden treats *heolden* as sp for *holden* 'loyal'; 'and his faithful companions.'

13068 *might*: B&L print *minte*; Madden and B&W have *mihte*.

13075 *encounter*: *finde* O; *iwinde* (?= *ifinde*) C; C has *hine* twice.

13078 *making peace*: *set . . . grið* O; *freondscipe* C.
          fight . . . him: *fihte him wið* O; *for to fihten* C.

13201 *the . . . darking*: *Bruttus beoð bolde* O [B&L]; om C.

13253 *bring . . . earth*: *grundien* C; *ʒou sarui: grundien*, which is gl in MED s.v. *grounden* v.6(b) 'strike sb. to ground'; overcome sb.; defeat', only in trans. form with a 15thc instance in Lydgate as the only other citation; Madden gives as literal sense 'fell you to the ground' (III, p. 508), with 'sink you' given in his translation; Hall gl 'bring you to the ground'. B&W gl 'triumph' and interpret 'prove ourselves worthy', derived from *grundien* in sense 'lay a foundation'. A similar verb occurs in L 15289 *folc unimete grunden an uolde* which appears to mean 'disembarked'. The simplest emendation would be *ʒe* for *we*: 'you will go down, descend', assuming error in the common ancestor of CO, which O has tried to rationalise by adding obj. *ʒou* and substituting *sarui* 'treat'.

13259 *he*: *þe* C; line reads *þat þe spere deore rof þorh þon swere* O.

13282 *or*: *oþer* O; *þa* C.

13300 *felling*: *fuld* O; *feollen* C: Madden emends: *feolden*.

13302 *fled*: *torned þe rugges* O; *afered* C: I emend to *alemed* 'driven away', as in L 4222.

13311 *taking . . . captive there*: following Madden's reading *lut þer of-nomen* rather than B&L *lut þer-of nomen* 'took few of them'.

13315 *horses*: *hors* O (13315–6); *hors* added in margin, later hand, C.

13385 *there*: *wa* C; O damaged; [B&L].

13460 *savage*: reading *bitele* C [B&W], rather than *bitere* O, emended in B&L.

13478 *support*: Madden (III, p. 75) reads *hele* C, B&L read *help* in text, *help* in fn; B&W read *hele* and gl 'strength', MED *hele* n.[1].

13487 *veteran of fame*: *har mon iblowen* C; . . . *man iblowe* O: Madden emends *har* C to *hard*; I read *har* = 'grey, old', MED s.v. *hōr* adj. 2(a) 'white or gray-haired'; 2(c) 'an old man' (cf. *Battle of Maldon* 169; *Beowulf* 1307);) B&W read *har* and gl 'doughty'.

13561a MS O (damaged) reads *þat hii an hiȝeng . . . en hire wepne*; line om C; I read *ȝarkien hire wepne*; B&W omit.

13587 *nation*: *leode* C [B&W]; O *londe*: read *þeode* [M]; C has *leode* twice in the line.

13642 *replied*: Madden prints *answarede* [B&W]; B&L print *answatede*.

13713 *out*: *vt* O; *at* C; [M].

13765 *Sextorius*: *Setor* C; O damaged: he is *Sexstorius* in 12663 and *Sextorius* in 13427; Madden would read *Sertor* (cf. Wace *Sertorius*) or *Sextor* B&W read *Setor* in text and *Seftor* in trans.

13775 *to see . . . death*: *þe he i-seh Beduer deaȝe* O; *þa his æm wes an deðe* C: reading *þa he i-seh his æmes deðe*.

13853 *flattened*: Madden alters his original transl. 'they felled the standards' [III, 108] to read *feollen* C as an impers. vb: 'the standards fell' [III, 509]; B&W trans 'banners fell'.

13865 *lurking*: *leouien* C; om O: ? read *leonien*; B&W read with C and gl 'actively defending himself'; *leonien* may = MED *lenen* v.(1) 1(d) *l.on* 'press. forward, advance'; 3 'crouch, lie in hiding'.

13867 *savage . . . sport*: *com wes swi sturne* C; *gome was wel kene* '(that) man, warrior was very brave' O: B&W emend C to *comp* 'contest'; M [III, p. 108] suggests '? read *gome*' transl. 'who was man exceeding stern'; B&L emend *gome*. B&W state that a sense 'man' would be syntactically difficult in relation to the following. Emending O to *gomen* 'game, sport, contest' achieves the same sense.

13885 *threat*: *ibeote* C; *dreade* O.

13888 *massive . . . dread*: *moche . . . moche care* O (damaged); half line om C: I have supplied 'dread'.

13889a The first half-line forms second half of 13888 in C; O reads *ne may no . . . telle ine boke ne in spelle*.

13919 *I'll*: *ich* O [M]; om C: C thus has only 13922 in direct speech; o reads 13920 *ȝou* (*heom* C) and continues the message in direct speech to 13922.

13925 *kinsman*: *Modred his may* O; *Modred his mæin* 'Modred's strength; military might' C (so B&W).

14015 *and . . . sorrow*: reading *and of sorȝen seoc* [Hall] for *of sorȝen and seoc* C; and *swiþe seak* O.

14033 *wish . . . evil*: *þe þe ufel unnen* C; O sophisticates: Hall emends to restore idiom . . . *on uuele unnen*.

14037 *the . . . best*: *þat me is leouest* O; om C.

14074 *miserable end*: *wæisið* C; B&W gl 'meet a fearful end'; *þis swikedom . . . (g)e* (damaged) O: ? read *fæisið (makien)* = 'die'.

14154 *running with*: *ȝurren* O; om C: *ȝurren* denotes the chattering of people, the whirring of ships' ropes in a storm; Emerson gl '(the stones) babbled (with streams of blood); Brandl and Zippel gl 'rattled'; B&W (following Madden) gl 'jarred'; I suggest reading *hurnen* (cf. 676 o), *vrnen* (cf. 5976) 'ran', MED *rennen* v.(1).

14159 *everything . . . gone*: *al ifaren* C in Madden, Brook, B&W; *il ifaren* 'had gone wrong' B&L; *ifaren* O.

14209a–10 Both lines taken from O; the first is not in C.

14215 *How . . . death*: *in woch wise ȝeo was dead* O; *whaðer heo weore on deðe* C.

and . . . departed: *and ou ȝeo hinne ◊ ende* O; om C: Emerson reads *and hu heo henne wende* 'how she departed', following O; I emend: *whiðer heo iwende*. In 14216 Emerson assumes the construction continues *whaðer* (emending *þa* C) 'or whether she had been (submerged in water)', and Brook follows; B&W read with C and trans 'whether she was dead . . . when she was herself submerged in the water', assuming a lacuna; 14216 is not in O. The expression 'anymore than if he/they were lost in/plunged in the sea' seems to be idiomatic, meaning 'no knowledge at all', of cf. 5659.

14230a, b Both lines from O; om C.

14234 *hoarfrost*: *rim* C; *ren* O: Madden suggests *rein* 'rain', which Emerson adopts.

14252 *conflict*: *wið* C; *weder* O: Bennett emends *wiðer* (no gl.), = 'hostility'; B&W read with C and trans *mêlée*; D&W treat *wiðe* as adv and gl 'whoever was joined in battle with one another'.

14355 *And . . . slain*: from MS O [Brook]; om C.

14257 *and the low*: from MS O [B&L, Brook); om C.

14541 MS C is corrupt, and has been partly emended by a later hand; O is burned away: *ichecele he lette soeðe* C with *children* supplied in margin in later hand; B&L read *eche child*, and I have supplied *adrenke mid wateren* after *seoðe*; in Wace the children are disembowelled: 13485 *enfanz en berz esbüeler*; the line may however have been nearly identical with 10465 (Gurmund's behaviour is similar to Childric's); *seoðe* may in fact be an error for **seokende* 'suckling'.

14599 *drew . . . strips*: *cuht heom swiðe narewe* C [B&L]; Madden reads *tuhte . . . narewe* [III, p. 511], which Hall emends to *tuhte heom in are medewe*; O burned.

14612 *crept*: *grupen* C 'groped', emended Stratmann, followed by Hall, to *crupen* 'crept'; O burned.

14698 *further*: *speden* supplied by B&L; om C; O burned.

14747 *and . . . grimaced at him*: *and . . . ennede ȝam an* O; *and heo grenneden him hon* added in margin in later hand, C.

14751 *to . . . many*: *ȝam . . . to roupe* O; om C.

14754 *taunts*: *scornes* O; *stanen* C; Le Saux thinks 'stones' is right, Madden accepts O.

14763 *wretched*: *wræstliche* C; om O.

14765 *derided*: *(heo maȝen iteled beon* C = 'reproached', with pun on 'tailed'; *and alle . . . les beren* O.

14863 *and to obey . . . refuse*: *ne . . . e louie nolleþ* 'and refuse to love/praise him' O; first half of line partly on erasure, *and heren h* added in margin second hand, *ine nulleþ* supplied by B&L.

14914 *þeh noma h . . . ne bede* O; *þeh na nam hine ne* (interlined by reviser) *bede* C.

14919 *utterly*: *and and unrihtes*, second *and* expuncted, probably in attempt to subpunct *n* and add 'u*n*' = *adu*n; *adunrihtes* O; Madden corrects his earlier conjecture and adopts *adunrihtes* (III, p. 512).

14936 *they governed*: purely conjectural: C omits second half-line; O damaged.

14953 *biting edge*: *þurh steles biten* C, perhaps for *bitele* 'sharp', but MED gl this instance under *bite* 1(a) 'blow with sharp weapon'; O damaged.

14955 *crowd . . . smaller*: reading *heþ* C as 'heap, crowd', this occurrence cited in MED under *heþ* 1(a) 'company of people'; (d) 'military strength'; other possible senses are: 'help' or 'hap': cf. lines 2051, 2948, 9149.

15054 *asking*: *bi-sohte* O [M]; *bi-þohte* C.

15066 *intended*: *ituht* C; O damaged; reading *itiht* 'intended' (or: *ituhte him* 'prepared').

15081–2 *the wisely . . . Edwin*: from MS O [B&L]; not in C.

15100 *and . . . beside*: from MS O; not in C.

15133 *As . . does*: this alignment in B&L assumes a half-line is lost; in fact the second half of 15132 C, not in O, is probably scribal, and 15133 C belongs in 15132, as in O.

15154 *gathered*: *.gadere* O, prob. for *togadere*; om C.

15180 *heaps*: *flockes* O; *fockes* C, *l* interlined, later hand = *folckes*.

15222 *from* (twice): *of (twice)* O; *a* (twice) C.

15223 *floated*: *wlæt* C; *fleot* O (cf. 10642); *wlæt* prob = *fleot* here (and prob also in 10642).

15228–31 Madden realigns here by reading the first half of 15229 as the second half of 15228, with the first half of 15230 as the completion of the second half of 15229, and so on to 15231 *cumen to þissen londe* for which he supplies, as second half-line: [*mid genge stronge*], following Wace 14168 *suvent appareilla navie/E suvent ot grant compainie*.

15262 *turned . . . well*: *þat tornde to mochel god* O; *seoþþen he þohten him swi god* C.

15289 *disembarked*: *grunden an uolde* C; *þe sipes he fulde* O: O looks like an attempted gloss, but *uolde* C could be a sp for *fulde*, and C then means 'he filled from the ground up'; cf. 13252 *grundien* (above). The usual formula involves *grund* sb plus *uolde* in sense 'felled': *uolde to grunden* 'overthrown, struck to the ground.'

15306 *trick*: *lisse* C; O damaged: Stratmann emends to *liste* (ES 3, 269).

15322 *with . . . strong-room*: *stið biwaled on eorðen* C; *þat was wel bi-walled*: Hall emends C to *on horden stið biwalled*.

15385 *windows*: *widewen* C; O damaged; [M].

15422 *transported*: *longien* C; O damaged: gl in MED as *longen* v. (4), also *longien* 'to summon (sb); bring (sth), citing this instance;

? = OED *long* v¹.4 'cause to pass over a long distance' (but earliest sense in OED is 1674).

15732 *families*: ginge C; om O: Madden suggests read *kinge*: '(of) kings'.

15772 *I . . . believe*: ne may ich hit ileue O; nulle he nauere icnawen.

15882 *yet another*: þe oþer C, presumably for (oðer) . . . þe or oðer . . . oðer 'at one time, at another'; perhaps scribe thought sense was 'the other peasant'; om O.

15886 *uppen þan monen* C ? 'under influence of the moon', cf. 6954 *monen* 'to the moon'; Hall emends to *monnen* 'upon men'; om O.

15912 *hardship*: hette C; . . (t)e O: 'violence' does not fit here, nor 'heat', and 'drought' might be appropriate (cf. 2017, 4365, 10199, 10342, 10925).

15947 *former days*: frimdæȝen 'early days' [M] C; . . . ne daȝe O, prob = *ferne daȝen* cf. C 13536 *ferndæȝen*: Hall reads *furndaȝen*.

before: bi-æften C; . . . afte(r) C: Ine (rightly) is accounted earlier than Athelstan in 15959, and *bi-æften* must mean 'previously' [H] rather than 'hereafter' [M].

15961 *the Pope's*: conjectural; his C; O damaged: Hall thinks that a preceding line has been lost in C.

15963 *stood*: istonde C: so Madden, Hall (B&L: *ist onde*); om O.

16014 *God's provision*: Godes dome CO, Hall proposes the emendation *Godes deme* 'God's ruler, judge' (i.e. the Pope).

16072 *four-and-a-half*: C; O has bote two ȝere.